The Handbook of International Macroeconomics

The Handbook of
International Macroeconomics

Edited by
FREDERICK VAN DER PLOEG

BLACKWELL
Oxford UK & Cambridge USA

Copyright © Basil Blackwell Ltd 1994

First published 1994
Reprinted 1994

Blackwell Publishers
238 Main Street,
Cambridge, Massachusetts 02142
USA

108 Cowley Road
Oxford OX4 1JF
UK

Library of Congress Cataloging-in-Publication Data

The handbook of international macroeconomics / edited by Frederick van
    der Ploeg
        p.   cm.
    Includes bibliographical references and index.
      ISBN 0–631–18026–5 (alk. paper). – ISBN 0–631–19062–7 (pbk.: alk. paper)
    1. International finance.   2. Monetary policy.   3. Macroeconomics.
I. Ploeg, Frederick van der, 1956–
HG3851.H347   1993
332'.042 – dc20

93–9823
CIP

British Library Cataloguing in Publication Data
A CIP catalogue record for this book is available from the British Library.

Typeset in 11 on 13 pt Times
by Times Graphics, Singapore
Printed in Great Britain by T.J. Press (Padstow) Ltd, Padstow, Cornwall.

This book is printed on acid-free paper

Contents

List of Figures

List of Tables

List of Contributors

Pierre-Richard Agénor, International Monetary Fund

George Alogoskoufis, Athens School of Economics and CEPR

David K. Backus, Stern School of Business, New York University

Giuseppe Bertola, Università di Torino, Princeton University, CEPR, and NBER

A. Lans Bovenberg, CentER, Tilburg University, OCFEB, Erasmus Universiteit Rotterdam, and CEPR

Daniel Cohen, Université Paris-I and ENS, Paris, CEPREMAP, and CEPR

Huw D. Dixon, University of York and CEPR

Bernard Dumas, HEC School of Management, Fuqua School of Business (Duke University), NBER, and CEPR

Barry Eichengreen, University of California at Berkeley

Robert P. Flood, International Monetary Fund

Alberto Giovannini, University Columbia, Ministero del Tesoro, CEPR, and NBER

Patrick J. Kehoe, University of Pennsylvania and Federal Reserve Bank of Minneapolis

Kenneth M. Kletzer, University of California, Santa Cruz

Finn E. Kydland, Carnegie-Mellon University

Frederick van der Ploeg, University of Amsterdam, Tinbergen Institute, and CEPR

Neil Rankin, University of Warwick and CEPR

Assaf Razin, Tel-Aviv University, NBER, and CEPR

Efraim Sadka, Tel-Aviv University

Partha Sen, Delhi School of Economics

Paul J.G. Tang, Tinbergen Institute

Bart Turtelboom, Columbia University and Katholieke Universiteit Leuven

Casper G. de Vries, Katholieke Universiteit Leuven and Erasmus Universiteit Rotterdam

Preface

The idea of preparing another handbook in the general area of international economics seemed at first an unnecessary venture. After all, it was only about seven years ago that the authoritative and comprehensive *Handbook of International Economics* was edited by Ronald W. Jones and Peter B. Kenen and published by North-Holland (1985). This handbook was and is put to good use by many teachers in both undergraduate and postgraduate courses in international economics throughout the world. It also provides an authoritative state of the art for researchers in the field of international economics. Although many collections of papers have been published subsequently, some teachers and PhD students still express a need for a more up-to-date handbook as the field has expanded rapidly during the last seven years. Rapid advances in theory and applied work have taken place in the areas both of international trade and of international monetary economics. In the general area of international trade a lot of research has been completed on increasing returns, imperfect competition and intra-industry trade.

The handbook consists of five parts: I Micro Foundations of International Macroeconomics; II Capital Taxation and Real Models; III International Monetary Regimes; IV Capital Markets, Money, and Exchange Rates; and V Debt, Deficits, and Growth.

It focuses, in contrast with Jones and Kenen's book, on the advances made during the last seven years in the field of international monetary economics. Since attention is not exclusively restricted to monetary issues and nominal exchange rates, it seemed more appropriate to call it a *Handbook of International Macroeconomics*. Coming from a small country myself, it is indeed very hard to imagine anything else but *open economy macroeconomics* (in contrast to the macroeconomics of a closed economy).

Some of the contributions in the book build on the original Jones and Kenen handbook. For example, this handbook contains chapters on the history of the international monetary system (Barry Eichengreen), the optimal exchange rate regime (George Alogoskoufis), international capital market equilibrium (Dumas), and stylized facts of nominal exchange rate returns (de Vries). The first two of these chapters begin with a discussion of the history and its implications for research in international macroeconomics and finance of the classical gold standard, the interwar years and Bretton Woods. The discussion is followed by a theoretical analysis of the desirability of monetary versus exchange rate targets and, more generally, of the optimal exchange rate regime within the context of a stochastic small open economy with an integrated capital market. The latter two chapters begin with an extensive discussion of the international capital asset pricing model and arbitrage arguments followed by a brief discussion of general equilibrium models. These discussions are followed by a presentation of stylized facts (unit roots, triangular arbitrage, cointegration, fat tails, skewness, volatility clusters, etc.) and appropriate econometric techniques for the empirical analysis of nominal exchange rate returns.

Other chapters in the handbook, however, are concerned with topics that are not covered by Jones and Kenen, often because the research results described have only been obtained during the last few years. Part I thus contains innovative chapters on the microeconomic foundations of international macroeconomics – temporary equilibrium models based on quantity constraints (Neil Rankin), the economics of imperfect competition (Huw Dixon), and theory and empirical evidence for international real business cycles (David Backus, Patrick Kehoe and Finn Kydland). This part of the handbook thus gives a flavor of how "European" neo-Keynesian, "Cambridge USA" New Keynesian and "fresh water" New Classical macroeconomics have affected recent theories of international macroeconomics. Part II is concerned with capital taxation in the global economy, paying particular attention to residence-based versus tax-based taxes, within the context of static general equilibrium models (Assaf Razin and Efraim Sadka) and of dynamic overlapping generations models (Lans Bovenberg). Part II is concerned with *real* models in international macroeconomics in the sense that money and nominal interest and exchange rates play no role.

Part III, in contrast, is concerned with *monetary* issues in international macroeconomics. Apart from the chapters by Eichengreen and Alogoskoufis mentioned above, there are innovative contributions on speculative attacks and balance of payments crises (Pierre Agénor and Robert Flood) and continuous-time models of exchange rates, bands and intervention policy (Giuseppe Bertola). These chapters focus on attacks on the currency and use of foreign reserves and policy switches to defend the currency on the one hand, and, on the other, the use of the theory of Brownian processes with reflecting barriers to explain the movement of exchange rates when central banks are committed to intervene in order to keep exchange rates within pre-specified bands (target zones). Part IV contains, apart from the contributions by Dumas and de Vries mentioned above, an up-to-date survey of the international aspects of the theory of currency substitution (using cash-in-advance as well as transactions costs models) and Gresham's law as well as a very detailed discussion of the empirical evidence for currency substitution (Alberto Giovannini and Bart Turtelboom).

The final part of the handbook begins with two thorough surveys on the bargaining and renegotiation aspects of sovereign immunity and international lending (Kenneth Kletzer) and on the macroeconomics of growth, credit rationing and the repudiation of external debt (Daniel Cohen). These chapters are followed by a survey of intertemporal theories of saving and investment and the implications for the current account within the context of classical growth theory, paying attention to among other topics the Harberger–Laursen–Metzler effect and the Feldstein–Horioka puzzle (Partha Sen). The final chapter surveys the new theories of endogenous growth (within the context of overlapping generations) and their implications for the global economy (Frederick van der Ploeg and Paul J. G. Tang). This last survey pays particular attention to the adverse consequences of loose budgetary policies on the rate of economic growth and external deficits and foreign debt, to the beneficial effects of supply side policies on the global rate of growth, and to issues of catch-up, development, and convergence of the level of income in poor countries to the level of income in rich countries.

In preparing the handbook we have attempted to cover the more exciting topics on the frontiers of research in international macroeconomics, those that lend themselves for teaching in graduate courses. All contributors have been asked to write their chapters in such a way that they can be used in graduate courses. Rather than having an exhaustive bibliography and discussion of every published model on the topic, the contributors have attempted to pick out an illustrative analytical model which can be used for teaching purposes and which gives the students a clue of how to go about doing research on their own. In some of the chapters an attempt is also made to confront recent theoretical developments with empirical evidence for a number of countries. Some contributors also attempt to indicate exciting directions for future research.

I am very much indebted to the contributors for the care they took in preparing their chapters and the time and effort they devoted to commenting on the chapters of other contributors. I am also grateful to a number of PhD students, in particular Roel Beetsma, Frank de Jong, Catrien Hooyman, Berthold Leeftinck, Jenny Ligthart, Eric Schaling, Sjak Smulders, Paul Tang, Eelke de Jong, and Lex Meijdam, who commented on and benefited from earlier drafts of some of the chapters. Finally, it is a pleasure to acknowledge the secretarial assistance I received from Robert Helmink and Josephine Ruitenberg.

Frederick van der Ploeg
University of Amsterdam,
Tinbergen Institute, and CEPR

PART I

MICRO FOUNDATIONS OF INTERNATIONAL MACROECONOMICS

1 Quantity-constrained Models of Open Economies

NEIL RANKIN

1 Introduction

In the 1980s the quantity-constrained modeling approach developed by Barro and Grossman (1971), Benassy (1975), Malinvaud (1977), and others in the 1970s found its main role to be as a tool for analyzing open economies. This trend was begun, in particular, by Dixit (1978) and Neary (1980), and the early phase of the literature is well summarized and surveyed by Cuddington et al. (1984) and by Neary (1990). In this chapter we focus on more recent developments, and in particular on the *intertemporal* quantity-constrained models which have extended the static one-period framework used until the mid-1980s.

The value of quantity-constrained equilibrium as a modeling technique for open economy macroeconomics derives from, perhaps, two sources. First, it adds the discipline of micro foundations which is lacking in traditional "directly postulated" macromodels, ensuring that thought is given to the exact number and structure of markets, to the process (Walrasian or non-Walrasian) within them used to resolve demands and supplies into actual exchanges, to agents' exact budget constraints (including intertemporal ones) and expectations, and to agents' objective functions and how they are maximized. Second, it adds the realism of unemployment and the scope for macroeconomic policy effectiveness which is lacking in – otherwise rigorously specified – Walrasian models. For example, the recent book by Frenkel and Razin (1987) uses intertemporal optimization and perfect foresight to model fiscal policy in open economies, but suffers from the major drawback that full employment is always guaranteed by the ubiquitous use of the Walrasian concept of equilibrium. A particular advantage of quantity-constrained equilibrium as applied to open economy macro-economics is that many of the questions we wish to answer (e.g. about the effects of oil price shocks, or of protectionism) are ones where "micro" and "macro" issues overlap, so that neither of the traditionally separate approaches to these is adequate by itself.

The criticism most often made of quantity-constrained models is that they treat some or all prices as fixed, yet fail to explain why this is so. There are several justifications for such an approach. Foremost is that fixed or sluggishly adjusting prices (either absolute or relative) are a fact of the real world, and appear to explain much macroeconomic behavior for which no superior explanation has yet been found. While it is very desirable to be able to explain rigid prices themselves, many major research programs on this topic during the last fifteen years (into implicit contracts, efficiency wages, imperfect competition, menu costs, to name but a few) have so far failed to produce a non-Walrasian paradigm which has been widely accepted as having all the features we could reasonably seek in a basis for macroeconomics. Quantity-constrained equilibrium, although it leaves unanswered this deeper question, does provide a rigorous method for exploring the *implications* of price inflexibilities. Its mechanisms are by now well understood, and it is versatile inasmuch as not all prices in the economy need be assumed fixed. In particular the common assumption used in intertemporal models is that current prices are fixed and future ones are flexible, which provides a simple but attractive method of capturing the notion of price rigidity as an essentially short-run phenomenon.

The work surveyed in this chapter falls naturally into two categories. First, roughly half the intertemporal models constructed have been "real" models, in that they exclude money. Price rigidities in these models are therefore all "real" (or "relative") price rigidities, rather than nominal rigidities. The advantage of excluding the complication of money is that the "real" side of the model can be more fully developed: for example physical investment by firms can be properly accommodated. Perhaps the most notable model of this sort is the one used in two papers by van Wijnbergen (1985, 1987). Hence in section 2 we examine a simplified version of the van Wijnbergen model and use it as a basis for a discussion of several other "real" models. The other papers in the literature have all been "monetary" models (as indeed has been the entire closed economy literature). Price rigidities here are therefore "nominal" (as well as real). An obvious advantage of a monetary model is that different nominal exchange rate regimes can be analyzed, since whether the exchange rate is fixed or floating, for example, is a question of monetary policy. However, the problem of why agents demand money now arises. This is a deep question which goes beyond issues of concern only for an open economy. Two simple alternative methods of deriving a demand for money have been employed: the "cash-in-advance" constraint, and the assumption that real balances provide utility. In section 3, where we deal with monetary models, we accordingly divide them into these two groups.

2 Real models

2.1 Short run and long run

Behind the move to consider intertemporal versions of quantity-constrained models has been a realization of the importance of intertemporal decision-making to macroeconomic behavior more generally. The first paper to construct an intertemporal disequilibrium model of a *closed* economy was that of Neary and Stiglitz (1983). Neary and Stiglitz use a two-period structure similar to that later adopted in many open economy models in order to examine the implications of rational expectations of future quantity constraints for macroeconomic policy. Their most notable result is that, when there is a regime of Keynesian unemployment in both periods, rational expectations *increase*, rather than – as in "new classical" models – reduce, policy effectiveness. This is striking proof of the fact that, as has often been pointed out,[1] rational expectations *per se* do not imply ineffectiveness: it is the nature of equilibrium in markets which is the critical factor.

One of the advantages of an intertemporal structure for an open economy quantity-constrained model, then, is that it permits us to see whether expectations of future quantity constraints can have similar effects in an open economy. Another aspect of expectations which it enables us to examine is whether rational expectations are necessarily optimal, in a welfare sense. This question is posed by Persson and Svensson (1983), who use a two-period open economy model with Keynesian unemployment in period 1 to show that over-optimistic expectations of the future productivity level raise welfare not only *ex ante* but also *ex post* relative to the case of perfect foresight. In contrast with Neary and Stiglitz's result, this depends on there being Walrasian equilibrium in period 2: the reason is that when productivity is discovered to be less than expected, price adjustment dampens the reduction in output (relative to its expected level) which this causes.

Perhaps the most important advantage of an intertemporal analysis for an open economy, however, arises from the fact that in recent work on the determinants of the current account of the balance of payments (see chapter 3 of this volume) intertemporal decisions have come to be seen as paramount. In this approach, a country's trade balance is seen as the gap between its savings and investment, which are the outcomes of intertemporal optimization decisions by, respectively, households and firms. The revival of interest in the Harberger–Laursen–Metzler effect of a terms of trade change on the trade balance is an example of this.[2] In this section, we shall focus in particular on the issue of the trade balance and its relation to fiscal policy, but in a more realistic context than the one used in much of this literature, namely one where unemployment is present. Our exposition will center on a version of the "real" model employed in two papers by van Wijnbergen (1985, 1987).

There are two standard structures for a country's goods markets which permit a variable real exchange rate, and both are used in the quantity-constrained literature. In the Salter–Swan framework the country has two output sectors, for traded and nontraded goods. The traded goods market is a Walrasian flex-price market in which the country is "small" and so a price-taker, while the nontraded goods market may or may not have a rigid price, leading to excess supply or demand. This is the structure used in Neary's (1980) original paper, and in Cuddington and Vinals (1986a, b) and Fender (1986), discussed below. In the alternative Mundell–Fleming framework the country produces a single specialized output. Being specialized means that there are no perfect substitutes produced elsewhere, so that the country is "large" in the world market for the good. Although it is traded internationally, its price may be rigid at some arbitrary level, since the downward-sloping demand curve for it means that demand does not go to zero or infinity if the price is set above or below a given world price. Van Wijnbergen (1985, 1987) uses the latter structure. Both have very similar implications, although there are some differences which will be pointed out in due course.

In any period t ($t = 1, 2$) there are thus two goods traded in the van Wijnbergen model: an imported consumption good, in the market for which the country is small, and which is used as the numeraire; and domestic output, whose price in terms of the imported good we denote as p_t. p_t is thus also the terms of trade. Labor is used as an input to production in both periods and paid a wage w_t. The key assumption which van Wijnbergen makes is that (w_1, p_1) are arbitrary and exogenous, causing excess supply or demand in the labor or output markets, while (w_2, p_2) adjust instantaneously to ensure Walrasian equilibrium in period 2. If period 1 is thought of as the short run and period 2 as the long run, this captures the widely accepted notion that price rigidity exists in the short but not in the long run. More specifically, it can be thought of as arising from price-setting behavior of a sort originally suggested by Green and Laffont (1981). Suppose prices are set one period in advance, at levels which are expected to clear markets if no unexpected shocks occur, but cannot be changed *ex post* when a random shock has been realized. Then period 1 of the model depicts the equilibrium after the realization of first-period shocks and given rational expectations of future shocks. Below, as well as considering this set-up, we shall begin by considering the case where (w_2, p_2) are also rigid. This represents more persistent price inflexibility than is allowed by van Wijnbergen, and is closer to the Neary–Stiglitz (1983) closed economy model.

2.2 The representative household

Let us begin by examining the optimization problem faced by a representative domestic household. The household's problem may be written as

$$\text{maximize} \quad u(h_1, f_1, h_2, f_2) \tag{1.1}$$

$$\text{subject to} \quad a = p_1 h_1 + f_1 + dp_2 h_2 + df_2 \tag{1.2}$$

where h_t, f_t are the consumptions of home goods and foreign goods in period t, a is the household's lifetime assets or wealth, and $d = 1/(1 + r)$ is the real discount factor. Households have access to the world capital market where they can borrow and lend at the world real interest rate r. The country is assumed to be small in this market, so that r, and thus d, is an exogenous variable. Since here we shall confine our analysis to disequilibrium regimes in which there is either excess supply or clearing in the goods market, quantity constraints on households' purchases of goods may be ignored. However, quantity constraints affect the household in the labor market, where they determine income and thus lifetime wealth:

$$a = p_1 y_1 - p_1 i - \tau_1 + d[p_2 y_2 - \tau_2] \tag{1.3}$$

where i is investment and y_t is output in period t. The household's income in period t comprises wages $w_t l_t$ and dividends π_t. When the wage is assumed flexible and thus the labor market clears, employment l_t equals labor supply. Since there is no utility of leisure, at any positive wage households will wish to supply their entire endowment of time, L, to the labor market, so that employment just equals the exogenous L. When, alternatively, the wage is assumed fixed and excess supply of labor occurs, l_t becomes an exogenous quantity constraint on the household, determined by firms' labor demand. Under our assumptions, in either case $w_t l_t$ is exogenous to the household. Dividends are also exogenous, and since they consist of output less wage costs,[3] both components of income may be aggregated, giving $y_1 - i$ in period 1 and y_2 in period 2. τ_t is a lump-sum tax levied by the government.

Van Wijnbergen uses duality theory to solve the household's problem, and places only weak restrictions on the utility function (1.1). However, little is lost in terms of results, and considerable ease of derivation is gained, if we work with the more familiar Marshallian demand functions and use a specific functional form such as the Cobb–Douglas function:

$$u = h_1^\alpha f_1^\beta h_2^\gamma f_2^\delta \qquad \alpha + \beta + \gamma + \delta = 1 \tag{1.4}$$

Note that Cobb–Douglas utility implies constant expenditure shares, so that from (1.2) and (1.4), $p_1 h_1 = \alpha a$ etc. The resulting demand functions may thus be written as (in explicit and schematic forms)

$$h_1 = \alpha a/p_1 = h_1(a, p_1) \tag{1.5a}$$

$$f_1 = \beta a = f_1(a) \tag{1.5b}$$

$$h_2 = \gamma a/dp_2 = h_2(a, p_2, d) \tag{1.5c}$$

$$f_2 = \delta a/d = f_2(a, d) \tag{1.5d}$$

The potential restrictiveness of Cobb–Douglas utility lies in the fact that, as can be seen from (1.5), all cross-price effects are zero. To be precise, goods are neither gross substitutes nor complements as income and substitution effects exactly cancel out. For present purposes, this greatly simplifies the derivation of the results, without prejudicing them.

2.3   The representative firm

Turning to the representative firm, the problem it faces is that of choosing labor and capital inputs to maximize profits, subject to possible quantity constraints on sales of output. In period 1, the capital stock k_0 is predetermined, so that labor is the only variable input. Since we are concerned with the case of excess goods supply in period 1, the firm in these circumstances faces an exogenous quantity constraint y_1 on output[4] and thus has to demand whatever employment level l_1 is determined by the production function $y_1(k_0, l_1)$. In fact we can omit an explicit formula for the firm's effective demand for labor since – as noted above – if output is known it is not necessary also to know employment in order to calculate households' goods demand, and in the formal solution of the model employment is determined as a residual. In period 2, the capital stock which matters for output is k_1, via the production function $y_2(k_1, l_2)$. k_1 is the outcome of investment undertaken in period 1 ($k_1 = i$ if we assume 100 percent depreciation of k_0), so that i will depend on the firm's expectations of period-2 variables.

Taking first the case of excess supply in period 2, the firm is subject to an exogenous expected quantity constraint $\bar{y}_2$ on its production and so faces the problem

$$\text{maximize} \qquad dp_2\bar{y}_2 - p_1 i - dw_2 l_2 \qquad (1.6)$$

subject to the sales constraint

$$\bar{y}_2 = y_2(i, l_2) \qquad (1.7)$$

This is a simple cost-minimization problem, which requires choosing (i, l_2) such that the ratio of the marginal products is equal to the ratio of the own-product prices $(p_1/dp_2, w_2/p_2)$. For illustration, suppose the production function has a Cobb–Douglas form $y_2 = Bk_1^\varepsilon l_2^{1-\varepsilon}$. Then we readily obtain

$$i = vy_2 = \bar{i}(y_2, dw_2/p_1) \qquad (1.8)$$

where $v \equiv B^{-1}[(1/\varepsilon - 1)p_1/dw_2]^{\varepsilon - 1}$. This is, of course, a simple accelerator-type demand for investment.

In the alternative case of Walrasian equilibrium in period 2, employment will be determined exogenously at L, enabling us now to express the firm's optimization problem as

$$\text{maximize} \qquad dp_2 y_2 - p_1 i \qquad (1.9)$$

subject to the production function

$$y_2 = y_2(i, L) \qquad (1.10)$$

To solve this we simply equate the (own-product) real interest rate p_1/dp_2 to the marginal product of capital, which with the Cobb–Douglas technology yields

$$i = \psi \left[\frac{dp_2}{p_1}\right]^{1/(1-\varepsilon)} = i\left[\frac{dp_2}{p_1}\right] \qquad (1.11)$$

where $\psi \equiv L(\varepsilon B)^{1/(1-\varepsilon)}$. This is a conventional demand function which relates investment by firms negatively to the real interest rate.

2.4 The government

The third agent in the economy is the government, which makes purchases of domestic output and finances them either through lump-sum taxation or borrowing. If it is assumed that the government and private sector have equal access to the world capital market, so that both can borrow and lend at the given world interest rate r, then Ricardian equivalence holds and there will be no difference between the two financing methods. Households will perceive a current tax cut which increases the budget deficit as implying higher future taxation. Hence, discounting this at the same interest rate as the government pays on its own debt, they will perceive no change in their net lifetime wealth. However, in van Wijnbergen (1987) a simple but plausible assumption which breaks this equivalence is employed. Suppose the government can borrow and lend at a lower world interest rate than private households can (which in practice may occur if it is perceived to offer a lower risk of default, though we do not model this here). Then – as we shall see – increased future taxation will be privately discounted at a higher rate of interest than the government pays, raising private net wealth. The government's intertemporal budget constraint we thus write as

$$p_1 g_1 + d_g p_2 g_2 - \tau_1 - d_g \tau_2 = 0 \qquad (1.12)$$

where in general we assume $d_g > d$.

2.5   Keynesian unemployment in the short run and in the long run

Given the microeconomic behavior described above, we now consider the macroeconomic equilibrium. First, we take a variant of the van Wijnbergen (1987) model in which not only (w_1, p_1) but also (w_2, p_2) are exogenous. We assume that the exogenous variables are such that excess supply in the labor and domestic output markets prevails in both periods. Such a configuration of market disequilibrium may be referred to as the K–K regime, since there is Keynesian unemployment in both periods.[5] When a market is in excess demand or supply, the rule which determines the quantity traded is the "short-side" rule: trade = min(demand, supply). Applying this to the present regime of general excess supply, output in both periods must be demand determined and so may be written as

$$y_1 = h_1(p_1, a) + h_1^*(p_1, a^*) + \bar{\imath}(y_2, dw_2/p_1) + g_1 \qquad \text{IS}_1 \quad (1.13)$$
$$y_2 = h_2(p_2, d, a) + h_2^*(p_2, d, a^*) + g_2 \qquad \text{IS}_2 \quad (1.14)$$

where

$$a = p_1 y_1 + d p_2 y_2 - p_1 \bar{\imath}\left(y_2, \frac{dw_2}{p_1}\right) - \left[1 - \frac{d}{d_g}\right]\tau_1 - \frac{d}{d_g} p_1 g_1 - d p_2 g_2 \quad (1.15)$$

and foreign variables are denoted by an asterisk. This system of two IS equations determines (y_1, y_2) contingent on the exogenous variables $(p_1, p_2, w_2, d, d_g, a^*)$. Foreign demands for home output (h_1^*, h_2^*) (i.e. for exports) are taken to have qualitatively (though not quantitatively) symmetric functional forms with home demands for foreign output (i.e. for imports). Since the country is "small," foreign wealth a^* is treated as exogenous. To obtain the equation for a, equation (1.15), we have used the government budget constraint (1.12) to substitute τ_2 out of (1.3). This is done on the assumption that out of the four policy instruments $(g_1, g_2, \tau_1, \tau_2)$, of which only three can be independent, it is τ_2 which acts as the residual. From (1.15) we see immediately that, when $d_g = d$, τ_1 has no effect on household wealth, which is, of course, the manifestation of Ricardian equivalence at work.

A neat diagrammatic representation of the equilibrium is possible. Substituting a from (1.15) into IS_1, IS_2 and using the explicit Cobb–Douglas functional forms for demands from (1.5) and (1.8), after regrouping terms we obtain the reduced-form IS curves

$$p_1y_1 = \frac{\alpha}{1-\alpha} dp_2[y_2 - g_2] + vp_1y_2 + \frac{1}{1-\alpha} \alpha^*a^*$$

$$+ \frac{1 - \alpha[d/d_g]}{1-\alpha} p_1g_1 - \frac{\alpha}{1-\alpha}\left[1 - \frac{d}{d_g}\right]\tau_1 \qquad IS_1 \qquad (1.16)$$

$$p_1y_1 = \frac{1-\gamma}{\gamma} dp_2[y_2 - g_2] + vp_1y_2 - \frac{1}{\gamma} \gamma^*a^*$$

$$+ \frac{d}{d_g} p_1g_1 + \left[1 - \frac{d}{d_g}\right]\tau_1 \qquad IS_2 \qquad (1.17)$$

This clearly gives us a pair of upward-sloping lines in (y_1, y_2) space. Since it would be reasonable to assume that the lifetime expenditure shares on domestic goods, (α, γ), are both less than one-half, IS_1 is steeper than IS_2 (figure 1.1).

Now consider the effect of an increase in g_1, i.e. a "temporary" increase in government spending. First, if $d_g = d$, then (1.16) and (1.17)

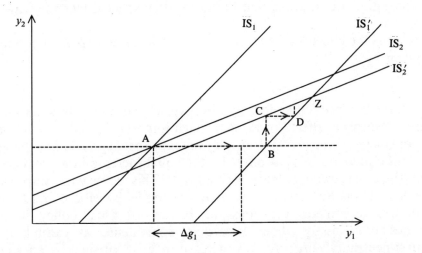

Figure 1.1   Equilibrium in the Keynesian–Keynesian regime.

show that both curves shift to the right by Δg_1. This yields $dy_1/dg_1 = 1$, which is the textbook "balanced-budget" multiplier. Such a result is not particularly surprising when it is remembered that, under $d_g = d$, government borrowing is equivalent to tax financing. If $d_g > d$, however, then IS_1 shifts to the right by more than Δg_1, while IS_2 shifts to the right by less. This is the case depicted in figure 1.1. It clearly follows that in the new equilibrium at Z, $dy_1/dg_1 > 1$, i.e., a genuine "multiplier" exists.

To understand the mechanism underlying this Keynesian multiplier, and to see how rational expectations of future output y_2 contribute to increasing it – as Neary and Stiglitz (1983) found for the closed economy – we can break down the multiplier process into a series of steps. Suppose initially that expectations of y_2 are unchanged following the shock. Then the familiar "static" multiplier process (in which the increase in government spending raises period-1 output, which raises income, which raises current consumption demand, and so on) will work itself out, moving the economy from A to B. With y_1 as at B, however, expectations of y_2 are too low: the extra demand created would imply the level of y_2 shown at C. If expectations now adjust to this, the anticipated increase in y_2 will induce higher spending in period 1 (both on consumption, because lifetime wealth has increased, and on investment, because firms' expected sales have increased), which will again be worked out through the static multiplier, moving the economy to D. This triggers a further increase in expected y_2, and so on, until full equilibrium is achieved at Z. Expectations of future quantity constraints play a clear role in increasing the size of the final multiplier. However, it is also clear that, without $d_g > d$, expectations of higher future taxes completely offset any increase in lifetime wealth due to the initial rise in y_1, so that the rationally expected increase in y_2 is zero.

What is the effect on the trade balance? The trade surplus in period 1 is given by

$$b = p_1 h_1^* - f_1 = \beta^* a^* - \beta a \qquad (1.18)$$

The trade balance b therefore moves inversely with private wealth a: a pure "absorption effect" working through imports. The effect on a may be considered using (1.15). If $d_g = d$, we know that (y_2, i) do not change, while the increase in y_1 is offset by the equal increase in g_1, leaving a and thus the trade balance unchanged. This somewhat surprising conclusion was first obtained in a similar model by Moore and Neary (1985). It completes the emerging picture of fiscal policy in the Keynesian economy under Ricardian equivalence as exhibiting a "quasi-neutrality" property: an increase in g_1 is satisfied by an equal increase in y_1, with no other variables affected. If $d_g > d$, however, then in (1.15) the increase in y_1 exceeds the increase in g_1, and also the increase in y_2 exceeds the increase in i,[6] so that private wealth a unambiguously increases and the trade balance deteriorates.

2.6 Keynesian unemployment in the short run and Walrasian equilibrium in the long run

We now turn to the exact disequilibrium configuration considered by van Wijnbergen (1985, 1987). Here there is still Keynesian unemployment in period 1 but it is now accompanied by Walrasian equilibrium in period 2. This regime is the one favored in the majority of the intertemporal disequilibrium papers.[7] The equilibrium conditions are very similar to IS$_1$, IS$_2$ above except that we replace IS$_2$ with a goods-market clearing equation GM$_2$, by equating y_2 to $y_2(i, L)$, and use the Walrasian demand function (1.11) for i rather than the quantity-constrained function (1.8). With Cobb–Douglas functional forms we then have (after regrouping terms as before)

$$p_1y_1 = \frac{\alpha}{1-\alpha} dp_2 \left[\phi\left[\frac{dp_2}{p_1}\right]^{\varepsilon/(1-\varepsilon)} - g_2 \right] + p_1\psi\left[\frac{dp_2}{p_1}\right]^{1/(1-\varepsilon)} + \frac{1}{1-\alpha} \alpha^* a^*$$

$$+ \frac{1-\alpha[d/d_g]}{1-\alpha} p_1 g_1 - \frac{\alpha}{1-\alpha}\left[1 - \frac{d}{d_g}\right]\tau_1 \qquad \text{IS}_1 \qquad (1.19)$$

$$p_1y_1 = \frac{1-\gamma}{\gamma} dp_2 \left[\phi\left[\frac{dp_2}{p_1}\right]^{\varepsilon/(1-\varepsilon)} - g_2 \right] + p_1\psi\left[\frac{dp_2}{p_1}\right]^{1/(1-\varepsilon)} - \frac{1}{\gamma} y^* a^*$$

$$+ \frac{d}{d_g} p_1 g_1 + \left[1 - \frac{d}{d_g}\right]\tau_1 \qquad \text{GM}_2 \qquad (1.20)$$

where $\phi[dp_2/p_1]^{\varepsilon/(1-\varepsilon)} = y_2$ ($\phi \equiv L\varepsilon^{\varepsilon/(1-\varepsilon)}B^{1/(1-\varepsilon)}$) and has been obtained by substituting investment demand (1.11) into the production function. This time the endogenous variables are (y_1, p_2) rather than (y_1, y_2), but IS$_1$, GM$_2$ still give rise to very similar upward-sloping loci in (y_1, p_2) space (figure 1.2).

Again we can study the impact of an increase in g_1. With $d_g = d$, both IS$_1$ and GM$_2$ shift to the right by Δg_1, yielding $dy_1/dg_1 = 1$ and the "quasi-neutrality" noted above. With $d_g > d$, IS$_1$ shifts to the right by more than Δg_1 and GM$_2$ by less, as shown in figure 1.2. Therefore dy_1/dg_1 is as before greater than unity. Rational expectations are once more pivotal in increasing the multiplier, but this time the transmission mechanism is somewhat different and may be explained as follows. With a constant expected p_2, the increase in y_1 from A to B increases household wealth and thus demand for y_2. This now raises the period-2 price, or the terms of trade. Once the rise in p_2 is anticipated, there is

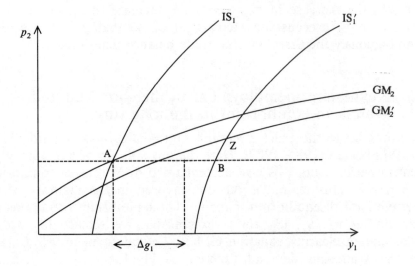

Figure 1.2   Equilibrium in the Keynesian–Walrasian regime.

a positive stimulus to investment, since producing for future sales has become more profitable, and this now has a further multiplier effect on y_1, and so on. Investment plays a more important role in this regime than in the previous one, since it is now the *only* channel by which future endogenous changes feed back onto current demand. If investment were excluded, no "intertemporal multiplier effect" would operate. As van Wijnbergen points out, it is also striking that fiscal policy *crowds in* investment in this model (as also in the previous regime), whereas conventional closed economy IS–LM analysis has schooled us to think that investment must be crowded out by a fiscal expansion.

What is the effect of an anticipated future increase in spending (higher g_2)? From (1.19) and (1.20), both IS_1 and GM_2 shift to the left. Since GM_2 shifts to the left by more provided that $(1 - \gamma)/\gamma > \alpha/(1 - \alpha)$, p_2 rises. To resolve the apparently ambiguous effect on y_1, note that if investment $\psi[dp_2/p_1]^{1/(1 - \varepsilon)}$ is shifted to the left-hand side, (1.19) and (1.20) may be viewed as an equation system determining the composite variables $(y_1 - i, y_2 - g_2)$. Since g_2 only enters this system via $y_2 - g_2$ itself, the composite variables are unaffected by a change in g_2. It then follows that $dy_2/dg_2 = 1$ and $dy_1/dg_2 = di/dg_2 > 0$ (this last since the rise in p_2 raises i). This unambiguously expansionary effect is interesting in view of the debate over whether anticipated fiscal policy is contractionary (see for example Blanchard and Fischer, 1989, ch. 10.4). This debate took place in "postulated" models; our use of micro foundations here suggests that the possibility of contraction has been over-emphasized.

2.7   Discussion

The empirical motivation for van Wijnbergen's (1987) analysis is the large fiscal deficits run by many countries, in particular the USA, during the 1980s. This is also the historical episode which interests Cuddington and Vinals (1986a, b), whose monetary models will be discussed in the next section. The van Wijnbergen model does indeed fit many aspects of the US experience. A large budget deficit initiated during Reagan's first term of office brought about a rapid recovery from the slump of the early 1980s, but also brought with it an appreciation of the real exchange rate and, in contrast to the prediction of conventional models, buoyant investment. At the same time a severe current account deficit arose. All these outcomes are explained by the model. To explain the rather different effects of the large fiscal deficits run in several European countries, van Wijnbergen suggests that a regime of first-period "classical" unemployment is more appropriate. This he models by assuming that p_1 is upwardly flexible and that w_1 is now indexed to consumer prices. An increase in g_1 is shown to cause a much smaller increase in output since firms are now operating on their Walrasian supply curves,[8] which is consistent with the failure of Keynesian reflationary measures in some European countries. It is also possible that investment now falls and the current account improves (as happened in the Netherlands), owing to the higher cost of capital and to the fall in wealth as increased taxes are not offset by the rise in current output.

Another "real" analysis in which investment plays an important role is that of Moore (1989). Moore considers inventory rather than fixed capital investment, though in all other respects his model is very close to van Wijnbergen's. However, the difference turns out to be an important one. Whereas investment in van Wijnbergen's model increases the fiscal multiplier and adds to the negative impact on the trade balance, in Moore's model it lowers the fiscal multiplier and results in a positive impact on the trade balance. The reason is that inventories lead to "production smoothing". An expansion of current demand can be met partly by running down inventories and so only part of it is met by increasing production. Households' wealth in fact falls, since the higher tax burden is no longer fully offset by the rise in output and income, and hence import demand falls, causing the trade balance to improve.[9]

We have so far discussed van Wijnbergen's model as a tool for analyzing fiscal deficits in the 1980s, which is the focus of his 1987 paper. In van Wijnbergen (1985), essentially the same model is used to study the effects of the 1974 oil price increase. Imported oil is introduced as a second input to production, and the question asked is into which regime an oil price increase will push the economy, assuming an initial situation of Walrasian equilibrium. An oil price rise has a negative effect on both the supply of and the demand for domestic output, and so the answer depends on which dominates. If the reduction in demand is bigger then excess supply, i.e. Keynesian unemployment, is the outcome, while excess demand, i.e. classical unemployment, is the result in the opposite case. The merit of the present model for analyzing this question is that it enables more of the very many factors which bear on demand and supply, including expectations of future variables, to be taken into account. Van Wijnbergen's argument is that the supply shock is more likely to have dominated in developed countries and the demand shock in less developed countries, because production technology is more oil intensive in the former. This argument is put forward to explain why Europe experienced unemployment which was unresponsive to traditional demand expansion policies, while less developed countries such as Korea were able to reflate out of recession. A related paper by Buffie (1986), although not using an intertemporal framework, provides a more detailed analysis of how production technology affects the regime. In Buffie's model unemployment turns out to be Keynesian or classical following a jump in the oil price according as the elasticity of substitution between value added and oil is (respectively) less than or greater than unity.

3   Monetary models

Although real models offer many valuable insights, no macroeconomic model is complete if it is impossible to examine monetary policy within it, which in the open economy context means, in particular, being able to examine the influence of the nominal exchange rate regime. An intertemporal structure sharpens the question of exactly how money should be introduced. The one-period models of the early literature generally used the "temporary equilibrium" approach in which money is the only asset and so the demand for money is the same as the demand for saving, or for future consumption. This is represented by including money in the utility function and interpreting the latter as a "partially indirect" utility function proxying utility of future consumption.[10] In multi-period models where there are already assets in the form of interest-bearing bonds, if there is to be a positive demand for non-interest-bearing money then money must have some role over and above being a store of value. Such a role would usually be taken to be a "transactions" role. One way of representing this formally is to impose Clower's (1967) "cash-in-advance" constraint, which makes it a rule that at the start of a period an agent must hold at least as much money as the value of her intended purchases during the period. This constraint was revived by Helpman (1981) for use in open economies, and his specification of it has been followed in most subsequent applications. An alternative approach is to represent the transactions services provided by money by including real money balances in agents' utility function. This was first used, in the economic growth context, by Sidrauski (1967), and Feenstra (1986) has recently studied the precise conditions necessary to justify it in more rigorous terms. We accordingly divide this section between models which rely on these two different approaches.

3.1   Cash in advance

3.1.1   Two countries with purchasing power parity

The first intertemporal quantity-constrained model to include money was that of Persson (1982). Persson's is a two-country model constructed in order to examine macroeconomic interdependence. The goods and labor market structure is the very simple one used by Dixit (1978). There is a single world output which is traded in a flex-price market so that purchasing power parity (PPP) $p_t = E_t p_t^*$ holds at all times (where E_t is the domestic-currency price of foreign currency). The money wage is rigid, making output an increasing function of price, $y(p_t)$, as in the textbook aggregate supply relation. Under the cash-in-advance specification households receive factor payments with a one-period lag and at the start of each peiod must decide how much to convert into bonds (domestic- and foreign-currency bonds being perfect substitutes, given no uncertainty and perfect foresight), how much to convert into foreign currency, and how much to hold as domestic currency. It is assumed that each country's goods must be paid for in the seller's currency.[11] Given the interest cost of holding more currency than is necessary to finance purchases, rational households will demand currency to exactly the value of their planned consumption of each country's output, so that in money market equilibrium each country's money supply just equals the nominal value of its output.

First, consider the determination of output under a floating exchange rate. Persson assumes that each government purchases g_t of its own country's output, for which it also needs to hold cash in advance. It raises this cash either by levying a lump-sum tax T_t on households at the start of the period or by issuing new money, so that the supply of domestic currency at the start of period t is $M_t = M_{t-1} - T_t + p_t g_t$. Money market equilibrium then requires

$$p_t y(p_t) = M_{t-1} - T_t + p_t g_t \qquad (1.21)$$

Equation (1.21) determines p_t directly, and so also y_t. Thus we see that, first, expectations of future variables are irrelevant to current output. The model is therefore essentially a static one as far as price and output are concerned. The intertemporal structure thus only matters for consumption and for the trade balance (which is just the gap between supply and demand). Second, foreign variables are irrelevant for domestic output. Under a floating exchange rate output is therefore insulated from foreign shocks. This insulation property holds despite perfect capital mobility, which in the textbook Mundell–Fleming model destroys the insulating properties of a floating regime. As in the Mundell–Fleming model, however, pure fiscal policy is unable to affect output. A tax-financed increase in g_t, since it leaves M_t (i.e. the right-hand side of (1.21)) unchanged, has no effect on p_t or y_t.

Next suppose the exchange rate is fixed ($E_t = 1$). Persson assumes that this is brought about by a rule for intervention in the foreign exchange markets such that the world money supply is held constant. For example, this may arise with an arrangement in which the country with a balance of payments surplus makes a gift of its currency to the deficit country, which then sells it to maintain the parity. In equilibrium world money demand must equal world money supply:

$$p_t[y(p_t) + y^*(p_t)] = M_{t-1} - T_t + p_t g_t + M^*_{t-1} - T^*_t + p_t g^*_t \qquad (1.22)$$

It is clear from this that any policy which raises the world money supply, i.e. the right-hand side of (1.22), such as an increase in g_t or a cut in T_t, will increase both countries' outputs. Under fixed exchange rates, therefore, insulation from foreign shocks no longer obtains, but it remains true that expectations of future variables are irrelevant for current outputs.

3.1.2   Nontraded goods

Cuddington and Vinals (1986a, b) extend Persson's (1982) model to include a nontraded sector (though they consider a small country rather than two countries). Their model thus constitutes an intertemporal version of Neary's (1980), just as Persson's constitutes an intertemporal version of Dixit's (1978). The first-period price of nontraded goods is fixed: in the 1986a paper this is assumed to cause excess supply in the nontradeables market, i.e. a Keynesian unemployment regime; in the

1986b paper it is assumed to cause excess demand, i.e. a classical unemployment regime. Under a fixed exchange rate, as shown by Neary (1980), a nontraded sector in excess supply restores the Keynesian multiplier to the model, this being absent from the one-sector model under a fixed exchange rate. This model is therefore an example of the use of the Salter–Swan structure to obtain Keynesian properties, as an alternative to the Mundell–Fleming structure used by van Wijnbergen. The cash-in-advance constraint again means that the money supply must equal the value of output, and so with two output sectors money market equilibrium now requires, in period 1,

$$p_1[y_{N1} + \rho_1 y_{T1}(\rho_1)] = M_0 - T_1 + p_1 g_{N1} \qquad (1.23)$$

Tradeables output y_{T1} is supply determined as before, depending only on the tradeables price, which (since there is an exogenous nontradeables price p_1) in turn depends only on the relative price or real exchange rate $\rho_1 \equiv E_1/p_1$.[12] However, with Keynesian unemployment, nontradeables output y_{N1} is demand determined. Under a regime of floating exchange rates (1.23) thus contains two endogenous variables (y_{N1}, ρ_1) and so is no longer sufficient by itself to tie down the equilibrium. This means that expected future variables and foreign variables are now able to affect domestic output, unlike in Persson's model. Pure fiscal policy remains essentially ineffective: if the government holds the current money stock M_1 (i.e. the right-hand side of (1.23)) constant, aggregate nominal output (i.e. the left-hand side of (1.23)), and thus also aggregate real output in nontradeables units, must clearly remain constant whatever value is chosen for g_{N1} – although its composition can be altered.

Cuddington and Vinals use their model primarily to study the "twin deficits" problem. In the 1986a paper the Keynesian unemployment regime is considered and is suggested – as by van Wijnbergen – to be a good representation of the USA in the early 1980s. In the 1986b paper, the classical unemployment regime is the one under scrutiny and is claimed to describe several European countries in the early 1980s. In the Keynesian regime it is found that a current government spending increase worsens, and an anticipated future increase improves, the current trade balance. It is the failure of monetary policy to accommodate the increase in nontradeables output which causes the exchange rate to appreciate and the current account to worsen: if the fiscal expansion is money financed rather than tax financed, the "quasi-neutral" outcome obtained by van Wijnbergen under Ricardian equivalence reappears. In the classical regime higher first-period spending has either no effect or a beneficial effect on the current account, depending on whether it is tax or money financed. This possibility of a *positive* trade balance effect under classical unemployment is broadly in line with van Wijnbergen's findings, cited earlier.

3.2   Utility of real balances

3.2.1   *The Mundell model revisited*

The restrictiveness of the simple cash-in-advance treatment of money demand when our main interest is in the determination of output is most clearly seen by comparing the above results with those of otherwise very similar models which use instead the utility-of-real-balances approach. A model identical to that of Persson (1982) save in its treatment of money demand is that of Rankin (1989). On the question of macroeconomic interdependence – the main focus of both papers – with a floating exchange rate Rankin finds that a current foreign fiscal expansion boosts, and a foreign monetary expansion depresses, output in the home country. These findings replicate the standard ones of Mundell (1968) for a two-country IS–LM model. In Persson's model, by contrast, under a floating exchange rate the cash-in-advance approach automatically excludes any effect of foreign macroeconomic policies on domestic output, as seen above. A difference from Mundell's standard findings obtained by Rankin is that an anticipated future foreign fiscal expansion *lowers* current home output, so that a permanent foreign fiscal expansion has an overall ambiguous effect on domestic activity (being just the sum of the two separate effects).

The earliest intertemporal quantity-constrained open economy model to use the utility-of-real-balances approach was that of Fender (1986). Since it includes a nontraded sector, this may be seen as a utility-of-real-balances version of the model of Cuddington and Vinals. Fender's is a small-country model and his concern is with monetary policy: the main novel result demonstrated is that an anticipated future monetary expansion may cause the current exchange rate to appreciate. In conventional models it *de*preciates, because the future exchange rate depreciates and the expectation of this requires a rise in the nominal interest rate to maintain the same rate of return for foreign investors (the "uncovered interest parity" (UIP) condition), which then lowers the current demand for domestic currency causing its price to fall. In Fender's model money demand depends also on lifetime wealth,[13] which rises since future tradeables output is stimulated by the future depreciation, and this has a counteracting positive effect on current demand for the currency which may outweigh the effect via the interest rate. A similar model, without a nontraded sector but including a second tradeables sector, is used by Fender and Yip (1989) to examine the employment effects of tariffs. The conventional presumption is that although tariffs boost employment under a fixed exchange rate by raising the price earned by import-competing firms, under a floating exchange rate they lower it, since the induced appreciation of the currency reduces the competitiveness of both sectors. Fender and Yip show that the latter result may be reversed if a sufficiently high proportion of initial employment is in the import-competing sector.

The question of macroeconomic interdependence has already been raised in discussing the papers by Persson (1982) and Rankin (1989). Interest in this question was revived in the 1980s by the over-valuation of the dollar, which cast doubt on the value of freely floating exchange rates, and by worries over the effects on the world economy of the high interest rates thought to be associated with large US budget deficits. Consequently calls for greater international macroeconomic policy coordination were heard, and tentative steps were taken towards this in the form of the Plaza and Louvre agreements of 1985 and 1987. It is still the case, however, that our understanding of interdependence is at a rudimentary stage compared with our understanding of own-country effects. A serious limitation of Persson's and Rankin's papers for analyzing interdependence is that the assumption of a single homogeneous product removes the possibility of real exchange rate changes. This limitation is overcome in further studies of interdependence by Svensson (1987), Svensson and van Wijnbergen (1989), and Rankin (1988). The first two are companion papers which use the same model to consider (respectively) fiscal and monetary spillovers. The model is based on a cash-in-advance approach to money demand but modified by the inclusion of stochastic shocks which are assumed to be known only after the money-holding decision has been made. This gives rise to an interest- and wealth-sensitive "precautionary" demand for money, which relaxes the unitary velocity of circulation imposed in simpler models and hence is closer to the utility-of-real-balances approach. The interesting findings in all three papers[14] are that the signs of international monetary and fiscal spillovers depend critically on substitutability between goods in consumers' preferences. Gross substitutability between domestic and foreign outputs leads to negative monetary spillovers and gross complementarity to positive monetary spillovers, while fiscal spillovers, although zero for current policy in the Keynesian regime, again depend on substitutability in the case of anticipated future policy or in other regimes. This is markedly different from the two-country IS–LM analysis of Mundell (1968), where fiscal policy has a positive spillover and monetary policy a negative one independently of the degree of substitutability.

3.2.2 Two countries with imperfect substitution between home and foreign goods

To demonstrate some of these findings we consider Rankin's (1988) model, which uses the familiar two-period fix/flex-price framework.[15] This is essentially a two-country monetary version of the van Wijnbergen model considered in section 2 (although it excludes investment and differing private/public discount rates). The home consumer faces the problem:

$$\text{maximize} \qquad u = c_1^\alpha \left[\frac{M_1}{P_2}\right]^\gamma c_2^\delta \left[\frac{M_2}{P_2}\right]^\zeta \qquad \alpha + \beta + \gamma + \zeta = 1 \qquad (1.24)$$

where

$$c_t = [\beta h_t^\rho + [1 - \beta] f_t^\rho]^{1/\rho} \qquad \rho < 1, 0 < \beta < 1 \qquad (1.25)$$

subject to the budget constraint

$$a = h_1 + e_1 f_1 + \frac{i d M_1}{p_2} + d h_2 + d e_2 f_2 + \frac{d M_2}{p_2} \qquad (1.26)$$

Utility thus includes real balances (deflated by the consumer price index P_2), and subutility over home and foreign goods incorporates a constant elasticity of substitution $1/(1 - \rho)$. (p_t now denotes the money price of home goods, e_t the real exchange rate, and i the nominal interest rate.) The lifetime budget constraint now includes final real balances and the forgone interest due to holding M_1.[16] This gives rise to the demand functions

$$h_1 = \frac{\alpha a}{1 + \phi(e_1)} = h_1(\underset{(+)}{a}, \underset{(?)}{e_1}) \qquad (1.27)$$

$$f_1 = \frac{\alpha a}{e_1} \frac{\phi(e_1)}{1 + \phi(e_1)} = f_1(\underset{(+)}{a}, \underset{(-)}{e_1}) \qquad (1.28)$$

$$h_2 = \frac{\delta a}{d[1 + \phi(e_2)]} = h_2(\underset{(+)}{a}, \underset{(?)}{e_2}, \underset{(-)}{d}) \qquad (1.29)$$

$$f_2 = \frac{\delta a}{d e_2} \frac{\phi(e_2)}{1 + \phi(e_2)} = f_2(\underset{(+)}{a}, \underset{(-)}{e_2}, \underset{(-)}{d}) \qquad (1.30)$$

$$\frac{M_1}{p_2} = \frac{\gamma a}{i d} = m_1(\underset{(+)}{a}, \underset{(-)}{i}, \underset{(-)}{d}) \qquad (1.31)$$

$$\frac{M_2}{p_2} = \frac{\zeta a}{d} = m_2(\underset{(+)}{a}, \underset{(-)}{d}) \qquad (1.32)$$

where

$$\phi(e_t) = \left[\frac{1}{\beta} - 1\right]^{1/(1-\rho)} e_t^{\rho/(\rho-1)} \tag{1.33}$$

Note that $\phi(.)$ is decreasing or increasing, respectively, as home and foreign goods are gross substitutes or complements ($\rho > 0$ or $\rho < 0$).

An interesting feature of all such utility-of-real-balances models is that the nominal interest rate depends only on the ratio of the two money supplies. To see this, note that under floating exchange rates M_1, M_2 are exogenous variables and that (1.31) and (1.32) may hence be treated as the money-market clearing, or LM, equations of the model. Dividing (1.32) by (1.30) then gives

$$i = \frac{\gamma}{\zeta}\frac{M_2}{M_1} \tag{1.34}$$

We may also use this to show the close connection between (M_1, M_2) and the equilibrium value of household wealth, a. Inverting (1.32) and substituting for i (note $d/p_2 \equiv 1/(1 + i)p_1$) gives

$$a = \frac{M_1 M_2}{[\zeta M_1 + \gamma M_2]p_1} \tag{1.35}$$

Thus (since p_1 is exogenous), both a and i in equilibrium depend only on the exogenous instruments of monetary policy, M_1, M_2. The *composition* of household wealth has not yet been mentioned. As in section 2 it consists of the present value of disposable income, but it also includes an initial endowment of real balances M_0/p_1. When we consolidate it with the intertemporal government budget constraint by using the latter to eliminate τ_2 (as was done in deriving (1.15) in section 2), we obtain

$$a = y_1 - g_1 + d[y_2 - g_2] + \frac{iM_1 + M_2}{[1 + i]p_1} \tag{1.36}$$

M_1 and M_2 enter because government spending may now be money financed as well as tax financed.

A useful condition in defining the overall equilibrium is the balance of payments constraint:

$$h_1^* - e_1 f_1 = -d[h_2^* - e_2 f_2] \tag{1.37}$$

This says that any first-period trade surplus of the home country must be matched by a second-period deficit of equal present value, i.e. that the country must balance its account with the rest of the world in an intertemporal sense. It is derived by eliminating a between (1.26) and

(1.36) and canceling terms using the IS_1 and GM_2 equations, which as in section 2 are given by

$$y_1 = h_1 + h_1^* + g_1 \qquad IS_1 \qquad (1.38)$$

$$\bar{y}_2 = h_2 + h_2^* + g_2 \qquad GM_2 \qquad (1.39)$$

A final equilibrium condition is provided by the assumption of perfect capital mobility, which implies the UIP equation

$$d = d^* e_1/e_2 \qquad UIP \qquad (1.40)$$

Here d is the real discount rate measured in home output units and d^* is the discount rate measured in foreign output units, so that arbitrage ensures that any difference between them must be made up by an expected real depreciation or appreciation, e_1/e_2.

Before looking at the equilibrium of the full two-country model, some remarks on the case of a small open economy may be of interest. We can solve the model under the assumption that the home country is "small" by treating the foreign country as "large" and so taking (a^*, d^*) to be exogenous. (A fuller examination of the small-country case can be found in Rankin (1988).) The model which results is essentially a micro foundations version of the textbook Mundell–Fleming model. A well-known implication of this model is that, under a floating exchange rate, perfect capital mobility makes fiscal policy completely ineffective, and we have seen that this conclusion carries over to Persson's (1982) and to Cuddington and Vinals' (1986a) cash-in-advance quantity-constrained models. However, in the present framework fiscal policy is still effective. The balanced-budget multiplier is in fact unity. The reason for this is easy to see from a modified "directly postulated" IS–LM model such as the following:

$$y = c(y - \tau) + g + b(y - \tau, e) \qquad IS$$

$$M/p = m(y - \tau, i^*) \qquad LM$$

In the standard analysis an increase in g (whether accompanied by an increase in τ or not) is unable to affect y because y is determined directly by the LM equation, given that (M, p, i^*) are exogenous. In the version here, however, as in our full model above, a difference is that money demand depends on income net of tax, $y - \tau$, rather than on gross income, as is more usually assumed. In the full model this emerges from the optimization process, as may be seen from inspecting (1.31) and (1.32), and so is not just an arbitrary assumption. It is immediate from the above equations that an equal increase in g and τ[17] must raise y by the same amount, to keep the LM in balance. This breakdown of the fiscal ineffectiveness result suggests that it is due to the special nature of the "postulated" money demand function assumed in the Mundell–Fleming approach or to the simple "quantity theory" form taken by money demand in the cash-in-advance approach. That ineffectiveness is not robust to plausible changes in the model has already been suggested by Branson and Buiter (1983).[18] Here we have further support for such a view.

We now return to the two-country version. Equilibrium may be depicted as the intersection of two curves – BB and GG – in (e_1, e_2) space. BB is the balance of payments constraint (1.37) with the demands substituted in from (1.27)–(1.30) (and by qualitatively symmetric analogs for demands by the foreign country). The UIP condition (1.40) causes (d, d^*) to drop out. GG is obtained by likewise substituting in the demands to GM_2 and to its similar foreign counterpart GM_2^*, and then combining GM_2, GM_2^* and UIP to eliminate (d, d^*):

$$e_1 = \frac{a}{a^*} \frac{\alpha\phi(e_1)/[1 + \phi(e_1)] + \delta\phi(e_2)/[1 + \phi(e_2)]}{\alpha^*\phi^*(1/e_1)/[1 + \phi^*(1/e_1)] + \delta^*\phi^*(1/e_2)/[1 + \phi^*(1/e_2)]} \quad \text{BB}$$

(1.41)

$$e_1 = \frac{\delta a}{\delta^* a^*} \frac{1 + \phi^*(1/e_2)}{1 + \phi(e_2)} \frac{[\bar{y}_2^* - g_2^*]e_2 - [\bar{y}_2 - g_2]\phi(e_2)}{[\bar{y}_2 - g_2] - [\bar{y}_2^* - g_2^*]e_2\phi^*(1/e_2)} \quad \text{GG}$$

(1.42)

Recalling (1.33), it can be seen that GG is upward sloping for positive, zero and small negative ρ, ρ^*.[19] BB, on the other hand, can be seen to be vertical in the "benchmark" case in which ρ, ρ^* are zero (ϕ, ϕ^* are then constants), but respectively downward or upward sloping when ρ, ρ^* are moved above or below zero. This is shown in figure 1.3. With e_1 determined by BB and GG, y_1 may finally be found from the IS_1 equation (1.38), which when the demand functions are substituted is

$$y_1 = \frac{\alpha a}{1 + \phi(e_1)} + \frac{\alpha^* a^* e_1 \phi^*(1/e_1)}{1 + \phi^*(1/e_1)} \quad IS_1$$

(1.43)

From this, y_1 is evidently increasing in e_1 for positive, zero and small negative ρ, ρ^*.

What is the impact of a foreign fiscal expansion on home output? We can see that g_1^* does not enter BB or GG, so that e_1, e_2 must remain unchanged. Then from (1.43) y_1 also remains unchanged: there is a zero spillover. This is just an extension of the "quasi-neutrality" already observed in the van Wijnbergen model. However, a different outcome

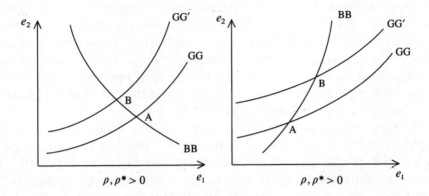

Figure 1.3   Equilibrium in the two-country model.

is obtained in the case of an anticipated future foreign fiscal expansion. An increase in g_2^* can be seen to leave BB unchanged but to shift GG left, causing a move from A to B in figure 1.3. Thus e_1 appreciates if $\rho, \rho^* > 0$ and depreciates if $\rho, \rho^* < 0$, with (from (1.43)) a negative or positive effect, respectively, on y_1. A *permanent* foreign fiscal expansion, i.e. an equal increase in g_1^* and g_2^*, thus has a negative or positive spillover on home output according as the countries' products are gross substitutes or complements in consumption.

A foreign monetary expansion, whether in M_1^* or M_2^*, may be represented by an increase in a^*, as shown by (1.35). This can be seen to shift both BB and GG to the left. e_1 then clearly appreciates for positive, zero and small negative ρ, ρ^*. The change in y_1 is hence ambiguous, as can be seen from (1.43): the increase in a^* has a positive "export multiplier" effect, but this is counteracted by the appreciation of the home country's exchange rate. By resorting to differentiation we can show that the positive effect dominates if and only if $\rho, \rho^* < 0$. Thus, as with fiscal policy, monetary policy has a negative or positive spillover according as countries' outputs are gross substitutes or complements.

4   Conclusions

Quantity-constrained equilibrium has proved to be a versatile tool for improving our analytical understanding of the macroeconomic transmission mechanisms at work in open economies. In the 1980s, unlike in the 1970s, most of the modeling questions which have arisen in quantity-constrained models have not been about the quantity-constrained equilibrium concept itself but about how best to represent the sectoral structure of an open economy, or how to incorporate financial aspects such as money and non-neutral bonds. The focus has also shifted from internal questions of modeling techniques to external questions of the real-world events which it is hoped to explain, such as the effects of fiscal deficits on the trade balance and on other countries or the effects of oil price shocks on open economies.

A number of gaps remain to be filled. The real models give an important role to investment but neglect financial considerations. A synthesis of investment, money and Ricardian nonequivalence has still to be made. Monetary models, although in principle permitting a comparison of nominal exchange rate regimes, have in practice nearly all focused on the case of floating exchange rates. The case of fixed exchange rates requires further exploration. Relaxation of the ubiquitous perfect capital mobility assumption would also be desirable. Implicitly, domestic and foreign bonds are imperfect substitutes in the stochastic models of Svensson (1987) and Svensson and van Wijnbergen (1989), but the role of imperfect substitutability is not the primary focus of these papers. An attempt to look at this more directly is made in Rankin (1992). A longer-run development of the literature would also be to consider applications of alternative non-Walrasian equilibrium concepts, in order to test how endogeneity of price setting can influence results. The work on imperfect competition in open economies (see chapter 2 in this volume), although still in its infancy, may be a natural successor.

Notes

1   For example by Begg (1982).
2   See, for example, Svensson and Razin (1983) and chapters 3 and 15 in this volume.
3   And, in period 1, less investment, which may be thought of as financed out of retained earnings.
4   Since domestic output is also used for investment, this would be altered if the firm were allowed to use its own output for investment. We are thus implicitly imposing a rule that it must buy its investment goods from other firms.
5   The other possible disequilibrium regimes are repressed inflation (excess demand in both markets) and classical unemployment (excess supply of labor, excess demand for goods). Here we opt to devote the available space to the more interesting Keynesian unemployment regime(s); see van Wijnbergen for an analysis of the others, and of the determination of the regime itself.
6   This follows from the fact that the firm is demand constrained: a higher value of $\bar{y}_2$ must make possible a higher maximized value of the firm, $dp_2 y_2 - p_1 i - dw_2 l_2$.

7 Persson and Svensson (1983), Cuddington and Vinals (1986a), Fender and Yip (1989), Moore (1989), Rankin (1988, 1989).

8 The reason output can increase at all, despite full wage indexation, is that a rise in p_1 lowers the real product wage more than it lowers the real consumption wage.

9 A contributory factor in generating this contrasting result is that Ricardian equivalence (i.e. $d_g = d$) is assumed by Moore. If this were relaxed, a counteracting expansionary force would be introduced.

10 The monetary temporary equilibrium concept goes back to Patinkin (1958). In the Walrasian context, Grandmont (1983) provides a definitive modern discussion.

11 This is referred to as the S-system, as opposed to the alternative B-system where the buyer's currency is used. The choice of system affects the results, and the S-system is closer to observed practice.

12 Normalizing the exogenous foreign price of tradeables to unity, the tradeables price just equals E_1 by the PPP condition.

13 A concrete example of this sort of money demand function is provided in (1.31) below.

14 All these analyses are for floating exchange rates.

15 The other two papers use an infinite-horizon framework with one-period predetermined prices. See Svensson (1986) for the original closed economy version.

16 This may be derived by writing down the two single-period budget constraints and eliminating bond holdings between them. An oddity of the cash-in-advance approach is that households incur no interest cost of holding money since they acquire money at the start of the period and spend it before the end. It is hence effectively firms who "hold" the money stock between periods.

17 Remember that, since Ricardian equivalence holds, any change in government spending must be considered as a balanced-budget change.

18 Their model is directly postulated and the mechanism is different: the exchange rate appreciates, lowering the consumer price index and so increasing the stock of real money balances.

19 The numerator and denominator of the third term in GG are positive provided that we assume (sufficient) quantitative symmetry between the two countries (whence $e_2 = 1$) and that consumers have a preference for their own country's product (from (1.33), $\phi(1) < 1$ if $\beta > 1/2$).

References

Barro, R.J. and H.I. Grossman (1971) "A general disequilibrium model of income and employment," *American Economic Review* 61, 82–93.

Begg, D.K.H. (1982) *The Rational Expectations Revolution in Macroeconomics*, Oxford, Philip Allen.

Benassy, J.-P. (1975) "Neo-Keynesian disequilibrium theory in a monetary economy," *Review of Economic Studies* 42, 503–23.

Blanchard, O.J. and S. Fischer (1989) *Lectures on Macroeconomics*, Cambridge, MA, MIT Press.

Branson, W.H. and W.H. Buiter (1983) "Monetary and fiscal policy with flexible exchange rates," in Bhandari and Putnam (eds) *Economic Interdependence and Flexible Exchange Rates*, Cambridge, MA, MIT Press.

Buffie, E.F. (1986) "Input price shocks in the small open economy," *Oxford Economic Papers* 38, 551–65.

Clower, R.W. (1967) "A reconsideration of the microfoundations of monetary theory," *Western Economic Journal* 6, 1–8.

Cuddington, J.T. and J.M. Vinals (1986a) "Budget deficits and the current account: an intertemporal disequilibrium approach," *Journal of International Economics* 21, 1–24.

—— and —— (1986b) "Budget deficits and the current account in the presence of classical unemployment," *Economic Journal* 96, 101–19.

——, P.-O. Johansson and K.-G. Lofgren (1984) *Disequilibrium Macroeconomics in Open Economies*, Oxford, Blackwell.

Dixit, A.K. (1978) "The balance of trade in a model of temporary equilibrium with rationing," *Review of Economic Studies* 45, 393–404.

Feenstra, R.C. (1986) "Functional equivalence between liquidity costs and the utility of money," *Journal of Monetary Economics* 17, 271–91.

Fender, J. (1986) "Monetary and exchange rate policies in an open macroeconomic model with unemployment and rational expectations," *Oxford Economic Papers* 38, 501–15.

—— and C.K. Yip (1989) "Tariffs and employment: an intertemporal approach," *Economic Journal* 99, 806–17.

Frenkel, J.A. and A. Razin (1987) *Fiscal Policies and the World Economy*, Cambridge, MA, MIT Press.

Grandmont, J.-M. (1983) *Money and Value*, Cambridge, Cambridge University Press.

Green, J. and J.-J. Laffont (1981) "Disequilibrium dynamics with inventories and anticipatory price-setting," *European Economic Review* 16, 191–221.

Helpman, E. (1981) "An exploration in the theory of exchange rate regimes," *Journal of Political Economy* 89, 865–90.

Malinvaud, E. (1977) *The Theory of Unemployment Reconsidered*, Oxford, Blackwell.

Moore, M.J. (1989) "Inventories in the open-economy macromodel: a disequilibrium analysis," *Review of Economic Studies* 56, 157–62.

—— and J.P. Neary (1985) "Déséquilibre intertemporel dans une économie ouverte," in P.Y. Henin, W. Marois and P. Michel (eds) *Déséquilibres en economie ouverte*, Paris, Economica.

Mundell, R.A. (1968) *International Economics*, New York, Macmillan.

Neary, J.P. (1980) "Non-traded goods and the balance of trade in a neo-Keynesian temporary equilibrium," *Quarterly Journal of Economics* 95, 403–29.

—— (1990) "Neo-Keynesian macroeconomics in an open economy," in F. van der Ploeg (ed.) *Advanced Lectures in Quantitative Economics*, London, Academic Press.

—— and J.E. Stiglitz (1983) "Towards a reconstruction of Keynesian economics: expectations and constrained equilibria," *Quarterly Journal of Economics* 98, suppl., 199–228.

Patinkin, D. (1958) *Money, Interest and Prices*, New York, Harper and Row.

Persson, T. (1982) "Global effects of national stabilisation policies under fixed and floating exchange rates," *Scandinavian Journal of Economics* 64, 165–92.

—— and L.E.O. Svensson (1983) "Is optimism good in a Keynesian economy?" *Economica* 50, 301–10.

Rankin, N. (1988) "Macroeconomic interdependence, floating exchange rates and product substitutability," *Greek Economic Review* 10, 162–84 (reprinted in A.S. Courakis and M.P. Taylor (eds) *Private Behaviour and Government Policy in Interdependent Economies*, Oxford, Oxford University Press, 1990).

—— (1989) "Monetary, fiscal and exchange intervention policy in a two-country intertemporal disequilibrium model," *European Economic Review* 33, 1463–80.

—— (1992) "Policy uncertainty and capital mobility in a small open economy," mimeo, Warwick University.

Sidrauski, M. (1967) "Rational choice and patterns of growth in a monetary economy," *American Economic Review* 57, 534–44.

Svensson, L.E.O. (1986) "Sticky goods prices, flexible asset prices, monopolistic competition and monetary policy," *Review of Economic Studies* 53, 385–405.

—— (1987) "International fiscal policy transmission," *Scandinavian Journal of Economics* 89, 305–34.

—— and A. Razin (1983) "The terms of trade and the current account: the Harberger–Laursen–Metzler effect," *Journal of Political Economy* 91, 97–125.

—— and S. van Wijnbergen (1989) "Excess capacity, monopolistic competition and international transmission of monetary disturbances," *Economic Journal* 99, 785–805.

van Wijnbergen, S. (1985) "Oil price shocks, private investment, employment and the current account: an intertemporal disequilibrium analysis," *Review of Economic Studies* 52, 627–45.

—— (1987) "Government deficits, private investment and the current account: an intertemporal disequilibrium analysis," *Economic Journal* 97, 596–615.

2 Imperfect Competition and Open Economy Macroeconomics

HUW D. DIXON

1 Introduction

There is now a large and established literature on imperfect competition in closed economies, surveyed by Dixon and Rankin (1994) and Silvestre (1993). The origins of this literature stemmed from the desire to make prices endogenous in the fix-price models of the 1970s (see, for example, Benassy, 1976, 1978; Negishi, 1979). The literature took off, however, with Hart's (1982) paper, which provided a simple and tractable model with a clear macroeconomic content. Since then, on both sides of the Atlantic there has been the development of the New Keynesian school of macroeconomics which seeks to put imperfect competition at the center of macroeconomic models (see *inter alia* Akerlof and Yellen, 1985; Mankiw, 1985; Blanchard and Kiyotaki, 1987; Benassy, 1987; Dixon, 1987, 1988). This approach provides the most coherent challenge to the Walrasian view of the New Classical macroeconomics.

It is worthwhile to state the case for imperfect competition in macroeconomic models. First, in a Walrasian framework (of whatever vintage) there is little or no scope in principle for macroeconomic policy to be effective or useful. From the two fundamental theorems of welfare economics, we know that Walrasian equilibria are Pareto optimal as long as there is a complete system of (spot and forward) contingent markets. If we start from a position of Pareto optimality, then typically there will be little or no role for government intervention of any kind, and in particular no role for macroeconomic intervention. With imperfect competition, in contrast, the equilibrium itself is not typically Pareto optimal – as in the prisoner's dilemma, agents acting strategically in their own interest will give rise to a socially suboptimal

(Pareto-inefficient) outcome. Imperfect competition provides a more satisfactory framework in which to evaluate the need for and effects of macroeconomic policy. Second, imperfect competition provides a more satisfactory model of wage and price determination than does the competitive "supply-and-demand" framework. There is a central paradox in competitive markets, where all agents are assumed to be price-takers, yet prices need to adjust to clear markets. No such paradox is present in imperfectly competitive models, where optimizing agents set wages and prices. Furthermore, imperfectly competitive models often *generalize* the competitive model in the sense that perfect competition is often a special or limiting case of imperfect competition. Last, but not least, there is the empirical observation that in many markets in many countries market power is exercised, whether we are talking about highly concentrated product markets or unionized labor markets.

The main theme to emerge from the literature in imperfect competition and macroeconomics is that the welfare properties of equilibrium and policy are radically different from the Walrasian case. First, imperfect competition in either the output or the labor market typically gives rise to a Pareto-inefficient equilibrium in which there is too little output and employment (one need only consider the standard models of the monopolist or monopoly union). Second, if we start from a situation where the market prices of output and/or labor exceed their social shadow price, any policy (monetary or fiscal) that raises output is more likely to have a welfare-improving effect than in Walrasian models. See, for example, the beneficial effects of monetary policy with menu costs (Akerlof and Yellen, 1985; Mankiw, 1985; Blanchard and Kiyotaki, 1987), and of fiscal policy (Benassy, 1991; Dixon, 1990b, 1991).

There has, as yet, been little literature developing the theme of imperfect competition in open economy models. This literature divides into three groups. First, there is the issue of exchange rate pass-through concerned with how prices respond to a devaluation of the exchange rate. Most of these models have been of a partial equilibrium nature, exploring an oligopolistic output market with home and foreign firms competing. A devaluation then alters the relative costs of home and foreign firms, leading also to changes in prices (see, for example, Aizenman, 1989; Dornbusch, 1987; Froot and Klemperer, 1989; Giovannini, 1988). By focusing on the product market, treating costs (such as wages) as unaffected by devaluation, these papers ignore any long-run general equilibrium effects of a devaluation. The only paper to evaluate pass-through in a general equilibrium imperfectly competitive framework is that of Campos (1991). Second, there is the issue of real-wage resistance. This has been explored in an open economy wage-bargaining model by Ellis and Fender (1987). Third, there is the issue of standard monetary and fiscal policy effectiveness under different nominal exchange rate regimes. This has been explored for a unionized economy under floating exchange rates by Dixon (1990a). Helpman (1988) also considers the effect of price controls on the macroeconomic impact of demand changes in a small open economy.

In this chapter we shall develop a simple general equilibrium macromodel of an open economy. We have chosen to focus on imperfect competition in the output market, leaving the labor market perfectly competitive. This is not because we believe that labor markets are actually competitive. Far from it. Rather, we want to show that, even with labor-market clearing, imperfect competition in the output market is on its own enough to generate substantially different welfare effects for policy. Indeed, throughout the chapter we shall focus on the welfare analysis of policy (and its contrast with the Walrasian case).

2   A two-sector model of a small open economy

We shall be considering a two-sector model of a small open economy. The precise interpretation of the two sectors will vary slightly. However, we can specify them broadly as follows.

1   The *domestic sector* consists of oligopolistic industries meeting domestic consumer demand. In the absence of any foreign competition, this will be a *nontraded* sector. Firms in this sector have market power, and an increasing returns to scale technology.

2   The *export sector* consists of perfectly competitive price-taking firms who supply a traded good to foreign and domestic consumers at exogenous world prices. Following Neary (1980), we abstract from the distinction between goods which are net exports and net imports. These firms are assumed to have diminishing returns to scale.

It should be immediately apparent that the presence of increasing returns to scale in the domestic sector marks a decisive shift away from the competitive paradigm, as has been seen in the new international trade theory. The government is assumed to spend money purchasing the output of the domestic sector. This expenditure is regarded as "waste." Whilst we recognize that this is not a very realistic assumption (most government expenditure goes on health and education), it serves to focus on the purely *macroeconomic* implications of fiscal policy. For similar reasons, the government raises a lump-sum tax (for the alternative treatments of taxation in imperfectly competitive models, see Molana and Moutos (1992)).

Clearly, the choice of model structure for this chapter is one of many possible ways of modeling an imperfectly competitive open economy. For example, we could have allowed unions in the labor market. We could have allowed for imperfect competition in the export sector. Perfect competition in the export sector is mainly for parsimony, since it means that we need not model the rest of the world in any detail. This chapter focuses on imperfect competition in the *output* market, in contrast with the existing papers in the open economy literature (Ellis and Fender, 1987; Dixon, 1990a). Clearly, the exercise of market power by unions can lead to real wages above the market clearing level, and hence to some form of involuntary unemployment. However, as we shall see, the presence of imperfect competition in the domestic sector output market is *in itself* a cause of distortion leading to Pareto suboptimality, and also it is enough to make possible welfare-improving monetary and fiscal policy. The implications of firm–union bargaining in the framework developed in this chapter are explored in Dixon and Santoni (1992).

2.1   Households

There is a continuum of measure H (or just plain H households) who each supply up to one unit of labor. Since we shall be assuming that households have suitable preferences for aggregation, we shall save notation by dealing with a single leviathan (or representative) household with H units of labor. This household consumes domestic sector output c^D, traded sector output c^T, and real money balances (where the latter can be derived as a mixed indirect utility function or proxy for an overlapping generations model (see Campos, 1991). Initial money balances are denoted M^0, and end-of-period balances M. Household preferences take the form

$$c^{-c}(1-c)^{-(1-c)}[u(c^D, c^T)]^c \left[\frac{M}{P(p^D, p^T)} \right]^{1-c} - \theta N \qquad (2.1)$$

where N is employment, θ is the disutility of work, u is a homothetic subutility function, and $P(p^D, p^T)$ stands for the corresponding cost-of-living function. Although much of the analysis of this chapter could be carried through for the general case of homothetic preferences (see, for example, Dixon, 1990a, 1992), we shall assume that u is Cobb–Douglas:

$$u(c^D, c^T) = (c^D)^{1-m}(c^T)^m[m^m(1-m)^{1-m}]^{-1} \qquad (2.2a)$$

$$P(p^D, p^T) = (p^D)^{1-m}(p^T)^m \qquad (2.2b)$$

The household's budget constraint is

$$p^D c^D + p^T c^T + M \leq wN + \Pi + M^0 - T$$

where w is the nominal wage rate, Π denotes nominal profits, and T stands for the lump-sum tax levied by the government. We can aggregate over total wage and profit income to denote the total (flow component) of household income as

$$Y = wN + \Pi \qquad (2.3)$$

where Y is of course to be determined. However, we can note that, *given Y*, the household follows a two-stage budgeting decision. In the first stage it allocates a proportion c of total funds $Y + M^0 - T$ to consumption and a proportion $1 - c$ to money balances ("saving"). For obvious reasons c is interpreted as the marginal propensity to consume. In the second stage, the household uses subutility function (2.2a) to allocate its total expenditure between the domestic sector and export sector outputs. Since u is itself Cobb–Douglas, the consumer budget shares of the goods produced by the domestic and export sectors are constant:

$$p^D c^D = (1-m)c(Y + M^0 - T) \qquad (2.4a)$$

$$p^T c^T = mc(Y + M^0 - T) \qquad (2.4b)$$

For obvious reasons we can identify the preference parameter m as the marginal propensity to import.

From (2.1) the labor supply decision is very simple. If the real wage exceeds θ, the household wishes to supply H units of labor; if it equals θ it is indifferent between work and leisure; if it is less than θ the household will not work. Throughout this chapter, we shall be assuming that the real wage equals θ, so that the labor market clears at a level of employment below H:

$$\frac{w}{P(p^D, p^T)} = \theta \qquad N < H \qquad (2.5)$$

The actual level of employment will be demand determined. We are assuming a single economy-wide labor market, with perfect labor mobility between sectors.

2.2   The export sector

In the export sector, perfectly competitive firms produce a traded good whose foreign currency price $p*$ in world markets is fixed. Hence the domestic currency price is

$$p^T = ep*$$

where e is the exchange rate, the quantity of domestic currency necessary to buy one unit of foreign currency. Aggregating over firms, employment in this sector is N^T, and output is given by

$$x^T = (N^T)^\alpha$$

Given the domestic wage w, the profit-maximizing levels of output and employment of the firm are

$$x^T = \left(\frac{ep*}{w}\, \alpha\right)^{\alpha/(1-\alpha)} \tag{2.6a}$$

$$N^T = \left(\frac{ep*}{w}\, \alpha\right)^{1/(1-\alpha)} \tag{2.6b}$$

2.3   The domestic sector

We shall assume initially that the goods produced by the domestic sector are not traded, although in section 7 we allow for foreign competition. We conceive of the domestic sector as consisting of a large number of identical industries, but formally we shall deal with one "representative" industry. In this industry there are a fixed number n of home firms who act as Cournot–Nash competitors (we allow for free entry and exit in section 6). Each firm i has an increasing returns technology:

$$x_i = N_i - \bar{N}$$

Industry demand is given by the sum of household and government demand. Household demand is given by (2.4a) and is unit elastic (given Y, to be determined below). We shall also assume that government expenditure G is fixed in *nominal* terms. This is realistic in the UK, and convenient, since this simplification rules out any "elasticity effect" of government expenditure (see Dixon and Rankin, 1994). Each firm acts as a Cournot competitor, choosing its output given the outputs of other firms in its industry. The firm's objective demand curve is thus

$$p^D = \frac{G + (1-m)c(Y + M^0 - T)}{\sum_{j=i}^{n} x_j} \tag{2.7a}$$

The firm's nominal profits are

$$(p^D - w)x_i - w\bar{N} \tag{2.7b}$$

The firm is assumed to maximize nominal profits, equation (2.7b), subject to the objective demand curve (2.7a). Nominal profit maximization is reasonable if there are many industries in the domestic sector, so that any one has little effect on the general price level.

Given unit-elastic industry demand, with n firms there is a unique symmetric Cournot–Nash equilibrium in which price is a mark-up on marginal cost w:

$$p^D = \frac{n}{n-1}w \tag{2.8a}$$

Demand in the domestic sector is given by

$$x^D = g + c^D$$

where c^D is derived from (2.8a) and (2.4a), whilst *real* government expenditure g is

$$g = G/p^D$$

Employment in the domestic sector is

$$N^D = x^D + n\bar{N}$$

A more useful way of writing the oligopolistic price equation is to express it in terms of the disutility of labor, using (2.5):

$$\frac{p^D}{P(p^D, p^T)} = \frac{n}{n-1}\theta \tag{2.8b}$$

This equation states that the real price of domestic output is a mark-up over the disutility of labor. Clearly, as n becomes larger, the mark-up tends to unity (the competitive price). This mark-up in the domestic sector, equation (2.8), represents the only distortion introduced in this model. The real price of output exceeds the marginal social cost θ of its production.

2.4   Balance of payments and nominal national income

The balance of trade surplus S in terms of domestic currency is simply the difference between the value of the total expenditure on the traded good and its output (often called net exports):

$$S \equiv ep^*x^T - mc(Y + M^0 - T) \tag{2.9}$$

The national income is equal to the sum of the total home consumption of outputs C, plus government expenditure G plus net exports S. From (2.9) and (2.4)

$$Y = C + G + S$$

$$= c(Y + M^0 - T) + G + [ep^*x^T - cm(Y + M^0 - T)]$$

Hence the equilibrium level of nominal national income is given by

$$Y = \frac{c(1 - m)}{1 - c(1 - m)}(M^0 - T) + \frac{ep^*x^T + G}{1 - c(1 - m)} \qquad (2.10a)$$

This equation gives the income–expenditure equilibrium, since Y can be seen either as income (wages and profits of the home households in the domestic and export sectors) or as the flow of expenditure on home-produced outputs by home and foreign households. As we shall see in section 3, x^T is in fact constant in equilibrium. If we have balanced trade, so that $S = 0$, then (2.10a) simplifies to

$$Y = \frac{1}{1 - c}[c(M^0 - T) + G] \qquad (2.10b)$$

These equations can be used to substitute for equilibrium national income Y in the previous equations (2.4) and (2.7).

Lastly, we have the equation for the expansion in the domestic money supply from the various agents' budget constraints:

$$M - M^0 = S - T + G \qquad (2.11)$$

This equation says simply that the three deficits (public, private, foreign) must all sum to zero. Monetary expansion (the gap between income and consumption) equals the budget deficit plus the balance of trade surplus.

3   Macroeconomic equilibrium

In this section we shall solve for equilibrium in the private sector *given* the exchange rate e and government policy (G, M^0, T). This is not a long-run equilibrium since we are not imposing balanced trade. We shall explore the long-run equilibrium in subsequent sections: section 5 achieves balanced trade through a floating exchange rate given the money supply; section 7 achieves balanced trade through changes in the domestic money supply given e. Because trade need not be balanced, we can consider the equilibrium in this section to be temporary or short run.

The model presented in section 2 is easily solved because it is recursive. It should be recalled throughout that we are treating e, M^0, G, and T as exogenous. Let us first take the wage and price equations ((2.2b), (2.5), (2.8b)):

$$p^T = ep*$$

$$P(p^D, p^T) = (p^D)^{1-m}(p^T)^m \tag{2.2b}$$

$$\frac{w}{P(p^D, p^T)} = \theta \tag{2.5}$$

$$\frac{p^D}{P(p^D, p^T)} = \frac{n}{n-1}\theta \tag{2.8b}$$

We can solve these for (p^D, w) which yields

$$p^D = ep*\left(\frac{n\theta}{n-1}\right)^{1/m} \tag{2.12a}$$

$$w = ep*\theta^{1/m}\left(\frac{n}{n-1}\right)^{(1-m)/m} \tag{2.12b}$$

What equations (2.12) tell us is that both the domestic wage and price become *pegged* to the price of tradeables $ep*$. This happens because from (2.5) and (2.8b) both p^D and w are fixed relative to the cost-of-living index $P(p^D, p^T)$. But since the price of tradeables is fixed at $ep*$, this ties down both p^D and w (see for a similar result Dixon, 1990a, proposition 1). Another way of expressing this is to note that both equations (2.5) and (2.8b) are homogeneous of degree zero in (p^D, p^T, w), so that both w and p^D are determined relative to p^T.

Having solved for nominal wages and prices, we can now solve for the output of the export sector, combining (2.6) with (2.12b):

$$X^T = \left(\frac{ep*}{w}\alpha\right)^{\alpha/(1-\alpha)} = \left[\alpha\left(\frac{n}{n-1}\right)^{(m-1)/m}\theta^{-1/m}\right]^{\alpha/(1-\alpha)} \tag{2.13}$$

Output in the traded sector is determined solely by the technology (α), preferences (m, θ), and the degree of competition in the *domestic* sector (n). Note that as n increases (the domestic sector is more competitive), the equilibrium output X^T increases. This is an interesting spillover (or "externality") from the imperfectly competitive sector to the competitive export sector which we shall explore in more detail in section 6. It is important to note for future policy analysis that equilibrium X^T is independent of both the exchange rate and government policy parameters (G, M^0, T). This is because the competitive firms' output depends only upon the own-product real wage w/ep^*. Since w is itself pegged to ep^* from (2.12b) it follows that the own-product real wage in the export sector is constant. Having determined X^T, it can be plugged into (2.10) to yield equilibrium Y.

Output and employment in the domestic sector follow straightforwardly. We know the level of demand and employment given Y and the nominal price level:

$$X^D = \frac{G + c(1 - m)(Y + M^0 - T)}{p^D} \qquad (2.14a)$$

$$N^D = X^D + n\bar{N} \qquad (2.14b)$$

Total employment N is simply the sum of employment in the two sectors:

$$N = N^T + N^D \qquad (2.15)$$

where N^T is derived directly from (2.13) using the production function. For the model to be consistent with labor market equilibrium, we need the total labor demand (2.15) to be less than total labor supply H. This implies that the right-hand side determinants of X^D should not be too large (these are G, M^0, e, p^*).

How does the equilibrium in this section contrast with the Walrasian equilibrium? We shall explore this issue further in section 5 when we examine the equilibrium with a floating exchange rate. However, to compare the imperfectly competitive equilibrium with the Walrasian equilibrium, we can take the limit as the number of firms tends to infinity. If we do this, the following are easily verified.

1   p^D and w are lower in the Walrasian limit. From (2.12) they are both lower relative to ep^*.
2   X^T is larger in the Walrasian limit. As a result of (1), the own-product wage w/ep^* declines, thus stimulating output X^T.
3   Y is higher in the Walrasian limit. Since from (2) tradeables exports increase, this increases nominal national income from (2.10a).
4   X^D, N^D are higher in the Walrasian limit as a result of lower nominal w, p^D from (1) and higher nominal demand from (3).

None of these four comparisons is surprising. In a general equilibrium system the imperfections in one market can spill over to affect other markets. Most importantly, here the market imperfection in the domestic sector spills over and lowers output in the export sector, which has repercussions on equilibrium nominal national income.

4   Macroeconomic policy under a fixed exchange rate

In this section we shall examine the effect of macroeconomic demand management, in terms of its impact both on output and employment and on welfare. The analysis is concerned with the short run, in the sense that we shall not be imposing the condition of balanced trade on the economy, nor following through the effects of any trade surplus or deficit on the domestic money supply using (2.11). We shall examine the long-run equilibrium with a floating exchange rate in section 5 and with an endogenous money supply in section 7.

The economy we are considering is Walrasian in all of its aspects except that the domestic sector is a Cournot oligopoly. This means that the equilibrium does not satisfy the first fundamental theorem of welfare economics. Indeed, the equilibrium is Pareto suboptimal, since the consumers' marginal rate of substitution between domestic sector and export sector output does not equal the marginal rate of transformation (the latter being 1:1). Hence the most significant difference between the Walrasian equilibrium and imperfectly competitive equilibrium will be in welfare analysis.

4.1   Monetary policy

Let us first consider the short-run impact of monetary policy. Since money is the only asset in the model, monetary policy should be conceived of as a "helicopter drop" exercise. From section 3, we know that, given the exchange rate e, domestic nominal wages and prices become fixed in nominal terms. The effects of monetary policy are therefore very easy to follow through. An increase in the nominal money supply will increase initial real balances, leading to an increased demand for both the domestic and traded outputs. The increased demand for domestic sector output will lead to a direct increase in output and employment. Increased output comes at the cost of leisure forgone as employment increases. However, since the price of output is "too high," there is a surplus gained in the form of profits. It is best to explore this more formally. The welfare of the representative household is given by the indirect utility function corresponding to (2.1), given the level of employment (2.15):

$$V(p^D, p^T, Y + M^0 - T, N) = \frac{Y + M^0 - T}{P(p^D, p^T)} - \theta N \qquad (2.16)$$

PROPOSITION 1   Under a fixed nominal exchange rate, an increase in M^0 leads to a Pareto-improving increase in output and employment.

PROOF   Since $P(p^D, p^T)$ is constant, we have

$$\frac{dV}{dM^0} = \frac{1}{P}\left(1 + \frac{dY}{dM^0}\right) - \theta \frac{dN}{dM^0}$$

Turning first to dN/dM^0, note that, since N^T is fixed, only N^D can vary with M^0 from (2.14):

$$\frac{dN^D}{dM^0} = \frac{c(1-m)}{p^D}\left(\frac{dY}{dM^0} + 1\right)$$

From the mark-up equation

$$\frac{\theta}{p^D} = \frac{1}{P(p^D, p^T)}\frac{n-1}{n}$$

so that

$$\frac{dV}{dM^0} = \left(1 + \frac{dY}{dM^0}\right)\left[\frac{n - c(1-m)(n-1)}{n}\right]P^{-1} > 0 \qquad (2.17)$$

where of course from (2.10a)

$$\frac{dY}{dM^0} = \frac{(1-m)c}{1 - c(1-m)}$$

Note that we use the term "Pareto improvement," since the nominal income of no agent (wage-earner, shareholder) goes down and prices are constant.

If we consider (2.17) it is clear that, as n increases, the welfare improvement decreases. The reason for this is that the "surplus" earned in the domestic sector declines as it becomes more competitive. This surplus stems from the fact that the disutility of labor (the marginal social cost of output) is less than the real price of output. This is depicted in figure 2.1. As the monetary expansion shifts demand from DD to DD', the shaded rectangle ABCD represents the difference between the value of the additional output and its cost. This is not the only source of welfare gain. The additional consumption of the traded output is bought (in the short run) with no cost in terms of increased employment since N^T is fixed. In the Walrasian limit only this factor is present, and the second term on the right-hand side reduces to $1 - c(1-m)$. The presence of imperfect competition clearly boosts the welfare gain from monetary expansion.

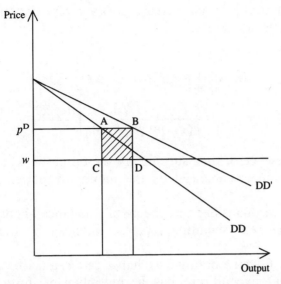

Figure 2.1 Imperfect competition and Pareto-improving monetary policy.

4.2 Fiscal policy

Let us turn to the consideration of fiscal policy. First, we shall deal with a *money-financed* increase in expenditure. As with monetary policy, since nominal prices are pegged to ep^*, the effects are fairly straightforward and Keynesian.

PROPOSITION 2   For a given nominal exchange rate and lump-sum tax T, the government expenditure multipliers are

$$\left.\frac{dc^D}{dg}\right|_T = \frac{c(1-m)}{1-c(1-m)}$$

$$\left.\frac{dN}{dg}\right|_T = \left.\frac{dx^D}{dg}\right|_T = \frac{1}{1-c(1-m)}$$

PROOF   The proof follows directly from (2.14). Note that since p^D is fixed the derivative of *real* government expenditure with respect to nominal expenditure is

$$\frac{dg}{dG} = \frac{1}{p^D} \qquad \qquad \square$$

Under a fixed exchange rate, there is a "crowding-in" effect in that the increase in government expenditure on the domestic sector output causes private sector expenditure (c^D, c^T) to increase. The welfare effects of a money-financed increase in G are very similar to the effects of a pure monetary policy:

$$\frac{dV}{dG} = \frac{dY}{dG}\left[\frac{1}{P(p^D, p^T)} - \theta \frac{dN}{dY}\right]$$

$$= \frac{1}{1 - c(1 - m)} \frac{1}{P(p^D, p^T)}\left[\frac{n - c(1 - m)(n - 1)}{n}\right]$$

Again the presence of the "surplus" in the domestic sector means that the welfare gain is enhanced by the monopoly power in the output market.

Lastly, we can consider the effects of a balanced-budget multiplier, with a government spending increase financed by lump-sum taxes ($G = T$).

PROPOSITION 3   Given a nominal exchange rate e, a tax-financed increase in government expenditure has a multiplier of unity and reduces welfare.

PROOF   From (2.10a)

$$\left.\frac{dY}{dG}\right|_{BB} = 1$$

(BB, balanced budget). That is, the increase in nominal national income equals the increase in government expenditure. Private disposable income is constant, and hence so is (c^D, c^T), so that welfare is decreased:

$$\left.\frac{dV}{dG}\right|_{BB} = -\theta \frac{dN}{dG} \qquad \square$$

This proposition shows that a tax-financed increase in government expenditure will leave private disposable income (and hence consumption) unchanged. However, the increased output demanded by the government is produced by more work and thus less leisure, which reduces welfare. In terms of national income accounts, there is an increase in tax revenue which is offset by the increase in wages and profits received in the domestic sector.

Under a fixed nominal exchange rate, then, the fact that nominal wages and prices are fixed in equilibrium gives the model a textbook Keynesian flavor as only output responds to changes in nominal aggregate demand brought about by monetary and fiscal policy. The presence of an imperfectly competitive output market in the domestic sector, however, is sufficient to make the welfare effects of policy different from the Walrasian case.

5 Macroeconomic policy under a floating exchange rate

In the previous section we analyzed the short-run effects of macroeconomic policy under a fixed exchange rate without any condition for balanced trade. There are two mechanisms in this simple framework which can bring about balanced trade: (a) an adjustment in the nominal exchange rate; (b) an endogenous change in the domestic money supply. In this section we consider the mechanism of a floating nominal exchange rate and in section 7 the latter mechanism.

Recalling (2.9), the balance of payments surplus S is

$$S = ep*X^T - cm(Y + M^0 - T) \tag{2.18}$$

Recall that from (2.13) the output of tradeables X^T is determined in equilibrium independently of e. From (2.10a) we have

$$Y + M^0 - T = \frac{1}{1 - c(1 - m)}(ep*X^T + M^0 + G - T)$$

Hence, solving (2.18) for $S = 0$ yields an expression for the nominal exchange rate:

$$e = \frac{cm}{1 - c}\frac{M^0 + G - T}{p*X^T} \tag{2.19}$$

This equation is very intuitive. The exchange rate will be higher when the marginal propensities to consume and import (c, m) are higher, when domestic nominal demand is higher (as indicated by $M^0 + G - T$), and when the output or foreign currency price of the export sector is larger.

We can now substitute the long-run equilibrium nominal exchange rate (2.19) into the equilibrium equations in section 3. From (2.12) we obtain

$$p^D = \frac{cm}{1 - c}\frac{M^0 - T + G}{X^T}\left(\frac{n\theta}{n - 1}\right)^{1/m} \tag{2.20a}$$

and likewise for w. The price of tradeables in domestic currency is

$$P^T = \frac{cm}{1 - c}\frac{M^0 + (G - T)}{X^T} \tag{2.20b}$$

The equilibrium cost-of-living index is given by

$$P(p^D, p^T) = \frac{cm}{1 - c}\frac{M^0 + (G - T)}{X^T}\left(\frac{n\theta}{n - 1}\right)^{(1 - m)/m} \tag{2.20c}$$

Equations (2.20) simply reflect the fact that domestic prices (and wages) are pegged to the domestic currency price of tradeables ep^*, which itself is determined by (2.19). If we combine equations (2.20) with the equation for nominal national income when there is balanced trade (equation (2.10b)), these price equations imply fixed domestic consumption of the domestic and traded good. The condition for balanced trade immediately implies that $c^T = X^T$. Turning to domestic sector output, this is obtained by combining (2.20c) with (2.4a) to yield (noting that Y is given by (2.10a)) an expression for consumption of home goods:

$$c^D = \frac{1-m}{m} X^T \left(\frac{n-1}{n\theta} \right)^{1/m} \tag{2.21}$$

where X^T is of course given by (2.13). c^D is in the long run independent of government policy (G, M^0, T) and is determined by household preferences, the export sector technology, and the degree of oligopoly.

The reasons behind the determination of c^D under balanced trade are simple enough. In equilibrium, nominal wages and prices are pegged to the nominal exchange rate e, which in effect fixes *relative* prices p^D/p^T. Furthermore, the output of tradeables in the export sector is determined by (2.13). Under balanced trade, domestic consumption of the traded good must equal its output, $c^T = X^T$. Given both relative prices and the quantity of the traded good to be consumed, the first-order tangency condition for utility maximization ties down the quantity of domestic output that must be consumed in any equilibrium, as depicted in figure 2.2. The ray through the origin IC is the income-expansion path depicting the allocation of expenditure between the domestic and traded goods as expenditure increases, given relative prices p^D/p^T. (It is linear because the subutility over consumption is homothetic.) On the horizontal axis is the quantity of the traded good X^T. The corresponding equilibrium consumption c^D of domestic output is obtained where the vertical broken line meets the income-expansion path at A. At this point, as depicted, the budget line bb is tangential to maximum utility u^*.

At this stage it is perhaps useful to compare the imperfectly competitive equilibrium with the Walrasian equilibrium. To do this, note that from (2.13) X^T is *increasing* in n. The Walrasian value for X^T is obtained by letting n approach infinity, which limit we denote by $X^T(w)$. Furthermore, note that imperfect competition alters *relative* prices, and hence the slope of budget constraints and the income-expansion path. From (2.20) we obtain

$$\frac{p^D}{p^T} = \left(\frac{n\theta}{n-1} \right)^{1/m}$$

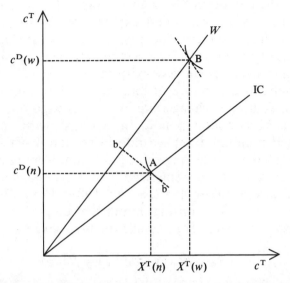

Figure 2.2   Equilibrium consumption with balanced trade.

Hence, as n increases, p^D falls relative to p^T, as we would expect. In figure 2.2, we have depicted the Walrasian income–expenditure path W, which lies "above" the imperfectly competitive income–expenditure path (IC), reflecting the fact that the optimal consumption of domestic output will be higher when its relative price is lower. Putting together the fact that X^T is larger and p^D/p^T is smaller in the Walrasian case, we can compare the consumption of domestic output in the Walrasian case ($c^D(w)$) with consumption of domestic output under imperfect competition ($c^D(n)$). The Walrasian equilibrium occurs at B and the imperfectly competitive equilibrium at A in figure 2.2. We have drawn in the corresponding budget line and indifference curves. As should be clear from figure 2.2 and the above arguments, c^D increases with n, i.e. decreases with the monopoly power of firms. This is easily verified directly from (2.21).

Under balanced trade, the welfare of the representative household is given by a simple expression. Using (2.20c) we obtain

$$V = \frac{Y + M^0 - T}{P(p^D, p^T)} - \theta N$$

$$= \frac{1}{cm}\left(\frac{n\theta}{n-1}\right)^{1-1/m} X^T - \theta N \qquad (2.22)$$

The first term on the right-hand side gives indirect utility from consumption and real balances. Since c^D, c^T and real balances are all tied down by the condition for balanced trade, this is *increasing* in the number of firms *n*, as we would expect from figure 2.2: imperfect competition reduces welfare. The second term on the right-hand side gives the disutility from work. This will tend to be increasing in *n*, since c^D and X^T and hence *N* increase with *n*.

Having analyzed the nature of long-run equilibrium with balanced trade under a floating exchange rate, we can now go on to analyze the effects of macroeconomic policy. In contrast with the case of a short-run fixed nominal exchange rate in section 4 which was rather Keynesian in its flavor, the long-run equilibrium is more classical. This mirrors the approach of the American New Keynesians in their closed economy analysis (Mankiw, 1992; Startz, 1989). From (2.22), in so far as policy does succeed in raising output and employment *N*, it must inevitably *reduce* welfare. Total employment is given by

$$N = N^D + N^T = c^D + g + N^T \tag{2.23}$$

where c^D is given by (2.21), N^T follows from (2.13), and *real* government expenditure *g* is given by

$$g = \frac{G}{p^D} = \frac{1-c}{cm} \frac{X^T G}{G + M^0 - T} \left(\frac{n\theta}{n-1}\right)^{-1/m} \tag{2.24}$$

Let us turn first to monetary policy. Since we are looking at long-run equilibrium with balanced trade we shall restrict ourselves to a balanced budget for the government (i.e. no monetary growth from (2.11)), so that $G = T$.

PROPOSITION 4   Monetary policy under a floating rate: assuming a balanced budget for the government

(a)   if $G = 0$, $dN/dM^0 = 0$;
(b)   if $G > 0$, $dN/dM^0 < 0$ and welfare is increasing in M^0.

PROOF   The proof follows directly from (2.23) and (2.24) given $G = T$. Since c^D and c^T are constant (as trade balances)

$$\frac{dN}{dM^0} = \frac{dg}{dM^0} = -\frac{g}{M^0} \le 0$$

Hence, if *G* (and hence *g*) is strictly positive, employment decreases and welfare increases with M^0.

In the absence of any fiscal policy ($G = T = 0$), money is neutral. This is because the equilibrium nominal exchange rate is proportional to M^0 (see (2.19)). In effect, *real money balances* are endogenously determined under balanced trade from (2.20c):

$$\frac{M^0}{P(p^{\mathrm{T}}, p^{\mathrm{D}})} = \frac{1-c}{cm} X^{\mathrm{T}} \left(\frac{n\theta}{n-1}\right)^{1-1/m} \tag{2.25}$$

A change in the domestic money supply simply leads to an equipro-portionate rise in the nominal exchange rate, and thus also in p^{D} and p^{T}. In the presence of government expenditure/taxation, the rise in nominal prices engendered by the rise in M^0 reduces *real* government expenditure and hence employment.

Turning to fiscal policy, we find that the multiplier for *real* government expenditure is unity, which follows from the fact that c^{D} and X^{T} are fixed in equilibrium. This holds irrespective of how government expenditure is financed (see Dixon, 1990a, p. 84, propo-sition 2), although in proposition 5 below we shall conduct the analysis with a balanced budget.

PROPOSITION 5   Under a floating nominal exchange rate with a balanced government budget

(a) $\mathrm{d}N/\mathrm{d}g = 1$;
(b)   welfare is decreasing in g.

PROOF   The proof follows directly from (2.23). Note that from (2.24) we have

$$\frac{\mathrm{d}N}{\mathrm{d}G} = \frac{\mathrm{d}N}{\mathrm{d}g} \frac{\mathrm{d}g}{\mathrm{d}G}$$

$$= \frac{1-c}{cm} \frac{X^{\mathrm{T}}}{M^0} \frac{n-1}{n\theta} > 0 \qquad \square$$

Thus whilst fiscal policy can increase output and employment, it must reduce welfare. If we compare the Keynesian results of section 4 with the more classical results of this section, we can see that whilst there is a short-run role for welfare-improving monetary and fiscal policy, in the long run the condition for balanced trade makes policy either neutral or effective and welfare reducing. Even though the long-run equilibrium is Pareto inefficient (due to imperfect competi-tion), output-increasing fiscal policy tends to *reduce* welfare.

6   Balanced trade with free entry and exit of firms

So far, we have treated the number of firms n as exogenous. However, at least since Weitzman (1982), many have argued that the combination of increasing returns with free entry and exit may play a special role in models with imperfect competition (for closed economy models with imperfect competition and free entry and exit see Snower (1983), Startz (1989), and Dixon and Lawler (1992)). In this brief section we outline the effects of introducing free entry and exit into the long-run balanced-trade equilibrium of section 5. The classical results of the previous section were obtained for the case of a fixed number of firms n. However, if government expenditure leads to more firms, then under Cournot competition this will make the economy more competitive. This will have important consequences for both the domestic and export sectors.

If we recall the analysis of section 2, each domestic sector firm i has the increasing (constant) returns technology $X_i = N_i - \bar{N}$, where $\bar{N} > 0$ ($\bar{N} = 0$) is a fixed cost of producing output. Nominal profits of firm i are then

$$\Pi_i = (p^D - w)X_i - w\bar{N} \qquad (2.26)$$

The mark-up in the typical domestic sector industry is given by

$$p^D = \frac{n}{n-1} w \qquad (2.8a)$$

Hence the free entry and exit condition of zero profits is that n satisfies

$$\frac{1}{n-1}X_i - \bar{N} = 0 \qquad (2.27a)$$

If we aggregate over firms i and ignore the fact that n is an integer, this simplifies to

$$n(n-1) = X^D/\bar{N} \qquad (2.27b)$$

From (2.27b) it is clear that, as total employment (output) in the domestic sector increases, more firms will want to enter the market and n will increase. As more firms enter the domestic sector, this will have knock-on general equilibrium effects in the whole economy.

Consider the long-run equilibrium conditions for $X^T, p^D/p^T$, and c^D in section 5. As n increases, X^T and c^D rise and p^D/p^T falls. If an increase in government expenditures induces entry, it will thus move the whole economy towards the Walrasian point W in figure 2.2. Whilst entry tends to bring the domestic price nearer to its competitive level relative to (w, p^T), it also induces an inefficiency since production becomes less efficient (the domestic sector has a subadditive cost function). If we focus on the domestic sector (where n is determined), we have two equations with two endogenous variables (X^D, n):

$$X^D \equiv c^D(n) + g$$

$$X^D = \bar{N}n(n-1) \tag{2.27b}$$

where c^D is expressed as a function of n. Total differentiation yields

$$\frac{dX^D}{dg} = \frac{\bar{N}(2n-1)}{\bar{N}(2n-1) - \partial c^D/\partial n} > 1 \tag{2.28a}$$

$$\frac{dn}{dg} = \frac{1}{\bar{N}(2n-1) - \partial c^D/\partial n} > 0 \tag{2.28b}$$

Together, the two equations (2.28) tell us that the real government expenditure multiplier on output is greater than unity, since additional expenditure induces entry. The multiplier for domestic sector employment will also be greater than unity:

$$N^D = X^D + n\bar{N}$$

$$\frac{dN^D}{dg} = \frac{dX^D}{dg} + \bar{N}\frac{dn}{dg}$$

$$= \frac{\bar{N}2n}{\bar{N}(2n-1) - \partial c^D/\partial n} > 1$$

In addition to the marginal workers needed to produce the extra output, dX^D/dg, there are also more workers needed to cover the fixed-cost element of the new firms. The output and employment multipliers for the export sector follow directly from (2.28b) and (2.13).

What of the welfare analysis of fiscal policy under balanced trade induced by a floating nominal exchange rate? The results here are rather complicated and in general ambiguous. We shall merely show that it is *possible* for an increase in government expenditure to increase social welfare by providing a numerical example. Under balanced trade, we are in fact able to express all the endogenous variables as functions of exogenous variables (α, m, c, θ, $\bar{N}$, g). However, although n is an endogenous variable under free entry and exit, as our analysis in section 5 showed, we can express the endogenous variables c^D, X^T, and N^T in terms of n and the exogenous variables. In fact, we can express social welfare as a function of (n, g) and then find the overall effect of g on welfare directly and via n. From (2.22) and (2.13), we obtain an expression for welfare:

$$V = \left[a_0 \left(\frac{n-1}{n} \right)^{a_1} - \theta^{1+a_2} N \right] \theta^{-a_2} \tag{2.29}$$

where

$$a_0 = (cm)^{-1} \alpha^{\alpha/(1-\alpha)}$$

$$a_1 = \frac{1-m}{m(1-\alpha)}$$

$$a_2 = \frac{1-m(1-\alpha)}{m(1-\alpha)}$$

Now, again from (2.13) we obtain an expression for employment in the traded sector

$$N^T = cma_0 \left(\frac{n-1}{n} \right)^{a_1} \theta^{-1/m(1-\alpha)} \tag{2.30}$$

and from (2.27b) and the definition of N^D we obtain

$$N^D = n^2 \bar{N} \tag{2.31}$$

Substituting (2.31) and (2.30) into (2.29) and using the monotonic transform of indirect utility (welfare) $\bar{V} = \theta^{a_2} V$, we have (after some considerable manipulation)

$$\bar{V} = a_0 \left(\frac{n-1}{n} \right)^{a_1} (1 - cma_0) - \theta^{1+a_2} n^2 \bar{N} \tag{2.32}$$

In effect, we have eliminated g from any direct effect on $\bar{V}$. This is because the only direct effect of g on $\bar{V}$ is via N^D, and from (2.31) we have expressed this in terms of n. Hence, from (2.32) we need only consider the size of $d\bar{V}/dn$ to determine the sign of $d\bar{V}/dg$:

$$\mathrm{sign}\left(\frac{d\bar{V}}{dg} \right) = \mathrm{sign}\left(\frac{d\bar{V}}{dn} \frac{dn}{dg} \right) = \mathrm{sign}\left(\frac{d\bar{V}}{dn} \right)$$

A general analysis of this is left to the reader. However, we consider a numerical example for which an increase in real government expenditure g can increase welfare.

EXAMPLE   Let $\alpha = c = m = 0.5$. Then $a_1 = a_0 = 2$, and $a_2 = 3$. Hence

$$\bar{V} = \left(\frac{n-1}{n} \right)^2 - \theta^4 \bar{N} n^2$$

and

$$\frac{d\bar{V}}{dn} = 2\left(\frac{n-1}{n^3} \right) - 2\theta^4 \bar{N} n \tag{2.33}$$

The difficulty in evaluating (2.33) is that n is endogenous, and so we cannot independently choose n, $\bar{N}$, and θ. However, it is easy to solve for n when $g = 0$. Under our parameter values, equations (2.13) and (2.21) yield

$$X^T = \frac{1}{2}\left(\frac{n-1}{n}\right)\theta^{-2} \qquad c^D = \frac{n-1}{n}\frac{1}{2\theta} \qquad (2.34)$$

With $X^D = c^D$ when $g = 0$, it follows from the free entry and exit condition (2.27b) that

$$n = (2\bar{N}\theta)^{-1/2} \qquad (2.35)$$

We can therefore examine the impact of an increase in n in the neighborhood of $g = 0$. First, consider the parameter values $\theta = 1/8$ and $\bar{N} = 1/4$. It is easily verified from (2.35) that the equilibrium number of firms is $n = 4$, and from that $d\bar{V}/dn > 0$. Again, for $\theta = 1/2$, $\bar{N} = 1/25$. In this case $n = 5$, and from (2.33) $d\bar{V}/dn > 0$. These two examples show that, if the government expenditure is entry inducing, then it can increase welfare even though we are in a long-run balanced-trade equilibrium and government expenditure is pure "waste."

7   Intra-industry trade and exchange rate pass-through

In this section we extend the model of the previous section to allow for intra-industry trade. We open up the domestic sector to allow for a foreign competitor. There will be two firms supplying the domestic sector, one "home" firm and one foreign firm which produces abroad. The foreign firm has an identical technology and pays wages w^* (in foreign currency) with no transport costs. For simplicity, we also assume that home consumers do not consume any of the export sector output (in terms of (2.1), $m = 0$), and since there is no entry we set $\bar{N} = 0$. The structure of this model is similar to that of Campos (1991).

The main goal of this section is to explore the effect of a devaluation in an imperfectly competitive trade environment. Much of the existing literature has focused on this in a purely *partial equilibrium* setting (e.g. Dornbusch, 1987; Froot and Klemperer, 1989). We shall explore this in a general equilibrium model. This, of course, also relates to the issue of real wage resistance which we shall briefly discuss. Lastly, in this section we shall assume a regime of fixed exchange rates for the long run, so that the domestic money supply will adjust to achieve balanced trade. This is in contrast with the assumption of a floating exchange rate assumed in the previous two sections.

7.1   Domestic sector equilibrium

The main difference in modeling the domestic sector from previous sections is that the duopolists will have *different* marginal costs. Hence, the symmetric equilibrium conditions in section 2 will not be generally applicable. The wages paid by foreign firms are given by ew^* in domestic currency. Furthermore, the level of imports will depend upon the market share of the foreign firm and is endogenously determined by the duopoly equilibrium. Throughout this section, we shall ignore the government sector, setting $G = T = 0$ (we are focusing on the policy instrument of devaluation). Total domestic consumption will be the sum of home firm output x and imports x^* from the foreign firm:

$$c^D = x + x^*$$

Since $m = 0$ in (2.1), all consumer expenditure is used for goods produced by the domestic sector. Let us define this total nominal expenditure Y^D, which will be a proportion c of total income (wages, profits, initial money balances). Y^D is of course endogenous and will be determined by the income–expenditure relations below. The "industry" demand curve for the domestic sector is

$$p^D = Y^D/c^D \tag{2.36}$$

Hence (nominal) profits for the home and foreign firm are given by

$$\Pi^h = \frac{x}{x + x^*} Y^D - wx \tag{2.37a}$$

$$\Pi^* = \frac{x^*}{x + x^*} Y^D - ew^*x \tag{2.37b}$$

Each firm chooses its own output to maximize nominal profits (in domestic currency), treating Y^D, e, w, and w^* as given. To justify this we need to appeal to the notion that we are looking at a *representative* industry in the domestic sector which is one of many, so that firm's actions have no effect on aggregate variables. The first-order conditions are

$$\frac{d\Pi^h}{dx} = \frac{x^*}{(x + x^*)^2} Y^D - w = 0 \tag{2.38a}$$

$$\frac{d\Pi^h}{dx^*} = \frac{x}{(x + x^*)^2} Y^D - ew^* = 0 \tag{2.38b}$$

From (2.38) we can directly obtain the relative outputs and market shares as functions of relative wages:

$$\frac{x^*}{x} = \frac{w}{ew^*} \tag{2.39a}$$

$$\frac{x^*}{x + x^*} = \frac{w}{w + ew^*} \tag{2.39b}$$

$$\frac{x}{x + x^*} = \frac{ew^*}{w + ew^*} \tag{2.39c}$$

Substituting (2.39) back into (2.38) yields the solutions for equilibrium outputs and price as functions of Y^D, w, and ew^*:

$$x = \frac{ew^*}{(w + ew^*)^2} Y^D \tag{2.40a}$$

$$x^* = \frac{w}{(w + ew^*)^2} Y^D \tag{2.40b}$$

$$p^D = w + ew^* \tag{2.40c}$$

These equations make intuitive sense, and when $w = ew^*$ yield the standard symmetric duopoly results.

The real wage for domestic households depends only upon p^D when $m = 0$; $P(p^D, p^T) = p^D$. Hence, from (2.40c) the labor market equilibrium (2.5) becomes

$$\frac{w}{p^D} = \frac{w}{w + ew^*} = \theta$$

which yields the equilibrium nominal wage

$$w = ew^* \frac{\theta}{1 - \theta} \tag{2.41}$$

Although the mechanism is different, the domestic nominal wage again is pegged to the nominal exchange rate e. The reason is that the domestic sector price is itself pegged to the domestic value of foreign wages, from (2.41) and (2.40c):

$$p^D = \frac{ew^*}{1 - \theta} \tag{2.42}$$

7.2   National income

We now solve the national income system for total nominal expenditure Y^D on the domestic sector and national income Y. The marginal/average propensity to import $\bar{m}$ comes directly from (2.39b), the foreign firms' market share, combined with (2.41):

$$\bar{m} = \frac{w}{ew^* + w} = \theta \tag{2.43}$$

As in previous sections, the fact that domestic wages are pegged to the nominal exchange rate ties down the output of the export sector:

$$X^T = \alpha^{\alpha/(1-\alpha)} \left(\frac{p^*}{w^*} \frac{1-\theta}{\theta} \right)^{\alpha/(1-\alpha)} \tag{2.44}$$

The flow component of home income Y in the form of wages and profits from the domestic and export sector is

$$Y = (1 - \bar{m})Y^D + ep^*x^T \tag{2.45}$$

Imports are of course $\bar{m}Y^D$. We can now solve for Y^D using the consumption function (2.4a) with $m = 0$ (recall that $G = T = 0$):

$$Y^D = c(Y + M^0)$$

$$= c((1 - \bar{m}))Y^D + (ep^*x^T) + cM^0$$

$$= \frac{c}{1 - c(1 - \bar{m})}(M^0 + ep^*x^T) \tag{2.46}$$

Hence, from (2.45) and (2.46), we obtain an expression for the national income of the home country

$$Y = \frac{c(1 - \bar{m})}{1 - c(1 - \bar{m})} M^0 + \frac{1}{1 - c(1 - \bar{m})} ep^*x^T \tag{2.47}$$

and the trade surplus is given by

$$S = ep^*x^T - \bar{m}Y^D \tag{2.48}$$

Solutions (2.46)–(2.48) are valid whether or not trade is balanced. In the long run with balanced trade, so that $S = 0$, Y is again given by (2.10b). Since we are holding e constant (at least after each devaluation), the new long-run equilibrium nominal money supply is given by

$$M^0 = \frac{1-c}{c\bar{m}} ep^*x^T \tag{2.49}$$

7.3   Devaluation and pass-through

We shall break up the analysis of devaluation into three Marshallian time "periods":

1   *very short run (VSR)* – domestic wages are fixed;
2   *short run (SR)* – domestic nominal wages and prices adjust to equilibrium, but trade need not be balanced;

3 *long-run (LR)* – trade balances through adjustment of the domestic money supply.

Most of the recent literature on imperfect competition and pass-through is partial equilibrium in outlook and has really dealt only with the VSR. Literature on real-wage resistance (e.g. Ellis and Fender, 1987) has examined the SR issues in the context of a bargaining model. With the exception of Campos (1991, 1992), this is the first attempt to examine the long run.

   In the VSR, the domestic wages w are treated as fixed, so that the effects are straightforward. A devaluation raises the (domestic currency) wages and marginal cost of the foreign firm. If we depict the two firms' reaction functions in (x, x^*) space, the foreign firm's reaction function r^* moves leftwards in figure 2.3 to r^{**}, and equilibrium moves from A to B. As can be seen from (2.40), devaluation of the exchange rate boosts x and reduces x^*, with the domestic price p^D rising since the slope of r is less than unity. The extent of pass-through in the VSR is

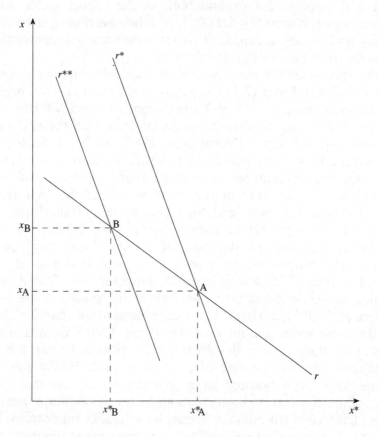

Figure 2.3 Pass-through in the very short run.

captured by the elasticity of p^D with respect to e:

$$\left.\frac{d \log p^D}{d \log e}\right|_w = \frac{ew^*}{w + ew^*} < 1$$

Hence, from (2.39c) the extent of pass-through is inversely related to the foreign firm's market share. This is perhaps counter-intuitive, and illustrates that the introduction of imperfect competition raises many possibilities, as was pointed out by Dornbusch (1987). If we contrast this with the competitive export sector, pass-through is 100 percent even in the VSR, since $p^T = ep^*$. Hence the relative price p^D/p^T falls.

In addition to the effects of a devaluation on prices (p^D, p^T) in the VSR, there are secondary knock-on effects to national income. These stem from two sources: the reduced import penetration of the domestic sector means that $\bar{m}$ falls in (2.46) and (2.47), thus boosting (Y^D, Y); second, the (domestic currency) earnings from the export sector (price and output are up) are increased. In the VSR, then, devaluation has a clear expansionary effect on the economy as output and employment expand both in the export sector and the domestic sector. Nominal prices (p^D, p^T), however, have risen relative to wages and money balances. This sets counteracting contractionary tendencies in train.

In the short run we allow wages to respond, employing equation (2.46) and (2.42). From (2.41), domestic nominal wages are pegged to the domestic currency value of foreign wages ew^* and will rise directly in proportion to the devaluation in order to restore the real wage θ. This *real-wage resistance* (Dornbusch, 1980, pp. 71–4; Sachs, 1980; Eichengreen, 1980; Ellis and Fender, 1987) leads to a *contractionary* effect from the devaluation. In essence, there has been 100 percent pass-through (via the labor market), and with fixed nominal domestic money balances this will lead to a decline in output. From (2.46) and (2.47), although export earning ep^*x^T will have risen in line with the devaluation and domestic prices, the "monetary" part M^0 will not. The output of the export sector will return to its initial value as w rises. The domestic sector, however, will find its output declining to below its initial value. Whilst the market share adjusts, the price p^D will have risen by a greater proportion than Y^D. Hence, total domestic sector output declines. If we started from a situation of balanced trade before devaluation, the situation after the short-run adjustments will be one of a trade surplus. Whilst the export earnings have been boosted in proportion to the devaluation, the impact of the contraction brought about by the devaluation means that imports have risen (in nominal terms) by a smaller proportion. Hence a specie-flow mechanism will lead to an increase in the domestic money supply until the long-run equilibrium is reached. From (2.49) we can see that the balanced-trade equilibrium level of the nominal domestic money stock is proportional to e. Hence the long-run increase in the domestic money supply will fully restore c^D, x, and x^* to their initial equilibrium values.

The effects of a devaluation of the exchange rate thus differ over time. In the long run, it can have no effect as the balanced-trade condition will ultimately tie down all of the real variables, as we saw in a slightly different model in section 5. We have not, of course, considered fiscal policy in this section, but the analysis would be much the same as in section 5. In the VSR, before the domestic labor market has time to respond, the effect of a devaluation on domestic output and employment is unambiguously positive. In the domestic sector, the output of the home firm rises, whilst output of the export sector also rises. However, real-wage resistance leads to a return of output of the export sector to its initial value, and the domestic sector output of home and foreign firms contracts due to a "real-balance" effect since prices have risen relative to the nominal money supply. To what extent is there a distinctive role in this story for imperfect competition? Not much, it seems to me, except in the VSR. In the VSR, the exact type of output market configuration will indeed influence the immediate rate of exchange rate pass-through. However, beyond that initial impact, the issue becomes dominated by the perennial factors to do with the labor market and real balances. To put all these factors together, as we have done, requires a coherent general equilibrium framework.

8   Conclusion

Whilst the theme of imperfect competition has been well developed during the last two decades in the context of a closed economy, its implications for open economies have received relatively little attention. In this chapter we have focused on the implications of imperfect competition in the domestic/nontraded output market of an open economy. The basic framework can easily be extended to embrace alternative configurations. I hope to have convinced the reader that both the positive and the welfare analysis of government policy under imperfect competition differ significantly from those under Walrasian equilibrium. In order to capture these differences fully it is necessary to model the components of the macroeconomy and their interrelationships carefully in a coherent general equilibrium setting. An alternative approach is developed by Abayasiri-silva (1992), who develops Ng's mesoeconomic approach (Ng, 1982) in an open economy setting.

References

Abayasiri-silva, K. (1992) "Aggregate supply functions in closed and open economies," *American Economic Review, Papers and Proceedings* 80, 379–85.

Aizenman, J. (1989) "Monopolistic competition, relative prices and output adjustment in the open economy," *Journal of International Money and Finance* 8, 5–28.

Akerlof, G. and J. Yellen (1985) "A near rational model of the business cycle, with wage and price inertia," *Quarterly Journal of Economics, Supplement* 100 (5), 823–38.

Benassy, J.-P. (1976) "A disequilibrium approach to monopolistic price setting and general monopolistic equilibrium," *Review of Economic Studies* 43, 69–81.

—— (1978) "A neo-Keynesian model of price and quantity determination in disequilibrium," in G. Schwodiauer (ed.) *Equilibrium and Disequilibrium in Economic Theory*, Dordrecht, Reidel.

—— (1987) "Imperfect competition, unemployment and policy," *European Economic Review* 31, 417–26.

—— (1991) "Microeconomic foundations and properties of a macroeconomic model with imperfect competition," in K. Arrow (ed.) *Issues in Contemporary Economics*, London, Macmillan, vol. 1, 121–38.

Blanchard, O. and N. Kiyotaki (1987) "Monopolistic competition and the effects of aggregate demand," *American Economic Review* 77, 647–66.

Campos, R. (1991) "Short-run and long-run effects of a devaluation in a macromodel of imperfect competition," mimeo, Warwick University.

—— (1992) "Essays on the macroeconomics of imperfect competition," PhD Thesis, Warwick University.

Cooper, R.N. (1971) "Currency devaluation in developing countries," Essays in International Finance 86, International Finance Section, Princeton University.

Dixon, H. (1987) "A simple model of imperfect competition with Walrasian features," *Oxford Economic Papers* 39, 134–60.

—— (1988) "Unions oligopoly and the natural range of employment," *Economic Journal* 98, 1127–47.

—— (1990a) "Macroeconomic policy with a floating exchange rate and a unionised non-traded sector," *Economic Journal* 100, suppl., 78–90.

—— (1990b) "Imperfect competition, unemployment benefit and the non-neutrality of money," *Oxford Economic Papers* 42, 402–13.

—— (1991) "Macroeconomic equilibrium and policy in a large unionised economy," *European Economic Review* 35, 1427–48.

—— (1992) "Macroeconomic price and quantity responses when product markets are heterogeneous," mimeo, York University.

—— and P. Lawler (1992) "Fiscal policy in a monopolistic economy," mimeo, Swansea University.

—— and N. Rankin (1992) "Imperfect competition and macroeconomics," *Oxford Economic Papers*, forthcoming.

—— and M. Santoni (1992) "Unions and oligopolies in a small open economy," mimeo, York University.

Dornbusch, R. (1987) "Exchange rates and prices," *American Economic Review* 77, 93–106.

—— (1980) *Open Economy Macroeconomics*, New York, Basic Books.

Eichengreen, B.J. (1980) "Protection, real wage resistance and employment," *Weltwirtschaftliches Archiv* 119, 429–52.

Ellis, C. and J. Fender (1987) "Bargaining and wage resistence in an open macroeconomic model," *Economic Journal* 97, 106–20.

Fender, J. and C. Yip (1992) "Open economy macroeconomics under imperfect competition: a two country model," mimeo, Birmingham University.

Froot, K.A. and P. Klemperer (1989) "Exchange rate pass-through when market share matters," *American Economic Review* 79, 636–54.

Giovannini, A. (1988) "Exchange rates and traded goods prices," *Journal of International Economics* 24, 45–68.

Gomez, A. (1992) "On the real effects of monetary expansions, price controls, and devaluation in a monopolistically competitive economy," mimeo, Warwick University.

Hanson, J.A. (1983) "Contractionary devaluation, substitution in production and consumption, and the role of labor market," *Journal of International Economics* 14, 179–89.

Hart, O. (1982) "A model of imperfect competition with Keynesian features," *Quarterly Journal of Economics* 97, 109–38.

Helpman, E. (1988) "The macroeconomic effects of price controls: the role of market structure," *Economic Journal* 98, 340–54.

Hirschman, A.O. (1949) "Devaluation and the trade balance: a note," *Review of Economics and Statistics* 31, 50–3.

Krugman, P. and L. Taylor (1978) "Contractionary effects of devaluation," *Journal of International Economics* 8, 445–56.

Mankiw, N.G. (1985) "Small menu costs and large business cycles: a macroeconomic model of monopoly," *Quarterly Journal of Economics* 100, 529–37.

—— (1992) "The reincarnation of Keynesian economics," *European Economic Review* 36, 559–65.

Molana, H. and T. Moutos (1992) "A note on taxation, imperfect competition and the balanced budget multiplier," *Oxford Economic Papers* 43, 68–74.

Neary, P. (1980) "Non-traded goods and balance of trade in a neo-Keynesian temporary equilibrium," *Quarterly Journal of Economics* 95, 109–39.

Negishi, T. (1979) *Microeconomic Foundations of Keynesian Macroeconomics,* New York, North-Holland.

Ng, Y.K. (1982) "Macroeconomics with non-perfect competition," *Economic Journal* 90, 598–610.

Rankin, N. (1989) "Monetary and fiscal policy in a "Hartian" model of imperfect competition," Centre for Economic Research Discussion Paper 8926.

Sachs, J. (1980) "Wage-indexation, flexible exchange rates and macroeconomic policy," *Quarterly Journal of Economics* 94, 731–47.

Snower, D.J. (1983) "Imperfect competition, underemployment and crowding out," *Oxford Economic Papers* 35, suppl., 245–70.

Startz, R. (1989) "Monopolistic competition, as the foundation for Keynesian macroeconomic models," *Quarterly Journal of Economics* 104, 737–52.

Silvestre, J. (1993) "The market power foundations of macroeconomic theory," *Journal of Economic Literature* 31, 105–41.

Weitzman, M. (1982) "Increasing returns and the foundations of unemployment theory," *Economic Journal* 92, 787–804.

3 Relative Price Movements in Dynamic General Equilibrium Models of International Trade

DAVID K. BACKUS, PATRICK J. KEHOE, AND FINN
E. KYDLAND

1 Introduction

Relative prices are a central feature of both the pure theory of
international trade and open economy macroeconomics. Although the
emphasis differs in the two branches of international economics, to a
great extent the same theory underlies theoretical and empirical work
in each. Applications of dynamic general equilibrium theory, or
international real business cycle theory, continue this tradition by
extending, at the aggregate level, several of the features of static trade
theory to dynamic and stochastic settings. What it adds, we think, is a
deeper understanding of the dynamics of trade and relative prices.

The Marshall–Lerner condition is, without question, the most
common link between trade theory and international macroeconomics.
In trade theory this elasticity condition on import demand functions
determines the direction of many comparative statics exercises and
serves as a stability condition on an otherwise static theory, telling us
whether a disequilibrium adjustment process will succeed in establishing equilibrium. In international macroeconomics the same condition
is used to establish a positive association between the trade balance and
the terms of trade or real exchange rate. This is the level at which the
theory is presented in most textbooks and, indeed, in the popular
Mundell–Fleming and Dornbusch macroeconomic models of open
economies.

The macroeconomic branch of international economics has also
developed insights that are largely independent of the theory of trade.
The absorption approach focused on the accounting relation between
saving, investment, and the balance of trade. What distinguishes this
work from static trade theory is its suggestion that the trade balance, or

the closely related current account, reflects the dynamic decisions by agents to lend or borrow in international capital markets (see chapters 1, 5, and 15 in this volume). A critical development for understanding the relation between trade and relative prices was the recognition that any dependence of the trade balance on the terms of trade implied, as a matter of accounting, a similar relation with international borrowing and lending. This connection was noted by Harberger (1950) and Laursen and Metzler (1950) and later incorporated by Obstfeld (1982) and Svensson and Razin (1983) into explicitly dynamic theories of the balance of trade. These later papers emphasized the influence of terms of trade movements on permanent income, and hence saving. They argued that persistent changes in the terms of trade have larger income effects than transitory changes, and thus give rise to potentially different relations between the trade balance and the terms of trade. The effect, in their analysis, is a comparison between two deterministic equilibria.

We approach trade and relative price dynamics from a somewhat different theoretical tradition, that of dynamic general equilibrium theory. As in much of static trade theory, we use competitive consumers and producers. Unlike that work, however, our theory is explicitly dynamic. And unlike the modern approach to the Harberger–Laursen–Metzler effect, we consider not comparisons between different deterministic equilibria, but properties of equilibria in stochastic theoretical economies. We consider in the theory the same experiment that applied economists consider in the data: we look at correlations between trade and relative price variables along an equilibrium path. Somewhat to our surprise, this approach leads to substantially different views of trade and price behavior than suggested by earlier work.

The application of dynamic general equilibrium theory to international trade has also led, in a rapidly growing number of papers, to attempts to quantify the theory's properties and compare them with properties of national economies. These attempts have led to a clearer understanding of which features of the data can be accounted for by the present state of theory and which remain anomalous. This quantitative approach generates sharper predictions than qualitative theory, and helps to focus further theoretical work on clearly defined issues.

We elaborate on the twin themes of theoretical development and quantitative properties in the rest of the chapter. We start, in section 2, by documenting some of the salient properties of aggregate trade and relative prices for a number of industrialized countries. These properties make explicit the objects of interest in theoretical economies and serve as a basis of comparison with the theory.

We develop the theory in a series of two-country worlds, highlighting as we go the roles played by different theoretical features. Section 3 is devoted to an exchange economy in which each country specializes in a single traded good. Here the variability of relative prices and the relation between prices and trade are governed by a single parameter: the elasticity of substitution between foreign and domestic goods. Some of the quantitative properties of this economy change when we consider preferences that are not additively separable between foreign and domestic goods and that favor consumption of home goods. This aspect of the theory is developed in section 4. We find, among other things, that agents' risk aversion plays a role in both the dynamics of trade and prices and the relation between these two variables.

In section 5 we compare this theory with alternatives based on the Marshall–Lerner condition and the Harberger–Laursen–Metzler effect. We show that our elasticity condition is not related to the Marshall–Lerner condition, which is always satisfied in our symmetric economy. With respect to the Harberger–Laursen–Metzler effect, we find that the persistence of shocks is orthogonal to the relation between relative prices and the balance of trade: for given preference parameters, the correlation between trade and prices is the same whether price changes last one period or a hundred. In both comparisons, dynamic general equilibrium theory provides a different perspective on trade and price fluctuations from earlier work.

In the remaining sections we consider extensions of the theoretical structure that change some of its quantitative features and broaden the theory's predictions. In section 6 we consider shocks to government spending as well as to aggregate endowments. As one might expect, this extension has the potential to change equilibrium co-movements considerably. We find, for example, that the sign of the relation between the trade balance and the terms of trade depends on the relative sizes of shocks to endowments and government spending, as well as the elasticity of substitution.

In section 7 we imbed the exchange structure of earlier sections into an economy with endogenous labor supply and capital formation. The critical element here is capital formation. With this modification, we find that the dynamics of trade now reflect, to a large extent, cyclical fluctuations in physical investment. The most striking result is an asymmetric cross-correlation function for the trade balance and the terms of trade, which we label the S-curve. This feature does not arise in exchange economies, where by construction investment is zero and the cross-correlation function is symmetric. In this sense the dynamics of capital formation play an important role in connecting the dynamics of the trade balance and the relative price of foreign to domestic goods.

We conclude with a few remarks on the strengths and weaknesses of existing dynamic general equilibrium theories of international trade and with suggestions for directions the theory might take in the future.

2 First look at the data for the terms of trade, net exports, and real output

Since the ultimate objective of our theory is to account for empirical regularities, we start by looking at some of the properties of international relative prices. We focus here on three variables. The terms of trade, denoted p, is the ratio of the import price deflator to the export price deflator, both taken from national income and product accounts. Net exports, denoted nx, is the ratio of exports minus imports, in current prices, to output in current prices. Real output, denoted y, is gross domestic product or gross national product, depending on the country, in base-year prices (generally 1985). All three variables are constructed with data taken from the OECD's *Quarterly National Accounts*.

In table 3.1 we report various properties of the terms of trade for three countries: Japan, the UK, and the USA. These statistics refer to Hodrick–Prescott filtered variables, and both the terms of trade and real output are logarithms. Many of the same properties are reported in Backus et al. (1991) and Blackburn and Ravn (1991) for additional developed countries and in Mendoza (1992) for developing countries. In table 3.1 the sample period runs from 1955:2 to 1989:4, which enables us to look separately at the periods before and after the collapse of Bretton Woods.

We see, for a start, that movements in the terms of trade have been both variable and persistent. The standard deviation of terms of trade fluctuations ranges from 2.71 percent in the UK to 5.97 percent in

Table 3.1 Properties of the trade balance and the terms of trade

Country	Period	Standard deviation (%)		Autocorrelation		Cross-correlation	
		p	nx	p	nx	(p, nx)	(p, y)
Japan	1955–89	5.97	0.97	0.87	0.77	– 0.46	– 0.09
	1955–70	2.17	0.98	0.73	0.66	– 0.55	0.41
	1971–89	7.76	0.94	0.87	0.83	– 0.51	– 0.27
UK	1955–89	2.71	1.08	0.76	0.66	– 0.54	0.20
	1955–70	1.51	0.78	0.38	0.54	– 0.15	0.56
	1971–89	3.38	1.21	0.79	0.65	– 0.60	0.10
USA	1955–89	2.99	0.45	0.82	0.80	0.30	– 0.09
	1955–70	1.31	0.30	0.65	0.79	0.28	0.47
	1971–89	3.84	0.55	0.84	0.80	0.30	– 0.23

p, the terms of trade, logarithm; nx, the ratio of net exports to output; y, real output, logarithm. Data are quarterly from the OECD's *Quarterly National Accounts*. Statistics refer to Hodrick–Prescott filtered variables.

Japan. Both here and in our earlier paper, variability of the terms of trade is considerably larger for Japan than we have found for other countries. We are unsure, at this point, how much of this additional variability reflects true relative price movement and how much reflects differences in the manner in which trade prices are constructed. Both Alterman (1991) and Graboyes (1991) raise questions concerning the quality of current trade prices in the USA, and these problems may be greater in earlier periods and other countries. Alterman (1991) estimates that improved price data exhibit about 30 percent less variability than those reported here. Nevertheless, we are probably on safe ground in claiming substantial variability of the terms of trade in all countries. Persistence is evident in the autocorrelations, which are generally in the neighborhood of 0.8. Table 3.1 also verifies that there has been much more variability of the terms of trade since the advent of floating exchange rates than before, a feature stressed by Mussa (1986) for real exchange rates (ratios of consumer price indexes converted at spot exchange rates). Standard deviations of the terms of trade are typically two to three times larger in the later period.

We also include, in table 3.1, correlations of the terms of trade with net exports and real output. With respect to net exports, we find greater coherence across periods but little across countries. The terms of trade and net exports have generally been positively correlated in the USA and negatively correlated in Japan and the UK. We see in table 3.2, which covers the post-Bretton Woods period for ten countries, that the

Table 3.2 The trade balance, the terms of trade, and government purchases

Country	Standard deviation (%)		Cross-correlations			
	y	g	(p, nx)	(g, nx)	(g, p)	(g, y)
Australia	1.47	1.90	−0.11	−0.15	0.15	0.17
Austria	1.27	0.45	−0.25	0.11	0.28	−0.23
Canada	1.49	1.16	−0.06	−0.15	−0.02	−0.22
France	0.91	0.66	−0.50	0.11	−0.45	0.24
Germany	1.47	1.22	−0.09	−0.11	−0.16	0.23
Italy	1.70	0.69	−0.66	0.11	−0.42	−0.01
Japan	1.48	1.54	−0.51	0.19	−0.35	0.02
Switzerland	1.94	1.01	−0.61	−0.15	−0.29	0.28
UK	1.60	1.07	−0.60	−0.06	−0.01	0.06
USA	1.93	1.47	0.31	−0.28	0.13	0.12

The sample period is 1971:1 to 1989:4.
p, the terms of trade, logarithm; nx, the ratio of net exports to output; y, real output, logarithm; g, real government purchases of goods and services, logarithm.
Data are quarterly from the OECD's *Quarterly National Accounts*. Statistics refer to Hodrick–Prescott filtered variables.

USA is an outlier in this regard: the correlation between the trade balance and the terms of trade is negative for every other country. With respect to output, there has been no regularity in the correlation with the terms of trade, either over time or across countries.

The contemporaneous correlation between net exports and the terms of trade fails to capture an important regularity that appears when we examine the complete cross-correlation function: the correlations, that is, between p_t and nx_{t+k} for various leads and lags k. The contemporaneous correlation refers to $k = 0$. For positive k the correlations pertain to net exports and past prices, and for negative k the reverse. We find (figure 3.1) for Japan and the UK that this function has an asymmetric S shape, which we call the S-curve. For Japan and the UK this feature appears not only in the postwar period as a whole, but in the pre- and post-Bretton Woods subperiods as well. For the USA the same pattern is evident only in the earlier period. Our earlier work (Backus et al., 1991, figure 1) documents this pattern in eight of 11 countries.

In the remainder of this chapter we examine these properties from the perspective of a series of successively more complex dynamic general equilibrium models, bringing additional data to bear when the theory suggests it. For now, we note that the terms of trade has been highly variable and persistent in all three countries, that its correlation with net exports is generally negative, and that the cross-correlation function for net exports and the terms of trade is often asymmetric (the S-curve property).

3   A dynamic exchange economy

One of the simplest dynamic general equilibrium models of a world economy has two countries who trade specialized endowments. Let time t run from an initial date 0 to a terminal date T, possibly infinite. The evolution of this endowment is stochastic, given by a "Debreu tree" that we describe in notation adapted from Lucas (1984). The state z^t, an element of the set Z^t, denotes the history of the economy from date 0 through t. Each of these possible states occurs with a probability $\pi(z^t)$. Country 1, which we call the home country, is endowed with a stream of positive quantities of the home good, denoted $\{y_1(z^t)\}$ or, in short-hand notation, simply (y_1). Likewise, country 2, the foreign country, is endowed with the positive sequence (y_2) of quantities of the foreign good. We denote the prices of the domestic and foreign goods in state z^t by $q_1(z^t)$ and $q_2(z^t)$. As in section 2, we define the terms of trade $p(z^t) = q_2(z^t)/q_1(z^t)$ as the relative price of imports to exports.

3.1   Consumer behavior

Each country is represented by a single consumer who stands in for a large number of like agents. The preferences of the consumer of country i are characterized by the expected utility function

$$u_i = \sum_{t=0}^{T} \beta^t \sum_{z^t \in Z^t} \pi(z^t) \, U[c_i(z^t)]$$

with $0 < \beta < 1$, $U(c) = c^{1-\gamma}/(1-\gamma)$, and $\gamma > 0$. We refer to γ as the risk aversion parameter. Both agents consume composites of the foreign and domestic goods described by the Armington aggregator functions

$$c_1(a_1,b_1) = G(a_1,b_1) \qquad c_2(b_2,a_2) = G(b_2,a_2)$$

with

$$G(a,b) = (\omega a^{1-\alpha} + b^{1-\alpha})^{1/(1-\alpha)}$$

where a_i and b_i are the quantities of the domestic and foreign goods consumed by the agent of country i. Thus the agents of each country consume a combination of foreign and domestic goods, as expressed in the function G. This theoretical device, due to Armington (1969), is widely used in computable static general equilibrium trade models. In this economy it is equivalent to giving consumers preferences over foreign and domestic goods directly. The two parameters $\alpha > 0$ and $\omega > 0$ govern the elasticity of substitution and shares of foreign and domestic goods. The elasticity is $\sigma = 1/\alpha$. With $\omega = 1$ the two consumers have identical preferences, and with $\omega > 1$ they exhibit a preference for home goods: if home and foreign goods sell for the same price, agents consume more of the home good than the foreign good. The budget constraint of the domestic agent is

$$\sum_{t=0}^{T} \sum_{z^t \in Z^t} [q_1(z^t)a_1(z^t) + q_2(z^t)b_1(z^t)] \le \sum_{t=0}^{T} \sum_{z^t \in Z^t} q_1(z^t)y_1(z^t)$$

The foreign agent faces an analogous constraint.

3.2   Competitive equilibrium

A competitive equilibrium in this economy consists of state-contingent quantities a_i, b_i and prices q_i such that (a) consumers maximize utility given prices and budget constraints and (b) quantities satisfy the resource constraints

$$y_1(z^t) = a_1(z^t) + a_2(z^t)$$

$$y_2(z^t) = b_1(z^t) + b_2(z^t)$$

for each state z^t. We find it convenient to compute an equilibrium using the Negishi–Mantel algorithm in which, for any initial distribution of resources, a competitive allocation is associated with a Pareto optimum. Each optimum is the solution to a problem of the form: for some choice of positive welfare weights (λ_1, λ_2), choose quantities (a_1, a_2, b_1, b_2) in each state to maximize $\Sigma_i \lambda_i u_i$, subject to the resource constraints. The supporting prices can then be identified with the Lagrange multipliers on the constraints or derived from consumers' first-order conditions. Backus (1992, section 2) describes this procedure in a similar context and discusses alternative decentralization schemes.

For the optimum problem, let us denote the Lagrange multipliers on the resource constraints in state z^t by $q_1(z^t)$ and $q_2(z^t)$ for the domestic and foreign goods respectively. The Lagrange multipliers correspond to prices in the associated competitive equilibrium. If, for each i, we define spot price functions Q_i by $q_i(z^t) = \beta^t \pi(z^t) Q_i(z^t)$, then the optimum problem separates into a number of identical problems, one for each state z^t, of the form

$$\max_{\{a_i, b_i\}} \beta^t \pi(z^t)(\lambda_1 U\{G[a_1(z^t), b_1(z^t)]\} + \lambda_2 U\{G[b_2(z^t), a_2(z^t)]\})$$

subject to the resource constraints. The first-order conditions for each state are

$$Q_1(z^t) = \lambda_1 \omega c_1[a_1(z^t), b_1(z^t)]^{\alpha - \gamma} a_1(z^t)^{-\alpha}$$
$$= \lambda_2 c_2[a_2(z^t), b_2(z^t)]^{\alpha - \gamma} a_2(z^t)^{-\alpha}$$

$$Q_2(z^t) = \lambda_1 c_1[a_1(z^t), b_1(z^t)]^{\alpha - \gamma} b_1(z^t)^{-\alpha}$$
$$= \lambda_2 \omega c_2[a_2(z^t), b_2(z^t)]^{\alpha - \gamma} b_2(z^t)^{-\alpha}$$

The terms of trade is $p(z^t) = q_2(z^t)/q_1(z^t) = Q_2(z^t)/Q_1(z^t)$.

In this section we restrict ourselves to the case of identical preferences, $\omega = 1$, for which the analysis can be done analytically. The equilibrium allocation is then

$$a_i(z^t) = s_i y_1(z^t) \qquad b_i(z^t) = s_i y_2(z^t)$$

for countries $i = 1, 2$, with consumption shares $s_i = \lambda_i^{1/\gamma}/\Sigma_j \lambda_j^{1/\gamma}$ that sum to unity. Backus (1992) describes how the welfare weights, and hence the shares, are related to the endowments. The properties of interest, however, do not depend on the choice of weights, and so we can skip this additional step. The supporting prices up to a factor of proportionality are

$$Q_i(z^t) = y_i(z^t)^{-\alpha}$$

and the equilibrium terms of trade are

$$p(z^t) = \left[\frac{y_2(z^t)}{y_1(z^t)}\right]^{-\alpha}$$

The trade balance in country 1 in units of the domestic good is

$$nx_1(z^t) = y_1(z^t) - [a_1(z^t) + p(z^t)b_1(z^t)]$$

In equilibrium the ratio of the trade balance to output (the form of the trade variable used in table 3.1) is

$$\frac{nx_1(z^t)}{y_1(z^t)} = (1 - s_1) - s_1\left[\frac{y_2(z^t)}{y_1(z^t)}\right]^{1-\alpha}$$

Along any equilibrium path for this economy the welfare weights λ_i are constant. Since the consumption shares s_i are functions of the welfare weights alone, they are constant as well. Thus fluctuations in both the trade balance and the terms of trade are driven, along any equilibrium path, only by movements in the endowment ratio y_2/y_1. In this sense, equilibrium prices and quantities are functions of a single state variable, the ratio y_2/y_1, and are thus indirectly related to each other.

3.3   Movements of the terms of trade and net exports

Although the theory is fairly simple, we can start to compare some of its properties with those of the data – in particular, the variability and persistence of the terms of trade p and the correlation of the terms of trade with net exports. It is clear that the variability of p is governed by the variability of the endowment ratio y_2/y_1 and the substitution parameter $\sigma = 1/\alpha$. A given amount of variability of the endowment ratio can produce as much price variability as we like if σ is small enough. As an example, consider the standard deviation of the US terms of trade reported in table 3.1: 3 percent, for the period as a whole. This refers to the standard deviation of the Hodrick–Prescott filtered logarithm. The standard deviation of the filtered logarithm of the ratio of Japanese to US output is about 2.2. To generate the amount of price variability we see in the USA, then, we need an elasticity of about $\sigma = 0.73$ (since $2.2/0.73 = 3.0$). This is only a rough calculation, since the data refer to a world with more than one country and in which a large part of the variability of output appears in investment, which is obviously absent here. But it is suggestive of the role played by the elasticity of substitution in generating relative price variability. As a rule, the theory can produce any amount of price variability we like if the elasticity of substitution is a free parameter.

With regard to persistence, the terms of trade inherits the autocorrelation properties of the endowment ratio. To continue our example, the autocorrelation of the Japan–US output ratio (i.e. the filtered logarithm) is 0.7, and so the autocorrelation of the terms of trade, in our theory, is also 0.7. This is slightly less than we see for the US terms of trade in table 3.1, but the discrepancy is not large, either economically or statistically.

The final issue concerns the relation between the trade balance and the terms of trade. The contemporaneous relation is summarized by proposition 1.

PROPOSITION 1   Let $\omega = 1$ in the Armington aggregator G. Then the relation between the trade balance nx_1/y_1 and the terms of trade p is governed by $\sigma = 1/\alpha$, the elasticity of substitution between foreign and domestic goods. If $\sigma > 1$ the two variables are positively related, and if $\sigma < 1$ they are negatively related.

More precisely, consider two states with endowment ratios $x = y_2/y_1$ and $x' = y_2'/y_1'$, with $x > x'$. Since p is a decreasing function of the endowment ratio, $p < p'$. Now consider the trade balance. If $\sigma > 1$ then $nx/y < nx'/y'$. In this case the state with higher p also has higher nx/y and the two variables are, in this sense, positively related. If $\sigma < 1$ the reverse is true. A similar result is implicit in Stockman and Svensson (1987, section 5.3). If $\sigma = 1$ the trade balance is constant, as noted recently by Cole and Obstfeld (1991). Except for nonlinearities and nonstationarities, the correlation is either $+1$ or -1 unless $\sigma = 1$, when the trade balance is constant and the correlation is not defined.

The dynamics of the relation between trade and prices, like the dynamics of prices, are determined completely by the dynamics of the endowment ratio. Except for nonlinearities and nonstationarities, the cross-correlation function for the trade balance and the terms of trade is the same as the autocorrelation function of the endowment ratio. By way of example, suppose the logarithm of the endowment ratio is AR(1), with autocorrelation $\rho > 0$. Then if $\sigma > 1$ the cross-correlation function for the trade balance and the terms of trade is tent-shaped: the contemporaneous correlation is $+1$ and the correlation between p_t and nx_{t+k} is $\rho^{|k|}$. If $\sigma < 1$ the function is V-shaped. Even with other autocorrelation patterns the cross-correlation function will be symmetric since the autocorrelation function is. The exchange economy is therefore incapable of reproducing the asymmetric correlation functions pictured in figure 3.1.

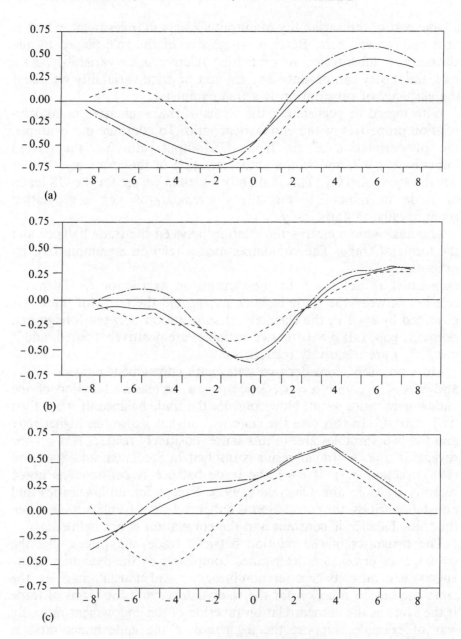

Figure 3.1   S-curves in the data: (a) Japan; (b) UK; (c) USA; ———,
all; ---, pre-Bretton Woods; _ . _ , post-Bretton Woods.

4   Preference for home goods

When consumers in the two countries have preferences that favor their respective home goods ($\omega > 1$ in the Armington aggregator G), the behavior of trade and prices changes somewhat. When preferences for domestic and foreign goods are not additively separable, we find that the risk aversion parameter γ, as well as the elasticity of substitution between foreign and domestic goods $\sigma = 1/\alpha$, plays a role in the relation between the trade balance and the terms of trade.

The simplest case is $\gamma = \alpha$: risk aversion γ is the inverse of the substitution elasticity for foreign and domestic goods ($\sigma = 1/\alpha$). With this restriction preferences, including the aggregator, are additively separable between the foreign and domestic goods, which simplifies the analysis considerably. We compute an equilibrium, as before, from an optimum. The reader may verify that the equilibrium allocations, for countries $i = 1,2$, are

$$a_i(z^t) = s_i^a y_1(z^t) \qquad b_i(z^t) = s_i^b y_2(z^t)$$

where the consumption shares $s_1^a = (\omega\lambda_1)^{1/\gamma}/[(\omega\lambda_1)^{1/\gamma} + \lambda_2^{1/\gamma}]$, $s_2^a = 1 - s_1^a$, $s_1^b = \lambda_1^{1/\gamma}/[\lambda_1^{1/\gamma} + (\omega\lambda_2)^{1/\gamma}]$, and $s_2^b = 1 - s_1^b$ are constant along any equilibrium path. The only difference from the symmetric case is that the consumption shares now differ across goods, with larger values of ω leading to larger shares of home good consumption s_1^a and s_2^b. The supporting prices are

$$Q_1(z^t) = [(\omega\lambda_1)^{1/\gamma} + \lambda_2^{1/\gamma}]^\gamma y_1(z^t)^{-\alpha}$$

$$Q_2(z^t) = [\lambda_1^{1/\gamma} + (\omega\lambda_2)^{1/\gamma}]^\gamma y_2(z^t)^{-\alpha}$$

and so the equilibrium terms of trade are

$$p(z^t) = \frac{Q_2(z^t)}{Q_1(z^t)} = \left(\frac{\omega s_1^b}{s_1^a}\right)^\gamma \left[\frac{y_2(z^t)}{y_1(z^t)}\right]^{-\alpha}$$

As before, the relative price p is driven by the endowment ratio. The only change is the factor of proportionality, which does not affect the properties of the logarithm of p. The variability of the terms of trade is determined by the variability of the endowment ratio y_2/y_1 and the elasticity of substitution $\sigma = 1/\alpha$.

The trade balance for country 1 in this economy, expressed as a ratio to domestic output, is

$$\frac{nx_1(z^t)}{y_1(z^t)} = (1 - s_1^a) - s_1^b \left[\frac{y_2(z^t)}{y_1(z^t)}\right]^{1-\alpha}$$

We can see that preference for home goods ($\omega > 1$) has the effect of damping fluctuations in the balance of trade, since larger values of ω imply smaller values of s_1^b. Co-movements, however, do not change: the sign of the effect of the endowment ratio on the balance of trade once more hinges on whether $\sigma = 1/\alpha$ is greater or less than unity and does not depend on any other parameters. Thus the properties described in the previous section for identical preferences ($\omega = 1$) apply to this economy as well.

It should be clear, then, that any influence of the home preference parameter ω on price behavior must operate through nonseparabilities between domestic and foreign goods – different values of α and γ. The allocation of goods between countries is influenced, in this case, by the sign of $\alpha - \gamma$. The first-order conditions do not admit a simple analytic solution, but the intuition behind the equilibrium allocation is fairly straightforward. As before, the variables of interest are functions of the endowment ratio $x = y_2/y_1$. In states with high values of x, the ratios of foreign to domestic good consumption b_i/a_i and the aggregate consumption ratio c_2/c_1 are also high: they are increasing functions, in other words, of the endowment ratio x. Neither property is surprising: if there is relatively more of the foreign good, then in equilibrium both agents consume relatively more, and aggregate consumption favors the country whose preferences weight the foreign good more (country 2, since $\omega > 1$). In simple terms, let the foreign and domestic goods be bananas and apples and suppose the foreign agent prefers bananas ($\omega > 1$) and the domestic agent prefers apples. Then the two statements are, first, that in states with relatively more bananas both agents consume relatively more bananas than apples and, second, that aggregate consumption by the foreign agent, who has a stronger preference for bananas, rises proportionately more than consumption by the domestic agent. Proofs of both of these statements are included in the appendix.

From this starting point we can deduce the effects on the relative price of the foreign good and the balance of trade. Consider the price. From the first-order conditions reported in the previous section we see that the terms of trade satisfy the relations

$$p = \omega^{-1}\left(\frac{b_1}{a_1}\right)^{-\alpha} = \omega\left(\frac{b_2}{a_2}\right)^{-\alpha}$$

where for convenience we have dropped explicit dependence of variables on the state z^t. Since b_1/a_1 and b_2/a_2 are increasing functions of the endowment ratio x, the terms of trade is a decreasing function. Thus an increase in the relative supply of the foreign good lowers its relative price. With somewhat greater effort we can characterize the magnitude of the decline. The first step is to relate the endowment ratio to b_1/a_1. The resource constraints imply

$$x = \frac{y_2}{y_1} = s_1^b\left(\frac{b_1}{a_1}\right) + (1 - s_1^b)\left(\frac{b_2}{a_2}\right) = [s_1^b + \omega^{2/\alpha}(1 - s_1^b)]\left(\frac{b_1}{a_1}\right)$$

where $s_1^b = b_1/y_2$ is the (possibly state-dependent) share of foreign good consumption by the agent of country 1. Thus, with $\omega > 1$, the proportional change in b_1/a_1 can be either greater than or less than the proportional change in x, depending on whether s_1^b increases or decreases with x. The second step follows from the first-order conditions for the foreign good:

$$\left(\frac{b_1}{b_2}\right)^\alpha = \left(\frac{s_1^b}{1 - s_1^b}\right)^\alpha = \frac{\omega\lambda_2}{\lambda_1}\left(\frac{c_2}{c_1}\right)^{\gamma - \alpha}$$

Since c_2/c_1 is an increasing function of the endowment ratio, s_1^b is increasing in x if $\gamma > \alpha$, decreasing if $\gamma < \alpha$, and constant if $\gamma = \alpha$ (this being the additively separable case described earlier). Thus the (absolute value of the) slope of the relation between the logarithms of the terms of trade p and the endowment ratio x is greater than α if $\gamma > \alpha$, less than α if $\gamma < \alpha$, and equal to α (as we have already seen) if $\gamma = \alpha$. Other things being equal, greater risk aversion tends to increase the variability of the terms of trade relative to that of the endowment ratio.

The contemporaneous relation between the trade balance and the terms of trade is characterized by proposition 2.

PROPOSITION 2   Let $\omega > 1$ (preference for home goods). Then there is a positive number σ^* such that if $\sigma > \sigma^*$ the trade balance nx_1/y_1 is positively related to the terms of trade p and if $\sigma < \sigma^*$ the two variables are negatively related. Furthermore, if $\gamma > 1$ then $\sigma^* < 1$.

Thus the risk aversion parameter γ has an influence on co-movements between the trade balance and the terms of trade. The proof consists largely of expressing the ratio of the trade balance to output in a convenient form. As in proposition 1, both the trade balance and the terms of trade are monotonic functions of the endowment ratio $x = y_2/y_1$. The terms of trade, for all parameter values, is decreasing in x. As for the trade balance, we let

$$\frac{nx_1}{y_1} = \frac{a_2 - pb_1}{y_1} = 1 - s_1^a\left[1 + \omega^{-1}\left(\frac{b_1}{a_1}\right)^{1-\alpha}\right]$$

With $\omega = 1$, s_1^a is constant. Since b_1/a_1, as we have shown, is increasing in the endowment ratio $x = y_2/y_1$, the proposition follows immediately with $\sigma^* = 1$. With $\omega > 1$ the dependence of s_1^a on x introduces an additional element of dependence on x. If $\gamma > 1$ and $\alpha < \gamma$, s_1^a is increasing in x. Thus, for $\alpha \leq 1$ the trade balance is decreasing in x. By continuity this is true for values of α slightly greater than 1 as well. For large values of α, however, the trade balance is increasing in x, as we show in the appendix (result 4). Thus there are numbers $\alpha^* > 1$ and $\sigma^* = 1/\alpha^* < 1$ that divide regions of positive and negative co-movement between the trade balance and the terms of trade.

In short, the economy is much like that of the previous section. Its similarities and differences are illustrated by the following example.

EXAMPLE   There are two states with unconditional probabilities (1/2, 1/2). (With two states nonlinearities are irrelevant since two points can always be connected by a straight line.) Let the aggregate endowments (y_1, y_2) of the domestic and foreign goods be $(1 + \varepsilon, 1 - \varepsilon)$ in state 1 and $(1 - \varepsilon, 1 + \varepsilon)$ in state 2, with $\varepsilon > 0$. Thus the standard deviations of y_1 and y_2 are ε and the standard deviation of the logarithm of the endowment ratio y_2/y_1 is, for small ε, approximately 2ε. The transition probabilities between states i and j are

$$[\pi_{ij}] = \begin{bmatrix} (1+\rho)/2 & (1-\rho)/2 \\ (1-\rho)/2 & (1+\rho)/2 \end{bmatrix}$$

The persistence parameter ρ governs the autocorrelation function for any random variable adapted to the state, with the k-order autocorrelation equal to ρ^k.

CASE 1: IDENTICAL PREFERENCES ($\omega = 1$)   The terms of trade are

$$p = (y_2/y_1)^{-\alpha}$$

which equals $[(1 + \varepsilon)/(1 - \varepsilon)]^{-\alpha}$ in state 1 and $[(1 - \varepsilon)/(1 + \varepsilon)]^{-\alpha}$ in state 2. The standard deviation of the logarithm of p, for small ε, is approximately $\alpha(2\varepsilon)$. With $\varepsilon = 0.05$ and $\alpha = 5$, the standard deviation is 0.500. The ratio of the trade balance to output is

$$tb = \frac{nx_1}{y_1} = \frac{1}{2} - \frac{1}{2}\left(\frac{y_2}{y_1}\right)^{1-\alpha} = \frac{1}{2}\left[1 - \left(\frac{y_2}{y_1}\right)^{1-\alpha}\right]$$

Thus for $\sigma = 1/\alpha < 1$ the correlation between p and tb is -1; for $\sigma > 1$ the correlation is $+1$. For $\alpha = 1$ the trade balance is zero in both states and the correlation is not defined. Note that the persistence parameter ρ has no bearing on this correlation. The cross-correlation function for the trade balance and the terms of trade has the form

$$corr(tb_t, p_{t+k}) = sign(\sigma - 1)\, \rho^{|k|}$$

where $\sigma = 1/\alpha$. As noted earlier, this function is symmetric in k.

CASE 2: PREFERENCE FOR HOME GOODS ($\omega > 1$)   To make this concrete, let $\varepsilon = 0.05$, $\omega = 2$, and $\gamma = 2$. With $\alpha = 5$ the standard deviation of the logarithm of the terms of trade is 0.497, slightly smaller than in the case of identical preferences. There is a critical value $\sigma^* = 0.885 < 1$ of the elasticity of substitution such that for $\sigma > \sigma^*$ the trade balance and the terms of trade are positively correlated, and for $\sigma < \sigma^*$ they are negatively correlated. The cross-correlation function is

$$\text{corr}(\text{tb}_t, p_{t+k}) = \text{sign}(\sigma^* - 1)\, \rho^{|k|}$$

which remains symmetric.

5   The Marshall–Lerner condition and the Harberger–Laursen–Metzler effect

The theory of the last two sections and its relation to time series data is relatively straightforward. We have found, however, that it gives us a very different understanding of the relation between trade and relative prices than either the widely cited Marshall–Lerner condition or the 1980s literature on the Harberger–Laursen–Metzler effect. In this section we compare our work with these other approaches and point out the differences between them.

5.1   A closer look at the Marshall–Lerner condition

The elasticity condition of proposition 1 is an example of a common result in price theory, that the sign of something depends on whether utility is more or less concave than the logarithm ($\sigma = 1$). In that sense there is nothing surprising about it. What we find interesting in the present setting is the difference between this condition and the Marshall–Lerner condition, often cited as the determining factor in the sign of the relation between the trade balance and the terms of trade. The Marshall–Lerner condition is the centerpiece of textbook treatments of this issue; among many other examples, see Dornbusch (1980, p. 59), Ethier (1988, pp. 402–7), and Krugman and Obstfeld (1991, p. 423).

The Marshall–Lerner condition applies to a static economy, but we can review its logic in a one-period version of our two-country world. Our treatment follows Kemp (1987). We start by deriving conditions on static import demand functions that allow us to express the balance of trade as an increasing function of the terms of trade. Among the conditions for equilibrium in the static economy are the resource constraint for the home good

$$a_1 + a_2 = y_1$$

and the first agent's budget constraint

$$a_1 + pb_1 = y_1$$

These conditions together imply balanced trade:

$$nx_1 = a_2 - pb_1 = 0$$

Utility maximization by both agents, subject to their respective budget constraints, results in import demand functions $a_2(p)$ and $b_1(p)$, say. These functions define net exports as a function of the terms of trade:

$$nx_1(p) = a_2(p) - pb_1(p)$$

This function is increasing in p if

$$\varepsilon + \varepsilon^* > 1$$

where

$$\varepsilon = -\frac{\partial b_1}{\partial p}\frac{p}{b_1}$$

and

$$\varepsilon^* = \frac{\partial a_2}{\partial p}\frac{p}{a_2}$$

are the domestic and foreign import elasticities. The inequality is the well-known Marshall–Lerner condition.

We now apply this analysis to our economy. The relevant import demand functions are

$$b_1(p) = \frac{y_1}{p + p^\sigma}$$

$$a_2(p) = \frac{y_2 p^{\sigma+1}}{p + p^\sigma}$$

where, as before, $\sigma = 1/\alpha$ is the elasticity of substitution between foreign and domestic goods. The import elasticities are therefore

$$\varepsilon = -\frac{1 + \sigma p^{\sigma-1}}{p + p^\sigma}$$

$$\varepsilon^* = \frac{p^\sigma(\sigma + p^{\sigma-1})}{p + p^\sigma}$$

Adding these two expressions together, we find that for all positive p and σ

$$\varepsilon + \varepsilon^* > 1$$

In other words, the Marshall–Lerner condition is always satisfied in this economy, regardless of the value of the elasticity of substitution between foreign and domestic goods. This example illustrates a more general result, cited by Ethier (1988, section A.3): that the Marshall–Lerner condition is always satisfied when consumers in the two countries have identical homothetic preferences.

Thus we see that the Marshall–Lerner condition has no connection with the elasticity condition of proposition 1 and therefore has no bearing on the correlation between the trade balance and the terms of trade for time series data generated by economies like ours. The difference in results stems, we think, from the difference between dynamic modeling and the static analysis that underlies the Marshall–Lerner condition. Despite the intuitive appeal of the latter, we find that when the dynamics are worked out explicitly we get a different interpretation of this property of the data.

5.2 Revival of the Harberger–Laursen–Metzler effect

The theoretical state of the art regarding the relation between the trade balance and the terms of trade, however, is not the Marshall–Lerner condition but the 1980s revival of the Harberger–Laursen–Metzler effect initiated by Obstfeld (1982) and Svensson and Razin (1983). These papers, and others that followed, start with the central insight of the absorption approach: that trade imbalances reflect differences between saving and investment. The theoretical economies of these two papers are deterministic but share with ours the feature that dynamics are explicit. They come to very different conclusions, however, regarding the factors that lead to a positive association between the trade balance and the terms of trade. These papers suggest that two factors are critical in determining the pattern of co-movements: the persistence of the shock and the form of dependence of the discount factor, or rate of time preference, on future utility. Transitory shocks typically lead, in their analysis, to movements in the terms of trade and the trade balance of opposite sign. We find, in contrast, that the relation between the trade balance and the terms of trade is independent of the dynamics of prices. Obstfeld (1982) and Svensson and Razin (1983) also find that the effect of permanent shocks depends on the behavior of the discount factor. As Svensson and Razin (1983, p. 100) put it: "A permanent terms-of-trade deterioration . . . causes a deterioration or improvement in the real trade balance, depending on whether . . . the rate of time preference decreases or increases, respectively, with the level of welfare." Obstfeld (1982) assumes that the rate of time preference is increasing in utility and therefore predicts a decline in the trade balance. In his words (1982, p. 251), "an economy specialized in production must experience a fall in aggregate spending and a current [account] surplus as a result of an unanticipated, permanent worsening in its terms of trade." In both papers there is no effect of a permanent change in price on the trade balance if the rate of time preference is constant. In our economies, the rate of time preference is constant, fixed by the discount factor β. The conclusion should then be that permanent movements in the terms of trade have no effect on the trade balance. We find, instead, that the relation between the trade balance and the terms of trade is determined by the elasticity of substitution, regardless of the persistence of shocks.

As in our analysis of the Marshall–Lerner condition, the difference between our approach and that of the Harberger–Laursen–Metzler literature stems, in part, from our definition of the issue. In our analysis, the relation between the trade balance and the terms of trade pertains to the correlation between these two variables for a single time series realization, like the quarterly series for Japan, the UK, and the USA described in table 3.1. This corresponds, in our theoretical economies, to the correlation between the two variables along an equilibrium path. In the analysis of Obstfeld (1982) and Svensson and Razin (1983), however, the Harberger–Laursen–Metzler effect pertains to a comparison between two different deterministic equilibria: one in which the terms of trade is high, and one in which it is low. Apparently these two thought experiments emphasize very different features of the theory. We would argue that our thought experiment is closer to what we have in mind when we compare theory and data. A closer look also suggests, as brought out by Backus (1992) and Stockman and Svensson (1987), that the theory requires explicit treatment of the stochastic structure of the economy, something that deterministic analysis obviously cannot provide.

One way in which these two points of view might be reconciled is to consider economies in which agents have more limited ability to hedge risk than they do in the complete market economies of sections 3 and 4. In the 1980s analysis of the Harberger–Laursen–Metzler effect, income effects play a central role. In our economies, however, there are no income effects along an equilibrium path. With complete markets each agent has a single, date-0 budget constraint. As a result, each has a state-invariant marginal utility of income, reflected in the constant welfare weights of our optimum problem. Backus (1992), Kehoe and Richardson (1985), and Mendoza (1992) suggest that some of the flavor of the Harberger–Laursen–Metzler literature may carry over to dynamic stochastic settings with some types of market incompleteness.

In short, we have found that explicit dynamic stochastic analysis of trade and relative prices leads to very different views of the factors determining their co-movements. Even the role of that textbook standard, the Marshall–Lerner condition, may need to be reconsidered.

6   Government spending

The theory thus far has focused on fluctuations in trade and prices arising from movements in endowments. Here we consider an extension to the exchange economy of section 3 in which, in addition, we have exogenous shocks to government spending. Related analyses have been provided by Baxter (1992), Buiter (1989), Hodrick (1988), Macklem (1991), Obstfeld (1989), Reynolds (1991), and Yi (1991). We find this extension both interesting in its own right and a useful step toward introducing a wide range of impulses into dynamic general equilibrium models of trade: shocks, for example, to taxes, tariffs, and possibly even monetary policies. To keep the analysis simple, we restrict ourselves to the case of symmetric preferences ($\omega = 1$ in the Armington aggregator G).

In this new economy the government is an additional consumer of goods. Let us say that in state z^t the government of country i consumes the quantity $g_i(z^t)$ of its home good. This spending is financed with lump-sum taxes, $\tau_i(z^t)$ say. An equilibrium then consists of quantities a_i and b_i, prices q_i, and government policies g_i, τ_i such that (a) agents maximize utility given prices and budget constraints, (b) quantities satisfy the resource constraints

$$y_1(z^t) - g_1(z^t) = a_1(z^t) + a_2(z^t)$$

$$y_2(z^t) - g_2(z^t) = b_1(z^t) + b_2(z^t)$$

and (c) policies satisfy governments' budget constraints.

With this structure, the economy is equivalent to one with "net endowments" $y_i - g_i$, rather than y_i, and we can apply most of the results of section 3 with little change. The equilibrium allocation includes

$$a_i(z^t) = s_i[y_1(z^t) - g_1(z^t)]$$

$$b_i(z^t) = s_i[y_2(z^t) - g_2(z^t)]$$

for $i = 1,2$, with consumption shares $s_i = \lambda_i^{1/\gamma}/\Sigma_j\lambda_j^{1/\gamma}$ for some choice of welfare weights λ_i. The equilibrium terms of trade are

$$p(z^t) = \left[\frac{y_2(z^t) - g_2(z^t)}{y_1(z^t) - g_1(z^t)}\right]^{-\alpha}$$

The variability of the terms of trade is governed, then, by the variability of the net endowment ratio and the elasticity of substitution $\sigma = 1/\alpha$. In practice, the addition of government purchases has little influence on the variance of p since g is only a fraction of output and is generally less variable. The same reasoning applies to persistence: introducing government purchases of goods and services does little to change our prediction that relative prices retain the persistence of output ratios.

The most interesting consequences of government purchases concern trade. If $w_i = y_i - g_i$ is the endowment net of government purchases, net exports in country 1 are

$$nx_1(z^t) = (1 - s_1)w_1(z^t) - \left[\frac{w_2(z^t)}{w_1(z^t)}\right]^{-\alpha} s_1 w_2(z^t)$$

$$= w_1(z^t)\left\{(1 - s_1) - s_1\left[\frac{w_2(z^t)}{w_1(z^t)}\right]^{1-\alpha}\right\}$$

The ratio of net exports to output is

$$\frac{nx_1(z^t)}{y_1(z^t)} = \left\{(1 - s_1) - s_1\left[\frac{w_2(z^t)}{w_1(z^t)}\right]^{1-\alpha}\right\}\frac{w_1(z^t)}{y_1(z^t)}$$

In our earlier analysis, g_1 was zero and the last term was therefore unity. As a result, the effect of the endowment ratio on the trade balance and the association between movements in the trade balance nx_1/y_1 and the terms of trade p depended only on the value of $\sigma = 1/\alpha$. For $\sigma < 1$ the association was positive; for $\sigma < 1$ the reverse. Here we find an additional factor, the ratio of the net endowment w_1 to total output y_1.

We can get some idea of the contributions of output and government spending shocks on trade and price fluctuations by considering special cases. Consider, first, the case in which g_1 is proportional to y_1. Then w_1/y_1 is constant, and the relation between the trade balance and the terms of trade is determined by σ, as it was in proposition 1. With $\sigma > 1$ (or $\alpha < 1$) the trade balance and the terms of trade are positively related along an equilibrium path; with $\sigma < 1$ they are negatively related. Alternatively, suppose outputs y_i are constant and g_1 is the only shock. Then the trade balance and the terms of trade are positively associated, regardless of the value of σ. This example is like many others in economics in which the co-movement between two endogenous variables depends on the source of their fluctuations.

This analysis suggests a second look at trade and price data, with special attention paid to government purchases. As we see in table 3.2, there has been little regularity across countries either in the variability of government purchases relative to that of real output or in the correlation between these two variables. The same statement applies to the correlations of government purchases with the trade balance and the terms of trade. That is not to say that government purchases have not played a role in trade and price behavior, but simply that this role is not simple enough to show up in summary statistics of this form. Froot and Rogoff (1991) document somewhat stronger indications of a relation between government spending and real exchange rates using different methods.

7   Trade and capital formation

In the exchange economies of sections 3 and 4 we compared properties of the data with analogous properties of trade and relative prices in simple theoretical economies. This analysis brought up two questions that deserve a closer look. We found, for one thing, that the variability of the terms of trade is governed by the variability of the output ratio and the elasticity of substitution between foreign and domestic goods. By choosing a sufficiently small elasticity the theory can generate literally any amount of relative price variability. The question, in this case, is whether price variability in the theory and price variability in the data are close for reasonable values of this elasticity. In another respect, we found that the exchange economy could not, for any choice of parameter values, mimic the data: the cross-correlation function for the trade balance and the terms of trade. In the data this function is generally asymmetric, a feature we documented in figure 3.1 and labeled the S-curve. In the exchange economy, however, the function is symmetric by construction, since both the trade balance and the terms of trade are functions of the same state variable. The question here is whether this property changes when we introduce physical capital formation.

The introduction of capital formation brings us closer to the theme of the absorption approach to the balance of payments: that fluctuations in trade reflect differences between saving and investment. At the level of accounting this connection is undeniable, but it also shifts one's attention away from within-period relative prices to the intertemporal decisions to save and invest. Thus Sachs (1981) argues that trade deficits often reflect investment booms and Stockman and Svensson (1987) tie both trade and relative prices to fluctuations in, among other things, fixed capital formation. We continue this tradition by introducing capital formation to an economy that is otherwise like our earlier ones. The structure is adapted from Backus et al. (1991). The emphasis, as in earlier sections, is on the dynamics of the trade balance and the terms of trade.

7.1 The theoretical two-country framework

The theoretical economy has the following elements. There are, as before, two countries that specialize in different goods. Preferences of the representative consumer in each country i are characterized by an expected utility function of the form

$$u_i = E_0 \sum_{t=0}^{\infty} \beta^t U(c_{it}, 1 - n_{it})$$

where c_{it} and n_{it} are consumption and hours worked in country i, $U(c, 1 - n) = [c^\mu (1 - n)^{1 - \mu}]^{1 - \gamma}/(1 - \gamma)$, and $\gamma \geq 0$. The primary difference in preferences from the economy of section 3 is the appearance of leisure in agents' utility functions.

Goods in the two countries, labeled a for country 1 and b for country 2, are produced using capital k and labor n with linear homogeneous production functions of the same form, $F(k, n) = k^\theta n^{1 - \theta}$. This gives rise to the date-t resource constraints

$$a_{1t} + a_{2t} = y_{1t} = z_{1t} F(k_{1t}, n_{1t})$$

$$b_{1t} + b_{2t} = y_{2t} = z_{2t} F(k_{2t}, n_{2t})$$

in countries 1 and 2 respectively. The quantity y_{it} denotes gross domestic product in country i, measured in units of the local good, and a_{it} and b_{it} denote uses of the two goods in country i. If k and n are constant, this reduces to the pure exchange setting of section 3, with productivity shocks giving rise to proportionate output fluctuations. The vector $z_t = (z_{1t}, z_{2t})$ is a stochastic shock to productivity whose properties will be described shortly.

Consumption, investment, and government spending in each country are composites of the foreign and domestic goods, with

$$c_{1t} + x_{1t} + g_{1t} = G(a_{1t}, b_{1t})$$

$$c_{2t} + x_{2t} + g_{2t} = G(b_{2t}, a_{2t})$$

where, as before, $G(a, b) = (\omega a^{1 - \alpha} + b^{1 - \alpha})^{1/(1 - \alpha)}$. The parameters α and ω are both positive, and the elasticity of substitution between foreign and domestic goods is $\sigma = 1/\alpha$. As noted earlier, this structure is widely used in static general equilibrium models of trade. Capital stocks evolve according to

$$k_{it+1} = (1 - \delta)k_{it} + x_{it}$$

where δ is the depreciation rate. Two differences between this economy and the exchange economy of sections 3–5 are the introduction of capital formation and the assumption here that government spending may have some foreign content.

Finally, the underlying shocks to our economy are independent bivariate autoregressions. The technology shocks follow

$$z_{t+1} = Az_t + \epsilon_{t+1}^z$$

where ϵ^z is distributed normally and independently over time with variance V_z. The correlation between the technology shocks z_1 and z_2 is determined by the off-diagonal elements of A and V_z. Similarly, shocks to government spending are governed by

$$g_{t+1} = Bg_t + \epsilon_{t+1}^g$$

where $g_t = (g_{1t}, g_{2t})$ and ϵ^g is distributed normally with variance V_g. Technology shocks z and government spending shocks g are independent.

7.2   Behavior of the terms of trade

With these elements, and the parameter values listed in table 3.3, we can approach the behavior of the terms of trade. The critical parameters, for our purpose, are the elasticity of substitution σ which we set equal to 1.5, and the steady state ratio of imports to gross domestic product, which we set equal to 0.15 by choosing ω appropriately. In this benchmark version of the economy foreign and domestic goods are better substitutes than they would be with Cobb–Douglas preferences ($\sigma = 1$) and imports are, on average, 85 percent of gross domestic product. The choice of elasticity is in the range of estimates from a large number of studies, as documented by Whalley (1985, ch. 4). Estimates of the elasticity are generally close to unity, often slightly larger. The import share is slightly larger than we see in the

Table 3.3   Benchmark parameter values

Preferences	$\beta = 0.99$	$\mu = 0.34$	$\gamma = 2.0$
Technology	$\theta = 0.36$	$\delta = 0.025$	$\sigma = 1/\alpha = 1.5$

Technology row, final column: import share = 0.15

$$A = \begin{bmatrix} a_{11} & a_{12} \\ a_{12} & a_{11} \end{bmatrix} = \begin{bmatrix} 0.906 & 0.088 \\ 0.088 & 0.906 \end{bmatrix}$$

Forcing processes

$$\text{var } \varepsilon_1^z = \text{var } \varepsilon_2^z = 0.00852^2 \qquad \text{corr}(\varepsilon_1^z, \varepsilon_2^z) = 0.258$$

$$g_t = 0$$

USA, Japan, or an aggregate of European countries (with intra-European trade netted out), but smaller than we see for most countries individually.

A number of properties of the theoretical economy with alternative parameter settings are reported in table 3.4. Consider, first, fluctuations in the terms of trade. The standard deviation of the terms of trade with our benchmark parameter values is 0.48 percent, which is a factor of 6 less than we see for the USA in table 3.1. With smaller values of σ the theoretical economy generates greater variability of the terms of trade. As illustrated in figure 3.2, the standard deviation of p gets larger as we decrease σ, and for σ less than 0.03 the standard deviation exceeds 2. Thus it appears that while the theory can produce as much variability in the terms of trade as we see in the data, it requires an elasticity of substitution much smaller than most existing estimates.

The value of σ required to match the variability of the terms of trade in US data is substantially smaller in this model (less than 0.03) than in our calculation in section 3 for the USA and Japan (for which we estimated than $\sigma = 0.73$ would be sufficient). Three factors account for most of this difference. The first is that the theoretical economy, in the benchmark case, has about 25 percent less variability in the output ratio than we calculated for Japan and the USA. Modifications of the theory that bring the magnitude of business cycles closer to the data will also bring the theory and data closer together with respect to price

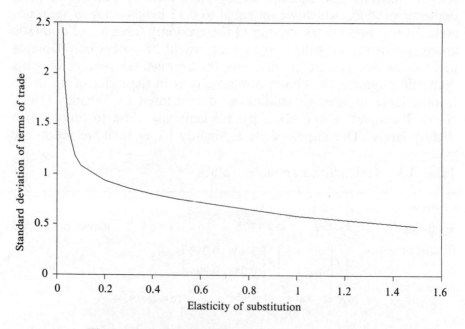

Figure 3.2   Variability of the terms of trade.

Table 3.4 Properties of theoretical economies with capital formation

Economy	Standard deviation (%)			Autocorrelation			Correlation		
	nx	y	p	nx	y	p	(nx, y)	(nx, p)	(y, p)
Benchmark	0.30	1.38	0.48	0.61	0.63	0.83	−0.64	−0.41	0.49
	(0.02)	(0.18)	(0.06)	(0.07)	(0.10)	(0.05)	(0.07)	(0.08)	(0.14)
Large	0.33	1.41	0.35	0.63	0.64	0.88	−0.57	−0.05	0.43
elasticity	(0.03)	(0.18)	(0.05)	(0.07)	(0.18)	(0.03)	(0.08)	(0.09)	(0.14)
Small	0.37	1.33	0.76	0.61	0.63	0.77	−0.66	−0.80	0.51
elasticity	(0.03)	(0.18)	(0.07)	(0.07)	(0.10)	(0.05)	(0.07)	(0.09)	(0.16)
Big share	0.63	1.37	0.58	0.59	0.64	0.83	−0.61	−0.41	0.52
	(0.04)	(0.18)	(0.08)	(0.07)	(0.10)	(0.04)	(0.07)	(0.07)	(0.13)
Small share	0.08	1.38	0.43	0.62	0.63	0.81	−0.65	−0.41	0.48
	(0.01)	(0.18)	(0.06)	(0.07)	(0.10)	(0.05)	(0.07)	(0.08)	(0.14)
Two shocks	0.33	1.33	0.57	0.62	0.65	0.78	−0.57	−0.05	0.39
	(0.03)	(0.15)	(0.07)	(0.08)	(0.08)	(0.06)	(0.15)	(0.17)	(0.17)
Government	0.16	0.17	0.30	0.67	0.67	0.67	−0.55	1.00	−0.55
shocks	(0.03)	(0.02)	(0.05)	(0.11)	(0.08)	(0.11)	(0.13)	(0.00)	(0.13)

Statistics are based on Hodrick–Prescott (1980) filtered data. Entries are averages over fifty simulations of 100 quarters each; numbers in parentheses are standard deviations.
Parameters are as in table 3.3, except for the following: large elasticity, $\sigma = 2.5$; small elasticity, $\sigma = 0.5$; big share, import share 0.25; small share, import share 0.05; two shocks, mean of $g = \text{diag}(0.2, 0.2)$, $B = \text{diag}(0.2, 0.2)$, $V_g = \text{diag}(0.95, 0.95)$, and $V_g = \text{diag}(0.004^2, 0.004^2)$; government shocks, as in two shocks plus $z_t = 1$, all t.

variability. The second factor is capital formation. If we eliminate capital (which we can do by setting $\theta = 0$ in the production function), the economy generates considerably greater price variability, despite less variability in the ratio of outputs. The final factor is the import share. If the import share is raised from 0.15 to 0.25, the variability increases substantially at every value of σ. For $\sigma = 1.5$, the benchmark value, the standard deviation of the relative price rises from 0.48 to 0.58.

7.3   Net exports and the terms of trade

A second property of the model is the contemporaneous correlation between net exports and the terms of trade. In the data this correlation has been positive for the USA and negative for Japan and the UK (see table 3.1). In the theoretical economy we find, for the benchmark parameter values, that the correlation is − 0.41. As we might expect from propositions 1 and 2, this correlation is sensitive to the elasticity of substitution. We see in figure 3.3 that the correlation increases with σ and is positive for elasticities greater than $\sigma^* = 2.76$. This feature, too, is strongly influenced by capital formation. In the model without capital ($\theta = 0$) the economy is much like that described in proposition 2, with

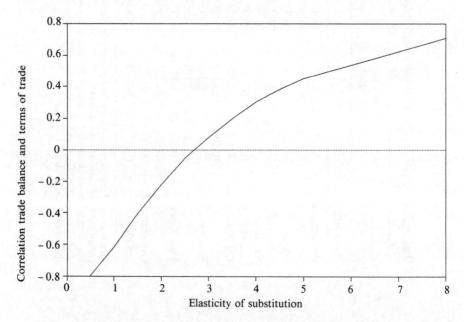

Figure 3.3   The trade balance and terms of trade.

a critical elasticity $\sigma^* = 0.94$. For $\sigma > \sigma^*$ the trade balance and the terms of trade are positively correlated; for $\sigma < \sigma^*$ the reverse.

A third property of interest is the impact of government spending on the correlation between the trade balance and the terms of trade. We see in table 3.4 that, with only shocks to government spending, the correlation between net exports and the terms of trade shifts from negative to positive. This mirrors a similar result in section 6. With shocks to both productivity z and government spending g we find that the former dominate, in the sense that the economy's properties are very similar to those with shocks to productivity alone.

Finally, we look at the complete cross-correlation function for net exports and the terms of trade. As pictured in figure 3.4, this correlation has the same asymmetric shape we documented for the data in figure 3.1. Some intuition for this behavior is provided by figure 3.5, in which we graph the dynamic responses to a one standard deviation shock to domestic productivity. Following this shock, output and the relative price of foreign goods both rise. Consumption also rises, but by less than output. Investment rises initially by much more than consumption, as resources are transferred to the home country to exploit its expected future productivity advantage. As capital accumulates, this resource transfer diminishes. The trade balance, which is the difference, at market prices, between output and the sum of consumption and

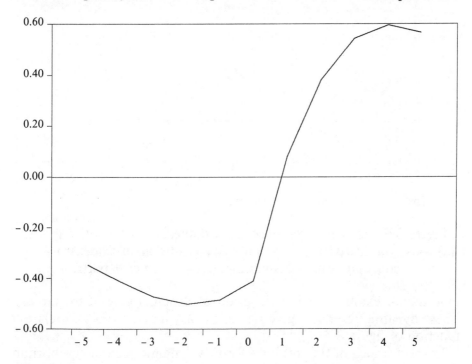

Figure 3.4 Cross-correlation function for the benchmark economy.

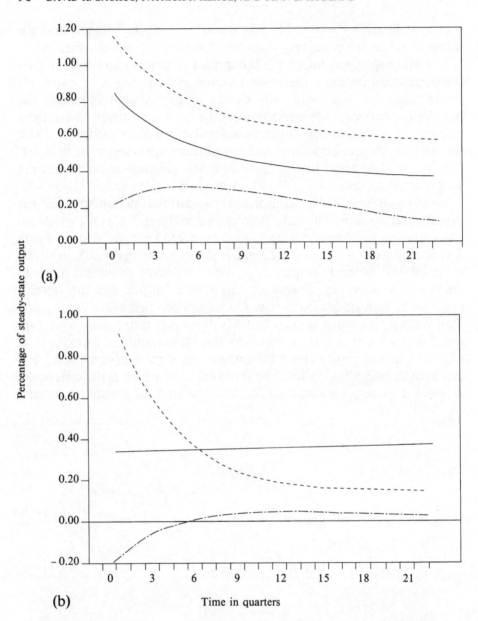

Percentage of steady-state output

(a)

(b)

Time in quarters

Figure 3.5 Dynamic responses to a domestic productivity shock:
(a) —— , productivity, ---, output, — . — , terms of trade; (b) —— ,
consumption, ---, investment, — . — , net exports.

investment, exhibits an initial period of deficit, followed by surplus.
These dynamic responses give rise to the asymmetric cross-correlation
function of figure 3.4.

In short, much of the intuition for this dynamic general equilibrium
trade model is available from the exchange economy of sections 3–5.

What the exchange economy misses completely is the dynamics of the relation between the trade balance and the terms of trade: the asymmetric cross-correlation function that we documented in the data and labeled the S-curve. The cross-correlation function between these two variables is symmetric in the exchange economy for all parameter values. In this section we have seen that the dynamics of capital formation provide a plausible basis for an asymmetric pattern.

8   Final thoughts

We have argued that a dynamic general equilibrium approach to aggregate trade theory provides both a new level of understanding of the interrelations between trade and price movements and a framework in which these relations can be quantified. With regard to the former, we have seen that the relation between trade and price variables is very different from that suggested by the Marshall–Lerner condition cited in most textbooks. With regard to the latter, we suggest that the dynamic relation between trade and the relative price of foreign goods can be understood as a consequence of the dynamics of capital formation. Thus the dynamics of trade variables are inseparable from the dynamics of the rest of the economy.

Future work will undoubtedly focus, however, not on these contributions but on dimensions in which the theory, in its current incarnation, provides a relatively poor approximation to the dynamics of actual economies. The most obvious example is the variability of the terms of trade. In the economy of section 7, and in Stockman and Tesar (1991) as well, the standard deviation of the terms of trade is substantially smaller than we estimate in the data. This discrepancy between theory and data helps to motivate theories in which monetary policy influences relative prices (Grilli and Roubini, 1992; Schlagen-hauf and Wrase, 1992) and in which international market segmentation, possibly in conjunction with imperfect competition, also play a part (Dumas, 1992; Giovannini, 1988; Lapham, 1990). Ongoing research will hopefully tell us how important each of these features is, and how they modify the lessons of the theory outlined above.

Appendix

The algebra for section 4 is straightforward but fairly tedious. We start by reducing the economy to two equations in two unknowns. The unknowns are the consumption shares of the first agent, $s_1^a = a_1/y_1$ and $s_1^b = b_1/y_2$. The first-order conditions and resource constraints then imply

$$\frac{s_1^a}{1 - s_1^a} = \omega^v \frac{s_1^b}{1 - s_1^b} \tag{A3.1}$$

and

$$\left(\frac{s_1^a}{1 - s_1^a}\right)^{\gamma} \frac{\lambda_2}{\omega \lambda_1} = \left(\frac{\omega + m^{1-\alpha}}{1 + \omega^{1+v} m^{1-\alpha}}\right)^{(\alpha - \gamma)/(1 - \alpha)} \tag{A3.2}$$

where $m = b_1/a_1 = x s_1^b/s_1^a > 0$ and $v = 2/\alpha > 0$. With these substitutions, the two equations determine s_1^a and s_1^b as functions of the endowment ratio $x = y_2/y_1$. Note that if either $\omega = 1$ or $\alpha = \gamma$ the right-hand side of (A3.2) is unity and s_1^a is constant.

Preliminaries

(a) If we differentiate the first equation we get

$$d\left(\frac{s_1^a}{1 - s_1^a}\right) = \frac{ds_1^a}{(1 - s_1^a)^2} = \omega^v \frac{ds_1^b}{(1 - s_1^b)^2}$$

or

$$\frac{ds_1^b}{s_1^b} = \frac{s_1^b}{s_1^a} \omega^v \frac{ds_1^a}{s_1^a}$$

Thus s_1^a and s_1^b are positively related and we can use this relation to substitute out any ds_1^bs we get.

(b) Differentiate the ratio s_1^b/s_1^a:

$$d\left(\frac{s_1^b}{s_1^a}\right) = \frac{s_1^b}{s_1^a}\left(\frac{s_1^b}{s_1^a}\omega^v - 1\right)\frac{ds_1^a}{s_1^a}$$

(c) Differentiate m:

$$\frac{dm}{m} = \frac{dx}{x} + \left(\frac{s_1^b}{s_1^a}\omega^v - 1\right)\frac{ds_1^a}{s_1^a}$$

(d) Inequalities. From (A3.1) and with $\omega > 1$:

$$s_1^a > s_1^b$$

$$\frac{s_1^b}{s_1^a}\omega^v - 1 = \frac{s_1^a - s_1^b}{1 - s_1^a} > 0$$

We now prove the propositions used in the text.

1   We show that s_1^a is increasing in x if $\gamma > \alpha$, decreasing if $\gamma < \alpha$. We differentiate (A3.2) and find, after rearrangement,

$$\gamma(w + m^{1-\alpha})(1 + w^{1+\nu}m^{1-\alpha})\frac{ds_1^a}{s_1^a} = (\alpha - \gamma)(1 - w^{2+\nu})(1 - s_1^a)m^{1-\alpha}\frac{dm}{m} \quad \text{(A3.3)}$$

If we substitute the expression for dm/m ((c) above) we get an equation of the form

$$A\frac{ds_1^a}{s_1^a} = B\frac{dx}{x} \quad \text{(A3.4)}$$

so that s_1^a is increasing in x if $B/A > 0$, decreasing otherwise. The coefficient of dx/x is

$$B = (\alpha - \gamma)(1 - \omega^{2+\nu})(1 - s_1^a)m^{1-\alpha}$$

Since $\omega > 1$, B has the same sign as $\gamma - \alpha$. The coefficient of ds_1^a/s_1^a is

$$A = \gamma(w + m^{1-\alpha})(1 + w^{1+\nu}m^{1-\alpha}) + (\gamma - \alpha)(1 - \omega^{2+\nu})(s_1^a - s_1^b)m^{1-\alpha}$$

Clearly, if $\gamma < \alpha$, A is positive and ds_1^a/dx is negative. If $\gamma > \alpha$, then

$$\frac{A}{\gamma} = (w + m^{1-\alpha})(1 + w^{1+\nu}m^{1-\alpha}) + \theta(1 - \omega^{2+\nu})m^{1-\alpha}$$

where $\theta = (s_1^a - s_1^b)(\gamma - \alpha)/\gamma < 1$. Combining terms makes it clear that A is positive in this case too. Thus the sign of ds_1^a/dx is the same as the sign of $\gamma - \alpha$.

2 An immediate corollary is that c_2/c_1 is increasing in x: the first-order conditions imply

$$\left(\frac{s_1^a}{1 - s_1^a}\right)^\alpha = \frac{\omega\lambda_2}{\lambda_1}\left(\frac{c_2}{c_1}\right)^{\gamma - \alpha}$$

The behavior of s_1^a with respect to x implies that the consumption ratio c_2/c_1 is increasing in x, as claimed in the text.

3 We now show that $b_1/a_1 = m$ is increasing in x. From (A3.3) we have

$$(\alpha - \gamma)(1 - w^{2+\nu})(1 - s_1^a)m^{1-\alpha}\frac{dm}{m} = \gamma(w + m^{1-\alpha})(1 + w^{1+\nu}m^{1-\alpha})\frac{ds_1^a}{s_1^a}$$

$$= \gamma(w + m^{1-\alpha})(1 + w^{1+\nu}m^{1-\alpha})\frac{B}{A}\frac{dx}{x}$$

From the definition of B,

$$A\frac{dm}{m} = \gamma(w + m^{1-\alpha})(1 + w^{1+\nu}m^{1-\alpha})\frac{dx}{x}$$

Since $A > 0$, m is increasing in x.

4 We turn to the dependence of the trade balance on x. As in the text,

$$\frac{nx_1}{y_1} = 1 - s_1^a(1 + \omega^{-1}m^{1-\alpha})$$

Differentiating, we find

$$d\left(\frac{nx_1}{y_1}\right) = -ds_1^a(1 + \omega^{-1}m^{1-\alpha}) - (1-\alpha)s_1^a\omega^{-1}m^{1-\alpha}\frac{dm}{m}$$

which is positive if

$$(1 + \omega^{-1}m^{1-\alpha})\frac{ds_1^a}{s_1^a} + (1-\alpha)\omega^{-1}m^{1-\alpha}\frac{dm}{m} < 0$$

From (A3.4) and (A3.5) we can show that this inequality holds for large enough α.

Note

We thank Ron Jones, Maury Obstfeld, and Chris Stefanadis for helpful comments and the National Science Foundation, the Institute for Empirical Macroeconomics, and the Center for Japan–US Business and Economic Studies faculty fellowship program for financial support.

References

Alterman, William (1991) "Price trends in U.S. trade: new data, new insights," in P. Hooper and J.D. Richardson (eds) *International Economic Transactions: Issues in Measurement and Empirical Research*, Chicago, IL, University of Chicago Press.

Armington, Paul (1969) "A theory of demand for products distinguished by place of production," *IMF Staff Papers* 27, 488–526.

Backus, David (1992) "Interpreting comovements in the trade balance and the terms of trade," *Journal of International Economics*, forthcoming.

——, Patrick Kehoe, and Finn Kydland (1991) "Dynamics of the trade balance and the terms of trade: the S-curve," *American Economic Review*, forthcoming.

Baxter, Marianne (1992) "Fiscal policy, specialization, and trade in the two-sector model: the return of Ricardo?" *Journal of Political Economy* 101, 713–44.

Blackburn, Keith, and Morten Ravn (1991) "Contemporary macroeconomic fluctuations: an international perspective," unpublished manuscript, January.

Buiter, Willem (1989) *Budgetary Policy, International and Intertemporal Trade in the Global Economy*, Amsterdam, North-Holland.

Cole, Harold, and Obstfeld, Maurice (1991) "Commodity trade and international risk-sharing," *Journal of Monetary Economics* 28, 3–24.

Dornbusch, Rudiger (1980) *Open Economy Macroeconomics*, New York, Basic Books.

Dumas, Bernard (1992) "Dynamic equilibrium and the real exchange rate in a spatially separated world," *Review of Financial Studies*, 5, 153–80.

Ethier, Wilfred J. (1988) *Modern International Economics*, 2nd edn, New York, Norton.

Froot, Kenneth, and Kenneth Rogoff (1991) "Government spending and the real exchange rate in the Bretton Woods era," unpublished manuscript.

Giovannini, Alberto (1988) "Exchange rates and traded goods prices," *Journal of International Economics* 24, 45–68.

Graboyes, Robert (1991) "International trade and payments data," *Federal Reserve Bank of Richmond Quarterly Review* 77, 20–31.

Grilli, Vittorio, and Nouriel Roubini (1992) "Liquidity and exchange rates," *Journal of International Economics* 32, 339–52.

Harberger, Arnold (1950) "Currency depreciation, income, and the balance of trade," *Journal of Political Economy* 58, 47–60.

Hodrick, Robert (1988) "U.S. international capital flows: perspectives from rational maximizing models," *Carnegie-Rochester Conference Series on Public Policy* 30, 231–88.

Kehoe, Patrick, and Paul Richardson (1985) "Dynamics of the current account: theoretical and empirical analysis," Federal Reserve Bank of Minneapolis Working Paper.

Kemp, Murray (1987) "Marshall–Lerner condition," In P. Newman, M. Milgate, and J. Eatwell (eds) *The New Palgrave: A Dictionary of Economics*, London, Macmillan.

Krugman, Paul, and Maurice Obstfeld (1991) *International Economics: Theory and Policy*, New York, Harper Collins.

Lapham, Beverly (1990) "A dynamic, general equilibrium analysis of deviations from the laws of one price," unpublished manuscript, Queen's University.

Laursen, Svend, and Lloyd Metzler (1950) "Flexible exchange rates and the theory of employment," *Review of Economics and Statistics* 32, 281–99.

Lucas, R. (1984) "Money in a theory of finance," *Carnegie-Rochester Conference Series on Public Policy* 21, 9–45.

Macklem, R. Tiff (1991) "Terms-of-trade disturbances and fiscal policy in a small open economy," Bank of Canada Working Paper 90–7.

Mendoza, Enrique (1992) "The terms of trade and economic fluctuations," unpublished manuscript, International Monetary Fund.

Mussa, Michael (1986) "Nominal exchange rate regimes and the behavior of real exchange rates," in K. Brunner and A. Meltzer (eds) *Real Business Cycles, Real Exchange Rates, and Actual Policies*, Carnegie-Rochester Conference Series, Amsterdam, North-Holland.

Obstfeld, Maurice (1982) "Aggregate spending and the terms of trade: is there a Laursen–Metzler effect?" *Quarterly Journal of Economics* 97, 251–70.

—— (1989) "Fiscal deficits and relative prices in a growing economy," *Journal of Monetary Economics* 23, 461–84.

Reynolds, Patricia (1991) "Capital formation, government spending and international economic fluctuations," unpublished manuscript, Northwestern University.

Sachs, Jeffrey (1981) "The current account and macroeconomic adjustment in the 1970s," *Brookings Papers on Economic Activity* 1, 201–68.

Schlagenhauf, Don, and Jeffrey Wrase (1992) "A monetary, open-economy model with capital mobility," unpublished manuscript, Arizona State University.

Stockman, Alan, and Lars E.O. Svensson (1987) "Capital flows, investment, and exchange rates," *Journal of Monetary Economics* 19, 171–201.

—— and Linda Tesar (1991) "Tastes and technology in a two-country model of the business cycle: explaining international comovements," unpublished manuscript.

Svensson, Lars, and Assaf Razin (1983) "The terms of trade and the current account: the Harberger–Laursen–Metzler effect," *Journal of Political Economy* 91, 97–125.

Whalley, John (1985) *Trade Liberalization Among Major Trading Areas*, Cambridge, MA, MIT Press.

Yi, Kei-Mu (1991) "Can government purchases explain recent U.S. net export deficits?" unpublished manuscript, presented at the NBER Universities Conference, May.

PART II

CAPITAL TAXATION AND REAL MODELS

4 International Fiscal Policy Coordination and Competition

ASSAF RAZIN AND EFRAIM SADKA

1 Introduction

This chapter addresses the issue of international tax competition among sovereign governments in the presence of fully integrated markets for capital and goods. To present a self-contained argument we start by examining the basic principles of international taxation. Concerning capital income (direct) taxation we distinguish between the residence principle and the source principle. According to the first principle households and firms are taxed on their worldwide income, uniformly, regardless of where income originates. This does not exclude taxes collected in the source country, as long as the residence country would credit these taxes. According to the second principle agents are taxed uniformly where income originates, regardless of their residence.

Concerning commodity (indirect) taxation, we distinguish between the destination principle and the origin principle. Under the first principle commodities are taxed uniformly regardless of whether they are imported or produced domestically. In contrast, under the second principle the uniform tax is applied to all goods that are produced in a particular country, regardless of their final destination.

International tax arbitrage imposes severe constraints on the ability of an individual fiscal authority to set tax rates on capital income and on commodities. To prevent profitable arbitrage, foreign and domestic residents must be indifferent between foreign and domestic assets on the one hand and between purchasing any tradeable commodity at home or abroad on the other. As a result various tax rates adopted by various countries should meet a particular restriction.

To complete the building blocks of the international tax competition model we examine the question of optimal tax strategy for a small open economy in a second-best (tax-distorted) world. To do this we apply the Diamond–Mirrlees production efficiency proposition to international taxation.

The analysis of Nash–Cournot international tax competition is carried out for three cases:

1   when each of the competing countries cannot exercise significant market power in setting its tax rates;
2   when the design of fiscal policy by each of the competing countries incorporates the indirect effect on world prices; and
3   when governments are unable to commit themselves to pre-announced paths of taxes for the entire future.

In each of these cases we examine the desirability of international tax harmonization in which tax rates are set cooperatively.

2   Principles of international taxation

The various structures of the national tax systems have important implications for the direction and the magnitude of international flows of goods and capital and, consequently, for the worldwide efficiency of resource allocation in the integrated world economy. Although there is probably no country which adheres strictly to a pure principle of international taxation, it seems nevertheless that two polar principles with a wide application can be detected, both in the area of direct taxation and in the area of indirect taxation.

2.1   Capital income (direct) taxation

Two polar principles of international income taxation are the *residence* (of the taxpayer) principle and the *source* (of income) principle. According to the residence principle, residents are taxed on their worldwide income uniformly, regardless of the source of income (domestic or foreign).[1] Thus, nonresidents are not taxed on incomes originating in the country. According to the source principle, all incomes originating in the country are taxed uniformly regardless of the place of residence of the recipients of these incomes. Thus, residents of the country are not taxed on their foreign-source income and nonresidents are taxed equally to residents on incomes originating in the country.

International capital market integration which enables a resident in one country to invest in other countries brings up the issue of international tax arbitrage. Such arbitrage has important implications for the viability of equilibrium in the capital markets.

To highlight this issue, consider the familiar two-country model ("home" country and "foreign" country) with perfect capital mobility. Denote interest rates in the home country and the foreign country by r and r^*, respectively. In general, the home country may have three different effective tax rates applying to interest income:

τ_{rD} tax rate levied on residents on domestic-source income;

τ_{rA} effective rate of *additional* tax levied on residents on foreign-source income (over and above the tax paid in the foreign country);

τ_{rN} tax rate levied on the income of nonresidents.

Correspondingly, the foreign country levies similar taxes, denoted by τ_{rD}^*, τ_{rA}^*, and τ_{rN}^*. We assume that these tax rates apply symmetrically to both interest income and interest expenses.

At an equilibrium, the home-country residents must be indifferent between investing at home or abroad. This implies that

$$r(1 - \tau_{rD}) = r^*(1 - \tau_{rN}^* - \tau_{rA}) \tag{4.1}$$

Similarly, at equilibrium, the residents of the foreign country must be indifferent between investing in their home country (the "foreign" country") or abroad (the "home" country), so that

$$r^*(1 - \tau_{rD}^*) = r(1 - \tau_{rN} - \tau_{rA}^*) \tag{4.2}$$

Hence, for the interest rates r and r^* to be positive (in which case we say that the capital market equilibrium is viable), the two equations (4.1) and (4.2) must be linearly dependent. That is,

$$(1 - \tau_{rD})(1 - \tau_{rD}^*) = (1 - \tau_{rN} - \tau_{rA}^*)(1 - \tau_{rN}^* - \tau_{rA}) \tag{4.3}$$

This constraint, which involves tax rates of the two countries, implies that, even though the two countries do not explicitly coordinate their tax systems between them, each nevertheless must take into account the tax system of the other in designing its own tax system.[2]

It is noteworthy that when both countries adopt one of the two aforementioned polar principles of taxation, residence and source, then condition (4.3) is fulfilled. To see this, observe that if both countries adopt the residence principle then

$$\tau_{rD} = \tau_{rA} + \tau_{rN}^* \qquad \tau_{rD}^* = \tau_{rA}^* + \tau_{rN} \qquad \tau_{rN} = 0 = \tau_{rN}^* \tag{4.4}$$

If both countries adopt the source principle, then

$$\tau_{rD} = \tau_{rN} \qquad \tau_{rD}^* = \tau_{rN}^* \qquad \tau_{rA} = \tau_{rA}^* = 0 \tag{4.5}$$

Evidently, the joint constraint (4.3) is fulfilled if either (4.4) or (4.5) holds. However, if the two countries do not adopt the same polar principle (or do not adopt either one of the two polar principles), then condition (4.3) is not in general met, and a viable equilibrium may not exist.

The structure of taxation also has important implications for the international allocation of investments and savings. If all countries adopt the residence principle (i.e. condition (4.4) holds), then it follows from either (4.1) or (4.2), the rate of return arbitrage conditions, that $r = r^*$. That is, the *gross* rates of return to capital are equated internationally. As the gross rate of return to capital is equal to the marginal product of capital, it follows that the marginal products of capital are equated internationally. Thus, the world's output (in the future) is maximized and worldwide production efficiency prevails.[3] However, if the tax rate on income from capital is not the same in all countries (i.e. $\tau_{rD} \neq \tau_{rD}^*$), then the *net* rates of return earned by savers vary across countries (i.e. $r(1 - \tau_{rD}) \neq r^*(1 - \tau_{rD}^*)$). As the net rate of return to capital is equated to the consumer's intertemporal marginal rate of substitution, it follows that the intertemporal marginal rates of substitution are not equated internationally. Thus, the world's allocation of savings is inefficient.

Alternatively, if all countries adopt the source principle (i.e. condition (4.5) holds), then it follows from either (4.1) or (4.2) that $r(1 - \tau_{rD}) = r^*(1 - \tau_{rD}^*)$. Thus, the intertemporal marginal rates of substitution are equated internationally and the world's allocation of savings is efficient. However, if the tax rate on income from capital is not the same in all countries, then $r \neq r^*$. That is, the marginal product of capital varies across countries and the worldwide allocation of investment is inefficient.

2.2   Commodity (indirect) taxation

Analogously to the residence and source principles of direct taxation, the two polar principles of indirect taxation (in particular, the value-added tax, VAT) are the destination principle and the source principle, respectively. According to the destination principle, a good or a service purchased by a resident is taxed uniformly whether produced domestically or imported. That is, imports are taxed while exports are exempted.[4] Put differently, all goods and services destined for final consumption in the country are taxed regardless of the source of production. According to the source principle, the tax is levied on all goods and services produced in the country irrespective of their final destination.

Analogously to international capital mobility which imposes the rate of return arbitrage conditions (4.1) and (4.2), trade in goods and services dictates the following price arbitrage conditions:

$$p(1 + \tau_D) = p^*(1 + \tau_X^* + \tau_M) \qquad (4.6)$$

and

$$p^*(1 + \tau_D^*) = p(1 + \tau_X + \tau_M^*) \qquad (4.7)$$

where p and p^* are the producer price of a tradeable good in the home and foreign country respectively. These prices are expressed in terms of a common (to both the home and the foreign country) untaxed numeraire.[5] The home country may employ three tax rates.

τ_D tax rate levied on the good if produced domestically and sold domestically;

τ_X tax rate levied on exports of the good;

τ_M *effective* tax rate levied on the imports of the good (in addition to the tax, if any, levied abroad).

Similarly, the foreign country may employ three tax rates: τ_D^*, τ_X^*, and τ_M^*. Conditions (4.6)–(4.7) implicitly assume that the good is produced and consumed in positive quantities in both countries. These conditions yield the following joint constraint which is imposed on both countries:

$$(1 + \tau_D)(1 + \tau_D^*) = (1 + \tau_X^* + \tau_M)(1 + \tau_X + \tau_M^*) \qquad (4.8)$$

As with direct taxes, it is straightforward to verify that either of the two polar principles, destination and source, when adopted by both countries, meets the joint constraint (4.8). Similarly, when the destination principle is adopted by both countries, worldwide production efficiency prevails (because producer prices are internationally equated) but the international allocation of consumption is generally inefficient (because consumer prices vary across countries).[6] On the other hand, when the source principle is adopted by both countries, the international allocation of consumption is efficient but the allocation of world production is not efficient.

3   Optimal taxation and capital movements

Apart from its major role in correcting various market failures (due to increasing returns and imperfect competition, external economies or diseconomies etc.), a government also levies taxes in order to redistribute income and finance the provision of public goods and public inputs. As these taxes are distortionary, the allocation of resources is not Pareto efficient. Thus, the optimal design of the fiscal policy is typically carried out in a second-best context.

When capital is free to move in or out of the country and the residence principle is applied in capital income taxation, it follows from the analysis of the preceding section that the marginal product of domestic capital will be equated to the world rate of interest and production efficiency will prevail. An interesting question is whether the fiscal policy should maintain production efficiency (a first-best solution in production) even though the overall allocation of resources in the economy is not Pareto efficient. A fundamental result of optimal tax theory suggests that, under certain conditions, production efficiency should still be maintained even though the (distortionary) tax structure can achieve only a second-best optimum.[7] Thus, capital should be free to move in and out of the country and residents should be taxed uniformly on their worldwide income (the residence principle).

3.1 A stylized two-period model

We demonstrate this fundamental result in a stylized two-period model with one composite good serving both for (private and public) consumption and for investment. In the first period the economy possesses an initial endowment of the composite good. Individuals can decide how much of their initial endowments to consume and how much to save in the first period. Saving is allocated to either domestic investment or foreign investment. In the second period, output (produced by capital and labor) and income from foreign investment are allocated between private and public consumption. For simplicity, we assume that government spending takes place in the second period. The government employs taxes on labor, taxes on income from domestic investments, and taxes on income from investments abroad in order to finance optimally, taking into account both efficiency and equity considerations, its public consumption and a uniform lump-sum subsidy for redistribution purposes.

Suppose there are H households. The utility function of household h is denoted by

$$u^h(c_{1h}, c_{2h}, L_h, G) \qquad h = 1, \ldots, H \tag{4.9}$$

where c_{1h}, c_{2h}, and L_h are first-period consumption, second-period consumption, and second-period labor supply, respectively, of household h, and G is second-period public consumption.

Denote the saving of household h in the form of domestic capital by K_h and saving in the form of foreign capital by B_h. We assume for concreteness that the patterns of capital flows are such that the country is a capital exporter (i.e. $\Sigma_h B_h \geq 0$). Thus the aggregate saving in the form of domestic capital is equal to the stock of capital in the second period. The budget constraints of household h in the first and second period are, respectively,

$$c_{1h} + K_h + B_h = I_h \tag{4.10}$$

and

$$c_{2h} = K_h[1 + r(1 - \tau_{rD})] + B_h[1 + \bar{r}(1 - \tau_{rA})] + (1 - \tau_w)wL_h + S' \tag{4.11}$$

where τ_{rD} is the tax on capital income from domestic sources, τ_{rA} is the tax on capital income from foreign sources, τ_w is the tax on labor income, S' is a lump-sum subsidy, r is the domestic rate of interest, $\bar{r}$ is the world rate of interest (net of taxes levied abroad), w is the wage rate, and I_h is the initial (first-period) endowment.

As was already pointed out in the preceding section, if residents can freely invest abroad, they must, at equilibrium, earn the same net return whether investing at home or abroad, i.e.

$$r(1 - \tau_{rD}) = \bar{r}(1 - \tau_{rA}) \tag{4.12}$$

With restrictions on capital flows, the latter equality does not have to hold. In such a case there is an infra-marginal profit on foreign investment resulting from the net interest differential. One possibility is for this profit to accrue to the investors. Another possibility is for the government to fully tax away this profit. (This is the equivalent capital-export tax version of the capital-export quota.) We adopt the second possibility, namely that the government chooses the level of the tax on income from foreign investments (τ_{rA}) so as to eliminate entirely the infra-marginal profits. This implies that, whether or not there are restrictions on foreign investment, the government chooses τ_{rA} so as to maintain equality (4.12).

Under this tax scheme the household is indifferent between investing at home (K_h) or abroad (B_h), caring only about the level of total investment ($K_h + B_h$). Therefore we can consolidate the two periodic budget constraints (4.10) and (4.11) into a single present-value budget constraint:

$$c_{1h} + q_{c2}c_{2h} = I_h + q_L L_h + S \tag{4.13}$$

where $q_{c2} = [1 + (1 - \tau_{rD})r]^{-1}$ is the consumer (after-tax) price of second-period consumption in present-value terms; $q_L = (1 - \tau_w)wq_{c2}$ is the consumer price of labor (net wage rate) in present-value terms; and $S = q_{c2}S'$ is the present value of the subsidy.

Maximizing the utility function u^h subject to the budget constraint (4.13) yields the consumption demand functions

$$c_{ih} = c_{ih}(q_{c2}, q_L, I_h + S, G) \qquad i = 1, 2 \tag{4.14}$$

the labor supply function

$$L_h = L_h(q_{c2}, q_L, I_h + S, G) \tag{4.15}$$

and the indirect utility function

$$v^h = v^h(q_{c2}, q_L, I_h + S, G) \tag{4.16}$$

In the second period, domestic output (Y) is produced by capital and labor according to a concave constant-returns-to-scale production function:

$$Y = F(K, L) \tag{4.17}$$

where $K = \Sigma_h K_h$ is the stock of domestic capital and $L = \Sigma_h L_h$ is the aggregate supply of labor.

Profit maximization implies that

$$r = F_K \qquad w = F_L \tag{4.18}$$

The resource constraints of this economy require that

$$\sum_h I_h = \sum_h c_{1h} + \sum_h B_h + \sum_h K_h \tag{4.19}$$

and

$$Y + (1 + \bar{r}) \sum_h B_h + \sum_h K_h = \sum_h c_{2h} + G \tag{4.20}$$

Substituting (4.10), (4.14), (4.15), (4.17), and (4.19) into (4.20) yields the following single equilibrium condition:

$$F\left[\sum_h I_h - \sum_h c_{1h}(q_{c2}, q_L, I_h + S, G) - B, \sum_h L_h(q_{c2}, q_L, I_h + S, G)\right]$$

$$+ (1 + \bar{r})B + \sum_h I_h - \sum_h c_{1h}(q_{c2}, q_L, I_h + S, G) - B$$

$$- \sum_h c_{2h}(q_{c2}, q_L, I_h + S, G) - G = 0 \tag{4.21}$$

where $B = \Sigma_h B_h$ is aggregate capital exports.

3.2   Optimal fiscal policy

The optimal fiscal policy is achieved by maximizing the social welfare function

$$W = W[v^1(q_{c2}, q_L, I_h + S, G), \ldots, v^H(q_{c2}, q_L, I_H + S, G)] \quad (4.22)$$

subject to the equilibrium condition (4.21). The control variables are the consumer prices q_{c2} and q_L (which implicitly define the tax rates τ_{rD} and τ_w), public consumption G, and the aggregate level of capital exports B. Notice that by referring to B as a control variable we do not mean that the government directly determines the level of capital exports. Rather, the government, through its tax policy, affects total savings ($\Sigma_h K_h + \Sigma_h B_h$) and domestic investments ($\Sigma_h K_h$). Capital exports B are then determined as a residual (the difference between total savings and domestic investments).

Maximizing (4.22) subject to (4.21) yields (among other conditions) the following first-order condition:

$$r = \bar{r} \qquad\qquad (4.23)$$

The latter condition holds if the government adopts a policy of letting capital move freely in and out of the country (condition (4.22)) and of employing the residence principle of taxation (i.e. $\tau_{rD} = \tau_{rA}$). In this case, investment is efficiently allocated between home and abroad. The intuition behind the result is that, if capital is perfectly mobile while labor is completely immobile, source-based capital taxes are completely shifted to labor. It is better to tax labor directly than to rely on an indirect labor tax. In other words the small open economy faces a completely elastic schedule of excess supply of capital and applies at the optimum no nonresident taxation.[8]

4   Tax competition and tax coordination: international price-taking behavior

If countries integrate their capital markets (e.g. Europe of 1992), then in the absence of full-fledged harmonization of their tax systems tax competition emerges as a real possibility.

International tax competition, or fiscal policy competition in general, has major effects on the resource allocation between countries and within each country. For example, the worldwide level of savings as well as its cross-country composition may be distorted by such competition. Similarly, the aggregate level of investment and its international allocation is potentially also inefficient. In general, the effects of tax competition on the allocation of resources can be decomposed into two elements. The first consists of indirect manipulation of the international terms of trade by various fiscal measures (other than explicit trade barriers such as tariffs and quotas), akin to the familiar "trade wars." The second element, which has received less attention, concerns the international and domestic misallocation of resources that is generated by tax competition in a tax distortion environment but with international price-taking behavior on the part of the competing governments.

This section focuses on the second element; the next section deals with terms of trade manipulation.

To simplify the exposition, we assume that the world economy consists of two countries, the home country (denoted by superscript H) and the foreign country (denoted by superscript F). We maintain the basic model of the preceding section with two periods, one composite good which can serve for private and public consumption and investment, and two factors: internationally mobile capital, and internationally immobile labor. To simplify the notation further, we assume that households within each country are identical. This enables us to consider a representative household in each country.

Consider first the home country. The household sector possesses a utility function

$$u^H(c_1^H, c_2^H, L^H, G^H) \tag{4.24}$$

Denoting saving in the form of domestic capital by S^{HH} and saving exported to country F by S^{HF}, the budget constraint of the household sector in the first period is

$$c_1^H + S^{HH} + S^{HF} = I^H \tag{4.25}$$

In the second period the budget constraint is

$$c_2^H = (1 - \tau_w^H)w^H L^H + S^{HH}[1 + (1 - \tau_{rD}^H)r^H]$$
$$+ S^{HF}[1 + (1 - \tau_{rA}^H)(1 - \tau_{rN}^F)r^F] \tag{4.26}$$

For ease of notation we specify the tax τ_{rA} in this section as applying to the return from investment abroad, net of the taxes paid abroad (whereas in section 2 τ_{rA} applied to the gross return).[9]

As before, the rate of return arbitrage in the home country implies that

$$(1 - \tau_{rD}^H)r^H = (1 - \tau_{rA}^H)(1 - \tau_{rN}^F)r^F \tag{4.27}$$

Hence, the second-period budget constraint may be rewritten as

$$c_2^H = (1 - \tau_w^H)w^H L^H + S^H[1 + (1 - \tau_{rD}^H)r^H] \qquad (4.28)$$

where

$$S^H = S^{HH} + S^{HF} \qquad (4.29)$$

is the *aggregate* saving of the private sector in country H. Now, the budget constraints for the first and second periods ((4.25) and (4.28)) can be consolidated into a single (present-value) lifetime budget constraint

$$c_1^H + q_{c2}^H c_2^H = I^H + q_L^H L^H \qquad (4.30)$$

where

$$q_{c2}^H = [1 + (1 - \tau_{rD}^H)r^H]^{-1}$$

and

$$q_L^H = (1 - \tau_w^H)w^H[1 + (1 - \tau_{rD}^H)r^H]^{-1}$$

are respectively the consumer prices of second-period consumption and labor, in present-value terms.

Maximization of the utility function (4.24) subject to the budget constraint (4.30) yields the demand for private consumption in the first period, $c_1^H(q_{c2}^H, q_L^H, I^H, G^H)$, and private consumption in the second period, $c_2^H(q_{c2}^H, q_L^H, I^H, G^H)$, the supply of saving, $S^H(q_{c2}^H, q_L^H, I^H, G^H)$, the supply of labor by the private sector in the second period, L^H $(q_{c2}^H, q_L^H, I^H, G^H)$, and the indirect utility function $v^H(q_{c2}^H, q_L^H, I^H, G^H)$.

Domestic output Y^H in the second period is produced by capital K^H and labor L^H according to a neoclassical constant-returns-to-scale production function:

$$Y^H = F^H(K^H, L^H) \qquad (4.31)$$

The stock of domestic capital is composed of the saving by domestic residents channeled to domestic uses (S^{HH}) and the saving by foreign residents channeled to country H (S^{FH}), i.e.

$$K^H = S^{HH} + S^{FH} = S^H - (S^{HF} - S^{FH}) \qquad (4.32)$$

where use is made of equation (4.29).

As usual, the marginal productivity conditions determine the (pre-tax) interest rate and the wage rate:

$$r^H = F_K^H(K^H, L^H) \qquad (4.33)$$

and

$$w^H = F_L^H(K^H, L^H) \qquad (4.34)$$

Country F is similar to country H, so that the corresponding equations are like country H equations, except that the superscripts F and H are interchanged. Of particular interest now is the rate of return arbitrage condition for residents of country F (the analog of (4.27)). Assuming interior solutions this becomes

$$(1 - \tau_{rD}^F)r^F = (1 - \tau_{rA}^F)(1 - \tau_{rN}^H)r^H \qquad (4.35)$$

The second-period resource constraint faced by country H is given by

$$G^H + c_2^H(q_{c2}^H, q_L^H, I^H, G^H) = F^H[K^H, L^H(q_{c2}^H, q_L^H, I^H, G^H)]$$

$$+ K^H + S^{HF}[1 + (1 - \tau_{rN}^F)r^F] - S^{FH}$$

$$\times [1 + (1 - \tau_{rN}^H)r^H] \qquad (4.36)$$

The condition states that total private and public consumption in the second period (i.e. $G^H + c_2^H$) is equal to the sum of (a) output generated by domestic capital which is financed by domestic saving (i.e. $I^H - c_1^H = S^H$) minus *net* capital exports (i.e. gross capital exports S^{HF} less gross capital imports S^{FH}) and labor; (b) domestic capital (i.e. K^H); and (c) the income from net capital exports (principal plus interest). Notice that by Walras's law the government budget constraint in each country is automatically satisfied.

Upon substituting (4.32) into (4.36) and employing the arbitrage condition (4.35), we conclude that country H has a single resource constraint as follows:

$$G^H + c_2^H(q_{c2}^H, q_L^H, I^H, G^H) = F^H[I^H - c_1^H(q_{c2}^H, q_L^H, I^H, G^H)$$

$$- (S^{HF} - S^{FH}), L^H(q_{c2}^H, q_L^H, I^H, G^H)]$$

$$+ I^H - c_1^H(q_{c2}^H, q_L^H, I^H, G^H)$$

$$+ S^{HF}(1 - \tau_{rN}^F)r^F - \frac{S^{FH}(1 - \tau_{rD}^F)r^F}{1 - \tau_{rA}^F} \qquad (4.37)$$

Tax competition works as follows. Each government designs its fiscal policy so as to maximize the welfare of its representative resident. In carrying out the optimization the government must take into account the resource constraints and the arbitrage conditions. It also takes as given all the fiscal instruments employed by other governments. In addition, each government is assumed to behave as a price-taker in the world market. That is, the government assumes that its actions have no effect on international prices (including interest rates). Put differently, at a given rate of interest (r^F), in the foreign country, country H assumes that it can export any quantity of capital (S^{HF}) and import any quantity of capital (S^{FH}). A similar behavior is adopted by country F. This leads to a *Nash equilibrium* between the two countries.

A world market equilibrium exists if world aggregate saving is equal to world aggregate stock of capital, i.e.

$$S^H + S^F = K^H + K^F \qquad (4.38)$$

Consider first the optimal policy design in the home country. The government chooses G^H, q_{c2}^H, q_L^H, S^{HF}, S^{FH}, r^H, w^H, τ_w^H, τ_{rD}^H, τ_{rA}^H, and τ_{rN}^H so as to maximize the utility function v^H, subject to the resource constraint (4.37), the definitions of q_{c2}^H and q_L^H in (4.30), and the relevant arbitrage condition (4.27). Notice that the other arbitrage condition (4.35) is irrelevant for country H because this condition has no effect on its economy (formally the endogenous variables in (4.35) appear nowhere else in the equations describing the economy of country H). In addition, r^H and w^H are given by the marginal productivity conditions (4.33) and (4.34).

The optimization problem can be simplified a great deal by solving the problem in two stages. First, the government chooses public consumption G^H, consumer prices of second-period consumption and labor (q_{c2}^H and q_L^H respectively), capital exports S^{HF}, and capital imports S^{FH} so as to maximize the indirect utility function (v^H) subject to just one constraint: the resource constraint (4.37). Then, in the second stage, the government sets r^H and w^H from (4.33) and (4.34) respectively, τ_{rD}^H and τ_w^H from (4.30), τ_{rN}^H from (4.35), and τ_{rA}^H from (4.27).

Carrying out the first stage of the optimization for country H, it follows from the first-order conditions with respect to capital exports (S^{HF}) and capital imports (S^{FH}) that

$$F_K^H = (1 - \tau_{rN}^F)r^F \qquad (4.39)$$

and

$$F_K^H = \frac{(1 - \tau_{rD}^F)r^F}{1 - \tau_{rA}^F} \qquad (4.40)$$

respectively. Obviously the terms on the right-hand sides of (4.39) and (4.40) must be equal to each other. In fact, this is an *equilibrium* condition rather than an optimality condition. To see this, observe that the term on the right-hand side of (4.39) is the return to capital exports while the term on the right-hand side of (4.40) is the unit cost of capital imports. Since country H takes these return and cost terms as exogenously given, then unless they are equal to each other unlimited gains can accrue to the country by back-to-back exports and imports of capital. Such unlimited gains are obviously inconsistent with the world market equilibrium.

Similarly, for country F we have

$$F_K^F = (1 - \tau_{rN}^H)r^H \tag{4.41}$$

and

$$F_K^F = \frac{(1 - \tau_{rD}^H)r^H}{1 - \tau_{rA}^H} \tag{4.42}$$

Since by (4.33) $F_K^H = r^H$, it follows from (4.35) and (4.40) that $\tau_{rN}^H = 0$ and, by symmetry, $\tau_{rN}^F = 0$. Also, (4.27) implies that $\tau_{rD}^H = \tau_{rA}^H$. It then follows from either (4.39) or (4.41) that

$$F_K^H = r^H = r^F = F_K^F \tag{4.43}$$

That is, tax competition leads to an equality between the marginal productivity of capital across countries H and F. This gross rate of return equalization implies that the world stock of physical capital is efficiently allocated between country H and country F. It then follows from (4.41) and (4.42) that $\tau_{rD}^H = \tau_{rA}^H$ and $\tau_{rD}^F = \tau_{rA}^F$. Since we have earlier shown that $\tau_{rN}^H = 0 = \tau_{rN}^F$, we conclude that each country taxes its residents on their worldwide income and exempts nonresidents from tax. To conclude, the residence principle of international taxation is adopted by each of the tax-competing countries and the worldwide allocation of investment is efficient.

Now, we address the issue of whether this tax competition Nash equilibrium is a second-best optimum (i.e. relative to the available tax policy tools). Or, can there be gains from concerted tax harmonization? Because capital is efficiently allocated between the two countries at this Nash equilibrium, no further gain from international trade in capital exists. Hence, we conclude that there are no gains from tax harmonization if the countries behave as price-takers.

5   Extensions: terms of trade manipulation and discretionary policy

We have so far assumed that the competing countries behave as price-takers in the world market. This assumption is certainly plausible if there are many competing countries and none of them is large enough to be able to exercise a nonnegligible market power.

Of course, if one of the competing countries is large relative to the world market, then it will not assume price-taking behavior. In this case, it will design its fiscal policies with a view to their effects on world prices. Put differently, it will attempt to manipulate world prices in its favor. This is akin to the familiar trade war[10] with the resulting inefficiencies in the worldwide allocation of resources. For instance, if we continue to assume a Nash–Cournot type of competition among the various countries (i.e. each country takes the fiscal policies of the other countries as exogenously given), then obviously the resulting equilibrium will not be second best (given the limited set of tax instruments available). The country which has some monopoly power will drive the world interest rate above its domestic marginal product of capital if it is a net exporter of capital, thereby preventing an efficient worldwide allocation of investments. If one (or more) of the other countries is also large enough relative to the world economy, then it will try to retaliate, with the final outcome impossible to determine *a priori*. In this case, international fiscal coordination will be a Pareto improvement.

Another issue is the ability of the governments to commit themselves to pre-announced paths of fiscal policies for the entire future. When they do commit themselves in this way, as we have assumed so far, international tax coordination is either redundant when the competing countries are price-takers or Pareto improving when they are able to extract some market power. If, however, governments are not pre-committed then it is quite possible that international tax coordination will be harmful. This possibility was first pointed out by Rogoff (1985).[11]

To demonstrate this point in a framework similar to that employed in this chapter, we draw on Kehoe (1989). In the absence of pre-commitment, each country will tax capital very heavily, because at each point of time the existing stock of capital is made up of *past* savings and is therefore perfectly inelastic. Hence, at each point of time a tax on the existing capital is a nondistortionary lump-sum tax. Kehoe describes a situation in which the decision of the private sector *where* to channel its savings, at home or abroad, is made *after* taxes are announced (even though the decision *how much* to save is made before taxes are announced). In this case, in the absence of international tax coordination, each government is deterred from taxing capital too heavily as it fears that capital will fly to other countries. With tax coordination, this fear no longer exists but the coordinated tax on capital is too heavy. Therefore international tax coordination is inferior to a full-fledged competition among sovereign tax authorities.

Notes

We thank Lans Bovenberg for useful comments on an earlier draft of this chapter.

1   A tax credit is usually given against taxes paid abroad on foreign-source income, to achieve an equal *effective* tax rate on income from all sources. See Frenkel et al. (1991) for a modern treatise on international taxation.

2   The issue of tax arbitrage is not unique to open economies. Tax arbitrage emerges also in closed economies if the relative tax treatment of various assets differs across individuals. In the open economy case tax arbitrage becomes more serious if different types of financing are treated differently. This enables individuals and corporations to arbitrage across different statutory tax rates. Another factor that increases the scope of tax arbitrage is the interaction between inflation and exchange rates, on the one hand, and differential tax treatments of inflation and exchange rate gains and losses on the other.

3   Efficiency emerges when corporate and individual taxes are fully integrated and interest income faces the same tax rate as equity income. Evidently, a nonuniform treatment of different components of the capital income tax base would violate efficiency.

4   More precisely, exports are zero rated rather than just exempted. The destination principle is difficult to apply if consumers are mobile across international borders (through, for example, mail orders). In this case cross-border shopping results in losses of tax revenue to the high-tax country.

5   The choice of a common numeraire for both countries implicitly assumes that the numeraire good or factor is internationally mobile.

6   Obviously, a nonuniform commodity tax structure may allow countries to violate the spirit of the destination principle implicitly. They can define commodities in such a way that the high-tax commodities are imported. This practice sneaks in through the back door border taxes such as import or export taxes.

7   See Diamond and Mirrlees (1971).

8   If rents cannot be fully taxed or the country manipulates world prices the choice of whether to adopt the source principle or the residence principle (or a mixture of the two principles) will depend on the interest rate elasticities of saving and investment (see Giovannini, 1990). See also Gordon (1986), Musgrave (1987), and Sinn (1990). Dixit (1985a, b) demonstrates a related result by showing that the production efficiency proposition implies no border taxes, such as import or export taxes.

9   This is why the net return on one ECU earned abroad is $(1 - \tau_{rA})(1 - \tau_{rN})$ in this section and $1 - \tau_{rA} - \tau_{rN}$ in section 2. This is merely an accounting difference.

10   For a modern survey see Dixit (1985a, b).

11   See also Canzoneri and Henderson (1988) and van der Ploeg (1988).

References

Canzoneri, Mathew B. and Dale W. Henderson (1988) "Is sovereign policy making bad?" in Karl Brunner and Alan Meltzer (eds) *Stabilization Policies in Labor*

Markets, Carnegie-Rochester Conference Series on Public Policy 28, Amsterdam, North-Holland, pp. 93–140.

Diamond, Peter A. and James Mirrlees (1971) "Optimal taxation and public production," *American Economic Review* 61, 8–17, 261–78.

Dixit, Avinash (1985a) "Tax policy in open economies," in Alan Auerbach and Martin Feldstein (eds) *Handbook on Public Economics*, Amsterdam, North-Holland, ch. 6, pp. 314–74.

—— (1985b) "Strategic aspects of trade policy," mimeo, Princeton University.

Frenkel, Jacob, Assaf Razin, and Efraim Sadka (1991) *International Taxation in an Integrated World*, Cambridge, MA, MIT Press.

Giovannini, Alberto (1990) "Reforming capital income taxation in open economies: theoretical issues," in Horst Siebert (ed.) *Reforming Capital Income Taxation*, Tubingen, Mohr.

Gordon, Roger H. (1986) "Taxation of investment and savings in a world economy," *American Economic Review* 76, 1087–1102.

Kehoe, Patrick J. (1989) "Policy cooperation among benevolent governments may be undesirable," *Review of Economic Studies* 56, 289–96.

Musgrave, Peggy (1987) "International tax competition and gains from tax harmonization," NBER Working Paper 3152 (October), Cambridge, MA.

van der Ploeg, Frederick (1988) "International policy coordination in interdependent monetary economies," *Journal of International Economics* 25, 1–23.

Rogoff, Kenneth (1985) "Can international monetary policy cooperation be counterproductive," *Journal of International Economics* 18, 199–217.

Sinn, Hans–Werner (1990) "Tax harmonization and tax competition in Europe," NBER Working Paper 3263 (February), Cambridge, MA.

5 Capital Taxation in the World Economy

A. LANS BOVENBERG

1 Introduction

The internationalization and liberalization of financial markets has increased the importance of tax rules, especially those regarding the taxation of capital income, in determining international capital and trade flows. In particular, taxes that affect domestic saving or invest-ment behavior may upset saving–investment balances, thereby setting in motion large international capital and trade flows. This chapter surveys the literature exploring the macroeconomic implications of capital income taxation in open economies and complements the analysis of chapter 4 in this volume. Futhermore, we develop an intertemporal equilibrium framework to analyze these issues and provide some suggestions for future research.

Capital income taxes can be levied according to two alternative principles, namely the residence and source principles. Under the residence principle, residents are taxed uniformly on their worldwide capital income irrespective of the particular jurisdiction where this income originates. Residence-based taxes reduce the after-tax return on domestic saving by driving a wedge between the rate of return on world financial markets and the after-tax rate of return received by residents in a particular country. Hence, residence taxes can be interpreted as taxes on the ownership of capital, i.e. saving.

Source-based taxes are levied on all capital income that originates in a particular jurisdiction irrespective of the country of residence of the saver who receives the capital income. These taxes raise the required return on domestic investment above the rate of return on world financial markets. Accordingly, source-based taxes amount to taxes on the location of capital, i.e. investment.[1]

In considering the choice between source-based and residence-based taxes, one can show that under certain conditions a small open economy should not apply any source-based capital income taxation at all but should adopt only capital income taxes that are residence based. The most important assumptions underlying this result are twofold. First, capital should be perfectly mobile internationally. Second, the government should be able to tax freely the immobile factors of production, and labor in particular.[2] The intuition is that a source-based tax on capital is completely shifted to the immobile factors (including labor) if perfect international capital mobility causes the supply of capital from abroad to become infinitely elastic. Hence, a source-based tax on capital income amounts to an implicit tax on labor if capital is perfectly mobile internationally. It is more efficient to reduce the return on labor (and that on the other immobile factors) directly by using an explicit labor tax rather than to rely on an implicit labor tax which distorts not only labor–leisure decisions but also international investment decisions (see, for example, Gordon, 1986). Another advantage of residence- over source-based taxes is that residence-based taxes can serve equity objectives. In particular, governments can adjust the tax rate on residence-based taxes according to the individual circumstances of the taxpayer (e.g. the total taxable income that accrues to the taxpayer).[3]

The optimal tax literature suggests that residence-based taxes on capital income, in contrast to source-based taxes, can be part of an efficient tax structure for a small open economy. The optimal mix between, on the one hand, taxes on labor income and, on the other hand, residence-based taxes on capital income is guided by the elasticity of labor supply and the intertemporal substitution elasticity of consumption. In particular, Sørensen (1990) has shown that the optimal rate of residence-based tax should be set according to the optimal tax rule for the mix between labor and capital income taxation in a closed economy (derived and interpreted by King (1980) and Sandmo (1985)) (see also Gordon, 1986).

In practice, a government may not be able to enforce residence-based taxes because it faces serious difficulties in monitoring the capital income earned by residents on foreign soil.[4] Technological advances in information technology and the associated liberalization and integration of world capital markets have caused these problems to become even more serious by reducing the transaction costs of hiding income and, more generally, raising gross capital flows. Therefore, governments increasingly require close cooperation from foreign authorities in the form of exchange of information (implying, for example, the loosening of bank secrecy laws) in order to include worldwide capital income of their residents in the domestic tax net. However, foreign authorities do not have an incentive to cooperate; from their perspective, cooperation amounts to a source-based tax, which increases the cost of capital to domestic firms and reduces domestic wages.[5] If capital-exporting countries cannot effectively enforce a residence-based tax on worldwide capital income, capital income taxes may vanish altogether (see, for example, Razin and Sadka, 1989; chapter 4 in this volume; and Gordon, 1990).[6]

The results from the optimal tax literature – that small open economies should adopt no source-based taxes and that capital income taxes should be eliminated altogether if countries cannot enforce residence-based taxes – assume that countries can freely set tax rates on labor.[7] In practice, however, countries may find it difficult to tax labor and capital income at different rates because of the need to devise administrative procedures to split the income of the self-employed. These difficulties may explain why small open economies continue to tax capital income despite the growing international mobility of capital and the increasing difficulties in enforcing taxes on foreign-source capital income.[8] In particular, source-based capital income taxes may protect the domestic base of the income tax by preventing residents from sheltering their labor income from tax by classifying it as capital income. Accordingly, countries may have to resort to source-based capital income taxes in the face of feasibility constraints on the use of various tax instruments.[9]

In examining the macroeconomic implications of source-based and residence-based capital income taxes, this chapter focuses on the effects on the external current account. In this connection, one can employ the identity between, on the one hand, the external current account balance and, on the other hand, the difference between domestic saving and domestic investment. Using this identity, Summers (1988) argues that, in a world with international capital mobility, it is crucial to distinguish between tax policies that primarily affect saving and policies targeted at domestic investment.[10] In particular, policies that reduce saving would initially worsen the external current and trade accounts by boosting short-run consumption. Policies that discourage investment, in contrast, would improve the external accounts initially by weakening domestic demand. This reasoning would suggest important differences between source-based capital income taxes, which increase the required return on domestic investment, and residence-based capital income taxes, which reduce the after-tax return to domestic saving. Indeed, numerical simulations by Mutti and Grubert (1985) and Goulder and Eichengreen (1989) largely confirm this intuition.

Feldstein and Horioka (1980), however, found a rather strong empirical correlation between domestic investment and domestic saving, even for small open economies that are integrated in world financial markets. These results suggest that domestic saving and investment are not determined independently (see also chapter 15 in this volume). Feldstein and Horioka interpreted their empirical findings as reflecting a low degree of international capital mobility. While more recent empirical studies more or less confirmed a strong correlation between investment and saving (see, for example, Frankel, 1989), theoretical studies have questioned the inference that the correlation between investment and saving is a valid measure for the degree of international capital mobility. To illustrate, Murphy (1986), Engel and Kletzer (1989), and Bovenberg (1989) formulate models in which imperfect substitution between commodities rather than low capital mobility explains the observed correlation between saving and investment. Intuitively, intratemporal international trade in commodities needs to affect the resource transfers implicit in intertemporal trade. Accordingly, mobility of financial capital is not a sufficient condition for *ex ante* saving–investment imbalances to give rise to significant intertemporal trade. An additional necessary condition for this to occur is that trade flows are elastic.

This chapter explores the distinct macroeconomic effects of capital income taxes by using an intertemporal equilibrium model of a small open economy. This model combines, on the one hand, adjustment costs affecting domestic investment and, on the other hand, overlapping generations determining domestic saving. The intertemporal equilibrium framework allows for an integrated analysis of traditional public finance issues, such as efficiency and (intergenerational) equity, and macroeconomic phenomena, such as investment, saving, trade and capital flows, and the accumulation of net foreign assets and the domestic capital stock. Moreover, the model enables one to explore the role of public debt policy in offsetting the effects of capital income taxes on the intergenerational distribution of resources.

In solving the model, we adopt the linearization technique developed in Judd (1982, 1985) for dynamic equilibrium models with perfect foresight. Using this technique, one can derive analytical solutions for the entire transition path in continuous time. The analytical solutions have an intuitive interpretation and explicitly reveal how several structural parameters influence the macroeconomic effects of capital income taxation.[11] In simulating the entire transition in continuous time, the modeling framework differs from most other analytical studies of open economies, which typically adopt two-period models (see, for example, Frenkel and Razin, 1986, 1987; van Wijnbergen, 1986).

2   Intertemporal equilibrium of a small open economy

2.1   Consumption and saving behavior

The saving and consumption side of the model consists of an overlapping generations model described by Buiter (1988), which is a combination of a version developed by Yaari (1965) and Blanchard (1984, 1985) and a version due to Weil (1989). Following the Yaari–Blanchard model, each household faces a constant probability of passing away, θ.[12] In the absence of an operative bequest motive, each household purchases (or sells) an annuity that pays a rate of return θ. New households that are *not* linked through operative intergenerational transfers to older households are born at a constant rate $n + \theta$.[13] This birth rate measures the heterogeneity, or economic disconnectedness, of the population (see Weil, 1989). Both the total population and the labor supply grow at the rate n because all households inelastically supply the same amount of labor.[14] At time $t \geq v$, the representative household of the generation born at time v maximizes the expected value of additive separable utility, adopting a subjective discount rate δ,

$$U(v, t) = \int_{t}^{\infty} u[c(v, s)] \exp[-\delta(s - t)] \exp[-\theta(s - t)] \, ds \qquad (5.1)$$

subject to a budget constraint

$$\dot{a}(v, t) = (r^* + \theta)a(v, t) + \omega(t) - c(v, t) \qquad (5.2)$$

where $c(v, t)$ and $a(v, t)$ represent, respectively, consumption and financial wealth per capita at time $t \geq v$ of the generation born at time v. A dot above a variable denotes a time derivative. In this chapter we assume that every living household supplies one unit of homogeneous labor per capita and receives the same lump-sum transfer per capita, which may vary over time. Hence, noncapital disposable income (which is the sum of before-tax wages and lump-sum transfers) per capita is age independent. It can be interpreted as the after-tax return to human capital and is denoted by $\omega(t)$. The intertemporal substitution elasticity of consumption is given by the reciprocal of the elasticity of marginal felicity, $\sigma = -cu''(c)/u'(c)$. The domestic economy is assumed to be small relative to the rest of the world. Accordingly, the real rate of return r is fixed by world capital markets. The after-tax rate of return r^* is given by

$$r^* = (1 - t_r)r \qquad (5.3)$$

where t_r represents the rate of residence-based tax on capital income. This tax applies uniformly to all returns on financial assets. Hence, interest income, accrued capital gains, and dividends are taxed at the same rate.

The optimization problem yields the following consumption function (see Buiter, 1988):

$$c(v, t) = \Delta[a(v, t) + h(t)]$$ (5.4)

$h(t)$ represents per capita human wealth at time t, which is identical for all agents alive at t because noncapital income does not depend on age:

$$h(t) = \int_{t}^{\infty} [\omega(s)] \exp[-(r^* + \theta)(s - t)]\, ds$$ (5.5)

Also the propensity to consume out of total wealth, Δ, is age independent because all agents feature the same time horizon:

$$\Delta = r^* + \theta - \frac{r^* - \delta}{\sigma} > 0$$ (5.6)

In this chapter we assume that the after-tax return r^* exceeds the discount rate. This implies that household consumption is rising over time and that financial wealth is positive.[15]

Following Blanchard (1984, 1985), we can aggregate across generations to arrive at expressions in terms of per capita aggregate variables

$$C(t) = \Delta[A(t) + H(t)] = \Delta W(t)$$ (5.7)

$$\dot{A}(t) = (r^* - n)A(t) + \omega(t) - C(t)$$ (5.8)

where the per capita aggregate variables are derived from the per capita generation-specific variables as follows:

$$X(t) = \int_{-\infty}^{t} x(v, t)(n + \theta) \exp[-(n + \theta)(t - v)]\, dv \qquad X = C, A \quad (5.9)$$

$$x = c, a$$

and $H(t) = h(t)$. $W(t) = A(t) + H(t)$ corresponds to per capita aggregate wealth at time t.

2.2   Production and investment

A neoclassical net production function represents a constant-returns-to-scale technology

$$y = f(k)$$ (5.10)

where y corresponds to output per capita (net of depreciation) of the single tradeable commodity and k stands for the capital–labor ratio.[16]

The marginal productivity condition for labor represents the demand for labor:

$$w = f(k) - kf'(k) \tag{5.11}$$

where w represents the before-tax wage rate and $f'(k) = df(k)/dk$. In addition to the production technology (5.10), the production sector faces a second technology constraint – the installation function. This function was introduced by Uzawa (1969) to model adjustment costs associated with investment.[17] With the labor force growing at the rate n and labor being immobile internationally, this installation function can be written as (see, for example, Bovenberg, 1986)

$$\dot{k} = k[g(x) - n] \qquad g'(x) > 0 \qquad g''(x) < 0 \tag{5.12}$$

where x is the ratio of net investment to the capital stock. Marginal installation costs rise with the rate of investment, which is reflected in the concavity of the installation function in investment. How rapidly costs increase is mirrored by the elasticity of the marginal productivity of investment σ_x, defined as

$$\sigma_x = -\frac{xg''(x)}{g'(x)} \tag{5.13}$$

For any given capital stock, the faster the capital stock expands, the more capital goods per additional unit of capital are required. The elasticity σ_x provides a measure for the degree of international mobility of the physical capital stock. A lower elasticity corresponds to a higher degree of international mobility of physical capital. In the short run, the physical capital stock is fixed. Hence, physical capital is immobile initially. In the long run, in contrast, physical capital is perfectly mobile internationally.

Firms are equity financed and maximize the present value of their after-tax cash flow subject to the installation function:

$$V = \int_0^\infty \{(1 - t_k)[f(k) - w] - xk\} \exp[-(r - n)t] \, dt \tag{5.14}$$

where t_k stands for the rate of source-based[18] tax on capital income.[19] Optimization gives rise to the optimal path for the shadow price of capital, q,[20]

$$\frac{\dot{q}}{q} = r - g(x) - \frac{(1 - t_k)f'(k)}{q} + \frac{x}{q} \tag{5.15}$$

and the implicit demand function for investment

$$qg'(x) = 1 \tag{5.16}$$

2.3   Government

The overlapping generations model causes Ricardian equivalence to fail. Accordingly, the intertemporal equilibrium is affected by how the government distributes the revenues from capital income taxes across (disconnected) generations. In examining the effects of capital income taxes, we assume that the government balances its budget at each point in time by providing a common (lump-sum) transfer to every living household.[21] This transfer can also be interpreted as a subsidy to labor because per capita labor supply is age independent and inelastic. Under the assumption that the government does not issue debt, the after-tax return to human capital (or after-tax labor earnings) amounts to

$$\omega = w + t_k kf'(k) + t_r rA \tag{5.17}$$

2.4   The model solution

In this chapter we explore the local behavior of the small open economy around the initial steady state by log-linearizing the model around the initial balanced growth path.[22] Unless otherwise indicated, a tilde $\sim$ above a variable stands for the change in this variable relative to its initial steady-state value. As regards the two tax rates, tildes are defined as follows:

$$\tilde{t}_i = \frac{d(1 - t_i)}{1 - t_i} < 0 \qquad i \equiv k, r \tag{5.18}$$

In the initial steady state, domestic residents own the entire domestic capital stock. Furthermore, the tax rates are zero on the initial balanced growth path. Hence, $r = r^*$ and $\omega = w$ in the initial steady state. The policies examined here are unanticipated and permanent and are implemented at $t = 0$. The model is solved recursively. First, the log-linearized investment model yields the time paths for the capital stock, the shadow price of capital, investment, and before-tax wages (see appendix 1). Combining these solutions with the government budget constraint, we derive the development of after-tax wages (see appendix 1), which is used to solve the saving side of the model (see appendix 2).

3   A residence-based tax

A residence-based tax imposed by a small open economy does not affect domestic investment because it does not drive a wedge between the required return on domestic investment and the fixed rate of return on world financial markets. Accordingly, the macroeconomic implications of a residence-based tax originate in the effects of the tax on saving and consumption behavior. In particular, the tax impacts saving through two channels: first, the intergenerational distribution of resources and, second, intertemporal substitution of consumption due to a lower after-tax return on domestic saving.

3.1   The intergenerational distribution

By reducing the after-tax return on financial wealth, a residence-based tax on capital income harms the owners of financial capital. Human capital, in contrast, benefits because the rate used to discount labor earnings declines, while the revenues from the residence-based tax are used to supplement labor earnings. The higher real value of human capital implies that the generations who are born after the residence-based tax is introduced gain. These generations start their lives without any financial capital and therefore depend entirely on labor earnings. Accordingly, the relative change in real wealth of the generations born at time $t \geq 0$, $\tilde{W}^*(t)$, corresponds to the relative change in real human wealth, $\tilde{H}^*(0)$, which is given by (see appendix 3)

$$\tilde{W}^*(t) = \tilde{H}^*(0) = -(r-n)\frac{A}{\omega}\frac{\tilde{rt}_r}{\Delta} \tag{5.19}$$

The (older) generations that are alive at the time the policy shock occurs are affected not only by changes in human wealth but also by changes in financial wealth. The overall effect on the real wealth position of these generations, $\tilde{W}^*(0)$,[23] is given by (see appendix 3)

$$\tilde{W}^*(0) = m^*\frac{A}{\omega}\frac{\tilde{rt}_r}{\Delta} \tag{5.20}$$

where m^* is defined as

$$m^* = n + \theta - \frac{r-\delta}{\sigma} > 0 \tag{5.21}$$

Hence, on average, current generations lose because the fall in financial wealth more than offsets the rise in real human wealth. Two factors importantly affect the magnitude of the redistribution of wealth away from older to younger generations. The first factor is the gap between the rate of return r and the discount rate δ (see appendix 2):

$$m^*\frac{A}{\omega} = \frac{(r-\delta)/\sigma}{r+\theta} \tag{5.22}$$

A larger gap between the real rate of return and the discount rate implies a steeper rise in consumption during the lifetime, which corresponds to a larger aggregate stock of financial capital in the steady state. The larger financial wealth is, the larger are the adverse effects of a residence-based tax on the currently alive who own this wealth at the time the unanticipated policy shock occurs.

The birth rate $n + \theta$ is the second major determinant of the intergenerational distributional effect. As the birth rate gets higher, the population becomes more heterogeneous and the current generations internalize less and less the higher value of human wealth.

3.2   Economy-wide consumption

The time path for aggregate consumption is characterized by three elements: the short-run and long-run changes in consumption and an adjustment speed m^* (see appendix 2):

$$\tilde{C}(t) = \tilde{C}(0) \exp(-m^*t) + \tilde{C}(\infty)[1 - \exp(-m^*t)] \qquad (5.23)$$

$$\tilde{C}(0) = -\frac{1}{\sigma} \frac{\delta + \theta \, \tilde{rt}_r}{r + \theta \, \Delta} \qquad (5.24)$$

$$\tilde{C}(\infty) = \frac{r - n}{m^*} \frac{1}{\sigma} \frac{\delta + \theta \, \tilde{rt}_r}{r + \theta \, \Delta} \qquad (5.25)$$

A residence-based tax unambiguously raises consumption initially. The larger the intertemporal substitution elasticity $1/\sigma$, the larger the initial boost to consumption. Intuitively, a higher intertemporal substitution elasticity renders consumption more sensitive to the lower after-tax rate of return. Following the initial rise, consumption starts to drop off and in the new steady state it has declined to a level below its initial steady-state value. The adjustment speed m^* corresponds to the absolute value of the stable root of the linearized saving system (see appendix 2). Expression (5.21) reveals that this adjustment speed is closely related to the birth rate. The higher the birth rate, the faster consumption converges toward its long-run equilibrium value.

3.3   Trade balance and net foreign assets

The effects on the trade balance can be written as the difference between domestic supply of and domestic demand for commodities:

$$\widetilde{TB} = \hat{y} - a_c \tilde{C} - a_1(\hat{x} + \hat{k}) \qquad (5.26)$$

Here, $\widetilde{TB}$ stands for the change in the trade balance relative to initial net domestic income. a_c and a_I denote the net income shares of, respectively, consumption and net investment in the initial steady state. Capital accumulation determines domestic supply according to

$$\tilde{y} = \alpha_k \tilde{k} \tag{5.27}$$

where α_k denotes the share of capital income (net of depreciation) in domestic income.

The residence-based tax impacts the trade balance only through its effect on consumption because it leaves unaffected investment demand and capital accumulation. Accordingly, the initial boost to domestic consumption worsens the trade balance in the short run. In the long run, however, the trade balance improves on account of lower consumption demand.

The consequences for net foreign assets are derived by subtracting the value of the domestic capital stock from financial assets owned by domestic households:

$$\tilde{F} = \tilde{A} - z(\tilde{q} + \tilde{k}) \tag{5.28}$$

Here, $z = \alpha_k - a_I \geq 0$ is the share of the cash flow of firms in (net) domestic income. $\tilde{F}$ and $\tilde{A}$ are defined as

$$\tilde{X} = (r - n)\frac{dX}{y} \qquad X = F, A \tag{5.29}$$

Since the residence-based tax does not affect the value of the domestic capital stock, the effect on the foreign asset position, $\tilde{F}$, corresponds to the effect on domestic financial wealth, $\tilde{A}$. The time path for net financial wealth is given by (see appendix 2)

$$\tilde{A}(t) = \tilde{A}(\infty)[1 - \exp(-m^*t)] \tag{5.30}$$

where

$$\tilde{A}(\infty) = a_c \tilde{C}(\infty) \tag{5.31}$$

The development over time of the ratio of net foreign assets to domestic income yields the effect on the growth-adjusted external current account balance:

$$\frac{\dot{\tilde{F}}}{r - n} = F + \widetilde{TB} \tag{5.32}$$

The residence-based tax unambiguously reduces saving, thereby worsening the external current account and negatively affecting net foreign assets. The magnitude of these effects depends importantly on the intertemporal elasticity of substitution.

3.4 Neutralizing the effects on the intergenerational distribution

The initial positive response of consumption is the result of, on the one hand, a positive substitution effect due to the lower after-tax return and, on the other hand, a negative income effect that originates in the redistribution away from the current generations. The government can actually neutralize the intergenerational distributional effects of the tax by employing public debt policy so that only the intertemporal substitution effect remains.

In order to leave the intergenerational distribution unaffected, the government provides a one-time subsidy to the owners of financial wealth at the time the unanticipated policy shock occurs. This subsidy should be debt financed and should offset the windfall loss suffered by capitalists.[24] Accordingly, the initial jump in public debt corresponds to the worsening of the real wealth position of the owners of financial capital (see appendix 3):

$$\tilde{B}(0) = - a_\omega(r - n)\frac{A}{\omega}\frac{r\tilde{t}_r}{\Delta} \tag{5.33}$$

where $a_\omega = 1 - \alpha_k$ denotes the share of (after-tax) labor earnings in net domestic income. $\tilde{B}$ is defined analogously to $\tilde{F}$ and $\tilde{A}$ as

$$\tilde{B} = (r - n)\frac{dB}{y} \tag{5.34}$$

In order to meet its budget constraint, the government reduces per capita transfers.[25] The public budget constraint is given by

$$\mathring{B}(t) = (r - n)\tilde{B}(t) + (r - n)\tilde{l}(t) \tag{5.35}$$

Here, $\tilde{l}(t)$ stands for the change in lump-sum transfers relative to net domestic income in the initial steady state. By using Laplace transforms, one can write the public budget constraint as[26]

$$\tilde{B}(0) = - (r - n)L_l(r - n) \tag{5.36}$$

In order to have all generations share equally in the cost of servicing the stock of public debt, the government chooses a constant path of transfers that meets (5.36):

$$\tilde{l} = - \tilde{B}(0) \tag{5.37}$$

This path for transfers implies that the ratio of public debt to income remains constant after its initial rise. Furthermore, the lower transfers exactly offset the positive effect of the residence-based tax on the real wealth position of human capital.

The combination of this public debt policy and the residence-based tax yields the following path for aggregate consumption:

$$\tilde{C}(t) = \tilde{C}(0) \exp(-m^*t) + \tilde{C}(\infty)[1 - \exp(-m^*t)] \qquad (5.38)$$

$$\tilde{C}(0) = -\frac{1}{\sigma}\frac{r\tilde{t}_r}{\Delta} \qquad (5.39)$$

$$\tilde{C}(\infty) = \frac{r-n}{m^*}\frac{1}{\sigma}\frac{r\tilde{t}_r}{\Delta} \qquad (5.40)$$

It appears from comparing this time path with that given by (5.23), (5.24), and (5.25) that the fluctuations in aggregate consumption are largest if the intergenerational distributional effects are eliminated. The reason is that the intergenerational distributional effects of a residence-based tax favor future generations at the expense of current generations. Hence, these income effects weaken the substitution effects of a lower after-tax return because they reduce initial consumption and boost long-run consumption.

3.5   Neutralizing the intertemporal substitution effects

The government can neutralize not only the income effects but also the intertemporal substitution effects of the tax. In particular, it can continue to tax the return on financial capital but at the same time allow a tax deduction for new saving. This policy experiment, in fact, effectively substitutes a destination-based consumption tax for a labor tax. Although this policy does not involve any intertemporal substitution effects, it does exert macroeconomic effects because it impacts the intergenerational distribution. In particular, it implies a capital levy on existing financial wealth and therefore a wealth transfer from older to younger generations.[27] Hence, consumption falls in the short run but rises in the long run. The trade balance improves initially and the economy accumulates additional financial assets in the form of net foreign assets.

4   A source-based tax

4.1   Investment and capital accumulation

A source-based tax on capital income affects not only domestic saving but also domestic investment. The investment system yields the following time path for the capital–labor ratio (see appendix 1):

$$\hat{k}(t) = \hat{k}(\infty)[1 - \exp(-mt)] \qquad (5.41)$$

m stands for the rate at which the capital intensity of production converges to its new steady-state value:

$$\frac{m}{r-n} = -\frac{1}{2} + \left[\frac{1}{4} + \frac{\alpha_k a_I (1 - \alpha_k)}{\sigma_x \sigma_k z^2}\right]^{1/2} \tag{5.42}$$

A less concave installation function, which reflects more elastic investment, yields a higher adjustment speed. The adjustment speed approaches infinity if adjustment costs are absent (i.e. $\sigma_x = 0$). This case corresponds to perfectly mobile physical capital. The case of a fixed factor, in contrast, is represented by a zero adjustment speed.

The long-run effect on the domestic capital stock $\tilde{k}(\infty)$ is given by

$$\tilde{k}(\infty) = \left(\frac{\sigma_k}{1 - \alpha_k}\right)\tilde{t}_k \tag{5.43}$$

Accordingly, source-based taxes reduce the domestic capital stock. The substitution elasticity between capital and the immobile factor (i.e. labor), σ_k, is an important determinant of the adverse effect on capital accumulation. The larger this elasticity, the less sensitive the marginal productivity of capital is with respect to the capital–labor ratio and therefore the more this ratio has to fall to raise the after-tax return of capital to the exogenous level in the rest of the world.

4.2 The intergenerational distribution

The impact on the intergenerational distribution depends importantly on how the source tax affects after-tax labor earnings over time. If the government does not adopt debt finance, after-tax labor earnings develop as follows:

$$\tilde{\omega}(t) = \tilde{\omega}(0) \exp(-mt) \tag{5.44}$$

$$a_\omega \tilde{\omega}(0) = -\alpha_k \tilde{t}_k \tag{5.45}$$

Initially, net labor earnings rise as the budgetary revenues from the capital income tax allow for larger transfers to labor. Over time, however, the gradual decline in the capital intensity of production reduces the marginal productivity of labor, thereby negatively affecting before-tax wages. Accordingly, following their initial rise, labor earnings start to fall. In the long run, labor earnings return to their initial steady-state level. Intuitively, capital can shift the entire long-run burden of the source-based tax to labor because physical capital is perfectly mobile in the long run. Indeed, in the long run a source-based tax on capital income constitutes an implicit tax on labor. Hence, a source-based tax on capital income that is returned as a transfer to labor does not affect after-tax labor earnings.[28]

The effect on human wealth of the generations who are alive at the time of the policy shock, $\tilde{H}(0)$, is computed by discounting the path of after-tax wages by the sum of the rate of return on financial capital and the probability of death:

$$a_\omega \tilde{H}(0) = -\frac{r+\theta}{m+r+\theta} \alpha_k \tilde{t}_k \tag{5.46}$$

A source-based tax raises the value of human capital. Human capital benefits most if sluggish capital decumulation causes before-tax wages to fall only slowly (i.e. m is small) and if the long-run changes in after-tax wages are discounted relatively heavily (i.e. $r + \theta$ is large). In that case, the eventual fall in before-tax wages occurs largely beyond the horizons of the currently alive.

The consequences for real wealth of the generations born at time $t \geq 0$, $\tilde{H}(t)$, are given by

$$\tilde{H}(t) = \tilde{H}(0) \exp(-mt) \tag{5.47}$$

Accordingly, the time path of after-tax earnings is the only determinant of the welfare position of generations that are born after the policy shock hits. Intuitively, these generations start their life without any financial capital and therefore depend entirely on labor income. The generations who are born immediately after the policy shock occurs gain most because they suffer least from lower before-tax wages on account of less capital-intensive production.

The welfare position of the older generations living at the time of the unanticipated policy shock is affected not only by the impact on human wealth but also by that on financial capital. The initial consequences for the value of financial capital indicate whether capitalists can shift the source-based tax:

$$\tilde{A}(0) = z\tilde{q}(0) = \frac{r-n}{r-n+m} \alpha_k \tilde{t}_k \tag{5.48}$$

The magnitude of the capital loss that is suffered by capitalists depends on the ratio of the adjustment speed, which is a measure of the international mobility of physical capital, and the effective discount rate $r - n$. The faster the capital–labor ratio falls, the more capital is able to shift the tax burden to labor. In fact, capital escapes the burden entirely if physical capital is perfectly mobile internationally (i.e. $m \to \infty$).

The consequences for the real wealth position of the current generations[29] are found by combining the effects on human and financial capital (expressions (5.47) and (5.48) respectively):

$$\frac{r+\theta}{\Delta} a_c \tilde{W}(0) = \frac{n+\theta}{r+\theta+m} \alpha_k \tilde{t}_k \tag{5.49}$$

A source-based tax harms current generations due to the redistribution away from capital to labor. Intuitively, current generations suffer a decline in real wealth because they own the entire domestic capital stock and therefore fully absorb lower capital earnings. However, they do not fully internalize higher transfers to labor as these transfers do, in part, accrue to future generations.

Current generations suffer most if the rate of birth $n + \theta$ is high and capital decumulation occurs only slowly (i.e. m is small). A low speed of capital decumulation causes capital earnings to rise only slowly after their initial fall, thereby depressing discounted capital earnings, which accrue to the currently alive. A high birth rate implies that the currently alive absorb only a small part of the higher return to human capital.

4.3   Consumption and saving

The source-based tax impacts consumption and saving because it affects the intergenerational distribution of resources. The time path for aggregate consumption is given by (see appendix 2)

$$\tilde{C}(t) = \tilde{W}(0) \exp(-m^*t) + m^* \frac{r+\theta}{r+\theta+m} \hat{\omega}(0) \left[\frac{\exp(-mt) - \exp(-m^*t)}{m^* - m} \right]$$

$$(5.50)$$

where $\tilde{W}(0)$ is given by (5.49). The time path of consumption is nonmonotonic (see figure 5.1). In particular, consumption falls initially

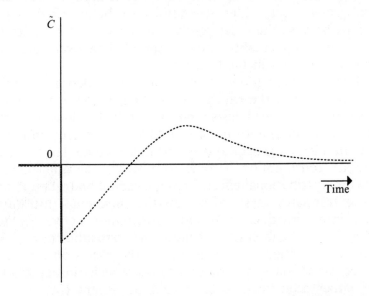

Figure 5.1   Source-based taxation and consumption.

on account of the worsening wealth position of the currently alive. Following its initial fall, however, consumption starts to recover. Intuitively, the development of consumption at each point in time depends on the relationship between the welfare of generations that are being born and the older generations. Economy-wide consumption rises if and only if newly born generations are wealthier than the preceding generations. The generations who are born immediately after the tax is introduced benefit from higher human wealth and, in contrast to older generations, do not suffer from lower capital earnings because they were not alive at the time the unanticipated policy shock occurred. Hence, the younger generations are better off than the older generations and consumption rises when they enter the population. A high rate of birth $n + \theta$ causes consumption to recover rapidly because it implies that the young generations, who benefit from the tax on capital income, rapidly constitute a large part of the population. When the older generations that were alive when the tax was introduced have become a sufficiently small part of the population, consumption rises above its initial steady-state level.

Eventually, however, consumption starts to decline and, on the new balanced growth path, it falls back to its initial steady-state value. The eventual fall in consumption is due to the declining trend in labor income. Near the new steady state, almost all living generations have been born after the tax was reduced. At that time, therefore, changes in human wealth are the major determinants of the relative wealth positions of the older and newly born generations. Near the new balanced growth path, older generations are better off than younger generations because the older generations benefit from higher human wealth, as per capita labor incomes are falling over time. Hence, consumption declines in the long run.

How large the fluctuations in consumption are depends importantly on the magnitude of the effects on the intergenerational distribution. The larger the adjustment costs (and the lower the adjustment speed of capital decumulation) and the birth rate are, the more substantial the redistribution across generations is and therefore the larger the swings in aggregate consumption become. Intuitively, the adjustment costs produce the distributional effects between capital and labor. A positive birth rate translates these effects on the functional distribution of resources into consequences for the distribution across generations. Accordingly, it is the interaction between nonzero adjustment costs and overlapping generations that gives rise to the effects on consumption. Indeed, consumption would remain constant at its initial steady-state level if either adjustment costs would be absent (i.e. $m \to \infty$) or households would internalize the welfare of their offspring (i.e. $n + \theta = 0$).

4.4   Trade balance and net foreign assets

A source-based tax impacts the trade balance through three channels: consumption and investment demand and the effect of domestic capital decumulation on the domestic supply of commodities. Substituting the expressions for capital accumulation and investment as well as the results for economy-wide consumption (5.50) into the definition of the trade balance (5.26), we derive for the initial trade balance response, which corresponds to the initial effect on the external current account,

$$\widetilde{TB}(0) = -\frac{m}{r-n}\, z\, \frac{\sigma_k}{1-\alpha_k}\, \tilde{\imath}_k - \left[\frac{n+\theta}{r+\theta+m}\right]\alpha_k\tilde{\imath}_k \qquad (5.51)$$

In the short run, demand effects determine the trade balance response. The reason is that domestic supply is fixed initially because labor supply is exogenous, while the physical capital stock is fixed in the short run on account of adjustment costs. It appears from (5.51) that a source-based tax unambiguously improves the trade balance in the short run. This initial improvement is due not only to weaker investment demand but also to a fall in initial consumption demand, reflecting a stronger saving performance. The effect of lower investment demand on domestic absorption is represented by the first term on the right-hand side of (5.51). The second term represents the positive saving effect of the source-based tax due to the intergenerational distributional effect. In particular, a source-based tax raises economy-wide saving because it benefits future generations at the expense of the currently alive.

After the trade balance improves initially, the improvement falls off for two reasons. First, domestic per capita supply declines on account of a lower capital–labor ratio. Second, consumption demand recovers (see above). The trade balance eventually deteriorates relative to the initial steady state. Intuitively, the dynamics of the trade balance reflect both the demand and supply effects of lower investment. The negative demand effects dominate in the short run and the trade balance improves. In the long run, the trade balance worsens due to adverse supply effects.

In the long run, the net foreign asset position improves. The increased net investment income received from abroad that corresponds to the improved foreign asset position allows the small open economy to afford a weaker trade balance in the long run.

4.5   Neutralizing the effects on the intergenerational distribution

Just as in the case of the residence-based tax, the government can neutralize the intergenerational distributional effects of a source-based tax by employing public debt policy. In particular, at the time that the unanticipated tax is implemented, it should provide a one-time wealth subsidy. This subsidy should be debt financed and should exactly offset the windfall losses suffered by capitalists. From the government budget constraint, one can find the (negative) discounted value of the transfers that are required to service the larger stock of public debt:

$$(r - n)L_l(r - n) = \frac{r - n}{r - n + m} \alpha_k \tilde{t}_k \qquad (5.52)$$

In order to confront all generations with the same absolute change in (*ex ante* or expected) welfare per capita, the government should aim at constant per capita labor earnings over time. The time path for transfers that meets both this condition and the intertemporal public budget constraint (5.52) is

$$\tilde{l}(t) = \alpha_k \tilde{t}_k \exp(- mt) \qquad (5.53)$$

4.6   Neutralizing the effects on the required return on new investment

The government can neutralize the effect of the source-based tax on investment behavior by allowing firms to expense their new investment spending from their capital income tax liability. A source-based tax combined with an immediate write-off for investment amounts to a tax on the cash flow of domestic firms. Just as a destination-based consumption tax does not affect the incentive to save for each individual household, so a cash-flow tax on investment leaves the incentive to invest unaffected.[30] However, both the destination-based consumption tax and the source-based cash-flow tax imply a capital levy on old capital. A destination-based consumption tax amounts to a capital levy on the stock of financial capital owned by domestic residents, while a source-based cash-flow tax implies a wealth tax on the owners of the domestic capital stock. Just as the destination-based consumption tax, the cash-flow tax harms current generations. This gives rise to macroeconomic effects. In particular, the cash-flow tax improves the trade balance in the short run as consumption demand falls. In the long run, a larger stock of foreign assets allows the economy to run a larger trade deficit corresponding to a higher level of domestic demand.

5   Conclusions and suggestions for future research

In this chapter we explored the macroeconomic implications of residence- and source-based taxes on capital income in small open economies. The analysis revealed that the two alternative types of capital income taxes yield different effects on domestic demand and the external accounts. This reflects mainly the differential effects of these taxes on the required return on investment and the after-tax return on saving. Whereas a residence-based tax depresses the return on domestic saving, a source-based tax raises the required return on domestic investment. Capital income taxes also influence the intergenerational distribution. In particular, they benefit younger generations at the expense of older generations, who own the stock of financial wealth. However, source-based taxes generally impose a smaller burden on older generations because capital can partly escape a source-based tax by moving abroad. Although it imposes the heaviest burden on older generations, a residence-based tax nevertheless depresses economy-wide saving on account of the intertemporal substitution effect associated with a lower after-tax return on saving. Accordingly, the substitution effect dominates the income effect and the trade balance worsens in the short run. In the long run, a smaller stock of foreign assets requires a stronger trade performance.

A source-based tax improves the initial trade performance by reducing investment and raising saving. Accordingly, larger saving on account of the intergenerational distributional effects strengthens the effects of weaker investment demand on the short-run trade balance. Investment falls because a source-based tax raises the required return on physical capital located domestically. Saving rises as a result of the intergenerational redistribution of resources away from current to future generations. In the long run, the trade performance worsens, as a smaller capital stock reduces domestic supply and as richer younger generations imply a higher level of consumption demand.

The analytical solutions reveal how various structural parameters impact the macroeconomic consequences of capital income taxes. In particular, a higher birth rate generates larger effects on the intergenerational distribution. The intertemporal substitution elasticity of consumption is an important determinant of the negative saving effects that are induced by a residence-based tax. The magnitude of the adverse investment effects of a source-based tax depends importantly on both the substitution elasticity between capital and labor in production and the adjustment costs in investment.

The model in this chapter could be extended in several directions. In particular, one could allow for positive tax rates in the initial steady state. In that case, an increase in capital income taxes generates first-order losses in overall efficiency. Bovenberg (1993) examines how the efficiency impact of source-based taxes affects domestic demand and the trade performance.[31] It appears that the efficiency losses associated with a higher source-based tax may reduce initial aggregate consumption and strengthen the initial trade performance. Intuitively, the efficiency losses yield lower incomes mainly in the longer run, when the capital–labor ratio has been reduced. Accordingly, households save more in order to smooth their consumption intertemporally in the face of the anticipation of lower long-run incomes. The importance of this consumption-smoothing effect depends importantly on the length of the planning horizon of the households, which is inversely related to the birth rate.

When exploring the macroeconomic effect of source-based taxes on capital income, Bovenberg (1993) also allows for foreign ownership of the domestic capital stock. The analysis reveals that foreign ownership may change the macroeconomic implications of capital income taxes owing to effects on the international distribution of resources.[32] In particular, if foreigners own the domestic capital stock in the initial equilibrium and if adjustment costs are high, foreigners rather than domestic residents at home absorb most of the burden of the source-based tax. The international distributional effect in favor of domestic residents boosts domestic consumption. The initial rise in consumption is especially large if the birth rate is high. In that case, the eventual decline in the marginal productivity of labor occurs largely beyond the horizons of the current generations at home. As regards the external accounts, an unanticipated source-based tax improves net foreign assets on impact. This allows the country to import additional resources from abroad. In fact, the trade balance may worsen not only in the long run but also in the short run if a high birth rate and substantial adjustment costs imply large benefits for the current generations at home.

The model assumes that labor supply is exogenous. Introducing endogenous labor supply would allow one to trade off labor–leisure distortions with distortions in the capital market. Sørensen (1990) introduces endogenous labor supply in an overlapping generations model that does not include adjustment costs in investment. When studying the macroeconomic effects of investment subsidies, Sen and Turnovsky (1990) incorporate endogenous labor supply in a model with an infinitely lived representative household (i.e. a zero birth rate).

We do not model imperfect substitution between commodities or assets in this chapter. As noted in the introduction, however, several studies have demonstrated that the existence of several commodities that are imperfectly substitutable may modify some of the results derived here because of effects on the terms of trade and the real exchange rate. To illustrate, Bovenberg (1989) shows that a source-based tax may worsen the trade balance in the short run if the intratemporal substitution elasticity between foreign and domestic commodities is small relative to the intertemporal substitution elasticity of consumption. Imperfect substitution between assets may require the introduction of uncertainty.[33]

In practice, one rarely finds pure residence-based or source-based taxes on capital income. In particular, capital income taxes typically discriminate across various forms of financing (see, for example, Sinn, 1987) and channels for international capital movements (e.g. portfolio versus direct investment). Nielsen and Sørensen (1991) incorporate various financing options within the modeling framework used in this chapter while assuming that all equity in domestic firms is held by domestic residents. They examine the effect of corporate taxes, which amount to source-based taxes on equity income, capital gains taxes, dividend taxes, and taxes on interest income. Their analysis could be extended to allow for foreign direct investment.

The framework used here could also be applied to study the strategic interaction between countries and, in particular, the potential welfare gains or losses from the international coordination of tax policies. For such a study, it is important to model correctly the objectives of the government (e.g. those regarding efficiency and equity) and the restrictions on the use of various instruments. The reason is that the costs of tax competition are likely to depend on the number of objectives as well as the number of tax instruments that are available to achieve these objectives. In this connection, one should recognize that imperfect information on the part of the tax authorities may limit the use of particular tax instruments, especially those that require the cooperation of foreign tax authorities.[34] In studying the strategic interactions between large countries, one should allow countries to influence the market interest rate and their terms of trade. If countries affect the world interest rate, they may impact foreign countries through effects on the intertemporal terms of trade and the foreign tax base.[35]

In order to do justice to the proponents of tax competition, one needs to model also imperfections in the political process, which may make tax coordination costly. Just as competition between private agents compels producers to develop and provide the goods and services that consumers want, tax competition may encourage governments to respond better to the desires of their constituents. The recent literature on time inconsistency of policies provides other arguments why the international coordination of tax policy may be undesirable. In particular, tax coordination may adversely affect the credibility of the commitment of governments not to tax capital. In view of these unresolved issues, it is likely that the taxation of capital income in open economies will generate more exciting academic research in the years to come.

Appendix 1: The investment system

Steady-state relationships

The elasticities in the log-linearized model are assumed to be fixed at their values in the initial steady-state equilibrium. In order to express these elasticities in terms of observable shares, we use two steady-state relationships ((A5.1) and (A5.4) below) that follow from (5.12) and (5.15) respectively.

On a balanced growth path, the capital–labor ratio is constant. Accordingly, (5.12) yields the following steady-state relationship:

$$g(x) = n \qquad\qquad (A5.1)$$

Setting the left-hand side of (5.15) equal to zero and using (A5.1), we derive

$$(r - n)q = (1 - t_k)f'(k) - x \qquad\qquad (A5.2)$$

On the initial balanced growth path the source-based tax is assumed to be zero (see section 2.4):

$$t_k = 0 \qquad\qquad (A5.3)$$

Substituting (A5.3) into (A5.2), we find the following steady-state relationship between the capital–output ratio and the share of the cash flow in output, z:

$$(r - n)\frac{qk}{f(k)} = z = \alpha_k - a_1 \qquad\qquad (A5.4)$$

The log-linearized model

The dynamic equations are found by log-linearizing (5.12) and (5.15) respectively:

$$\dot{\tilde{k}} = g'(x)x\tilde{x} \qquad\qquad (A5.5)$$

$$\dot{\tilde{q}} = -\frac{(1 - t_k)f''(k)k}{q}\tilde{k} + \frac{(1 - t_k)f'(k) - x}{q}\tilde{q}$$

$$-\frac{(1 - t_k)f'(k)}{q}\tilde{t}_k + \frac{x}{q}\tilde{x} - g'(x)x\tilde{x} \qquad\qquad (A5.6)$$

In order to eliminate $\tilde{x}$ from (A5.5) and (A5.6), we use the following log-linearized version of (5.16):

$$\tilde{q} = \sigma_x\tilde{x} \qquad\qquad (A5.7)$$

Then the steady-state elasticities in (A5.5) and (A5.6) are rewritten by eliminating $g'(x)$ from (5.16), eliminating q from (A5.4), imposing (A5.3), and using the definition of σ_k:

$$\sigma_k = -\frac{f'(k)}{f''(k)k}(1 - \alpha_k) \qquad\qquad (A5.8)$$

This procedure gives rise to the two-dimensional investment system

$$
\begin{bmatrix} \dot{\tilde{k}} \\ \dot{\tilde{q}} \end{bmatrix} = (r-n) \begin{bmatrix} 0 & \dfrac{a_I}{\sigma_x z} \\[2ex] \dfrac{\alpha_k}{z} & \dfrac{1-\alpha_k}{\sigma_k} & 1 \end{bmatrix} \begin{bmatrix} \tilde{k} \\ \tilde{q} \end{bmatrix}
$$

$$
+ (r-n) \begin{bmatrix} 0 \\[1ex] -\dfrac{\alpha_k}{z} \end{bmatrix} [\tilde{t}_k] \tag{A5.9}
$$

The solutions

The long-run solution for the *capital–labor ratio* (5.43) is derived by setting the left-hand side of (A5.9) equal to zero and solving for $\tilde{k}(\infty)$. Expression (5.42) for the *adjustment speed m* to the new long-run equilibrium is computed as the absolute value of the stable (i.e. negative) root of the first elasticity matrix on the right-hand side of (A5.9). Accordingly, m is the negative root of the following characteristic equation:

$$
m(m+r-n) - \frac{\alpha_k}{z} \frac{a_I}{z\sigma_x} \frac{1-\alpha_k}{\sigma_k} (r-n)^2 = 0 \tag{A5.10}
$$

The initial jump of the *unit value of the domestic capital stock, $\tilde{q}(0)$*, is found by substituting the solution for the capital–labor ratio (from (5.41) and (5.43)) into the first row of (A5.9):

$$
\frac{m}{r-n} \frac{\sigma_k}{1-\alpha_k} \tilde{t}_k \exp(-mt) = \frac{a_I}{\sigma_x z} \tilde{q}(t) \tag{A5.11}
$$

Using (A5.10) to eliminate the elasticities σ_x and σ_k, we arrive at (5.48).

The changes in *after-tax labor earnings* due to a source-based tax are derived by substituting (5.11) into (5.17) to eliminate w and log-linearizing the resulting equation:

$$
a_\omega \hat{\omega} = \alpha_k \frac{1-\alpha_k}{\sigma_k} \tilde{k} - \alpha_k \tilde{t}_k \tag{A5.12}
$$

where (A5.3) and (A5.8) have been used to rewrite the elasticities. Expressions (5.44) and (5.45) are derived from (A5.12) by substituting the time path for the capital–labor ratio (from (5.41) and (5.43)).

The relative change in *human wealth* (5.46) follows from log-linearizing the definition of human wealth

$$
H(t) = \int_t^\infty \omega(s) \exp[-(r^*+\theta)(s-t)] \, ds \tag{A5.13}
$$

according to

$$\tilde{H}(0) = (r^* + \theta) \int_0^\infty \tilde{\omega}(t) \exp[-(r^* + \theta)t]\, dt - \frac{r^*}{r^* + \theta}\tilde{t}_r \qquad (A5.14)$$

Substituting (5.44) and (5.45) into (A5.14), we find (5.46).

Appendix 2: The saving system

Dynamic equations

The saving system consists of two dynamic equations in aggregate consumption C and financial wealth A. The dynamic equation for consumption is found by differentiating (5.7) with respect to time:

$$\dot{C}(t) = \Delta[\dot{A}(t) + \dot{H}(t)] \qquad (A5.15)$$

Δ is constant over time because the after-tax return r^* remains constant after the residence-based tax is introduced at $t = 0$. The time derivatives on the right-hand side of (A5.15) are rewritten by using the time derivative of (A5.13)

$$\dot{H}(t) = (r^* + \theta)H(t) - \omega(t) \qquad (A5.16)$$

and (5.8). This yields

$$\dot{C}(t) = \frac{r^* - \delta}{\sigma} C(t) - \Delta(n + \theta)A(t) \qquad (A5.17)$$

The dynamic equation for financial wealth is derived by substituting (5.17) into (5.8) in order to eliminate ω:

$$\dot{A}(t) = (r - n)A(t) - \omega_1(t) - C(t) \qquad (A5.18)$$

where

$$\omega_1(t) = w(t) + t_k f'(k)k \qquad (A5.19)$$

Steady-state relationships

In order to manipulate the elasticities, in this appendix we derive a number of steady-state relationships. Imposing the steady-state condition on (A5.17), we find the following expression linking A and C on a balanced-growth path:

$$A = \frac{(r^* - \delta)/\sigma}{\Delta(n + \theta)} C \qquad (A5.20)$$

The steady-state value of human wealth is given by (using (A5.13))

$$H = \frac{\omega}{r^* + \theta} \qquad (A5.21)$$

The steady-state relationship between consumption and after-tax labor earnings is found by substituting (A5.20) and (A5.21) into (5.7):

$$\frac{\omega}{C} = \frac{a_\omega}{a_c} = \frac{m^*(r^* + \theta)}{\Delta(n + \theta)} \tag{A5.22}$$

where m^* is defined in (5.21). Expression (5.22), which links A and ω, is found by combining (A5.20), (A5.21), and (A5.22) and using $r = r^*$ in the initial steady state.

The log-linearized model

Log-linearizing (A5.17) and (A5.18) produces the saving system

$$\begin{bmatrix} \check{C}(t) \\ \check{A}(t) \end{bmatrix} = \begin{bmatrix} \dfrac{r^* - \delta}{\sigma} & -\dfrac{(n + \sigma)\Delta}{a_c(r - n)} \\ -(r - n)a_c & r - n \end{bmatrix} \begin{bmatrix} \tilde{C}(t) \\ \tilde{A}(t) \end{bmatrix}$$

$$+ \begin{bmatrix} 0 & \dfrac{\theta + \delta}{\sigma\Delta} r^* \\ (r - n)a_\omega & 0 \end{bmatrix} \begin{bmatrix} \omega_1(t) \\ \tilde{t}_r \end{bmatrix} \tag{A5.23}$$

where the time path for after-tax labor earnings, $\tilde{\omega}_1(t)$, is derived from theinvestment system (see equations (5.44) and (5.45)).

The saving system (A5.23) is solved by using Laplace transforms. The Laplace transform $L_p(s)$ of a function $p(t)$ is defined by

$$L_p(s) = \int_0^\infty \exp(-st)\, p(t)\, dt \tag{A5.24}$$

In this appendix we use the following expression for the Laplace transform of the time derivative of a function $p(t)$:

$$L_{\dot{p}}(s) = \int_0^\infty \exp(-st)\, \dot{p}(t)\, dt = sL_p(s) - p(0) \tag{A5.25}$$

Taking the Laplace transforms of (A5.23) and using (A5.25), one can solve for the Laplace transforms of consumption and financial wealth according to

$$D(s) \begin{bmatrix} L_{\check{C}}(s) \\ L_{\check{A}}(s) \end{bmatrix} = \begin{bmatrix} s - (r - n) & -\dfrac{(n + \theta)\Delta}{a_c(r - n)} \\ -(r - n)a_c & s - \dfrac{r - \delta}{\sigma} \end{bmatrix} \begin{bmatrix} \tilde{C}(0) + \dfrac{1}{s}\dfrac{\theta + \delta}{\sigma\Delta}\tilde{r}\tilde{t}_r \\ a_\omega(r - n)L_{\omega_1}(s) + \tilde{A}(0) \end{bmatrix} \tag{A5.26}$$

where the determinant $D(s)$ of the elasticity matrix is defined by $\qquad$ (A5.27)

$$D(s) = [s - (r + \theta)](s + m^*)$$

and where we have used $r = r^*$ as the residence-based tax is zero in the initial steady state.

The solutions

The short-run change in financial wealth, $\tilde{A}(0)$, is given from the investment system by (5.48). To pin down the *initial change in consumption*, $\tilde{C}(0)$, we use the condition that $L\tilde{c}(r + \theta)$ is bounded.[36] This implies that the first row of the right-hand side of (A5.26) should be zero, which gives rise to

$$\frac{a_c}{\Delta}\left[\tilde{C}(0) + \frac{1}{\sigma}\frac{\delta + \theta}{r + \theta}\frac{\tilde{r}_r}{\Delta}\right] = \frac{\tilde{A}(0)}{r - n} + L_{\tilde{\omega}_I}(r + \theta) \qquad (A5.28)$$

Equation (A5.28) yields (5.24) because $\tilde{\omega}_I = \tilde{A}(0) = 0$ in case the residence-based tax is introduced.

The long-run solutions for consumption and financial wealth when the residence-based tax is introduced (i.e. expressions (5.25) and (5.31)) are found by setting the left-hand side of (A5.26) equal to zero and solving for $\tilde{C}(\infty)$ and $\tilde{A}(\infty)$. The adjustment speed m^* is the absolute value of the negative root of the first elasticity matrix on the right-hand side of (A5.26).

The *time path for aggregate consumption* when the source-based tax is introduced (expression (5.50)) is derived by substituting (A5.28) into the first row of (A5.26) to eliminate the initial change in financial wealth:

$$L_{\tilde{c}}(s) = \frac{s - (r + \theta)}{D(s)}\tilde{C}(0) + \frac{\Delta(n + \theta)a_\omega}{D(s)a_c}[L_{\tilde{\omega}_I}(r + \theta) - L_{\tilde{\omega}_I}(s)] \qquad (A5.29)$$

By using (5.44) and (5.45), we can write the last term in square brackets on the right-hand side of (A5.29) as

$$\frac{L_{\tilde{\omega}_I}(r + \theta) - L_{\tilde{\omega}_I}(s)}{[s - (r + \theta)]} = \frac{\tilde{\omega}_I(0) - \tilde{\omega}_I(\infty)}{(m + r + \theta)(m + s)} + \frac{\tilde{\omega}_I(\infty)}{(r + \theta)s} \qquad (A5.30)$$

Substituting (A5.27), (A5.30), and (A5.22) into (A5.29) yields

$$L_{\tilde{c}}(s) = \frac{1}{s + m^*}\tilde{C}(0) + \frac{m^*}{s(s + m^*)}\tilde{\omega}_I(\infty)$$

$$+ \frac{m^*}{(s + m)(s + m^*)}\frac{r + \theta}{r + \theta + m}[\tilde{\omega}_I(0) - \tilde{\omega}_I(\infty)] \qquad (A5.31)$$

Inverting the Laplace transforms, we arrive at (5.50).

The initial relative change in consumption, $\tilde{C}(0)$, corresponds to the effect on the real wealth position of the currently alive. Expression (5.49) for this effect is found by using (A5.28). If $\tilde{t}_r = 0$, the last term on the right-hand side of (A5.28) is related to the effect on human wealth by

$$L_{\tilde{\omega}_I}(r + \theta) = \frac{\tilde{H}(0)}{r + \theta} \qquad (A5.32)$$

Substituting (A5.32), (5.46), and (5.48) into (A5.28), we arrive at (5.49).

Appendix 3: Welfare analysis of the residence-based tax

The utility of a household born at time v is defined by expression (5.1) in section 2. Assuming an iso-elastic utility function, one can write felicity $u(c)$ as

$$u(c) = \frac{1}{1-\sigma} c^{1-\sigma} \qquad (A5.33)$$

The time path for consumption of a household born at time v is given by

$$c(v, s) = c(v, t) \exp\left[\frac{r^* - \delta}{\sigma}(s-t)\right] \qquad s \geq t \geq v \qquad (A5.34)$$

Substituting (A5.33) and (A5.34) into (5.1) yields

$$U(v, t) = [c(v, t)]^{1-\sigma} \frac{\Delta}{1-\sigma} \qquad (A5.35)$$

The welfare effect of a residence-based tax is found by linearizing (A5.35):

$$\tilde{W}^*(v, t) = \tilde{c}(v, t) - \frac{\tilde{\Delta}}{1-\sigma} \qquad (A5.36)$$

Here, $\tilde{W}^*(v, t)$ is the relative change in real wealth that corresponds to the change in (*ex ante*) utility enjoyed by a household born at v beyond time $t \geq v$. In other words, the welfare of the household would not be affected if one reduced wealth by $\tilde{W}^*(v, t)$.

Linearizing (5.4) and (5.6), we find

$$\tilde{c}(v, t) = \tilde{\Delta} + \alpha_H \tilde{H}(t) \qquad (A5.37)$$

$$\tilde{\Delta} = \frac{1-\sigma}{\sigma} \frac{r\tilde{t}_r}{\Delta} \qquad (A5.38)$$

where α_H is the wealth share of human wealth in the initial steady state. We have put $r = r^*$ in the initial steady state and $h(t) = H(t)$. Furthermore, it has been assumed that financial wealth A is not affected by the residence-based tax. The reason is that generations born at $t \geq 0$ start life without any financial wealth, while the financial wealth of those that are alive at $t = 0$ is fixed in the short run. Substituting (A5.37) and (A5.38) into (A5.36) we arrive at

$$\tilde{W}^*(v, t) = \alpha_H \tilde{H}(t) + \frac{1}{\Delta} r\tilde{t}_r \qquad (A5.39)$$

The relative change in human wealth is found by log-linearizing (5.17)

$$\tilde{\omega}(t) = -\frac{A}{\omega} r\tilde{t}_r \qquad (A5.40)$$

and substituting (A5.40) into (A5.14). Substituting the result into (A5.39), we arrive at the following expression for the welfare effect:

$$\tilde{W}^*(v, t) = -\alpha_H \left(\frac{A}{\omega} r\tilde{t}_r + \frac{1}{r+\theta} r\tilde{t}_r\right) + \frac{1}{\Delta} r\tilde{t}_r \qquad (A5.41)$$

where the steady-state relationship $r = r*$ has been used.

Combining the steady-state expressions (A5.20), (A5.21), and (A5.22), we find expression (5.22)

$$\frac{A}{\omega} = \frac{A}{(r* + \theta)H} = \frac{(r* - \delta)/\sigma}{m*(r* + \theta)} \tag{A5.42}$$

and the wealth share of human wealth in the initial steady state:

$$\alpha_H = \frac{m*}{n + \theta} \tag{A5.43}$$

Substituting (A5.42) and (A5.43) into (A5.41), we arrive at the welfare effect for current generations given by expression (5.20). The welfare effect for generations born after the residence-based tax is introduced (expression (5.19)) is found by setting the human wealth share α_H in (A5.41) equal to 1, as these generations do not own any financial wealth at the beginning of their lives.

The welfare effect for owners of financial wealth is used to find expression (5.33), which corresponds to the public debt that is needed to offset this welfare effect. This jump in public debt is found by setting the human wealth share in (A5.41) equal to zero.

Notes

The author thanks Ben Heydra, Søren Bo Nielsen, and Hans-Werner Sinn for helpful comments on an earlier version of this chapter.

1 For an empirical analysis of how actual capital income tax provisions affect the saving and investment tax wedges in the USA and Japan, see Bovenberg et al. (1990).

2 Another important assumption is that the capital-importing country cannot affect the effective tax rate levied by foreign governments on domestically sourced capital income earned by foreign residents. This implies that the foreign (capital-exporting) country either exempts foreign-source income or adopts a deduction system under which foreign taxes are treated as a regular expense. If the foreign (capital-exporting) country adopts a credit system and the domestic tax rate does not exceed the foreign rate, the effective foreign tax rate depends inversely on the domestic tax rate because in that case the capital-exporting country provides a credit for taxes paid to the capital-importing country as long as this does not imply a refund (i.e. a negative effective foreign tax rate). If the capital-exporting country adopts such a credit system, the government of a small capital-importing country should set its source-based tax rate on capital income equal to the tax rate adopted by the capital-exporting country. In this way, the capital-importing country exploits the opportunity to tax the Treasury of the capital-exporting country without affecting the incentive to invest domestically (see, for example, Gordon, 1990; Sørensen, 1990). If the capital-exporting country allows tax credits on the basis of gross taxes rather than on the basis of taxes net of subsidies,

capital-importing countries should simultaneously tax and subsidize capital income (see Gersovitz, 1985).

3   However, a graduated rate structure for capital income aimed at income redistribution can give rise to unintended distributional effects if the effective tax rate on capital income depends on the financial arrangements for holding financial wealth. The reason is that individuals facing high tax rates tend to hold their wealth in lightly taxed assets, while individuals facing low rates use highly taxed financial arrangements. This process is generally known as tax arbitrage (see, for example, Steuerle, 1985; Gordon and Slemrod, 1988).

4   Another problem surrounding residence-based taxation is that it may induce savers to change their country of residence. The optimal tax literature has largely abstracted from the endogenous choice of country of residence.

5   This may explain why capital-exporting countries allow residents to credit taxes on foreign source income that are paid to the capital-importing country. By granting such a credit, residence countries effectively pay source countries for monitoring the capital income of their residents. The difficulties in monitoring capital income on foreign soil may also explain why capital-exporting countries tax the foreign earnings of domestic corporations only when these earnings are repatriated (see, for example, Mutèn, 1983). Hartman (1985) demonstrated that this tax deferral implies that the tax rate of the capital-importing country determines the incentive to invest in that country – at least for mature subsidiaries that finance marginal investments from their retained earnings. Accordingly, under deferral, corporate income taxes become effectively source- rather than residence-based. See also Tanzi and Bovenberg (1990).

6   Giovannini (1989) argues in favor of increased cooperation across countries in order to allow countries to apply the residence principle. The required cooperation would include full exchange of information, a review of bank secrecy laws, and the elimination of tax deferral.

7   Giovannini (1989) assumes that governments cannot tax labor income but have to rely on capital income taxes to raise public revenue. In this case, the welfare effects of residence- and source-based taxes depend on the relative magnitude of, respectively, saving and investment distortions. The intertemporal elasticity of substitution in consumption affects the saving distortion, while the investment distortion is determined by the substitution elasticity between labor and capital in domestic production.

8   Governments may also adopt source-based taxes if they provide public services to domestic investment for which it cannot charge firms more directly. These benefit taxes should reflect the marginal costs of providing these services. Furthermore, the relationship between public services and capital income should be rather close in order for capital income to be a reasonable proxy for the use of public services.

9   Slemrod (1990) emphasizes administrative constraints on how governments can tax income and commodities in practice. He argues that these constraints explain why most of the results derived by the theory of optimal taxation have not been applied in practice.

10   See also Sinn (1985, 1986) and Slemrod (1988).

11   For numerical studies of intertemporal equilibrium models of open economies with international capital mobility, see, for example, Lipton and Sachs (1983),

Goulder and Eichengreen (1989), Bovenberg and Goulder (1989), Keuschnigg (1990), and Søderlind (1990).

12   One can also interpret this constant probability of death as the probability that a dynasty expires. By allowing for $\theta < 0$, one can allow for intra-dynasty growth.

13   Weil (1989) interprets this birth rate as the rate at which new dynasties enter the domestic economy. This rate depends on the proportion of newly born children who are not "loved."

14   Hence, the birth rate $n + \theta$ and the death rate θ are distinct in this model. Blanchard (1984, 1985), in contrast, assumes that the birth rate equals the death rate (i.e. $n = 0$), while Weil (1989) abstracts from death (i.e. $\theta = 0$).

15   Bovenberg (1993) also examines the case $r^* < \delta$.

16   Throughout the rest of this chapter, variables are to be understood as dated at time t unless indicated otherwise.

17   Following Lucas (1967), Summers (1981) models adjustment costs in an alternative way. His formulation, however, leads to similar results for the optimal investment rule.

18   The corporate income tax is mainly source based. In particular, the corporate tax system in the host country (i.e. the country where the investment occurs) determines the effective corporate tax rate on marginal investment if foreigners finance these investments through portfolio capital flows. Even in the case of direct investments, the corporate tax may be effectively source based, for example if the residence country has a territorial system of corporate taxation.

19   The tax is assumed to be assessed on income net of true economic depreciation.

20   The cost of capital to firms is r rather than r^* because accrued capital gains are taxed at the same rate as interest income. For an alternative approach, see Nielsen and Sørensen (1991).

21   However, we introduce public debt financing when we explore policies that offset the effects of capital income taxes on the intergenerational distribution of resources.

22   For similar approaches, see for example Judd (1985) and Bovenberg (1986).

23   This effect is the weighted average of the welfare effects for generations with different ages. The older generations bear the heaviest burden because they own the most financial wealth. The youngest generations, who depend mainly on human wealth, may actually benefit from a residence-based tax.

24   This policy essentially amounts to exempting the initial stock of financial wealth from the residence-based tax and shifting the revenues from taxing the return on new saving forward in the form of higher debt-financed transfers. Transfers are increased before tax revenues accrue in order to compensate the older generations for the lower return on their (new) saving. Note that debt policy affects neither capital accumulation nor the interest rate in the small open economy.

25   This policy can also be interpreted as an increase in taxes on labor because per capita labor supply is exogenous and independent of age.

26   The Laplace transform of $G(t)$ is $L_G(s)$, where $L_G(s) = \int_0^\infty exp(-st)\ G(t)\ dt$. Intuitively, the Laplace transform of $G(t)$ is the present value of the flow $G(t)$ discounted at s.

27   See Bovenberg (1993). Auerbach and Kotlikoff (1987) examine these effects on the intergenerational distribution in a closed economy framework.

28   This neutrality result holds only for infinitely small increases in the tax. If the initial source-based tax on capital income is positive, a further rise in the tax causes after-tax labor earnings to fall in the long run. In this case, the source-based tax yields first-order losses in efficiency. See Bovenberg (1993).

29   How the tax impacts the welfare of currently alive generations with different ages depends on how the ownership of the domestic capital stock is distributed across different age groups when the policy shock occurs.

30   In other words, the cash flow tax yields a zero effective tax rate on investment.

31   When analyzing source-based taxes, Bovenberg (1993) is able to separate the impact on efficiency from that on the intergenerational distribution of resources. The reason is that the intergenerational distribution does not affect the physical capital stock at home and therefore does not impact the efficiency losses due to a source-based tax, which originate in the tax wedge between the social and private return to the domestic capital stock. However, in the case of a residence-based tax, one cannot easily separate the consequences for efficiency from intergenerational equity effects because the intergenerational distribution impacts financial wealth and therefore the distortions due to a residence-based tax. See also Auerbach and Kotlikoff (1987) for the measurement of the pure efficiency effect of tax reforms in an overlapping generations model.

32   Also Bovenberg and Goulder (1993) emphasize the importance of cross-ownership in determining the macroeconomic effects of capital income taxes on the external accounts. Using a two-country model with overlapping generations, Sibert (1990) shows how the macroeconomic effects of capital income taxes may depend on the initial current account and net foreign asset positions.

33   See, for example, Slemrod (1988). Goulder and Eichengreen (1989) and Bovenberg and Goulder (1993) allow for imperfect substitutability of assets without explicitly introducing uncertainty.

34   For example, countries may find it difficult to adopt statutory corporate tax rates that exceed those abroad if multinational corporations can use transfer prices to shift profits across jurisdictions. Similarly, if the tax rate on labor exceeds that on capital, the private sector may be able to shelter labor income as capital income. See also section 1.

35   See Gordon (1983) for a study of the channels through which jurisdictions can impose externalities on other jurisdictions. For an application of this framework to capital income taxation in open economies, see Sørensen (1991).

36   See, for example, Judd (1982). The latter paper explains the use of Laplace transforms to solve for linearized perfect foresight models.

References

Auerbach, Alan J. and Lawrence J. Kotlikoff (1987) *Dynamic Fiscal Policy*, Cambridge, Cambridge University Press.

Blanchard, Olivier J. (1984) "Current and anticipated deficits, interest rates and economic activity," *European Economic Review* 25, 7–27.
—— (1985) "Debt, deficits and finite horizons," *Journal of Political Economy* 93, 223–47.
Bovenberg, A. Lans (1986) "Capital income taxation in growing open economies," *Journal of Public Economics* 31, 347–77.
—— (1989) "The effects of capital income taxation on international competitiveness and trade flows," *American Economic Review* 79, 1045–64.
—— (1993) "Investment promoting policies in open economies: the importance of intergenerational and international distributional effects," *Journal of Public Economics* 51, 3–54.
—— and Lawrence H. Goulder (1993) "Promoting investment under international capital mobility: an intertemporal general equilibrium analysis," *Scandinavian Journal of Economics* 95, 133–56.
Bovenberg, A. Lans, Krister Andersson, Kenji Aramaki, and Sheetal K. Chand (1990) "Tax incentives and international capital flows: the case of the United States and Japan," in A. Razin and J. Slemrod (eds) *Taxation in the Global Economy*, Chicago, IL, University of Chicago Press.
Buiter, Willem H. (1988) "Death, birth, productivity growth and debt neutrality," *Economic Journal* 89, 279–93.
Engel, Charles, and Kenneth Kletzer (1989) "Saving and investment in an open economy with non-traded goods," *International Economic Review* 30, 735–52.
Feldstein, Martin, and C. Horioka (1980) "Domestic savings and international capital flows," *Economic Journal* 90, 314–28.
Frankel, Jeffrey A. (1989) "Quantifying international capital mobility in the 1980s," NBER Working Paper 2856, Cambridge, MA.
Frenkel, Jacob, and Assaf Razin (1986) "Fiscal policies in the world economy," *Journal of Political Economy* 94, 564–94.
—— and —— (1987) *Fiscal Policies and the World Economy,* Cambridge, MA, MIT Press.
Gersovitz, Mark (1985) "The effects of domestic taxes on foreign private investment," in N. Stern and D. Newberry (eds) *Taxation in Developing Countries*, Washington, DC, World Bank.
Giovannini, Alberto (1989) "National tax systems vs. the European capital market," *Economic Policy* 9, 345–86.
Gordon, Roger H. (1983) "An optimal taxation approach to fiscal federalism," *Quarterly Journal of Economics* 48 (4), 567–86.
—— (1986) "Taxation of investment and savings in a world economy," *American Economic Review* 76 (5), 1086–1102.
—— (1990) "Can capital income taxes survive in open economies?" NBER Working Paper 3416, Cambridge, MA.
—— and Joel Slemrod (1988) "Do we collect any revenue from taxing capital income?" in L.H. Summers (ed.) *Tax Policy and the Economy*, Cambridge, MA, MIT Press.
Goulder, Lawrence H. and Barry Eichengreen (1989) "Savings promotion, investment promotion and international competitiveness," in R. Feenstra (ed.) *Trade Policies for International Competitiveness*, Chicago, IL, University of Chicago Press.

Hartman, David D. (1985) "Tax policy and foreign direct investment," *Journal of Public Economics* 26, 107–21.

Judd, Kenneth L. (1982) "An alternative to steady-state comparisons in perfect foresight models," *Economic Letters* 10, 55–9.

——(1985) "Short-run analysis of fiscal policy in a simple perfect foresight model," *Journal of Political Economy* 93, 298–319.

Keuschnigg, Christian (1990) "The transition to a cash flow income tax," paper presented at a workshop on applied general equilibrium modelling at the University of Bern, March.

King, M. (1980) "Savings and taxation," in G. Hughes and G. Neal (eds) *Public Policy and the Tax System*, London, Allen and Unwin.

Lipton, David, and Jeffrey Sachs (1983) "Accumulation and growth in a two-country model," *Journal of International Economics* 15, 135–59.

Lucas, R.E. (1967) "Adjustment costs and the theory of supply," *Journal of Political Economy* 75, 321–34.

Murphy, R.G. (1986) "Productivity shocks, non-traded goods and optimal capital accumulation," *European Economic Review* 30, 1081–95.

Mutèn, Leif (1983) "Some topical issues concerning international double taxation," in Sijbren Cnossen (ed.) *Comparative Tax Studies: Essays in Honor of Richard Goode*, Amsterdam, North-Holland.

Mutti, Jack, and Harry Grubert (1985) "The taxation of capital income in an open economy: the importance of resident–nonresident treatment," *Journal of Public Economics* 27, 291–309.

Nielsen, Søren Bo, and Peter B. Sørensen (1991) "Capital income taxation in a growing open economy," *European Economic Review* 34, 179–97.

Razin, Assaf, and Efraim Sadka (1989) "International tax competition and gains from tax harmonization," NBER Working Paper 3152, Cambridge, MA.

Sandmo, A. (1985) "The effects of taxation on savings and risk taking," in A. Auerbach and M. Feldstein (eds) *Handbook on Public Economics*, Amsterdam, North-Holland.

Sen, Partha, and Stephen J. Turnovsky (1990) "Investment tax credit in an open economy," *Journal of Public Economics* 42, 277–99.

Sibert, Anne C. (1990) "Taxing capital in a large, open economy," *Journal of Public Economics* 41, 297–317.

Sinn, Hans-Werner (1985) "Why taxes matter: Reagan's accelerated cost recovery system and the US trade deficit," *Economic Policy* 1, 240–50.

——(1986) "The 1986 US tax reform and the world capital market," *European Economic Review* 32, 325–33.

——(1987) *Capital Income Taxation and Resource Allocation*, Amsterdam, North-Holland.

Slemrod, Joel (1988) "Effects of taxation with international capital mobility," in H. Aaron, H. Galper, and J.A. Pechman (eds) *Uneasy Compromise: Problems of a Hybrid Income-Consumption Tax*, Washington, DC, Brookings Institution.

——(1990) "Optimal taxation and optimal tax systems," *Journal of Economic Perspectives* 4 (1), 157–78.

Søderlind, Paul (1990) "The Swedish tax reform from an intertemporal perspective," Institute for International Economic Studies Seminar Paper 465, Stockholm.

Sørensen, Peter B. (1990) "Optimal capital taxation in a small capital-importing economy," in V. Tanzi (ed.) *Public Finance, Trade, and Development*, Proceedings of the 44th Congress of the International Institute of Public Finance, Istanbul, Detroit, MI, Wayne State University Press.

—— (1991) "Welfare gains from international fiscal coordination," in R. Prud-'homme (ed.) *Public Finance with Several Levels of Government*, Proceedings of the 46th Congress of the International Institute of Public Finance, Brussels, The Hague, Public Finance.

Steuerle, C.E. (1985) *Taxes, Loans, and Inflation: How the Nation's Wealth Becomes Misallocated*, Washington, DC, Brookings Institution.

Summers, Lawrence H. (1981) "Capital taxation and corporate investment: a *q*-theory approach," *Brookings Papers on Economic Activity* 1, 67–127.

—— (1988) "Tax policy and international competitiveness," in J.A. Frenkel (ed.) *International Aspects of Fiscal Policies*, Chicago, IL, Chicago University Press.

Tanzi, Vito, and A. Lans Bovenberg (1990) "Is there a need for harmonizing capital income taxes within EC countries?" in H. Siebert (ed.) *Reforming Capital Income Taxation*, Tübingen, Mohr.

Uzawa, H. (1969) "Time preference and the Penrose effect in a two-class model of economic growth," *Journal of Political Economy* 77, 628–52.

Weil, Philippe (1989) "Overlapping families of infinitely lived agents," *Journal of Public Economics* 38, 183–98.

van Wijnbergen, Sweder (1986) "On fiscal deficits, the real exchange rate, and the world rate of interest," *European Economic Review* 30, 1013–24.

PART III

INTERNATIONAL MONETARY REGIMES

6 History of the International Monetary System: Implications for Research in International Macroeconomics and Finance

BARRY EICHENGREEN

1 Introduction

What do practicing economists specializing in international macroeconomics have to learn from the history of the international monetary system? That is the question which the present chapter poses and endeavors to answer.

History, according to Voltaire, is nothing but a pack of tricks that we play upon the dead. I argue in this chapter that it offers considerably more to the living. International economics is replete with theories predicting differences in the behavior of real and financial variables under different exchange rate regimes. The predictions of competing theories are contradictory and impossible to verify on the basis of logical consistency alone. For that, empirical evidence is required. The history of the international monetary system is the obvious – in fact the only – source of systematic evidence on macroeconomic performance under different exchange rate regimes. International macroeconomists seeking to confront theories with data are drawn inescapably to historical evidence. Ineluctably, empirical research on alternative exchange rate systems is historical research.

This chapter suggests some implications of the history of the international monetary system for research in international macroeconomics and finance. Its first half reviews the last century of international monetary history, summarizing the basic facts with which practicing economists must be familiar if they are to make effective use of historical evidence. The references to the literature provided in this section can serve as a guide to further reading.

The second half of the chapter furnishes an overview of the statistical record of the last hundred years of international monetary experience.

I focus on the association, much debated among theorists, between the exchange rate regime and the business cycle. Issues include whether output volatility is exacerbated by flexible exchange rates; whether changes in the stability of the economic environment are associated with switches between fixed and flexible rates; and whether the coherence of cyclical fluctuations across countries is higher under fixed or flexible exchange rates. Findings reported in this section challenge conventional wisdom derived from theory and from the last three decades of international monetary experience. They reveal the limitations of the idea that periods of fixed exchange rates are associated with output stability, and of the notion that exchange rate flexibility minimizes the international transmission of business-cycle disturbances.

This half of the chapter contrasts three exchange rate regimes: the classical gold standard from 1880 to 1913 characterized by fixed nominal exchange rates and essentially no capital controls; the Bretton Woods system from 1950 to 1970 characterized by pegged nominal exchange rates but also pervasive capital controls; and the post-Bretton Woods period from 1973 to 1990 of flexible exchange rates. As a check on the findings that emerge from this comparison, I also consider macroeconomic performance under the different exchange rate regimes that prevailed between the two world wars: free floating from 1922 through 1926, pegged rates from 1927 through 1931, and dirty floating from 1932 through 1936.

The chapter concludes with an agenda for research.

2   Historical overview

2.1   The classical gold standard

The gold standard is often seen as the normal mode of organizing international monetary affairs before 1913. This conventional view is incorrect. As late as the second half of the nineteenth century, the currencies and exchange rates of different countries were still regulated in different ways. Some countries clung to bimetallism; others were on the silver standard. Only Great Britain was on the gold standard for an extended period of time. The *de facto* gold standard established by England in 1717 resulted from a policy error: Sir Isaac Newton, then Master of the Mint, set too high a silver price of gold and drove all full-bodied English silver coins from circulation. Silver nonetheless retained its legal tender status until 1774. The official British policy of bimetallism was only definitively abandoned in 1816, and full gold convertibility was only established in 1821.

What accounts for the century-long lag between the establishment of *de facto* and *de jure* gold standards in Britain, and for the delay before other countries followed? Until the technological changes of the late eighteenth and early nineteenth centuries, gold standards were difficult to operate.[1] The metal was too valuable to support a monetary system that relied exclusively on gold coin. The smallest such coin, weighing barely two grams, could represent a week's wages for a laborer. Smaller pieces were too easily lost and consequently were not readily accepted.

Hence the attraction of bimetallism, under which small denomination silver coins circulated alongside gold. The drawback of bimetallism was that mineral discoveries constantly altered the market prices of silver and gold, disrupting efforts to maintain official exchange rates between them. This was an inconvenience many governments were nonetheless willing to tolerate until steam power was introduced into the Mint in the first half of the nineteenth century. This new technology facilitated the circulation of token coins. Gold coin commanded its market value, but the monetary value of token coins could now safely exceed the value of their metal content, since steam-powered machinery rendered them costly to counterfeit.

Starting in 1870, there was widespread movement onto gold.[2] Germany adopted the gold standard in 1871, having taken her Franco-Prussian war reparations in specie.[3] The bimetallic countries of Europe, including the members of the Latin Monetary Union, followed her lead. In the USA, where greenbacks had been inconvertible since the outbreak of the American Civil War, the Coinage Act of 1873, which restored convertibility *de facto*, omitted any mention of coining silver dollars. The USA officially resumed gold convertibility in 1879. In 1880 the gold standard was operating over much of the world.

Bilateral exchange rates were fixed only indirectly, since countries declared parities against gold rather than foreign currencies. But with domestic currency convertible into gold and specie imports and exports unrestricted, arbitrage in the international gold market constrained the fluctuation of bilateral rates. Exchange rates could rise or fall only to the gold points (given by the costs of shipping, insurance and short-term credit), at which it became profitable to engage in gold market arbitrage. This arbitrage limited bilateral rates to narrow bands.[4] Though some developing countries remained on silver and others suspended gold convertibility repeatedly, allowing their currencies to depreciate, from the perspective of the industrial countries this was as close to a system of fixed exchange rates as the historical record offers.[5]

Capital controls were largely absent during this period. Governments sometimes attempted to influence the direction of international lending, but they rarely limited the access of their citizens to gold and foreign exchange whether for current or capital account transactions.

Possessing at best limited information on the magnitude of foreign lending, governments did not target the current account of the balance of payments. Exchange rate stability and the absence of current account targeting combined to produce an exceptionally large volume of international capital flows throughout the classical gold standard years.[6]

Figures 6.1 and 6.2 display four major exchange rates against the dollar during the classical gold standard period. (In these figures, as in figures 6.3–6.7, part (a) depicts the classical gold standard period, part (b) the interwar years, and part (c) the post-Second World War period.) For visual convenience, each exchange rate is normalized to 100 in a benchmark year at the middle of the period.[7] The vertical scale differs in the various parts, which is itself an important source of information about relative volatility.

Japan, as is evident from figure 6.1(a), was not a member of the gold standard world until after the turn of the century. But the dollar exchange rates of the other major industrial countries were very stable following the resumption of *de facto* gold convertibility in USA in 1873. Figure 6.2 shows how stable. The mark, franc, and sterling rates against the dollar fluctuated within a band that ranged from 101.1 to 99.1 percent of parity.

Exchange rate stability implied the convergence of price-level movements. Figure 6.3(a) shows the close co-movement of wholesale price indexes, again with the notable exception of Japan. It reveals how two decades of deflation following 1870 were reversed after the mid-1890s. The pre-1896 deflation reflected the tendency for money supplies (figure 6.4) to grow less quickly than output (figure 6.5).[8] Money growth then accelerated, reflecting the impact of a series of gold discoveries on the level of international reserves.

The contrast between the two halves of the classical gold standard period is less evident in figure 6.6(a) where long-term interest rates are plotted.[9] Long-term rates were remarkably stable and similar across countries. Their stability over time reflected the stabilizing impact on price levels of the gold standard, in conjunction with confidence that gold convertibility would be maintained. Their coherence across countries reflected the tendency for exchange rate stability and freedom from capital controls to integrate capital markets internationally.[10]

The outlier in figure 6.6 is the USA. Long-term interest rates in the USA remained high in the 1870s as a result of the country's late resumption of gold convertibility, and rose again in the first half of the 1890s, reflecting the effects of the 1893 financial crisis and fears in 1895 that William Jennings Bryan's populist presidential campaign would lead to devaluation and inflation. The credibility of the US commitment to gold was an open question; hence interest rates were not forced to European levels. These same facts are evident in

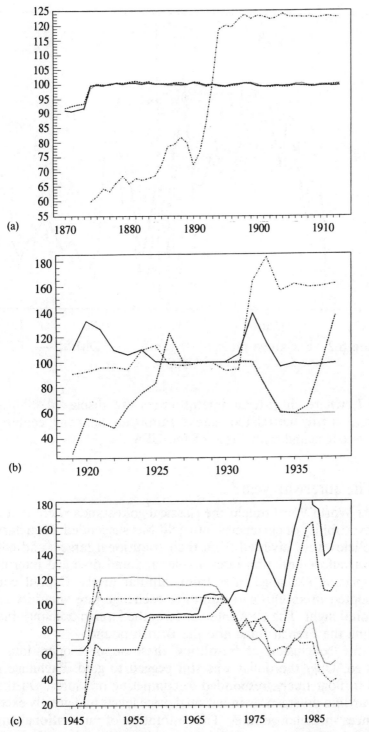

Figure 6.1 Exchange rates: ·-·-, yen/$; ····, DM/$; ---- FF/$;
—, UK£/$.

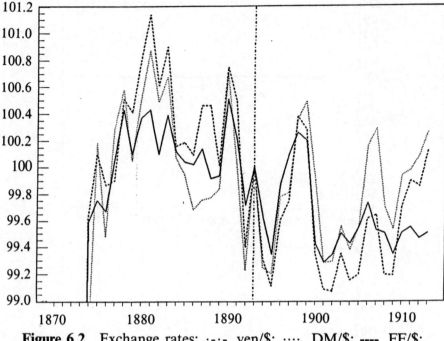

Figure 6.2   Exchange rates: ·---, yen/$; ····, DM/$; ----, FF/$;
—, UK£/$

figure 6.7, where short-term interest rates are displayed. Short-term rates were highly correlated across European financial centers, but much less correlated with those of the USA.

2.2   The interwar years

The First World War brought the classical gold standard era to a close. The convertibility of currencies into gold was suspended. Monetary and fiscal policies were diverted from their traditional targets and enlisted in the war effort. Inflation rates accelerated and diverged internationally, displacing exchange rates from familiar levels. Capital controls were adopted in an effort to minimize exchange rate volatility and to stem capital flight. The USA intervened in the foreign exchange market, supporting the French franc and the British pound.

With the conclusion of hostilities, these support operations were terminated. Only the dollar was still pegged to gold. Exchange rates, allowed to float freely, responded to competing pressures. On the one hand, wartime divergences in national price levels had greatly exceeded divergences in exchange rates. The restoration of international equilibrium therefore seemed to require further divergences in exchange rates, specifically an additional fall in the depreciated European currencies

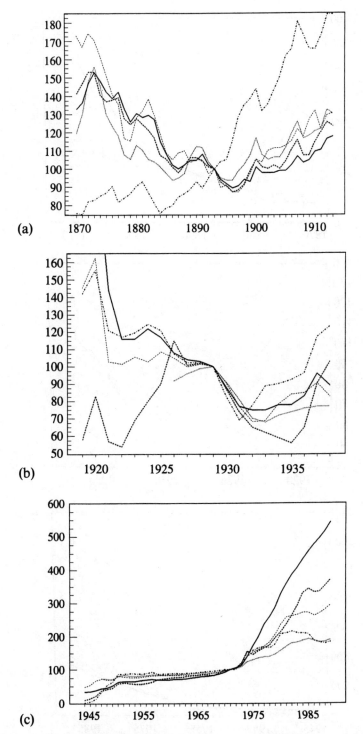

(a)

(b)

(c)

Figure 6.3   Wholesale price index: ·–·–, Japan; ····, Germany;
----, France; —, UK; ---, USA.

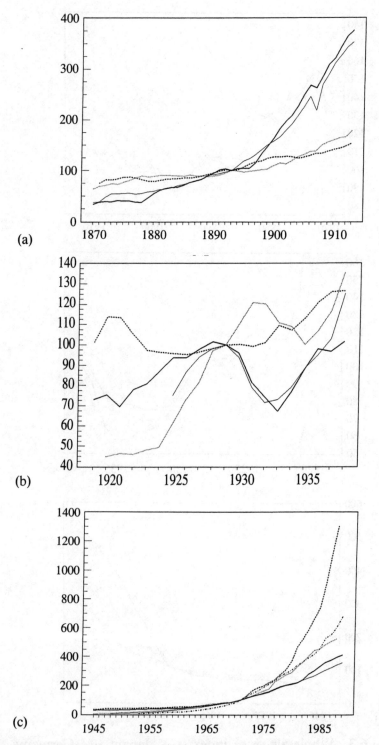

Figure 6.4 Money supply: ·-·-, Japan; —, Germany; ·····, France; ----, UK; —, USA.

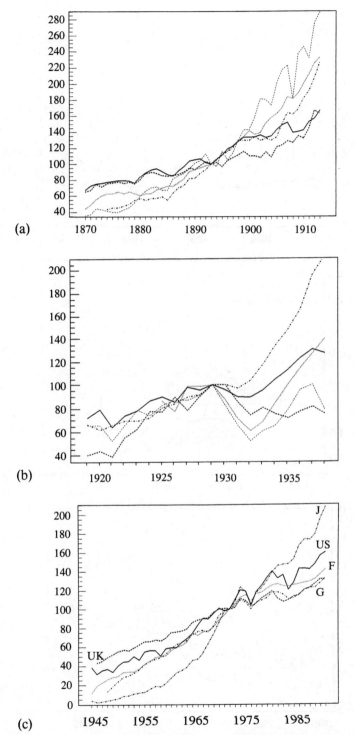

(a)

(b)

(c)

Figure 6.5 Industrial production: ·--·, Japan (J); ·····, Germany (G);
----, France (F); ——, UK; ----, USA.

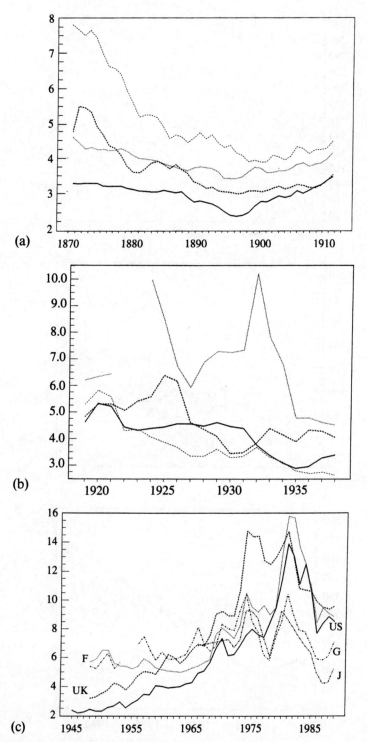

Figure 6.6   Long-term interest rates: ·--·, Japan (J); ····, Germany
(G); ----, France (F); —, UK; ----, USA.

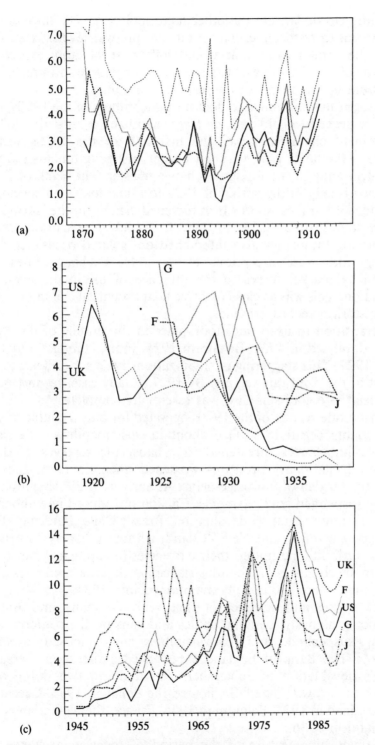

Figure 6.7 Short-term interest rates: ····, Japan (J); ·····, Germany (G); ----, France (F); —, UK; ----, USA.

against the US dollar. On the other hand, policymakers affirmed their commitment to restoring exchange rates to pre-war levels. In anticipation of the capital gains that would follow, speculators expecting a return to gold at the pre-war parity had the incentive to purchase and thereby bid up the prices of depreciated currencies.

Exchange rates continued to float until the middle of the 1920s, when they were pegged to gold and, *de facto*, stabilized against the dollar.[11] A prominent characteristic of the first half of the 1920s was the freedom of the float. With very few exceptions, governments refrained from intervening in the foreign exchange market. The Bank of France intervened briefly in the spring of 1924 to inflict losses on speculators who had sold francs short. It intervened again in the spring and summer of 1925 in an effort to stem the franc's depreciation. Belgian and German authorities also intervened on isolated occasions.[12] But these episodes were exceptions to the rule. Exchange rates were governed by market forces in the presence of minimal government intervention. This was as close to a free float absent official intervention as the historical record provides.

The transition to fixed rates took place in the middle of the 1920s. Sweden stabilized in 1924, Britain in 1925, France (*de facto*) in 1926, Italy in 1927. This staggering of stabilizations makes it difficult to date the start of the fixed rate regime. By 1927, in any case, reconstruction of the fixed rate gold standard was essentially complete.[13]

The fixed rate regime of the 1920s operated for only a couple of years before doubts began to surface about its sustainability.[14] Persistent payments imbalances threatened to exhaust the reserves of deficit countries. Deflationary pressures worsened unemployment and augmented the burden of mortgage debts. As early as 1929 Argentina and Uruguay suspended gold payments. Canada introduced new monetary restrictions tantamount to devaluation. Brazil, Chile, Paraguay, Peru, Venezuela, Australia, and New Zealand, without officially suspending gold convertibility, permitted their currencies to slip below par. It was mainly in the countries of the industrial center that the fixed rates of the gold standard were successfully maintained into 1931.

In the spring and summer of that year, Germany and Austria, experiencing domestic banking panics and runs on their international reserves, suspended gold convertibility and imposed exchange controls.[15] The Bank of England experienced a run soon thereafter. Sterling's devaluation in September 1931 induced two dozen other countries to follow.[16] The USA floated the dollar in 1933. Czechoslovakia devalued in 1934, Belgium in 1935, France, the Netherlands, and Switzerland in 1936.

A distinguishing feature of the period of renewed exchange rate flexibility after 1931 was pervasive government intervention in the foreign exchange market. In contrast to the first half of the 1920s, when exchange rates had also floated, now governments continually attempted to influence exchange rate movements. They established special Treasury or central bank accounts (known as exchange equalization funds) to limit exchange rate fluctuations. Increasingly they imposed capital controls to minimize the impact of international capital flows on exchange rate movements.

Figure 6.1(b) displays the behavior of exchange rates between the wars. Just as during the classical gold standard years, the major exchange rates were stable between 1927 and 1931. Again Japan was an outlier, reflecting her delayed return to the gold standard in 1930. But exchange rates fluctuated widely both before 1925 and after 1931. The coherence of price levels across countries (figure 6.3) was as high between 1926 and 1931 as it had been before the First World War, although deflation was more pronounced, reflecting, especially after 1929, the collapse of money supplies in the USA, Germany, and other countries. Neither long- nor short-term interest rates displayed the same stability and coherence across countries between 1926 and 1931 as had been customary before the First World War, reflecting the imperfect credibility of governments' stated commitments to gold convertibility.

2.3   Bretton Woods and its aftermath

This interwar experience was viewed as fundamentally unsatisfactory by observers looking back from the vantage point of the Second World War. Floating exchange rates, they concluded, tended to be destabilized by speculators. The global macroeconomy, they believed, was destabilized by haphazard exchange rate changes.[17] In reaction against these drawbacks of floating rates, the Bretton Woods System was constructed. The new design represented a compromise between the American position that rates should be fixed once and for all, and the British desire to retain the option of changing them to reconcile payments balance with full employment.[18] The Bretton Woods compromise was to accept the priority attached by the Americans to fixed rates but also to incorporate the escape clause demanded by the British. The USA pegged to gold, while other countries effectively pegged to the dollar. Although exchange rates would be pegged within 1 percent bands and controls on current account transactions would be removed, countries would be able to change the par value of their currencies to correct "fundamental disequilibria." The term was left vague as a way of skirting residual differences between the Americans and the British.

As under the nineteenth-century gold standard, parity changes were most prevalent in the developing world.[19] Exchange rate adjustments by the industrial countries were exceptional. Their common correlate was the incompatibility of the exchange rate with the targets of domestic policy. A high level of deficit spending by government figures in the French devaluation of 1957, the British devaluation of 1967, and the American devaluation of 1971 alike. In each case, military exigencies or employment targets delayed fiscal retrenchment.

But, as already emphasized, within the OECD exchange rate adjustments were very much the exception to the rule. As under the nineteenth-century gold standard, 1950–70 was a period of essentially fixed exchange rates for the industrialized countries. But in contrast with late nineteenth-century experience, capital controls were pervasive. With the notable exception of the US dollar, the major currencies remained inconvertible until 1958. At that point convertibility for current account transactions was restored, but controls were retained on purchases of foreign currency for capital account transactions.[20] The UK, which experienced recurrent balance of payments crises, maintained an array of controls on direct and portfolio investment abroad. The interest equalization tax imposed by the USA in 1963 was motivated by the desire to reconcile domestic stimulus with an increasingly worrisome external position. But surplus as well as deficit countries utilized capital controls during the Bretton Woods years. In 1961 and again in 1970, for example, the Bundesbank imposed discriminatory measures meant to discourage foreign residents' purchases of German assets in order to limit the deutschemark's appreciation.[21]

The dollar's 1971 and 1973 devaluations brought the Bretton Woods era to a close. The causes of the dollar crisis continue to be debated, although most observers now agree that deficit spending associated with the Vietnam War fueled the inflation which eroded the competitiveness of US exports and the demand pressure which stimulated imports. External deficits were the result. The willingness of foreign countries to absorb dollar reserves, in part because they viewed a stable dollar as the linchpin of the fixed rate system, put off the day of reckoning but did not eliminate it.[22]

Once the devaluation of the dollar brought down Bretton Woods, there was little desire to erect a new fixed rate system in its place. Starting in 1973, exchange rates were allowed to float and, as in the 1930s, were subjected to sporadic intervention. A 1976 amendment to the International Monetary Fund (IMF) Articles of Agreement acknowledging this reality authorized member countries to maintain floating rates but to intervene in the market. Thus the period from 1973 through 1990 marks another era of dirty floating.

Floating was less free in Europe than in other parts of the industrial world. From the beginning, European policymakers were dissatisfied with the new arrangements. The European economies were more open to international transactions than was the USA. It was in Europe where currency warfare in the 1930s had set the stage for other hostilities. Consequently it was in Europe where resistance to floating was most intense. The progress of European economic integration contributed to opposition to floating through the operation of the Common Agricultural Policy (CAP) of the European Community (EC). Since the CAP set minimum domestic currency prices of agricultural commodities in each country, exchange rate changes created incentives for cross-border transactions, greatly increasing the cost of operating the system – hence the pressure to stabilize exchange rates within Europe to ease the administration of the CAP.

Policymakers moved toward an agreement to stabilize exchange rates within Europe while permitting them to fluctuate against the dollar. Since EC members traded heavily with one another, this offered Europe the best of both worlds: exchange rate stability *vis-à-vis* their principal trading partners, and insulation through exchange rate adjustments from destabilizing impulses emanating from the rest of the world. The first attempt was the Snake, adopted in 1972 to limit the fluctuation of European currencies. The dollar and the deutschemark were allowed to float against one another, while other European countries attempted to stabilize their currencies against the deutchemark within 2¼ percent bands.

The Snake in practice resembled dirty floating: countries made sporadic efforts to stabilize their exchange rates, but the 2¼ bands were not continuously observed. France, for example, left the Snake in 1973, rejoined in 1975, and left again in 1976. The system failed to limit the volatility of exchange rates successfully and by the end of the 1970s had come to be regarded as a failure. In 1979 the principal members of the EC therefore agreed to a new initiative to stabilize exchange rates among themselves: the European Monetary System. The first stage in the evolution of this arrangement, from 1979 to 1983, was characterized by little policy convergence, wide inflation differentials, and frequent exchange rate realignments.[23] The second, from 1984 through 1988, was marked by a convergence of monetary policies, a narrowing of inflation differentials, and a progressive stabilization of exchange rates. The third stage, beginning in 1989, saw interest differentials between the principal members diminish greatly as capital controls were relaxed and finally eliminated. Thus, while exchange rates between the USA, Japan, and Europe have continued to float throughout the post-1972 period, exchange rates within Europe have reflected the influence of both floating and pegged rate regimes, with growing weight on the latter as the period progressed.

Figure 6.1(c) displays the movement of the four major exchange rates after the Second World War. It shows that each of these currencies, aside from the Japanese yen, was devalued or revalued against the dollar during the Bretton Woods years. The 1950s and 1960s nonetheless stand out as a period of exchange rate stability compared with what followed. Exchange rate volatility after 1972 is comparable with that for the first half of the 1920s or the 1930s. Figure 6.3 suggests that Bretton Woods had many of the implications of a gold standard for price performance: inflation was moderate and national price levels moved together before 1971 but not thereafter, reflecting monetary convergence in the first subperiod and monetary divergence in the second (figure 6.4). Long-term interest rates (figure 6.6) showed more stability and a greater tendency to move together under Bretton Woods than during the post-Bretton Woods float. But while long-term interest differentials across countries were roughly the same between 1950 and 1970 as they had been between 1880 and 1913, their stability over time was dramatically superior in the earlier period.

3   Statistical overview

The charts of section 2 point to striking differences across exchange rate regimes and suggest a variety of testable hypotheses. This section presents summary statistics on the behavior of some of the variables under the different regimes. Simple statistics turn out to be quite subversive to conventional notions derived from the theoretical literature and from recent international monetary experience. They throw into question the idea that fixed exchange rates are associated with output stability, and the notion that exchange rate flexibility limits the transmission of business-cycle disturbances internationally.

This analysis generalizes to the classical gold standard, the interwar years, and the first half of the Bretton Woods period the approach taken by Baxter and Stockman (1989) in their study of the 1960s, 1970s, and 1980s. I consider the entire Bretton Woods period, defined as the twenty-one years from 1950 through 1970, rather than focusing, as did these previous authors, on the 1960s alone.[24] With the passage of time, we now possess five additional years of data on the post-1972 float, rendering the period's sample length more closely comparable with the entire Bretton Woods period.[25] Whereas Baxter and Stockman employ quarterly data starting in 1960, comparisons over long historical periods necessarily entail the use of annual observations. Although this suppresses information on very short-term fluctuations, it allows me to utilize broader and more representative measures of economic activity like gross domestic product (GDP) rather than the industrial production index that Baxter and Stockman employ.[26]

Most of the time series studied are nonstationary, and so they must be detrended before their means and variances can be analyzed. Following Baxter and Stockman, two filters are applied: removal of a linear trend from the logarithm of the variable, and first differencing the logarithm of the variable. The first-difference filter provides more information on the high-frequency business-cycle movements in the underlying series, the linear filter on low-frequency shifts.

3.1   The volatility of gross domestic product

Figure 6.8 displays the volatility of GDP, as measured by the standard deviations of the detrended series, for subperiods corresponding to different exchange rate regimes. Standard deviations are measured in percent per year.[27] A point on the 45° line indicates no difference in the volatility of GDP across the periods.

In figures 6.8(a) and 6.8(c), the Bretton Woods years 1950–70 are displayed on the horizontal axis, and the floating years 1973–90 on the vertical axis. The observations in figure 6.8(a), where the first-difference filter is used, are clustered evenly around the 45° line, suggesting little change in output volatility at business-cycle frequencies. An unweighted average of standard deviations across countries suggests that output volatility rose slightly following the shift from fixed to floating rates (from 1.72 to 1.98 percent). This change in standard deviations is statistically insignificant, however, at standard confidence levels.[28] In figure 6.8(c), where the linear filter is used, the observations suggest if anything a slight reduction in output volatility at lower frequencies in the post-Bretton Woods period. In this case the arithmetic average of standard deviations falls (from 2.52 to 2.33 percent) with the shift from Bretton Woods to floating. Again, however, the difference across samples is statistically insignificant at standard confidence levels.

This evidence is at odds with that of Baxter and Stockman, who reported a noticeable increase in volatility following the shift to floating using both detrending methods. The present results, indicating that the shift from pegged to floating rates was accompanied by either a slight rise or a slight fall in output volatility depending on whether the first-difference or linear filter is used, are less definitive. Instead, this chapter's results paint essentially the same picture as those of Bordo (1993). Using data on gross national product (not GDP) drawn from other sources and the first-difference filter, Bordo found that output volatility fell with the transition from Bretton Woods to floating.[29]

The contrast reflects the fact that Baxter and Stockman only analyzed the second half of Bretton Woods. When I compare 1960–70 alone with the post-1972 float, like Baxter and Stockman I find that the average standard deviation rises following the transition to floating, regardless

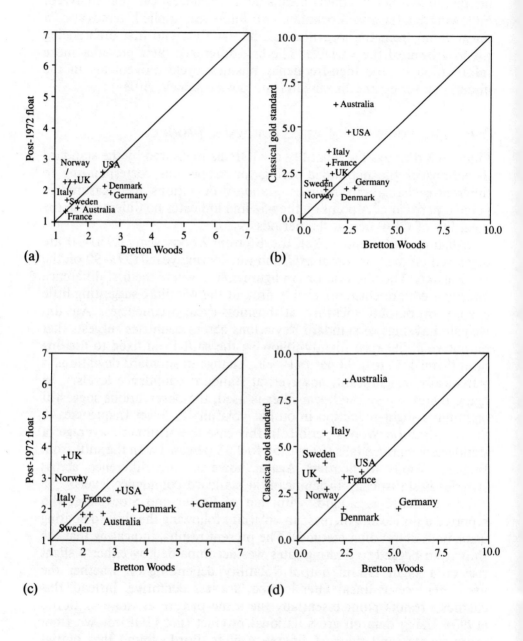

Figure 6.8 Variability of gross domestic product under different exchange rate regimes: (a), (b) standard deviation of gross domestic product, first-difference filter; (c), (d) standard deviation of gross domestic product, linear filter.

of how the data are detrended.[30] When I extend the Bretton Woods period back to 1950, however, I find that the Bretton Woods period becomes increasingly turbulent, suggesting no change in output volatility following the transition to floating (or even, if the linear filter is used, the possibility that output was actually more volatile under Bretton Woods than under the post-1972 float). This conclusion is further strengthened, as Bordo shows, when the Bretton Woods period is extended back to 1946. (With data starting in 1950, only the linear filter suggests that output was more volatile under Bretton Woods. But with data starting in 1946, as Bordo shows, this conclusion holds for the first-difference filter as well.)

What accounts for these differences? The first half of the Bretton Woods period was characterized by unusual output volatility for a number of reasons. Postwar growth was first marked by dramatic increases in output as infrastructure was repaired and idle capacity was put back to work. It was then disrupted by shortages of raw materials and capital equipment until the Marshall Plan came on stream. It was further perturbed by the recession that accompanied postwar adjustment in the USA, by the 1949 devaluations, and by the Korean War boom. These events are especially evident at high frequencies; hence Bordo finds higher output volatility in 1946–70 than in 1974–89 because he uses the first-difference filter, which emphasizes high-frequency movements. In addition, in several European countries, such as Germany and Denmark, growth associated with postwar reconstruction remained unusually rapid for much of the 1950s before decelerating subsequently. These secular shifts are evident at lower frequencies – hence my evidence of high GDP volatility in the 1950s when the first-difference filter is used.

The conclusion that output volatility has been no greater – indeed, that it may have been lower – under floating than fixed rates is reinforced by figures 6.8(b) and 6.8(d), which compare Bretton Woods (again on the horizontal axis) with the classical gold standard years 1880–1913 (on the vertical axis). The simple arithmetic average of standard deviations of detrended GDP is some 50 percent larger under the gold standard than under Bretton Woods. This is true regardless of which filter is used.[31] Germany and Denmark, in which, as described above, output was relatively volatile in the first post-Second World War decade, are the only exceptions to this regularity. Thus, historical comparisons not limited to the post-Second World War period provide little support for the notion that output volatility is lower under fixed than floating rates.[32]

These conclusions speak to at least three distinct theoretical literatures in international macroeconomics. One, associated with work on the classical gold standard and the European Monetary System, emphasizes the role of fixed rates as a disciplining device on policy-makers (Giavazzi and Pagano, 1988; Goodfriend, 1988). Its premise is that erratic policy is the predominant source of the destabilizing impulses perturbing output, and that under fixed rates the balance of payments constraint reins in policymakers. The evidence here that fixed rates exhibit no particular association with output stability suggests either that policymakers find ways of evading balance of payments discipline under fixed rates or that destabilizing policy is not the predominant source of output volatility. In section 3.4 below I suggest that the second interpretation fits the facts better.

A second literature to which these results are relevant concerns the determinants of the exchange rate regime. Some theories of regime selection suggest that fixed rates prevail when the underlying environ-ment is relatively stable (see Floyd (1985) and De Kock and Grilli (1989) for arguments and further references). Their premise is that increases in output volatility raise the costs of maintaining fixed rates and encourage a shift to floating. The evidence here that output was not particularly stable in periods of fixed rates is difficult to reconcile with this view.

A third literature to which these results direct attention is that stressing the importance of capital controls in reconciling exchange rate stability with macroeconomic turbulence. Giovannini (1989) has argued that capital controls were essential for reconciling stable rates with divergent macroeconomic performance in the European Monetary System of the 1980s. He suggests that capital controls played a similar role in the operation of the Bretton Woods system. Eichengreen (1993) similarly attributes the ability of the preconvertible Bretton Woods system to accommodate high levels of output volatility partly to the maintenance of controls on both current and capital account transac-tions. The results from the classical gold standard period suggest that capital controls are only part of the story. Controls were absent during the gold standard years, yet the system had no difficulty in accommo-dating levels of output volatility even higher than those that prevailed in the control-ridden 1950s or in Europe in the 1980s.

Thus, contrary to the implications of some recent analyses of post-1960 data, there is no simple association between the exchange rate regime and the volatility of GDP. There is no evidence that output volatility increased with the shift from pegged to floating rate regimes after 1972; if anything, the opposite may have been true.

3.2   Cross-country correlations

Various theories of international transmission suggest that business cycles should be more synchronized internationally under fixed than floating rates. They show that expansionary monetary policies have stimulative cross-country output effects under fixed rates. They demonstrate that expansionary fiscal policies can also have such effects, although international transmission is likely to be weakened by the existence of offsetting real exchange rate and interest rate effects (see Swoboda and Dornbusch, 1973; Mussa, 1979).

Figures 6.9(a) and 6.9(b) show the correlations of each country's GDP with that of the USA, the center country, for Bretton Woods (on the horizontal axis) and the post-1972 float (on the vertical axis). The results are sensitive to the choice of detrending method: the first-difference filter indicates a rise in the correlation after 1972, while the linear filter provides less evidence of an effect.

Again, these findings are different from those of Baxter and Stockman. Using the first-difference filter they found a decline, not a rise, in the cross-country correlation of output movements with the shift from fixed to flexible rates. (Neither study offers much evidence of a shift when the linear filter is used.) One potential explanation for the conflict is that the two studies use different measures of economic activity (industrial production versus GDP). I therefore replicated my analysis for the Bretton Woods years and the post-1972 float using annual industrial production indexes in place of GDP, but found that my previous conclusions continued to hold.[33] Another potential explanation is that my analysis of Bretton Woods incorporates data from the 1950s as well as the 1960s. In the 1950s, capital controls were especially prevalent, enhancing the autonomy enjoyed by domestic policymakers and limiting the international transmission of cyclical disturbances.[34] I again replicated the analysis, limiting the GDP time series to 1960–70. This too failed to overturn the finding of a higher cross-country correlation of output movements under the post-1972 float than under Bretton Woods.

A last possible explanation for the contrast is the use here of annual rather than quarterly observations. That Baxter and Stockman's evidence of an increase in the cross-country correlation is stronger when the first-difference filter, which emphasizes high-frequency movements, is used is consistent with this interpretation. This suggests that to the extent that fixed rates strengthen the cross-country coherence of business-cycle fluctuations, this occurs mainly at high frequencies.[35]

The rejection of capital controls as an explanation for the unusually low cross-country coherence of business cycles under Bretton Woods is reinforced by parallel results for the classical gold standard years. Capital controls were all but absent during the gold standard period, yet cross-country correlations with US output are even lower than under Bretton Woods.

One might argue, of course, that the low cross-country correlation

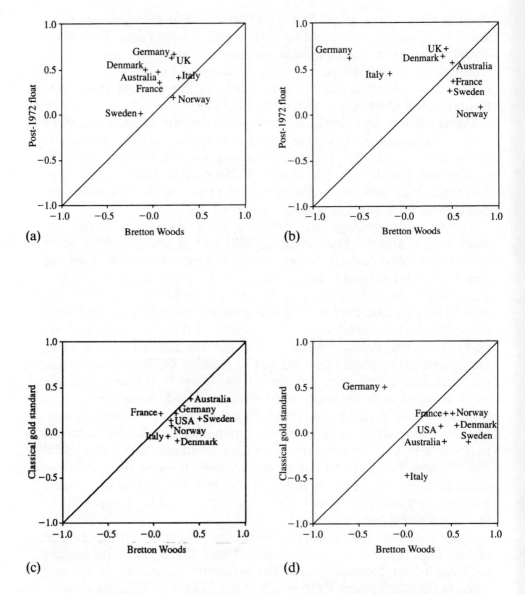

Figure 6.9 Cross-country correlations of gross domestic product under different exchange rate regimes: (a) correlation of gross domestic product with USA, first-difference filter; (b) correlation of gross domestic product with USA, linear filter; (c) correlation of gross domestic product with UK, first-difference filter; (d) correlation of gross domestic product with UK, linear filter.

reflects the fact that the USA played a less dominant role in the world economy before the First World War than after the Second World War. For much of this period, the USA was a capital importer rather than a capital exporter. It was not yet a major exporter of manufactured goods. For all these reasons one would expect business cycles in the USA to have had less of an effect on business cycles in other countries.

Figures 6.9(c) and 6.9(d) therefore present correlations of GDP growth rates with the UK rather than the USA. Regardless of which filter is used, the correlation is lower under the classical gold standard than during the Bretton Woods years.[36] That industrial country business cycles were not only more volatile under the gold standard than under subsequent fixed rate regimes but more idiosyncratic as well makes it all the more remarkable that the gold standard functioned so smoothly for as long as it did.[37]

The findings of the last two sections should temper empiricists' enthusiasm for theories mechanically linking the exchange rate regime to either the volatility of the business cycle or the international synchronization of output fluctuations. Comparisons of the classical gold standard, Bretton Woods, and the post-1972 float suggest that robust empirical regularities linking output fluctuations to the exchange rate regime are few and far between. The nagging question is whether the periods considered here are not representative and whether, if a larger sample were available, other regularities would surface.

3.3 Interwar comparisons

To probe this question, I extended the analysis to the interwar period. Recall that three exchange rate regimes can be distinguished between the wars: free floating, managed floating, and pegged rates. With data for this period it is therefore possible not just to augment the sample but to contrast the performance of pegged rates against alternative floating rate regimes featuring different degrees of intervention.

Following Eichengreen (1990), I divided the interwar years into a trio of five-year periods corresponding to different exchange rate regimes: 1922–6 (free floating), 1927–31 (pegged rates), and 1932–6 (managed floating). I then repeated the analysis of previous sections.[38] In this case the two filters produce similar results; in particular, since the periods are so short, the linear filter provides little additional information on low-frequency shifts.

Figures 6.10(a) and 6.10(c) display the standard deviation of output

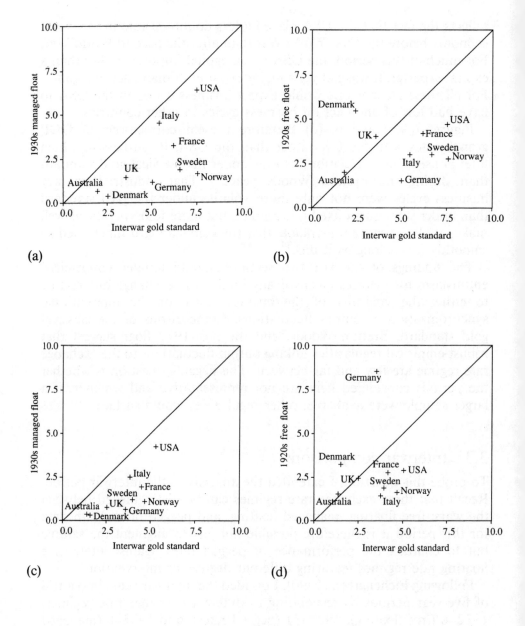

Figure 6.10 Variability of gross domestic product under different interwar exchange rate regimes: (a), (b) standard deviation of gross domestic product, first-difference filter; (c), (d) standard deviation of gross domestic product, linear filter.

under the interwar gold standard and the dirty float of the 1930s. For all countries output was more volatile under pegged rates. Again, this challenges any presumption of an association of pegged rates with output stability, either because fixed exchange rates discipline policy-makers or because output volatility increases the costs of maintaining a nominal exchange rate peg.

It is tempting to dismiss the interwar gold standard years as special since they span the onset of the Great Depression, an episode of exceptional turbulence. They are more difficult to dismiss, however, when placed alongside the finding (in section 3.1) that output was more volatile under the fixed rates of the classical gold standard than under the post-1972 float. Thus, we have several independent observations of greater output variability under fixed than floating rates. Figures 6.10(b) and 6.10(d), where results for the first half of the 1920s are shown, speak to the question of how much the freedom of the float matters. Recall that floating between 1922 and 1926 was virtually free of government intervention in the foreign exchange market, in contrast with the managed float of the 1930s when such intervention was widespread. Figure 6.10 shows that output was less volatile under free floating in the first half of the 1920s than under the fixed rates that followed. Only Denmark and – when the linear filter is used – Germany are exceptions to this generalization. (That these same two countries are the only ones for which, using the linear filter, volatility did not increase with the shift from the Bretton Woods system to the post-1972 float is presumably a coincidence.) Moreover, output was more volatile under the free float of the early 1920s than under the managed float of the early 1930s.[39] Analysis of this period therefore supports our conclusion of no simple association between the exchange rate regime and the volatility of GDP.

What about our heretical conclusions regarding transmission? In this respect interwar data, unlike comparisons across other historical periods, are consistent with conventional wisdom. Business cycles were more highly synchronized across countries under fixed than under floating rates. This is true whether fixed rates are compared with the managed float of the 1930s (figures 6.11(a) and 6.11(c)) or the free float of the 1920s (figures 6.11(b) and 6.11(d)). For once there is a direct correspondence between the freedom of the float and a summary statistic. The correlation of output fluctuations in other countries with those in the USA was higher under fixed rates than under managed floating, and higher under managed floating than under freely flexible rates.[40]

What accounts for the difference between the interwar years and other historical periods in the strength of international transmission under alternative exchange rate regimes? Theory suggests that flexible

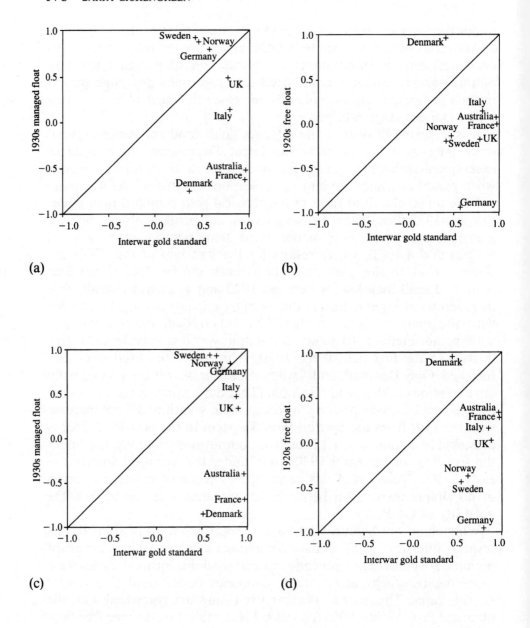

Figure 6.11 Cross-country correlations of gross domestic product under different interwar exchange rate regimes; (a), (b) correlation of gross domestic product with USA, first-difference filter; (c), (d) correlation of gross domestic product with USA, linear filter.

exchange rates provide better insulation against monetary disturbances than against real shocks. One would find the kind of association between the synchronization of output fluctuations across countries and stability of exchange rates that is evident between the wars if destabilizing impulses were primarily of monetary origin. This, of course, is the very argument made by Friedman and Schwartz (1963), among others, about the 1920s and 1930s. If other periods were dominated instead by real disturbances (including shifts in fiscal policy), then one would not expect to find the same association of business-cycle synchronization and pegged exchange rates.

3.4   Components of national income

Additional evidence on the nature of disturbances and on implications of the exchange rate regime for the business cycle can be gleaned from the behavior of components of national income. I follow Baxter and Stockman in analyzing consumption and government spending but also explore the behavior of investment and net exports of goods and services (the current account of the balance of payments).[41] I first consider the implications of this disaggregation for output and exchange rate stability, before briefly considering the light it sheds on international transmission.

The variability of two of these four components of national income, expressed as a share of the total, behaves similarly across regimes. The standard deviation of the consumption share of national income is quite stable across the classical gold standard, the Bretton Woods period, and the post-1972 float, for which it averages 2.48, 2.28, and 2.15 percent, respectively. The standard deviation of the investment share of national income is equally stable across regimes, averaging 2.12 under the gold standard, 2.16 under Bretton Woods, and 2.34 under the post-1972 float. Neither does the correlation between these two components differ noticeably across regimes. There is little evidence, then, that private sector behavior, to the extent that it is captured by these measures of consumption and investment, was profoundly different under the different exchange rate regimes.

Larger differences across exchange rate regimes are evident in the behavior of government spending and the current account. The government spending share of national income was more stable, as measured by the standard deviation, under the classical gold standard than under Bretton Woods, and under Bretton Woods than under the post-1972 float (see figures 6.12(a) and 6.12(b)).[42] This suggests that the nature of fiscal policy may have figured in the success with which the classical gold standard, and to a lesser extent Bretton Woods, accommodated output volatility. Activist fiscal policy was unknown

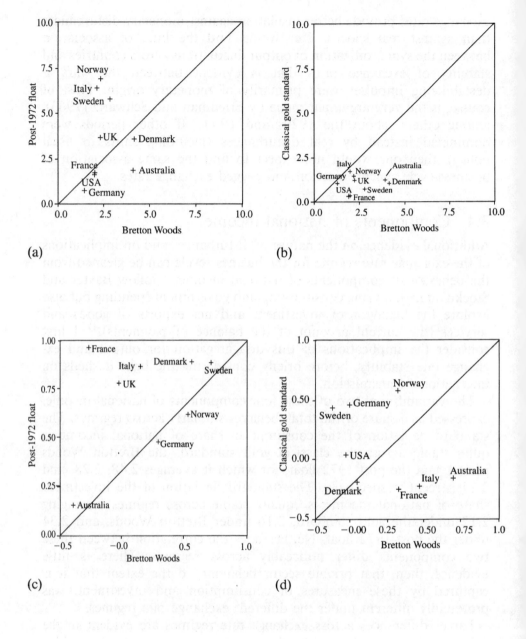

Figure 6.12 Standard deviations and cross-country correlations of government spending ratios: (a), (b) standard deviation of government spending ratio; (c) correlation of government spending ratio with USA; (d) correlation of government spending ratio with UK.

during the classical gold standard years (when major swings in the budgetary position were essentially limited to the outbreak of wars) and was only developed with a lag following the Second World War. Thus, fiscal policy was not employed in an effort to stabilize output at the risk of destabilizing the exchange rate. De Kock and Grilli (1989) invoke 150 years of British history to suggest that fiscal disturbances (typically associated with the outbreak of major wars) prompted Britain's repeated switches from fixed to floating rates. By implication they suggest that a passive fiscal response to disturbances is a correlate of the smooth operation of fixed rate systems. The international evidence presented here is consistent with their view.

Differences across exchange rate regimes are also evident in the behavior of the current account. The standard deviation of the current account balance as a share of national income is essentially the same under the classical gold standard and the post-1972 float, but only half as large during the Bretton Woods period.[43] An interpretation of these results is that, under the classical gold standard, government policies were subordinated to maintenance of the gold standard. The fiscal position was held stable while monetary policy was adjusted to maintain exchange rate stability. The credibility of governments' commitment to gold convertibility induced capital to flow in stabilizing directions to finance imbalances in the current account, imbalances that were magnified by the instability of the underlying environment and the absence of policy measures designed to limit output volatility.[44] Hence fixed rates were rendered compatible with swings in the current account and with a volatile business cycle. Under Bretton Woods, policy instruments were directed increasingly to other targets. Sometimes governments sought to use those policies to stabilize output. But the imperfect credibility of the authorities' commitment to fixed rates weakened stabilizing capital flows, forcing policymakers, in order to support the fixed rate system, to target the current account of the balance of payments as well. Relative to the gold standard, output was stabilized, but only to a degree, since policymakers were forced periodically to divert their efforts to targeting the current account instead. Following the transition to floating, large current account imbalances were allowed to re-emerge. The further decline in output volatility following this transition may have reflected the removal of the external constraint on policy.

According to this interpretation, then, what may have occurred over time was a shift from the use of policy to target the balance of payments to its use in targeting output and employment. The result was an increase in exchange rate instability but a decline in output volatility. Thus, what we have observed may not have been independent effects of the exchange rate regime on the stability of output but rather changes in accompanying policies leading to changes in both output and exchange rate volatility.

What are the implications of this disaggregated perspective for our findings on international transmission? Few regularities are apparent in cross-regime comparisons of consumption and investment. It is not clear that these components of national income have grown more or less correlated across countries, either over time or with shifts between fixed and floating rates. But the government spending ratio is more highly correlated across countries under the post-1972 float than under Bretton Woods, and more correlated internationally under Bretton Woods than under the classical gold standard (this is shown in figures 6.12(c) and 6.12(d)).[45] Thus, the greater international coherence of business cycles under the post-1972 float than under Bretton Woods, and under Bretton Woods than under the classical gold standard, may reflect the same reorientation of accompanying policies, specifically a rise over time in the cross-country correlation of fiscal impulses.

4   Implications for research

This chapter has provided a historical overview of the last century of international monetary experience, together with a preliminary investigation of the characteristics of business cycles under different exchange rate regimes. Some historical episodes, such as the interwar years, prove to be fairly congenial to the predictions of widely accepted theoretical models. Business-cycle fluctuations were more highly correlated across countries under the fixed exchange rates of the interwar gold standard, for example, than under the floating rate regimes immediately preceding and following. They were more correlated internationally under managed than free floating. But even the interwar period highlights the limited support lent to the predictions of mainstream theory by evidence drawn from the historical record. For instance, interwar data do not support the notion that cyclical fluctuations are necessarily less volatile under fixed than under floating rates.

Longer-run historical comparisons are even more subversive of modern conventional wisdom. Comparisons of the post-1972 float with the entire Bretton Woods period and the classical gold standard years do not support theories positing a positive association of fixed exchange rates with output stability or with the international synchronization of business cycles. If anything, the opposite appears to have been the case.

The question is whether this contrast is attributable to the exchange rate regime itself or to changes in accompanying policies. Analysis of components of national income suggests a role for fiscal variables in supporting exchange rate stability in earlier periods and perhaps also in reducing output volatility more recently. It suggests that increases over time in the international synchronization of fiscal impulses is responsible for the observed increase in the international synchronization of business cycles.

Thus it is tempting to argue that the decline over time in output volatility that has accompanied the shift from fixed to flexible rates reflects not the effect of the exchange rate regime *per se* but changes in accompanying policies. But before interpreting this conclusion too narrowly, it is worth observing that elimination of the exchange rate constraint may have facilitated that very reorientation of accompanying policies.

These preliminary explorations suggest an agenda for research. Extending the historical analysis to a larger sample of countries, developing as well as industrial, would serve to test the generality of this chapter's provisional conclusions. The different nominal exchange rate regimes might be broken up into subperiods in which accompanying policies differed, such as the preconvertible Bretton Woods years (1950–8) and the period of Bretton Woods convertibility (1959–70), facilitating investigation of explanations for the different behavior of output under different fixed rate regimes. Data of finer periodicity would facilitate more precise statements about the characteristics of business cycles under different exchange rate systems.

Equally important would be to identify the disturbances that provide the impulse for business cycles under different exchange rate regimes. Theories alluded to in section 3 predict that the discipline of fixed exchange rates is conducive to a lower incidence of demand disturbances, and that an unusual incidence of supply disturbances may occasion a shift from fixed to floating rates. Attempting to identify supply and demand disturbances using an approach like that of Blanchard and Quah (1989) could shed light on these issues. Going on to distinguish real from nominal and fiscal from monetary disturbances would help to explain why the association between the strength of international transmission and the exchange rate regime is more evident between the wars than in other historical periods. It would go some way toward testing our provisional explanation attributing changes in output stability under different exchange rate regimes to accompanying changes in fiscal policy.

Possessing information on the incidence of disturbances, it would then be possible to address the question of what determines the exchange rate regime. Most analysis of the implications for macroeconomic aggregates of alternative exchange rate arrangements takes the choice of regime as exogenous. This creates a selectivity problem for business-cycle analysis: observers may conclude that flexible exchange rates amplify business-cycle fluctuations when in fact it is the unusual amplitude of cyclical fluctuations that gives rise to flexible rates. An adequate general equilibrium analysis requires that both the choice of exchange rate regime and its effects be treated as endogenous. History can then provide the initial conditions that help to identify the resulting dynamic general equilibrium system.

Notes

I thank Luisa Lambertini and Carolyn Werley for research assistance and Micheal Bordo for helpful comments.

1   This discussion follows Redish (1990).
2   A useful chronology of events is given by Hawtrey (1931).
3   Details may be found in O'Farrell (1913) and Gavin (1992).
4   On the mechanics of the gold standard, see Bloomfield (1959). More specialized accounts that are also helpful include Sayers (1936), Whale (1937), and Lindert (1969). Clark (1984), Officer (1986), and Giovannini (1993) are representative of the recent literature in which the effectiveness of these arbitrage conditions is discussed.
5   Among the more important recent contributions to the literature on the gold standard at the periphery is de Cecco (1984). See also Ford (1962) on the gold standard in Argentina, Fritsch (1989) on Brazil, and Fetter (1931) on Chile. Britain itself had been forced to suspend convertibility due to crises in earlier years (Frenkel and Dornbusch, 1984), but not after 1870.
6   Fishlow (1985) estimates that international lending as a share of global GNP was perhaps three times as large during the final decades of the gold standard as during the lending bursts of the 1920s and 1970s. See Bloomfield (1963a, b) and Edelstein (1982) for additional information. Bayoumi (1990) and Eichengreen (1991a) run regressions of investment on savings *à la* Feldstein and Horioka (1980) for a variety of historical periods, finding a much lower correlation between the two variables, suggestive of higher levels of capital mobility, during the gold standard years.
7   For the classical gold standard period, exchange rates on London are drawn from Ohkawa et al. (1974) for Japan and from Mitchell (1988) for other countries, with dollar rates computed by triangular arbitrage. Interwar rates from the Board of Governors of the Federal Reserve System (1943) are linked to those provided by *International Financial Statistics* (*IFS*) for subsequent years. The French series is expressed in old francs for the entire period.
8   For each country M1 or M2 is used depending on availability. Money supplies are drawn from Friedman and Schwartz (1963) for the USA, from Capie and Webber (1985) for the UK, and from Saint Marc (1984) for France. The industrial production indices are drawn from Mitchell (1976, 1983), and are linked to *IFS* starting in 1950.

9   Long-term rates are taken from Macauley (1938), Homer (1977), and Mitchell (1976), linked to International Monetary Fund (various issues) for recent years. For the USA, Macauley's AAA railroad bonds for 1870–1921 are linked to Homer's long US government bonds for 1922–50. For the UK, 3 percent consols for 1870–1974 are taken from Mitchell and Homer. For France, Homer provides 3 percent *rentes* for 1870–1947 and 5 percent *rentes* for subsequent years; for Germany he provides high grade bond yields through 1949 and tax-free 4 percent bond yields through 1953, which are linked to the government bond yields reported by IMF. All Japanese data are taken from *IFS*.

10   McKinnon (1988) argues that exchange rate stability was conducive to capital market integration, while Eichengreen (1992) emphasizes the credibility of the pre-war commitment to gold. Giovannini (1993) provides systematic evidence on the credibility of the gold standard parities, showing that whenever the French franc and the German mark depreciated against the pound sterling, French and German interest rates declined relative to British rates as if investors regarded that depreciation as temporary and expected it to be reversed. This same relationship between the exchange rate and the interest rate differential did not hold for the USA, however, as if the dollar's gold standard parity was not regarded as fully credible, especially during the first half of the 1890s, a point also stressed by Eichengreen (1992). Sources and implications of this lack of credibility in the USA are developed in the next paragraph of the text.

11   This discussion of interwar exchange rate regimes draws on Eichengreen (1991b), where additional details are provided.

12   Dulles (1929) remains the classic account of the "battle of the [French] franc." Useful introductions to the Belgian and German experiences are Shepherd (1936) and Bresciani-Turroni (1937) respectively.

13   Perhaps the best overview of the construction of the interwar gold standard system is Palyi (1972).

14   For analyses of this period, see Clarke (1967) and Eichengreen (1992).

15   Basic sources on the financial crisis in Austria and Germany emphasizing international monetary aspects are Ellis (1941) and James (1986).

16   On the 1931 devaluations, see Cairncross and Eichengreen (1983). A recent account which discusses the politics in detail is Kunz (1987).

17   The definitive statement to this effect is Nurkse (1944). An influential modern account in the same tradition is Kindleberger (1973). For readers desiring additional detail, Brown (1940) may be recommended.

18   The most authoritative account of the Bretton Woods negotiations remains Gardner (1956). A subsequent analysis incorporating recent research in international relations is Ikenberry (1993).

19   Two of the most important studies of developing-country exchange rate experience under Bretton Woods are Cooper (1971) and Edwards and Santaella (1993). The generalization in the text leaves aside the realignments touched off by the 1949 devaluation of sterling. The subsequent devaluations, which involved nearly every industrial country but Japan, Switzerland, and the USA, were needed to set the stage for a viable system of fixed rates. (On the 1949 devaluations see Polak (1951).) Hence the empirical analysis discussed in section 3 takes the start of the Bretton Woods period as 1950.

20 A good summary of the evolution of Bretton Woods institutions is Tew (1988).

21 For details on the use of capital controls under Bretton Woods, see Giovannini (1989) and Obstfeld (1993).

22 As Robert Triffin argued (see Triffin, 1960), the world's growing demand for international liquidity inevitably led foreign countries to absorb dollar claims, but ultimately undermined the US government's ability to defend the $35 gold price. Two recent analyses of the debate over the collapse of Bretton Woods are Garber (1993) and Genberg and Swoboda (1993).

23 The following periodization draws on Giavazzi and Giovannini (1989), the definitive account of the operation of the European Monetary System.

24 The rationale for starting in 1950 rather than, say, 1945 is to omit the wave of realignments that occurred in 1949. See note 19 above.

25 Baxter and Stockman's sample ended in 1985, whereas ours continues through 1990.

26 Subsequent discussion explains when one or more of these innovations has substantive implications for the results.

27 Data are drawn from Maddison (1982) and *IFS*. For the gold standard period, we also utilize the Romer (1989) estimates of GNP, explaining in subsequent notes how much difference this substitution makes.

28 Formal statistical tests on data such as these should be interpreted cautiously, since they assume, strictly speaking, that the individual national observations are independent from one another, which is unlikely to hold in practice. Still, at a more heuristic level, the scatter diagram suggests little systematic difference in output volatility.

29 The standard deviations are 2.7 and 2.3 percent respectively. Bordo's results are for GNP per capita rather than overall GNP, but since population growth rates fluctuated little over the cycle this normalization is of little consequence.

30 The relevant statistics are 1.61 percent for 1960–70 and 1.98 percent (as before) when the first-difference filter is used, and 1.38 percent versus 2.33 percent when the linear filter is employed.

31 For readers concerned that this result may reflect spurious volatility in the US historical statistics, it is reassuring that the conclusion continues to hold when the Romer data are substituted for Maddison's US output series.

32 The average standard deviations for the gold standard and the post-1972 float are 3.77 and 2.33 percent respectively when the linear filter is used, versus 2.94 and 1.98 percent when the first-difference filter is employed. For another analysis that reaches broadly similar conclusions, see Bordo (1981).

33 Given the limitations of the available industrial production data, the Bretton Woods period was redefined as 1954–70 for this portion of the analysis.

34 The previous section provided grounds for skepticism that the prevalence of capital controls could explain differences in output volatility across different fixed rate regimes. This leaves open the question of whether they can explain differences in the correlation across countries of output under different fixed rate regimes, although I am about to argue that the data provide little support for this hypothesis either.

35 Again, this conclusion is consistent with the findings of Bordo (1993).

36 This continues to be the case when the Romer series is substituted for Maddison's output estimates for the USA. Interestingly, US GNP is nega-

tively correlated with UK output when the Romer series is used, a result which holds with both filtering methods, while the Maddison series is positively correlated in both cases.

37 I have suggested elsewhere that this testifies to the powerful influence of stabilizing international capital flows due to the unquestioned credibility of governments' commitment to gold convertibility. See Eichengreen (1992).

38 A similar analysis, using data on industrial production rather than GNP and employing only the linear filter, is reported in Eichengreen (1990).

39 The cross-country average of standard deviations falls from 4.85 to 2.36 when the first-difference filter is used and from 2.84 to 1.44 when the linear filter is employed. In both cases the difference in sample variances is statistically significant at the 95 percent confidence level.

40 Again, these are arithmetic averages of individual country correlations, which come to 0.67, 0.19, and − 0.05 respectively when the first-difference filter is used, and 0.79, 0.18, and − 0.02 when the linear filter is employed.

41 Baxter and Stockman focus on government consumption rather than overall government spending. Data limitations do not permit one to make the same distinction for earlier historical periods.

42 The three standard deviations average 1.0, 2.5, and 3.6 percent respectively.

43 Standard deviations averaged 2.19 percent under the gold standard and 2.11 percent under the post-1972 float, but only 1.37 percent under Bretton Woods.

44 For support, see notes 10 and 37 and the citations provided by those references.

45 This regularity holds whether the USA or the UK is the reference country. For the USA (UK), the correlation coefficient rises from − 0.07 (0.07) under the gold standard to 0.19 (0.20) under Bretton Woods to 0.71 (0.65) under the post-1972 float.

References

Baxter, Marianne, and Alan Stockman (1989) "Business cycles and the exchange rate regime: some international evidence," *Journal of Monetary Economics* 23, 377–400.

Bayoumi, Tamim (1990) "Saving–investment correlations: immobile capital, government policy, or endogenous behavior?" *IMF Staff Papers* 37, 360–87.

Blanchard, Olivier, and Danny Quah (1989) "The dynamic effects of aggregate demand and supply disturbances," *American Economic Review* 79, 655–73.

Bloomfield, Arthur I. (1959) *Monetary Policy under the International Gold Standard, 1880–1913*, New York: Federal Reserve Bank of New York.

—— (1963a) "Short-term capital movements under the pre-1914 gold standard," Princeton Studies in International Finance 11, Princeton, NJ, International Finance Section, Department of Economics.

—— (1963b) "Patterns of fluctuation in international investment before 1914," Princeton Studies in International Finance 21, Princeton, NJ, International Finance Section, Department of Economics.

Board of Governors of the Federal Reserve System (1943) *Banking and Monetary*

Statistics, 1914–1941, Washington, DC, Board of Governors.

Bordo, Michael (1981) "The classical gold standard: some lessons for today," *Federal Reserve Bank of St Louis Review* 63, 1–17.

—— (1993) "The Bretton Woods international monetary system: an historical overview," in Michael Bordo and Barry Eichengreen (eds) *A Retrospective on the Bretton Woods System*, Chicago, IL, University of Chicago Press, pp. 3–108.

Bresciani-Turroni, Constantino (1937) *The Economics of Inflation*, London, Allen and Unwin.

Brown, W.A. (1940) *The International Gold Standard Reinterpreted, 1913–1934*, New York, National Bureau of Economic Research.

Cairncross, Alec, and Barry Eichengreen (1983) *Sterling in Decline*, Oxford, Blackwell.

Capie, Forrest, and Alan Webber (1985) *A Monetary History of the United Kingdom, 1870–1982, vol. 1, Data, Sources and Methods*, London, Allen and Unwin.

de Cecco, Marcello (1984) *The International Gold Standard: Money and Empire*, 2nd edn, London, Frances Pinter.

Clark, Truman A. (1984) "Violations of the gold points, 1890–1914," *Journal of Political Economy* 92, 791–823.

Clarke, S.V.O. (1967) *Central Bank Cooperation, 1924–1931*, New York, Federal Reserve Bank of New York.

Cooper, Richard N. (1971) "Currency devaluation in developing countries," *Essays in International Finance* 86, Princeton, NJ, International Finance Section, Department of Economics.

De Kock, Gabriel, and Vittorio Grilli (1989) "Endogenous exchange rate regime switches," NBER Working Paper 3066, Cambridge, MA.

Dulles, E.L. (1929) *The French Franc, 1914–1928*, New York, Macmillan.

Edelstein, Michael (1982) *Overseas Investment in the Age of High Imperialism*, New York, Columbia University Press.

Edwards, Sebastian, and Julio A. Santaella (1993) "The Bretton Woods System, the IMF, and some devaluation controversies in the developing countries," in Michael Bordo and Barry Eichengreen (eds) *A Retrospective on the Bretton Woods System*, Chicago, IL, University of Chicago Press, pp. 405–60.

Eichengreen, Barry (1990) "International monetary instability between the wars: structural flaws or misguided policies?" in Yoshio Suzuki, Jinichi Miyake, and Mitsuaki Okabe (eds) *The Evolution of the International Monetary System*, Tokyo, University of Tokyo Press, pp. 71–115.

—— (1991a) "Trends and cycles in foreign lending," in Horst Siebert (ed.) *Capital Flows in the World Economy*, Tübingen, Mohr, pp. 3–28.

—— (1991b) "The comparative performance of fixed and flexible exchange rate regimes: interwar evidence," in Niels Thygesen, Kumaraswamy Velupillai, and Stefano Zambelli (eds) *Business Cycles: Theories, Evidence and Analysis*, London, Macmillan, pp. 229–72.

—— (1992) *Golden Fetters: The Gold Standard and the Great Depression, 1919–39*, New York, Oxford University Press.

—— (1993) "Three perspectives on the Bretton Woods System," in Michael Bordo and Barry Eichengreen (eds) *A Retrospective on the Bretton Woods System*, Chicago, IL, University of Chicago Press, pp. 621–58.

Ellis, Howard S. (1941) *Exchange Control in Central Europe*, Cambridge, MA,

Harvard University Press.

Feldstein, Martin, and Charles Horioka (1980) "Domestic saving and international capital flows," *Economic Journal* 90, 314–28.

Fetter, Frank (1931) *Monetary Inflation in Chile*, Princeton, NJ, Princeton University Press.

Fishlow, Albert (1985) "Lessons from the past: capital markets during the 19th century and the inter-war period," *International Organization* 39, 383–439.

Floyd, John E. (1985) *World Monetary Equilibrium: International Monetary Theory in an Historical-Institutional Context*, Philadelphia, PA, University of Pennsylvania Press.

Ford, Alec (1962) *The Gold Standard, 1880–1914: Britain and Argentina*, Oxford, Clarendon.

Frenkel, Jacob A. and Rudiger Dornbusch (1984) "The gold standard and the Bank of England in the crisis of 1847," in Michael Bordo and Anna Schwartz (eds) *A Retrospective on the Classical Gold Standard, 1821–1931*, Chicago, IL, University of Chicago Press, pp. 233–64.

Friedman, Milton, and Anna Schwartz (1963) *A Monetary History of the United States, 1867–1960*, Princeton, NJ, Princeton University Press.

Fritsch, Winston (1989) *External Constraints on Economic Policy, Brazil 1890–1930*, Pittsburgh, PA, University of Pittsburgh Press.

Garber, Peter (1993) "The collapse of the Bretton Woods fixed exchange rate system," in Michael Bordo and Barry Eichengreen (eds) *A Retrospective on the Bretton Woods System*, Chicago, IL, University of Chicago Press, pp. 461–94.

Gardner, Richard N. (1956) *Sterling–Dollar Diplomacy*, Oxford, Clarendon.

Gavin, Michael (1992) "Intertemporal dimensions of international economic adjustment: evidence from the Franco-Prussian war indemnity," *American Economic Review*, forthcoming.

Genberg, Hans, and Alexander K. Swoboda (1993) "The provision of liquidity in the Bretton Woods System," in Michael Bordo and Barry Eichengreen (eds) *A Retrospective on the Bretton Woods System*, Chicago, IL, University of Chicago Press, pp. 269–316.

Giavazzi, Francesco, and Alberto Giovannini (1989) *Limiting Exchange Rate Flexibility: The European Monetary System*, Cambridge, MA, MIT Press.

—— and Marco Pagano (1988) "The advantage of tying one's hands: EMS discipline and central bank credibility," *European Economic Review* 32, 1055–82.

Giovannini, Alberto (1989) "How do fixed exchange rate regimes work? Evidence from the gold standard, Bretton Woods and the EMS," in Marcus Miller, Barry Eichengreen, and Richard Portes (eds) *Blueprints for Exchange Rate Management*, New York, Academic Press, pp. 13–42.

—— (1993) "Bretton Woods and its precursors: rules versus discretion in the history of international monetary regimes," in Michael Bordo and Barry Eichengreen (eds) *A Retrospective on the Bretton Woods System*, Chicago, IL, University of Chicago Press, pp. 109–54.

Goodfriend, Marvin (1988) "Central banking under the gold standard," *Carnegie Rochester Conference Series on Public Policy* 29, 85–124.

Hawtrey, Ralph G. (1931) *The Gold Standard in Theory and Practice*, London, Longmans, Green.

Homer, Sydney (1977) *A History of Interest Rates*, New Brunswick, NJ, Rutgers

University Press.

Ikenberry, G. John (1993) "The political origins of Bretton Woods," in Michael Bordo and Barry Eichengreen (eds) *A Retrospective on the Bretton Woods System*, Chicago, IL, University of Chicago Press, pp. 155–200.

International Monetary Fund (various years) *International Financial Statistics*, Washington, DC, IMF.

James, Harold (1986) *The German Slump: Politics and Economics, 1924–36*, Oxford, Clarendon.

Kindleberger, Charles P. (1973) *The World in Depression, 1929–39*, Berkeley, CA, University of California Press.

Kunz, Diane B. (1987) *The Battle for Britain's Gold Standard in 1931*, London, Croom Helm.

Lindert, Peter H. (1969) "Key currencies and gold, 1900–1913," Princeton Studies in International Finance 24, Princeton, NJ, International Finance Section, Department of Economics.

Macauley, Frederick (1938) *The Movements of Interest Rates*, New York, National Bureau of Economic Research.

Maddison, Angus (1982) *Phases of Capitalist Development*, New York, Oxford University Press.

McKinnon, Ronald I. (1988) "An international gold standard without gold," mimeo, Stanford University.

Mitchell, B.R. (1976) *European Historical Statistics*, London, Macmillan.

—— (1983) *International Historical Statistics*, London, Macmillan.

—— (1988) *British Historical Statistics*, Cambridge, Cambridge University Press.

Mussa, Michael (1979) "Macroeconomic interdependence and the exchange rate regime," in R. Dornbusch and J. Frenkel (eds) *International Economic Policy: Theory and Evidence*, Baltimore, MD, Johns Hopkins University Press, pp. 160–204.

Nurkse, Ragnar (1944) *International Currency Experience*, Geneva, League of Nations.

Obstfeld, Maurice (1993) "The adjustment mechanism," in Michael Bordo and Barry Eichengreen (eds) *A Retrospective on the Bretton Woods System*, Chicago, IL, University of Chicago Press, pp. 201–68.

O'Farrell, Horace H. (1913) *The Franco-Prussian War Indemnity and its Economic Results*, London, Harrison.

Officer, Lawrence (1986) "The efficiency of the dollar–sterling gold standard, 1890–1908," *Journal of Political Economy* 94, 1038–74.

Ohkawa, Kazushi, Miyoshei Shinohara, and Mataji Umemura (1974) *Estimates of Long-term Economics Statistics of Japan since 1868 [Choki Keizai Tokei]*, Tokyo, Oriental Publishing.

Palyi, Melchior (1972) *The Twilight of Gold, 1914–1936*, Chicago, IL, Henry Regnery.

Polak, J.J. (1951) "Contribution of the September 1949 devaluations to the solution of Europe's dollar problem," *IMF Staff Papers*, 1–32.

Redish, Angela (1990) "The evolution of the gold standard in England," *Journal of Economic History* 50, 789–805.

Romer, Christina (1989) "The prewar business cycle reconsidered: new estimates of gross national product, 1869–1908," *Journal of Political Economy* 97, 1–37.

Saint Marc, Michele (1984) *Histoire monétaire de la France, 1800–1980*, France:

Presses Universitaires de France.

Sayers, Richard S. (1936) *Bank of England Operations, 1890–1914*, London, P.S. King.

Shepherd, Henry L. (1936) *The Monetary Experience of Belgium, 1913–1936*, Princeton, NJ, Princeton University Press.

Swoboda, Alexander, and Rudiger Dornbusch (1973) "Adjustment, policy and monetary equilibrium in a two-country model," in M. Connolly and A. Swoboda (eds) *International Trade and Money*, London, Allen and Unwin, pp. 229–61.

Tew, Brian (1988) *The Evolution of the International Monetary System, 1944–88*, 4th edn, London, Hutchinson.

Triffin, Robert (1960) *Gold and the Dollar Crisis*, New Haven, CT, Yale University Press.

Whale, P.B. (1937) "The working of the prewar gold standard," *Economica* 11, 18–32.

7 On Inflation, Unemployment, and the Optimal Exchange Rate Regime

GEORGE ALOGOSKOUFIS

1 Introduction

The main industrial economies have long experiences with regimes of both fixed and managed exchange rates. The bimetallic system that prevailed before the dominance of the international gold standard (1871–1914) was essentially a system of flexible exchange rates, as the relative price of gold and silver was variable. The gold standard itself was a system of fixed exchange rates. The interwar period saw a variety of exchange rate arrangements, from fully flexible exchange rates to exchange rate management, as well as an attempted but failed restoration of the gold standard. The Bretton Woods system of fixed but adjustable exchange rates prevailed from 1950 until the early 1970s, but it broke down to give way to a system of generalized floating and exchange rate management.[1] Since the late 1970s the economies of the European Community (EC) have adopted their own system of fixed but adjustable exchange rates and are now in the process of establishing a full-blown monetary union, by "irrevocably" fixing their exchange rates.

The fact remains that a variety of exchange rate regimes exists in the world today. Even a cursory look at the current exchange rate arrangements of the members of the International Monetary Fund (IMF) suggests a bewildering variety. For example, of the 154 members of the IMF whose arrangements were classified in June 1991, 85 were unilaterally pegging, either to the US dollar, the French franc, the Special Drawing Right or a basket of currencies, 10 of the members of the EC participated in a cooperative exchange rate regime (the European Monetary System (EMS)), and the remaining 59 followed more flexible arrangements such as independent floating or exchange rate adjustment rules according to various indicators. Among the industrial economies that are members of the Organization for Economic Cooperation and Development (OECD), five, namely Austria and the non-EC Nordic countries, were pegging to a currency basket, ten participated in the EMS, and eight followed an independent system of managed floating.

What are the implications of alternative exchange rate regimes for macroeconomic performance, and in particular inflation and unemployment? Why do countries with similar economic structure and relatively integrated financial markets, such as the OECD countries, opt for different monetary and exchange rate regimes, and why do they periodically revert from fixed to managed exchange rates and vice versa? Is there such a thing as an "optimal" monetary and exchange rate regime for an open economy? These are questions that have kept international macroeconomists busy for a long time.[2]

In this chapter I start by examining the implications of alternative monetary and exchange rate regimes for a single open economy, in a world of high capital mobility. I also examine the optimal choice of regime in the light of unanticipated nominal and real disturbances that cannot be taken into account in the periodic setting of nominal wages. I pay particular attention to the time inconsistency of optimal discretionary policy, and discuss rules versus discretion. Fixed exchange rate regimes, accompanied by an anti-inflationary international monetary standard, can be seen as one way of escaping from the inflationary consequences of the time-inconsistency problem of optimal discretionary policy, but they imply other costs that emanate from the lack of freedom to react to previously unanticipated real macroeconomic disturbances. The issue is ultimately empirical, as it involves a difficult cost–benefit calculus of comparing the costs of the inflationary bias that may result from discretionary policy with the costs of the higher variance of unemployment that may accompany a fixed exchange rate regime.

The chapter is organized as follows. Section 2 sets up one of the simplest possible models of an open economy. This is a competitive model of an economy producing an internationally traded commodity that is a perfect substitute for the commodities produced in other economies. The law of one price is assumed to hold. Interest-bearing bonds are also assumed to be perfect substitutes internationally. Thus, differences in nominal interest rates reflect only expectations of changes in the exchange rate. With regard to labor markets it is assumed that nominal wages are fixed for one period. Wages are set before current disturbances have been realized, based on rational expectations by wage-setters. The realization of disturbances affects prices, real wages, and unemployment, and creates incentives for the monetary authorities to react in order to bring about the desired balance between the unemployment and inflation effects. Since this is a monetary model of the exchange rate, the type of model that has dominated the recent literature, monetary and exchange rate policy are perfect substitutes under full information.

Section 3 examines two celebrated fixed rules for monetary policy in an open economy, namely a fixed rate of growth for the domestic nominal money supply and a fixed nominal exchange rate.

A domestic money supply rule allows an economy to choose its own average inflation rate. It completely insulates it from world price shocks, which are reflected in the nominal exchange rate. In addition, permanent productivity shocks do not affect unemployment but only cause fluctuations in the inflation rate. Shocks to money demand, such as exogenous velocity shifts, and foreign interest rate shocks cause fluctuations in both unemployment and inflation. The same holds for transitory productivity shocks.

In contrast with domestic money supply rules, under a fixed nominal exchange rate domestic inflation is equal to foreign inflation. Fluctuations in real wages and unemployment are only driven by shocks to world inflation and domestic productivity shocks. Although the equilibrium rate of unemployment is independent of the monetary regime, its fluctuations around equilibrium are not.

Section 4 concentrates on optimal exchange rate management in the face of nominal and real macroeconomic disturbances. The authorities are assumed to be solely concerned with inflation and unemployment. I distinguish between two cases. In the first, the "natural" rate of unemployment is deemed to be efficient, so that the authorities have no incentive to try systematically to reduce unemployment below the "natural" rate. In the second case the authorities are assumed to consider the "natural" rate of unemployment as inefficiently high, in which case they have an incentive to try systematically to reduce unemployment through unanticipated inflation.

In the first case, optimal monetary and exchange rate policy dominates both a fixed rate of growth for the money supply and fixed exchange rates. It implies an average rate of growth of the domestic money supply equal to the long-run rate of growth of output, but it allows for deviations in response to shocks in money demand and productivity. It is very similar to a zero inflation target, with deviations only in response to unanticipated productivity shocks that also cause deviations of unemployment from its efficient "natural" rate. Under this optimal policy, the exchange rate completely counteracts foreign inflation, by continuous appreciations if foreign inflation is positive. In addition, it partly counteracts productivity disturbances, in order to balance the cost of deviations of unemployment from its "natural" rate with that of deviations of inflation from zero.

I also examine the case of exchange market intervention under uncertainty, i.e. when the authorities cannot directly observe nominal and real shocks but only prices such as foreign inflation, interest rates, and exchange rates. In such a case, optimal exchange market intervention involves "leaning against the wind," i.e. monetary policy tightening in the light of depreciations of the exchange rate and vice versa. The reason is that the exchange rate contains information about productivity disturbances. A depreciation signifies a negative productivity shock, i.e. a fall in output, which necessitates some contraction in the money supply in order partly to control the concomitant rise in inflation. An appreciation partly signifies a positive supply shock which requires some accommodation.

The problem with these optimal policies is that they cannot fully explain some of the key characteristics of our experience. In particular, countries that have the option of exchange rate management do not end up with zero average inflation, but more frequently with positive and persistently high inflation. The seminal work of Kydland and Prescott (1977) and Barro and Gordon (1983a, b) suggests that, if the "natural" rate of unemployment is inefficient or other inefficiencies such as the need for seigniorage revenue (Calvo, 1978) are present, there are incentives for the authorities to try systematically to generate unanticipated inflation. Then, equilibrium inflation will rise to the point where such incentives no longer exist. Allowing for an inefficiently high "natural" rate of unemployment dramatically changes one's perception about the optimal monetary and exchange rate regime. Optimal exchange rate management allows the authorities partly to counteract the unemployment and inflation consequences of unanticipated shocks, but it may also result in a high equilibrium inflation rate, which is proportional to the inefficiency of the "natural" rate of unemployment. In fact, the more the authorities care about unemployment, the higher will be the equilibrium rate of inflation for a given inefficiency of the "natural" rate. This is because the incentives of domestic policymakers systematically to surprise the private sector are a function of this labor market inefficiency, and equilibrium inflation rises to the point where these incentives are no longer there.

Thus, the question of whether managed exchange rates dominate fixed exchange rates becomes an empirical one. If the inefficiency of the "natural" rate of unemployment dominates foreign inflation and the variability of productivity (more generally real) shocks, which exchange rate management serves partly to neutralize, then fixed exchange rates are the optimal exchange rate regime. If world inflation is high and real shocks have a high variability, exchange rate management dominates.

Section 4.5 investigates the role of credibility in the cost of transition from exchange rate management to a fixed exchange rate regime. If the private sector is uncertain about the true intentions of the authorities, an announced change in regime is initially going to be only partly believed. Thus, a high inflation economy that decides to join a low inflation fixed exchange rate regime may find that its wage inflation rate will not be reduced overnight, because expectations may take time to adjust. In the transition, there will be unanticipated price deflation which will raise unemployment above the "natural" rate. Depending on the horizon of the authorities, and their initial credibility, such transitional costs may even stop them from engaging in an otherwise desirable regime change.

The important point from this examination of the literature is that no monetary and exchange rate regime completely dominates under all circumstances. What favors fixed exchange rates is a nominal anchor that ensures low international inflation (e.g. a commodity standard or the dominance of an anti-inflationary foreign central bank), low variability of real shocks, and inefficiently high "natural" rates of unemployment. In times of high international inflation, say because of the absence of an international nominal anchor, or in periods with a high variance of real shocks, more countries will have an incentive to opt for an independent monetary policy, i.e. exchange rate management. In any case, because monetary and exchange rate management trades off the cost of unemployment against the cost of inflation, no monetary regime is going to be entirely satisfactory by itself, as it cannot eliminate both inflation and unemployment.

In section 5 I briefly discuss the extent to which the results for a single economy carry over to interdependent economies, and provide a brief survey of the role of asymmetries between countries for the choice between alternative exchange rate regimes. The last section contains conclusions.

2   A simple open economy macromodel

In this section I present a simple log-linear model of an open economy which will serve as the basis for the discussion of monetary policy and exchange rate regimes in the remainder of this chapter. This model is among the simplest available in open economy macroeconomics but has constituted the basic framework used for the theoretical analysis of monetary policy and exchange market intervention in open economies. One of the reasons for its popularity is that it has important analytical and notational advantages as it has a small number of parameters and its main properties are not misleading, in the sense that they carry over to more general models of open economies.[3]

2.1 The supply side

Consider an open economy that produces one internationally traded commodity. Capital will be assumed fixed in the short run, and output is given by a short-run production function of the type

$$y_t = \beta l_t + \mu_t \qquad (7.1)$$

where y is the logarithm of output, l is the logarithm of employment, and μ is a measure of productivity. β is the exponent of labor and is less than unity. Productivity is assumed to folow a random walk with drift:

$$\mu_t = g + \mu_{t-1} + v_t^\mu \qquad (7.2)$$

where g is the average (or expected) rate of growth of productivity and v^μ is a normally distributed productivity shock with zero mean and variance σ_μ^2.

Firms determine employment by equalizing the marginal product of labor to the real wage. This yields the following employment function:

$$l_t = -\frac{1}{1-\beta}(w_t - p_t - \mu_t) \qquad (7.3)$$

where w is the logarithm of the nominal wage and p is the logarithm of the price level.

The nominal wage is set at the beginning of each period and remains fixed for one period (Gray, 1976; Fischer, 1977). The objective of wage-setters is to stabilize expected employment around a target employment level $\tilde{n}$. Thus, wages in each period are set to minimize

$$E_{t-1}(l_t - \tilde{n})^2 \qquad (7.4)$$

where E_{t-1} is the operator of rational expectations, conditional on information available up to the end of period $t-1$. The minimization of (7.4) is subject to the labor demand function (7.3). From the first-order conditions for a minimum of (7.4) subject to (7.3), the nominal wage is given by

$$w_t = E_{t-1}p_t + E_{t-1}\mu_t - (1-\beta)\tilde{n} \qquad (7.5)$$

Substituting (7.5) in the labor demand function (7.3), and the resulting equation in the production function, we get the following relation between employment, output, and unanticipated shocks:

$$l_t = \tilde{n} + \frac{1}{1-\beta}(p_t - E_{t-1}p_t + v_t^\mu) \qquad (7.6)$$

$$y_t = \beta\tilde{n} + \mu_t + \frac{\beta}{1-\beta}(p_t - E_{t-1}p_t + v_t^\mu) \qquad (7.7)$$

An unanticipated rise in prices reduces the real wage and causes firms to employ more labor. Thus both aggregate employment and output rise above their equilibrium rate. On the other hand, an unanticipated shock to productivity increases the marginal product of labor, and given the real wage causes firms to employ more labor. Thus, employment rises above $\tilde{n}$, and output rises on account of both the higher employment and the higher productivity.

Subtracting (7.6) from the labor force n, using the approximation that $u \approx n - l$, and adding and subtracting $p_{t-1}/(1 - \beta)$, we get the following expression for the short-run determination of unemployment:

$$u_t = \tilde{u} - \frac{1}{1-\beta}(\Delta p_t - E_{t-1}\Delta p_t + v_t^\mu) \tag{7.8}$$

where $\tilde{u} = n - \tilde{n}$. $\tilde{u}$ can be thought of as the equilibrium or "natural" rate of unemployment in this model. Thus, (7.8) is the well-known expectations-augmented "Phillips curve." Unemployment deviates from its equilibrium rate only to the extent that there are unanticipated shocks to inflation or productivity. Anticipated shocks to inflation and productivity are reflected in wages (equation (7.5)) and do not affect unemployment.

2.2 The demand side

The remainder of the model consists of three equilibrium conditions. The first is the equilibrium condition in the money market. The money supply is willingly held. Money demand is a function of "permanent" income $\tilde{y}$ and the domestic nominal interest rate. It is given by

$$(m-p)_t = \tilde{y}_t - \alpha i_t + k_t \tag{7.9}$$

where m is the logarithm of the nominal money supply, i is the domestic nominal interest rate, and k is a shock to money demand. Given our assumption that productivity shocks are permanent, $\tilde{y} = \beta\tilde{n} + \mu_t$. shock k_t will be assumed to follow a simple random walk:

$$k_t = k_{t-1} + v_t^k \tag{7.10}$$

where v^k has zero mean and variance σ_k^2.

The second equilibrium condition is international bond arbitrage. Domestic and foreign bonds will be assumed perfect substitutes, in which case interest rate differentials only reflect expectations of changes in exchange rates. This assumption will be utilized throughout this survey. The uncovered interest parity condition is given by

$$i_t = i_t^* + E_t e_{t+1} - e_t \tag{7.11}$$

where i^* is the foreign nominal interest rate and e is the logarithm of the domestic exchange rate (units of domestic currency per unit of foreign currency).

The final equilibrium condition in the model is international goods arbitrage. Domestic goods will be assumed to be perfect substitutes for foreign goods, and goods prices are assumed equal in a common currency:

$$p_t = e_t + p_t^* \qquad (7.12)$$

where $p*$ is the log of the foreign price level.[4]

3   Monetary versus exchange rate targets

In this section we shall examine the implications of two well-known open-loop policy rules, namely the policy of a fixed rate of growth for the domestic money supply, and the policy of a fixed nominal exchange rate. Note that the money market equilibrium condition and uncovered interest parity imply that the money supply and the nominal exchange rate cannot be independent of each other. Thus, a rule for the money supply will make the exchange rate endogenous, and a rule for the exchange rate will make the money supply endogenous. This is a well-known implication of the monetary approach to the exchange rate (Mundell, 1963).[5]

3.1   A fixed rate of growth for the money supply

We start by considering the implications for inflation and unemployment of the famous Friedman (1960) rule of a constant x percent rate of growth for the domestic money supply. After substituting the goods and bonds market arbitrage conditions in the money demand function (7.9), we get the following first-order difference equation for the nominal exchange rate:

$$\left(F - \frac{1+\alpha}{\alpha}\right)e_t = -\frac{1}{\alpha}(m_t - p_t^* - \beta\tilde{n} - \mu_t + \alpha i_t^* - k_t) \qquad (7.13)$$

where F is the forward shift expectations operator, i.e. $Fe_t = E_t e_{t+1}$. Since the exchange rate is a jump variable, this equation must be solved forward. The minimum state variables solution of (7.13) is given by

$$e_t = \frac{1}{1+\alpha} \sum_{j=0}^{\infty} \left[\frac{\alpha}{1+\alpha}\right]^j E_t(m_{t+j} - p_{t+j}^* - \beta\tilde{n} - \mu_{t+j} + \alpha i_{t+j}^* - k_{t+j}) \qquad (7.14)$$

The current nominal exchange rate depends on the expected future path of the fundamentals, namely the domestic money supply, output and money demand shocks, and foreign prices and interest rates.[6]

To get a closed-form solution we need to make additional assumptions about the evolution of foreign prices and interest rates. I shall assume that foreign prices follow a random walk with drift π^* and that the foreign interest rate follows a simple random walk. With these assumptions, together with the assumptions about productivity and money demand shocks in (7.2) and (7.10), and a fixed rate of growth x for the domestic money supply, (7.14) implies that

$$e_t = \frac{\alpha}{1 + \alpha}(x - \pi^* - g) + (m_t - p_t^* - \beta\tilde{n} - \mu_t + \alpha i_t^* - k_t) \qquad (7.15)$$

From (7.15)

$$E_t\Delta e_{t+1} = x - \pi^* - g \qquad (7.16)$$

$$e_t - E_{t-1}e_t = -(\Delta p_t^* - \pi^*) + \alpha\Delta i_t^* - v_t^\mu - v_t^k \qquad (7.17)$$

where Δ is the first-difference expectations operator, i.e. $\Delta e_{t+1} = E_t(e_{t+1} - e_t)$. Obviously, $\Delta e_t = e_t - e_{t-1}$.

From (7.16), the expected exchange rate depreciation is equal to the difference between the rate of growth of the money supply and the sum of world inflation and domestic output growth. From the goods arbitrage condition, the expected rate of domestic inflation is equal to the difference between the rate of growth of the money supply and productivity. Thus, to the extent that the authorities wish to aim for price stability, they ought to equate x to the real rate of growth g.[7]

From (7.17), unanticipated depreciations of the exchange rate are only functions of shocks to world inflation and interest rates, and domestic productivity and money demand.

Substituting (7.15) in the goods arbitrage condition (7.12) and taking first differences, and in the "Phillips curve" (7.8), we get the following expressions for domestic inflation and unemployment under fixed money growth targets:

$$\Delta p_t = x - g + \alpha\Delta i_t^* - v_t^\mu - v_t^k \qquad (7.18)$$

$$u_t = \tilde{u} - \frac{1}{1 - \beta}(\alpha\Delta i_t^* - v_t^k) \qquad (7.19)$$

Under fixed monetary targets, domestic inflation deviates from average inflation $x - g$ only to the extent that there are foreign interest rate shocks and domestic productivity and money demand shocks. On the other hand, the only permanent shocks that cause deviations of unemployment from its natural rate are shocks to world nominal interest rates and domestic money demand. Domestic productivity shocks do not affect unemployment because they are fully reflected in the nominal exchange rate and prices.

The reason for the latter result is the assumption that productivity shocks are permanent. If productivity shocks were temporary they would affect unemployment as they would not be fully reflected in the nominal exchange rate and prices owing to the fact that a reversal of the shock would be expected in the future. This is the reason why Bean (1983) and Alogoskoufis (1989a) found that productivity shocks affect deviations of unemployment from its natural rate in models with transitory shocks.

For example, if we were to assume that productivity shocks are temporary, the closed-form solution for the exchange rate is independent of them. It takes the form

$$e_t = \frac{\alpha}{1+\alpha}(x - \pi^*) + (m_t - p_t^* - \beta\tilde{n} + \alpha i_t^* - k_t) \qquad (7.15')$$

The reason is that temporary productivity shocks do not affect permanent output and therefore money demand.

The solutions for inflation and unemployment take the form

$$\Delta p_t = x + \alpha\Delta i_t^* - v_t^k \qquad (7.18')$$

$$u_t = \tilde{u} - \frac{1}{1-\beta}(\alpha\Delta i_t^* - v_t^\mu - v_t^k) \qquad (7.19')$$

Temporary productivity shocks have no effect on the nominal exchange rate and prices and thus cause temporary changes in unemployment.[8]

3.2   A fixed nominal exchange rate

In the case of fixed nominal exchange rates, from the uncovered interest parity condition, domestic interest rates are the same as in the rest of the world. The money supply becomes endogenous and is given by

$$m_t = \bar{e} + p_t^* - \alpha i_t^* + \beta\tilde{n} + \mu_t + k_t \qquad (7.20)$$

The rate of change of the money supply is

$$\Delta m_t = \Delta p_t^* + \alpha\Delta i_t^* + g + v_t^\mu + v_t^k \qquad (7.21)$$

The rate of change of the money supply is determined by foreign inflation and changes in foreign interest rates, the average rate of growth of domestic productivity, and domestic productivity and money demand shocks.

What shocks affect inflation and unemployment under fixed exchange rates? From the goods arbitrage condition (7.12), and the

"Phillips curve" (7.8), inflation and unemployment under fixed exchange rates are given by

$$\Delta p_t = \Delta p_t^* \qquad (7.22)$$

$$u_t = \tilde{u} - \frac{1}{1-\beta}(\Delta p_t^* - \pi^* + v_t^\mu) \qquad (7.23)$$

Under fixed exchange rates, domestic inflation is equal to foreign inflation, and deviations of unemployment from its natural rate are only affected by foreign price shocks and domestic real shocks.

3.3   Monetary versus exchange rate targets

We see from the preceding analysis that neither fixed monetary nor fixed exchange rate targets completely insulate unemployment from all types of shocks.

Under domestic money supply targets, nominal shocks such as changes in world nominal interest rates and domestic monetary shocks cause fluctuations in unemployment. Permanent real shocks do not cause fluctuations in unemployment if they are recognized to be such, but temporary real shocks do. On the other hand, in principle at least, domestic monetary targets allow the domestic economy to choose its own average inflation rate by choosing the average rate of growth of the money supply.

Under fixed exchange rates, inflation is determined by foreign inflation only. Unemployment deviates from its natural rate in response to foreign inflation shocks and domestic real shocks. Although fixed exchange rates insulate the domestic economy from domestic nominal shocks, they do not insulate it from foreign price shocks and domestic real shocks.

How are we to choose then between fixed and flexible exchange rates? The comparison between open-loop monetary targets and fixed exchange rates is only a first step in this direction. Typically the monetary authorities are concerned with both inflation and unemployment. They would find it very hard to stick to open-loop policies of the type that we have examined in this section, because when they observe a shock that would tend to affect unemployment they would be tempted to change interest rates, and thus exchange rates, in order to strike a balance between changes in unemployment and inflation. Thus, monetary and exchange rate activism rather than fixed monetary targets has been the main characteristic of flexible exchange rate regimes because of such incentives. Is monetary and exchange rate management superior to open-loop rules such as those we have just examined? If yes, what are the characteristics of optimal exchange rate management? If not, which of the two types of fixed targets is preferable? These are the questions that will occupy us in the remainder of this survey.

4 Optimal exchange rate management

I now turn to monetary and exchange rate management in response to disturbances that were unanticipated at the time that wages were set. Because of the close interdependence between monetary and exchange rate policy in this class of monetary models, I shall only consider exchange rate management. Obviously this exchange rate management takes place through unsterilized exchange market interventions. To investigate the implications of particular exchange rate policies for exchange market intervention, we have to substitute the rule for the exchange at the left-hand side of equation (7.14) and solve for the path of the money supply that would be consistent with this exchange rate rule. Alternatively, we could utilize the uncovered interest parity condition only and solve for the path of exchange rate differentials implied by a particular rule. By and large I shall avoid these manipulations when I can, as they are tedious and offer few insights. Thus, for the most part, I shall be treating the exchange rate as a directly controllable policy instrument.[9]

To investigate optimal exchange rate management on the part of the authorities one must parameterize their preferences between inflation and unemployment. In accordance with much of the literature, I shall assume a quadratic loss function that penalizes both inflation and unemployment. This will take the form

$$\Lambda_t = \frac{1}{2}(\Delta p_t)^2 + \frac{\theta}{2}u_t^2 \qquad (7.24)$$

where θ measures the weight of unemployment relative to inflation in the preferences of the authorities.

The exchange rate management regime that we shall investigate differs from the open-loop policies that we investigated in the previous section in that the authorities can respond to shocks that were unanticipated by wage-setters when wages were set. Thus, the set-up is as follows. Wages are set at the beginning of period t, based on information available up to the end of period $t-1$. Then the shocks are realized and the authorities observe them and set the exchange rate to minimize the loss function (7.24). As will become obvious later, the nature of these interactions differs dramatically according to whether the "natural" rate of unemployment is viewed by the authorities as efficient or inefficiently high.

4.1   Optimal exchange rate management with an efficient "natural" rate

We shall start by assuming that the "natural" rate of unemployment is efficient. In the context of the model of section 2, this can be represented by the assumption that $\tilde{n}$, the target employment level of wage-setters, is equal to n, the effective labor force. In such a case the authorities have no incentive to try and reduce unemployment below its equilibrium rate. As there is no conflict between the unemployment targets of wage-setters and the monetary authorities, the policy game can be seen as a cooperative one in which the exchange rate is adjusted to minimize deviations of the unemployment rate from what wage-setters were aiming at, in response to unanticipated disturbances. The authorities are of course prevented from fully eliminating such deviations in the unemployment rate because of their additional concern with inflation.

Assuming that $\tilde{n} = n$, i.e. $\tilde{u} = 0$, and after substituting the "Phillips curve" (7.8) and the goods arbitrage condition (7.12) in the objective of the authorities (7.24), we get

$$\frac{1}{2}(\Delta e_t + \Delta p_t^*)^2 + \frac{\theta}{2(1-\beta)^2}(\Delta e_t - E_{t-1}\Delta e_t + \Delta p_t^* - E_{t-1}\Delta p_t^* + v_t^\mu)^2 \quad (7.25)$$

From the first-order conditions for a minimum of (7.25)

$$\Delta e_t = -\Delta p_t^* - \frac{\theta}{(1-\beta)^2}(\Delta e_t - E_{t-1}\Delta e_t + \Delta p_t^* - E_{t-1}\Delta p_t^* + v_t^\mu) \quad (7.26)$$

Taking expectations of (7.14), conditional on information available at the end of period $t-1$, we end up with

$$E_{t-1}\Delta e_t = -E_{t-1}\Delta p_t^* = -\pi^* \quad (7.27)$$

or

$$E_{t-1}\Delta p_t = 0 \quad (7.28)$$

The equilibrium expectations of domestic inflation are equal to zero, and the domestic exchange rate is expected to keep appreciating to counteract foreign inflation. Since wage-setting ensures that unemployment is expected to be at its efficient "natural" rate, the authorities are not expected to have any incentives to try and affect unemployment. They are expected to concentrate on the inflation objective and eliminate domestic inflation.

Substituting (7.27) in (7.26), the actual changes in the exchange rate are given by

$$\Delta e_t = -\Delta p_t^* - \phi v_t^\mu \quad (7.29)$$

where $\phi = \theta/[\theta + (1-\beta)^2] < 1$.

Exchange rate depreciations deviate from what was expected only in response to foreign inflation shocks and domestic real shocks. Foreign inflation shocks are fully counteracted because they affect unemployment and inflation through exactly the same channels as the exchange rate. Real shocks, however, are only partly counteracted because they have no direct impact on inflation and because of the authorities' concern with both unemployment and inflation.

From (7.15), the relation between changes in the exchange rate and the rate of growth of the domestic money supply is given by

$$\Delta m_t = \Delta e_t + \Delta p_t^* + \Delta \mu_t - \alpha \Delta i_t^* + \Delta k_t \tag{7.30}$$

From the optimal exchange rate policy

$$E_{t-1}\Delta m_t = x = g \tag{7.31}$$

$$\Delta m_t = g - \alpha \Delta i_t^* + (1 - \phi)v_t^\mu + v_t^k \tag{7.32}$$

The optimal exchange rate policy implies that on average the rate of growth of the money supply must be equal to the rate of growth of productivity. However, it should fully accommodate shocks to money demand and partly accommodate real shocks.

Equilibrium inflation and unemployment under the optimal policy are given by

$$\Delta p_t = -\phi v_t^\mu \tag{7.33}$$

$$u_t = -\psi v_t^\mu \tag{7.34}$$

where $\psi = (1 - \beta)/[\theta + (1 - \beta)^2]$.

In the presence of real shocks, the authorities cannot completely eliminate fluctuations in both unemployment and inflation. In fact, the optimal response is to allow the shocks to partly affect both unemployment and inflation, the weights depending on the relative concern of the authorities for these two targets. Note that in the extreme case where the authorities are not concerned with unemployment ($\theta = 0$), real shocks are not reflected in inflation at all ($\phi = 0$). In the other extreme where the authorities are not concerned with inflation (as $\theta \to \infty$), then real shocks are only reflected in inflation and do not affect unemployment. In general, however, both inflation and unemployment will be affected by real shocks under optimal exchange rate management. The expected per-period loss of the authorities is given by

$$E_{t-1}\Lambda_t = \frac{\phi}{2}\sigma_\mu^2 \tag{7.35}$$

This is positive, reflecting the fact that the authorities have only one instrument and two targets, and the best they can do is partly to attain each target.

In conclusion, in the idealized case where the equilibrium unemployment rate is efficient, exchange rate management dominates fixed exchange rates or fixed money supply targets. The average inflation rate is zero, the average deviations of unemployment from its "natural" rate are zero, and fluctuations in inflation and unemployment only reflect unanticipated real shocks.

4.2   Optimal exchange market intervention under uncertainty

The optimal policy analyzed in section 4.1 has demanding informational requirements. In particular, it requires the authorities to observe real shocks fully. In practice, however, the authorities may have little direct information on real and nominal shocks. What the authorities usually observe is not shocks themselves but market prices and, with a longer lag and less accurately, quantities. Thus, a large part of the literature on optimal exchange rate management has concentrated on the case where the authorities rely on the information embodied in market prices, and in particular financial market prices.

Under imperfect information, the interchangeability between the exchange rate and the money supply as policy instruments breaks down. This is because using the exchange rate as a policy instrument destroys its role as a signal of nominal and real shocks. As a result, a large part of the literature has explicitly examined exchange market intervention under uncertainty, concentrating on rules of the form[10]

$$\Delta m_t = \lambda_0 + \lambda_1 \Delta e_t + \lambda_2 \Delta p_t^* + \lambda_3 \Delta i_t^* \tag{7.36}$$

Equation (7.36) is a contingent, or closed-loop, policy rule that allows the money supply to react to all the independent price signals available to the authorities. The parameter λ_1 is interpreted as the coefficient of exchange market intervention.

Substituting (7.36) in the equation describing the equilibrium relation between the money supply and the exchange rate (equation (7.30)) we get that

$$\Delta e_t = -\frac{1 - \lambda_2}{1 - \lambda_1} \Delta p_t^* + \frac{\alpha + \lambda_3}{1 - \lambda_1} \Delta i_t^* + \frac{1}{1 - \lambda_1} (\lambda_0 - \Delta \mu_t - \Delta k_t) \tag{7.37}$$

We see from (7.37) that an observation of the exchange rate, in conjunction with foreign prices and interest rates, yields an observation of the sum of nominal and real shocks. Then, from optimal signal extraction, the rational expectation of the real and nominal shocks is given by

$$E_t v_t^\mu = \omega(\Delta\mu_t + \Delta k_t - g) \qquad \omega = \frac{\sigma_\mu^2}{\sigma_\mu^2 + \sigma_k^2} < 1 \qquad (7.38a)$$

$$E_t v_t^k = (1 - \omega)(\Delta\mu_t + \Delta k_t - g) \qquad (7.38b)$$

where from (7.37) we have that

$$\Delta\mu_t + \Delta k_t - g = -g - (1 - \lambda_1)\Delta e_t - (1 - \lambda_2)\Delta p_t^* + (\alpha + \lambda_3)\Delta i_t^* \qquad (7.39)$$

We can use (7.30) to substitute out the exchange rate in terms of the money supply and foreign and domestic shocks in the loss function of the authorities. By minimizing with respect to the money supply, after utilizing (7.38a), (7.38b), and (7.39), and comparing coefficients with (7.36), we have that

$$\lambda_1 = 1 - \frac{1}{\omega\phi} < 0 \qquad (7.40a)$$

$$\lambda_2 = \lambda_1 \qquad (7.40b)$$

$$\lambda_3 = -\alpha \qquad (7.40c)$$

$$\lambda_0 = g \qquad (7.40d)$$

Optimal exchange market intervention involves leaning against the wind, i.e. a monetary tightening in the light of exchange rate depreciations and vice versa. The reason is that an exchange rate depreciation signifies a negative productivity and output shock, which necessitates some contraction in the money supply in order to equilibrate the money market without a very high rise in inflation. An appreciation, on the other hand, partly signifies a positive supply shock which calls for some monetary relaxation.

To understand the optimal exchange market policy, substitute (7.40a)–(7.40d) in the exchange rate equation (7.37). Then we get

$$\Delta e_t = -\Delta p_t^* - \phi\omega(v_t^\mu + v_t^k) \qquad (7.41)$$

It is easy to see by comparing (7.41) and (7.29) that the optimal exchange policy differs from the case of perfect information only in that it allows the exchange rate partly to react to nominal shocks as well as real shocks. This is because the authorities do not observe nominal and real shocks separately, but only their sum. The expression that post-multiplies ϕ in (7.41) is the rational expectation of the real shock, given that only the sum of the two shocks is observed. Thus, since $0 < \omega < 1$, the exchange rate over-reacts to nominal shocks and under-reacts to real shocks, compared with the full information case.

The expected (average) welfare loss of the authorities is obviously higher under imperfect than under full information.

208   GEORGE ALOGOSKOUFIS

4.3   Optimal exchange rate management with an inefficient "natural" rate

One of the most unsatisfactory features of the models of the previous two sections is the assumption that the "natural" rate of unemployment is efficient. There is a widespread belief, even in economies with relatively low unemployment rates, that unemployment represents a market failure and is typically undesirably high.

In addition, the optimal policies examined in the previous two sections suggest that the equilibrium inflation rate when the authorities have monetary autonomy is equal to zero. There is no drift in prices in the equilibria we analyzed as the mean inflation rate is zero. Inflation deviates from zero only in response to white-noise real shocks, and therefore is itself a white-noise process. However, what we seem to observe is that periods of exchange rate management are associated with quite high and persistent inflation, even among the OECD industrial economies (see for example Alogoskoufis and Smith, 1991; Alogoskoufis, 1992).

It turns out from the seminal work of Kydland and Prescott (1977) and Barro and Gordon (1983a, b) that the two problems above are interrelated. If one allows the equilibrium unemployment rate to be inefficiently high, then the equilibrium inflation rate ceases to be equal to zero and in fact becomes positive and proportional to the "natural" rate of unemployment. Exchange rate management may no longer be the best monetary regime because of the time inconsistency of optimal exchange rate policy.[11]

To highlight these ideas, which have come to dominate current thinking about exchange rate regimes, assume that the target employment level of wage-setters is lower than the effective labor force ($\tilde{n} < n$). Then the equilibrium unemployment rate $\tilde{u}$ is positive, and the authorities have incentives systematically to depreciate the exchange rate and create unanticipated inflation in order to reduce unemployment below its inefficiently high "natural" rate.

The loss function of the authorities takes the form

$$\frac{1}{2}(\Delta e_t + \Delta p_t^*)^2 + \frac{\theta}{2}\left[\tilde{u} - \frac{1}{1-\beta}(\Delta e_t - E_{t-1}\Delta e_t + \Delta p_t^* - E_{t-1}\Delta p_t^* + v_t^\mu)\right]^2$$

(7.42)

From the first-order conditions for a minimum of (7.42),

$$\Delta e_t = -\Delta p_t^* + \frac{\theta}{1-\beta}\tilde{u} - \frac{\theta}{(1-\beta)^2}(\Delta e_t - E_{t-1}\Delta e_t + \Delta p_t^* - E_{t-1}\Delta p_t^* + v_t^\mu)$$

(7.43)

From (7.43),

$$E_{t-1}\Delta e_t = -\pi^* + \frac{\theta}{1-\beta}\tilde{u} \qquad (7.44)$$

$$E_{t-1}\Delta p_t = \frac{\theta}{1-\beta}\tilde{u} \qquad (7.45)$$

$$E_{t-1}u_t = \tilde{u} \qquad (7.46)$$

One can see that, when the "natural" rate of unemployment is inefficiently high, expected and therefore equilibrium inflation is positive and proportional to the equilibrium unemployment rate. The factor of proportionality is the product of the relative aversion of the authorities to unemployment and the elasticity of labor demand. If expectations of inflation by wage-setters were lower that what is implied by (7.45), the authorities would have an incentive to create surprise inflation even in the absence of any shocks. Thus, expectations would not turn out to be rational. Inflationary expectations rise to the point where there are no further incentives for the authorities to create surprise inflation in the absence of shocks. This is the well-known "inflationary bias" of discretionary policy analyzed by Barro and Gordon (1983a, b).

Although the authorities have *ex ante* incentives to promise to wage-setters that they are not going to produce surprise exchange rate depreciations to reduce unemployment below its "natural" rate, if wage-setters believe them the authorities will have *ex post* incentives to devalue. Optimal policy is time inconsistent (Kydland and Prescott, 1977). A Nash equilibrium involves expectations of inflation on the part of wage-setters that make the best response of the authorities equal to the expected inflation rate. The source of the problem is the inability of the authorities to pre-commit not to use unanticipated depreciations in a regime of managed floating.[12]

What about actual inflation and unemployment? They both deviate from what was expected only as a result of real shocks. From the first-order condition (7.43) and (7.44), the equilibrium rate of exchange rate depreciations is equal to

$$\Delta e_t = -\Delta p_t^* + \frac{\theta}{1-\beta}\tilde{u} - \phi v_t^\mu \qquad (7.47)$$

Exchange rate depreciations deviate from what was expected in response to world inflationary shocks and domestic real shocks.

Equilibrium inflation and unemployment are given by

$$\Delta p_t = \frac{\theta}{1-\beta}\tilde{u} - \phi v_t^\mu \qquad (7.48)$$

$$u_t = \tilde{u} - \psi v_t^\mu \qquad (7.49)$$

Optimal exchange rate management in response to unanticipated shocks results in the same type of reaction of unanticipated inflation as with an efficient "natural" rate, and deviations of unemployment from the "natural" rate also take the same form.

The per-period expected welfare losses of the authorities under exchange rate management are given by

$$E_{t-1}\Lambda_t^{M} = \frac{1}{2}\left[\frac{\theta}{1-\beta}\frac{1}{\psi}\tilde{u}^2 + \phi\sigma_\mu^2\right] \qquad (7.50)$$

where superscript M denotes optimal exchange rate management.

The inefficiently high "natural" rate of unemployment imposes two types of costs on the authorities. First it imposes unemployment costs, because the authorities cannot systematically reduce unemployment below the "natural" rate. Second it imposes inflation costs, as it affects inflationary expectations and therefore average inflation. Given that the authorities cannot systematically reduce unemployment, they would prefer a regime that guaranteed zero average inflation. The per-period expected welfare losses under such a hypothetical regime, in which the authorities behave as if the "natural" rate was efficient, are given by

$$E_{t-1}\Lambda_t^{P} = \frac{1}{2}[\theta\tilde{u}^2 + \phi\sigma_\mu^2] \qquad (7.51)$$

where superscript P denotes the hypothetical pre-commitment regime in which the authorities do not try to reduce unemployment systematically below the "natural" rate.

The welfare losses are obviously higher in the discretionary regime of exchange rate management as

$$E_{t-1}(\Lambda_t^{M} - \Lambda_t^{P}) = \frac{1}{2}\frac{\theta^2}{(1-\beta)^2}\tilde{u}^2 > 0 \qquad (7.52)$$

The authorities would clearly like to find ways to pre-commit to lower inflation, as this could reduce their welfare losses.[13]

4.4   Fixed versus managed exchange rates

One possible way to pre-commit to low inflation is to enter a low inflation international fixed exchange rate regime. After credible entry into a fixed exchange rate regime, expected and actual depreciations are zero and domestic inflation is equal to foreign inflation. Assume for simplicity that $\theta^* = 0$, in which case $\Delta p_t^* = 0$. Then domestic inflation is also equal to zero. The per-period welfare loss of the authorities when they have pre-committed to a zero-inflation fixed exchange rate regime is equal to

$$E_{t-1}\Lambda_t^F = \frac{\theta}{2}\left[\tilde{u}^2 + \frac{1}{(1-\beta)^2}\,\sigma_\mu^2\right] \qquad (7.53)$$

Exchange rate management does not necessarily dominate fixed exchange rates when the authorities have a credibility problem such as the one we analyzed. The authorities lose the option of reacting optimally to domestic real shocks but solve their credibility problem *vis-à-vis* their private sector, and thus reduce their average inflation rate. Which of the two forces dominates depends on the relative strength of the two distortions, namely the inefficiency of the high "natural" rate of unemployment which produces the high inflation problem and the inefficiency arising from pre-set nominal contracts that cannot take account of real shocks.

Subtracting (7.53) from (7.50), the per-period difference in welfare losses between a regime of discretionary exchange rate management and a regime of fixed exchange rates is given by

$$E_{t-1}(\Lambda_t^M - \Lambda_t^F) = \frac{\theta}{2}\left[\phi\tilde{u}^2 - \frac{\phi}{(1-\beta)^2}\,\sigma_\mu^2\right] \qquad (7.54)$$

A zero-inflation fixed exchange rate regime would dominate exchange rate management if

$$\tilde{u} > \frac{\sigma_\mu}{1-\beta} \qquad (7.55)$$

To give a numerical example, with β being about 0.7 and a standard deviation in productivity growth of the order of 0.02 (which is not atypical), the inefficiency in the "natural" rate of unemployment must exceed 6.6 percentage points to make joining a fixed exchange rate regime worthwhile. If the standard deviation of productivity growth is 0.01, then joining a fixed exchange rate regime would be worthwhile even with an inefficiency in the "natural" rate of unemployment slightly above 3.3 percentage points.

Of course if foreign inflation is not equal to zero but say $\pi^* > 0$, (7.55) becomes

$$\tilde{u} > \left(\frac{\sigma_\mu^2}{(1-\beta)^2} + \frac{\pi^{*2}}{\theta\phi}\right)^{1/2} \qquad (7.55')$$

Equation (7.55') requires higher inefficiencies in the "natural" rate of unemployment than (7.55) does to make fixed exchange rate regimes dominate optimal exchange rate management.

In conclusion, the issue of whether exchange rate management dominates fixed exchange rate regimes from the point of view of a single open economy is empirical. It depends on the variability of real shocks *vis-à-vis* the inefficiency in the equilibrium rate of unemployment. It also depends on the extent to which there are alternative ways of pre-committing to low inflation via domestic institutional solutions such as independent anti-inflationary central banks and reputational mechanism (see Rogoff, 1985, 1987; Canzoneri and Henderson, 1988; among others).

4.5   Credibility and regime changes

I finally turn to the problem of the transition from a regime of managed exchange rates to a fixed exchange rate regime. I shall abstract from unanticipated disturbances to concentrate on the uncertainty on the part of wage-setters about the true intentions of the authorities when they announce a change in regime.[14]

Assume that an economy has operated under managed exchange rates and high inflation for some time. At time t_0 the authorities announce that from next period they will enter a fixed exchange rate regime. Assume for simplicity that inflation of the other countries participating in the regime is zero. The question that arises is whether domestic inflation will fall immediately to zero without any transitional unemployment costs or whether the transition will be gradual and will involve an additional unemployment cost. A related question is whether in such a case it is still worthwhile to enter a fixed exchange rate regime.

To investigate this question we shall assume that the authorities are not fully credible when they make their initial announcement. We define as ω_0 the wage-setters' prior probability (or belief) that the authorities will carry out the change in regime announced at t_0. Thus, ω_0 is a measure of the initial *credibility* of the authorities, which will be assumed exogenous.

The credibility of the authorities will not remain constant. It will be revised in the next period as the wage-setters observe whether there has been an exchange rate depreciation or not. The revised credibility will be the posterior probability defined as

$$\omega_1 = 0 \tag{7.56a}$$

if the nominal exchange rate was devalued at t_{0+1} and

$$\omega_1 = \frac{\omega_0}{\omega_0 + (1 - \omega_0)\kappa} \tag{7.56b}$$

if the nominal exchange rate remained constant at t_{0+1}. κ is the probability that the authorities did not devalue the exchange rate, although there has not been a permanent change in regime. We shall in fact assume for simplicity that if the regime did not change the authorities cannot resist the temptation not to devalue. Therefore $\kappa = 0$. Thus, if the nominal exchange rate remains constant at t_{0+1}, the change in regime becomes fully credible ($\omega_1 = 1$).

We shall examine what happens to inflation and unemployment in periods t_0, t_{0+1}, t_{0+2}, and beyond.

At time t_0 there is still exchange rate management, and wages have been set on the basis of expectations based on such a regime. Therefore unemployment is at $\tilde{u}$ and inflation is equal to $\theta\tilde{u}/(1-\beta)$. The welfare loss of the authorities is given by (7.50), with $\sigma_\mu^2 = 0$, as we have assumed.

At time t_{0+1}, after the announcement of a change in regime, wage and domestic price inflation is going to be determined by

$$\Delta w_{t_{0+1}} = \Delta p_{t_{0+1}} = E_{t_0}\Delta e_{t_{0+1}} = (1-\omega_0)\Delta e_{t_{0+1}}^C \tag{7.57}$$

where superscript C denotes the expected exchange rate depreciation when the political authorities "cheat" and do not carry out the change in regime, engaging instead in exchange rate management.

If the change in regime is implemented, the exchange rate will remain constant. If it is not, the optimal rate of depreciation for the authorities will be given by (7.43). By substituting (7.57) in (7.43), assuming no unanticipated shocks, after some rearrangement we find that

$$\Delta e_{t_{0+1}}^C = \frac{\theta(1-\beta)\tilde{u}}{(1-\beta)^2 + \omega_0\theta} > 0 \tag{7.58}$$

From (7.58) and (7.57) it is obvious that expectations will not coincide with actual policy in the period after the announcement. Thus, if the authorities carry out the change in regime, expectations about the rate of depreciation of the exchange rate, and therefore inflation, will turn out to have been too high. Real wages and unemployment will rise above their equilibrium rate. On the other hand, if the authorities "cheat" and do not carry out the change in regime, depreciation and inflation expectations will turn out to have been too low, i.e. $(1-\omega_0)\Delta e_{t_{0+1}}^C$, and the unemployment rate will fall below equilibrium.

At the end of period t_{0+1} (and beyond), wage-setters will know what has happened. If the exchange rate has remained constant, the new regime will have obtained full credibility ($\omega_1 = 1$), future expectations of depreciation and inflation will be zero, and the unemployment rate will fall back to equilibrium. If the exchange rate has depreciated as in (7.58), the change in regime will have zero credibility ($\omega_1 = 0$) and inflation expectations will return to $\theta\tilde{u}/(1-\beta)$. The unemployment rate will rise back to equilibrium. Thus, when the authorities do not have full credibility, a change from a managed to a fixed exchange rate regime is going to be accompanied by a gradual fall in wage inflation and a temporary rise in unemployment. If the credibility of the initial announcement is full, i.e. $\omega_0 = 1$, expectations of inflation converge immediately to zero and unemployment does not rise above its equilibrium rate. Obviously, the higher the initial credibility of the authorities, the lower the wage inflation and unemployment rates in the transitional period.

The loss of the authorities in the transitional period is given by

$$\Lambda_1 = \frac{\theta}{2}\, u_1^2 \qquad (7.59)$$

Clearly,

$$\frac{\partial \Lambda_1}{\partial \omega_0} < 0 \qquad (7.60)$$

Thus, the higher the initial credibility of the authorities, the lower the cost of the transition to a fixed exchange rate regime.

In the second period the new regime obtains full credibility. Inflation falls to zero (world inflation) and unemployment returns to equilibrium.

What will determine whether the authorities will engage in a change in regime, from managed to fixed exchange rates? Clearly, they will have to weigh the costs of transition against the future benefits from low inflation.

Let us assume that the authorities have announced in period t_0 that they will enter a regime of fixed exchange rates. If this announcement is partly credible, it will affect the expectations of wage-setters and inflation. If they carry out the change in regime they will suffer a transitional loss, but the new regime will then result in zero inflation, rendering welfare gains equal to $\frac{1}{2}[\theta\tilde{u}/(1-\beta)]^2$ (with $\pi^* = 0$) in all subsequent periods. On the other hand, if they "cheat" and do not fix the nominal exchange rate, they will achieve a welfare gain in period t_{0+1} equal to

$$\Lambda_1 - \Lambda_C > 0$$

where Λ_C refers to the welfare loss for the authorities if they "cheat" and engage in exchange rate management as in (7.58) instead of keeping the exchange rate fixed.

The present value of the welfare losses for the authorities if they cheat is going to be equal to

$$\frac{1+\rho}{\rho}(\Lambda^M - \Lambda^F) > 0$$

where ρ is the rate of time preference of the authorities. The authorities will cheat if and only if

$$\Lambda_1 - \Lambda_C > \frac{1+\rho}{\rho}(\Lambda^M - \Lambda^F) \qquad (7.61)$$

Clearly, the higher the pure rate of time preference, the higher the probability that the authorities will cheat. If the pure rate of time preference is zero, the authorities will never cheat. The effects of the initial credibility on this inequality are ambiguous, as higher credibility reduces both the welfare loss Λ_1 and the welfare loss Λ_C.

One final question that needs to be addressed with regard to credibility and reputation is whether there is a need for institutional reform. For example, is it necessary to enter formally in an international fixed exchange rate regime? Why not announce unilaterally that the nominal exchange rate will remain fixed and keep it fixed, without engaging in additional "institution-building." One of the main arguments in favor of building new institutions or entering into international agreements is that this may increase the credibility of the initial announcement and therefore reduce the initial costs of transition to low inflation.

5 Exchange rate regimes in interdependent economies

We have now completed our examination of the issues relevant for the choice of exchange rate regime for a single open economy. In this section we provide a short discussion of the implications of the analysis for the choice of exchange rate regimes in interdependent economies.

The extra complication that arises once one starts thinking about interdependent economies is the so-called $N-1$ problem. A bilateral exchange rate is the relative price of two currencies, so that there are two countries taking an interest in the determination of this relative price. Under what conditions would it be optimal for *both* countries to opt for a fixed exchange rate rather than engage in non-cooperative monetary policies?

In the case where the two economies are exactly symmetric, it can be shown that a fixed exchange rate regime is optimal (Alogoskoufis (1989b) provides an example). Since fixed exchange rates insulate each economy from all shocks apart from foreign inflation and domestic productivity shocks, when the productivity shocks are common the optimal response of monetary policy will be the same for both economies. Thus, there will be no incentive for any of them to engage in exchange rate management as optimal responses of inflation to real shocks are the same for both economies. In addition, none of them is subjected to unwarranted foreign price shocks.

This result can be confirmed by looking at the optimal inflation rate given by (7.48). In a two-country world, equilibrium inflation with optimal discretionary monetary policy would imply that

$$\Delta p_t = \frac{\theta}{1-\beta} \tilde{u} - \phi v_t^\mu \tag{7.62a}$$

$$\Delta p_t^* = \frac{\theta}{1-\beta} \tilde{u}^* - \phi v_t^{\mu\cdot} \tag{7.62b}$$

$$\Delta p_t = \Delta e_t + \Delta p_t^* \tag{7.62c}$$

The unstarred variables denote the domestic economy, and the starred variables the foreign economy.

Substituting (7.62a) and (7.62b) in (7.62c) we see that in equilibrium

$$\Delta e_t = \frac{\theta}{1-\beta}(\tilde{u} - \tilde{u}^*) - \phi(v_t^\mu - v_t^{\mu\cdot}) \tag{7.63}$$

In a symmetric world where the "natural" rate of unemployment and the productivity shocks are the same for both economies, fixed exchange rates constitute the optimal monetary regime.

In the case where there are asymmetries, however, this result does not follow. Canzoneri and Henderson (1988, 1991), Alogoskoufis (1989b), Giavazzi and Giovannini (1989b), and others have investigated asymmetries in the type of shocks faced by each economy and other structural characteristics such as the natural rate of unemployment, preferences between inflation and unemployment, and economic size. If the only asymmetry is different productivity shocks, exchange rate management becomes the optimal regime (Alogoskoufis, 1989b). After all this is a key implication of the "optimum currency area" literature of the 1960s (Mundell, 1961). Once you introduce additional asymmetries, however, it is no longer the case that managed exchange rates necessarily dominate.

Consider for example the case where the relative shock $v_t^\mu - v_t^{\mu\cdot}$ has a zero mean and variance τ^2, and $\tilde{u} - \tilde{u}^* = \tilde{u} > 0$. In this case the authorities of the domestic economy, which has a more inefficient labor market, may find it optimal to forgo responding appropriately to unanticipated productivity shocks, and peg their currency to the currency of the foreign economy. In this way, they ensure a lower equilibrium inflation rate, a benefit that may outweigh the cost of a higher variability in unemployment. The foreign economy, on the other hand, determines its monetary policy optimally. It is not affected by the fixed exchange rate as it chooses its own monetary policy optimally. In such a case, fixed exchange rates are preferred by one of the two economies, while the other is indifferent.

Additional or different asymmetries may change the ranking of fixed versus flexible exchange rates.

It is widely recognized now that fixed exchange rate regimes have operated asymmetrically (see Eichengreen, 1987, 1989; Giovannini, 1986, 1989; Giavazzi and Giovannini, 1989a, b; and others). This was either by design, as in the case of the Bretton Woods system of fixed but adjustable exchange rates, or by default, as in the case of the international gold standard and the EMS.

In the case of the international gold standard the asymmetry stemmed from the special role of sterling as an international reserve currency, which in turn depended on the role of Britain in international trade and the City of London in the international financial system (see Eichengreen (1985, 1987) as well as the classic treatments of Brown (1940) and Bloomfield (1959)). Similarly under Bretton Woods the same role was performed by the US dollar. The role of the dollar was made official by the arrangement whereby the USA undertook to stabilize the price of gold in dollars, while the other central banks undertook to stabilize the exchange rate of their currency to the US dollar. The asymmetry arises in these two regimes from the fact that one of the countries has a free hand in determining its monetary policy while the others are concerned about their international reserves (see Eichengreen (1987), Giavazzi and Giovannini (1989b) and Giovannini (1989) who employ a model in which central banks are not concerned about inflation and unemployment but about nominal interest rates and international reserves).

It is only in the EMS, however, that the type of model that is utilized in this chapter can be seen as an explanation of the leading role of West Germany and the Bundesbank (Giavazzi and Giovannini, 1987, 1989a; Giavazzi and Pagano, 1988). The asymmetry of the EMS is not so much the special role of the deutschemark in the international monetary system, but the anti-inflationary credibility of the Bundesbank. By pegging to the deutschemark the other EC countries import this anti-inflationary credibility and sacrifice the flexibility of reacting optimally to real shocks.

6   Conclusions

The results in this chapter suggest that international monetary and exchange rate regimes have important implications for the level and variability of inflation. Although the equilibrium rate of unemployment does not depend on the monetary and exchange rate regime, its variability around equilibrium does.[15]

The choice between fixed and flexible exchange rates depends on two sets of factors. The first set is the domestic incentives to create unanticipated inflation, such as an inefficiently high "natural" rate of unemployment or high public debt. To the extent that there are insufficient domestic institutional mechanisms to pre-commit the monetary authorities to low inflation, fixed exchange rate regimes offer a way to affect expectations of wage-setters and keep inflation down. The second set of factors has to do with the variability of idiosyncratic real shocks that call for differences in monetary policy across countries, in order to keep the variability of unemployment rates low. This set of factors calls for domestic monetary autonomy, and therefore managed exchange rates. From the point of view of a single open economy the choice involves balancing these two sets of factors. It will depend on the extent to which the domestic economy can find domestic ways to pre-commit to low average inflation (such as central bank independence) and the extent to which the option of joining a credibly anti-inflationary international exchange rate regime is available. From the point of view of interdependent economies, the establishment of fixed exchange rate regimes requires lengthy consultations and coordination. History suggests that this process may be more likely to succeed in the case of pronounced monetary and financial asymmetries, although in principle it is hard to see why. In a completely symmetric world, fixed exchange rates are the optimal regime, as the world needs one monetary policy. In the case where asymmetries exist, which regime dominates is an open question. The highly simplified models examined in this chapter suggest that if there are differences in either labor market inefficiencies or preferences between inflation and unemployment that cause differences in domestic equilibrium inflation rates, the high inflation country may find it optimal to follow the monetary policy of the low inflation country by fixing its exchange rate, even at the expense of higher variability in domestic unemployment due to idiosyncratic domestic real shocks. The low inflation country provides the public good of low inflation but has the option of responding optimally to its own real shocks. All successful fixed exchange rate regimes, such as the gold standard, Bretton Woods and the EMS, were built around an anti-inflationary anchor. Both the gold standard and Bretton Woods collapsed when the anti-inflationary anchor was broken and the variability of relative real shocks increased, as a result of the First World War in the first case and the Vietnam War and the Great Society program in the second. It remains to be seen whether the EMS will be further strengthened in the form of the European Monetary

Union, or whether it will collapse. It also remains to be seen whether monetary cooperation at the world level, i.e. between the USA, Europe, and Japan, will be further strengthened or whether it will collapse as the world becomes more symmetric.

Notes

The research on which this chapter is based has had the benefit of financial assistance from the CEPR International Macroeconomics and FIMIE programs, supported through Ford Foundation (no. 890-0404), Alfred P. Sloan Foundation (no. 88-4-23), and EC Commission (SPES) research grants. Financial support from the ESRC is also gratefully acknowledged.

1 Much more detail on the gold standard, the interwar period and Bretton Woods may be found in chapter 6 in this volume.

2 Marston (1985), in one of the most recent comprehensive surveys of optimal stabilization policy in open economies, examined the choice of exchange rate regimes in his last section. Since his survey, developments such as the general recognition of the important role of the time-inconsistency problem have modified, and even reversed, some of the conclusions of the earlier literature.

3 A more general model that allows for imperfect competition and persistent deviations from the law of one price is examined in Alogoskoufis (1993, ch. 6).

4 As noted before, the law of one price is used here for reasons of analytical and notational simplicity and does not bias the nature of the results. For a thorough doctrinal and empirical investigation of this parity condition see Dornbusch (1988).

5 For early influential contributions to the monetary approach see Frenkel (1976) and Dornbusch (1976). See also the surveys of Frenkel and Mussa (1985), Obstfeld and Stockman (1985), and Levich (1985).

6 Equation (7.14) is a well-known equation in the context of the monetary approach to exchange rate determination. See for example Bilson (1978).

7 g is the rate of growth of both output and productivity in this model, as the labor force is assumed constant.

8 If money demand was assumed to be a function of current rather than permanent output, these effects would still go through, as productivity shocks would have less than a proportional effect on the nominal exchange rate and prices, owing to the expectation that they would be reversed in the future. See Alogoskoufis (1989a) for an example of this.

9 There is a large literature on the optimal choice of monetary policy instrument, following Poole (1970) and Sargent and Wallace (1975). There is an equally large literature on optimal exchange rate management. This includes among others Boyer (1978), Buiter (1979), Henderson (1979), Cox (1980), Roper and Turnovsky (1980), Frenkel and Aizenman (1982), Turnovsky (1983), Aizenman and Frenkel (1985), and a number of papers in Bhandari (1985). The relation between wage indexation and the exchange rate regime is explored by among others Flood and Marion (1982), Marston

220   GEORGE ALOGOSKOUFIS

(1984), Aizenman and Frenkel (1985), and Alogoskoufis (1990). In this chapter we shall for the most part abstract from the issue of optimal wage indexation. We shall also abstract from the recent literature on currency bands (Krugman, 1988; Krugman and Miller, 1991) which is surveyed by Bertola in chapter 9.

10 Most of the literature on exchange rate management referred to above has assumed uncertainty and investigated rules of the form of (7.36). However, it is worth noting that for the most part this literature treats unemployment as the sole objective of the authorities. Thus, optimal exchange rate policy turns out to be "accommodative," by producing exaggerated changes in the exchange rate and the price level. For example, Turnovsky (1985), and this is typical, considers the minimization of the variance of output as the sole objective of the authorities. The same holds for Aizenman and Frenkel (1985) and Alogoskoufis (1989a), who consider only the minimization of the distortions due to unemployment.

11 See Giavazzi and Giovannini (1987), Giavazzi and Pagano (1988), and Horn and Persson (1988) for this point in the context of models of open economies.

12 This credibility problem of the authorities can be solved through reputational mechanisms, as the interaction between the monetary authorities and wage-setters is repeated over time (see Barro and Gordon, 1983a). It can also be solved through some domestic institutional reform that would pre-commit the domestic authorities to low inflation. A classic example is central bank independence, with a constitution that would make price stability its only objective and/or the appointment of "conservative" central bankers (Rogoff, 1985).

13 Reputational mechanisms could sustain equilibria like P. If the authorities "cheated" in one period, expectations would revert to M in subsequent periods. As a result, their one-period gain would be reduced by the present value of future losses in the form of (7.52). Thus, if the one-period gain from "cheating" fell short of the present value of future losses from reversion to the discretionary policy, an economy could end up with the pre-commitment outcome. Incurring the costs of entering a low inflation fixed exchange rate regime, the solution we shall examine below, is another way of pre-commiting to low inflation (Giavazzi and Giovannini, 1987, 1989a; Horn and Persson, 1988).

14 The example in this section is built around the more elaborate examples of Backus and Driffill (1985a, b) and Barro (1986) for a closed economy with two types of policymakers.

15 Note, however, that the investigation by Baxter and Stockman (1989) failed to identify higher variability of employment under fixed exchange rate regimes. This could be a failure of this type of model or could be due to the endogenous choice of regime. For example, it could be that fixed exchange rate regimes prevail when there is a low variability of real shocks, and managed exchange rate regimes dominate when there is a high variability. In such circumstances the variability of unemployment will differ less across regimes than the variability of real shocks.

References

Aizenman, J. and J.A. Frenkel (1985) "Optimal wage indexation, foreign exchange intervention, and monetary policy," *American Economic Review* 75, 402–23.

Alogoskoufis, G.S. (1989a) "Monetary, nominal income and exchange rate targets in a small open economy," *European Economic Review* 33, 687–705.

—— (1989b) "Stabilization policy, fixed exchange rates and target zones," in M. Miller, B. Eichengreen, and R. Portes (eds) *Blueprints for Exchange Rate Management*, London, Academic Press.

—— (1990) "Monetary policy and the informational implications of the Phillips curve," *Economica* 57, 107–17.

—— (1992) "Monetary accommodation, exchange rate regimes and inflation persistence," *Economic Journal* 102, 461–80.

—— (1993) *The Macroeconomics of Interdependence and Exchange Rate Regimes*, Oxford, Oxford University Press (forthcoming).

—— and R. Smith (1991) "The Phillips curve, the persistence of inflation and the Lucas critique: evidence from exchange rate regimes," *American Economic Review* 81, 1254–75.

Backus, D. and J. Driffill (1985a) "Rational expectations and policy credibility following a change in regime," *Review of Economic Studies* 52, 211–21.

—— and —— (1985b) "Inflation and reputation," *American Economic Review* 75, 530–8.

Barro, R.J. (1986) "Reputation in a model of monetary policy with incomplete information," *Journal of Monetary Economics* 17, 3–20.

—— and D. Gordon (1983a) "Rules, discretion and reputation in a model of monetary policy," *Journal of Monetary Economics* 12, 101–22.

—— and —— (1983b) "A positive theory of monetary policy in a natural rate model," *Journal of Political Economy* 91, 589–610.

Baxter, M. and A.C. Stockman (1989) "Business cycles and the exchange rate regime: some international evidence," *Journal of Monetary Economics* 23, 377–400.

Bean, C.R. (1983) "Targeting nominal income: an appraisal," *Economic Journal* 93, 806–19.

Bhandari, J.S. (ed.) (1985) *Exchange Rate Management under Uncertainty*, Cambridge, MA, MIT Press.

Bilson, J. (1978) "Rational expectations and the exchange rate," in J. Frenkel and H.G. Johnson (eds) *The Economics of Exchange Rates*, London, Addison-Wesley.

Bloomfield, A. (1959) *Monetary Policy under the International Gold Standard, 1880–1914*, New York, Federal Reserve Bank of New York.

Boyer, R. (1978) "Optimal foreign exchange market intervention," *Journal of Political Economy* 86, 1045–56.

Brown, W.A. (1940) *The International Gold Standard Reinterpreted, 1914–34*, New York, National Bureau of Economic Research.

Buiter, W. (1979) "Optimal foreign exchange market intervention with rational expectations," in J. Martin and A. Smith (eds) *Trade and Payments Adjustment under Flexible Exchange Rates*, London, Macmillan.

Calvo, G. (1978) "On the time consistency of optimal policy in a monetary economy," *Econometrica* 46, 1411–28.

Canzoneri, M.B. and D. Henderson (1988) "Is sovereign policymaking bad?" *Carnegie-Rochester Conference Series on Public Policy* 28, 93–140.

—— and —— (1991) *Monetary Policy in Interdependent Economies*, Cambridge, MA, MIT Press.

Cox, W.M. (1980) "Unanticipated money, output and prices in a small open economy," *Journal of Monetary Economics* 6, 359–84.

Dornbusch, R. (1976) "Expectations and exchange rate dynamics," *Journal of Political Economy* 84, 1161–76.

—— (1988) "Purchasing power parity," in *The New Palgrave Dictionary of Economics*, London, Macmillan (reprinted in Dornbusch, R. (1988) *Exchange Rates and Inflation*, Cambridge, MA, MIT Press.

Eichengreen, B. (1985) *The Gold Standard in Theory and History*, London, Methuen.

—— (1987) "Conducting the international orchestra: Bank of England leadership under the classical gold standard," *Journal of International Money and Finance* 6, 5–29.

—— (1989) "Hegemonic stability theories of the international monetary system," in R. Cooper, B. Eichengreen, R. Henning, G. Holtham, and R. Putnam (eds) *Can Nations Agree?*, Washington, DC, Brookings Institution.

Fischer, S. (1977) "Wage indexation and macroeconomic stability," *Carnegie-Rochester Conference Series on Public Policy* 5, 107–47.

Flood, R.P. and N.P. Marion (1982) "The transmission of disturbances under alternative exchange rate regimes with optimal indexing," *Quarterly Journal of Economics* 97, 43–66.

Frenkel, J.A. (1976) "A monetary approach to the exchange rate: doctrinal aspects and empirical evidence," *Scandinavian Journal of Economics* 78, 200–24.

—— and J. Aizenman (1982) "Aspects of the optimal management of exchange rates," *Journal of International Economics* 13, 231–56.

—— and M. Mussa (1985) "Asset markets, exchange rates and the balance of payments," in R.W. Jones and P.B. Kenen (eds) *Handbook of International Economics*, vol. II, Amsterdam, North-Holland.

Friedman, M. (1960) *A Program for Monetary Stability*, New York, Fordham University Press.

Giavazzi, F. and A. Giovannini (1987) "Models of the EMS: is Europe a greater Deutsche-mark area?" in R. Bryant and R. Portes (eds) *Global Macroeconomics: Policy Conflict and Cooperation*, London, Macmillan.

—— and —— (1989a) *Limiting Exchange Rate Flexibility: The European Monetary System*, Cambridge, MA, MIT Press.

—— and —— (1989b) "Monetary policy interactions under managed exchange rates," *Economica* 56, 199–213.

—— and M. Pagano (1988) "The advantage of tying one's hand: EMS discipline and central bank credibility," *European Economic Review* 32, 1055–75.

Giovannini, A. (1986) "Rules of the game during the international gold standard: England and Germany," *Journal of International Money and Finance* 5, 467–83.

—— (1989) "How do fixed exchange rate regimes work? Evidence from the gold standard, Bretton Woods and the EMS," in M. Miller, B. Eichengreen and R. Portes (eds) *Blueprints for Exchange Rate Management*, London, Academic Press.

Gray, J.A. (1976) "Wage indexation: a macroeconomic approach," *Journal of*

Monetary Economics 2, 221–35.

Henderson, D.W. (1979) "Financial policies in open economies," *American Economic Review, Papers and Proceedings* 69, 232–9.

Horn, H. and T. Persson (1988) "Exchange rate policy, wage formation and credibility," *European Economic Review* 32, 1621–36.

Krugman, P. (1988) "Target zones and exchange rate dynamics," NBER Working Paper 2481, Cambridge, MA.

—— and M. Miller (1991) *Exchange Rate Targets and Currency Bands*, Cambridge, Cambridge University Press.

Kydland, F.E. and E.C. Prescott (1977) "Rules rather than discretion: the inconsistency of optimal plans," *Journal of Political Economy* 85, 473–91.

Levich, R. (1985) "Empirical studies of exchange rates: price behavior, rate determination and market efficiency," in R.W. Jones and P.B. Kenen (eds) *Handbook of International Economics*, vol. II, Amsterdam, North-Holland.

Marston, R.C. (1984) "Real wages and the terms of trade: alternative indexation rules for an open economy," *Journal of Money, Credit and Banking* 16, 285–301.

—— (1985) "Stabilization policy in open economies," in R.W. Jones and P.B. Kenen (eds) *Handbook of International Economics*, vol. II, Amsterdam, North-Holland.

Mundell, R.A. (1961) "Optimum currency areas," *American Economic Review* 51, 509–17.

—— (1963) "Capital mobility and stabilization policy under fixed and flexible exchange rates," *Canadian Journal of Economics* 29, 475–85.

Obstfeld, M. and A.C. Stockman (1985) "Exchange-rate dynamics," in R.W. Jones and P.B. Kenen (eds) *Handbook of International Economics*, vol. II, Amsterdam, North-Holland.

Poole, W. (1970) "Optimal choice of monetary policy instruments in a simple stochastic macromodel," *Quarterly Journal of Economics* 84, 197–216.

Rogoff, K. (1985) "The optimal degree of commitment to an intermediate monetary target," *Quarterly Journal of Economics* 100, 1169–90.

—— (1987) "Reputational constraints on monetary policy," *Carnegie-Rochester Conference Series on Public Policy* 26, 141–81.

Roper, D.E. and S.J. Turnovsky (1980) "Optimal exchange market intervention in a simple stochastic macromodel," *Canadian Journal of Economics* 13, 296–309.

Sargent, T.J. and N. Wallace (1975) "Rational expectations, the optimal monetary instrument and the optimal money supply rule," *Journal of Political Economy* 83, 241–54.

Turnovsky, S.J. (1983) "Wage indexation and exchange market intervention in a small open economy," *Canadian Journal of Economics* 16, 574–92.

—— (1985) "Optimal exchange market intervention: two alternative classes of rules," in J.S. Bhandari (ed.) *Exchange Rate Management under Uncertainty*, Cambridge, MA, MIT Press.

8 Macroeconomic Policy, Speculative Attacks, and Balance of Payments Crises

PIERRE-RICHARD AGÉNOR AND ROBERT P. FLOOD

1 Introduction

A fundamental proposition of open economy macroeconomics is that viability of a fixed exchange rate regime requires maintaining long-run consistency between monetary, fiscal and exchange rate policies. "Excessive" domestic credit growth leads to a gradual loss of foreign reserves and ultimately to an abandonment of the fixed exchange rate, once the central bank realizes that it is incapable of defending the parity any longer. Over the past decade, a large formal literature has focused on the short- and long-run consequences of incompatible macroeconomic policies for the balance of payments of a small open economy in which agents are able to *anticipate* future decisions by policymakers. In a pioneering paper, Krugman (1979) showed that under a fixed exchange rate regime domestic credit creation in excess of money demand growth leads to a sudden speculative attack against the currency that forces the abandonment of the fixed exchange rate and the adoption of a flexible rate regime. This attack always occurs *before* the central bank would have run out of reserves in the absence of speculation and takes place at a well-defined date.

Krugman's analysis drew, in part, on the Salant and Henderson (1978) model of a price-fixing scheme in which the government uses a stockpile of an exhaustible resource to stabilize its price – a policy that eventually ends in a speculative attack in which private agents suddenly acquire the entire remaining government stock.[1] Because of the nonlinear nature of his model, however, Krugman was unable to derive an explicit solution for the time of collapse. Later work by Flood and Garber (1984a) showed how such a solution could be derived in a linear model.

In recent years, the original Krugman–Flood–Garber insight has been amended or extended in various directions. This chapter reviews these extensions and advances, and examines areas that may warrant further attention.[2] The remainder of the chapter is organized as follows. Section 2 sets out a single-good full-employment small open economy model that specifies the basic theoretical framework used for analyzing balance of payments crises. Section 3 examines various extensions of this framework: the nature of the post-collapse exchange regime; uncertainty regarding the credit policy rule and the level of reserves that triggers the regime shift; imperfect asset substitutability and sticky prices; real effects of anticipated crises; external borrowing and capital controls; and switches in the macroeconomic policy mix. Section 4 examines some perspectives for future research. Finally, section 5 draws together the major policy implications of the literature for macroeconomic policy under a fixed exchange rate regime.

2   A basic framework

The process leading to a balance of payments crisis can be analyzed in the context of a simple continuous-time perfect foresight model.[3] The model is a log-linear formulation that allows an explicit calculation of the time of occurrence of the crisis by assuming that the exchange rate in the post-collapse regime is allowed to float permanently. This framework allows us to present the basic insights of the literature, which have been shown to carry through in more complex models where agents' decision rules are constrained by intertemporal solvency requirements.[4]

2.1   A model of a small open economy

Consider a small open economy whose residents consume a single tradeable good. Domestic supply of the good is exogenous, and its foreign-currency price is fixed (at, say, unity). The domestic-price level is equal, through a purchasing power parity condition, to the nominal exchange rate. Agents hold three categories of assets: domestic money (which is not held abroad) and domestic and foreign bonds, which are perfectly substitutable. There are no private banks, so that the money stock is equal to the sum of domestic credit issued by the central bank and the domestic-currency value of foreign reserves held by the central bank. Foreign reserves earn no interest, and domestic credit expands at a constant growth rate. Finally, agents are endowed with perfect foresight.

The model is defined by the following set of equations:[5]

$$m_t - p_t = \phi\bar{y} - \alpha i_t \qquad \phi, \alpha > 0 \qquad (8.1)$$

$$m_t = \gamma D_t + (1 - \gamma)R_t \qquad 0 < \gamma < 1 \qquad (8.2)$$

$$\dot{D}_t = \mu \qquad \mu > 0 \qquad (8.3)$$

$$p_t = e_t \qquad (8.4)$$

$$i_t = i^* + \dot{e}_t \qquad (8.5)$$

All variables except interest rates are measured in logarithms. m_t denotes the nominal money stock, D_t domestic credit, R_t the domestic-currency value of foreign reserves held by the central bank, e_t the spot exchange rate, p_t the price level, $\bar{y}$ exogenous output, i^* the foreign interest rate (assumed constant) and i_t the domestic interest rate.

Equation (8.1) relates the real demand for money positively to income and negatively to the domestic interest rate. Equation (8.2) is a log-linear approximation to the identity defining the money stock as the stock of reserves and domestic credit, which grows at the rate μ (equation (8.3)). Equations (8.4) and (8.5) define, respectively, purchasing power parity and uncovered interest parity.

Setting $\delta = \phi\bar{y} - \alpha i^*$ and combining equations (8.1), (8.4), and (8.5) yields

$$m_t - e_t = \delta - \alpha\dot{e}_t \qquad \delta > 0 \qquad (8.6)$$

Under a fixed nominal exchange rate regime, $e_t = \bar{e}$ and $\dot{e}_t = 0$ so that

$$m_t - \bar{e} = \delta \qquad (8.6')$$

which indicates that the central bank accommodates any change in domestic money demand through the purchase or sale of foreign reserves to the public.[6] Using equations (8.2) and (8.6′) yields

$$R_t = \frac{\delta + \bar{e} - \gamma D_t}{1 - \gamma} \qquad (8.7)$$

and, using (8.3),

$$\dot{R}_t = -\frac{\mu}{\theta} \qquad \theta \equiv \frac{1 - \gamma}{\gamma} \qquad (8.8)$$

Equation (8.8) indicates that if domestic credit expansion is excessive (i.e. if it exceeds the fixed demand for money, δ, given in equation (8.6′)), reserves are run down at a rate proportional to the rate of credit expansion. Any finite stock of foreign reserves will therefore be depleted in a finite period of time.

Suppose that the central bank announces at time t that it will stop defending the current fixed exchange rate after reserves reach a lower bound $\bar{R}$, at which point it will withdraw from the foreign exchange market and allow the exchange rate to float freely thereafter.[7] With a positive rate of domestic credit growth, rational agents will anticipate that without speculation reserves will eventually fall to the lower bound and will foresee therefore the ultimate collapse of the system. To avoid losses at the time of collapse, speculators will force a crisis *before* this point is reached. The problem is to determine the exact moment at which the fixed exchange rate regime is abandoned or, equivalently, the time of transition to a floating rate regime.

2.2 The shadow floating exchange rate

The length of the transition period can be calculated by using a process of backward induction, which has been formalized by Flood and Garber (1984a). In equilibrium, under perfect foresight, agents can never expect a discrete jump in the level of the exchange rate since a jump would provide them with profitable arbitrage opportunities. As a consequence, arbitrage in the foreign exchange market requires the exchange rate that prevails immediately after the attack to equal the fixed rate prevailing at the time of the attack. Formally, the time of collapse is found at the point where the "shadow floating rate," which reflects market fundamentals, is equal to the prevailing fixed rate. The shadow floating rate is the exchange rate that would prevail if reserves had fallen to the minimum level and the exchange rate were allowed to float freely. As long as the fixed exchange rate exceeds (i.e. is more depreciated than) the shadow floating rate, the fixed rate regime is viable; beyond that point, the fixed rate is not sustainable.

If the shadow floating rate falls below the prevailing fixed rate, speculators would not profit from purchasing the government's entire reserves stock and precipitating the adoption of a floating rate regime, since they would experience an instantaneous capital loss on their purchases. Symmetrically, if the shadow floating rate is above the fixed rate, speculators would experience an instantaneous capital gain. Neither anticipated capital gains nor losses at an infinite rate are compatible with a perfect foresight equilibrium. Speculators will compete with each other to eliminate such opportunities. This type of behavior leads to an equilibrium attack, which incorporates the arbitrage condition that the pre-attack fixed rate should equal the post-attack floating rate.

A first step, therefore, is to find the solution for the shadow floating exchange rate, which can be written as

$$e_t = \kappa_0 + \kappa_1 m_t \qquad (8.9)$$

where κ_0 and κ_1 are as yet undetermined coefficients and, from equation (8.2), $m_t = \gamma D_t + (1 - \gamma)\bar{R}$ when reserves reach their lower level.[8]

Taking the rate of change of equation (8.9) and noting from equation (8.2) that under a floating rate regime $\dot{m}_t = \gamma \dot{D}_t$ yields

$$\dot{e}_t = \kappa_1 \gamma \mu \tag{8.10}$$

In the post-collapse regime, therefore, the exchange rate depreciates steadily and proportionally to the rate of growth of domestic credit. Substituting (8.10) in (8.6) yields, with $\delta = 0$ for simplicity,

$$e_t = m_t + \alpha \kappa_1 \gamma \mu \tag{8.11}$$

Comparing equations (8.11) and (8.9) yields

$$\kappa_0 = \alpha \gamma \mu \qquad \kappa_1 = 1$$

From equation (8.3), $D_t = D_0 + \mu t$. Using the definition of m_t given above and substituting in equation (8.11) yields

$$e_t = \gamma(D_0 + \alpha\mu) + (1 - \gamma)\bar{R} + \gamma\mu t \tag{8.12}$$

2.3   Date of speculative attack

The fixed exchange rate regime collapses when the prevailing parity $\bar{e}$ equals the shadow floating rate e_t. From (8.12) the exact time of collapse T is obtained by setting $\bar{e} = e_t$, so that

$$T = \frac{\bar{e} - \gamma D_0 - (1 - \gamma)\bar{R}}{\gamma\mu} - \alpha$$

or, since from equations (8.2) and (8.6') $\bar{e} = \gamma D_0 + (1 - \gamma)R_0$,

$$T = \frac{\theta(R_0 - \bar{R})}{\mu} - \alpha \tag{8.13}$$

where R_0 denotes the initial stock of reserves.

Equation (8.13) indicates that, the higher the initial stock of reserves is, the lower the critical level, or the lower the rate of credit expansion is, the longer it will take before the collapse occurs. Without speculation, $\alpha = 0$ and the collapse occurs when reserves are run down to the minimum level. Setting $\alpha = 0$ in equation (8.13) yields the time of "natural collapse," as defined by Grilli (1986, p. 154). The interest rate (semi-) elasticity of money demand determines the size of the downward shift in money demand and reserves that takes place when the fixed exchange rate regime collapses and the nominal interest rate jumps to reflect an expected depreciation of the domestic currency. The larger α is, the earlier is the crisis.[9]

The analysis therefore implies that the speculative attack always occurs *before* the central bank would have reached the minimum level of reserves in the absence of speculation. To determine the stock of reserves just before the attack (i.e. at T^-) use equation (8.7) to obtain, with $\delta = 0$,[10]

$$R_{T-} \equiv \lim_{t \to T^-} R_t = \frac{\bar{e} - \gamma D_{T-}}{1 - \gamma}$$

where $D_{T-} = D_0 + \mu T^-$, so that

$$R_{T-} = \frac{\bar{e} - \gamma(D_0 + \mu T^-)}{1 - \gamma} \tag{8.14}$$

Using equation (8.13) yields

$$\bar{e} - \gamma D_0 = \gamma\mu(T^- + \alpha) + (1 - \gamma)\bar{R} \tag{8.15}$$

Combining (8.14) and (8.15) finally yields

$$R_{T-} = \bar{R} + \mu\alpha/\theta \tag{8.16}$$

Figure 8.1 illustrates the process of a balance of payments crisis under the assumption that the minimum level of reserves is zero.[11] Figure 8.1(a) portrays the behavior of reserves, domestic credit, and the money stock before and after the regime change, while figure 8.1(b) displays the behavior of the exchange rate. Prior to the collapse at T, the money stock is constant, but its composition varies since domestic credit rises (at the rate μ) and reserves decline at the rate μ/θ. An instant before the regime shift, a speculative attack occurs and both reserves and the money stock fall by $\mu\alpha/\theta$. Since $\bar{R} = 0$, the money stock is equal to domestic credit in the post-collapse regime. In figure 8.1(b) the exchange rate is shown to remain constant at $\bar{e}$ until the collapse occurs. The path continuing through AB followed by a discrete exchange rate jump BC corresponds to the "natural collapse" scenario ($\alpha = 0$). With speculation, the transition occurs earlier at A, preventing a discrete change in the exchange rate from occurring. Speculators, who foresee reserves running down to their critical level, avoid losses that would result from the discrete exchange rate change by attacking the currency at the point where the transition to the float is smooth – i.e. where the shadow floating exchange rate equals the prevailing fixed rate.[12]

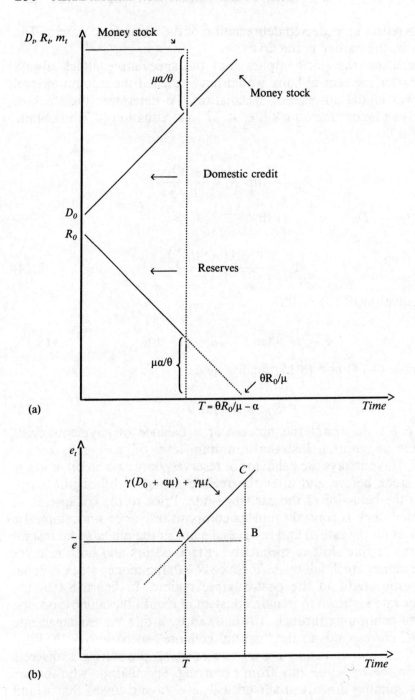

Figure 8.1   The process of balance of payments crisis.

3   Extensions to the basic framework

The analytical literature on balance of payments crises has refined and extended the basic theory presented above in several directions. In this section we examine major areas in which this literature has developed. We first consider alternative assumptions regarding the post-collapse exchange rate regime and focus, in particular, on the case of a (perfectly anticipated) temporary post-collapse period of floating followed by re-pegging. Second, we consider the introduction of uncertainty in government policy. The role of imperfect asset substitutability and sticky prices is then assessed. The real effects associated with an anticipated exchange rate crisis are subsequently examined in a model with endogenous output, sticky prices, forward-looking wage contracts, and external trade. The focus then switches to the role of foreign borrowing and the imposition of capital controls as policy measures undertaken to postpone (or prevent) the occurrence of a balance of payments crisis. Finally, we examine the issue of policy switches – i.e. changes in the macroeconomic policy mix aimed at avoiding the collapse of a fixed exchange rate.

3.1   Alternative post-collapse regimes

The focus of the early theoretical literature on balance of payments crises has been on the transition from a fixed exchange rate to a post-collapse floating exchange rate. Various alternative scenarios, however, are suggested by actual experience. For instance, the central bank can devalue the currency (Blanco and Garber, 1986),[13] implement a dual exchange rate arrangement, or adopt a crawling peg regime following the breakdown of the fixed rate system (Dornbusch, 1987). In general, one would expect the timing of a crisis to depend on the particular exchange arrangement agents expect the central bank to follow after a run on its reserve stock. A particularly interesting case – often observed in practice – corresponds to a situation in which, after allowing the currency to float for a certain period of time, the central bank returns to the foreign exchange market and fixes the exchange rate at a new and more depreciated level (Obstfeld, 1984). In what follows, we study this case as an illustration of the type of modifications of the basic structure needed for an analysis of alternative post-collapse regimes, as well as the effect of the length of a transitory arrangement on the time of occurrence of the crisis.

Suppose that the length of the transitory period of floating, denoted by τ, and the level $\bar{e}_1 > \bar{e}_0$ to which the exchange rate will be pegged at the end of the transition are known with certainty.[14] The time T at which the speculative attack occurs is calculated, as before, by a process of backward induction. However, this principle now imposes two restrictions rather than one. First, as before, the initial fixed rate $\bar{e}_0$ must coincide with the relevant shadow floating rate, i.e. $\bar{e}_0 = e_T$. Second, at time $T + \tau$ the pre-announced new fixed rate $\bar{e}_1$ must also coincide with the interim floating rate $\bar{e}_1 = e_{T+\tau}$. This last requirement acts as a terminal condition on the exchange rate differential equation.

Recall that in the last section, when the central bank's policy was assumed to involve abandonment of the fixed rate and adoption of a permanent float thereafter, the shadow floating rate was given by equation (8.11). Now, under a transitory floating regime, the shadow rate is given by

$$e_t = \kappa_0 + \kappa_1 m_t + A \exp(t/\alpha) \qquad T \le t \le T + \tau \qquad (8.17)$$

where A is a constant to be determined.[15] The complete solution must therefore specify values for both T and A. These solutions are obtained by imposing $\bar{e}_0 = e_T$ and $\bar{e}_1 = e_{T+\tau}$ on equation (8.17).[16] The solutions for T and A are

$$T = \frac{\bar{e}_0 - \kappa_0 - \kappa_1 \gamma D_0 - \Omega}{\kappa_1 \gamma \mu} \qquad (8.18a)$$

$$A = \Omega \exp(-T/\alpha) \qquad (8.18b)$$

where $\Omega = [(\bar{e}_1 - \bar{e}_0) - \kappa_1 \gamma \mu \tau]/[\exp(\tau/\alpha) - 1]$.

Equation (8.18a) indicates that the collapse time is linked to the magnitude of the expected devaluation $\bar{e}_1 - \bar{e}_0$ and the length of the transitional float.[17] Crises occur earlier the greater the anticipated devaluation is: equation (8.18a) shows that the higher the anticipated post-devaluation exchange rate, the sooner the speculative attack occurs ($\partial T/\partial \bar{e}_1 < 0$).[18] The relationship between the collapse time and the length of the floating rate interval depends, in general, on the parameters of the model: $\partial T/\partial \tau < 0$ for small τ and $\partial T/\partial \tau > 0$ for large τ. If the transitional float is sufficiently brief, however, a speculative attack on the domestic currency will occur as soon as the private agents realize that the current exchange rate cannot be enforced forever.

3.2   Uncertainty and the timing of speculative attacks

A basic assumption in the framework developed above was that there exists some binding threshold level, known by all agents, below which foreign reserves are not allowed to fall. The attainment of this critical level implied a permanent shift from a fixed exchange rate system to a floating rate regime. In practice, however, agents are only imperfectly informed of central bank policies. In particular, they may not know precisely the threshold level of reserves that triggers the regime shift. In circumstances in which uncertainty about current and future central bank policy prevails, the assumption of perfect foresight may be difficult to defend.

In addition, the implication of the perfect foresight model developed above for the behavior of the domestic nominal interest rate appears to be contradicted by experience. In the model, the nominal interest rate stays constant until the moment when the speculative attack occurs – at which point it jumps to a new level which reflects the behavior of the expected rate of depreciation of the floating exchange rate. In practice, interest rates have tended to increase sharply in the periods preceding the collapse of a fixed exchange rate regime (see Agénor et al., 1991). Uncertainty over the depreciation rate, as modeled below, may help to account for such a rise.

Uncertainty in the theory of balance of payments crises has been introduced in various forms but has focused essentially on two aspects: first, uncertainty regarding the reserve limit that triggers the crisis; and second, uncertainty regarding domestic credit growth. The first source of uncertainty relates to the observation that private agents are generally uncertain about how much of its potential reserves the central bank is willing to use to defend its fixed exchange rate target. Uncertainty of this type was first examined by Krugman (1979), who emphasized the possibility of alternating periods of crises and recoveries of confidence in the existing parity.[19] A general result, however, seems to be that speculative behavior is quite sensitive to the specification of the process that produces the critical level of foreign reserves. Depending on whether the threshold level is stochastic or fixed but unknown to agents, currency speculation reveals itself as, respectively, a speculative outflow distributed over several periods of time or a sudden speculative attack on the currency (Willman, 1989).

Uncertainty about domestic credit growth was first introduced by Flood and Garber (1984a), in a discrete-time stochastic model.[20] In their framework, credit is assumed to depend on a random component.[21] In each period, the probability of regime change in the next period is found by evaluating the probability that domestic credit in the next period is sufficiently large to result in a discrete depreciation should a speculative attack take place. In the Flood–Garber framework, a fixed rate regime will collapse whenever agents find it profitable to attack the currency. The condition for a profitable attack is now that the post-collapse exchange rate e_t be *larger* than the prevailing fixed rate $\bar{e}$. Profits of speculators are equal to the exchange rate differential multiplied by the reserve stock used to defend the fixed rate regime. Since these are risk-free profits earned at an infinite rate (speculators could always sell foreign exchange back to the central bank at the fixed rate if the attack is unsuccessful), the stock of reserves will come under attack if $e_t > \bar{e}$. Formally, the probability at time t of an attack at (say) time $t+1$, denoted $_t\pi_{t+1}$, is given by

$$_t\pi_{t+1} = \text{prob}_t(e_{t+1} > \bar{e}) \tag{8.19}$$

The specific nature of the process driving e_t will determine the exact form of $_t\pi_{t+1}$. From equation (8.19), the expected rate of depreciation of the exchange rate between t and $t+1$ is given as

$$E_t e_{t+1} - e_t = {}_t\pi_{t+1}[E_t(e_{t+1}|e_{t+1} > \bar{e}) - \bar{e}] \tag{8.20}$$

where $E_t(e_{t+1}|e_{t+1} > \bar{e})$ denotes the conditional expectation of e_{t+1}.

The expected rate of exchange rate depreciation given by equation (8.20) will change to the extent that the value of the variables forcing e_t change. The expected rate of change of the exchange rate increases prior to the collapse because both $_t\pi_{t+1}$ and $E_t(e_{t+1}|e_{t+1} > \bar{e})$ rise with the imminent occurrence of the crisis.[22] The probability of an attack next period, $_t\pi_{t+1}$, rises because the increasing value of the state variable (domestic credit) makes it increasingly likely that an attack will occur at $t+1$. The quantity $E_t(e_{t+1}|e_{t+1} > \bar{e})$ represents the value agents expect the exchange rate to take next period, given that there will be a speculative attack at $t+1$. That value depends, in turn, on the value agents expect domestic credit to take next period, given that an attack will occur at $t+1$. The value of domestic credit, as well as its conditional expectation, rises from period to period. The conditional expected rate of change of the exchange rate therefore also rises. As a result, the domestic nominal interest rate increases with the approach of the crisis – a phenomenon consistent with the empirical evidence alluded to above.

The Flood–Garber stochastic approach has given rise to a number of empirical applications.[23] The introduction of uncertainty in collapse models has several implications for the predictions of these models, beyond being consistent with rising interest rates prior to the crisis. First, the transition to a floating regime becomes stochastic, implying that the collapse time is a random variable which cannot as before be determined explicitly, since the timing of a potential future speculative attack is unknown. Second, there will in general always be a nonzero probability of a speculative attack in the next period, a possibility which, in turn, produces a forward discount on the domestic currency – a phenomenon known as the "peso problem" (Krasker, 1980).[24] Available evidence suggests indeed that the forward premium – or, as an alternative indicator of exchange rate expectations in developing countries, the parallel market premium – in foreign exchange markets tends to increase well before the regime shift. Third, the degree of uncertainty about the central bank's credit policy plays an important role in the speed at which reserves of the central bank are depleted (Agénor and Delbecque, 1991; Claessens, 1991). In a stochastic setting, reserve losses exceed increases in domestic credit because of a rising probability of regime collapse, so that reserve depletion accelerates on the way to the regime change. Such a pattern has often been observed in actual crises.

3.3   Imperfect substitutability and sticky prices

The basic framework developed above assumed that domestic and foreign bonds were perfect substitutes and that prices in the post-collapse regime were perfectly flexible. Extension of the model to a world of sticky prices and imperfect asset substitutability provides the possibility to assess the effect of changes in the speed of market adjustment on the collapse time. A simple way to introduce sluggish price adjustment in the basic framework consists in dropping the assumption of perfect substitutability between domestic and foreign goods – which yields the purchasing power parity condition (8.4) – and specifying a Dornbusch-type price equation in which aggregate demand is inversely related to the real exchange rate and the real interest rate (see Agénor et al., 1991). A fairly general result that emerges then is that the higher the degree of price flexibility, the earlier the crisis occurs. Essentially, this result derives from the anticipatory element that movements in prices incorporate in the sticky-price regime. Under perfect substitutability between domestic and foreign goods, the domestic price level remains constant (at the prevailing fixed exchange rate) until the crisis occurs, at which point it rises by the amount of exchange rate depreciation. By contrast, when the speed of adjustment to aggregate excess demand is less than infinite, a perfectly anticipated future collapse of the fixed exchange rate regime has an immediate impact on the behavior of domestic prices. Prices begin to rise gradually – or as soon as agents become aware that the exchange rate is not viable indefinitely – so as to prevent any jump when the regime switch occurs. The higher the degree of price inertia, the longer it takes for prices to adjust and ensure a "smooth" transition – and therefore the longer will be the time elapsed before the collapse.

The effect of price flexibility on the collapse time discussed above has also been highlighted by Blackburn (1988) and Blackburn and Sola (1991). In addition, they also examine the role of imperfect asset substitutability in the collapse process. Their analysis shows that the higher the degree of capital mobility, the earlier the crisis occurs. As in Willman's (1988) model, imperfect substitutability between domestic and foreign bonds implies that it is essentially the accumulating trade balance deficit that leads to depletion of foreign reserves and eventually causes the balance of payments crisis. Because of the potential impact of government spending on external deficits, it is therefore not just monetary policy but rather the overall macroeconomic policy mix that is of importance in the analysis of an exchange rate collapse.

3.4   Real effects of an anticipated collapse

The literature on balance of payments crises focused initially on the financial aspects of such crises and largely ignored the real events that were occurring simultaneously. Existing evidence suggests, however, that balance of payments crises are often associated with large current account movements during the periods preceding, as well as during the periods following, such crises. Typically, large external deficits tend to emerge as agents adjust their consumption pattern – in addition to adjusting the composition of their holdings of financial assets – in anticipation of a crisis. As suggested by the experience of Argentina, Chile, and Mexico, for instance, movements in the real exchange rate and the current account can be quite dramatic in the periods preceding exchange rate crises (Agénor et al., 1991). Such movements may provide an additional explanation as to why (in addition to uncertainty, discussed above) speculative attacks are generally preceded by a period during which official foreign reserves are lost at increasing rates.

The real effects of a potential exchange rate crisis have been investigated by Flood and Hodrick (1986) and Willman (1988) in economies with sticky prices and contractually predetermined wages.[25] Following Willman, assume that domestic output is demand determined, positively related to the real exchange rate, and inversely related to the real interest rate. The trade balance depends positively on the real exchange rate but is negatively related to domestic output. Prices are set as a mark-up over wages and imported input costs. Nominal wages are determined through forward-looking contracts, as in Calvo (1983). Under perfect foresight, an anticipated future collapse will affect wages immediately, and therefore prices, the real exchange rate, output, and the trade balance. At the moment the collapse occurs, the real interest rate falls because of the jump in the rate of depreciation of the exchange rate. As a result, output increases while the trade balance deteriorates. But since wage contracts are forward looking, anticipated future increases in prices are discounted back to the present and affect current wages. Consequently, prices start adjusting before the collapse occurs. The real interest rate falls gradually, and experiences a downward jump at the moment the collapse takes place, as indicated above. The decline in the (*ex post*) real interest rate has an expansionary effect on domestic activity before the collapse occurs. However, output also depends on the real exchange rate. The steady rise in domestic prices results in an appreciation of the domestic currency and this has a negative impact on economic activity that may outweigh the positive output effect resulting from a lower real interest rate. The net impact of an anticipated collapse on output may well be negative if relative price effects are strong. The continuous loss of competitiveness, unless it is associated with a fall in output, implies that the trade balance deteriorates in the periods preceding the collapse of the fixed exchange rate regime. The trade deficit increases further at the moment the crisis occurs and returns gradually afterwards to its steady-state level, following a gradual depreciation of the real exchange rate.

In the model described above, the real exchange rate appreciates until the time of collapse, at which point it starts depreciating smoothly. This feature of the model seems to account fairly well for the steady real appreciation and subsequent depreciation observed during crisis episodes in countries such as Argentina in 1980–1. By contrast, in the models developed by Calvo (1987) and Connolly and Taylor (1984), the real exchange rate depreciates markedly at the time of the crisis – a feature of the collapse process that is difficult to rationalize under perfect foresight. In both models, the price of traded goods is fixed at the time of a speculative attack. It cannot jump because the exchange rate is continuous (as a result of the asset-price continuity assumption) and the world price of traded goods is assumed constant. Consequently, a sharp real depreciation at the time of the crisis must be attributed, under perfect foresight, to a substantial *fall* in the nominal price of nontraded goods – an assumption that implies an implausible degree of downward price flexibility.

3.5   Borrowing, controls, and the postponement of a crisis

Countries that have faced balance of payments difficulties have often had recourse to external borrowing to supplement the amount of reserves available to defend the declared parity, or have imposed restrictions on capital outflows in an attempt to limit losses of foreign exchange reserves. In the basic model developed above, it has been assumed that there is a critical level, known by everyone, below which foreign reserves are not allowed to be depleted. However, such a binding threshold may not exist. A central bank facing a perfect capital market can – at least in principle – increase foreign reserves at its disposal by borrowing. Negative (net) reserves are therefore also feasible.

In fact, perfect access to international capital markets implies that, at any given point in time, central bank reserves can become in principle infinitely negative without violating the government's intertemporal solvency constraint. Unlimited access to borrowing could therefore avoid a regime collapse indefinitely. The rate of growth of domestic credit cannot, however, be *permanently* maintained above the world interest rate, because it would lead to a violation of the government budget constraint (Obstfeld, 1986a). In this sense, an over-expansionary credit policy would still, ultimately, lead to the collapse of a fixed exchange rate regime.[26] Moreover, even with perfect capital markets the timing of borrowing matters considerably for the nature of speculative attacks. Suppose that the interest cost of servicing foreign debt exceeds the interest rate paid on reserves. If borrowing occurs just before the fixed exchange rate would have collapsed without borrowing, the crisis is likely to be postponed. If borrowing occurs long enough before the exchange rate regime would have collapsed in the absence of borrowing, the crisis would occur earlier. The reason why the collapse is brought forward is, of course, related to the servicing cost of foreign indebtedness on the public sector deficit, which raises the rate of growth of domestic credit (Buiter, 1987).

In practice, most countries face borrowing constraints on international capital markets. The existence of limited access to external financing has important implications for the behavior of inflation in an economy where the private sector is subject to an intertemporal budget constraint. Consider, for instance, a country that has no possibility to borrow externally and in which the central bank transfers its net profits to the government. If a speculative attack occurs, the central bank will lose its stock of reserves, and its post-collapse profits from interest earnings on those reserves will drop to zero. As a consequence, net income of the government will fall and the budget deficit will deteriorate. If the deficit is financed by increased domestic credit (a typical situation if access to external borrowing is limited) the post-collapse inflation rate will exceed the rate that prevailed in the pre-collapse fixed exchange rate regime, raising inflation tax revenue so as to compensate for the fall in interest income (van Wijnbergen, 1988, 1991).

As indicated earlier, capital controls have often been used to limit losses of foreign exchange reserves and postpone a regime collapse. Such controls have been imposed either *permanently* or *temporarily* after the central bank had experienced significant losses or at times when the domestic currency came under heavy pressure on foreign exchange markets.[27] A simple way to introduce permanent controls in the above setting is to rewrite equation (8.5) as

$$i_t = (1 - \rho)(i^* + \dot{e}_t) \qquad 0 < \rho < 1 \qquad (8.5')$$

This equation states that deviations of the domestic interest rate from uncovered interest parity are accounted for by the existence of capital controls, which are modeled here as a proportional tax ρ on foreign interest earnings.[28] Using (8.5') and solving the model as before, the collapse time can be shown to be

$$T = \frac{\theta(R_0 - \bar{R})}{\mu} - (1 - \rho)\alpha \qquad (8.13')$$

Equation (8.13') indicates that the higher the degree of capital controls (the higher ρ), the longer it will take for the regime shift to occur. This is because controls dampen the size of the expected future jump in the domestic nominal interest rate and the associated shift in the demand for money.

The effect of temporary capital controls on the timing of a balance of payments crisis has been studied by Bacchetta (1990), Dellas and Stockman (1988), and Wyplosz (1986). In Wyplosz's model the domestic country expands credit at an excessive rate. Capital movements are subject to restrictions, and residents are not allowed to hold foreign currency assets (or to lend to nonresidents), but nonresidents are free from controls. There are only two assets, domestic money and foreign money. Nonresidents monitor reserve levels, provoking a "crisis" when reserve levels equal nonresident holdings of domestic currency. The currency is then devalued, setting off a new cycle. The analysis shows that in the absence of capital controls a fixed rate regime would be viable only if the central bank maintained a levei of uncertainty high enough to force risk-averse speculators to commit only limited amounts of funds in anticipation of a crisis.[29]

However, even with perfect foresight the fixed rate regime might still be viable if interest rates are endogenous – a feature that is absent in Wyplosz's model. Interest rates have an equilibrating role that eliminates the incentive for a run on reserves. For instance, if the public anticipates a devaluation it will shift out of domestic money. The authorities may accommodate the public, say, by bond sales at interest rates that reflect these expectations; such bond sales avert the need to shift into foreign assets. The implication of the analysis, nevertheless, is that without capital controls interest rates are likely to display substantial variability.[30]

Temporary restrictions on capital movements may also have real effects in the process leading to a balance of payments crisis, as shown by Bacchetta (1990). In a rational world, agents will anticipate the introduction of controls as soon as they realize the fundamental inconsistency between the fiscal policy and the fixed exchange rate. However, it is now critical to distinguish between the case in which the policy change is anticipated and the case in which it is not. If controls take agents "by surprise," capital outflows will increasingly be substituted by higher imports once such controls are put in place, leading eventually to a deterioration in the current account until a "natural" collapse occurs. The accelerated rate of depletion of foreign reserves through the current account will therefore precipitate the crisis, defeating the initial objective of controls. If capital controls are pre-announced – or if agents are able to "guess" correctly the exact time at which controls will be introduced – a speculative attack may occur just *before* the controls are imposed, as agents attempt to readjust their portfolios and evade restrictions. Such an attack will, again, defeat the very purpose of capital controls by in fact precipitating the regime collapse.

3.6 Policy switches and the avoidance of a collapse

Early models of balance of payments crises have generally been limited to the consideration of an exogenous rate of credit growth which, often implicitly, has been taken to reflect "fiscal constraints." The apparently ineluctable nature of a regime collapse that such an assumption entails runs into a conceptual difficulty – namely, why is it that policymakers do not attempt to prevent the crisis by adjusting their fiscal and credit policies? For instance, there is nothing in the basic model developed above that requires the central bank to float the currency and abandon the prevailing fixed exchange rate at the moment reserves hit their critical lower bound. Instead, the central bank could choose to change its credit policy rule so as to make it consistent with a fixed exchange rate target. Some recent models of balance of payments crises have indeed considered this type of endogenous change in monetary policy. Drazen and Helpman (1988) and Edwards and Montiel (1989), in particular, have argued that the assumption that the authorities choose to adjust the exchange rate instead of altering the underlying macroeconomic policy mix can only provide a temporary solution. Ultimately, if the new exchange rate regime is inconsistent with the underlying fiscal policy process, there will be a need for a new policy regime.

In fact, the mere expectation of a change in the macroeconomic policy mix may precipitate the collapse of a fixed exchange rate. Flood and Garber (1984b), for instance, showed in the context of a model of the gold standard how an attack on a price-fixing scheme can be self-fulfilling. This self-fulfilling aspect was applied to exchange rate regimes by Obstfeld (1986b). The collapse, in these models, results from an indeterminacy of equilibrium that may arise when agents expect a speculative attack to cause an abrupt change in government macroeconomic policies. Suppose, for instance, that a country fixes its exchange rate and maintains a stable credit policy in "normal times." In the event of a speculative attack, the country will stop fixing the exchange rate and will increase the rate of growth of domestic credit. Evidently, the private sector can be in equilibrium with either policy. If an attack never occurs, the fixed exchange rate will survive indefinitely. If there is an attack, the system may collapse. The indeterminacy arises because the authorities' credit policy is *not* exogenous to the collapse.

More generally, uncertainty about the post-collapse credit rule can threaten the viability of a fixed exchange rate regime. A simple way to introduce policy uncertainty in the basic model developed above is to allow two possibilities with respect to the credit growth rule (Willman, 1987). Assume that there is a probability q that the monetary authority will maintain the existing rule given by equation (8.3) and float the currency from the moment the stock of foreign exchange reserves has been depleted to zero, and a probability $1 - q$ that the authorities will adopt a zero-growth rule consistent with the prevailing fixed exchange rate:

$$\dot{D}_t = 0 \qquad\qquad (8.3')$$

Using equation (8.3') and solving as before, the collapse time can now be shown to be equal to

$$T = \frac{\theta(R_0 - \bar{R})}{\mu} - \alpha q \qquad\qquad (8.13'')$$

The earlier result (equation (8.13)) corresponds to a probability of adherence to the pre-collapse credit rule equal to unity. If that probability is zero, a speculative attack never occurs and the system collapses "naturally." The smaller q is – the greater the probability that the central bank alters the credit rule (8.3) – the longer it takes before the collapse occurs.

As an alternative way to examine the effect of a possible future credit policy switch, suppose that, instead of equation (8.3), the process driving domestic credit is stochastic:

$$dD_t = \mu \, dt + \sigma \, dz_t \qquad\qquad (8.3'')$$

where dz_t is a standard Wiener process and σ is a constant.[31] To derive the solution equation for the shadow floating exchange rate (with, for simplicity, a zero lower bound on reserves and $\delta = 0$), set $R_t = 0$ in equation (8.2) and use equations (8.4) and (8.5) in (8.1) to get

$$e_t = \gamma D_t + \alpha \dot{e}_t \qquad\qquad (8.21)$$

Assume that the central bank announces that, after allowing the exchange rate to float initially, it will again fix the exchange rate if a higher limit on domestic credit $\bar{D}$ – which is common knowledge – is reached.[32] The shadow floating rate can now be shown to be[33]

$$e_t = \gamma D_t + \gamma \alpha \mu \{1 - \exp[\tilde{\lambda}(D_t - \bar{D})]\} \qquad (8.22)$$

where $\tilde{\lambda}$ is the positive root of the quadratic equation in λ

$$\frac{\lambda^2 \alpha \sigma^2}{2} + \lambda \gamma \alpha \mu - 1 = 0 \qquad (8.23)$$

The collapse time T, which is stochastic, is now a "first passage" time which may be studied using methods given, for instance, in Feller (1966, pp. 174–5).

4   Some research perspectives

The important developments in the recent literature on speculative attacks has examined and clarified a variety of issues and assumptions made in the earlier models. For instance, the recent trend towards using optimizing models with properly defined budget constraints has undoubtedly helped to highlight the role of intertemporal solvency requirements faced by private agents and policymakers. There remain, however, a number of substantive issues to be addressed. In this section, we focus our attention on the following topics: new state space methods for studying speculative attacks and other policy-switching models, and the role of reputational factors as a deterrent to speculative attacks.[34]

4.1   State space methods

In the last few years economists have changed their approach to situations in which policymakers alter their policy rules or operating procedures when some target variable crosses a limit or "barrier." The new approach, which is due to Krugman (1991), studies issues – such as speculative attacks – using methods adapted from the options-pricing literature.[35] The basic ideas are unchanged from the earlier literature (agents, in particular, are still required to formulate probability distributions concerning future government decisions) but in the new literature the timing of the authorities' actions is not the primary focus. The analysis centers, rather, on agents' reactions to the current state of the system, given their knowledge of the possibility of profit opportunities generated by the policymaker's decisions, triggered themselves by the movement of some policy-targeted variable.

An important part of this literature has focused on exchange rate target zones, in which a policy authority announces lower and upper bands within which it will allow the exchange rate to float *vis-à-vis* another currency or a basket of currencies. This description fits well with actual practice in the Bretton Woods system or in the European Monetary System. One of the important insights in this literature is that a credible zone would stabilize the exchange rate inside the zone, the so-called "honeymoon effect" (Krugman, 1991). However, when the zone loses full credibility – because of, for instance, the possibility of a speculative attack (Flood and Garber, 1991) – the honeymoon effect is lessened (Krugman and Rotemberg, 1990).

An interesting, and promising, direction in this literature has been the extension of the Krugman model to a multi-state variable framework by Miller and Weller (1991). Such models are not analytically solvable but may be studied through computer simulations, using methods borrowed from the options-pricing literature.

4.2   Reputation as a deterrent to speculative attacks

Recent developments in macroeconomics have emphasized the game-theoretic aspects of macroeconomic policy and, in particular, the role of credibility factors in the context of exchange rate management.[36] A fruitful line of enquiry could be to examine the effect of exchange rate credibility on balance of payments crises. A fixed exchange rate regime will, in general, never carry full credibility. Official pronouncements notwithstanding, there is always a risk that when official reserves are being depleted a country will opt to alter its exchange rate rather than its monetary and/or fiscal policy. When agents perceive that the authorities' commitment – and ability – to maintain a fixed exchange rate is weak, speculative attacks may occur, regardless of whether the rate of credit growth is "excessive" or not. Such attacks may take place, in particular, when the competitiveness of a high-inflation country has been eroded by adherence to the nominal exchange rate parity. This will typically reduce the degree of confidence in the existing exchange rate and will raise expectations that the currency will be devalued, therefore precipitating a speculative attack. Lack of credibility can therefore be self-fulfilling. An important issue, in this context, is the extent to which reputational factors (such as membership in a currency union, or the appointment of a "conservative" central banker, as suggested by Rogoff, 1985) may mitigate the credibility problem and ensure the viability of a fixed rate regime (see Wood, 1991).

5 Conclusions

This chapter has provided an overview of recent theoretical developments in the literature on speculative attacks in foreign exchange
markets and balance of payments crises. A simple analytical model was
developed to describe the process leading to such crises. The analysis
showed that, under perfect foresight about the policy rule pursued by
the monetary authorities, an exchange rate regime shift from a fixed to
a floating regime is preceded by a speculative attack on the currency.
Moreover, the timing of such attacks is entirely predictable; intertemporal arbitrage ensures that the regime shift occurs "smoothly." Its
timing was shown to depend on the stock of foreign reserves committed
by the central bank to the defense of the fixed exchange rate regime, as
well as the critical level of reserves which triggers the abandonment of
the declared parity.

The second part of the chapter extended the basic analytical model
in various directions, while the third part discussed some possible areas
for future research, notably some recent analytical techniques that are
being used for studying speculative attacks models, as well as the role
of reputational factors as a deterrent to speculative attacks.

The literature on speculative attacks provides some major
implications for macroeconomic policy under a fixed exchange rate
regime which can be summarized as follows. Balance of payments crises
are often the equilibrium outcome of maximizing behavior by rational
agents faced with a fundamental inconsistency between monetary and
exchange rate policies, rather than the result of "exogenous" shocks. In
the periods preceding an eventual collapse, speculative attacks are likely
to occur recurrently, reflecting alternative periods of confidence and
distrust in the ability of the central bank to defend the official parity, and
changes in the degree of uncertainty regarding actual and future central
bank policies. Measures such as foreign borrowing and capital controls
may temporarily enhance the viability of a fixed exchange rate, but will
not prevent the ultimate collapse of the system if a consistent – and
sustainable, in the light of the intertemporal budget constraint faced by
the government – macroeconomic policy mix is not adopted.[37] The more
delayed fundamental policy adjustments are, the higher will be the
potential costs (in terms of lost output, for instance) of a regime collapse.

Notes

This chapter draws on a previous paper written jointly with Jagdeep S. Bhandari. Helpful
comments on that paper were provided by Peter Garber, Mohsin Khan, Mark Taylor, and Alpo
Willman.

1   See also Salant (1983) for extensions of the Salant–Henderson model. A crucial distinction between attacks in resource markets and the foreign exchange market is the possibility of external borrowing to supplement the central bank's reserves, an issue that is discussed below.

2   Agénor et al. (1991) provide a review of recent experiences of a group of developed and developing countries that faced exchange rate and balance of payments crises.

3   The continuous-time formulation is convenient but not entirely innocuous. For some of the complications that arise in a discrete-time model of speculative attacks, see Obstfeld (1986a).

4   The basic behavioral equation of the model – the money demand function – can be explicitly derived from a choice-theoretic framework. Optimizing models of balance of payments crises have been developed by Bacchetta (1990), Calvo (1987), Claessens (1988, 1991), Obstfeld (1986a), Penati and Pennachi (1989), van Wijnbergen (1988, 1991), and Willman (1991).

5   In what follows, a dot over a variable denotes its time derivative.

6   Since capital is perfectly mobile, the stock of foreign reserves can jump discontinuously as private agents readjust their portfolios in response to current or anticipated shocks.

7   Before time t, the public had assumed that the central bank would continue to defend the fixed exchange rate indefinitely, even if reserves became negative. A possible rationale for the existence of a lower bound on the central bank's reserves stock is provided by Willman (1991).

8   In general, the exchange rate solution can be derived – assuming no bubbles – by using the forward expansion of (8.6):

$$e_t = \gamma D_t + (1 - \gamma)\bar{R} - \delta + \alpha \dot{e}_t = \frac{\gamma}{\alpha} \int_t^\infty \exp\left(\frac{t-k}{\alpha}\right)[D_k + (1 - \gamma)\bar{R} - \delta]\, dk$$

or, using equation (8.3),

$$e_t = \frac{\gamma}{\alpha} \int_t^\infty \exp\left(\frac{t-k}{\alpha}\right)[D_t + (k - t)\mu + (1 - \gamma)\bar{R} - \delta]\, dk$$

which expresses the shadow floating exchange rate as the "present discounted value" of future fundamentals. Integration by parts yields equation (8.12) below.

9   Note also that the larger the initial proportion of domestic credit in the money stock (the higher γ), the sooner the collapse. γ, however, appears in our reduced form as an artifact of log-linearization, and is used in the model only to convert the exogenous credit growth rate to a money supply growth rate.

10 R_t is discontinuous at time T. It is positive as approached from below and jumps down to $\bar{R}$ at T.

11 Recall that R denotes the logarithm of the stock of foreign reserves, so that it is simply an accounting convention to set $\bar{R} = 0$.

12 The analysis above has been extended to consider the case where the pre-collapse regime is a crawling peg arrangement, and the case where speculative runs occur as buying rather than selling attacks. See Connolly and Taylor (1984), Dornbusch (1987), and Grilli (1986).

13 For other models in which a reserve crisis is followed by a devaluation, see Grilli (1986) who also considers the case where a speculative attack forces a

revaluation of the domestic currency. See also Otani (1989), Rodriguez (1978), and Wyplosz (1986).

14 Note that the new fixed exchange rate, to be viable, must be greater than (i.e. more depreciated) or equal to the rate that would have prevailed had there been a permanent post-crisis float.

15 The last term on the left-hand side of equation (8.17) represents a "speculative bubble" component that was ruled out from the solution (8.9) by imposing the transversality condition $A = 0$. Imposing the terminal condition $\bar{e}_1 = e_{T+\tau}$ requires now using the condition $A \neq 0$.

16 Formally, these restrictions are given by

$$\bar{e}_0 = \kappa_0 + \kappa_1 \gamma (D_0 + \mu T) + A \exp(T/\alpha)$$

$$\bar{e}_1 = \kappa_0 + \kappa_1 \gamma [D_0 + \mu(T + \tau)] + A \exp\left(\frac{T + \tau}{\alpha}\right)$$

Direct manipulations of these equations yield the solutions for A and T given in equations (8.18a) and (8.18b).

17 Note that equations (8.18a) and (8.18b) yield a solution for the collapse time that is equivalent to (8.13) with $\bar{R} = 0$ and for $\tau \to \infty$, since $(1 - \gamma)R_0 = \bar{e}_0 - \gamma D_0$.

18 If e_1 is high enough, it is possible that $T \leq 0$. In this case, the speculative attack occurs at the moment when investors learn that the fixed exchange rate cannot be defended indefinitely.

19 The issue has also been examined by Cumby and van Wijnbergen (1989), Otani (1989), and Willman (1989). Uncertainty about the overall stance of macroeconomic policy is examined below.

20 Uncertainty on domestic credit growth has also been introduced by, among others, Dornbusch (1987), Grilli (1986), and Obstfeld (1986b) who shows that as a result of uncertainty there may be circumstances when a system is attacked even though it is fundamentally viable. See the discussion below.

21 The reason why the government might want to execute "surprise" injections of domestic credit has not been satisfactorily explained in the literature. A possible link between the timing of a surge in domestic credit and seigniorage considerations is suggested by Penati and Pennachi (1989).

22 If the probability density function of e_{t+1}, viewed at time t, is denoted $g_t(e_{t+1})$, then

$$_t\pi_{t+1} = \int_{\bar{e}}^{\infty} g_t(e_{t+1})\, de_{t+1}$$

$$E_t(e_{t+1} \mid e_{t+1} > \bar{e}) = \int_{\bar{e}}^{\infty} g_t(e_{t+1}) e_{t+1}\, de_{t+1}$$

23 See Cumby and Wijnbergen (1989) for Argentina, Blanco and Garber (1986), Connolly and Fernandéz (1987), and Goldberg (1990) for Mexico, and Grilli (1990) for the USA during 1894–6. Econometric formulations of collapse models are examined in detail in Agénor et al. (1991).

24 In the Flood–Garber model, increments to credit follow an exponential distribution, so that $g_t(e_{t+1})$ defined above is an exponential function. This assumption implies that a particularly large increment to credit may cause reserves losses so large that a transition to floating occurs immediately, even if central bank reserves are large. By contrast, Dornbusch (1987) uses a

uniform distribution for credit growth with an upper limit. The existence of a maximum rate of increase implies that, if reserves are large, there will be no immediate possibility of a regime shift.

25 Other models focusing on real exchange rate effects of an anticipated collapse include Claessens (1991), Connolly and Taylor (1984), and Calvo (1987). Frenkel and Klein (1991) also analyze the real effects of alternative macroeconomic adjustment policies that aim at preventing a balance of payments crisis.

26 The relation between speculative attacks and the solvency of the public sector in an economy with interest-bearing debt has also been examined by Ize and Ortiz (1987).

27 In developing countries, capital controls have often had a permanent nature; see, for instance, Edwards (1989) for Latin American countries. Temporary controls have typically been used in industrial countries, notably in Europe.

28 The tax is assumed set at a level that is low enough not to impede international capital flows.

29 In Wyplosz's model, therefore, exchange controls succeed in salvaging the fixed exchange rate regime by imposing a ceiling on the potential volume of speculative transactions. By contrast, Dellas and Stockman show that the threat of capital controls may generate (self-fulfilling) speculative attacks instead of serving to deter them. The same point is emphasized by Bacchetta (1990) as discussed below.

30 For instance, the repeated imposition of temporary controls may well lead to a (variable) risk premium in domestic interest rates that would reflect the risk to investors that capital controls would be imposed in the future.

31 Equation (8.3″) is the continuous-time analog of a random walk with trend. Note also that when the variance of domestic credit is zero (i.e. $\sigma = 0$) the model reduces to the deterministic case. See the discussion by Bertola in chapter 9 of this volume.

32 Such a policy announcement may not, of course, be credible. We abstract from this complication here.

33 For details about the solution procedure, see Froot and Obstfeld (1991). Note that for $\bar{D} \rightarrow \infty$, equation (8.22) yields solution (8.12) with $\bar{R} = 0$

34 Further discussions of potentially fruitful research areas are provided in Agénor et al. (1991) and Blackburn and Sola (1991).

35 See chapter 9 by Bertola in this volume for an introduction to this literature.

36 See Blackburn and Christensen (1989) for a general review of these issues, and Andersen and Risager (1991).

37 In fact, the imposition of capital controls may even "backfire" by bringing forward the collapse of the fixed exchange rate if the measure is anticipated well in advance by private agents. Similarly, foreign borrowing may precipitate an exchange rate crisis if the associated increase in the cost of servicing the public debt raises the rate of growth of domestic credit.

References

Agénor, Pierre-Richard, and Bernard Delbecque (1991) "Balance of payments crises in a dual exchange rate regime with leakages," unpublished, Washington, DC, International Monetary Fund, March.

—— , Jagdeep S. Bhandari, and Robert P. Flood (1992) "Speculative attacks and models of balance of payments crises," NBER Working Paper 3919, Cambridge, MA, November. Condensed version published in *IMF Staff Papers* 39, 357–94.

Andersen, Torben M. and Ole Risager (1991) "The role of credibility for the effects of a change in the exchange-rate policy," *Oxford Economic Papers* 41, 85–98.

Bacchetta, Philippe (1990) "Temporary capital controls in a balance-of-payments crisis," *Journal of International Money and Finance* 9, 246–57.

Blackburn, Keith (1988) "Collapsing exchange rate regimes and exchange rate dynamics: some further examples," *Journal of International Money and Finance* 7, 373–85.

—— and Michael Christensen (1989) "Monetary policy and credibility: theories and evidence," *Journal of Economic Literature* 27, 1–45.

—— and Martin Sola (1991) "Speculative currency attacks and balance of payments crises: a survey," University of Southampton Discussion Paper 9204, December.

Blanco, Herminio, and Peter M. Garber (1986) "Recurrent devaluation and speculative attacks on the Mexican peso," *Journal of Political Economy* 94, 148–66.

Buiter, Willem H. (1987) "Borrowing to defend the exchange rate and the timing of and magnitude of speculative attacks," *Journal of International Economics* 23, 221–39.

Calvo, Guillermo A. (1983) "Staggered contracts and exchange rate policy," in Jacob A. Frenkel (ed.) *Exchange Rates and International Macroeconomics*, Chicago, IL, University of Chicago Press.

—— (1987) "Balance of payments crises in a cash-in-advance economy," *Journal of Money, Credit and Banking* 19, 19–32.

Claessens, Stijn (1988) "Balance-of-payments crises in a perfect foresight optimizing model," *Journal of International Money and Finance* 7, 363–72.

—— (1991) "Balance of payments crises in an optimal portfolio model," *European Economic Review* 35, 81–101.

Connolly, Michael B. and Arturo Fernandéz (1987) "Speculation against the pre-announced exchange rate in Mexico: January 1983 to June 1985," in Michael Connolly and Claudio Gonzaléz-Vega (eds) *Economic Reform and Stabilization in Latin America*, New York, Praeger, pp. 161–74.

—— and Dean Taylor (1984) "The exact timing of the collapse of an exchange rate regime and its impact on the relative price of traded goods," *Journal of Money, Credit and Banking* 16, 194–207.

Cumby, Robert E. and Sweder van Wijnbergen (1989) "Financial policy and speculative runs with a crawling peg: Argentina 1979–1981," *Journal of International Economics* 27, 111–27.

Dellas, Harris, and Alan Stockman (1988) "Self-fulfilling expectations, speculative attacks, and capital controls," Working Paper 138, University of Rochester New York, June.

Dornbusch, Rudiger (1987) "Collapsing exchange rate regimes," *Journal of Development Economics* 27, 71–83.

Drazen, Allan, and Elhanan Helpman (1988) "Stabilization with exchange rate management under uncertainty," in Elhanan Helpman, Assaf Razin, and Efraim

Sadka (eds) *Economic Effects of the Government Budget*, Cambridge, MA, MIT Press.

Edwards, Sebastian (1989) *Real Exchange Rates, Devaluation and Adjustment*, Cambridge, MA, MIT Press.

—— and Peter J. Montiel (1989) "Devaluation crises and the macroeconomic consequences of postponed adjustment in developing countries," *IMF Staff Papers* 36, 875–904.

Feller, William (1966) *An Introduction to Probability Theory and its Applications*, vol. 2, New York, Wiley.

Flood, Robert P. and Peter M. Garber (1984a) "Collapsing exchange rate regimes: some linear examples," *Journal of International Economics* 17, 1–13.

—— and —— (1984b) "Gold monetization and gold discipline," *Journal of Political Economy* 92, 90–107.

—— and —— (1991) "Linkages between speculative attack and target zone models of exchange rates," *Quarterly Journal of Economics* 106, 1367–72.

—— and Robert J. Hodrick (1986) "Real aspects of exchange rate regime choice with collapsing fixed rates," *Journal of International Economics* 21, 215–32.

Frenkel, Michael, and Martin Klein (1991) "Balance of payments crises and fiscal adjustment measures," *Journal of Macroeconomics* 13, 657–73.

Froot, Kenneth, and Maurice Obstfeld (1991) "Stochastic process switching: some simple solutions," *Econometrica* 59, 241–50.

Goldberg, Linda S. (1990) "Predicting exchange rate crises: Mexico revisited," NBER Working Paper 3320, Cambridge, MA, April.

Grilli, Vittorio (1986) "Buying and selling attacks on fixed exchange rate systems," *Journal of International Economics* 20, 143–56.

—— (1990) "Managing exchange rate crises: evidence from the 1890's," *Journal of International Money and Finance* 9, 135–82.

Ize, Alain, and Guillermo Ortiz (1987) "Fiscal rigidities, public debt, and capital flight," *IMF Staff Papers* 34, 311–32.

Krasker, William (1980) "The 'peso' problem in testing efficiency of forward exchange markets," *Journal of Monetary Economics* 6, 269–76.

Krugman, Paul (1979) "A model of balance of payments crises," *Journal of Money, Credit and Banking* 11, 311–25.

—— (1991) "Target zones and exchange rate dynamics," *Quarterly Journal of Economics* 106, 669–82.

—— and Julio Rotemberg (1990) "Target zones with limited reserves," NBER Working Paper 3418, Cambridge, MA, August.

Miller, Marcus H. and Paul Weller (1991) "Exchange rate bands with price inertia," *Economic Journal* 101, 1380–99.

Obstfeld, Maurice (1984) "Balance of payments crises and devaluation," *Journal of Money, Credit and Banking* 16, 208–17.

—— (1986a) "Speculative attack and the external constraint in a maximizing model of the balance of payments," *Canadian Journal of Economics* 19, 1–22.

—— (1986b) "Rational and self-fulfilling balance of payments crises," *American Economic Review* 76, 72–81.

Otani, Kiyoshi (1989) "The collapse of a fixed rate regime with a discrete realignment of the exchange rate," *Journal of the Japanese and International Economies* 3, 250–69.

Penati, Alessandro, and George Pennacchi (1989) "Optimal portfolio choice and the collapse of a fixed-exchange rate regime," *Journal of International Economics* 27, 1–24.

Rodriguez, Carlos (1978) "A stylized model of the devaluation–inflation spiral," *IMF Staff Papers* 25, 76–89.

Rogoff, Kenneth (1985) "The optimal degree of commitment to an intermediate monetary target," *Quarterly Journal of Economics* 100, 1169–89.

Salant, Stephen W. (1983) "The vulnerability of price stabilization schemes to speculative attack," *Journal of Political Economy* 91, 1–38.

—— and Dale W. Henderson (1978) "Market anticipation of government policy and the price of gold," *Journal of Political Economy* 86, 627–48.

Wood, Paul R. (1991) "Balance-of-payments crises with an optimizing central bank," mimeo, Board of Governors of the Federal Reserve System, Washington, DC.

van Wijnbergen, Sweder (1988) "Inflation, balance of payments crises, and public sector deficits," in Elhanan Helpman, Assaf Razin, and Efraim Sadka (eds) *Economic Effects of the Government Budget*, Cambridge, MA, MIT Press.

—— (1991) "Fiscal deficits, exchange rate crises, and inflation," *Review of Economic Studies* 58, 81–92.

Willman, Alpo (1987) "Speculative attacks on the currency with uncertain monetary policy reactions," *Economics Letters* 25, 75–8.

—— (1988) "The collapse of the fixed exchange rate regime with sticky wages and imperfect substitutability between domestic and foreign bonds," *European Economic Review* 32, 1817–38.

—— (1989) "Devaluation expectations and speculative attacks on the currency," *Scandinavian Journal of Economics* 91, 97–116.

—— (1991) "Why there is a lower bound on the central bank's foreign reserves," *Finnish Economic Papers* 4, 113–29.

Wyplosz, Charles (1986) "Capital controls and balance of payments crises," *Journal of International Money and Finance* 5, 167–79.

9 Continuous-time Models of Exchange Rates and Intervention

GIUSEPPE BERTOLA

1 Introduction

This chapter provides an introduction to continuous-time modeling tools, and to recent stochastic models of exchange rate determination emphasizing dynamic nonlinearities. Introductory surveys of recent contributions are already available in Krugman (1991a), Miller and Weller (1991a), and Svensson (1992a), and the economic structure and motivation of such models are quite similar to those of earlier work in a certainty setting surveyed by Obstfeld and Stockman (1985). But recent contributions obtain novel technical and economic insights in a continuous-time stochastic framework which readers might find unfamiliar and even forbidding at first. Since discrete-time counterparts to the new results would be very cumbersome to derive and ultimately not as clear, the payoffs of advanced techniques in terms of analytical neatness are well worth the effort of getting acquainted with the formalities of continuous-time stochastic modeling.

Accordingly, this chapter approaches the subject matter from a rather technical angle. Formal tools and results (which may be of use in a variety of fields) are discussed separately from their economic applications in the specific context of international finance. Deterministic and stochastic models are treated symmetrically in two separate sections, and the economic motivation of each exercise is discussed after rather than before its technical aspects. This somewhat dry structure aims at highlighting economic intuition in a simple formal setting on the one hand, and at providing a simple introduction to new and powerful technical tools on the other. If stochastic models were approached right away, it would be difficult to see the economics through a veil of technicalities. Conversely, a relatively formal treatment of the simple mathematics of certainty eases the approach to the unfamiliar formalities of stochastic models, and a firm grasp of the intuition for simple economic problems carries over to technically more complex frameworks.

The chapter has three substantive sections. Section 2 treats exchange rate determination in a certainty setting. Basic technical notions and formal tools are reviewed in section 2.1, while section 2.2 interprets formal assumptions and results in the economic context of arbitrage-free exchange rate and official intervention models. The similarly structured section 3 extends technical and economic insights to the case of uncertainty: section 3.1 offers an introductory treatment of stochastic processes and stochastic integration, leaving all discussion of the underlying economics to the brief section 3.2. Section 4 reviews recent work on "target zones" and regime switches. Space prevents an exhaustive survey of this large and still growing literature. Little more than an annotated bibliography is offered below, sketching the basic Krugman (1991b) model first and then outlining various directions along which it has been extended in the literature. Details are omitted, but the rather thorough treatment of technical aspects in the previous sections should enable readers to approach the original contributions knowledgeably and to work on similar matters if so inclined. The concluding section 5 briefly summarizes recent research, outlines how similar technical tools and results may be applied to different economic problems, and discusses questions of substance still open in the exchange rate context.

2   Certainty

Most readers are probably familiar with the technical tools and economic insights relevant to exchange rate dynamics under certainty, and in particular with the excellent survey by Obstfeld and Stockman (1985). The treatment here differs from Obstfeld and Stockman's in that simpler economic problems are considered, while the mathematical treatment is more formal. Section 2.1 deals with purely mathematical notions; economic interpretations and intuition are treated separately in section 2.2 to highlight the distinction between formal results obtained from equally formal assumptions on the one hand and the economic soundness and relevance of the assumptions and results on the other.

2.1   Integration

Functional equations are essential to the subject matter at hand, and it is instructive to consider a very simple case first. Consider a scalar variable t, taking values on the real line, and two scalar-valued functions $x(.)$ and $f(.)$ linked by the relationship

$$x(t) = f(t) + \alpha \frac{dx(t)}{dt} \tag{9.1}$$

for all t. This is an abstract mathematical requirement for now, and will be given an economic interpretation in the following section. The $x(.)$ function is the unknown in our problem, and *endogenous* to the model behind equation (9.1), while $f(.)$ is part of the problem data and hence *exogenous*.

The problem is that of finding $\{x(t)\}$ such that (9.1) is satisfied over some range of t values, for a given scalar α and a given $\{f(t)\}$ (the braces notation refers to the whole path of a variable as a single mathematical object). The functional solution $x(.)$ can be found by integration of (9.1). Recall the fundamental theorem of calculus: given a function $y(\tau)$,

$$\int_t^T y'(\tau)\, d\tau = \int_t^T dy(\tau) = y(T) - y(t) \tag{9.2}$$

where both equalities are definitional if the expressions on their sides are well defined. Separating the endogenous function and its derivatives from the exogenous $f(.)$ and multiplying both sides by the positive quantity $\exp[-(\tau-t)/\alpha]/\alpha$ we obtain

$$\exp\left(-\frac{\tau-t}{\alpha}\right)\frac{x(\tau)}{\alpha} - \exp\left(-\frac{\tau-t}{\alpha}\right)\frac{dx(\tau)}{d\tau} = \exp\left(-\frac{\tau-t}{\alpha}\right)\frac{f(\tau)}{\alpha} \tag{9.3}$$

The left-hand side of this relationship is the derivative with respect to τ of $-\exp[-(\tau-t)/\alpha]x(\tau)$, and integrating between t and T as in (9.2) yields

$$x(t) = \int_t^T \exp\left(-\frac{\tau-t}{\alpha}\right)\frac{f(\tau)}{\alpha}\, d\tau + \exp\left(-\frac{T-t}{\alpha}\right)x(T) \tag{9.4}$$

If we restrict attention to functions $x(t)$ such that

$$\lim_{T\to\infty} \exp\left(-\frac{T-t}{\alpha}\right)x(T) = 0 \tag{9.5}$$

(a purely mathematical requirement for now; see below for a discussion of the economic reasoning that might rationalize it), as T diverges to infinity we get

$$x(t) = \int_t^\infty \exp\left(-\frac{\tau-t}{\alpha}\right)\frac{f(\tau)}{\alpha}\, d\tau \tag{9.6}$$

The constant α and the $\{f(\tau)\}$ function are exogenously given, and hence the expression in (9.6) is indeed a solution to our problem if the integral converges.

In applications, it is of course desirable to compute closed-form expressions for the integral in (9.6). Consider for example the exogenous function

$$f(t) = \begin{cases} \theta t & \text{if } t < \bar{f}/\theta \\ \bar{f} & \text{otherwise} \end{cases} \tag{9.7}$$

Taking $\theta > 0$ for concreteness, $\{f(t)\}$ grows steadily until it reaches $\bar{f}$ and is constant forever after that. It is plotted against t in figure 9.1 as

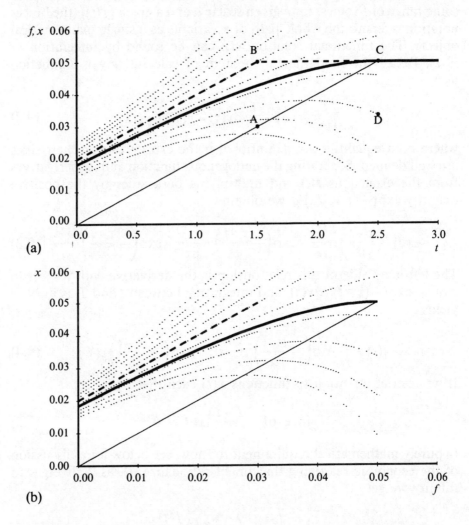

(a)

(b)

Figure 9.1 A regime switch under certainty: $\alpha = 1.0$, $\theta = 0.02$.

a thin solid line going through points A and C.

For all $t \geq \bar{f}/\theta$, integration of (9.6) yields $x(t) = \bar{f}$. Inserting (9.7) in (9.4) and solving a simple integral, it would also be easy to compute the $\{x(t); \ t \leq \bar{f}/\theta\}$ path which solves our problem in the region where f grows linearly. However, it is instructive to step back momentarily from the integral representation (9.6) and view the problem at hand as that of finding a *functional* solution to the problem posed by (9.1) and (9.7). In the interval $(-\infty < t \leq \bar{f}/\theta)$, $f(t)$ in (9.7) is a single-valued differentiable function of time with $df/dt = \theta$. Hence, we can express the dependence of x on t through f, and bypass the t dimension of the problem by writing $x(t) = x[f(t)]$. Recalling the change-of-variable rule

$$\frac{dx[f(t)]}{dt} = \frac{dx}{df}\frac{df}{dt} \tag{9.8}$$

equation (9.1) can be written

$$x(f) = f + \alpha x'(f)\theta \tag{9.9}$$

for $f < \bar{f}$. This is an easy differential equation, solved by functions in the form $x(f) = \alpha\theta + f + C \exp(f/\alpha\theta)$ for any value of C. The dotted lines in figure 9.1 represent several such solutions for various C values.

To determine C, note that $\{x(.)\}$ must approach $x(\bar{f}/\theta) = \bar{f}$ as t approaches $\bar{f}/\theta$: otherwise, the derivative $dx(t)/dt$ would not exist at $t = \bar{f}/\theta$ and (9.1) would fail. Using (9.9) in

$$\lim_{f \to \bar{f}} x(f) = \bar{f} \tag{9.10}$$

we have $C = -\alpha\theta \exp(-\bar{f}/\alpha\theta)$. Thus, the solution (9.6) to (9.1) and (9.5) can be written as a function of f

$$x(f) = \alpha\theta + f - \alpha\theta \exp\left(\frac{f - \bar{f}}{\alpha\theta}\right) \tag{9.11}$$

for $f \leq \bar{f}$. This is plotted in figure 9.1(b) by a thick solid line. Reinstating the t index,

$$x(t) = \alpha\theta + f(t) - \alpha\theta \exp\left[\frac{f(t) - \bar{f}}{\alpha\theta}\right]$$

which is plotted against t as a thick solid line in figure 9.1(a).

The solution has several noteworthy features. First, if the rate of increase of $f(t)$ for $t < \bar{f}/\theta$ could be extrapolated to the infinite future, then integration of (9.6) would yield

$$\tilde{x}(t) = \int_t^\infty \exp\left(-\frac{\tau-t}{\alpha}\right) \frac{f(t)+\theta(\tau-t)}{\alpha} \, d\tau = f(t) + \alpha\theta \qquad (9.12)$$

which is the broken 45° line in figure 9.1. Since $C < 0$, the expression in (9.12) lies above the $x(.)$ function that solves our problem for every $f < \bar{f}$ and for every $t < \bar{f}/\theta$ in figure 9.1(a). Second, the distance between $x(.)$ and $\tilde{x}(.)$ increases with f since $\alpha\theta > 0$, and the thick solid line bends down and away from the 45° line as f reaches its upper limit $\bar{f}$. Third, the broken line meets its upper boundary *smoothly*: not only does $x(t_-) = x(t_+)$ as required by (9.10), but also $x'(t_-) = x'(t_+)$ and $x'(\bar{f}_-) = x'(\bar{f}_+) = 0$. As both $\{x(t)\}$ and $\{f(t)\}$ are continuous at $t = \bar{f}/\theta$, the first derivative of the endogenous function $\{x(.)\}$ must also be continuous to satisfy (9.1).

2.2 Money demand and arbitrage-free equilibrium

Conditions like (9.1) and (9.5) are easily rationalized in simple monetary-approach models of exchange rate determination, where economic interpretations are available for the $f(t)$ dynamics assumed in (9.7) and for the character of the resulting $\{x(t)\}$ solution. Omitting time indexes for now, let money demand take the form

$$M^d = PY \exp(-\alpha i) \qquad (9.13)$$

where Y is a scale parameter, i is the short-term nominal interest rate, and P is the price level. In its simplicity, this relationship does make sense as a representation of transactions-motivated money demand. For given i, real money demand M^d/P is proportional to Y, which indexes the volume of monetary transactions and, in a fully specified model, would depend on income or wealth and on the transaction technology. For given Y, money demand is a decreasing function of the nominal return i on interest-bearing assets (the opportunity cost of money holdings). While the negative effect of high interest rates on money demand may take a variety of forms in specific models, a constant semielasticity α to the nominal interest rate is analytically convenient and empirically realistic.[1]

Viewing the exchange rate as the relative price of two monies, let the country under consideration interact with the rest of the world in two ways. First, its currency can be freely exchanged with another currency at exchange rate X. Second, goods traded in the market where its money provides transaction services are perfectly substitutable to, and freely exchangeable with, those traded abroad. The foreign price level can be normalized to unity choosing foreign currency as the numeraire and, to rule out arbitrage opportunities, it must be the case that

$$P = X \tag{9.14}$$

$$i = i^* + \frac{\dot{X}}{X} \tag{9.15}$$

where a dot denotes a time derivative. Condition (9.14) imposes that the price of perfectly substitutable goods be the same when expressed in the same currency; with a unitary foreign price level, the exchange rate X measures units of home currency per unit of foreign currency (the standard – outside the UK – convention from the point of view of the home country). By (9.15), holding each currency entails the same opportunity cost, so that it would not be profitable to move funds across currencies for the purely speculative purpose of performing the reverse transaction in the immediate future.

In equilibrium, of course, money demands must equal money supplies. Denote home money supply by M and foreign money supply by M^*, and let foreign money demand M^{*d} be given by an expression similar to (9.13) with scale Y^*. Imposing $M^d = M$ and $M^{*d} = M^*$, taking logs, and rearranging yields an equation identical to (9.1) above with

$$f(t) = \ln\left[\frac{M(t)Y^*(t)}{M^*(t)Y(t)}\right] = m(t) - m^*(t) + y^*(t) - y(t) \tag{9.16}$$

if lower-case variables denote natural logarithms. In (9.1), $x(t)$ is now the natural logarithm of the exchange rate at time t, α is the semielasticity of money demand with respect to the nominal interest rate, and the exogenous function $f(t)$ is the logarithm of the ratio of relative money supplies to the ratio of the scale of transactions in the two countries.

The expression in (9.16) indexes *fundamental* determinants of the exchange rate's level: stock money supplies, and transaction-motivated stock money demands. In static equilibrium, the relative price of currencies should be that which eliminates excess demand for either money stock. But monies are assets in intertemporal models, as emphasized by for example Svensson (1985). In (9.1), the exchange rate x depends on its own rate of change as well as on the current level of f. This illustrates an economic insight valid in much more general models than that under consideration: in an international setting, the relative demand for two currencies (and, in equilibrium, their relative price) depends on prospects of appreciation or depreciation as well as on current transaction motives. As money competes with interest-bearing assets in agents' financial portfolios, demand for currencies depends both on their current desirability as a vehicle of transactions and on their expected future price. Hence speculative capital-gain-seeking motives have a role in exchange rate determination.

2.2.1 Bubbles

Condition (9.5), however, restricts attention to those $\{x(t)\}$ paths along which money is ultimately held for transaction purposes. In fact, it allows the exchange rate to be expressed in (9.6) as the present discounted value of future fundamentals, i.e. of future transaction services and future stock supplies. If (9.5) were not satisfied along an exchange rate path, the level of $\{x(t)\}$ would depend on purely speculative motives, with one currency valued above the other just because it is expected to be even more overvalued in the future. Such exchange rate paths contain a "bubble," or a process that satisfies an equation like (9.1) regardless of the fundamental's level.

Integrating (9.1), it is always possible to write

$$x(t) = \int_t^\infty \exp\left(-\frac{\tau - t}{\alpha}\right)\frac{f(\tau)}{\alpha}\,d\tau + \lim_{T\to\infty} \exp\left(-\frac{T-t}{\alpha}\right)x(T) \equiv F(t) + B(t)$$

(9.17)

where $F(t)$ is given by (9.6) and satisfies (9.1) by construction. The difference between (9.17) and the fundamental-based solution (9.6)

$$B(t) \equiv \lim_{T\to\infty} \exp\left(-\frac{T-t}{\alpha}\right)x(T)$$

must then satisfy the *homogeneous* differential equation $B(t) = \alpha dB(t)/dt$, which has solutions in the form

$$B(t) = B(0)\exp(t/\alpha)$$

as functions of t.[2]

Bubbles grow exponentially over time in the certainty framework under consideration, and exchange rate paths which violate (9.5) embark on trajectories like those plotted as dotted lines in figure 9.1. The no-arbitrage condition (9.1) is always satisfied along such paths. To rule out a self-fulfilling conviction of endless appreciation one has to assume, first, that (at least) one agent in the economy under consideration does indeed look forward to the ultimate infinite-horizon implications of the trajectory implied by the initial condition (which is of course inappropriate if all agents and speculators are finitely lived and hence infinite in number over an infinite time horizon: see Tirole, 1982); second, that the limiting behavior of a bubble path would be inconsistent with some basic equilibrium conditions. In the framework under consideration, with certainty and a bubble on fiat money, a bubble would annihilate one currency's real value as prices expressed in the two currencies diverge from each other. This would eventually violate a no-arbitrage condition if currencies are at least partly backed in real terms.[3]

2.2.2   Intervention and nonlinearities

Turning now to economic interpretations for paths like that illustrated in figure 9.1, it is useful to introduce a distinction between the dynamics of the variables included in the "fundamentals" definition (9.16). All fundamental variables are modeled above as exogenous to exchange rate determination: but while some are best interpreted as acts of nature beyond anybody's control, others may be viewed as policy actions, whose dynamic effects are interesting to discuss in the light of the formal results above.

The distinction is tenuous, since all variables likely to appear on the right-hand side of (9.16) are subject to policy decisions or "interventions" of some type as well as to uncontrolled dynamics of different character and origin. Money supply is a most likely policy instrument, however, and it is a useful exercise to view the "fundamental" path in figure 9.1 as tracking the quantity of money in the home country of our model, taking M^*, Y, and Y^* as given and (for simplicity) constant. We are then modeling exchange rate determination in a country that fixes the exchange rate after a period of sustained money creation. The inflationary policy is known to cease as soon as its continuation would depreciate the exchange rate beyond $\bar{f}$, and the public's money demand takes this into account.

With this interpretation, the simple formal setting of section 9.1 usefully illustrates economic intuition and formal insights common to models of infrequent intervention, regime switches, and nonlinear exchange rate dynamics. A basic economic mechanism is responsible for the character of the solution. By equation (9.1), which we now view as a reasonable no-arbitrage requirement in an intertemporal context, exchange rate determination is *forward looking*. Ruling out bubbles, the current level of the exchange rate in (9.6) and its dynamic path are determined by not only the current but also the future relative usefulness for transactions of two currencies. "Stabilizing" speculation tends to anticipate future fundamental developments, and the (discounted) future dynamics are reflected in current exchange rates.

From this perspective, it is easy to interpret the qualitative features of the $\{x(t)\}$ solution in figure 9.1. Forward-looking agents know that post-stabilization fundamental levels will be lower than they would be if no stabilization ever occurred. Hence, the pre-stabilization exchange rate (plotted by the thick solid line) is always lower than that which simply extrapolates to infinity the current rate of money creation (plotted by the broken line). Further, future fundamentals are discounted at rate $1/\alpha$ in (9.6). Hence, eventual stabilization becomes more and more relevant to current exchange rates as it comes closer in time, and the solution bends further and further away from the hypothetical free-float exchange rate. It is also not surprising that the exchange rate should go through the stabilization smoothly. A fully expected exchange rate jump at $t = \bar{f}/\theta$ would obviously be inconsistent with equilibrium, as none of the agents faced by the portfolio management process behind (9.13) would want to hold other than an infinitely negative amount of the currency undergoing a step depreciation. As $x(t)$ and (by assumption) $f(t)$ are continuous upon stabilization, $\dot{x}(t)$ cannot jump either for (9.1) to hold at $t = \bar{f}/\theta$ and, in the light of (9.15), the path of the interest rate differential $i - i^*$ is continuous at the intervention point.

2.2.3   Exchange rate paths and interventions

If at some time $t < \bar{f}/\theta$ the exchange rate took a value $\hat{x}(t)$ different from that given in (9.11), equation (9.1) would subsequently require it to follow a path like those plotted by dotted lines in the figure. Such paths can be written in the form (9.7) for some integration constant $\hat{C}$ different from the C which solves (9.10). They deviate from the solution derived above by the quantity $(\hat{C} - C)\,\exp(f/\alpha\theta)$ which, with $f/\theta = t$, diverges exponentially at rate $1/\alpha$: a *bubble* in terms of the discussion above.[4] Like all bubbles, such solutions do not violate instantaneous arbitrage. Only their failure to join the (asymptotically) bubble-free limiting solution at $t = \bar{f}/\theta$ rules them out in equilibrium.

However, the dotted lines in figure 9.1 are not qualitatively different from the thick solid line, and each of them could in fact be validated by different assumptions as to the dynamics of $\{f\}$. The bubble-free exchange rate in (9.6) is determined by the whole future path of fundamentals. When focusing on a situation of initial fundamental growth and eventual stabilization (or "intervention"), one needs to specify not only the pre-stabilization behavior of fundamentals (a logarithmic trend in the example above), but also the time *and* level of the intervention (respectively $\bar{f}/\theta$ and $\bar{f}$ above). If one of the last two is kept constant, varying the other will validate a different dotted line as the pre-stabilization exchange rate function. The inflationary policy represented by the upward trend θ might still be assumed to stop as the exchange rate and the fundamental reach $\bar{f}$; but if this need not occur at $\bar{f}/\theta$, then (for example) the straight broken line in figure 9.1 may plot the bubble-free exchange rate path: the fundamental might grow up to point A, then jump to point B, and stay constant thereafter to prevent the exchange rate from exceeding $\bar{f}$. Any of the other dotted lines which reach $\bar{f}$ could be similarly validated by smaller (or larger) fundamental jumps occurring sooner (or later). Symmetrically, one could consider the family of policies that freeze the exchange rate at $t = \bar{f}/\theta$ but specify post-stabilization fundamental and exchange rate levels different from $\bar{f}$: for the same pre-stabilization fundamental path, any of the dotted lines could be validated by a final fundamental jump (e.g. a jump from point C to point D). If the fundamental path is allowed to jump, then ruling out discontinuities in the exchange rate's level does *not* imply continuity of its time derivative (and of interest rate differentials). For example, an upward f jump of size $\alpha\theta$ from A to B would offset the drop from θ to zero of the fundamental's and the exchange rate's rate of change, consistently with a continuous exchange rate, and rule out arbitrage opportunities. Similarly, a downward fundamental jump from C to D would offset the shift from a locally appreciating exchange rate path to stabilization at level D.

The effect of the form of intervention on exchange rate dynamics is worth emphasizing, for two reasons. First, the literature reviewed in section 4 below is often less than explicit as to the nature of the "interventions" considered, and this might engender some confusion as to relationships between formal results, economic assumptions, and empirical reality. Second, and looking back to slightly older literature, the economic mechanisms under consideration are essentially the same as those underlying earlier contributions on regime collapses and announced policy changes, where jumps in money supply and other policy variables played an important role.[5]

In an exercise symmetric to that above, i.e. a transition from fixed to flexible exchange rates, continuity of interest rate differentials would be particularly unrealistic, as exchange rate crises have important interest rate effects (see chapter 8 and the references given there). One should then identify the formal assumptions responsible for the result in the simple model above and scrutinize their economic realism, paying particular attention to the economic nature of the "interventions" under consideration. Recall that money supply is a natural candidate for the switching dynamics exemplified by the fundamental path of figure 9.1. Still, monetary authorities can affect money supply in more than one way. The stock of (fiat) money M issued by a country's monetary authorities satisfies the central bank's nominal accounting identity

$$M = D + R \qquad (9.18)$$

where D, *domestic credit*, denotes credit extended by the central bank to domestic residents (notably the government) and R, *reserves*, reflects the domestic-currency value of amounts owed to the issuer of home currency by foreigners (notably foreign central banks). To any movement in M must then correspond some combination of movements in D and R: a change in M accompanied by a change in R is referred to as *unsterilized* intervention in the literature; *sterilized* intervention swaps D with R; and *open market operations* move D and M in the same direction.[6] Given Y, Y^*, and M^*, only the outstanding money stock M matters for exchange rate determination in the simple monetary model. Hence sterilized intervention, which leaves M unchanged, has no effects on $x(.)$. Reserve movements may still be relevant to the feasibility of sterilized intervention, however, and to the likelihood of (future) unsterilized intervention – which matters for future exchange rates and, given forward-looking speculation, current rates as well.

Since most of a central bank's domestic assets reflect credit extended to the country's fiscal authorities, the behavior of D has obvious policy relevance and, in the long run, ultimately determines that of M if the range of variation of reserves is limited by sustainability concerns. In models of collapsing exchange rate regimes, the potential exchange rate and price level effects of an upward-sloping domestic credit path are neutralized by reserve expenditure (unsterilized intervention) to keep money supply consistent with a fixed exchange rate. The flow nature of government deficits and domestic credit changes makes it natural to model D as a continuous process. This does not imply that fundamentals should be continuous across regime changes, however: the stock R of reserves can jump via unsterilized intervention for a given D, as in the case of speculative attacks when such stock outflows have to occur to prevent arbitrage opportunities. If money market fundamentals jump, interest rates also jump to preserve money market equilibrium, and the exchange rate path is continuous but not smooth across regimes. The broken line in figure 9.1 plots a time-reversed "collapsing" exchange rate path. As the formerly floating exchange rate is fixed at $\bar{f}$ at point A, and f jumps up (a stock inflow of reserves), the interest rate differential drops discretely from θ to zero; if time was running from right to left in the figure, the experiment would correspond exactly to that considered by models of collapsing exchange rate regimes.

3   Uncertainty

This section extends the formal and economic framework above to an uncertainty setting. Uncertainty does not introduce really new essential economic insights, and the formal tools employed in explicitly stochastic models can be viewed as natural extensions of the more familiar ones reviewed above. But the extension is still worth pursuing in both respects. From a substantive point of view, allowing for realistic uncertainty makes it possible to derive a theoretical model's empirical implications explicitly. At a formal level, the technicalities of stochastic calculus are new and exciting, and useful in many applications other than those considered here.

The treatment again starts with an abstract review of mathematical concepts and techniques, postponing discussion of the assumptions' realism and of the economic intuition behind formal results to sections 3.2 and 4. Of course, the economics of the problem are quite the same as those of the certainty model above, and readers might want to interpret formal assumptions and results along the lines of section 2.2 even before reaching the end of section 3.1.

3.1   Stochastic processes

Consider first how uncertainty might be introduced in a situation where numbers such as $\{x\}$ and $\{f\}$ are associated with a time index $\{t\}$. If $x(.)$ and $f(.)$ were single-valued functions of t, as in section 2.1, then their behavior would be perfectly predictable by anybody with access to a clock and a calendar. We thus need to consider mathematical objects that depend not only on t but also on some other, imperfectly observable index. The objects of our analysis are then *stochastic processes*: random functions of time, or collections of random variables indexed by t.[7] Endogenous and exogenous variables are real-valued functions $\{x(t; \omega)\}$ and $\{f(t; \omega)\}$ with arguments t, taking values in some subset of the real line, and ω, an unobservable *state of nature*. States of nature are elements of some specified set; their role is the purely formal one of indexing the unknown, and they need not have numerical interpretations. The notions of *probability* and (conditional) *expectation* make this concept operative: the exact value of ω is not known or there would be no uncertainty as to $\{f\}$ and $\{x\}$, but the likelihood of different ωs can be evaluated quantitatively by probability assessments reflecting the degree of uncertainty as to which particular ω rules the behavior of $\{f\}$ and $\{x\}$.

Rather than developing such concepts in full generality, consider a specific and very powerful formal framework. The basic building block for a class of stochastic processes which admit a stochastic counterpart to the functional relationships studied in section 2.1 is a *standard Brownian motion* or Wiener process, denoted $\{W(t)\}$ in what follows. This process can be defined by its probabilistic properties: $W(0; \omega) = 0$ for "almost all" ω, in the sense that the probability is one that the process takes value zero at $t = 0$; fixing ω, $\{W(t; \omega)\}$ is continuous in t with probability one; fixing $t \geq 0$, probability statements about $W(t; \omega)$ can be made viewing $W(t)$ as a normally distributed random variable, with mean zero and variance t as of time zero: realizations of $W(t)$ are quite concentrated for small values of t, while more and more probability is attached to values far from zero for larger and larger values of t. Most importantly, similar properties hold if enough is known about ω to eliminate all uncertainty as to the values of $W(t)$ for t less than or equal to some t_1. If the realization of $\{W(t); 0 \le t \le t_1\}$ is known with certainty, then probability statements on $\{W(t); t_1 \le t \le T\}$ can be made viewing $W(t) - W(t_1)$ as a normally distributed random variable with zero mean and variance $t - t_1$.

The Wiener process is a random walk defined on infinitesimal time and state steps, a simple and powerful way to model uncertainty: nature takes infinitely frequent random steps, and probabilistic assessments of events far into the future are more uncertain inasmuch as the number of random steps taken in the meantime is larger.[8] Normality of discrete time increments follows by a central limit theorem, as each such increment contains infinitely many independent random steps. Independent increments endow the Wiener process with the Markov property, whose importance in applications cannot be overstressed. In simple terms,[9] a stochastic process is *Markov* in levels if the value it takes at some time τ contains all the information necessary to form probability assessments on the values it takes for $t > \tau$. This is obviously true of $\{W\}$ since, once $W(\tau; \omega)$ is known, for $t > \tau$ $W(t; \omega)$ is normally distributed with mean $W(\tau)$ and variance $t - \tau$, regardless of what path ω might have determined for $t < \tau$. Independence of the process's increments has one important and somewhat disconcerting implication: for a fixed ω, the path $\{W(t)\}$ is continuous but (with probability one) *not* differentiable at any point t. This is awkward but, after a moment's thought, quite intuitive. A process with differentiable sample paths would have locally predictable increments, as extrapolation of the recent past would eliminate all uncertainty about the behavior of the process in the immediate future. For increments to be independent over any t interval, including arbitrarily short ones, the direction of movement must be random at arbitrarily close t points. A typical sample path then turns so frequently as to be nondifferentiable at any t point and has *infinite variation*: the absolute value of its increments over infinitesimally small subdivisions of an arbitrarily short time interval is infinite.

It is far from trivial to show that the Wiener process can be constructed from some underlying set of ωs and an associated probability structure. Each ω indexes one among the continuous functions which map a t into real numbers, and the probability (measure) defined on this functional space is defined so as to satisfy the above properties. From this perspective, nondifferentiable paths may be taken to reflect the fact that, among all continuous functions, those which are differentiable at some t are so few as to receive negligible probability weight. Such formalities can remain in the background of applied work. Still, it is helpful to view the Wiener process (and the functions of it constructed and manipulated below) as a function of time *and* "states of nature," and stochastic problems as functional problems similar in spirit to those considered in section 2.1 above. In particular, a stochastic process is conceptually single valued as a function of t and ω, so stochastic problems are akin to that posed by the first portion of the path in figure 9.1 with $\{f\}$ and $\{x\}$ one-to-one functions of t.

3.1.1 Stochastic calculus

Functions mapping the realizations of $\{W\}$ into real numbers depend on t and on ω through their argument, and hence are stochastic processes. They can be manipulated by stochastic calculus tools developed by the Japanese mathematician T. Itô on the pattern of Leibnitz's functional calculus.[10] While stochastic and nonstochastic calculus are quite similar in spirit, the special nature of the functions treated by the latter introduce some important formal differences: since Brownian paths are never differentiable, it is not possible to apply the standard calculus tools recalled in (9.2) and (9.8) to functions of Wiener processes.

However, mathematical operators with similar properties are available. Given a process $\{A(t)\}$ with finite variation, a process $\{y(t)\}$ which satisfies certain regularity conditions, and a Wiener process $\{W(t)\}$, an *Itô process* $\{z(t)\}$ is defined by the integral equation

$$z(T; \omega) = z(t; \omega) + \int_t^T y(\tau; \omega)\, dW(\tau; \omega) + \int_t^T dA(t; \omega) \qquad (9.19)$$

where $\int y\, dW$ is a *stochastic* or Itô integral, whose exact definition need not concern us here.[11] Integration modulates the raw randomness of the Wiener process's increments $dW(t)$ by a "weight" function $\{y(t)\}$, itself a stochastic process in general. The formal properties of Itô integrals are similar to those of more familiar integrals. Stochastic integrals of linear combinations can be written as linear combinations of stochastic integrals, and the *integration by parts* formula (Harrison, 1985, pp. 72–3)

$$z(t)x(t) = z(0)x(0) + \int_0^t z(\tau)\, dx(\tau) + \int_0^t x(\tau)\, dz(\tau) \qquad (9.20)$$

holds when z and x are processes in the class defined by (9.19) and one of them has finite variation. The stochastic integral has one additional important property. By the unpredictable character of the Wiener process's increments, for any $\{y(t)\}$ such that the expression is well defined

$$E_t \left[\int_t^T y(\tau) \, dW(\tau) \right] = 0$$

where the *conditional expectation* operator $E_t[.]$ denotes integration over states of nature using the probability weights which reflect all relevant information available as of time t (information which, in turn, is summarized by the current level of the processes under consideration if they are Markov).

Using the differential form suggested by (9.2), we write from (9.19)

$$dz(t) = y(t) \, dW(t) + dA(t) \tag{9.21}$$

and we are led to seek a stochastic equivalent of the change-of-variable rule (9.8). If $f(.)$ is a twice continuously differentiable function from real numbers into real numbers, and $\{z(t)\}$ is an Itô process in the form (9.19), then $\{f[z(t)]\}$ can itself be written in the form (9.19) as

$$f[z(T)] = f[z(t)] + \int_t^T f'[z(\tau)]y(\tau) \, dW(\tau) + \int_t^T f'[z(\tau)] \, dA(\tau)$$
$$+ \frac{1}{2} \int_t^T f''[z(\tau)][y(\tau)]^2 \, d\tau$$

or, in differential form,

$$df[z(t)] = f'[z(t)]y(t) \, dW(t) + f'[z(t)] \, dA(t)$$
$$+ \frac{1}{2} f''[z(t)][y(t)]^2 \, dt \tag{9.22}$$

Comparing Itô rule (9.22) with (9.8), we see that when applied to an Itô process the change-of-variable operation takes not only the first but also the second derivative into account. Heuristically, the order of magnitude of $dW(t)$ increments is higher than that of dt if uncertainty is present in every dt interval, no matter how small. Independent increments also imply that the sign of $dW(t)$ is just as likely to be positive as negative, and by Jensen's inequality the curvature of $f(z)$ influences locally nonrandom behavior even in the infinitesimal limit:

$$E_t(df[z(t)]) \lesseqgtr f'[z(t)] \, E_t[dz(t)] \qquad \text{as} \qquad f''[z(t)] \lesseqgtr 0$$

Taking conditional expectations in (9.22) where $E_t[dW(t)] = 0$ by the unpredictability of the Wiener process, we have

$$E_t(df[z(t)]) = f'[z(t)] \, dA(t) + \frac{1}{2} f''[z(t)][y(t)]^2 \, dt$$

This conditional expectation is itself a stochastic process. Its value depends on what information is available at the time it is formed, and any such information depends in turn on what ω "state of nature" rules the behavior of the processes under consideration.

We are now ready to state a counterpart to the basic relationship (9.1). In the presence of uncertainty, a linkage is posited among the realizations of three stochastic processes rather than among three functions of time:

$$x(t; \omega) = f(t; \omega) + \alpha \frac{E_t[dx(t; \omega)]}{dt} \tag{9.23}$$

with the equality holding for all t and all ω in some specified set. Again taking the process $\{f(.)\}$ as given, we want to solve for a process $\{x(.)\}$ whose level and conditional expected differential satisfy (9.23). As long as we keep in mind that the objects under consideration are stochastic processes in the form (9.19) and we equip ourselves with the appropriate technical tools, we can follow the formal steps of section 2.1 in our search for such a solution. The nonstochastic problem could be approached either by integrating the relationship (9.23) or by rewriting the problem as one that involves a function of f rather than of time. Similar approaches are valid in the stochastic context.

Using the differential form of (9.20) with $\{z(t)\} = \exp[-(\tau - t)/\alpha]$, equation (9.23) can be rearranged to read

$$d\left[-\exp\left(-\frac{\tau - t}{\alpha} \right) x(\tau) \right] = \exp\left(-\frac{\tau - t}{\alpha} \right) \left[\frac{f(\tau)}{\alpha} \right] dt - \exp\left(-\frac{\tau - t}{\alpha} \right)$$
$$(dx(\tau) - E_t[dx(\tau)])$$

Integrating as in (9.19) the increment $x(T) - x(t)$ may be expressed as an ordinary integral of the first term on the right-hand side plus a stochastic integral against expectational errors.[12] Taking expectations conditional on time t information, the stochastic integral vanishes by definition, and slight rearranging yields

$$x(t) = E_t\left[\int_t^T \exp\left(-\frac{\tau - t}{\alpha} \right) \frac{f(\tau)}{\alpha} d\tau \right] + \exp\left(-\frac{T - t}{\alpha} \right) E_t[x(T)] \tag{9.24}$$

If we let T diverge to infinity and require that

$$\lim_{T \to \infty} \exp\left(-\frac{T - t}{\alpha} \right) E_t[x(T)] = 0 \tag{9.25}$$

we have the formal equivalent of (9.6) in a stochastic context: for all t (and ω) our solution should satisfy

$$x(t) = E_t\left[\int_t^\infty \exp\left(-\frac{\tau - t}{\alpha} \right) \frac{f(\tau)}{\alpha} d\tau \right] = \int_t^\infty \exp\left(-\frac{\tau - t}{\alpha} \right) \frac{E_t[f(\tau)]}{\alpha} d\tau$$
$$\tag{9.26}$$

where the second equality follows from the fact that double integrals in either order are both well defined if one of them is and are equal to each other ("Fubini's theorem," see for example Harrison, 1985, p. 131). Like (9.6), equation (9.26) represents the solution in terms of exogenous quantities. Such integral representations are not very useful for characterization purposes, however. In section 3.1.2 we discuss closed-form solutions for stochastic versions of the problem proposed and solved in section 2.1.

3.1.2   Stabilization

There is more than one way to specify a stochastic counterpart to the dynamics of figure 9.1, where $\{f(t)\}$ moves upwards for a while and is stopped at some point. Even ruling out fundamental jumps, choosing a cutoff level $\bar{f}$ is not the same as choosing a stabilization time if f depends on ω as well as on t: in a stochastic setting, we could either specify a time and let the level be random or specify a stabilization level and let it occur at a random time. The latter assumption is more tractable because, if the change in dynamic behavior is triggered by f hitting $\bar{f}$, then it is possible for $\{f(t)\}$ to be a Markov process in levels; as will be apparent below, this makes it possible to bypass the time dimension of the problem.

As a simple example, consider a process with initial condition $f(0) = 0$ and differential

$$df(t) = \theta \, dt + \sigma dW(t) \qquad (9.27)$$

This is the differential of a continuous-time random walk with drift, perhaps the simplest Markov process in levels. The distribution of its increments is independent not only of variables other than its current level (which makes it Markov) but of the level itself as well. If $\sigma = 0$ then (nonstochastic) integration yields $f(t) = \theta t$, as in equation (9.7) and figure 9.1. With $\sigma > 0$, if (9.27) always holds up to time τ then integration of (9.27) as in (9.19) yields

$$f(\tau) = f(t) + (\tau - t)\theta + [W(\tau) - W(t)]\sigma \qquad (9.28)$$

and $f(\tau)$ is normally distributed with mean $f(t) + \theta(\tau - t)$ and variance $(\tau - t)\sigma^2$ on the basis of the information available at t. The distribution of $f(\tau)$ depends on $f(t)$ only (and on parameters) in this case, and the same Markov property holds even if there exist times when (9.27) is relaxed, provided that at any such time the differential of the $\{f(t)\}$ process is uniquely determined by its level.

If $\{f(t)\}$ is Markov, each of the conditional expectations on the right-hand side of equation (9.26) can be written as a function of $f(t)$.

Thus, the left-hand side can be expressed in terms of $f(t)$ as well and, as in section 2, we can work with $x(f)$ instead of $x(t)$. Itô's rule (9.22) yields

$$dx(f) = x'(f)(\theta\, dt + \sigma\, dW) + \tfrac{1}{2}x''(f)\sigma^2\, dt \qquad (9.29)$$

in the $f < \bar{f}$ region where (9.27) holds true. Taking expectations and considering (9.23) we have a second-order ordinary differential equation:[13]

$$x(f) = f + \alpha[x'(f)\theta + \tfrac{1}{2}\sigma^2 x''(f)] \qquad (9.30)$$

This is solved by functions in the form

$$x(f) = \alpha\theta + f + C_1 \exp(\lambda_1 f) + C_2 \exp(\lambda_2 f) \qquad (9.31)$$

where λ_1 and λ_2 are the two solutions of the quadratic equation

$$\frac{1}{2}\sigma^2\lambda^2 + \theta\lambda - \frac{1}{\alpha} = 0 \qquad (9.32)$$

With $\alpha\sigma^2 > 0$, the roots of this equation are real and have opposite sign; put $\lambda_1 > 0$, $\lambda_2 < 0$.

Several functions in the form (9.31) are plotted in figures 9.2(b) and 9.3(b) as dotted lines, for a variety of C_1, C_2 pairs. Each such function satisfies (9.23) by construction. Turning to determination of the C_1 and C_2 constants of integration, consider first that in the absence of any dynamic change at $\bar{f}$ we would have

$$x(t) = \int_t^\infty \exp\left(-\frac{\tau-t}{\alpha}\right)\frac{E_t[f(\tau)]}{\alpha}\,d\tau$$

$$= \int_t^\infty \exp\left(-\frac{\tau-t}{\alpha}\right)\frac{f(t)+\theta(\tau-t)}{\alpha}\,d\tau$$

$$= \alpha\theta + f(t) \qquad (9.33)$$

This relationship is plotted by broken lines in figures 9.2 and 9.3, and coincides with (9.12): since the Brownian component $W(\tau)$ enters linearly in (9.28) and has symmetric positive and negative realizations, randomness of the $\{f\}$ path has no effect on this calculation. When the dynamics change at $\bar{f}$, conversely, nonzero values of C_1 or C_2 in (9.31) reflect the asymmetric character of future f realizations. Those paths that would make f exceed $\bar{f}$ are truncated; but as $f(t)-\bar{f}$ tends to negative infinity, the probability that $f(\tau)=\bar{f}$ for any given $\tau>t$ becomes arbitrarily small, and the solution should approach the broken line for $f\to-\infty$. Thus, $C_2 = 0$, or else the relevant exponential term in (9.31) would diverge when unboundedly negative values are considered for f.

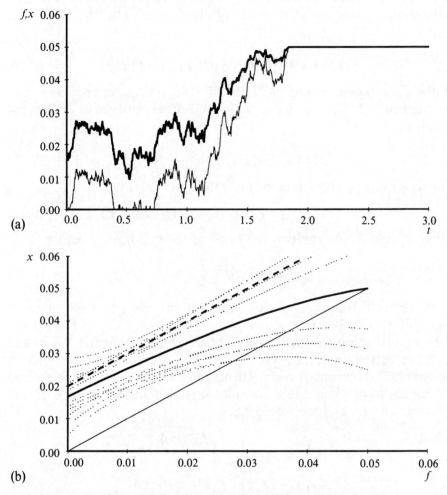

Figure 9.2   Absorption under uncertainty: $\alpha = 1.0$, $\theta = 0.02$, $\sigma = 0.02$.

To obtain a stochastic counterpart to the exercise in figure 9.1, we relax (9.27) when $f = \bar{f}$. In the nonstochastic case the tendency of $\{f(t)\}$ to drift upwards is canceled upon reaching the $\bar{f}$ limit, and $df(\tau) = 0$ for all $\tau > \bar{f}/\theta$. In the presence of uncertainty, the $\{f(t)\}$ process drifts upwards but also fluctuates randomly, and we may or may not want to suppress the random as well as the trend component of $\{f(t)\}$'s dynamics upon reaching $\bar{f}$. If we do set $df = 0$ forever after $\bar{f}$ is reached for the first time, then $\bar{f}$ is an absorbing barrier (see figure 9.2); if we instead allow f to fluctuate (downwards) after hitting $\bar{f}$, we shall be modeling a reflecting barrier at $\bar{f}$ (as in figure 9.3). In both cases, f does not jump upon changing its dynamic behavior. Hence, solutions must be such that neither x nor $E_t(dx)/dt$ jump upon going through the transition point, or else (9.23) would fail at $\bar{f}$.

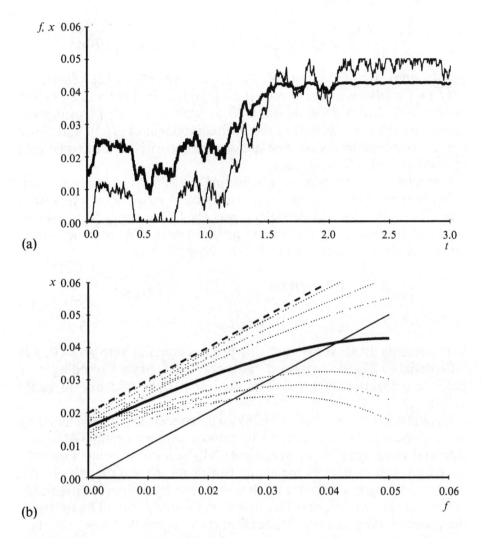

Figure 9.3   Reflection under uncertainty: $\alpha = 1.0$, $\theta = 0.02$, $\sigma = 0.02$.

3.1.3   Absorption versus reflection

Consider first the absorption case of figure 9.3: if $f(t^*) = \bar{f}$, then $df(\tau) = 0$ and $f(\tau) = \bar{f}$ (with certainty) for all $\tau > t^*$. Simple integration of (9.26) yields $x(\tau) = \bar{f}$ for all $\tau > t^*$ in this case; imposing that $\lim_{f \to \bar{f}} x(f) = f$ yields

$$C_1 = -\alpha\theta \exp(-\lambda_1 \bar{f})$$

and selects the thick solid line in the figure as the problem's solution. To verify that (9.23) is satisfied at $\bar{f}$, consider that

$$\frac{E[dx(\bar{f})]}{dt} = x'(\bar{f})\theta + \frac{1}{2}x''(\bar{f})\sigma^2 = (1 - \alpha\theta\lambda_1)\theta - \frac{1}{2}\alpha\theta\lambda_1^2\sigma^2$$

equals zero by definition of λ_1 as a root of (9.32). However, $x'(\bar{f}) = 1 - \alpha\theta\lambda_1$ equals zero only if $\sigma = 0$ and, as in section 2, $\lambda_1 = 1/\alpha\theta$. With $\sigma > 0$, $E(dx)$ depends on $x''(.)$ as well as on $x'(.)$. Absorption eliminates the noise as well as the drift component of $\{f(t)\}$, and hence a linear combination of the first *and* second derivatives must equal zero to prevent $E(dx)$ from jumping.

Consider next the case of a reflecting barrier: f is prevented from going further when reaching $\bar{f}$ but is allowed to move downwards from there. Formally, we can define the process $U(t) = \sup_{\tau \leq t}[\theta\tau + \sigma W(\tau)]$, whose realization at t is the highest previous peak of a continuous-time random walk with differential (9.27), and write f as

$$f(t) = \begin{cases} \theta t + \sigma W(t) & \text{if } U(t) < \bar{f} \\ \\ \bar{f} + \theta t + \sigma W(t) - U(t) & \text{otherwise} \end{cases} \tag{9.34}$$

It is not difficult to verify that this process starts at zero at $t = 0$, has differential (9.27) for $f < \bar{f}$, and "bounces" off $\bar{f}$, never exceeding it. A possible realization of $\{f(t)\}$ is plotted as a thin solid line in figure 9.3(a).

Given (9.34) the integral in (9.26) might conceivably be evaluated by brute force, computing the conditional expectations on the right-hand side and integrating them over time.[14] In section 2, doing so would have been just as easy as bypassing t to relate x and f directly. In the presence of ongoing uncertainty, however, the latter approach is vastly preferable. To see this, consider how complicated it would be to depict the problem along the time dimension (as in figure 9.1) when the data and solution are stochastic processes. A stochastic counterpart to figure 9.1 would in principle need an extremely complex ω dimension, along which *all* continuous functions of time $f(t)$ would be plotted along with the corresponding $x(t)$ solutions.

In differential form, (9.34) can be written

$$df(t) = \theta \, dt + \sigma \, dW(t) - dU(t) \qquad f(0) = 0$$

The (upper) *regulator* $\{U(t)\}$ defined above is the (unique) process which is continuous, never decreases, increases only when $f(t) = \bar{f}$, and keeps $f(t) \leq \bar{f}$ (Harrison, 1985, p. 20). Monotonicity of the increments rules out infinite variation, and hence $\{U(t)\}$ can be included in the $\{A(t)\}$ component of (9.19). Applying the change-of-variable rule (9.22) and taking conditional expectations, we have

$$E_t[dx(f)] = x'(f)[\theta\, dt - dU(t)] + \tfrac{1}{2}x''(f)\sigma^2\, dt \qquad (9.35)$$

For $f < \bar{f}$, the solution takes the form (9.31) since $dU = 0$, and reasoning based on (9.33) still leads to $C_2 = 0$. As to C_1, note that the future evolution of $\{f(t)\}$ is stochastic in (9.26) even when $f = \bar{f}$. Hence, the condition $\lim_{f \to \bar{f}} x(f) = x(\bar{f})$ does not help to determine C_1 as its right-hand side is not as easy to evaluate as in the absorption cases. However, the solution should satisfy (9.30) for f arbitrarily close to $\bar{f}$, and also (9.35) at $f = \bar{f}$, where dU may be positive (and indeed will be whenever $f = \bar{f}$, by the infinite-variation property of the Wiener process). By continuity of $\{x\}$ and $\{f\}$, (9.29) evaluated at $f = \bar{f}$ and (9.30) can both hold true only if $x'(\bar{f}) = 0$.[15] Thus, we may compute C_1 imposing $x'(\bar{f}) = 0$, to find $C_1 = -\exp(-\lambda_1\bar{f})/\lambda_1$, and write the solution to (9.23) and (9.25) as

$$x(f) = \alpha\theta + f - \frac{\exp[\lambda_1(f - \bar{f})]}{\lambda_1} \qquad (9.36)$$

The relationship (9.36) between $x(t)$ and $f(t)$ is plotted by a thick solid line in figure 9.3. It is qualitatively similar to the nonstochastic solution discussed in section 2.1: the $x(.)$ solution never exceeds the 45° line (9.33) appropriate for the unregulated case; it bends progressively farther away from it as $f \to \bar{f}$; and it meets the upper boundary smoothly to first order. Further, in figure 9.3 the solution lies below $\bar{f}$ even when $f = \bar{f}$: f paths can never exceed $\bar{f}$ but, with $\sigma > 0$ and a reflecting barrier, will surely fall below $\bar{f}$ after reaching it. And, in both figures 9.2(a) and 9.3(a) the endogenous variable is less volatile than the exogenous process when the latter's fluctuations are unchecked by the regulator. Formally, f movements are "dampened" when reflected into x movements by the $x(f)$ function plotted in parts (b) of the figures, which is everywhere flatter than a 45° line.

3.2   Economic interpretation

The simple economics of section 3.1 are readily adapted to the present formal framework. Let behavioral relationships in the form (9.13) apply, with their straightforward (if simplistic) economic interpretation in terms of money's transaction role. If at least some of the variables appearing in the definition (9.16) of "fundamentals" follow a stochastic process of the type introduced in (9.19) and exemplified by (9.34) then the formal results above may be used to characterize no-arbitrage equilibria.

The introduction of uncertainty is inconsequential to the no-arbitrage condition in (9.14), which holds instantaneously for any ω. The interest rate parity condition in (9.15), conversely, is intrinsically forward looking and needs to take into account market participants' attitude towards risk if the future is uncertain. However, Frankel (1986) and Svensson (1992b) show that reasonable degrees of risk aversion have negligible effects in the context of macroeconomic models of exchange rate determination. It is then an acceptable approximation to suppose that arbitrage opportunities are ruled out by

$$i = i^* + \frac{1}{dt} E(dx) \qquad (9.37)$$

or that market participants are indifferent in equilibrium between holding funds in domestic-currency-denominated assets over a short interval of time dt (and earning interest i) or exchanging initial holdings into foreign currency, earning interest i^*, and converting the proceeds back into domestic currency at the random log-exchange rate $x(t + dt)$.[16]

The model has now the same formal structure as that considered in section 2.2, with (9.23) and (9.25) in place of (9.1) and (9.5). Specific assumptions as to the behavior of $\{f(t)\}$ and the character of the corresponding solution have much the same economic interpretation as their nonstochastic counterparts. If in figure 9.1 an upward-sloping and eventually stabilized fundamental path could be taken to represent an inflationary period followed by a permanent commitment to fixed exchange rates, in figures 9.2 and 9.3 random components of money supply disturb the linear growth path, and concerns about excessive depreciation still induce authorities to halt money creation whenever fundamentals reach $\bar{f}$. Under the absorption assumption of figure 9.2, the resulting model is a simple version of those in Flood and Garber (1983), Froot and Obstfeld (1991a), Smith and Smith (1990), Smith (1991), and Miller and Sutherland (1991). In the reflecting case of figure 9.3, randomness leads to downward movements even after stabilization, and the model describes an ongoing structural relationship (the one-sided target zone of Delgado and Dumas, 1990) rather than a one-time experiment.

The economic intuition for the character of the $x(f)$ solution plotted in the figures is quite similar to that outlined in the nonstochastic context above, again with a crucial role for the forward-looking nature of exchange rate processes. By equation (9.26) the exchange rate reflects (only) those speculative forces that are ultimately motivated by currency use in transactions. Hence, stabilizing speculation tends to anticipate future fundamental developments and affects the equilibrium exchange rate's level and dynamic behavior. The exchange rate paths of figures 9.2 and 9.3 are noticeably less volatile than both the corresponding f path and the hypothetical freely floating exchange rate process. Intuitively, an upward movement towards $\bar{f}$ implies a less than proportional shift of all future expected fundamentals when their range of variation is known to be truncated at $\bar{f}$. As revision of expectations is dampened by knowledge that intervention will occur at $\bar{f}$, the current level of the f process has a lesser effect on its expected future evolution (and on the forward-looking exchange rate) than in the uncontrolled or free-float case. Movements towards $\bar{f}$ have very small effects on the exchange rate in the neighborhood of $\bar{f}$, where regulation looms particularly large and, in the limit, $x'(\bar{f}) = 0$. The boundary behavior of $x(f)$ and of its first derivative follows formally from no-arbitrage conditions and from the assumed continuity of the fundamental's sample path, as noted above.[17] Further intuition is suggested by economic considerations: since $\{f\}$ can only move down when $f = \bar{f}$, any first-order dependence of x on f would imply certain appreciation at that point; the resulting incentive to take unbounded positions in the currency would be inconsistent with equilibrium (see Krugman (1991b) and Froot and Obstfeld (1991a) for similar arguments). The expectation of *uncertain* appreciation implied by the negative second-order derivative $x''(f)$ in (9.30) is instead consistent with a finite exchange rate, since a negative $Et(\mathrm{d}x)$ is offset by a positive interest rate differential $i - i^*$.

As to the character of intervention, it may be interesting to note that the regulator process $\{U(t)\}$ is smallest among those processes which keep the fundamentals below $\bar{f}$ with probability one (Harrison, 1985, p. 20). This suggests a possible economic rationale for the dynamics assumed in (9.34): if the authorities were interested in obtaining $f(t) \leq \bar{f}$ using the least amount of control in the cumulative sense, then "fundamentals" might indeed feature reflection at $\bar{f}$. But the considerations in section 2.2 above also apply in a stochastic context. The economic rationale for the crucial relationship (9.23), the nature and eventual sustainability of the "intervention" leading to (occasional or permanent) stabilization at $\bar{f}$, and the possibility of different assumptions as to the fundamentals' time path (possibly to include discontinuities) all deserve to be discussed in the richer setting of a stochastic model, whose obvious advantages in terms of realism make it possible to address such issues with attention to the economic relevance and empirical soundness of many possible assumptions. The remainder of the chapter reviews recent work on these issues.

4 Target zones and regime switches

Recent modeling of exchange rate determination is motivated by the character of real-life intervention policies. Policymakers are obviously concerned with nominal exchange rate stability, but not so much as to choose irrevocably fixed parities: limits to exchange rate variability are traded off against the authorities' desire for monetary sovereignty and exchange rate management. These conflicting objectives do appear to result in periods of relatively wide exchange rate fluctuations alternating with sudden freezes, in qualitative accord with the simple models above. Williamson and Miller (1987) and others have argued at a theoretical level that resolving the policy tradeoff in this fashion might optimally allow some monetary policy flexibility while ensuring exchange rate stability and keeping in check speculative pressures on "weak" currencies. Indeed, real-life "fixed" exchange rate regimes never specify a single price at which the monetary authorities of participating countries are committed to buy and sell foreign exchange. When the specie content of currencies was fixed as under the gold standard, transport and insurance costs for bullion prevented would-be arbitrageurs from exploiting small exchange rate fluctuations. Whether for historical continuity or for more substantial reasons, exchange rate arrangements for fiat currencies mimic the "gold points" of the gold standard (see chapter 6 in this volume). Fluctuation bands for bilateral exchange rates of the order of a few percentage points are or were featured by the post-war Bretton Woods system, by the exchange rate mechanism of the European Monetary System (EMS), and by the unilateral exchange rate targets of Nordic currencies.

The economic insights afforded by models of exchange rate determination and official intervention are useful for studying such formal fluctuation bands and the interest and exchange rate data they generate, as well as possible informal "target zone" arrangements. This section briefly reviews theoretical and empirical applications in this area.

4.1   The basic target zone model

Following Krugman (1991b) and Froot and Obstfeld (1991a), consider a monetary model of exchange rate determination and let authorities be firmly committed to prespecified, common-knowledge limits $[\underline{x}, \bar{x}]$ for the logarithmic exchange rate process $\{x(t)\}$. If the no-bubble condition (9.25) holds and the fundamental process $\{f\}$ is Markov in levels (which will have to be checked below for specific models), then, by equation (9.26), the exchange rate can be written as a function $x(f)$. Under these conditions, a commitment to maintain exchange rates within prespecified points implies that fundamentals should be similarly restrained within a fluctuation band $[\underline{f}, \bar{f}]$ of their own, such that

$$x(\bar{f}) = \bar{x} \qquad x(\underline{f}) = \underline{x} \tag{9.38}$$

As in section 3, we consider a simple fundamental process with stochastic differential

$$df(t) = \theta\, dt + \sigma\, dW(t) + dL(t) - dU(t) \qquad (9.39)$$

where $\{U(t)\}$ and $\{L(t)\}$ are nondecreasing regulator processes which increase only when fundamentals are at the limits of their fluctuation band, and then only by as much as necessary to prevent those limits from being trespassed. By this definition, and by the properties of the Brownian increment dW, the fundamental process is indeed Markov: the probability distribution of $\{f(t)\}$ increments only depends on its current level and on parameters.

To give an economic interpretation to our assumptions, recall from (9.16) that

$$f(t) = m(t) - m^*(t) + y^*(t) - y(t) \qquad (9.40)$$

The dynamics in (9.39) are appropriate if the variables on the right-hand side of (9.40) all follow constant-parameter Itô processes, with one or both of the money supplies being adjusted (via unsterilized intervention or open market operations) when necessary to prevent the exchange rate exceeding its boundaries. Following Krugman, all fundamentals could be taken to be constant except $y(t)$, with dynamics $dy(t) = \theta\, dt + \sigma\, dW(t)$ to represent exogenous liquidity shocks, and $m(t)$, with $dm(t) = dL(t) - dU(t)$ representing occasional intervention at the margins of the target zone. When the exchange rate tends to depreciate beyond $\bar{x}$, the "home" central bank intervenes to buy its own currency and sell reserves (the other country's currency) and/or domestic credit assets. Symmetrically, an incipient appreciation beyond $\underline{x}$ leads to a sale of domestic currency.

The mathematical tools discussed in earlier sections make it possible to find the $\{x(t)\}$ process and the $\underline{f}, \bar{f}$ intervention points consistent with its never leaving the $[\underline{x}, \bar{x}]$ band. Since the differential equation (9.30) should be satisfied at all interior points of the fluctuation bands of the exchange rate and fundamental, the general form of $x(f)$ is that given in (9.31). Arguments similar to those above imply that $x'(\bar{f}) = 0$, $x'(\underline{f}) = 0$. These and (9.38) determine $\bar{f}, \underline{f}, C_1$, and C_2. One C constant is positive, the other negative, and the resulting $x(f)$ function has the S-shape plotted in figure 9.4(b) as a thick solid line. (The dotted lines in the figure plot solutions in the form (9.31) for different C constants, and may be disregarded for now.)

Marginal intervention truncates above at $\bar{f}$ the fundamental paths that would lead to excessive depreciation, and truncates below at $\underline{f}$ the paths that would lead to excessive appreciation. As the fundamental process approaches its upper limit, the latter truncation is less likely to occur in the near future; the present *discounted* value of fundamentals

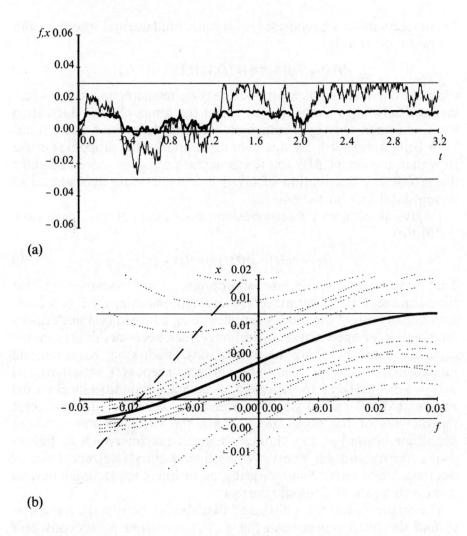

(a)

(b)

Figure 9.4   The basic target-zone model: $\alpha = 1.0$, $\theta = 0.02$, $\sigma = 0.04$.

becomes progressively lower than it would be in the absence of regulation: and the target zone solution bends downwards away from the exchange rate function (9.33) corresponding to a free-float fundamental process with $dU(t) = dL(t) = 0$ at all t (a broken line in the figure). Getting closer and closer to the upper barrier, it becomes more and more likely (and eventually certain) that intervention will soon stop $\{f\}$ at $\bar{f}$, and the $x(f)$ relationship bends down more and more, eventually becoming flat. Symmetric reasoning applies to the region neighboring the lower intervention point. Since the figure is drawn for positive within-band drift, however, quantitative effects are asymmetric. With $\theta > 0$, stronger expectational biases are induced by truncation at the upper intervention point, and the thick solid line lies below the broken line through most of the band.

4.2   Implications

Stabilizing-speculation effects in forward-looking exchange rate determination have a crucial role in the above model. At a qualitative level, such phenomena could of course be studied in much simpler settings; but the target zone model yields implications that are readily comparable with empirical evidence. Not only formal commitments to exchange rate stability such as the Bretton Woods system or the EMS, but also informal "target zone" agreements specify limits for realized exchange rate fluctuations rather than more sophisticated (and perhaps less easily verifiable) indicators of exchange rate volatility. Inasmuch as such limits are enforced by the occasional marginal interventions assumed by the target zone model, its observable implications can usefully be confronted with empirical data from such arrangements.

An attempt to relate theoretical insights and empirical evidence needs to address the fact that "fundamentals" are unobservable as such. Theory is vague as to the real-life counterpart of the $y(t)$ money demand scale variable and, even if one were willing to take a stand on this, the relevant data would typically not be available at the same frequency as short-run exchange rate phenomena. As long as the exchange rate can be expressed as a function $\{x[f(t)]\}$ of an (unobservable) fundamental process with drift θ and volatility σ, however, Itô's change-of-variable rule (9.22) yields

$$\mathrm{d}x(t) = (x'[f(t)]\theta + \tfrac{1}{2}\sigma^2 x''[f(t)]) \, \mathrm{d}t + x'[f(t)]\sigma \, \mathrm{d}W(t) \quad (9.41)$$

and the "bending" property of the target zones solution has quite general implications for (observable) interest and exchange rates (see Svensson (1991b) and Bertola and Caballero (1992) for technical details and formal solutions). First, in (9.41) the instantaneous volatility of observable exchange rate changes is proportional to the absolute value of the $x(f)$ function's slope, and $|x'(f)|$ is large in the middle of the band and declines to zero at its limits (see figure 9.4). Second, the predictable component multiplying $\mathrm{d}t$ in equation (9.41) is the expected rate of depreciation, and can be shown to be negative (positive) in the upper (lower) portion of the exchange rate's fluctuation band: quite intuitively, x is expected to appreciate when nearing the upper limit of the band, to depreciate when it nears the lower limit. Under uncovered interest parity, the model implies an exact relationship between two observables: the exchange rate's position in the band, and instantaneous (or very short-term) interest rate differentials.

Interest rate differentials of longer maturity depend on the exchange rate's position within the band in qualitatively similar ways (see Svensson, 1991b). If one looks further and further ahead, however, current levels provide less and less information on future exchange rates: as initial conditions come to be dominated by the cumulative importance of random fluctuations in the fundamentals and exchange rates the probability distribution of exchange rates within the band eventually settles down into its unconditional *ergodic* distribution. The latter's shape yields further observable implications. The unconditional density of x is inversely related to the absolute size of the drift and standard deviation in (9.41): intuitively, x is likely to be observed at points where its drift and standard deviation are relatively small (in figure 9.4, for example, the exchange rate spends most of the time at the upper boundary of its fluctuation band). If the fundamental's drift θ and standard deviation σ are constant as assumed above, then it is not difficult to see from (9.41) and figure 9.4 that exchange rates should most probably be observed at the boundaries of its fluctuation band, where their volatility is lowest.

Summing up, the simple target zone model outlined above has three interrelated observable implications. First, exchange rates should be more volatile in the interior of their fluctuation band than at its edges. Second, interest rate differentials should be negatively related to the exchange rate's distance from its lower (most appreciated) bound. Third, exchange rate observations should tend to cluster in the neighborhood of the fluctuation band's margins. Empirical work on exchange rate "bands" has found little support for these features.[18] Such findings have of course led to a relaxation of the basic model's stringent assumptions: that interventions have infinitesimal size and known direction, that fundamentals follow a random walk in the interior of the fluctuation band, and that equilibrium exchange rates are determined by instantaneous clearing of both money and goods markets.

4.3 Interventions and realignments

Two extensions regarding the character of infrequent interventions have been pursued. First, marginal regulation of $\{f\}$ is not the only intervention policy capable of maintaining $\{x\}$ within prespecified boundaries. Second, real-life exchange rate bands are not irrevocable commitments on the part of the authorities: rather, they are subject to *realignments*.

The first point is made by Flood and Garber (1991), who let the fundamental jump back discretely when reaching prespecified trigger points $\underline{F}$ and $\bar{F}$: from $\underline{F}$ up to $\underline{f}$, from $\bar{F}$ down to $\bar{f}$. With constant θ and

σ, $x(f)$ should still satisfy (9.30) and take the form (9.31) when intervention is not taking place. Exchange rate jumps would violate (9.23) and the values of C_1 and C_2 are determined by the boundary conditions

$$x(\underline{F}) = x(\underline{f}) \qquad x(\overline{F}) = x(\overline{f}) \qquad (9.42)$$

Such no-jump conditions are familiar from earlier models of arbitrage-free exchange rate dynamics,[19] and the Flood and Garber model usefully clarifies the interpretation of smooth-pasting properties: for given $\underline{x}$, $\overline{x}$, the exchange rate function for the jump-intervention case coincides with that plotted in figure 9.4, but turns back towards the interior of the band after reaching its boundaries. The first derivative of the differentiable $x(.)$ function in the form (9.31) vanishes at its (local) extrema, namely at the boundaries of the exchange rate's (not of the fundamental's) fluctuation band.

Absent arbitrage opportunities, intervention cannot excite exchange rate jumps if its timing and size are certain; with a continuous $\{x\}$, a jump in $E(\mathrm{d}x)$ must occur at times when expected jumps occur in f, and the interest rate differential is discontinuous. Intervention may not be fully expected, however, and exchange rates do jump in reality when *realignments* occur, i.e. when a commitment to intervene is abandoned by the authorities. In the framework set out above, realignments may be modeled as occasional step changes in $\{f\}$ and/or in the points that trigger intervention by the authorities. For a finite exchange rate to satisfy (9.23) in the imminence of an exchange rate jump, the $E(\mathrm{d}x)$ term in (9.23) should have the same order of magnitude as $\mathrm{d}t$. Svensson (1991b, d) models realignments as jumps in exchange rates, fundamentals, and band boundaries, which occur with infinitesimal probability $\delta \, \mathrm{d}t$ regardless of the exchange rate's and fundamental's position in the band. Such independence assumptions eliminate any expectational effects of the type discussed above, leaving the shape of $x(f)$ unaffected. Conversely, Miller and Weller (1989) and Bertola and Caballero (1992) assume that realignments occur with finite probability at common-knowledge points f^*, where jumps in either direction may take place with known probability. Then, the likelihood of a devaluation in the near future does depend on the fundamental's position relative to the relevant "trigger" f^*, and the shape of the $x(f)$ relationship depends on the relative likelihood of movements in either direction. Specifically, suppose that upon reaching $\overline{f}$ the fundamental path might jump to f_1 with probability p or to f_2 with probability $1 - p$. To prevent arbitrage, the $x(f)$ function should satisfy no-expected-jump conditions in the form[20]

$$x(\bar{f}) = x(f_1)p + x(f_2)(1 - p) \qquad (9.43)$$

which make it possible to determine C_1 and C_2 in (9.31). An "intervention" jump to $f_1 > \bar{f}$ represents a realignment, or the failure on the part of the authorities to bring f to f_2 and enforce the upper boundary $\bar{f}$ of the fundamentals' fluctuation band. A large value of p reverses the signs of the integration constants, and reverses the target zone model's implications as well: while interventions meant to limit exchange rate fluctuations are associated with stabilizing speculation and with a relatively flat relationship between exchange rates and fundamentals, interventions in the realignment direction symmetrically excite destabilizing speculation. The expected discounted integral of future fundamentals diverges from the free-float locus when destabilizing fundamental jumps become more likely over the relevant horizon, and the relationship between exchange rates and fundamentals becomes steeper as the exchange rate approaches the band's boundaries (see Bertola and Caballero, 1992).

4.4   Reserves and other state variables

It may of course be desirable to let variables other than f affect the level and dynamics of the exchange rate. Work in this direction has been motivated at a theoretical level by a desire to relate the infrequent "interventions" of mathematical models to the dynamics of foreign exchange reserves, and at a more applied level by the fact that empirical relationships between interest rate differentials, exchange rates, and central parities appear far from being as sharp as simpler models would imply.

In the framework outlined above, "interventions" are infrequent nonlinear changes in the dynamic behavior of fundamentals. The economic nature of such infrequent changes is irrelevant to their expectational effects. Still, dynamic discontinuities are most naturally interpreted in terms of m or m^*, and many contributions identify them with unsterilized intervention or foreign exchange reserve expenditure.[21] As reserves cannot become unboundedly positive or negative in reality, the current level of reserves has a bearing on the size and direction of interventions. Under the maintained assumption that (9.23) should hold at every point in time and that $\{f\}$ has constant drift and standard deviation when interventions and realignments are not taking place, some contributions explore the long-run sustainability of prespecified intervention rules in the once-and-for-all framework of earlier "collapse" models, where intervention ceases forever once a country's reserves are exhausted. A paradox may arise in a stochastic setting, where random fundamental movements may deplete reserves even though, on average, they would *increase* over time if the intervention regime continued. In the event, the run on reserves that would eliminate arbitrage opportunities cannot occur because the exchange rate is expected to appreciate upon regime collapse (see Buiter and Grilli (1991) and Obstfeld's discussion of their paper). In reality, however, there is no well-defined limit on reserves if the authorities can borrow abroad, and a structurally strong currency should enable them to do so at will. Buiter and Grilli (1991) resolve the paradox by allowing rational speculators (or the authorities themselves) to do what the central bank is artificially prevented from doing in collapse models, namely finance a temporary shortfall of reserves without a collapse. Appropriate "collapse scenarios" may also restore equilibrium: Delgado and Dumas (1990) let a central bank remain ready to buy foreign exchange when reserves are exhausted, implementing a "one-sided" target zone like that depicted in figure 9.3, and Krugman and Rotemberg (1991) make similar assumptions in the gold standard context. The substantive issue in this context is, of course, the size of reserve stocks required to prevent collapse: see Delgado and Dumas (1990) and Dumas and Svensson (1991) for a neat derivation of the expected time to collapse as a function of reserve stocks and intervention rules.

The end of intervention or of a specific regime might be better modeled as a temporary and recurring event (as in Blanco and Garber, 1986) rather than as the once-and-for-all absorbing regime change of stylized collapse models. In the model of Bertola and Caballero (1991), reserve stocks may be depleted or replenished by stabilizing interventions and realignments, and the relative likelihood of "stabilizing" versus "destabilizing" interventions depends on the level of reserves. Thus, the current stock of reserves is relevant to forward-looking exchange rate determination, and acts as a natural second state variable in determining the position and shape of the $x(f)$ function. More generally, work on reserves makes it clear that the character of a given country's intervention policy need not remain constant over time, and that variables other than traditional "fundamentals" may well matter for exchange rate determination if they affect the direction and likelihood of future interventions. This insight is relevant to applied work: while exchange rates and interest rate differentials would be driven by a single source of randomness and stable functions of each other if the fundamental $\{f(t)\}$ process were Markov in levels as assumed above, empirical relationships between observable exchange rates and interest rate differentials are far from being as clean as simple models would imply (see Flood et al. (1991) for an exhaustive review of the evidence). From the economic point of view, of course, there is no reason why a single-variable Markov assumption should be appropriate: just as reserves should matter in the stylized framework above, in reality the character of the (continuous and infrequent) dynamics of fundamentals should be affected by changes in the policy stance of the government regarding the tradeoff between domestic credit creation and exchange rate stability, as well as by such changes in the dynamic behavior of $y - y^*$ as might occur for exogenous reasons.

It would be desirable to model these aspects explicitly, of course, but it is not easy to combine realistic models of economic policy with the rigorous rational expectations framework of stochastic models. Bertola and Svensson (1991) let the size and/or likelihood of realignments follow a stochastic process that is not perfectly correlated with that followed by fundamentals. While the economic determinants of such fluctuations are left unspecified, the extension delivers a nondeterministic relationship between the exchange rate's position in the band (which is not independent of devaluation risk in a forward-looking market) and interest rate differentials (which reflect devaluation risk as well as the expected rate of within-band depreciation). Rose and Svensson (1991) find that the devaluation risk obtained by fitting the model to exchange and interest rate data has explanatory power for the actual occurrence of devaluations, and further work sheds some light on the economic determinants of fundamental and devaluation risk fluctuations.[22]

4.5   Different driving processes

Other contributions relax the simplifying assumption that fundamentals should follow a random walk between interventions. Exchange rate stabilization concerns may well lead to such sudden changes in the dynamic behavior of fundamentals as those which occur at the boundaries of target zones, but the policy component of fundamentals' dynamics is often interpreted as (sterilized or unsterilized) official intervention, which quite clearly can and does occur when the exchange rate is not at the boundaries of its fluctuation band. Presumably, such intramarginal intervention reflects the authorities' desire to "lean against the wind" and control exchange rate fluctuations, introducing *mean reversion* in the $\{f(t)\}$ process or a tendency for fundamentals to move away from the limits of their fluctuation band and towards the current central parity.

To model official concern as to the level of exchange rates in the interior as well as at the margins of fluctuation bands, several contributions derive counterparts to differential equation (9.30) for fundamental processes which, unlike the random walk in (9.27), let the probabilistic character of $\{f\}$'s increments depend on its current level.

Analytical solutions are available for simple mean-reverting forms of the drift term $dA(t)$ in the Itô differential (9.21). Froot and Obstfeld (1991b) and Delgado and Dumas (1991) let fundamentals follow a Ornstein–Uhlenbeck process, with $dA(t) = -\rho f(t)\, dt$. Pesenti (1990) studies (possible) regulation of a switching-drift process, with $dA(t)$ taking different values depending on whether $\{f\}$ is above or below the level targeted by the monetary authorities. Such persistent efforts on the authorities' part to bring the exchange rate back in line have expectational effects, of course, which interact with those of expected regulation at the margins of "imperforate" fluctuation bands and those of infrequent drift switches as well. Lewis (1990) proposes another complex and perhaps realistic mixture of continuous and discontinuous dynamics in f, with infrequent interventions of infinitesimal size becoming more likely as Brownian dynamics bring $\{f\}$ farther from a central reference value.

With mean-reverting fundamental dynamics, the $x(f)$ relationship is not as steep as in the random walk case, since outlying f values have smaller effects on the distribution of future fundamentals. Exchange rates tend to revert to the mean not only because of within-band fundamental mean reversion but also because of marginal reflection if nonlinear "target zone" limits are imposed on a mean-reverting fluctuation. The exchange rate function is still S-shaped in this case and pastes smoothly to the boundaries of the fluctuation zone. However, nonlinear boundary effects may be irrelevant if the mean-reverting tendency of fundamentals is so strong as to make it extremely unlikely that the boundaries of the target zone will ever be approached. Quite interestingly, Lindberg and Söderlind (1991a) find support for this in Swedish target zone data.

4.6   Different equilibrium conditions

The simple monetary model of section 2.2 assumes immediate and continuous absence of arbitrage on two possible margins: both price levels and interest rates should always be in line with each other when expressed in a common currency. In financial markets, information flows efficiently and transaction costs are small; thus the assumption of continuous market clearing is not unreasonable for nominal exchange rates and interest rates. But assumptions of instantaneous frictionless adjustment are empirically unappealing for goods' prices, since prices of individual goods and aggregate price levels respond quite slowly to exchange rate changes.

In theory, deviations for purchasing power parity may occur and persist because international shipments of goods are costly (as in Dumas, 1992) or because of adjustment costs for nominal prices (as in, for example, Daniel, 1986). Concerns about imperfect price flexibility are addressed by Miller and Weller (1989, 1990, 1991a, b) and others in stochastic versions of the Dornbusch "overshooting" models, where "sticky" price levels revert slowly (rather than instantaneously) towards the level that would satisfy the $P = X$ no-arbitrage relation in (2.14). Miller and Weller succinctly summarize the structure of their models in their 1991a survey and provide a detailed discussion of their results in their 1991b paper. What follows reviews the additional economic insights and technical difficulties introduced by sticky prices and makes an effort to relate the assumptions and results of these models to those of monetary approach models.

Consider a model with the same structure as that introduced in section 2.2 above but replace the assumption that $p = x$ with the dynamic relationship

$$dp(t) = [x(t) - p(t)]\phi \, dt \qquad \phi > 0 \qquad (9.44)$$

Equation (9.44) captures the notion of slow or sticky price adjustment in a simple way: with $p(t)$ denoting the logarithm of the price level in the home country and a unitary foreign price level, only a fraction $\exp(-\phi)$ per unit time of any price level divergence is eliminated by price (and/or quantity) adjustments. If money demand takes the form (9.13) and uncovered interest parity holds, then instantaneous clearing of the home and foreign money markets requires

$$p(t) = f(t) + \alpha \frac{E_t[dx(t)]}{dt} \qquad f(t) \equiv m(t) - y(t) - [m^*(t) - y^*(t)] \quad (9.45)$$

Of course, the scale of money demand (y, y^* in the notation used here) may in general depend on the real exchange rate $x - p$ once it is allowed to vary over time. To keep the model as close as possible to those discussed above, however, it will be convenient still to view y, y^* as exogenously given. The equilibrium condition (9.45) is then similar to that above, but the price level p replaces the exchange rate level x. The latter need not satisfy instantaneous no-arbitrage conditions: rather, equilibrium requires the exchange rate *path* to be consistent with the price level's dynamic path. If the real money stock is high but expected to decrease as p increases, then money-market clearing requires a low interest rate and, by uncovered interest parity, an appreciating exchange rate path (the celebrated overshooting result of Dornbusch, 1976).[23]

Indeed, equation (9.45) can be rearranged to give an expression for the expected instantaneous rate of depreciation and, retracing the steps leading to equation (9.26), integration yields

$$x(t) = \int_t^T \frac{E_t[f(\tau) - p(\tau)]}{\alpha} \, d\tau + E_t[x(T)] \qquad (9.46)$$

To rule out instantaneous arbitrage, expected cumulative depreciation from t up to some future time T must be equal to the expected *undiscounted* integral of log-deviations of money demand and supply "fundamentals" from the price level (which, though not an exogenous process, is predetermined with respect to the exchange rate). Equation (9.45) holds with probability one at all times, and hence must be expected to hold at arbitrarily remote horizons as of time t. Economic constraints on the limiting behavior of $\{p(\{t\})$, $\{f(t)\}$, and $\{E_t[dx(t)]\}$ make it possible to pin down the exchange rate's level, with a role symmetric to that of the no-bubble condition (9.25) in the monetary model above.

For purposes of illustration, take $f(t)$ to follow a driftless and (for now) unregulated Itô process:

$$f(\tau) = f(t) + \sigma W(\tau - t) \qquad (9.47)$$

Adding and subtracting $f(t) = E_t[f(T)]$ in (9.46) and taking T to positive infinity, we obtain

$$x(t) = f(t) + \int_t^\infty \frac{E_t[f(\tau) - p(\tau)]}{\alpha} \, d\tau \qquad (9.48)$$

provided that, as a counterpart of the no-bubble condition (9.25),

$$\lim_{T \to \infty} E_t[x(T) - f(T)] = 0 \qquad (9.49)$$

This condition rules out expectations of permanent deviation between the fundamental determinants of (nominal) money demand and the price of money, once again requiring exchange rate behavior to be ultimately rationalized by monies' transaction role. For the expectation in (9.46) to be well defined in the limit, of course, the price level process must be cointegrated with the nonstationary process followed by fundamentals in (9.46). Equation (9.49) imposes the stronger condition that the exchange rate and fundamentals processes must have the same asymptotic mean: in the nonstochastic Dornbusch (1976) model, a steady state with $f(t) = p(t) = x(t)$ would surely be reached over an infinite time horizon. A similar condition holds in expectation in the stochastic driftless case under consideration.[24]

Like the similar but discounted expressions in (9.6) and (9.25), (9.48) is a formal solution to the exchange rate determination problem. With sticky prices, the (nominal) exchange rate deviates from its fundamental determinants in $f(t)$ even when the $\{f(t)\}$ process has driftless unregulated dynamics. The predetermined price level process $p(t)$ only slowly adjusts to innovations in $f(t)$ and, to ensure money-market clearing, the level of $x(t)$ needs to "overshoot" in response to nominal innovations.[25] Sticky prices imply rich forward-looking dynamics even when the exogenous $\{f\}$ dynamics take such a simple form as (9.47). It is then understandably quite difficult to use this class of models, rather than the simpler monetary models, to study the effects of nonlinear interventions or regime shifts on the fluctuations of nominal or real exchange rates. Even when the bivariate process $\{f(\tau), p(\tau)\}$ is Markov in levels and we can write $x(t) = x[f(t), p(t)]$ from (9.48), the rate of change of p depends on the level of x through the slow-adjustment assumptions made in (9.44), and application of a multivariate version of the change-of-variable rule (9.22) yields a nonlinear partial differential equation of x with no closed-form solution.

In their work, Miller and Weller let a Brownian noise term affect price dynamics, and take f to be constant in the absence of interventions. This reduces (to one) the number of state variables relevant to exchange rate determination; the differential equation to be solved, while still nonlinear, is then ordinary rather than partial and can be solved using the numerical techniques discussed and implemented by Sutherland (1991). Inasmuch as money market equilibrium and uncovered interest parity are maintained assumptions, the properties of forward-looking exchange rates in nominal or real target zones are qualitatively similar to those outlined in the previous sections (see Miller and Weller (1991a) for a summary and survey).[26] The exchange rate function still "bends" as it approaches points where intervention is known or expected to take place, and boundary conditions similar to those discussed above are valid at the intervention points.

4.7   Bubbles and indeterminacies

Like their nonstochastic counterpart (9.5), conditions (9.25) and (9.49) rule out self-fulfilling "bubble" paths which satisfy the appropriate differential equation but violate the boundary conditions implied by the behavior of the fundamental process. As noted above, such paths (plotted as dotted lines in the figures) are not qualitatively different from those implied by infrequent interventions. The presence of uncertainty makes for a more complex but not essentially different situation. For given (in terms of t and ω) behavior of fundamentals in the absence of intervention (e.g. in the interior of a target zone), it is possible to specify an "intervention" policy that validates any such exchange rate solution.

It is particularly important to note that if intervention is made contingent on the current or future level of the exchange rate (rather than of exogenous fundamentals), then expressing the current exchange rate in terms of future expected fundamentals may well be uninformative. Equations like (9.6) or (9.26) uniquely pin down bubble-free exchange rates in terms of the fundamental's process (as a function of time, or of time and "state of the world"). But if fundamentals in turn depend on exchange rates, these equations collapse to formal identities like (9.4) and (9.24) which tell us little as to exchange rate determination. Such self-fulfilling expectational equilibria were originally identified by Obstfeld (1984) in the context of collapsing exchange rate models, and are in fact always a possibility in forward-looking models with passive interventions.

"True" bubbles are deviations of exchange rates from expressions such as (9.6) or (9.26). In a stochastic context, to satisfy a homogeneous counterpart to the basic no-arbitrage condition (9.23) they must have *submartingale* properties, a stochastic counterpart to the explosive behavior of nonstochastic bubble paths (see for example Karatzas and Schreve, 1988, p. 11). As this implies positive probability for arbitrarily large deviations from initial levels, such processes are ruled out by definition in models that specify both an exogenously given fundamentals process and credible (by assumption) limits to exchange rate fluctuations. As in Buiter and Pesenti (1990), however, fundamental intervention policies might not be exogenous and might be allowed to depend on the level of the bubble contained in the exchange rate process. A large multiplicity of solutions then arises, compounding the indeterminacy of intervention policies which maintain the exchange rate within predetermined boundaries with the many possible "bubble" paths in an uncertainty setting. Selection of one among these solutions should ultimately be justified by empirical arguments.

5   Interventions in exchange rates and other contexts

In his seminal 1987 working paper, Krugman noted that infrequent interventions (or "trigger strategies") are realistic in many economic contexts and posed two questions: how do [such policies] affect the dynamics of market behavior, and are they welfare improving? All of this chapter is concerned with the first question, to which recent work has provided not one but many answers. The techniques and models reviewed above provide a general insight: even when exogenous processes have (locally) linear dynamics, expectations of future interventions (or changes in the dynamics of the driving processes) introduce dynamic nonlinearities in endogenous forward-looking processes. The specific character of such phenomena, however, depends on the form of intervention policies, on their economic nature, and on the economic and institutional environment in which expectations are formed and equilibria are determined. These insights are important not only for exchange rate determination but also for any economic problem when expectations play an important role. For example, Bertola and Drazen (1993) study the expectational effects of stochastic fiscal stabilization policies, and Balduzzi et al. (1992a, b) introduce dynamic nonlinearities in otherwise standard models of asset-price and interest rate determination.

Focusing on the consequences (rather than on the causes) of "interventions" in expectational economic models, recent work has not shed as much light on the answer to the second question above. Rigorous welfare analysis requires firm microeconomic foundations or, in the specific context of exchange rate determination, realistic and meaningful models of money's role in a modern economy. In the flexible-price model outlined in section 2.2, of course, money is fully neutral, and it is hard to see why policy should target nominal exchange rates. Market imperfections which prevent instantaneous price adjustment may rationalize such policies: however, slow price adjustment has quite different implications if it is due to costs of adjusting quantities in a competitive market as in Dumas (1989) or to price adjustment costs as in, for example, Daniel (1986). In the former case, monetary policy should still be neutral; in the latter, there is room for monetary policy to improve welfare.

As a shortcut, one might proceed under *ad hoc* "stickiness" assumptions such as (9.44). Even then, however, it is not easy to make a theoretical case for the occasional intervention policies studied in much recent literature. In the light of many drastic changes in exchange rate regimes, and of realignments and exchange rate crises in particular, there can be little doubt that infrequent "interventions" are relevant to exchange rate dynamics. It is less clear that formal fluctuation bands or informal target zones reflect commitments to intermittent interventions, as declared fluctuation limits might simply represent vague (but verifiable) commitments to partial exchange rate stability. The infrequent component of intervention policies might be rationalized by linear costs of intervention, as in Avesani (1990) and Corbae et al. (1990). Yet, it is not clear what might give rise to such costs, and in their absence Beetsma and van der Ploeg (1991) find (not surprisingly) that nonlinear target zone limits to exchange rate volatility are inferior to linear "leaning against the wind" rules in terms of optimizing nominal and real exchange rate variability.

In a similar vein, Svensson (1992c) proposes a linear model of mean-reverting intervention to characterize the tradeoff between exchange rate stability and monetary independence, and to address realistic time-consistency issues as well (see, for example, Giavazzi and

Pagano, 1988, and chapter 7 in this volume). Such issues are obviously important in a forward-looking model of policy where not only the authorities' current actions but also expectations about their future stance (or about "interventions") are relevant to the exchange rate's level and dynamics. Any declaration of future policy is subject to scrutiny on the agents' part and, if the commitment to intervention is not irrevocable, then intervention will be expected to occur only if it is in the authorities' best interest at the time when it is supposed to take place. The presence of "bands" need not free monetary policy from exchange rate stability concerns and, in both theoretical and empirical work, "intervention" should probably be modeled as occurring continuously, possibly (but not necessarily) in linear fashion. Not only the agents but also the authorities should be aware that current fundamental movements have a bearing on their future probability distribution. Intervention policies and the behavior of fundamentals between interventions should be jointly modeled. This is a difficult theoretical problem. Fortunately, models of exchange rate determination are becoming complex and realistic enough to be confronted with real-life evidence, in search of empirical resolutions of theoretical ambiguities.

Notes

An early draft was written at IGIER in Milan. For help and comments I thank Rami Amir, Pierluigi Balduzzi, Leonardo Bartolini, Roel Beetsma, Bill Branson, Bernard Dumas, Silverio Foresi, Cindy Miller, Marcus Miller, Serena Ng, Paolo Pesenti, Christina Terra, participants in the SPES Workshop on Exchange Rate Target Zones at CEPR, and especially Lars Svensson. Any errors are mine.

1   Branson and Henderson (1985, p. 798) discuss money demand functional forms in intertemporal models where real money balances enter the objective function. Relationships between nominal money demand and asset returns under a variety of transaction technologies are discussed by Feenstra (1986) and Balduzzi and Foresi (1991).

2   A differential equation is homogeneous when all its terms involve one and only one level or derivative of the unknown function. The difference between the expressions in (9.17) and (9.6), which both solve the nonhomogeneous equation (9.1), must satisfy the homogeneous equation obtained from (9.1) by deleting $f(t)$.

3   The argument is due to Obstfeld and Rogoff (1983). Given purchasing power parity, it applies equally well to exchange rates as to price levels.

4   As fundamentals are a function of time only in this simple model, deterministic bubbles are "intrinsic" (i.e. they depend on the same state variables as fundamentals) in the terminology of Froot and Obstfeld (1991a).

5   See Obstfeld and Stockman (1985), especially sections 2.2 and 2.3, and their references, starting from Dornbusch (1976) and Krugman (1979).

6   The liabilities side of the balance sheet also contains the central bank's net (nominal) worth. This changes over time if the domestic-currency value of R is altered by exchange rate fluctuations rather than by interventions. It would also be affected by *helicopter drops*, i.e. changes in M which occur at unchanged D and R.

7   What follows simply tries to convey some intuition as to the formal meaning of notions which may be unfamiliar to the reader, and is by no means a rigorous introduction to stochastic processes in continuous time. Good references are Stokey and Lucas (1990), chs 7 and 8 for an introduction to probability notions; Harrison (1985) for an accessible applications-oriented treatment of stochastic calculus; and Karatzas and Schreve (1988) for an exhaustive exposition of formal results.

8   In fact, a good way to get acquainted with continuous-time stochastic processes is by building them up from discrete-time discrete-state-space processes, as in Dixit (1991).

9   See Karatzas and Schreve (1988, pp. 74–89) for a formal probabilistic treatment.

10   See Karatzas and Schreve (1988), pp. 394–8 for references to theoretical and applied technical work. Continuous-time methods are commonplace in engineering and physics, and in finance: see Merton (1990) and references therein. Recent work on microeconomic adjustment policies and on their macroeconomic consequences also make intensive use of these tools; see Bertola and Caballero (1990) and their references.

11   For technical details, see Karatzas and Schreve (1988), especially chapter 3. A formal definition of stochastic integrals and a statement of the regularity conditions to be imposed on $\{y(t)\}$ can be found on pp. 137–45.

12   By the martingale representation theorem (Karatzas and Shreve, 1988, p. 184), a right-continuous process whose increments cannot be predicted from observation of a Wiener process can be written as a stochastic integral with respect to that same Wiener process.

13   Karatzas and Schreve (1988, p. 271ff., 367ff., 427ff.) show that differential equations such as (9.30) admit stochastic representations similar to (9.26) in much more general settings than the present one.

14   The distributions which would make this possible involve combinations of truncated-normal random variables and are discussed in Harrison (1985, pp. 7–15) and Smith and Spencer (1991).

15   See Froot and Obstfeld (1991a) for further informal arguments, and their appendix for a formal proof.

16   Note that x denotes the logarithm of the exchange rate, and hence condition (9.37) reflects *logarithmic* "risk neutrality." If dX is random, then $E(dx) \neq E(dX/X)$ by Jensen's inequality (or Itô's lemma): in words, the logarithmic rate of growth does not coincide with the proportional growth rate of levels, and thus (9.37) is not the no-arbitrage relationship implied by risk neutrality. In fact, truly risk-neutral agents would be unable to reach market equilibrium (Siegel's 1972 paradox): since $XE[d(1/X)] \neq -E(dX)/X$, arbitrage could not be ruled out in terms of both X and $1/X$. The logarithmic no-arbitrage condition does hold symmetrically in terms of each currency's value and is invariant to choice of numeraire.

17   Dumas (1990) objects to use of the "smooth pasting" or "super contact" terminology in no-arbitrage models because conditions of this type follow from "value matching" conditions like (9.10) and do not have the independent role they would have in an optimizing context. Still, in an optimization problem a condition similar to (9.23) would be satisfied by a co-state variable, which has a "value" or "asset" interpretation and as such is subject to no-arbitrage constraints. Given (9.23) and continuity of $\{f(t)\}$, smooth pasting follows for purely formal reasons; given continuity and smooth pasting, (9.23) follows for equally formal reasons. Either set of conditions may be viewed as substantial, or as a purely formal consequence of the other.

18   Svensson (1991d), Lindberg and Söderlind (1991a, b), and others study data from the Swedish pegging scheme. Data generated by the operation of the exchange rate mechanism in the EMS are studied by Bertola and Caballero (1990), Bartolini and Bodnar (1991), Rose and Svensson (1991), Dominguez and Kenen (1992), Frankel and Phillips (1991), Weber (1991), Pesaran and Samiei (1992), and most exhaustively by Flood et al. (1991) and Svensson (1991a). Pessach and Razin (1990) explore the applicability of such models to Israeli data.

19   See chapter 8 in this volume; Flood and Garber (1983, 1984); Blanco and Garber (1986); and other work surveyed and referred to by Obstfeld and Stockman (1985).

20   Once again, condition (9.43) rules out expected arbitrage opportunities in exchange rate logarithms while Siegel's paradox prevents the formulation of similar conditions for exchange rate levels.

21   Of course, money supply dynamics may also affect the drift and noise component of fundamentals. In the central bank's accounting identity (9.18), the counterpart of (continuous or discontinuous) money supply development may be foreign exchange reserves expenditure or domestic credit changes or both.

22   See Lindberg et al. (1991), Svensson (1991a), and Frankel and Phillips (1991). Lindberg et al. find that the devaluation risk implied by fitting the model to Swedish data can be meaningfully related to such observables as competitiveness and the timing of elections.

23   If the real exchange rate affects the scale of money demand, then undershooting rather than overshooting may occur; see Miller and Weller (1991a). Also note that the exchange rate level would have to satisfy equilibrium constraints if slow price adjustment were rationalized from first principles, as in Dumas (1989), rather than postulated in the ad hoc fashion of (9.44). It would be interesting, but quite difficult, to specify forward-looking processes for real and nominal exchange rates so as simultaneously to clear goods and money markets.

24   If the $\{f(t)\}$ process had nonzero drift θ, then we would have $p(t) = x(t) = f(t) + \alpha\theta$ in a nonstochastic steady state, and the expectational counterpart to this condition would hold in the stochastic case. Lyons (1990) considers complex and realistic sticky price models where θ itself may be stochastic.

25   As noted by Froot and Obstfeld (1991b, n. 2), slow price adjustment introduces a special form of mean reversion in the process driving exchange rates: the price level which deflates nominal money demand depends on past

exchange rates, and hence on past innovations to the (nominal) fundamental process. A solution is available if f follows the linear process in (9.47). Since f increments are independent of its current level, x is always on the convergent saddlepath of a simple Dornbusch (1976) overshooting model:

$$x(t) = f(t) + \frac{1}{\alpha\lambda}[p(t) - f(t)]$$

where λ is the negative solution to $\alpha\lambda^2 - \phi - \alpha\phi\lambda = 0$. Defining $\rho \equiv (\phi + \alpha\phi\lambda)/\alpha\lambda$, we have

$$d[f(t) - p(t)] = -\rho[f(t) - p(t)]\,dt + \sigma dW(t)$$

This is the stochastic differential of a mean-reverting *Ornstein–Uhlenbeck* process, for which

$$E_t[f(\tau) - p(\tau)] = [f(t) - p(t)]\exp[-\rho(\tau - t)]$$

(Karatzas and Schreve, 1988, p. 358). Using this in (9.48) it is straightforward to verify that the saddlepath solution satisfies (9.45) and (9.49).

26 Of course, money market equilibrium and uncovered interest parity are not unquestionable in principle. The latter, in particular, is not robust to more general assumptions as to the financial market's attitudes towards risk. However, Svensson (1992b) and Frankel (1986) show that risk-determined deviations from uncovered interest parity are trivially small under reasonable parametric assumptions, and Frankel and Phillips (1991) find that survey data on exchange rate expectations behave much as interest rate differentials do.

References

Avesani, Renzo G. (1990) "Endogenously determined target zones and central bank optimal policy with limited reserves," mimeo, Università di Trento.

Balduzzi, Pierluigi, and Silverio Foresi (1991) "Money, liquidity, and optimal portfolio choices," Working Paper, New York University.

——, Giuseppe Bertola, and Silverio Foresi (1992a) "Nonlinearities in asset prices and infrequent noise trading," Princeton University Financial Research Center Memorandum 131.

——, ——, and —— (1992b) "Target changes and the term structure of interest rates," Working Paper, Princeton University.

Bartolini, Leonardo, and Gordon M. Bodnar (1991) "Target zones and forward rates in a model with repeated realignments," *Journal of Monetary Economics*, forthcoming.

Beetsma, Roel, and Frederick van der Ploeg (1991) "Exchange rate bands and optimal monetary accumulation under a dirty float," Working Paper, University of Amsterdam.

Bertola, Giuseppe, and Ricardo J. Caballero (1990) "Kinked adjustment costs and aggregate dynamics," in Olivier J. Blanchard and Stanley Fischer (eds) *NBER Macroeconomics Annual 1990*, Cambridge, MA, MIT Press.

——, and —— (1991) "Sustainable intervention policies and exchange rate dynamics," in P. Krugman and M. Miller (eds) *Exchange Rate Targets and*

Currency Bands, Cambridge, Cambridge University Press.
—— and —— (1992) "Target zones and realignments," *American Economic Review* 82 (3), 520–36.
—— and Allan Drazen (1993) "Trigger points and budget cuts: explaining the effects of fiscal austerity," *American Economic Review* 83 (1) 11–26.
—— and Lars E.O. Svensson (1991) "Stochastic devaluation risk and the empirical fit of target zone models," *Review of Economic Studies*, forthcoming.
Blanco, Herminio, and Peter M. Garber (1986) "Recurrent devaluations and speculative attacks on the Mexican peso," *Journal of Political Economy* 94, 148–66.
Branson, William H. and Dale W. Henderson (1985) "The specification and influence of asset markets," in R. Jones and P.B. Kenen (eds) *Handbook of International Economics* vol. 2, Amsterdam, North-Holland, ch.15.
Buiter, Willem H. and Vittorio U. Grilli (1991) "Anomalous speculative attacks on fixed exchange rate regimes: possible resolutions of the gold standard paradox," in P. Krugman and M. Miller (eds) *Exchange Rate Targets and Currency Bands*, Cambridge, Cambridge University Press.
—— and Paolo A. Pesenti (1990) "Rational speculative bubbles in an exchange rate target zone," CEPR Discussion Paper 479.
Corbae, Dean, Beth Ingram, and Guillermo Mondino (1990) "On the optimality of exchange rate band policies," Working Paper, University of Iowa.
Daniel, Betty C. (1986) "Optimal purchasing power parity deviations," *International Economic Review* 27 (2), 483–511.
Delgado, Francisco, and Bernard Dumas (1990) "Monetary contracting between central banks and the design of sustainable exchange-rate zones," NBER Working Paper 3440, Cambridge, MA.
—— and —— (1991) "Target zones, broad and narrow," in P. Krugman and M. Miller (eds) *Exchange Rate Targets and Currency Bands*, Cambridge, Cambridge University Press.
Dixit, Avinash K. (1991) "A simplified exposition of the theory of optimal control of Brownian motion," *Journal of Economic Dynamics and Control* 15, 657–73.
Dominguez, Kathryn M. and Peter B. Kenen (1992) "Intramarginal intervention in the EMS and the target-zone model of exchange-rate behavior," *European Economic Review* 36, 1523–32.
Dornbusch, Rudiger (1976) "Expectations and exchange rate dynamics," *Journal of Political Economy* 84, 1161–76.
Dumas, Bernard (1989) "Pricing physical assets internationally: a non linear heteroskedastic process for equilibrium real exchange rates," Working Paper, University of Pennsylvania.
—— (1990) "Super contact and related optimality conditions," *Journal of Economic Dynamics and Control* 15, 675–85.
—— (1992) "Dynamic equilibrium and the real exchange rate in a spatially separated world," *Review of Financial Studies* 5, 153–80.
—— and Lars E.O. Svensson (1991) "How long do unilateral target zones last?" Working Paper, IIES and Wharton School.
Feenstra, Robert C. (1986) "Functional equivalence between utility costs and the utility of money," *Journal of Monetary Economics* 17, 271–91.
Flood, Robert P. and Peter M. Garber (1983) "A model of stochastic process switching," *Econometrica* 15, 537–52.

—— and —— (1984) "Collapsing exchange rate regimes: some linear examples," *Journal of International Economics* 17, 194–207.

—— and —— (1991) "The linkage between speculative attack and target zone models of exchange rates: some extended results," in P. Krugman and M. Miller (eds) *Exchange Rate Targets and Currency Bands*, Cambridge, Cambridge University Press.

——, Andrew K. Rose, and Donald J. Mathieson (1991) "An empirical exploration of exchange rate target zones," *Carnegie-Rochester Series on Public Policy* 35, 7–66.

Frankel, Jeffrey A. (1986) "The implications of mean–variance optimization for four questions in international macroeconomics," *Journal of International Money and Finance* 5, S53–75.

—— and Steven Phillips (1991) "The European Monetary System: credible at last?" Working Paper, University of California at Berkeley.

Froot, Kenneth A. and Maurice Obstfeld (1991a) "Exchange rate dynamics under stochastic regime shifts: a unified approach," *Journal of International Economics* 31, 203–29.

—— and —— (1991b) "Stochastic process switching: some simple solutions," *Econometrica* 59, 241–50; also in P. Krugman and M. Miller (eds) *Exchange Rate Targets and Currency Bands*, Cambridge, Cambridge University Press.

Giavazzi, Francesco, and Pagano, Marco (1988) "The advantage of tying one's hands: EMS discipline and central bank credibility," *European Economic Review* 32, 1055–74.

Harrison, J. Michael (1985) *Brownian Motions and Stochastic Flow Systems*, New York, Wiley.

Karatzas, Iannis, and Steven E. Schreve (1988) *Brownian Motion and Stochastic Calculus*, New York, Springer.

Klein, Michael W. (1990) "Playing with the band: dynamic effects of target zones in an open economy," *International Economic Review* 31, 757–72.

—— and Karen K. Lewis (1990) "Learning about intervention target zones," NBER Working Paper 3674, Cambridge, MA.

Krugman, Paul R. (1979) "A model of balance-of-payments crises," *Journal of Money, Credit and Banking* 11, 311–25.

—— (1987) "Trigger strategies and price dynamics in equity and foreign exchange markets," NBER Working Paper 2459, Cambridge, MA.

—— (1991a) "Exchange rates in a currency band: a sketch of the new approach," in P. Krugman and M. Miller (eds) *Exchange Rate Targets and Currency Bands*, Cambridge, Cambridge University Press.

—— (1991b) "Target zones and exchange rate dynamics," *Quarterly Journal of Economics* 106, 669–82.

—— and Marcus Miller (eds) (1991) *Exchange Rate Targets and Currency Bands*, Cambridge, Cambridge University Press.

—— and Julio Rotemberg (1991) "Speculative attacks on target zones," in P. Krugman and M. Miller (eds) *Exchange Rate Targets and Currency Bands*, Cambridge, Cambridge University Press.

Lewis, Karen K. (1990) "Occasional intervention to target rates," NBER Working Paper 3398, Cambridge, MA.

Lindberg, Hans, and Paul Söderlind (1991a) "Target zone models and the intervention policy: the Swedish case," IIES Seminar Paper 496.

—— and —— (1991b) "Testing the basic target zone model on Swedish data," IIES Seminar Paper 488; *European Economic Review*, forthcoming.

——, Lars E.O. Svensson, and Paul Söderlind (1991) "Devaluation expectations: the Swedish krona 1982–1991," IIES Seminar Paper 495, *Economic Journal, forthcoming*.

Lyons, Richard K. (1990) "Whence exchange rate overshooting: money stock or flow?" *Journal of International Economics* 29, 369–84.

Merton, Robert (1990) *Continuous-Time Finance*, Oxford, Blackwell.

Miller, Marcus, and Alan Sutherland (1991) "Britain's return to gold and entry into the EMS: joining conditions and credibility," in P. Krugman and M. Miller (eds) *Exchange Rate Targets and Currency Bands*, Cambridge, Cambridge University Press.

——, and Weller, Paul A. (1989) "Exchange rate bands and realignments in a stationary stochastic setting," in M. Miller, B. Eichengreen, and R. Portes (eds) *Blueprints for Exchange Rate Management*, New York, Academic Press.

—— and —— (1990) "Currency bubbles which affect fundamentals: a qualitative treatment," *Economic Journal* 100, suppl., 170–9.

—— and —— (1991a) "Currency bands, target zones, and price flexibility," *IMF Staff Papers* 38, 184–215.

—— and —— (1991b) "Exchange rate bands with price inertia," *Economic Journal* 101, 1380–99.

Obstfeld, Maurice (1984) "Balance-of-payments crises and devaluation," *Journal of Money, Credit and Banking* 16, 208–17.

—— and Kenneth Rogoff (1983) "Speculative hyperinflations in maximizing models: can we rule them out?" *Journal of Political Economy* 91, 675–87.

—— and Alan C. Stockman (1985) "Exchange rate dynamics," in R. Jones and P.B. Kenen (eds) *Handbook of International Economics*, vol. 2, Amsterdam, North-Holland, ch. 18.

Pesaran, M. Hashem, and Hossein Samiei (1992) "An analysis of the determination of deutsche mark/French franc exchange rate in a discrete-time target zone," *Economic Journal* 102, 388–401.

Pesenti, Paolo A. (1990) "Perforate and imperforate currency bands: exchange rate management and the term structure of interest rate differentials," Economic Growth Center Discussion Paper 626, Yale University.

Pessach, Shula, and Assaf Razin (1990) "Targeting the exchange rate: an empirical investigation," Working Paper, International Monetary Fund; also NBER Working Paper 3662, 1991.

Rose, Andrew K. and Lars E.O. Svensson (1991) "Expected and predicted realignments: the FF/DM exchange rate during the EMS," IIES Seminar Paper 485; NBER Working Paper 3685; CEPR Discussion Paper 552.

Siegel, Jeremy J. (1972) "Risk, interest rates and the forward exchange," *Quarterly Journal of Economics* 86, 303–9.

Smith, Gregor W. (1991) "Solution to a problem of stochastic process switching," *Econometrica* 59, 237–9.

—— and R. Todd Smith (1990) "Stochastic process switching and the return to gold, 1925," *Economic Journal* 100, 164–75.

—— and Michael G. Spencer (1991) "Estimation and testing in models of exchange-rate target zones and process switching," in P. Krugman and M. Miller (eds) *Exchange Rate Targets and Currency Bands*, Cambridge, Cambridge University Press.

Stokey, Nancy L. and Robert Lucas (1990) *Recursive Methods in Economic Dynamics*, Cambridge, MA, Harvard University Press.

Sutherland, Alan (1991) "Target zone models with price inertia: some testable implications," Working Paper, University of York.

Svensson, Lars E.O. (1985) "Currency prices, terms of trade and interest rates," *Journal of International Economics* 18, 17–41.

—— (1991a) "Assessing target zone credibility: mean reversion and devaluation expectations in the EMS," IIES Seminar Paper 493.

—— (1991b) "Target zones and interest rate variability," *Journal of International Economics* 31, 27–54.

—— (1991c) "The simplest test of target zone credibility," *IMF Staff Papers* 38, 655–65.

—— (1991d) "The term structure of interest rates in a target zone: theory and Swedish data," *Journal of Monetary Economics* 28, 87–116.

—— (1992a) "An interpretation of recent research on exchange rate target zones," *Journal of Economic Perspectives* 6 (4), 119–44.

—— (1992b) "The foreign exchange risk premium in a target zone with devaluation risk," *Journal of International Economics* 33, 21–40.

—— (1992c) "Why exchange rate bands? Monetary independence in spite of fixed exchange rates," IIES Working Paper, Stockholm University.

Tirole, Jean (1982) "On the possibility of speculation under rational expectations," *Econometrica* 50, 1163–81.

Weber, Axel A. (1991) "Stochastic process switching and intervention in exchange rate target zones: empirical evidence from the EMS," CEPR Discussion Paper 554.

Williamson, John, and Miller, Marcus H. (1987) *Targets and Indicators: A Blueprint for the International Coordination of Economic Policy*, Washington, DC, Institute for International Economics.

PART IV

CAPITAL MARKETS, MONEY, AND
EXCHANGE RATES

10 Partial Equilibrium versus General Equilibrium Models of the International Capital Market

BERNARD DUMAS

1 Introduction

As a representation of international capital market equilibrium, one model has clearly failed. It is the model featuring independently and identically distributed (iid) random shocks and a homogeneous, or quasi-homogeneous, population of consumer-investors, differing at most by their risk aversions and endowments.[1] We review in section 2 the stylized facts which lead one to believe that the predictions of the model are incorrect or that its assumptions are so grossly violated that its predictions could not possibly be correct.

In this iid–homogeneous investors model, financial markets are essentially Arrow–Debreu complete in the sense that an unconstrained Pareto optimum prevails. Investors are able to insure all the risks that they wish to insure. Surprises are hedged away. Hence, along the equilibrium path, the economy is guaranteed a very tranquil ride. This is the main stylized fact that is contradicted by the data.

The major issue is how to search for, and how to identify, the right model that will replace the failed one. Apart from some attempts at modifying the form of the investors' utility function,[2] the main directions of research aim to relax the assumption that the investor population is homogeneous or that investors can hedge away all surprises. Markets may be incomplete, segmented, or imperfect.

The financial market is incomplete when some securities that at least some investors would like to trade (or to hold) are not available for trading to anyone. The incompleteness may be postulated (exogenous) or endogenous. When it is endogenous, it may arise from the inability to write contracts for which the outcome (the state or the state variable) is observable by the parties to the contract or verifiable by third parties in charge of enforcing the contract, such as members of the judicial system. Or it may arise from the absence of law or enforcement mechanisms, public or private, as is often the case when contracts involve parties residing in different countries.

Financial markets are segmented when some individuals (e.g. nationals of some countries) are prevented from trading (or holding) some securities. The distinction between incompleteness and segmentation is a fine one; it may turn out to be a vacuous one. Ultimately, when incompleteness or segmentation is fully endogenized, models will be classified according to the assumed cause of either phenomenon, not according to which one is being considered.

The financial market is imperfect when frictions, such as transactions costs or holding costs, cause the equilibrium to differ from the perfect market outcome. It seems plausible that a financial market bridging several countries is less perfect than a financial market designed by one country. Imperfections would seem particularly relevant to the modeling of the multi-country economy.[3] Imperfections in the financial markets are themselves a source of incompleteness and/or segmentation, since transactions costs prevent some individuals from holding or trading securities that they otherwise would hold or trade.

Most forms of incompleteness, segmentation, or imperfection in the financial market generate a form of heterogeneity in the investor population. For instance, transactions costs cause investors to differ from each other according to their inventory of securities. Heterogeneity of the investing public may also arise from imperfections that exist *outside* the financial market. For example, when the law of one price does not hold worldwide in the goods market, the prices of commodities to which investors of different countries have access are unequal. When the price differences are stochastic, they create a form of heterogeneity among investors that has been the focus of a generalization of the capital asset pricing model (CAPM) which we review in section 3 below.[4]

Furthermore, the form of incompleteness/segmentation/imperfection or heterogeneity postulated in a model dictates the relevant set of state variables that is needed to describe the evolution of the economy. For instance, in the presence of transactions costs, the wealths of investors, which are traditional state variables in the frictionless investment–consumption problem, no longer suffice to describe the state of the economy. Because the several forms of current wealth are no longer perfect substitutes, each investor's detailed holdings must be considered as separate state variables.

Much of research activity aims to tie equilibrium rates of return on the financial market to a number of state variables. Since returns are not iid, their *conditional* probability distribution has become the focus of research. This is a twofold endeavor. First, one must identify the state variables that can serve to condition returns (i.e. that have some power to predict returns). Second, one must verify whether the conditional distribution satisfies some asset-pricing restrictions. For instance, can the first moments of returns be made to match *time-varying risk premia* built on second moments, as the conditional form of the CAPM would suggest they should? The search for the relevant state variables, which will account for the time variability of asset returns, is also a search for the relevant model specification.

When searching for the correct model type, the orthodox method in economics calls for general equilibrium (GE) models of each type to be developed and empirically tested. GE models are superior guides to policy because they permit comparative statics and dynamics. From the empirical standpoint, they have the decisive advantage that each GE model dictates the list of variables that describe the state of the economy. The only practical problem that remains when setting out to test a GE model is that some state variables may not be observable; a search for proxy variables must then be undertaken. But there is no interrogation as to which state variables ought to be used as instruments.

However, GE models of the international capital market appear to be very complex to solve. One can run, instead, tests of somewhat aggregated first-order conditions which make up partial equilibrium models. The various CAPMs are examples of these. State variables are found by means of trial and error. I will regard the empirical analysis of partial equilibrium models as heterodox but, possibly, more pragmatic and useful than would be the orthodox method of testing GE models after they have been fully worked out.

The question that I would like to discuss in this chapter is the following: which of two different lines of attack (the orthodox GE method or the heterodox CAPM method) is more likely to help us identify the relevant state variables in order to have a clue as to the correct model type? I want to review the kit of models developed so far and assess the potential for success.

The remainder of the chapter is organized as follows. In section 2 I review briefly the stylized facts of international financial life which ought to be explained or must, at the very least, be incorporated in models of the international economy. In section 3 I review International CAPMs that take into account deviations from purchasing power parity (PPP) between consumers of various countries of residence. In section 4 I survey the empirical tests of CAPMs and their results. In section 5 I describe some GE models. Section 6 concludes as far as GE models are concerned.

2   The stylized facts

Several anomalies are listed below. These are unlikely ever to be explained by the neoclassical model featuring a homogeneous investor population and iid shocks. Future models of the international economy must, at the very least, take these anomalies into account. The final goal would be to explain them with the right mix of incompleteness/ segmentation/imperfection.

1   Violations of uncovered interest rate parity (and attendant predictability of spot exchange rate changes) are well documented. I review this evidence briefly in section 4.1 below. The violations are such that they are unlikely to be explainable as risk premia.

2   Currencies remain undervalued/overvalued relative to their purchasing power parity level for very long periods of time. Deficits/ surpluses of balances of trade are also persistent. The long-term reversion of currencies toward PPP is so slow that it is barely detectable by statisticians. In fact, the hypothesis was entertained and not rejected that real exchange rates may follow a martingale process (Adler and Lehmann, 1983). At the very least, we can say that changes in real exchange rates have a large permanent component (Campbell and Clarida, 1987; Huizinga, 1987). Volatile changes in deviations from PPP translate into large differences in real interest rates between countries.

   Can PPP deviations of this magnitude be relative price deviations? Or do they represent violations of the law of one price? Giovannini (1988), Marston (1990), and Engel (1991), among others, have shown that the law of one price is grossly violated, because competition between firms is imperfect.

3   Studies of the US economy have revealed that the time series of consumption is too smooth for consumption to be determined by wealth and for wealth to be the present value of future consumption. Stock market studies have shown that consumption is also too smooth to serve as a basis for pricing financial assets, as the neoclassical theory of marginal utility says it should. I return to that issue in section 5.1. On the international scene, the evidence is that the correlation of consumption across countries is extremely low, whereas the theory of complete integrated markets says it should be equal to unity.[5]

4   Investors' portfolios exhibit strong home equity preference. French investors devote almost all their portfolio to French securities, whereas traditional portfolio theory would have them hold the world market portfolio. The evidence on this issue is presented in Eldor et al. (1988),

French and Poterba (1991), Cooper and Kaplanis (1991), Howell and Cozzini (1990, 1991), Broadgate Consultants (1991), and Tesar and Werner (1992). Because extant economic theory overrates the investors' willingness to invest abroad, it is not easily able to explain savings in relation to terms of trade. Neither does it explain well the high degree of correlation between savings and investment noted by Feldstein and Horioka (1980). One issue of interest is the following. Have PPP deviations and exchange rate behavior, noted under 2 above, something to do with the observed home equity preference?

3   International capital asset pricing models and uncovered interest rate parity

3.1   Heterogeneity created by consumption goods prices: the international capital asset pricing model

Siegel (1972) first raised the question of asset pricing when investors live in different countries and deviations from PPP are the source of heterogeneity among them. Under risk neutrality, he reasoned, forward prices are equal to expected future spot prices.[6] But, if a forward exchange rate, expressed in dollars per franc, is equal to the expected value of the future spot exchange rate, also in dollars per franc, how then can the forward exchange rate in terms of francs per dollar be equal to the expected value of the future spot in francs per dollar? The answer is that, for as long as the future spot rate is random, the two equalities cannot both be true, because of Jensen's inequality. This simple observation is called "the Siegel paradox."

For two decades, international macroeconomists eschewed Siegel's question and went to the extreme of postulating, in an *ad hoc* way, that the logarithm of the forward exchange rate was equal to the expected value of the logarithm of the future spot rate. No known utility function, with which to endow consumer investors, risk neutral or otherwise, can produce such a result at equilibrium.[7] The goal was to do away with Siegel's paradox. Empiricists and statisticians (McCulloch, 1975) pointed out that, for the real-world degree of volatility of exchange rates, the "Jensen inequality term" was of small magnitude anyway.

In 1974, Solnik (1974) confronted directly the problem of deriving restrictions on equilibrium rates of return that would prevail in a world capital market populated by risk-averse investors who would differ in their consumption prices. A logical antecedent to the Solnik model is the closed economy CAPM expressed in nominal terms which has been derived by Friend et al. (1976). Calling ρ_i the rate of return on security

i, over a short holding period, expressed in real terms (i.e. adjusted for inflation), the classic CAPM of Sharpe (1964), Lintner (1965), and Mossin (1966) says that, in equilibrium, there must exist two numbers η and θ, common to all securities, such that, for all securities (all i),

$$E(\rho_i) = \eta + \theta \, \mathrm{cov}(\rho_i, \rho_m) \tag{10.1}$$

where ρ_m is the real rate of return on the market portfolio. The two numbers η and θ may be interpreted as the (possibly shadow) real rate of return and as the market average degree of risk aversion respectively. Observing that the real rate of return ρ_i is given by

$$\rho_i = \frac{1 + R_i}{1 + \pi} - 1 \tag{10.2}$$

where R_i is the nominal rate of return and π the rate of inflation, we can substitute (10.2) into (10.1) and apply the rules of stochastic calculus (Itô's lemma) to obtain

$$E(R_i) - E(\pi) + \mathrm{var}(\pi) - \mathrm{cov}(R_i, \pi) = \eta + \theta \, \mathrm{cov}(R_i - \pi, R_m - \pi) \tag{10.3}$$

or, rearranging terms,

$$E(R_i) = \eta + E(\pi) - (1 - \theta) \, \mathrm{var}(\pi) - \theta \, \mathrm{cov}(\pi, R_m) + (1 - \theta) \, \mathrm{cov}(R_i, \pi)$$
$$+ \theta \, \mathrm{cov}(R_i, R_m) \tag{10.4}$$

In equation (10.4), the first four terms of the right-hand side sum to the nominally riskless rate of return r if one is available.[8] Hence, we can rewrite (10.4) in the following form:

$$E(R_i) = r + (1 - \theta) \, \mathrm{cov}(R_i, \pi) + \theta \, \mathrm{cov}(R_i, R_m) \tag{10.5}$$

This simple nominal CAPM provides us with a simple lesson. Risky inflation produces a separate premium in nominal returns. This premium receives a coefficient equal to one minus the market risk aversion; it would therefore be present even if investors were risk neutral ($\theta = 0$). Another version of the same lesson is that the coefficient on the covariance with inflation and the coefficient on the covariance with the market sum to unity. This restriction on the coefficients of the CAPM comes from the fact that investors evaluate returns in real terms (i.e. in terms of consumption units). They do not suffer from "money illusion."

As portfolio theory does generally, the work of Solnik (1974) produced two insights concerning the international equilibrium. One was a CAPM, or a restriction on securities returns; the other was a description of investors' holdings in equilibrium.

A special case of some relevance is the one in which,[9] in each of the respective local currencies, the inflation rate is nonrandom: the French inflation rate, measured as a percentage increase in the francs consumer index, is nonrandom; so is the US inflation rate measured in dollars etc. We call this case "the Solnik special case" and we consider its implications in various respects.

Observe that the rate of inflation over a period in any country may be measured in any currency. For instance, we can measure the French inflation rate in dollar units, using the following translation formula:

$$\pi_{\text{Fra}}^{\$} = (1 + \pi_{\text{Fra}}^{\text{FF}})(1 + v_{\text{FF}}^{\$}) - 1 \qquad (10.6)$$

where $v_{\text{FF}}^{\$}$ is the relative change in the dollar–franc spot exchange rate over the period. Equation (10.6) is a formula used merely to change units of measurement. It contains no economic assumption.[10] In Solnik's special case, the rate of inflation in France measured in francs is nonrandom, but the rate of inflation in France measured in dollars is random, reflecting, as it does then, exclusively the randomness in the exchange rate.

Consider now the rates of return R_i of all securities and all the country rates of inflation, all expressed in the same unit, say the current dollar. If need be, the securities, rates of return that are expressed in foreign currency units may be translated into dollars using the following formula, which is analogous to the formula used for inflation rates:

$$R_i = (1 + R_i^*)(1 + v) - 1 \qquad (10.7)$$

where R_i^* is the rate of return on security i expressed in the nondollar currency and v is the rate of change of the spot exchange rate expressed in dollars per unit of nondollar currency.

In the absence of PPP, the rates of inflation in the various countries, all expressed in dollars, are unequal and their differences are random. This is the kind of heterogeneity that we must have among investors in order to represent realistically an international world in which people appreciate differently the real returns from the same securities. Each country or each national group of consumer-investors, of country l say, has its own rate of inflation π^l. In Solnik's special case, it reflects entirely the random fluctuations of each currency against the dollar; the US rate of inflation is the only one that is not random in dollar units.

The international (nominal) CAPM, expressed in dollars, may now be derived in the following way. For each national group of investors a first-order condition similar to equation (10.5) holds:

$$E(R_i) = r + (1 - \theta^l)\operatorname{cov}(R_i, \pi^l) + \theta^l \operatorname{cov}(R_i, R_p^l) \qquad (10.8)$$

where r is the dollar, nominally riskless, interest rate and R_p^l is the dollar rate of return on the optimal portfolio held by the investors of country l: $R_p^l = \Sigma_i x_i^l R_i$ (x_i^l being the weight allocated by investors of country l to security i). In order to aggregate the first-order conditions (10.8) over all the investor groups, we divide both sides of (10.8) by θ^l, multiply them by W^l (each country's wealth), sum them over all national investor groups, and finally divide them by $\Sigma_l W^l/\theta^l$, to get

$$E(R_i) = r + \theta \sum_l \left(\frac{1}{\theta^l} - 1\right) W^l \frac{\text{cov}(R_i, \pi^l)}{W} + \theta \, \text{cov}(R_i, R_m) \quad (10.9)$$

$$W = \sum_l W^l \qquad \frac{1}{\theta} = \frac{\Sigma_l W^l/\theta^l}{W}$$

The international nominal CAPM (10.9) now contains as many "inflation premia" as there are national investor groups.

In Solnik's special case, US investors do not contribute a term to the dollar CAPM because for them $\pi^l = 0$. The inflation premia that do exist simply reflect covariances with exchange rates $(\text{cov}(R_i, \pi^l)$ $= \text{cov}(R_i, v^l))$. They are premia for bearing the foreign exchange risk which is statistically contained in any investment.

Relaxing Solnik's assumption only causes the various inflation rates π^l to reflect not only the random fluctuation in exchange rates but also the randomness in the various local currency inflation rates, in accordance with formula (10.6). Furthermore, the inflation premium corresponding to US investors would not be zero as their $\text{cov}(R_i, \pi^l)$ would generally differ from zero.[11] Observe that the coefficients of all the premia (inflation and market premia) sum to unity, as they did in (10.5), because of the absence of money illusion.

The dollar rate of return from a foreign currency deposit is given by a formula which is a special case of (10.7); it is equal to $(1 + r_j^*)$ $(1 + v_j) - 1$, where r_j^* is the nominal rate of interest on foreign currency j. Applying (10.9) to foreign currency deposits gives

$$r_j^* + E(v_j) = r + \theta \sum_l \left(\frac{1}{\theta^l} - 1\right) W^l \frac{\text{cov}(v_j, \pi^l)}{W} + \theta \, \text{cov}(v_j, R_m) \quad (10.10)$$

This equation is the form taken under risk aversion by the well-known uncovered interest rate parity (UIRP) relation which relates the interest rates on two different currencies.

Consider now a change of currency unit. We switch to a different currency in terms of which to express the CAPM. The translation formula for rates of return is equation (10.7), where v is the rate of change of the dollar value of the currency into which we are switching. Substituting (10.7) into (10.9) and using the rules of stochastic calculus, we get

$$E(R_i^*) + E(v) + \text{cov}(R_i^*, v) = r + \theta \sum_l \left(\frac{1}{\theta^l} - 1 \right) W^l \frac{\text{cov}(R_i^* + v, \pi^{*l} + v)}{W}$$

$$+ \theta \, \text{cov}(R_i^* + v, R_m^* + v)$$

or[12]

$$E(R_i^*) = r - E(v) + \theta \sum_l \left(\frac{1}{\theta^l} - 1 \right) W^l \frac{\text{cov}(v, \pi^{*l} + v)}{W} + \theta \, \text{cov}(v, R_m + v)$$

$$+ \theta \sum_l \left(\frac{1}{\theta^l} - 1 \right) W^l \frac{\text{cov}(R_i^*, \pi^{*l})}{W} + \theta \, \text{cov}(R_i^*, R_m^*) \qquad (10.11)$$

By virtue of (10.10), the first four terms of the right-hand side of (10.11) sum to r^*, the rate of interest on the currency we are translating into. Hence we have

$$E(R_i^*) = r^* + \theta \sum_l \left(\frac{1}{\theta^l} - 1 \right) W^l \frac{\text{cov}(R_i^*, \pi^{*l})}{W} + \theta \, \text{cov}(R_i^*, R_m^*) \quad (10.12)$$

which is an international CAPM exactly identical to (10.9) but with a different intercept r^* instead of r. Changing currency unit preserves the CAPM, as would be expected in the absence of money illusion.

Adler and Dumas (1983) observed that the international CAPM (10.9) may be reduced to the ordinary nominal CAPM (10.5) as far as equities are concerned. This reduced international CAPM applies to equity rates of return "hedged against exchange risk." Consider supplementing each equity investment with a basket of currencies, held short, such that the net return – equity rate of return plus or minus the returns from currencies – is rendered independent of PPP deviations:

$$R_i = \sum_j \gamma_{ij}(r_j^* + v_j) + \zeta_i \qquad \text{for all } i \qquad (10.13)$$

$$\sum_j \gamma_{ij} = 1 \qquad E(\zeta_i) \neq 0$$

$$\text{cov}[\zeta_i(\pi^l - \pi^{\text{USA}})] = 0 \qquad \text{for all } l$$

The coefficients γ_{ij} are chosen in such a way that ζ_i is independent of all PPP deviations, $\pi^l - \pi^{\text{USA}}$.[13] The coefficients γ_{ij} may be interpreted as "exposures" of the equities to exchange risk.[14] The net returns ζ_i are equity returns hedged against exchange risk. Adler and Dumas show that the following restriction holds for all i and any l:

$$E(\zeta_i) = (1 - \theta) \, \text{cov}(\zeta_i, \pi^l) + \theta \, \text{cov}(\zeta_i, R_m) \qquad (10.14)$$

The CAPM (10.14) prices equity rates of return relative to all currency rates of return.

3.2   Portfolio holdings in equilibrium

Sercu (1980)[15] has given a lucid description of equilibrium portfolio holdings in the Solnik model.[16] Consider inverting the first-order condition system (10.8) to obtain the composition x^l of the portfolio held by investors of country l taken as a whole. Observe that, for $\theta^l = 1$, the portfolio composition is independent of the investor's country of residence, since π^l disappears from the first-order conditions. An investor with unit risk aversion[17] is nationless, as it were. His portfolio is universally efficient.

Black's (1976) "separation theorem" states that, assuming short sales are allowed, the set of mean–variance-efficient portfolios is included in the set of linear combinations of just two efficient portfolios. The idea then comes of decomposing the portfolio of the investor of any country (with any value of risk aversion θ^l) into two components. We already know that the unit risk aversion portfolio is universally efficient. The other component will have to be specific to the investors of each country. Call Ω the variance–covariance matrix of nominal dollar rates of return ($\Omega_{i,j} = \mathrm{cov}(R_i, R_j)$) and ω^l the vector of covariances of dollar rates of return with country l's nominal inflation measured in dollars ($\omega_j^l = \mathrm{cov}(R_j, \pi^l)$). Finally, call μ the vector of dollar excess returns ($\mu_i = E(R_i) - r$). Then, from (10.8), the portfolio composition x^l may be written[18]

$$x^l = \frac{1}{\theta^l}\Omega^{-1}\mu + \left(1 - \frac{1}{\theta^l}\right)\Omega^{-1}\omega^l \qquad (10.15)$$

In equation (10.15), the first portfolio component $\Omega^{-1}\mu$ is identifiable as the unit risk aversion portfolio; we verify that its composition is independent of l, the country of the investor. The composition of the second one, $\Omega^{-1}\omega^l$, is formally identical to the vector of coefficients of a multiple regression of π^l on all the securities' returns R_i. This makes it easy to interpret. This portfolio is designed as a hedge of the investor's home inflation, since the correlation of its nominal return with home inflation is maximum. In the Solnik special case, in which home inflation is nonstochastic when expressed in the investor's currency, the hedge portfolio is simply made up 100 percent of the investor's home-currency deposit.

This simple decomposition gives us a picture of securities holdings in world capital market equilibrium. We are aided in this description by table 10.1. All investors in the world hold the unit risk aversion

Table 10.1 Dollar amounts held in the portfolios

	RA1 portfolio	*France*	*UK* ...	*USA*	*World market portfolio*
Equities Wx_m		0	0	0	Wx_m
Currencies					
FF	$-(1-1/\theta^{\mathrm{Fra}})W^{\mathrm{Fra}}$	$(1-1/\theta^{\mathrm{Fra}})W^{\mathrm{Fra}}$			0
UK£	$-(1-1/\theta^{\mathrm{UK}})W^{\mathrm{UK}}$		$(1-1/\theta^{\mathrm{UK}})W^{\mathrm{UK}}$ 0		0
.		0	.		
US$	$-(1-1/\theta^{\mathrm{USA}})W^{\mathrm{USA}}$			$(1-1/\theta^{\mathrm{USA}})W^{\mathrm{USA}}$ 0	
Total	W/θ		$W(1-1/\theta)$		W

portfolio RA1 which generally contains equities[19] as well as currency deposits. Each country devotes to it a fraction $1/\theta^l$ of its wealth.

In the Solnik special case, they devote the remainder, $1-1/\theta^l$, of their wealth to their home-currency deposit exclusively. Hence, equities are held as part of the RA1 portfolio only. In equilibrium, all the equity holdings must sum to the world market portfolio of equities. The relative composition of the equity part of the RA1 portfolio, which is also the relative composition of the equity part of any investor's portfolio, must therefore be identical to the composition of the world market portfolio of equities, no matter what may be the structure of the variances and covariances of returns. At equilibrium, all investors hold equities in the same proportions.[20]

Currency deposits, on the other hand, are forms of borrowing (when they are held negatively) and lending. For every borrower there must be a lender; they net out to zero. If French people invest a fraction $1-1/\theta^{\mathrm{Fra}}$ of their wealth into franc deposits, as a "hedge portfolio," then the world at large must be borrowing the same amount, as part of their RA1 portfolio. This observation provides the equilibrium composition of the currency part of the RA1 portfolio; it provides also the relative size of the equity and currency parts of this portfolio.

In the typical case in which every country's risk aversion is greater than unity, the people of the various countries hold their home-currency deposits positively ($1-1/\theta^l > 0$). The RA1 portfolio therefore typically contains currencies negatively. This portfolio, which is universally efficient, has the same composition as the world market portfolio as far as equities are concerned, but contains some currency financing.[21]

3.3   The lessons of international portfolio theory

International portfolio theory has produced two results which, in principle, are testable: a CAPM equation and a detailed description of portfolio holdings in equilibrium. Section 4 will be devoted to empirical tests of various CAPMs applied to international securities returns. We now discuss the implication for UIRP and the verisimilitude of portfolio holdings.

If the financial market is integrated, the CAPM (10.9) applies, of course, to all securities. When applied to currency deposits, it takes the form (10.10) which is a relationship between short-term nominal interest rates quoted on two different currencies or equivalently, between the short-maturity forward premia and the expected spot exchange rate. It provides the deviation from the traditional UIRP which prevails when investors are risk averse and PPP does not hold. In section 4 below, we examine the empirical evidence on UIRP to see whether it is likely to be compatible with (10.10) written in various ways.

We can now return to Siegel's paradox by taking the limit $\theta^l \to 0$ in (10.10) to reach risk neutrality. It is obvious from (10.10) or (10.9) that the equilibrium collapses. When investors are risk neutral and PPP does not hold, they disagree infinitely about the required returns; no equilibrium exists.

If PPP prevails, however, the correct CAPM is (10.5) which, when applied to currency deposits, gives

$$r_i^* + E(v_i) = r + (1 - \theta) \operatorname{cov}(v_i, \pi) + \theta \operatorname{cov}(v_i, R_m) \qquad (10.16)$$

where π is world inflation measured in the same currency unit as exchange rates and rates of return. If $\theta = 0$, we still have $r_i + E(v_i) = r + \operatorname{cov}(v_i, \pi)$. There exists an equilibrium but the equilibrium relationship between interest rates incorporates an inflation premium which is a deviation from nominal UIRP, the reason being that investors care about real returns. This inflation premium resolves the Siegel paradox.[22] Whether $\theta = 0$ or not, equation (10.16) is perfectly symmetric; the expected rate of return of investing in dollars measured in currency i is[23]

$$r - E(v_i) + \operatorname{var}(v_i) = r_i^* + (1 - \theta) \operatorname{cov}(- v_i, \pi - v_i)$$
$$+ \theta \operatorname{cov}(- v_i, R_m - v_i) \qquad (10.17)$$

which is equivalent to (10.16) itself.

Turning now to equilibrium portfolio holdings, the lesson of international portfolio theory is rich is precision. But is it compatible with casual empiricism? In section 2 we pointed out that investors' actual portfolios exhibit strong home equity bias. The theory predicts that investors would exhibit strong home-currency preference in the sense that they would hold their home-currency deposits as a hedge, or a riskless asset. But the theory also says that they all hold equity in the same relative composition as in the world market portfolio. This is true strictly only in the Solnik special case, which is probably not far from the truth. It would not be true if home-currency inflation in the investors' country of residence were random. Although this should be settled empirically, we can surmise that home inflation risk is unlikely to be a convincing justification for home equity preference.

Exchange risk and PPP deviations turn out not to be a relevant explanation for home equity bias.[24] This is because, in the model, people can hedge away exchange risk. The availability of currency deposits in all currencies (or forward exchange contracts) renders the investor population homogeneous once again.[25]

Evidently, a number of features of the actual international capital market that would help explain home equity bias are missing from the model. Capital market segmentation, in various forms, is an obvious candidate.[26] Research should be undertaken to identify the nature and sources of segmentation. Sovereign risk has been studied in papers on the less developed country debt crisis but has not been modeled as a source of capital market segmentation. Asymmetric information, along the lines of Admati (1985) or Diamond and Verrechia (1981), should find an application in international finance. French people may possess more direct information on the state of the French economy and French firms than do American investors, and *vice versa*. Local information would be a form of insider information leading investors to invest less abroad, and possibly also to modify the composition of their foreign portfolio.

Considering the paucity of data on actual portfolio holdings, it would be useful to draw the implications of international portfolio theory for international capital flows, as these are recorded in the balance of payments.[27] If securities rates of return are assumed to be iid over time, the theory predicts a modicum of transactions in securities. As in the classic one-country theory, rebalancing occurs following the realizations of rates of return. Since investors wish to maintain fairly fixed fractions of wealth invested in the various equity securities, a high realization of return on a security produces an increase in the value of portfolio holdings of that security, leading to a desire to sell it. At that point, explicit treatment of physical investment by firms and households becomes necessary. If physical capital is perfectly flexible, the desire to sell is accommodated by a reduction (or a reduced increase) in the firm's capital stock (by means of dividend distribution and/or share repurchase). The investor hardly needs to transact.

In the international model, portfolios differ across investors in their currency components. This gives some play to exchange rates. Following the realization of a large increase in the value of the franc, French people wish to sell it to buy other currencies and equities. The foreigners' franc debt has increased in value; they want to pay some back. These two desires are compatible.

There would be more action on the capital flow front if rates of returns were not iid. Strictly speaking, the model that we have exposited so far is not compatible with non-iid returns because we have not incorporated in the investors' first-order conditions (10.8) intertemporal hedging terms à la Merton (1971, 1973). If we were to consider the model, nonetheless, as an approximation of a dynamic model and were to make use of it as a workhorse, simply by replacing the expected values, variances, and covariances of returns by their conditional counterparts, the capital flow issue would not be clarified until after the joint stochastic process for rates of return and other "information" variables had been identified. For instance, an increase in a security's conditionally expected rate of return would cause investors to buy that security and the issuing firm simultaneously to increase its physical capital. But a temporary increase in return would induce a smaller value of this flow than would a permanent one.[28]

Soon, it appears that a proper study of international capital flows requires a worked out GE model with explicit treatment of monetary and fiscal policy, capital formation by firms, price and wage rigidity etc. so that one knows which variables drive the stochastic process for rates of return.

3.4   Other capital asset pricing models applicable to international returns

In the previous sections, the traditional one-country CAPM has been shown not to survive, without amendment, the transfer to a world of heterogeneous investors. Other CAPM types are different in this respect. The consumption CAPM of Breeden (1978) or the arbitrage pricing theory (APT) of Ross (1976) may be applied to international data without change.

Consider first the consumption CAPM. Breeden (1978)[29] has shown that securities' real rates of return satisfy a first-order condition involving any investor's rate of consumption. This condition holds generally, in a multi-period as much as in a one-period setting, in a complete or an incomplete market for as long as the investor optimizes his portfolio and his consumption. It only requires that the investor have access to the securities to which the condition is applied. According to this condition, there exist two numbers η and θ such that

$$E(\rho_i) = \eta + \theta \operatorname{cov}(\rho_i, \chi) \qquad (10.18)$$

where χ is the investor's real consumption rate. Translation of this real CAPM into a nominal CAPM gives

$$E(R_i) - E(\pi) + \operatorname{var}(\pi) - \operatorname{cov}(R_i, \pi) = \eta + \theta \operatorname{cov}(R_i - \pi, c - \pi) \quad (10.19)$$

where c is the investor's nominal consumption rate. Finally, interpreting some terms as summing to the nominal rate of interest, we get

$$E(R_i) = r + (1 - \theta) \operatorname{cov}(R_i, \pi) + \theta \operatorname{cov}(R_i, c) \qquad (10.20)$$

This condition holds from the point of view of any national group of investors.[30] It can be used provided that the group's rate of consumption is observable, or under some other auxiliary assumptions that give the model some empirical content. Equation (10.20) would be the ideal device to determine to which securities each category of investors has access and thereby to track down segmentations. However, the consumption CAPM has failed empirically as a pricing device[31] mostly because consumption is observed infrequently and its observed behavior is so much smoother than that of wealth. The variable c has little variation over time and the term $\operatorname{cov}(R_i, c)$ fails to explain the cross-section of returns. Using the consumption CAPM, Wheatley (1988) has not detected segmentation in the world equity market. Hansen and Hodrick (1983) have used (10.20) as a point of departure but have found a way, under some auxiliary assumption, to avoid the need to measure consumption. We return to their work in section 4.3.

Ross's (1976) APT may be applied to international data even if the world population is made heterogeneous by PPP deviations. Ross postulates that securities rates of return satisfy a factor structure such as

$$R_i = E(R_i) + f\beta_i + \varepsilon_i \qquad (10.21)$$

where β_i is a vector of coefficients and f is a vector of K common random factors; $E(f) = 0$; $E(\varepsilon_i) = 0$; $E(fe_i) = 0$. Some structure (often a diagonal structure) is imposed on the variances and covariances of the security-specific residuals ε_i, while the number of securities in the market is increased to infinity, and the number of factors remains fixed at K. By virtue of the law of large numbers, any portfolio made up of the large number of securities will have a negligible ε risk. Only the factor risks are "nondiversifiable." Ross shows that, in order to bar arbitrage, there must exist a pricing relationship between expected returns and the nondiversifiable risks β:

$$E(R_i) = r + \lambda\beta_i \qquad (10.22)$$

where λ is a vector of market prices of risk applicable to all securities.

Solnik (1983a) and Levine (1989) have shown that a relationship such as (10.22) still holds after a change of reference currency.[32]

4   Comparing empirical methods

Because the CAPM is a partial equilibrium incompletely specified model, it is not directly testable without some auxiliary assumptions. Mostly, what is needed is the specification of the external state variables that move the probability distribution of returns period after period. Since the model by itself, in contrast with a fully specified GE model, contains no clue as to the choice of these instrumental variables, one uses it purely as a "fishing net." The test of performance for a particular set of variables is how well they help to predict returns and to what extent the conditional expected values, variances, and covariances so obtained satisfy the CAPM restriction.[33]

4.1   Constant risk premia

Many tests of UIRP have been conducted by regressing spot exchange rate movements on earlier interest rate differentials (or forward premia). For instance, Cumby and Obstfeld (1984) tested the following equation:

$$ln\ S_{t+1} - ln\ S_t = a + b(ln\ F_t - ln\ S_t) + u_{t+1} \qquad (10.23)$$

where S_t and F_t are a pair of spot and forward exchange rates at time t. Under the strict UIRP hypothesis,[34] we would have $a = 0$ and $b = 1$. Amending the strict UIRP to include a risk premium, and adding the hypothesis that risk premium is constant over time, we should still have $b = 1$. For most currencies over the floating rate period, Cumby and Obstfeld found estimates of b that were much smaller, and significantly smaller, than 1 and many times also smaller than 0. Moreover, they found evidence of heteroskedasticity in the residuals u. For this reason it is hard to justify the assumption that risk premia are constant.

Fama (1984) asked the question: would a justifiable risk premium be sufficiently variable to account for the finding $b \ll 1$? To throw some light on this question, he broke the right-hand side of equation (10.23) in the following way:

$$ln\ S_{t+1} - ln\ S_t = a + (ln\ F_t - ln\ S_t) + (b-1)(ln\ F_t - ln\ S_t) + u_{t+1} \qquad (10.24)$$

The terms of the right-hand side of (10.24) can be interpreted: the second term is, of course, the forward premium; the sum of the first three terms equals the conditionally expected change in the (log) spot exchange rate, $E_t(\ln S_{t+1}) - \ln S_t$, while the sum of the first and third terms $a + (b-1)(\ln F_t - \ln S_t)$ is the conditional risk premium. In this interpretation, a finding of $b < 0.5$ implies that the conditional risk premium varies over time more than the conditionally expected change in the exchange rate, or that the unconditional variance of the risk premium is greater than the unconditional variance of the expected change.[35] For instance, if $b = 0.4$, the conditional expected change varies as much as 0.4 times the forward premium, while the conditional risk premium varies as much as -0.6 times the forward premium. In absolute value, 0.6 is greater than 0.4. Also, note the signs: the conditional risk premium would have to covary negatively with the conditional expected change. These features of a risk premium are unlikely to be found in a GE model.

The finding that $b \neq 1$ implies that exchange rate changes are predictable from the knowledge of forward premia. D. Hsieh has pointed out, however, that this in-sample predictability of exchange rates frequently does not translate into the ability to predict out of sample. Some assumptions of the statistical theory underlying the tests must therefore be violated. Hsieh (1991) suspects that the assumption of linearity, built into equation (10.23), ought to be investigated. He uses nonlinear methods in an attempt to achieve out-of-sample predictability.

One alternative to the constancy of the risk premium has been suggested by Frankel (1982). He assumed that the variance–covariance matrix of exchange rates is constant over time. This assumption does not imply a constant risk premium because the supply of assets denominated in the various currencies varies over time. Frankel (1982), and later Engel and Rodrigues (1988) as well as Engel et al. (1991), test the following equation:

$$R_{t+1} - r_t = \theta_t \Omega x_t + u_{t+1} \qquad (10.25)$$

where the left-hand side term is a vector of excess return on several securities over the time period t to $t+1$, x_t is a vector of asset supplies at time t, and u is a vector of unanticipated returns. Equation (10.25) is tested under the restriction that the matrix Ω is constant and is equal to the variance–covariance matrix of the unanticipated returns u. The advantage of the method is that no restriction is imposed on the price of risk, θ_t. The vector of asset supplies is identified with the supplies of government bonds denominated in the various currencies.[36] The test rejects the restriction.

4.2 Instrumental variables

In this section I try to establish an inventory of the variables that have

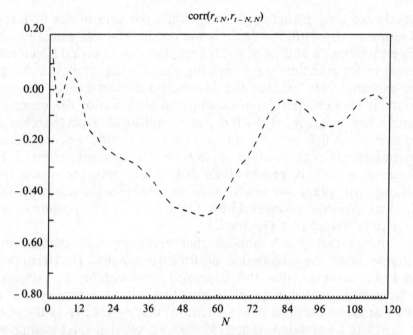

$$\text{corr}(r_{t,N}, r_{t-N,N})$$

Figure 10.1 Sample estimates of first-order autocorrelations of
N-month real returns (continuously compounded) on the equally
weighted New York Stock Exchange portfolio. The estimates are
obtained by regressing the N-month return on its lagged value, using
monthly observations with overlapping return horizons.
Source: Kandel and Stambaugh, 1988

been used by researchers to predict returns, in the one-country as well
as in a multi-country setting.

Stambaugh (1986) and Fama and French (1988a, b) among others
pointed out that stock market returns are predictable (which means
"non-iid") on the basis of past returns and a few "information
variables." Figure 10.1, which is a diagram borrowed from Kandel and
Stambaugh (1988), summarizes the empirical dependence on past
returns; the diagram shows the serial correlation in relation to the
length of the holding period. The serial dependence is particularly
strong for rates of return calculated over longer holding periods.[37] As
much as 15–25 percent of the variation of 3–5 year stock returns is
predictable from past returns.[38] Notice that the serial correlation is
mostly positive over shorter holding periods (below and of the order of
one year) and negative for longer holding periods, reflecting reversion
in stock prices.[39]

In the one-country context, Fama and Schwert (1977), Rozeff (1984),
Keim and Stambaugh (1986), Fama and French (1988b), and Campbell
and Shiller (1988) have also shown empirically that stock returns are

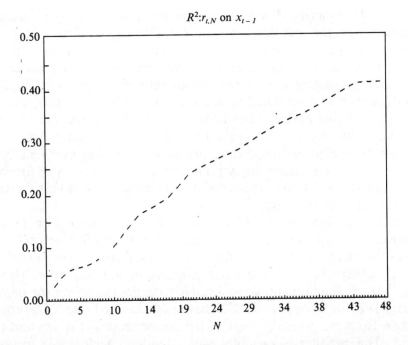

Figure 10.2 R^2 values in regressions of N-month real returns (continuously compounded) on the equally weighted New York Stock Exchange portfolio on three predictive variables (the Baa yield minus the Aaa yield, the Aaa yield minus the T-bill yield, and the dividend–price ratio). For each N, the R^2 value is obtained in a regression using monthly observations with overlapping return horizons.

Source: Kandel and Stambaugh, 1988

predictable on the basis of one or several of the following variables: the dividend yield,[40] the short-term rate of interest, the spread between long and short bond yields (which is a term structure premium), the spread between corporate and government bonds (which is a default risk spread), and a number of dummy variables such as one for the month of January and for some days of the week. Figure 10.2, also borrowed from Kandel and Stambaugh (1988), summarizes the empirical dependence of longer-holding-period rates of return on these variables.[41]

Cutler et al. (1991)[42] proceeded to verify whether other variables had any forecasting ability for stock returns in the international context. In view of the fact that the historical record for stock markets of countries other than the USA is typically comparatively short (of the order of 20–30 years), international studies cannot very well consider rates of return over very long holding periods. Cutler et al. examined one-month holding period returns and cumulated them to holding periods of up to 48 months. Their sample included stock market indexes observed over the period 1960–88 for thirteen countries and ten bilateral foreign exchange rates from 1974 to 1988, as well as commodities, such as gold and silver, and real assets. In most cases, they found a positive autocorrelation of rates of return over holding periods shorter than or equal to one year and negative autocorrelation for longer holding periods (one to four years). The stock returns were predictable, but weakly so, on the basis of own-dividend yields.[43]

As far as foreign exchange rates are concerned, the results summarized in section 4.1 above imply predictability on the basis of forward premia. Predictability has also been found on the basis of past forecast errors of the forward rates.[44]

Bekaert and Hodrick (1992) used a vector autoregression (VAR) framework to study simultaneously stock returns and foreign exchange returns in relation to some predictive variables. They looked at monthly observations of the stock markets of four countries (USA, Japan, UK, Germany) and three foreign exchange rates over the period January 1981 to December 1989. They also examined rates of return of equities, from the points of view of the deutschemark, the yen and the pound. The predictive variables were dividend yields and forward exchange premia. VARs were estimated for two countries at a time; the corresponding two dividend yields were included in the VAR. Bekaert and Hodrick concluded, with confidence level of the order of 0.99, that the VAR is capable of predicting monthly rates of return. They also calculated the autocorrelations of longer holding period returns implied by the monthly VAR model with its estimated coefficients, in order to study the link between short-term and longer-term predictability. Interestingly, for some countries at least, they were able to replicate in this way patterns of autocorrelations such as the ones described above: positive autocorrelations over a few months, negative autocorrelations over periods of more than one year.[45]

Using a number of combinations of variables that include the US and Japanese dividend yields, short-term rates, and long-term/short-term rate spreads, Campbell and Hamao (1992) report an R^2 equal to 0.065 for Japan and an R^2 equal to 0.10 for the USA over the period 1971–87.

Harvey (1991) affords a comparison between various sets of predictive variables. The study covers seventeen countries over the period December 1969 to May 1989. One set of predictive variables is "the common set" which includes the lagged world stock market rate of return,[46] a dummy variable for the month of January, the US dividend yield, the US term structure premium, and a US default risk spread. But several "local instrument sets" are also examined which reflect own-country effects. Harvey concludes that "the common information variables appear to capture the bulk of the predictable variation in the country returns." Comparing the common information regressions with the completely local information regressions, almost all countries show a lower R^2 using pure local information. The two local information variables that are the most helpful (but only marginally so) are the lagged own-country returns and the local dividend yields.

The various empirical asset pricing studies that will be reviewed in the next sections use similar sets of instrumental variables.

4.3   Latent variables models

Hansen and Hodrick (1983) with foreign exchange market data and Gibbons and Ferson (1985) with stock market data were the first to use a statistical model called the "latent variable model." To explain this statistical model, let me use as a point of departure the consumption CAPM which we rewrite in its conditional form:

$$E_{t-1}(R_i) = r_{t-1} + (1 - \theta_{t-1}) \operatorname{cov}_{t-1}(R_i, \pi) + \theta_{t-1} \operatorname{cov}_{t-1}(R_i, c) \quad (10.26)$$

The subscript $t-1$ in equation (10.26) refers to the values of moments and parameters conditioned on the values of the information variables at time $t-1$. In most tests, the inflation premium $\operatorname{cov}_{t-1}(R_i, \pi)$ is neglected and some portfolio p is used to interpret θ, leading to

$$E_t(R_i) - r_t = [E_t(R_p) - r_t]\beta_i \quad (10.27)$$

where $\beta_i = \operatorname{cov}_{t-1}(R_i, c)/\operatorname{cov}_{t-1}(R_p, c)$. The assumption is made that β_i is constant over time. Equation (10.27) then says that the time variations of all securities' expected returns have one factor in common: $E_{t-1}(R_p) - r_t$. Some way must be found of deciding empirically whether one factor accounts for expected returns. To this end, postulate that the excess return on portfolio p is linearly related to a number of instrumental variables z:

$$R_{p,t} - r_t = \sum_j \delta_j z_{j,t} + u_t \quad (10.28)$$

with the condition

$$E(u \mid z) = 0 \quad (10.29)$$

which implies

$$E(uz) = 0 \quad (10.30)$$

Substituting (10.28) into (10.27) gives

$$E(h \mid z) = 0 \quad (10.31)$$

where h is defined by

322   BERNARD DUMAS

$$R_{i,t} - r_{t-1} = \beta_i\left(\sum_j \delta_j z_{j,t-1}\right) + (u_t\beta_i + h_{i,t}) \tag{10.32}$$

Equation (10.31) implies

$$E(h_i z) = 0 \tag{10.33}$$

Equations (10.30) and (10.33) put together, of course, imply

$$E[(u\beta_i + h_i)z] = 0 \tag{10.34}$$

which means that the residual of (10.32) is orthogonal to the instruments.

The latent variable method proceeds as follows. First, estimate (10.32) as an unconstrained regression:

$$R_{i,t} - r_{t-1} = \sum_j \gamma_{ij} z_{j,t-1} + \varepsilon_{i,t} \tag{10.35}$$

Then, re-estimate (10.32) constraining the coefficients γ_{ij} to be of the form $\gamma_{ij} = \beta_i \delta_j$. Finally, compare the goodness of fit (the χ^2) of the two regressions. If their difference is significant statistically, the pricing model is rejected.

Using this method, Hansen and Hodrick (1983) rejected the consumption CAPM on foreign exchange rates, using lagged forward premia as instruments. But Hodrick and Srivastava (1984) accepted it on the same data, using past forecast errors of forward rates as instruments.

Giovannini and Jorion (1987, 1989) used this method also to run tests of the adequacy of the consumption CAPM, applied jointly to foreign exchange and stock markets. They rejected the model on the basis of weekly observations of spot exchange rates of seven currencies, one-week Eurocurrency interest rates and US stock market returns on a value-weighted index, over the period August 3, 1973, to December 28, 1984. They also tried to relax the assumption that the βs are constant by allowing them to vary linearly with rates of interest. The model was no longer rejected. Variation in βs may be worth investigating. We return to that issue in the next sections.

Campbell and Hamao (1992) and Bekaert and Hodrick (1992) report results of models with one, two or three latent variables, pertaining to pairs of countries. The data on USA–Japan reject the model while the data on USA–UK and USA–Germany do not. Three-country systems also reject the one- and two-latent variable models.

In order to allow it to vary over time, Cumby (1987) explicitly models covariance with consumption in a linear relation with a set of instrumental variables.[47] He also rejects the consumption CAPM on international data.

The latent variable method begs one issue. Suppose that one finds that the model is accepted with the meaning that some time variation of θ_t or $E_t(R_p) - r_t$ can account for risk premia. The issue that is not addressed is whether the implied variance of this variable is or is not excessive relative to the variance one would expect from a fully specified portfolio optimization model based on risk aversion.[48]

4.4 The arbitrage pricing theory and multi-factor capital asset pricing models

The difference is subtle between latent variable models and empirical implementations of the APT. Ross's (1976) original intent in constructing the APT was to allow more degrees of freedom than there were in the classic one-premium CAPM. To this end, he proposed the introduction of several factors which would generate as many risk premia.

The factors could be either prespecified observable variables, in which case the factor loadings were to be estimated by regression, or nonspecified or latent, in which case the factor structure and loadings were to be estimated by some form of factor analysis.

Just as the CAPM may be stated in terms of unconditional or conditional moments, so can the APT. It suffices to rewrite equation (10.22) as

$$E_{t-1}(R_i) = r_{t-1} + \lambda_{t-1}\beta_i \qquad (10.36)$$

where the conditional expected excess returns on assets, $E_{t-1}(R_i) - r_{t-1}$, and the prices of risk λ vary over time, perhaps in relation to a number of instrumental variables z. Connor and Korajczyck (1991) have shown that the variable risk premia λ_{t-1} may be interpreted as conditionally expected excess returns on portfolios whose rates of return mimic the factors f.[49]

As in the latent variable approach, the factor loadings β_i are always assumed constant. When the factors are unspecified variables, therefore, there is practically no difference conceptually between the APT in its conditional form and the latent variable approach with several latent variables.[50]

When the factors are prespecified observable variables, it is important to distinguish two sets of variables which play different roles in the statistical analysis. The first set is the set of variables[51] f which are priced factors in the pricing equation. These need not predict returns over time; they need only serve as common variables that explain contemporaneously a wide cross-section of returns. Alternatively, an optimization-based theory may point to the priced factors; for instance, in the classic CAPM the single priced factor is the market. The second set is the set of predetermined or instrumental variables z to which the variations of $E_t(R_i) - r_t$ and λ_t will be related. In some CAPMs[52] it would be stipulated that the zs are lagged versions of the βs; but that is not always so. In fact, many of the variables that we have identified in section 4.2 as useful instruments were also recognized by APT investigators Chen et al. (1986) as useful factors.

In the case of prespecified factors, empirical implementations of the APT rely on a two-pass method. First, to estimate the βs, deviations of rates of return from their conditionally expected values are regressed on factors in a times series fashion. Second, the conditionally expected returns are confronted in a cross-section with the calculated βs.

Gultekin et al. (1989) report on a study which relies on the unconditional version of the APT, using both prespecified as well as latent factors. The data concern the stock markets of the USA and Japan over two periods of time: January 5, 1977, to December 31, 1980, and January 7, 1981, to December 26, 1984. Trading of Japanese securities by foreigners was liberalized on January 1, 1981. Gultekin et al. formed twenty-two portfolios of US and Japanese stocks and estimated the risk coefficients λ for these two categories of securities separately, based on the same set of prespecified factors. Their main test was a test of equality of the λs between the two categories of stocks. Rejection of the null hypothesis of equality indicates capital market segmentation between the USA and Japan. For most testing procedures used, the null is clearly rejected over the first period and not rejected over the second period. The technique has been able to detect segmentation during a period where we know it is present.

Korajczyck and Viallet (1992) studied rates of return on foreign currency investments in relation to latent common factors that account for a large part of the variance of returns across the foreign exchange *and* equity markets. If currencies and equities are priced on an integrated market, both the APT and, for example, the CAPM (10.10) indicate that the changes in a common set of risk premia should be able to account for changes over time in expected returns, to the exclusion of any other variable. Therefore, if excess returns on foreign currencies are regressed on a set of regressors which includes forward premia (interest rate differentials), as in Cumby and Obstfeld (1984),[53] but includes also the excess returns on the factor-mimicking portfolios, the forward premia should receive a coefficient that is not significantly different from zero; such is their null hypothesis. They used monthly observations of eight foreign exchange rates against the dollar over the period January 1974 to December 1988. They built their factor structure from these eight currencies and as many as 8000 to 11,000 equity securities traded in various stock exchanges of the world.[54] They reject the null hypothesis. The APT with constant βs does not adequately explain excess returns on currencies.

Ferson and Harvey (1991b) investigate a CAPM/APT model in which the factors include the world market portfolio and a number of prespecified common variables f such as the price of oil. They call them "the world economic risk factors." Separately, they introduce "aggregate information variables" z such as those listed in section 4.2 above. They first estimate the βs with respect to the world market and the economic risk variables. The originality of the work of Ferson and Harvey[55] is that they allow for variations in these βs. They simply recompute them at the end of each sixty-month period. The βs, that is, are assumed not to vary over the subperiods, in the tradition of Fama and MacBeth (1973). They also demonstrate that the information variables have predictive power for rates of return. The second step would be to test a conditional CAPM/APT. The difficulty with the technique is that there is no way of knowing whether a sixty-month updating frequency for βs is an adequate one. The only way of answering that question is to account explicitly for variations of the second moments.

4.5 Autoregressive conditional heteroskedasticity

Autoregressive conditional heteroskedasticity (ARCH) is a statistical model that serves to estimate a process for the second moments. It implies persistence in the second moment, a feature which seems present in many economic time series. The simplest ARCH model for the univariate series $\{y_t\}$ is written

$$y_t = \phi y_{t-1} + \varepsilon_t$$

$$\varepsilon_t \sim N(0, h_t)$$

$$h_t = \omega + \alpha \varepsilon_{t-1}^2$$

where $|\phi| < 1$, $\omega > 0$, and $\alpha \geq 0$. A more sophisticated version (called generalized ARCH in mean) is[56]

$$y_t = \phi y_{t-1} + \gamma h_t + \varepsilon_t$$

$$\varepsilon_t \sim N(0, h_t)$$

$$h_t = \omega + \alpha \varepsilon_{t-1}^2 + \beta h_{t-1}$$

ARCH models are typically estimated by means of maximum likelihood.

Chan et al. (1992) have used[57] a multivariate version of GARCH to test whether the covariance with foreign markets generates a significant risk premium in the CAPM applied to domestic stocks. They implement the following equation system:

$$r_{dt+1} = \alpha_d + \beta_{dv}w_{dt}h_{dt+1} + \beta_{dc}(1 - w_{dt})h_{ct+1} + \theta_{d1}\varepsilon_{dt} \qquad (10.37)$$

$$+ \theta_{d2}\varepsilon_{dt-1} + \varepsilon_{dt+1}$$

$$r_{ft+1} = \alpha_f + \beta_{fv}w_{ft}h_{ft+1} + \beta_{fc}(1 - w_{ft})h_{ct+1} + \theta_{f1}\varepsilon_{ft} \qquad (10.38)$$

$$+ \theta_{f2}\varepsilon_{ft-1} + \varepsilon_{ft+1}$$

$$\varepsilon_t = \begin{bmatrix} \varepsilon_{dt+1} \\ \varepsilon_{ft+1} \end{bmatrix} \sim N(0, H_{t+1}) \qquad H_{t+1} = \begin{bmatrix} h_{dt+1} & h_{ct+1} \\ h_{ct+1} & h_{ft+1} \end{bmatrix} \qquad (10.39)$$

$$H_{t+1} = P'P + F'H_tF + G'\varepsilon_t\varepsilon_t'G \qquad (10.40)$$

In equations (10.37) and (10.38), r_d and r_f denote domestic or foreign equity return; w_d, w_f denote the composition of the benchmark portfolio as between domestic and foreign stocks and the h are time-varying conditional variances and covariances. The weights w are observable, being the relative capitalizations of the various markets. They use daily stock returns on indexes from the USA, and Japan (Nikkei) or Europe, Asia and the Far East (Morgan Stanleys' EAFE). They find that the conditional covariance of the US return with the Nikkei return has a significant positive effect on the US conditional expected returns, but that the conditional variance of the US return has no effect. In another test, they find no evidence that the prices of risk, βs in the notation of (10.37) and (10.38), differ between US and Japanese shares or that segmentation exists between the two markets.

4.6   The full conditional version of the capital asset pricing model

Harvey (1991) has discovered a method that allows one to remain agnostic concerning the time variation of conditional second moments, so that they can vary in an unspecified way in tests of the classic CAPM. He first specifies a model for the conditional first moments. He assumes that investors process information using a linear filter:

$$R_{jt} - r_{t-1} = z_{t-1}\delta_j + u_{jt} \qquad (10.41)$$

$$E(u_{jt} \mid z_{t-1}) = 0 \qquad (10.42)$$

Here u_{jt} is the investor's forecast error for the return on asset j, z_{t-1} is a row vector of predetermined instrumental variables which are known to the investor, and δ_j is a column vector of time-invariant forecast coefficients. A similar assumption is made concerning $R_{mt} - r_{t-1}$, the excess return on the market portfolio. Given the assumptions, the classic CAPM (without inflation premium) may be written

$$z_{t-1}\delta_j = \theta_{t-1}E(u_{jt}u_{mt} \mid z_{t-1}) \qquad (10.43)$$

$$\theta_{t-1} = \frac{z_{t-1}\delta_m}{E(u^2_{mt}\,|\,z_{t-1})} \tag{10.44}$$

Equation (10.44) illustrates that θ_{t-1} is an unspecified function of z_{t-1}. Now, define

$$h_{jt} = u^2_{mt}z_{t-1}\delta_j - u_{jt}u_{mt}z_{t-1}\delta_m \tag{10.45}$$

and notice that the CAPM equation (10.43) can be written

$$E(h_{jt}\,|\,z_{t-1}) = 0 \tag{10.46}$$

In this form, the "market price of covariance risk" θ_{t-1} has been substituted out between the pricing equations for individual assets and the pricing equation for the market. At no time has it been necessary to specify the behavior of second moments. Equations (10.42) and (10.46) constitute an overidentified system of moment conditions which can be optimized with respect to parameter choice and tested using the generalized method of moments. On the basis of data that we have already described (section 4.2), Harvey finds that the classic CAPM is rejected in individual country tests.

Dumas and Solnik (1991) follow the lead of Harvey but test the international nominal CAPM, equation (10.9):[58]

$$E_{t-1}(R_i) - r_{t-1} = \sum_l \lambda^l_t \operatorname{cov}_{t-1}(R_i, v^l) + \theta_{t-1} \operatorname{cov}_t(R_i, R_m) \tag{10.47}$$

where, as we recall, v^l stands for the change in exchange rate l over the period t to $t+1$. The λ^l are baptized "market prices of foreign exchange risk" while θ is the market price of covariance risk in the terminology of Harvey. Because the international CAPM is a multi-factor, or multiple-risk premia, CAPM, the substitution approach of Harvey, to eliminate θ_t, is not applicable. Dumas and Solnik retain and later relax Harvey's assumption (10.41) concerning the conditional first moments of returns but also assume that the market prices of risk are related to the instrumental variables z:[59]

$$\lambda^l_{t-1} = z_{t-1}\phi^l \qquad \theta_{t-1} = z_{t-1}\phi_m \tag{10.48}$$

Here the ϕ are time-invariant vectors of weights.
Now, define

$$h_{jt} = z_{t-1}\delta_j - z_{t-1}\sum_{l=1}^{L}\phi^l u_{jt}u_{n+l,t} - z_{t-1}\phi_m u_{jt}u_{mt} \tag{10.49}$$

h_{jt} is a disturbance that is unrelated to the information z_{t-1} under the null hypothesis that (10.47) holds. We form the vector of residuals $\varepsilon_t = (u_t, h_t)$ and impose the overidentified moment conditions $E(z\varepsilon) = 0$.

Dumas and Solnik examine simultaneously monthly data concerning four national stock market indexes and three exchange rates over the period 1970–91. The main result is that the overidentifying restrictions of the classic CAPM are rejected while those of the international CAPM (10.47) are not. In a test of (10.43) against (10.47), rejection occurs, which means that the foreign exchange risk premia in (10.47) are significant.

4.7 Implied pricing kernels

All existing CAPMs, whether static or intertemporal, may be written in the form

$$E_t[m_{t+1}(R_{t+1} - r_t)] = 0 \qquad (10.50)$$

where $R_{t+1} - r_t$ is a vector of excess returns and m_{t+1} is a marginal rate of substitution between consumption at time t and consumption at time $t+1$. Hansen and Jagannathan (1991) have pointed out that there always exists a linear combination m^*_{t+1} of available returns such that

$$E_t[m^*_{t+1}(R_{t+1} - r_t)] = 0 \qquad (10.51)$$

m^*_{t+1} is called a "pricing kernel." The various CAPMs are economic theories capable of restricting the dimension of the rate of return basis in terms of which m^*_{t+1} is expressed. Hansen and Jagannathan also show that the variance of m^*_{t+1} is a lower bound on the variance of m_{t+1} that would be capable of rationalizing the observed variance of asset returns.

De Santis (1991), Bekaert and Hodrick (1992), and Bansal et al. (1992) apply this idea, or generalizations thereof, to international stock returns. De Santis finds that adding securities of a capital market to the pricing kernel projection space helps in explaining returns in another capital market. This may be indicative of market segmentation.

4.8 Conclusion: what have we learned from empirical capital asset pricing models?

From the standpoint of economic science, CAPM tests are somewhat heterodox. Because the CAPM is a partial equilibrium model, most CAPM tests require auxiliary *ad hoc* assumptions, i.e. assumptions that are neither dictated by the economic theory being tested nor separately testable. For instance, the test of the international CAPM by Dumas and Solnik (1991), described in section 4.6, relies on the assumption that the prices of risk are linearly related to the instrumental variables. Or, the latent variable method, described in section 4.3, is based on the assumption that the βs of individual securities relative to consumption c are constant.

Wheatley (1989) has cogently illustrated the potential pitfalls of *ad hoc* untestable assumptions in his critique of latent variable tests. He pointed out, first, that the assumption of constant βs cannot be verified separately since the benchmark c is unobserved. As in any joint test, if the *ad hoc* assumption of β constancy is actually false, the test could mistakenly reject the theoretical restriction that a single unobserved benchmark is the basis for pricing when it is in fact true. More striking is Wheatley's argument that the test could mistakenly accept the hypothesis. He argues that, for any data set whatsoever, there exists an infinity of portfolios p that verify exactly a CAPM restriction similar to (10.27), with $\beta_i = \mathrm{cov}(R_i, R_p)/\mathrm{var}(R_p)$. If one of these portfolios happens to yield constant βs for all securities, then the econometrician mistakenly concludes that the validity of (10.27) implies a single unobserved benchmark.

Similar arguments can presumably be made concerning tests of any partial equilibrium relationship which, by construction, is incompletely specified. It is frequently impossible, strictly speaking, to test a part of the economic system without testing the whole. In principle, a GE model should be specified and tested. However, the assumptions of existing GE models may be utility theoretic (not *ad hoc*) but they are, at present, many times more restrictive than the *ad hoc* assumptions mentioned so far. Given their heroic assumptions, the likelihood that available GE models are close to the truth is so small that it is hardly worth the effort of testing them at this early stage.

In the meantime, if one accepts some level of pragmatism, CAPMs may afford a glimpse of the truth. The results reported above have given us some information concerning the degree of integration between stock markets of the world. Except for Gultekin et al. (1989), little evidence of segmentation has been found in stock returns.[60] The low degree of correlation in consumption between countries (stylized fact 3) could therefore be due not to segmentation between countries but to worldwide market incompleteness. The counterpoint to such a hypothesis is that home equity preference (stylized fact 4) would seem to be a form of segmentation *per se*. Theoreticians should perhaps take that information into account when building future models.

We have also learned that PPP deviations probably play a significant role in pricing assets on the international capital market. However, we have seen theoretically that, provided investors are willing to hedge exchange risk, PPP deviations, in principle, should not be an explanation for home equity preference.

Finally, we have learned that existing CAPMs can be made compatible with the evidence on the risk premium in the foreign exchange market. Several tests reported above[61] are able to fit the same CAPM simultaneously to stock market and foreign exchange market data. However, it may be that the degree of time variation of market prices of risk necessary to achieve that goal is not compatible with any known GE model. Fama's (1984) question is not yet answered.

An argument can be made in favor of continuing to test CAPMs at the same time that GE models become richer. Indeed, when a CAPM is rejected, there may be no point in building a GE model around it. On the other hand, some empirical paradoxes become truly apparent only in empirical tests of, or by reference to, GE models. Such is the case for the equity premium puzzle of Mehra and Prescott (1985),[62] or the foreign exchange risk premium puzzle.[63]

5   General equilibrium models without money

In discussing international capital flows, in section 3.3 above, we rapidly came to the conclusion that a partial equilibrium purely financial model such as the one of portfolio theory would probably not be able to account for international capital flows. For that purpose, we need to know the behavior of physical variables (consumption, investment, employment). As Frankel (1992) pointed out in this context, "Bonds are not perfect substitutes for equities or for factories, and the latter are clearly not perfect substitutes across countries." The same conclusion would be reached by someone attempting to understand the role of financial markets in the international transmission of shocks and business cycles.

5.1   The difficulty with general equilibrium models

It may be argued that the construction of international GE models is premature at this point. In a one-country setting, stochastic GE models that have been built on existing financial models are as yet unable to account for the relationship between financial and real variables.

Consider, for instance, the relationship between consumption and wealth, as measured in the stock market. An investor-consumer who maximizes the expected utility of his lifetime consumption stream would smooth his consumption. He would let his consumption rate depend on his lifetime anticipated income stream or, equivalently, on his wealth. The volatility of his consumption should be of the same order of magnitude as that of his wealth, and both volatilities should be no greater than that of income. The data, however, tell a different story. The volatility of wealth, measured in the stock market, is several times larger than the volatility of consumption which in turn, is, approximately equal to the volatility of income.[64]

This observation explains the empirical failure of the consumption CAPM. It is also at the heart of the "equity premium puzzle" pointed out by Mehra and Prescott (1985). Given the empirically observed stochastic behavior of consumption, which is very smooth, the excess expected return of equities relative to riskless assets seems excessive. The risk in the economy, as measured by the volatility of consumption, is not large enough to account for it, unless one assumes that relative risk aversion is as large as 40.[65]

The GE models that have been built in the international context have had two goals. They aim to explain the volatility of real exchange rates and the relationship between them and trade/capital flows. They all suffer from the shortcoming that they yield theoretical risk premia that are too small compared with empirical risk premia. We can classify international GE models into two categories: models without frictions and models with frictions.

5.2 General equilibrium models without frictions

In these models, traded goods prices satisfy the law of one price between countries. Deviations from PPP are accounted for by the existence of nontraded goods that are produced and consumed in each country specifically. The initial work in this area was done by Dornbusch (1983), Stulz (1987), Devereux (1988), Stockman and Dellas (1989), and Stockman and Tesar (1990). A stochastic model with nontraded goods is exposited in another chapter of this volume.[66]

To avoid repetition within the book, I simply summarize the conclusions that emerge from this literature: (a) nontraded goods stochastic equilibrium models are capable of explaining a relatively low degree of cross-correlation in consumption between countries and high correlations between saving and investment within countries; (b) they are capable of explaining persistent deviations from PPP and comparatively volatile real exchange rates; (c) they are capable of explaining home equity preference.[67]

I dwell on this third point, first to explain it, and second to relate it to a similar point made in the finance literature. The explanation goes thus. Investors living in one country know that they will have to consume the home good which they alone consume. They therefore hold the equity of the firms producing the home good as a consumption hedge.

The reasoning is a special case of the observation, made by Adler and Dumas (1983) and repeated above in section 3.2, that investors would generally hold equities as part of their hedge portfolio, which is, as we recall, specific to each national investor group.[68]

While the point is evidently correct, theoretically speaking, I cannot see how the data on home equity preference (reviewed in section 2) can be matched that way. The Adler and Dumas (1983) paper contains some empirically based calculations of optimal hedge portfolios for developed country investors.[69] These reflect the actual behaviors of equity prices and inflation in each country during the 1970s. The inflation index used is the consumer price index which contains a large share of nontraded goods. In practically *all* cases, the optimal hedge portfolio is 99 percent made up of the home-currency short-term bank deposit. Empirically speaking, that is, the hedge portfolio weights falling on equities are not of the order of magnitude capable of explaining the strong home equity preference observed in the real world.

Pure inflation risk (measured in the investor's home currency), as distinct from exchange risk, is too small – and is too little correlated with exchange rates and equities – to be a factor in the portfolio choices of investors of the countries considered. Solnik's special case was very close to the truth in these countries.[70] There is every reason to think that the same empirical observation could be made today, inflation risk having been further reduced.

5.3   General equilibrium models with frictions

The empirical work of Giovannini (1988), Marston (1990), Engel (1991), and others, quoted in section 2, made clear that traded goods do not sell for the same price in different countries; the law of one price is not satisfied in the goods markets.

Dumas (1992) set out to build a stochastic model that endogenizes deviations from the law of one price. The device that is used for this purpose is a "shipping cost."[71] The world economy is made of two countries, each with its own capital stock, K and K^*. Shipping physical resources from one country to the other is costly. The cost is assumed to be proportional to the physical amount transferred; a fraction $1 - s$ of physical resources is expended in transportation. In this model, the single good is sometimes traded, sometimes not traded.

In each country, the physical resources may at will be consumed, invested in the local production process, or transferred abroad. The local production process is risky, with constant risk and constant returns to scale. The correlation between the output shocks in the two countries is zero. Households only consume the physical resources currently available in their country, an assumption which is inherited from the international CAPM model of section 3.1 above. Households' utility functions are isoelastic.

The shipping cost is the only friction present in the model. Financial markets are fully integrated and frictionless. Perfect competition is assumed in all markets. Equilibrium is calculated as a central planning problem.

The price variable of interest in the model is the price p of physical resources currently located in one country relative to physical resources currently located in the other; this price reflects the deviation from the law of one price and is called "the real exchange rate." It is at once the relative price of goods and the relative price of the equities of the firms operating in the two countries. The exchange rate fluctuates around the value unity (parity); it stays within a band, the width of which is determined by the transportation loss factor. Figure 10.3 shows the relationship between the logarithm of the exchange rate, $\ln p$, and the logarithm of the physical imbalance: $\omega = \ln K - \ln K^*$.

The author's main purpose in building the model was to derive endogenously the stochastic process for law of one price deviations within the band that would be compatible with financial market equilibrium. The process obtained is not a martingale; it displays reversion in the mean. It also displays a strong degree of heteroskedasticity;[72] the conditional variance is equal to zero at the edges of the band and is largest at the central point. The behavior of the variance causes the real exchange rate process to be centrifugal,

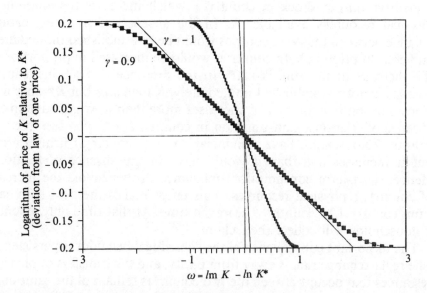

Figure 10.3 The function $\ln p(\omega)$: —, autarky; ■, costly trade $(1 - \gamma$ is the investors' risk aversion).

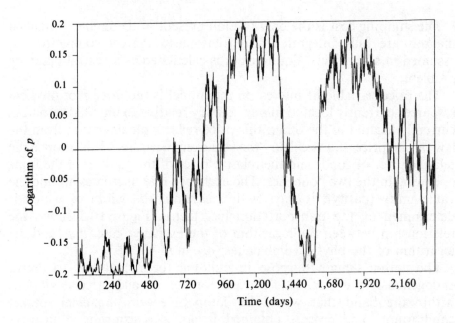

Figure 10.4 Sample path of the real exchange rate.

probabilistically speaking, despite reversion in the mean; the chance of a move away from parity is greater than that of a move towards parity. Figure 10.4 shows a simulated sample path of the process.

The rationale for the centrifugal behavior is the following. Consider a positive output shock in country 1 which increases the amount of physical resources available, K. In the absence of frictions, capital balance between the two countries would be re-established immediately and consumption in both countries would be increased in proportion to the increase in the sum $K + K^*$. In the presence of frictions, capital balance is not re-established immediately; K increases but K^* does not. Consumption in country 1, c, increases more than it would have in the absence of frictions. Consumption in country 2, c^*, increases because country 2 households have a financial claim on country 1 firms' output but it increases less than it would have in the absence of frictions. Hence, short-term consumption imbalance further favors the increase of country 1 physical resources. This effect makes the next shipment from country 1 to country 2 nearer in time. At that time only, country 2 households will collect their claim.

The important consequence of the centrifugal behavior is persistence. The real exchange rate is away from parity, and the transfers of physical resources that occur between the two countries remain of the same sign, for periods of time that are "very long."[73] The variance of the exchange rate is persistent as well. These features accord well with facts. In particular, they imply positive serial correlation in observations of the real exchange rate over the shorter run. Over the longer run, shipments "push back" the real exchange rate to the inside of the band and the serial correlation beomes negative.

The Dumas (1992) paper also derives an expression for the real interest rate differential, and the risk premia that it incorporates, that is entirely based on the slope of the $\ln p$ function in figure 10.3. The expression accounts for the Cumby and Obstfeld (1984) empirical finding, reviewed above, that exchange rate changes are related to the interest rate differential by a coefficient that is less than unity. But the coefficient is not sufficiently far from unity to account fully for the empirical findings.[74]

6   Issues and conclusions regarding general equilibrium models

The two GE models that have been briefly discussed are embarrassingly rudimentary. No doubt their extreme simplicity has something to do with their inability to resolve the puzzles of international finance. Therefore a laundry list of what is missing in these models may be appropriate at this point. Such a list could conveniently be summarized by three items: imperfectly adjustable prices, imperfect competition, and money.

Imperfectly adjustable nominal prices of goods are the hallmark of the barriers that exist between countries. The role of each country's money as a unit in terms of which prices are sticky cannot be overemphasized Mussa (1986) compared the behavior over time of the prices of goods in US and Canadian cities. The behavior of prices in Toronto was closer to their behavior in Vancouver than to their behavior in Detroit. As a matter of fact, the behavior of Canadian prices expressed in Canadian dollars was more similar to the behavior of US prices expressed in US dollars than to the behavior of US prices translated into Canadian dollars.

Sticky prices would go a long way toward "explaining" the wide PPP deviations that accompany the daily movements in nominal exchange rates. Even if prices are simply posited to be sticky, some device must still be invoked to prevent commodity arbitrage between countries; otherwise no deviations from the law of one price would materialize. The "shipping costs" of Dumas (1992) could serve as such a device. It would be useful to study the dynamics of the real exchange rate in the presence of sticky prices and shipping costs.

The reasons why prices are sticky have long been debated in macroeconomics. They have to do with consumer search, imperfect competition, locational advantage, and corporate firms' strategies. These factors take special meanings in the international setting.[75] The evidence is that import/export firms do not pass through to their customers the exchange rate movements that they suffer or benefit from. They prefer to smooth them out and to price their goods "to the market."[76] International trade is an intertemporal corporate decision.[77]

As we have seen, the segmentation in the goods market coincides with the borders of monetary zones (Mussa, 1986). Some recent evidence (Bayoumi, 1990; Sinn, 1991; Bayoumi and Rose, 1992) seems to indicate that the same is true for capital markets. The "home equity preference" mentioned in section 2 may be, in fact, a preference for the equities issued in the monetary zone (not specifically the country) that the investor lives in.[78] If this evidence is right, it makes it essential to have at our disposal a GE monetary model of the international economy with several currencies.

There are at least two obstacles on the way to this goal. First, the microeconomics of money is at a standstill. There is no consensus as to which form of market incompleteness, or restriction to market access, is the main motivation for holding money. Some of the existing GE models (Lucas, 1982; Svensson, 1985) use the cash-in-advance formulation, with its somewhat artificial timing for the access to markets. Others (e.g. Labadie, 1986; Sibert, 1989) have recourse to the overlapping generations formulation. Others still enter money in the utility function (Stulz, 1987). Most of the existing models let prices adjust freely;[79] the law of one price prevails between countries. There is need for a microeconomic theory of money that would give a role to money as a unit of account, in terms of which local goods prices are kept rigid.

The second obstacle is a technical one. When money balances are present in portfolios, an equilibrium is not a Pareto optimum. Hence the equilibrium must be calculated directly, without recourse to the equivalent central planning program. The solution of monetary models is a formidable computational problem. Lucas (1982), for instance, has been forced to assume a high degree of similarity between the households of different countries; essentially, they differ only in the currency that they wish to hold.[80] Thanks to this simplifying assumption, Lucas's equilibrium is a "pooling equilibrium" in which, except for money, households' portfolios are identical across countries.

Notes

The author is affiliated with the HEC School of Management. He is Research Professor at Duke University (Fuqua School of Business) and a Research Associate of the NBER and the CEPR. This paper is a personal statement, not a survey. No attempt is made at exhaustivity. Some of my colleagues will find that their work is not quoted, even though it may fall under the general topic covered here. I beg to be forgiven. The comments of Bruno Solnik were very helpful.

1   The assumption is also frequently made that the investors' lifetime utility functions are time additive.

2   Moving away, that is, from the assumption of time separability or the von Neumann–Morgenstern property of state separability.

3   At the same time, the cross-border segment of the world financial market may be less imperfect than any of the purely national market segments.

4   Another departure from the basic model can be formulated by postulating that the shocks external to the system are not iid and follow, instead, some given stochastic process. However, if at least some external shocks are not observable to the econometrician, a theory based on a postulated process for these shocks quickly becomes tautological, in the sense that it may always be possible to postulate the right process which will account for almost any observed behavior of financial prices. As a research strategy it would seem preferable first to try iid external shocks with a design of the economy such that financial market returns will not be iid in equilibrium, to match observation. If that line of research fails, it will then be time to investigate non-iid outside shocks.

5   See Grossman and Shiller (1982), Leme (1984), Scheinkman (1984), and Obstfeld (1986, 1989).

6   Equivalently, since covered interest rate parity always holds, this is a statement that the rates of interest on two currencies differ by the expected exchange rate change, which is uncovered interest rate parity.

7   It is not wrong to compare the logarithm of the forward rate with the expected value of the logarithm of the future spot rate, but then some other term – a sort of premium – must also enter the equation if compatibility with equilibrium is to be maintained.

8   If none is available, call r the shadow nominally riskless return.

9   This was the assumption made in Solnik's work.

10 The following relationship would be a statement of relative PPP:

$$\pi_{\text{USA}}^{\$} = (1 + \pi_{\text{Fra}}^{\text{FF}})(1 + v_{\text{FF}}^{\$}) - 1$$

Note the difference with (10.6). $\pi_{\text{USA}}^{\$}$ is the dollar rate of inflation *in the USA*.

11 See Adler and Dumas (1983).

12 We use the fact that the coefficients of all the premia sum to unity to cancel $\text{cov}(R_i, v)$ between the two sides of the equation.

13 In the Solnik special case, this reduces to a requirement that ζ_i be made independent of all exchange rate movements v_l.

14 The set of coefficients γ_{ij} is invariant under a translation of returns from one currency of reference to the other.

15 As well as Ross and Walsh (1983).

16   Sercu (1980) also relaxed an assumption made by Solnik unnecessarily, namely that securities' rates of return expressed in their respective currencies would be independent of exchange rates (which is $\gamma_{ii} = 1$; $\gamma_{ij} = 0$, $j \neq i$).

17   His von Neumann–Morgenstern utility function would be the logarithmic function. We could call his portfolio "the logarithmic portfolio."

18   The holding of dollar deposits is equal to the fraction $1 - \Sigma_i x_i^l$ of the investor's wealth.

19   I include under "equities" all securities which are in positive net supply.

20   When the Solnik special case does not prevail, investors also hold equities as part of their hedge portfolios. There is no simple relationship between each investor's portfolio and the world market portfolio.

21   Currencies in the RA1 portfolio are an investment, albeit a negative one, as much as equities. The best proof is that the amount invested in them depends on risk aversion (and on expected returns). Naturally, the diversification motive also plays a role in the currency investment but that is not a sufficient reason to regard the currency financing in the portfolio purely as an exchange risk hedge of the equity investment. For descriptive purposes, it could be helpful to decompose the RA1 portfolio into an equity component hedged against exchange risk and a pure investment in currencies (this would be done by partitioning the matrix Ω and then inverting it). But such a decomposition would be uninteresting, since all investors would hold the two subparts in the same proportion.

22   This was first noted in print by Frenkel and Razin (1980).

23   The inflation premium serves to resolve the paradox even if world inflation measured in dollars, π, happens to be nonrandom (so that the premium from the dollar point of view happens to be zero). If PPP prevails, world inflation, when measured in nondollar currency i, *is* random and a premium appears in the translated equation (10.17). That premium does the job of explaining away the Siegel paradox.

24   In particular, differences in consumption baskets *per se* do not explain home equity bias. I supplement this discussion in section 5.2 below. There, I also briefly consider nontraded goods.

25   Black (1990) pointed out that Japanese investors provide cheap hedging of yen risk to American investors and *vice versa*. If his risk aversion is greater than 1, each investor wishes to hold his home currency positively as part of his hedge portfolio. Foreigners can therefore short the home currency at little cost.

26   The main academic contribution to the theory of capital market segmentation is Errunza and Losq (1985). Most of the literature on segmentation takes segmentation as a given and works out its consequences. At best, it classifies the various forms of segmentation. It does not explain it. The drawback is that no guidance is provided as to which form of segmentation constitutes a reasonable assumption.

27   Unfortunately, international portfolio theory does not recognize the distinction, which is made in balance of payments statistics, between capital flows of a portfolio nature and direct investment.

28   In section 4 below I discuss empirical work in which the process for rates of return is taken into account.

29   See also Lucas (1978, equation (6)).

30   Stulz (1981) has examined the aggregation of this condition over all national investor groups, in the absence of PPP.
31   See Hansen and Singleton (1982), or Breeden et al. (1989).
32   For the dissenting view, see Ikeda (1991).
33   We have already pointed out that, when returns are not IID, for consistency one should really be using a multi-period CAPM in the manner of Merton (1971, 1973).
34   Or, rather, a logarithmic version of it, in order to avoid the Siegel paradox.
35   To learn about the connection between regression tests such as (10.23) and variance bounds tests, see Frankel and Stock (1987), Froot (1987), and Cochrane (1991).
36   For the method to be correct, however, x_t must include all assets.
37   For a methodological critique of the Fama–French approach, see Richardson (1990). The reader is cautioned that the successive points of the curve of figure 10.1 are not observed independently; they are calculated from the same data; the pattern displayed by the curve may therefore be somewhat misleading.
38   Serial dependence in a single series may be captured not only by running distributed-lag regressions but also by a Lo and MacKinlay (1988) test, which is based on a ratio of two variances measured on various period lengths. The approach can be extended to a multivariate context.
39   Please note that reversion does not necessarily result from reversion in the expected value (mean reversion). It can also result from changes in variance; reversion is induced when variance becomes larger as one moves away from the reversion point.
40   The Fama–French study is concerned with the behavior of stock indexes. I am referring here to the dividend yield on the index.
41   For a critique, see Forster and Smith (1992). Again, the reader is cautioned that the successive points of the curve are not statistically independent.
42   Earlier, Gultekin (1983) and Solnik (1983b) had examined whether short-term interest rates predict stock returns in each country separately.
43   See also Solnik (1992).
44   See Hodrick (1987) for a survey of this evidence.
45   This was achieved without taking into account the variability of the conditional variance of monthly returns.
46   Harvey's purpose was to exploit parsimoniously the serial dependence found in Fama and French (1988a).
47   This is in the same spirit as the work of Giovannini and Jorion who allowed βs to vary in relation to the rate of interest.
48   See section 4.7 below.
49   Consider a portfolio j such that $\beta_{jj} = 1$ and $\beta_{jk} = 0$ ($k \neq j$). Equation (10.22) applied to portfolio j reads

$$E(R_j) = r + \lambda_j$$

50   However, different researchers utilize different estimation techniques. The latent variable model is frequently estimated with the generalized method of moments, which places severe limitations on the number of assets that can be considered simultaneously, whereas the APT model is usually estimated by means of a factor analytic technique, which is a two-step method. First the

factor analytic structure is estimated and then the expected returns are compared cross-sectionally with the loadings (βs).

51   In the notation of equation (10.21).

52   Such as the multi-period CAPM of Merton (1971, 1973) which can also be written in the form (10.36).

53   See section 4.1.

54   All returns are translated into dollars. Currency translation effects are common to all stocks. There is a strong suspicion that the factor-mimicking portfolios reflect mostly currencies.

55   See Ferson and Harvey (1991a) for their work on US securities returns.

56   The adjective "generalized" refers to the presence of the h_{t-1} term in the equation for h_t and the expression "in mean" refers to the presence of the h_t term in the "mean equation," the first equation of the system.

57   Hamao et al. (1990) also use a GARCH formulation to model returns in several countries. Although they use an ARCH-in-mean formulation, their main goal is not to test for the significance of risk premia but to describe spillover effects from one market to another. Engel and Rodrigues (1988) and Engel et al. (1991) use ARCH to allow variations in the variance–covariance matrix of the Frankel (1982) asset supply CAPM, discussed above in section 4.1.

58   Dumas and Solnik make the approximation that the Solnik special case applies. The replacement of π^l by v^l in the following equation is due to that.

59   In contrast with the latent variable model, they are forced to assume an exact relationship.

60   Roll (1992) finds that different behaviors of twenty-four national equity markets can largely be explained by industry specialization and exchange rate fluctuations.

61   For example Giovannini and Jorion (1987, 1989) or Dumas and Solnik (1991). But see Korajczyck and Viallet (1992).

62   See section 5.1.

63   Backus et al. (1990) and Sibert (1989) have built GE models of the foreign exchange risk premium and calibrated it. They have done for the exchange risk premium what Mehra and Prescott had done for the equity premium. As Fama suspected, they find that the theoretical premium is much too small to account for the empirical results of Cumby and Obstfeld (1984).

64   Shiller (1981) made the same, and largely equivalent, point concerning the volatility of wealth compared with the volatility of dividends.

65   Weil (1989) suggested that this paradox arises from the assumed time additivity of lifetime utility. He used instead the Epstein and Zin (1989) lifetime utility. But, with that utility specification, it is still true that consumption at any given time is proportional to wealth. Constantinides (1990) suggested a lifetime utility with habit formation. Past consumption serves as a standard below which people hate to let their current consumption fall. In that case, current consumption is a function of wealth *and* past consumption. This is equivalent to introducing a friction which slows down consumption adjustments.

66   Chapter 3.

67 In chapter 3 it is shown that the model is also capable of rationalizing empirical patterns in the relationship between real exchange rates and balances of trade.

68 This is an example of a point that can be made in the simple context of portfolio theory without recourse to a full-fledged GE model.

69 The article gives the time average of hedge portfolios calculated monthly, conditional on the various currencies' interest rates.

70 Recall that, when that special case is valid, investors hold no equity whatever as part of the hedge portfolio.

71 This device is analogous to the "installation costs" that have been invoked by Abel (1979) to endogenize Tobin's q, the ratio of the equity value of installed capital to its replacement value.

72 Note that the heteroskedasticity in the exchange rate is endogenous. Output shocks in each country are assumed homoskedastic.

73 With proportional transactions costs, trade is choppy. That is an unpleasant aspect of the model but one that washes out with some degree of time aggregation.

74 Uppal (1993) has shown that the same model is capable of generating some degree of home equity preference.

75 See chapter 2 in this volume.

76 Krugman (1987), Marston (1990).

77 Dixit's (1989a, b) "hysteresis" model of entry into a foreign market (which takes after Baldwin (1986) and Baldwin and Krugman (1989)) has been extended to a GE setting by Dumas (1988). Dixit (1989b) and Dumas both find that equilibrium prices are specific to the local market and differ from production cost even though perfect competition is assumed.

78 There is presumably a link between the segmentation in the goods market along monetary borders and the segmentation of the capital market. But we have seen in section 3 that exchange risk, real or nominal, is not likely to be the source of home equity preference, as long as investors are able to hedge it by borrowing and lending currencies.

79 An exception is Svensson and van Wijnbergen (1989).

80 In addition, claims to future monetary transfers are assumed tradeable.

References

Abel, A.B. (1979) *Investment and the Value of Capital*, New York and London, Garland Publishing.

Adler, M. and B. Dumas (1983) "International portfolio choice and corporation finance: a synthesis," *Journal of Finance* 38, 925–84.

—— and B. Lehmann (1983) "Deviations from purchasing power parity in the long run," *Journal of Finance* 38, 1471–87.

Admati, A. (1985) "A noisy rational expectations equilibrium for multi-asset security markets," *Econometrica* 53, 629–57.

Backus, D., A.W. Gregory, and C.I. Telmer (1990) "Accounting and forward rates in markets for foreign currency," Working Paper 439, Federal Reserve Bank of Minneapolis.

Baldwin, R. (1986) "Hysteresis in trade," Working Paper, Massachusetts Institute of Technology, April.

—— and P. Krugman (1989) "Persistent trade effects of large exchange rate shocks," *Quarterly Journal of Economics* 104, 635–54.

Bansal, R., D.A. Hsieh, and S. Viswanathan (1992) "A new approach to international arbitrage pricing," Working Paper, Duke University.

Bayoumi, T. (1990) "Savings–investment correlations: immobile capital, government policy, or endogenous behavior?" *IMF Staff Papers* 37, 360–87.

—— and A. Rose (1992) "Domestic saving and intranational capital flows," *European Economic Review*, forthcoming.

Bekaert, G. and R.J. Hodrick (1992) "Characterizing predictable components in excess returns on equity and foreign exchange markets," *Journal of Finance* 47, 467–508.

Black, F. (1972) "Capital market equilibrium with restricted borrowing," *Journal of Business* 45, 444–54.

—— (1990) "Equilibrium exchange rate hedging," *Journal of Finance* 45, 899–908.

Breeden, D.T. (1978) "An intertemporal asset pricing model with stochastic consumption and investment opportunities," *Journal of Financial Economics* 7, 265–96.

——, M.R. Gibbons, and R.H. Litzenberger (1989) "Empirical tests of the consumption-oriented CAPM," *Journal of Finance* 44, 231–62.

Broadgate Consultants (1991) *"International Investments Trends."*

Campbell, J.Y. and R. Clarida (1987) "The dollar and real interest rates," in Karl Brunner and Allan Meltzer (eds) *Empirical Studies of Velocity, Real Exchange Rates, Unemployment and Productivity*, Carnegie-Rochester Conference Series on Public Policy 27, Amsterdam, North-Holland, pp. 103–40.

—— and Y. Hamao (1992) "Predictable stock returns in the United States and Japan: a study of long-term capital market integration," *Journal of Finance* 47, 43–70.

—— and R. Shiller (1988) "The dividend–price ratio and expectations of future dividends and discount factors," *Review of Financial Studies* 1, 195–228.

Chan, K.C., G.A. Karolyi, and R.M. Stulz (1992) "Global financial markets and the risk premium on U.S. equity," Working Paper 92-19, College of Business, Ohio State University.

Chen, N.-F., R. Roll, and S.A. Ross (1986) "Economic forces and the stock market," *Journal of Business* 59, 383–403.

Cochrane, J.H. (1991) "Volatility tests and market efficiency: a review essay," *Journal of Monetary Economics* 27, 463–85.

Connor, G. and R.A. Korajczyk (1991) "Risk and return in an equilibrium APT: application of a new test methodology," *Journal of Financial Economics* 21, 255–89.

Constantinides, G. (1990) "Habit formation: a resolution of the equity premium puzzle," *Journal of Political Economy* 98, 519–43.

Cooper, I. and E. Kaplanis (1991) "What explains the home bias in portfolio investment?" Discussion Paper, London Business School.

Cumby, R. (1987) "Consumption risk and international asset returns: some empirical evidence," NBER Working Paper 2383, Cambridge, MA.

—— and M. Obstfeld (1984) "International interest rate and price level linkages under flexible exchange rates: a review of recent evidence," in J.F.O. Bilson and

R.C. Marston (eds) *Exchange Rate Theory and Practice*, Chicago, IL, University of Chicago Press.

Cutler, D.M., J.M. Poterba and L.H. Summers (1991) "Speculative dynamics," *Review of Economic Studies* 58, 529–46.

De Santis, G. (1991) "Volatility bounds for stochastic discount factors: tests and implications for international stock returns," manuscript, University of Chicago.

Devereux, M.B. (1988) "Non-traded goods and the international transmission of fiscal policy," *Canadian Journal of Economics* 21, 265–78.

Diamond, D.W. and R.E. Verrechia (1981) "Information aggregation in a noisy rational expectations economy," *Journal of Financial Economics* 9, 221–35.

Dixit, A. (1989a) "Entry and exit decisions under uncertainty," *Journal of Political Economy* 97, 620–38.

—— (1989b) "Hysteresis, import penetration, and exchange rate pass-through," *Quarterly Journal of Economics* 104, 205–28.

Dornbusch, R. (1983) "Real interest rates, home goods, and optimal external borrowing," *Journal of Political Economy* 91, 141–53.

Dumas, B. (1988) "Perishable investment and hysteresis in capital formation," Working Paper, Wharton School of the University of Pennsylvania.

—— (1992) "Dynamic equilibrium and the real exchange rate in a spatially separated world," *Review of Financial Studies* 5, 153–80.

—— and B. Solnik (1991) "The world price of exchange rate risk," Working Paper, HEC School of Management.

Eldor, R., D. Pines and A. Schwartz (1988) "Home asset preference and productivity shocks," *Journal of International Economics* 25, 165–76.

Engel, C. (1991) "Is real exchange rate variability caused by relative price changes? An empirical investigation," Working Paper, Federal Reserve Bank of Kansas City.

—— and A.P. Rodrigues (1988) "Tests of international CAPM with time-varying covariances," *Journal of Applied Econometrics* 4, 119–38.

——, J. Frankel and K. Froot (1991) "The constrained asset share estimation (CASE) method: testing mean-variance efficiency of the U.S. stock market," Working Paper, Massachusetts Institute of Technology.

Epstein, L.G. and S.E. Zin (1989) "Substitution, risk aversion, and the temporal behavior of consumption and asset returns: a theoretical framework," *Econometrica* 57, 937–69.

Errunza, V. and E. Losq (1985) "International asset pricing under mild segmentation: theory and test," *Journal of Finance* 40, 105–24.

Fama, E.F. (1984) "Forward and spot exchange rates," *Journal of Monetary Economics* 14, 319–38.

—— and K. French (1988a) "Permanent and temporary components of stock prices," *Journal of Political Economy* 96, 246–73.

—— and —— (1988b) "Dividend yields and expected stock returns," *Journal of Financial Economics* 22, 3–26.

—— and J.D. MacBeth (1973) "Risk, return and equilibrium: empirical tests," *Journal of Political Economy* 71, 607–36.

—— and G.W. Schwert (1977) "Asset returns and inflation," *Journal of Financial Economics* 5, 115–46.

Feldstein, M. and C. Horioka (1980) "Domestic saving and international capital flows," *Economic Journal* 90, 314–29.

Ferson, W.E. and C.R. Harvey (1991a) "The variation of economic risk premiums," *Journal of Political Economy* 99, 385–415.

—— and —— (1991b) "The risk and predictability of international equity returns," Working Paper, University of Chicago.

Forster, F.D. and T. Smith (1992) "Assessing goodness of fit of asset pricing models: the distribution of the maximal R^2," Working Paper, Duke University, Fuqua School of Business.

Frankel, J.A. (1982) "In search of the exchange risk premium: a six-currency test of mean–variance efficiency," *Journal of International Money and Finance* 1, 255–74.

—— (1992) "Measuring international capital mobility: a review," *American Economic Review* 82, 197–202.

—— and J. Stock (1987) "Regression vs. volatility tests of foreign exchange markets," *Journal of International Money and Finance* 6, 49–56.

French, K. and J. Poterba (1991) "Investor diversification and international equity markets," *American Economic Review* 81, 222–6.

Frenkel, J.A. and A. Razin (1980) "Stochastic prices and tests of efficiency of foreign exchange markets," *Economic Letters* 6, 165–70.

Friend, I., Y. Landskroner and E. Losq (1976) "The demand for risky assets under uncertain inflation," *Journal of Finance* 31, 1287–98.

Froot, K.A. (1987) "Tests of excess forecast volatility in the foreign exchange and stock markets," NBER Working Paper 2362, Cambridge, MA.

Gibbons, M.R. and W.E. Ferson (1985) "Testing asset pricing models with changing expectations and an unobservable market portfolio," *Journal of Financial Economics* 14, 217–36.

Giovannini, A. (1988) "Exchange rates and traded goods prices," *Journal of International Economics* 24, 45–68.

—— and P. Jorion (1987) "Interest rates and risk premia in the stock market and in the foreign exchange market," *Journal of International Money and Finance* 6, 107–23.

—— and —— (1989) "Time variation of risk and return in the foreign exchange and stock markets," *Journal of Finance* 44, 307–26.

Grossman, S.J. and R.J. Shiller (1982) "Consumption correlatedness and risk measurement in economies with non-traded assets and heterogeneous information," *Journal of Financial Economics* 10, 195–210.

Gultekin, N.B. (1983) "Stock market returns and inflation: evidence from other countries," *Journal of Finance* 38, 49–66.

——, M.N. Gultekin and A. Penati (1989) "Capital controls and international capital market segmentation: the evidence from the Japanese and the American stock markets," *Journal of Finance* 44, 849–69.

Hamao, Y., R.W. Masulis and V. Ng (1990) "Correlations in price changes and volatility across international stock markets," *Review of Financial Studies* 3, 281–308

Hansen, L.P. and R.J. Hodrick (1983) "Risk averse speculation in the forward foreign exchange market: an econometric analysis of linear models," in Jacob A. Frenkel (ed.) *Exchange Rates and International Macroeconomics*, Chicago IL, University of Chicago Press.

—— and R. Jagannathan (1991) "Implications of security market data for models of dynamic economies," *Journal of Political Economy* 99, 225–62.

—— and K. Singleton (1982) "Generalized instrumental variables estimation of nonlinear rational expectations models," *Econometrica* 50, 1269–85.

Harvey, C. (1991) "The world price of covariance risk," *Journal of Finance* 46, 111–58.

Hodrick, R.J. (1987) *The Empirical Evidence on the Efficiency of Forward and Futures Foreign Exchange Markets*, Chur, Harwood Academic.

—— and S. Srivastava (1984) "An investigation of risk and return in forward foreign exchange," *Journal of International Money and Finance* 3, 5–29.

Howell, M. and A. Cozzini (1990) *International Equity Flows*, London, International Equity Research, Salomon Brothers.

—— and —— (1991) *International Equity Flows*, London, International Equity Research, Salomon Brothers.

Hsieh, D.A. (1991) "Using nonlinear methods to search for risk premia in currency futures," mimeo, Fuqua School of Business, Duke University.

Huizinga, J. (1987) "An empirical investigation of the long-run behavior of real exchange rates," in Karl Brunner and Allan Meltzer (eds) *Empirical Studies of Velocity, Real Exchange Rates, Unemployment and Productivity*, Carnegie-Rochester Conference Series on Public Policy 27, Amsterdam, North-Holland, pp. 149–214.

Ikeda, S. (1991) "Arbitrage asset pricing with exchange risk," *Journal of Finance* 46, 447–55.

Kandel, S. and R.F. Stambaugh (1988) "Modeling expected stock returns for long and short horizons," Working Paper, Wharton School of the University of Pennsylvania.

Keim, D. and R.F. Stambaugh (1986) "Predicting returns in the stock and bond markets," *Journal of Financial Economics* 17, 357–90.

Korajczyck, R. and C. Viallet (1992) "Equity risk premia and the pricing of foreign exchange risk," *Journal of International Economics* 33, 199–220.

Krugman, P. (1987) "Pricing to market when the exchange rate changes," in S.W. Arndt and J.D. Richardson (eds) *Real Financial Linkages among Open Economies*, Cambridge, MA, MIT Press, pp. 49–70.

Labadie, P. (1986) "Competitive dynamics and risk premia in an overlapping generations model," *Review of Economic Studies* 53, 139–52.

Leme, P. (1984) "Integration of international capital markets," mimeo, University of Chicago.

Levine, R. (1989) "An international arbitrage pricing model with PPP deviations," *Economic Inquiry* 27, 587–99.

Lintner, J. (1965) "The valuation of risky assets and the selection of risky investment in stock portfolios and capital budgets," *Review of Economics and Statistics* 47, 103–24.

Lo, A.W. and A.C. MacKinlay (1988) "Stock market prices do not follow random walks: evidence from a simple specification test," *Review of Financial Studies* 1, 41–66.

Lucas, R.E. (1978) "Asset prices in an exchange economy," *Econometrica* 46, 1429–46.

—— (1982) "Interest rates and currency prices in a two-country world," *Journal of Monetary Economics* 10, 335–60.

Marston, R.C. (1990) "Pricing to market in Japanese manufacturing," *Journal of International Economics* 29, 217–36.

McCulloch, J.H. (1975) "Operational aspects of the Siegel paradox" *Quarterly Journal of Economics* 89, 170–2.

Mehra, R. and E.C. Prescott (1985) "The equity premium: a puzzle," *Journal of Monetary Economics* 15, 145–61.

Merton, R.C. (1971) "Optimum consumption and portfolio rules in a continuous-time model," *Journal of Economic Theory* 3, 373–413.

—— (1973) "An intertemporal capital asset pricing model," *Econometrica* 41, 867–87.

Mossin, J. (1966) "Equilibrium in a capital asset market," *Econometrica* 34, 768–83.

Mussa, M. (1986) "Nominal exchange rate regimes and the behavior of real exchange rates," *Carnegie-Rochester Series on Public Policy* 25.

Obstfeld, M. (1986) "Capital mobility in the world economy: theory and measurement," *Carnegie-Rochester Conference Series on Public Policy* 31, 1–24.

—— (1989) "How integrated are world capital markets? Some new tests," in G. Calvo, R. Findlay and J. de Macedo (eds) *Debt, Stabilization and Development*, Oxford, Blackwell, pp. 134–55.

Richardson, M. (1990) "Temporary components of stock prices: a skeptic's view," Working Paper, Wharton School of the University of Pennsylvania.

Roll, R. (1992) "Industrial structure and the comparative behavior of international stock market indexes," *Journal of Finance* 42, 3–42.

Ross, S.A. (1976) "The arbitrage theory of capital asset pricing," *Journal of Economic Theory* 13, 341–60.

—— and M.W. Walsh (1983) "A simple approach to the pricing of risky assets with uncertain exchange rates," *Research in International Business and Finance* 3, 39–54.

Rozeff, M. (1984) "Dividend yields are equity risk premiums," *Journal of Portfolio Management* 68–75.

Scheinkman, J. (1984) "General equilibrium models of economic fluctuations: a survey of theory," mimeo, University of Chicago.

Sercu, P. (1980) "A generalization of the international asset pricing model," *Revue de l'Association Française de Finance* 1, 91–135.

Sharpe, W. (1964) "Capital asset prices: a theory of market equilibrium under conditions of risk," *Journal of Finance* 19, 425–42.

Shiller, R. (1981) "Do stock prices move too much to be justified by future dividends?" *American Economic Review* 71, 421–36.

Sibert, A. (1989) "The risk premium in the foreign exchange market," *Journal of Money, Credit and Banking* 21, 49–65.

Siegel, J. (1972) "Risk, interest and forward exchange," *Quarterly Journal of Economics* 86, 303–9.

Sinn, S.A. (1991) "Measuring international capital mobility: a critical note on the use of saving and investment correlations," mimeo, Institut für Welwirtschaft, Kiel.

Solnik, B. (1974) "An equilibrium model of the international capital market," *Journal of Economic Theory* 8, 500–24.

—— (1983a) "International arbitrage pricing theory," *Journal of Finance* 38, 449–57.

—— (1983b) "The relation between stock prices and inflationary expectations: the international evidence," *Journal of Finance* 38, 35–48.

——(1992) "Using the predictability of international asset returns," Working Paper, HEC School of Management, August.

Stambaugh, R. (1986) "Discussion," *Journal of Finance* 41, 601–2.

Stockman, A.C. and H. Dellas (1989) "International portfolio nondiversification and exchange rate variability," *Journal of International Economics* 26, 271–89.

——and L. Tesar (1990) "Tastes and technology in a two-country model of the business cycle: explaining international comovements," Working Paper 16–90, University of California, Santa Barbara.

Stulz, R. (1981) "A model of international asset pricing," *Journal of Financial Economics* 9, 383–406.

——(1987) "An equilibrium model of exchange rate determination and asset pricing with nontraded goods and imperfect information," *Journal of Political Economy* 95, 1024–40.

Svensson, L.E.O. (1985) "Currency prices, terms of trade and interest rates: a general-equilibrium asset pricing, cash-in-advance approach," *Journal of International Economics* 18, 17–42.

——and S. van Wijnbergen (1989) "Excess capacity, monopolistic competition, and international transmission of monetary disturbances," *Economic Journal* 99, 785–805.

Tesar, L.L. and I.M. Werner (1992) "Home bias and the globalization of securities markets," Working Paper, Graduate School of Business, Stanford University, July.

Uppal, M. (1992) "Deviations from purchasing power parity and capital flows," *Journal of International Money and Finance* 11, 126–44.

——(1993) "A general equilibrium model of international portfolio choice," *Journal of Finance* 48, 529–53.

Weil, P. (1989) "The equity premium puzzle and the risk-free rate puzzle," *Journal of Monetary Economics* 24, 401–21.

Wheatley, S.M. (1988) "Some tests of international equity market integration," *Journal of Financial Economics* 21, 177–212.

——(1989) "A critique of latent variable tests of asset pricing models," *Journal of Financial Economics* 23, 325–38.

11   Stylized Facts of Nominal Exchange Rate Returns

CASPER G. DE VRIES

1   Motivation

Upon returning to the USA from a sabbatical leave in several European countries a colleague was audited by the IRS (the US tax office). To her amazement the audit contained a nice surprise as it appeared that she had grossly understated her deduction for business expenses. Being an economics professor, she inquired about the reasons and found out the auditor had simply added all her European bills without regard for currency and exchange rates. While in some parts of Europe currency unions are actively debated, it may be still a while before we have a single world currency and the IRS can simply go ahead. At present, there are almost as many currencies as countries, and since the breakdown of the Bretton Woods arrangement the most actively internationally traded currencies experience considerable movements of their exchange rates at all frequencies.

While the disregard or ignorance of the IRS may seem a little incredible, there are a number of well-known and less well-known stylized facts about the empirical behavior of exchange rates that are often ignored in empirical and theoretical economics research. For example, the highly interesting target zone literature commonly employs the small-scale monetary model which, just as most other reduced-form structural models, has been firmly rejected as a parsimonious modeling device. This gives the theoretical predictions an unnecessary disadvantage in confrontation with the data (the theory may fail not for its essential contribution). The success story of, for example, neoclassical growth theory was made by the way it explained and integrated

Kaldor's empirical regularities. The purpose of this chapter is therefore to collect and expose the empirical regularities which have been found in the movements of exchange rates, so as to provide a skeleton for future empirical and theoretical work. The present chapter thereby complements the theory of chapter 10 in this volume.

The focus of the chapter is necessarily kept quite narrowly on the high frequency, nominal exchange rate behavior of the well-traded currencies. In this way we can provide an in-depth statistical treatment, develop a sound economic intuition, and collect new ideas for future research. Related variables such as forward and futures rates, interest rates, commodity prices, and asset prices will be treated when the occasion arises. The behavior of the exchange rates of minor currencies, such as black market rates, receive a similar treatment. Exchange rate models are extensively dealt with in chapter 10 of this volume and the reader is urged not to read this as a chapter on measurement without theory. The regularities of the relation between exchange rate regimes and macro variables like gross domestic product (GDP) or employment are treated in chapter 6 by Eichengreen. The main purpose of this essay is, nevertheless, to provide the student and researcher with a number of facts about nominal exchange rates on which future research can, and perhaps should, be based.

Before we set out, we like to note that over the years a number of high quality surveys on the topic have appeared. The interested reader is urged to consult Mussa (1979), Levich (1985), and Frankel and Meese (1987). A comprehensive account of the econometrics of exchange rates is provided by Taylor (1986), Diebold (1988), and Baillie and McMahon (1989). Hodrick (1987) gives an excellent survey of the efficiency issue. De Grauwe (1989) discusses on an intuitive level exchange rate behavior from the broader macro and historical–institutional perspective. For a number of reasons, we believe, the present chapter may have a positive clearing price. First, international finance is a rapidly developing field, so that a number of important new results are not adequately covered by the previous essays. Second, included in this chapter are a number of statistical techniques which are essential for researchers in the area but are not always easily accessible. Third, this chapter emphasizes the distributional aspects of exchange rate movements and what we can learn from this economically, which is typically not the approach taken in the economics literature.

Section 2 collects a number of stylized facts which are the stepping stones for exchange rate modeling. A number of these facts are singled out for an in-depth treatment in section 3, i.e. the unit root property, the fat tail property, and the clustering phenomenon. Section 4 includes a number of technical results that are useful for the researcher.

2   Empirical regularities

Before we can report on empirical regularities we have to define the variables of our interest, which in turn depend on the type of questions we face. The spot foreign exchange rate, for example, seems the obvious candidate variable for trade-related questions, because the exchange rate is the variable that clears the market for exports and imports. As of today, however, there are several economic arguments which suggest that for many questions the foreign exchange rate return rather than the exchange rate level is the relevant economic variable.[1] The major causes of short-run foreign exchange rate movements are international capital movements. For example, the net daily turnover on all foreign exchange markets of the world in April 1989 was 540 billion US dollars on average, which was 40 percent more than the total mass of all foreign official reserves of which only 3 percent was trade related. A basic presumption in finance is that investors equalize returns, corrected for uncertainty. Given the predominance of capital movements it seems therefore logical to focus on the returns rather than the levels.

There are two additional benefits from concentrating on the returns. Numeraire conventions are an important factor favoring the logarithmic transformation. The British and the continental notations are the same for the logarithm of the exchange rate, except for the sign. Hence, the sample moments are "identical" under the two conventions. In this way, Siegel's paradox, due to Jensen's inequality, i.e. $1/E(x) \neq E(1/x)$ in general (see chapter 10), is circumvented. Another problem is the denomination of a currency. However, when exchange rate returns are used, one obtains a unit-free measure.

The stylized facts are classified as follows. First, several facts constitute so called no (possibility of) arbitrage conditions, and consequently have direct economic content. Second, other facts are mere statistical regularities for which we currently lack a good economic explanation. A third category comprises some "negative" results, artifacts say, i.e. regularities which are commonly hypothesized but for which not much empirical support has been found.

2.1   No-arbitrage conditions

2.1.1   Unit root property

That returns are the variables on which we want to focus our attention for our economic investigations is corroborated by the first stylized fact. FACT 1 (UNIT ROOT PROPERTY)   The logarithm of the nominal exchange rate for two freely floating currencies is nonstationary, while the first difference is stationary.[2]

Let $s(t) = \log S(t)$ where $S(t)$ is the spot rate and log stands for the natural logarithm; then fact 1 can be restated as follows. The first-order autoregressive stochastic process $\{s(t)\}$

$$s(t) = \lambda s(t-1) + \varepsilon(t) \qquad \lambda = 1 \tag{11.1}$$

with $\{\varepsilon(t)\}$ stationary contains a unit root $\lambda = 1$. The knife-edge value induces the nonstationarity of $\{s(t)\}$ (note that $\{s(t)\}$ would be stationary for $|\lambda| < 1$). Table 11.1 reports a number of test results of $H_0: \lambda = 1$ for

Table 11.1   Unit root tests

	τ	τ_μ	$Z(l = 2)$	$Z(l = 10)$	$Z^*(l = 2)$	$Z^*(l = 10)$
Log-levels	0.823	− 0.068	0.672	1.194	− 1.005	− 0.849
Returns	− 12.106	− 12.618	− 19.201	− 18.664	− 19.377	− 19.065

The test statistics are the Dickey–Fuller statistics τ, τ_μ (see Fuller, 1976) for the model $x_t = c + x_{t-1} + \beta(x_{t-1} - x_{t-2})$ with c zero or unrestricted, and the Phillips statistics $Z(l)$, $Z^*(l)$ (see Phillips, 1987) for the model $x_t = c + x_{t-1}$ with c zero or unrestricted and truncation lag l. The variable x_t refers to either the log exchange rate level or first differences.
Source: Hols and de Vries, 1991

475 Thursday closing quotations of the Canadian–US dollar spot exchange rate from 1973 to 1983. Because $s(t)$ will be nonstationary under the null hypothesis, the usual critical values of the t tests do not apply. Appropriate critical values are provided in table 11.2. Both

Table 11.2   Unit root simulations

		Probability of a smaller value	
Test statistic	*Distribution*	*0.025*	*0.975*
τ	Normal	− 2.26	1.66
τ	Cauchy	− 1.98	1.36
τ_μ	Normal	− 3.12	0.23
τ_μ	Cauchy	− 3.85	0.28

This table corresponds to table 8.5.2 in Fuller (1976) for the normal distribution and sample size $n = 474$; in addition it gives the critical values if the innovations are Cauchy distributed. It is based on 10,000 replications (see Gielens and de Vries, 1990).
Source: Hols and de Vries, 1991

tables are taken from Hols and de Vries (1991) but are representative for the area (cf. Baillie and McMahon, 1989, ch. 4).

While any student with some experience in applied econometrics would be cautious with reporting exactly $\lambda = 1$ as a fact of life, economic intuition strongly favors this specific value. In efficient markets all information at time $t-1$ is incorporated in the price $s(t-1)$, $\varepsilon(t)$

captures the unanticipated elements, and hence equation (11.1) is indeed a "no-arbitrage condition" (see LeRoy, 1989). (See section 3 for a slight modification of this statement due to the interest differential.) It has some amazing implications. For example, if we are willing to make the additional assumption, which was often made in the older literature, that the $\varepsilon(t)$ are independent and identically distributed (iid), then $s(t)$ follows a random walk and hence $s(t)$ eventually crosses any level $s \in R$, with obvious ramifications for exchange-rate-related variables. These issues are elaborated on further in section 3.

2.1.2   Triangular arbitrage condition

The following two no-arbitrage conditions are the centerpieces of the international money market. The highly automated information processing allows for efficient trade and arbitrage between different financial centers. Direct purchase of a particular foreign currency or indirect purchase via a third currency (financial center) should cost the same.

FACT 2 (TRIANGULAR ARBITRAGE CONDITION)   If the logarithm of two different dollar spot rates, say the deutschemark–US dollar rate $s_1(t)$ and the inverse British pound–US dollar rate $-s_2(t)$ are added, this yields the logarithmic deutschemark–British pound cross rate $s_3(t)$:

$$s_1(t) - s_2(t) = s_3(t) \tag{11.2}$$

Because this equality holds very well in practice, and because some of the univariate statistical properties are common to all exchange rates, it should be the case that these statistical properties are invariant under addition (see also fact 9). This might be a very useful fact for any axiomatic approach to the distribution of exchange rates which, as of today, is nonexistent. *Inter alia*, note that equations like (11.2) in a multivariate context restrict the dimensionality of the covariance matrix of equation (11.1), i.e. imply a singular multivariate distribution.

2.1.3   Parity conditions

Let $F(t)$ be the forward foreign currency rate at time t of a forward contract with delivery date $t+1$, let $I(t)$ and $I^*(t)$ be the domestic and foreign one-period nominal interest rates, and let $C(t)$, $P(t)$ denote the prices of a foreign currency call and put option with exercise price X that expire at $t+1$. Now, investing in a local bond with a return of $1 + I(t)$ should yield the same as investing in a bond of equal quality abroad and exchanging the future proceeds at the current forward rate, i.e. $[1 + I^*(t)]F(t)/S(t)$. Similarly, directly buying a forward contract for future exchange against rate $F(t)$ should cost the same as taking an indirect hedge through buying a call selling (writing) a put, i.e. a so-called "reversal," and bringing forward the cost of borrowing the difference $C(t) - P(t)$. To see that this reversal duplicates a forward contract, note that the trader using the options market gains (loses) dollar for dollar by the amount that the future spot rate is above (below) the exercise price X; similarly a trader using the forward market gains (loses) the difference between the future spot rate and the forward rate.

FACT 3 (PARITY CONDITIONS)   The relations for covered interest rate parity

$$\frac{F(t)}{S(t)} = \frac{1 + I(t)}{1 + I^*(t)} \tag{11.3}$$

and put–call parity

$$F(t) = X + [C(t) - P(t)][1 + I(t)] \tag{11.4}$$

hold for all major traded currencies.

The covered interest rate parity condition is often stated in the following approximate format:

$$f(t) - s(t) = I(t) - I^*(t) \tag{11.5}$$

where $f(t) = \log F(t)$. Discrepancies in these relations arise owing to transactions costs, bid–ask spreads, and capital controls (see for example Levich, 1985; Baillie and McMahon, 1989, ch. 5). Usually some wedge between the left-hand side and right-hand side of equations (11.3) and (11.4) exists, suggesting arbitrage opportunities. Most of the time, however, transactions costs, albeit small, prevent a profitable roundtrip. While (11.3) usually holds up very well if offshore (Euromarket) interest rates are used, this is not the case for onshore interest rates. The discrepancy is mostly due to the existence of capital controls. During times of strains within for example the European Monetary System (EMS), the disparity usually increases due to the risk of a realignment, which renders the forward market thin. For futures contracts a condition similar to (11.3) holds.

2.1.4   Cointegration of spot and forward rates

Evidently, equations (11.3) and (11.4) can be combined to yield an arbitrage relation between interest rates and currency options. An interesting "new" fact arises from combining facts 1 and 3. To introduce this new fact we need a new concept. Recall the definition of stationarity in note 2, and the fact that while $s(t)$ is found to be nonstationary the return $s(t) - s(t - 1)$ is stationary. This univariate differencing to obtain a stationary series can be generalized to a multivariate setting. Two nonstationary random variables, say $s(t)$ and $f(t)$, are said to be cointegrated if some linear combination $x(t) = s(t) + af(t)$, say, is stationary; a is said to be the cointegrating "vector" (in the univariate case one could say that $s(t)$ and $s(t-1)$ are cointegrated if $f(t)$ is replaced by $s(t)$ and a is set at -1). If there does not exist such a linear combination, the two variables are not cointegrated. Now suppose that the interest differential on the right-hand side of equation (11.5) is a stationary random variable and recall fact 1. We then have the following.

FACT 4 (COINTEGRATION)   The spot rate $s(t)$ and the accompanying forward rate $f(t)$ are cointegrated with cointegrating vector $a = -1$, while different (freely floating) spot rates are typically not cointegrated.

If $s(t)$ and $f(t)$ are cointegrated, then $f(t)$ and $s(t+k)$ will be cointegrated as well. To see this, suppose that $f(t)$ and $s(t+k)$ were not cointegrated; then $s(t+k) - f(t)$ would be nonstationary and hence, in combination with fact 1, it follows that both $s(t+k)$ and $f(t)$ could wander infinitely far away from each other. This implies infinitely high risk premia, defying the existence of a forward market (a direct analytical proof is to add the stationary increment $s(t+k) - s(t)$ to the difference $s(t) - f(t)$). Thus $s(t+k) - f(t)$ being stationary makes sense. Hence, Granger (1986) concluded that in an efficient market contracts which are related to the same asset should be cointegrated. Evidence of this cointegration relation is reported in table 11.3. The table reports ordinary least squares estimates for the equation

$$s(t+k) = a + bf(t) + \varepsilon(t+k)$$

with k equal to the number of trading days during a thirty-day forward contract. The table is based on Baillie and McMahon (1989, ch. 4), who also test against nonstationarity of the residuals. Except for the

Table 11.3   Cointegration between $s(t+k)$ and $f(t)$

Country	â	b̂
UK	− 0.0187	1.0135
West Germany	− 0.0301	0.9802
France	− 0.0379	0.9852
Italy	− 0.0892	0.9886
Switzerland	− 0.0298	0.9756
Japan	− 0.8347	0.8476
Canada	− 0.0095	0.9599

Estimates are based on a sample of US dollar daily foreign exchange quotations in New York over the period 1980–5.
Source: Baillie and McMahon, 1989, ch. 4

dollar–yen rate, the results are convincing. See Hakkio and Rush (1989) for additional evidence.

We started the discussion of fact 4 by assuming that the interest differential in equation (11.5) is stationary, and in combination with the nonstationarity of $s(t)$ we found that $f(t)$ has to be cointegrated with $s(t)$. Vice versa, given that $f(t)$ and $s(t)$ are cointegrated, and if nominal interest rates are nonstationary, then $I(t)$ and $I^*(t)$ are cointegrated as well. Thus cointegration between one set of variables induces important stochastic restrictions on other sets of variables. The noncointegrating feature of different (freely floating) spot rates is also important, as it yields indirect support for the efficient market hypothesis discussed in the next section. On the other hand, this observation does not apply to cross rates (recall equation (11.2)). Moreover, it does not apply to different (cross) rates from currency blocs like the EMS.

2.1.5 News dominance and calendar effects

Related to the spot and forward rate movements is the following fact on the relative importance of the innovations.

FACT 5 (NEWS DOMINANCE)   The variation in the spot returns $s(t + 1) - s(t)$ is much larger than the variation in the forward premium $f(t) - s(t)$, and *ipso facto* the interest differential.

If the realized spot return is decomposed into an anticipated part and an unanticipated or news part, and if we identify the anticipated part with the forward premium, then fact 5 says that the news factor dominates. That $|f(t) - s(t)|$ is small relative to $|s(t + 1) - s(t)|$ is not too surprising given the way the forward market operates. Banks which provide forward contracts hardly take any open positions but instead try to reverse their position by an opposite contract. Thus banks basically perform a clearing or matching function and hence the risk premium can be relatively small. The interest rate parity condition (11.5) implies that the same conclusion applies to the relative variability of the spot returns *vis-à-vis* the interest differential. We also note that the interest differentials, and hence the forward premiums, are usually autocorrelated.

FACT 6 (CALENDAR EFFECTS)   There are significant time of trade effects, such as the day of the week, on the location and scale of the process.

In particular, positive Wednesday and negative Thursday dummies for the mean, and positive Monday dummies for the variance, are found in the data, see for example Taylor (1986) and Baillie and McMahon (1989). These effects are often due to institutional factors. For example the opposite Wednesday–Thursday effects on the mean are caused by different delays in settlement for dollar and nondollar contracts, and the positive Monday effect on the scale arises from uncertainty induced by market closure over the weekend. The institutional set-up of the currency market also explains why psychological barriers, i.e. fewer trades take place in the neighborhood of rounded numbers such as a deutschemark–US dollar rate of 2.00, seem to exist in dollar rates, while the inverse rates do not exhibit this pattern. The reason is that all quotations on the Reuter's screens are given on a per dollar basis. This, though, does not of course explain the existence of such psychological barriers in itself (see De Grauwe and Decupere, 1992). In the context of security prices it has been observed that rounding effects may seriously bias estimates of the moments. Care has to be taken, when multiple time series such as the forward rate and the related future spot rate are investigated, that the series are appropriately matched. Typically high frequency data are not equally spaced in time, and this may affect the results. Also, there may be simply too many data to check the recording consistency by hand, and hence appropriate filters may have to be employed. Wasserfallen (1989) and Goodhart and Figliuoli (1991) discuss the properties of data recorded at the highest possible frequency.

2.2   Statistical regularities

We turn our attention to regularities which have a sound statistical basis but for which no convincing economic explanation has been established. On first sight the unit root scheme (11.1) leaves disappointingly little room for further investigations, because no other variables than the lagged rate appear on the right-hand side. As it turns out, though, a lot more can be said about the stationary innovations $\varepsilon(t)$. The evidence is classified according to the features of the unconditional and the conditional distribution, and we start with the former.

2.2.1   Fat tail phenomenon

FACT 7 (FAT TAIL PHENOMENON)   Exchange rate returns, irrespective of the regime, when standardized by their scale exhibit more probability mass in the tails than distributions such as the standard normal distribution.

Loosely speaking this means that extremely high and low realizations occur more frequently than under the hypothesis of normality. *Ipso facto* one has to exercise care in removing so-called outliers so as not to reject the good with the bad. A related fact is that the density of the

returns is more peaked than the normal density. A popular measure for
the latter fact is the kurtosis, but note that a positive kurtosis does not
necessarily indicate the fat tail phenomenon as is sometimes supposed
(see section 3). The distinction between thin-tailed distributions like the
normal distribution and fat-tailed distributions is that the former have
tails which decline exponentially, while the latter distributions have
tails which decline by a power. A simple condition, known as a regular
variation at infinity, operationalizes the fat tail property. Let $F(t)$ be a
distribution function. Then if

$$\lim_{t \to \infty} \frac{1 - F(tx)}{1 - F(t)} = x^{-\alpha} \qquad \alpha > 0 \qquad (11.6)$$

holds for some α and positive x, $F(t)$ is said to be regularly varying with
tail index α. Loosely speaking, α can be identified with the number of
moments that exist (in case of the Student t distribution α equals the
degrees of freedom), and thus represents a measure of tail fatness.
Semiparametric estimates of α for three different periods are recorded
in table 11.4, which is based on Koedijk et al. (1992). Parametric

Table 11.4   Tail indexes α

	Period		
	Fix (62–71)	Float (73–84)	Float (73–91)
No. of observations	485	605	962
Deutschemark	1.20	3.45	3.51
	(0.86, 1.52)	(2.53, 4.37)	(2.75, 4.28)
Pound	1.14	3.21	3.58
	(0.82, 1.45)	(2.35, 4.06)	(2.80, 4.36)
Yen	1.26	2.74	2.74
	(0.91–1.60)	(2.01–3.47)	(2.15–3.34)
Guilder	2.42	3.35	3.45
	(1.75, 3.08)	(2.45, 4.24)	(2.70, 4.21)
Canadian dollar	1.59	2.66	2.99
	(1.15–2.03)	(1.95–3.37)	(2.34–3.64)

Estimates are based on weekly return data of US dollar exchange rates. The method of estimation
is the Hill estimator (see section 3) and asymptotic standard errors are recorded in parentheses.
Source: Koedijk et al., 1992

estimates reported in Westerfield (1977) and Boothe and Glassman
(1987) reveal the same message but are hampered by the non-
nestedness of the different parametric models. This is not the case for
the semiparametric approach.

From table 11.4 it is apparent that exchange rate returns are heavily fat tailed, and the more so the more they are regulated. The economic intuition behind this fact is an odd basket of arguments, some of which may have to be thrown out on second thought. For example, the overshooting property maintains that, as floating rates carry the burden of adjustment in the presence of sticky commodity prices and wages, exchange rates tend to overshoot. Also, some of the other properties presented below, i.e. additivity and volatility clustering, are connected with the fat tail property. In general, though, one finds that, the more a rate is left to float freely, the thinner the tails – see table 11.4 where the αs for the float are significantly higher than the αs for the period of almost fixed exchange rates. This corroborates the Friedman presumption that the free float produces a smoother adjustment than the other regimes.

2.2.2   Skewness and additivity

The second statistical fact relates to the third central moment of the unconditional distribution.

FACT 8 (SKEWNESS)   Exchange rate returns of currencies which experience similar monetary policies exhibit no significant skewness, while dissimilar policies tend to generate skewness.

Skewness appears in the data if an exchange rate predominantly drifts one way or another. This is often caused by a disparity between monetary policies, like a hyperinflation versus a deflationary policy. Less extremely, within the EMS the weaker currencies were repeatedly devalued *vis-à-vis* the stronger currencies because of the devaluation bias inherent to a system of semi-fixed currencies. The following fact is somewhat more surprising.

FACT 9 (ADDITIVITY)   The distribution of the largest returns when aggregated over time or across exchange rates is invariant up to a location and scale adjustment.

The precise meaning of this statement will only become clear from the concepts introduced in section 3. The additivity property, in combination with the existence of all moments, is the defining characteristic of the normal distribution. Mandelbrot (1963a, b) first observed that the property was also present in non-normal fat-tailed distributed return series. The additivity property across different exchange rates follows almost directly from fact 2, the triangular arbitrage condition, and fact 7, the fat tail property, because, if two (independent) random variables have distributions which are regularly varying, i.e. satisfy (11.6), then the distribution of the sum is regularly varying as well (see section 3).

2.2.3   Volatility clusters and GARCH

The conditional distribution, i.e. the distribution of $\varepsilon(t)$ in equation (11.1) given the observed history $\{\varepsilon(t-1), \ldots, \varepsilon(t-n)\}$, is dominated by the following fact.

FACT 10 (VOLATILITY CLUSTERS)   Periods of quiescence and turbulence tend to cluster together.

Again, this fact was already observed by Mandelbrot but was more or less neglected until recently. Return series were often subjected to tests of serial dependence, but such tests focused primarily on the autocorrelation properties in the mean or location of the process and relied on the popular autoregressive moving-average (ARMA) representation of time series. However, not much of such dependence could be detected The clusters of volatility regularity suggest, instead, that autocorrelation in the scale of the process $\{\varepsilon(t)\}$ is the more typical feature.[3] The convenient generalized autoregressive conditional heteroskedasticity (GARCH) scheme developed at the beginning of the 1980s was instrumental in popularizing this fact in economic modeling. By letting the conditional variance depend on the past squared innovations, it directly captures the effect that, once the market is heavily volatile, it is more likely to remain so than to calm down, and vice versa.

Formally, the GARCH(1, 1) model reads as follows (see also section 3):

$$\varepsilon(t) = X(t)\,H(t)^{1/2} \tag{11.7}$$

$$H(t) = \omega + \lambda\varepsilon(t-1)^2 + \beta H(t-1) \tag{11.8}$$

where $X(t)$ are iid innovations. Some typical parameter estimates for the case when $X(t)$ is Student t distributed with v degrees of freedom are reported in table 11.5.

The GARCH parameters are significantly different from zero in all cases, and hence volatility clusters are clearly present. Also, as will become evident from the discussion in section 3, the parameter estimates of (λ, β, v) corroborate the fat tail phenomenon of fact 7 and are in line with the results of table 11.4. Specifically, the intra-EMS rates again display fatter tails. Hence, the explanation for fact 7 may just be the volatility cluster effect. Unfortunately, this shifts the problem towards explaining fact 10, because the economics behind the latter fact are not well understood yet. Note, however, that taken together the absence of dependence in the mean and positive autocorrelation in the scale of the process is not inconsistent with risk-neutral agents arbitraging in the levels of the returns.[4] The converse, i.e. fact 10 implicitly rejecting risk aversion, is not necessarily true though (see for example LeRoy, 1973). General specification tests, which were derived

Table 11.5   The GARCH model

Exchange rate	Parameter		
	λ	β	v
French franc/US dollar	0.15	0.79	6.56
Yen/US dollar	0.08	0.90	5.91
Deutschemark/US dollar	0.11	0.86	14.93
Belgium franc/French franc	0.71	0.21	2.46
Belgium franc/yen	0.17	0.63	4.44
Belgium franc/deutschemark	0.58	0.39	3.06

The results for the first three exchange rates are taken from Baillie and McMahon (1989, ch. 4, with permission of Cambridge University Press) and are based on a sample of 1,200 daily observations, while the last three are based on 500 weekly observations reported by De Ceuster (1992). Details of the estimations are given in these studies.

as a byproduct from chaos theory, have confirmed that nonlinearities in the data-generating process are clearly present. But so far this has not led to serious amendments of the ARCH model. The well-known deterministic nonlinear chaos models have not made much inroad because their deterministic features and data requirements for falsification render them unsuitable for economic analysis.

2.3   Artifacts

There are a number of relationships which make sense on the basis of economic principles but for which the empirical evidence is only marginal. Some of these relations are nevertheless frequently hypothesized in theoretical work, because they are so "convenient" or because they are part and parcel of current paradigms. Needless to say, empirical work which is based on such a theoretical exposé often fails because one of the maintained hypotheses is grossly at variance with the data (this is, of course, not a necessity). In this section we collect a number of these "artifacts." We remind the reader that our focus is on the high frequency behavior of freely traded currencies and that the artifacts may become facts in a different context (e.g. purchasing power parity (PPP) fails on high frequency data, while it cannot be rejected on very low frequency data).

2.3.1   Uncovered interest rate disparity

One form of the efficient market hypothesis, i.e. when the market uses all relevant information and uses this information correctly to determine exchange rates, in conjunction with risk neutrality implies that the forward rate is an unbiased predictor of the future spot rate:

$$f(t) = E[s(t+1)] \qquad (11.9)$$

where $E(.)$ is the expectations operator given the information set at time t. Combining equations (11.5) and (11.9) then yields the uncovered interest rate parity condition.

FACT 11 (UNCOVERED INTEREST RATE DISPARITY)   This condition

$$E[s(t+1)] - s(t) = I(t) - I^*(t) \qquad (11.10)$$

is usually rejected by the empirical material.

Tests of equation (11.10) are marred by the non-observability of $E[s(t+1)]$, the overlapping data problem (see Hansen and Hodrick, 1980), conditional heteroskedasticity (see Hodrick, 1987, ch. 3), and cointegration (see Hakkio and Rush, 1989). Nevertheless, the unbiasedness hypothesis has been rejected time and time again (see Baillie and McMahon, 1989, ch. 6; Hodrick, 1987, ch. 3; Fama, 1984). This is not necessarily evidence against market efficiency, only against the particular model of market equilibrium on which the tests are based. In particular, the unbiasedness hypothesis (11.9) almost always presupposes risk-neutral agents. Therefore research has turned to testing efficient market models which generate a nonzero risk premium, such as the consumption-based capital asset pricing model (CAPM). To this end the ARCH-type error structure is employed because its conditional heteroskedasticity conveniently captures the idea of a time-varying risk premium. To date, however, this research is largely inconclusive (see Frankel and Meese, 1987). Other explanations are based on market inefficiency, expectational failures, and nonergodicity of the data due to Peso problems. To conclude, the hunt for a plausible econometric specification generating a risk premium that explains the failures of (11.9) or (11.10) is still on.

2.3.2 No purchasing power parity

From the trade balance point of view one would expect an intimate relation between relative prices and exchange rates. Let $p(t)$ and $p^*(t)$ denote the logarithm of the domestic and foreign price levels. PPP is said to prevail in absolute terms if

$$s(t) = p(t) - p^*(t) \qquad (11.11)$$

and in relative terms if

$$\Delta s(t) = \Delta p(t) - \Delta p^*(t) \qquad (11.12)$$

where Δ is the difference operator.

FACT 12 (NO PURCHASING POWER PARITY)   Neither form of PPP holds in the short run, while there is some evidence favoring (relative) PPP in the long run.

The absence of PPP in the short run follows from the fact that aggregate price levels or indexes are relatively sticky in the short run, owing to, for example, the periodic fixing of wage contracts. This, in combination with equation (11.1), renders the failure of (11.11) or (11.12) a small surprise. In other words, the real exchange rate $q(t)$ where

$$q(t) = s(t) + p^*(t) - p(t) \qquad (11.13)$$

is indistinguishable from a unit root process in the short run. But persistent deviations have been observed over much longer horizons than, say, a year. Only over time horizons of, for example, a century have terms of trade effects caused by say relative productivity changes been detected (see Frankel and Meese, 1987). Also, currencies which experience a hyperinflation *vis-à-vis* stable currencies usually have depreciating exchange rates, corroborating fact 8. But again, in general, detection of PPP is deterred by statistical features of the data, like unit roots and cointegration, and these have only recently been tackled head on.

Fixed and semi-fixed regimes exhibit a number of interesting idiosyncrasies. A celebrated relationship exists between the trade balance $B(t)$ and the logarithmic (real) exchange rate. Disaggregating $B(t)$ into domestic and foreign demand and supply, rewriting this equation into elasticity format, and differentiating with respect to $q(t)$ yields a "positive" effect of a devaluation on the trade balance if the Marshall–Lerner condition is satisfied, i.e. the sum of the absolute demand elasticities must exceed unity. Received wisdom has it that the elasticity condition holds, albeit not in the short run owing to price rigidities which produce an initial deterioration of $B(t)$, i.e. the typical J-curve effect. Recent econometric investigations which directly evaluate the connection between $q(t)$ and $B(t)$, instead of the indirect evidence produced by estimating trade elasticities, however, do not find any definite relationship (see Rose, 1991). Given the absence of PPP stated in fact 12, this is not too surprising. A relatively new phenomenon is the S-shaped behavior of exchange rates within the target zone. This is extensively discussed in chapter 9 of this volume by Bertola.

A typical aspect of pegged exchange rates is the nth currency problem. Because n currencies only generate $n-1$ exchange rates relative to a numeraire currency (and all other cross rates follow from the triangular arbitrage condition (11.2)), this leaves one degree of freedom: with $n-1$ relative prices, the level of the nth currency stock can be chosen freely. This turned out to be the case under the Bretton Woods agreement whereby the USA took its liberties until the other countries were no longer willing to swallow the increase in dollars. A similar degree of freedom exists within the EMS. And one of the questions is whether Germany plays the nth country role – the so-called German dominance hypothesis. This is briefly discussed in section 3.

2.3.3   Ineffectiveness of sterilized intervention

The pressure on fixed or managed exchange rates which builds up as a result of, for example, diverging inflation rates is often countered through official interventions. One could say that the foreign exchange market is an asset market with sanctioned insider trading. Nevertheless, the intentions of the central banks are often revealed indirectly through their publicly announced targets concerning other variables such as the interest rate. While unsterilized intervention may be effective because it changes the money supply, the effectiveness of sterilized intervention hinges on the nonsubstitutability of foreign and domestic assets.

FACT 13 (INEFFECTIVENESS OF STERILIZED INTERVENTION)   Most evidence shows that sterilized intervention has no effect or only temporary effects on the exchange rate.

2.3.4   Inelastic currency substitution

Alternative means for managing exchange rates are capital controls. A special case of this is the use of dual exchange rates. Under a dual exchange rate regime, different parts of the balance of payments are cleared against different rates. This, of course, induces the possibilities for (illegal) arbitrage. If exchange controls drive too big a wedge between the official rate and the shadow free market rate, the latter comes into the open in the form of a black market rate. Often such a market is unofficially tolerated, to take away the greatest strains from the system. Another arbitrage scheme is currency substitution which occurs when some of the roles of the local currency are partly taken over by a foreign currency.[5] Indirect currency substitution is said to occur when other foreign assets are being substituted for other domestic assets, as in the case of bond substitution.

FACT 14 (INELASTIC CURRENCY SUBSTITUTION)   The elasticity of direct currency substitution is not very high.

Habit formation, legal restrictions, and the fact that the rate of return on money is dominated by other assets severely limit the possibilities and rationale for direct currency substitution (see de Vries (1988) for estimates of the elasticity of substitution). It must be said, though, that in countries where one would *a priori* expect a high elasticity, as in the case of a hyperinflation, a lack of good data material has prevented reliable measurement of the elasticity of currency substitution. Evidently, within one jurisdiction, the elasticity of substitution between coins, paper money, and plastic money is very high. Nevertheless, there is evidence that even during hyperinflations substitute monies are not used on a large scale (see Barro, 1972). Much more detailed evidence on currency substitution may be found in chapter 12 of this volume.

2.3.5 Volatility and trade

Considerable attention has been devoted to the impact of (conditional) exchange rate variability on the volume of international trade. This activity notwithstanding, we have the following conclusion.

FACT 15 (NO VOLATILITY IMPACT ON TRADE) There does not appear to exist an unambiguous relationship between (conditional) exchange rate (return) volatility and international trade.

The failure to turn up the presumed negative relationship is due to several factors. Theoretical models that incorporate the possibilities for hedging and employ a general equilibrium setting do not necessarily imply that exchange rate volatility is detrimental to trade (see Viaene and de Vries, 1992). The measurement of the volatility effects, moreover, is not easy. For example, inclusion of a volatility measure in a regression purporting to explain trade flows may be marred by the constructed regressor problem. The measurement of the conditional volatility could conceivably be improved by exploiting the fact of volatility clustering through an ARCH-type representation. On the other hand, longer term volatility as signified by the sustained increases and decreases in the value of the US dollar during the 1980s has left its imprints on trade. Goldstein and Kahn (1985) provide a survey of the other trade, price, and exchange rate issues.

2.3.6 No fundamentals

The relation between the exchange rates and other macroeconomic variables in general, except those which appear in the no-arbitrage conditions, can be succinctly worded as follows.

FACT 16 (NO FUNDAMENTALS) The predictions from (high frequency) reduced-form exchange rate models do not outperform simple no-change forecasts.

Note that this fact is in conformity with the unit root property stated in fact 1. While we shall see that equation (11.1) is just a simple no-arbitrage condition, it took a long time before it was put to test, given the economist's focus on structural models, and its full implications are still being assessed. The most damaging evidence against the fundamentals approach was delivered by Meese and Rogoff (1983). Meese and Rogoff compared out-of-sample forecasts of reduced-form structural models (using actual realized values of the explanatory variables) with the no-change forecast of a random walk. Table 11.6

Table 11.6   Root mean square forecast errors

Exchange rate	Forecast horizon	Random walk	Monetary model
US dollar/deutschemark	1 month	3.72	3.17
	6 months	8.71	9.64
US dollar/yen	1 month	3.68	4.11
	6 months	11.58	13.38
US dollar/pound	1 month	2.56	2.82
	6 months	6.45	8.90

Exchange rates are in logarithms; hence the forecast error is approximately in percentage terms. The monetary model derives from the logarithmic difference of the domestic quantity equations and the logarithmic PPP relation (see section 3.1).
Source: Meese and Rogoff, 1983, table 1, with permission of Elsevier Science Publishers

summarizes some of their results. The absence of a fundamentals model also impairs the recently popular tests for excess exchange rate volatility based on variance bounds or bubbles, because these are all conditional on using the correct fundamentals model. Lack of knowledge of this model renders such tests virtually inapplicable. The macro oriented exchange rate literature after the demise of Bretton Woods has largely been an epitaph on the fundamentals models of exchange rates. This has nevertheless been a positive process, because it stimulated the inquiry into the behavior of $\varepsilon(t)$, generated numerous of the facts recounted above, and has been useful for economic modeling as is evidenced by the other chapters in this volume.

3   Theory

3.1   Arbitrage and unit roots

In this section we single out the three dominant statistical issues, i.e. nonstationarity, fat tails, and volatility clusters, for further investigation. This is not to say that the other facts are of lesser importance, but these are extensively treated elsewhere. Turning to the topic of this section, we wish to remind the reader of facts 1 (unit roots), 16 (no fundamentals), and 4 (cointegration). We shall first argue why economists have not been able to develop a convincing model of high frequency exchange rate behavior on the basis of economic fundamentals. Fortunately, this does not imply that economics has nothing to say. In fact, consistent with most economic theories, arbitrage arguments strongly suggest that we should not be able to find the stone of economic wisdom for predicting exchange rate levels. Instead, economic theory does suggest something about the way returns behave and vice versa.

3.1.1   Impossibility of profitable trading systems

To see the no-arbitrage argument, recall the fact recounted above that almost no exchange in the foreign exchange market is trade related but instead most transactions are investment motivated. Now contemplate the following experiment. Suppose one is teaching a class and offers to sell the contents of one's wallet through an English auction such as is used in selling antiques, without revealing the actual contents beforehand. Two students, however, are granted the right to see the true contents before the auction. When played in practice, one usually finds the two informed students bidding against each other while the uninformed hardly participate. When the uninformed students are asked to guess the true contents after the bidding has ceased, most students call the winning bid, as they realize that the two informed have an incentive to outbid each other until the true value of the contents is reached. Thus all information gets reflected in the price and the market is said to be efficient. Similarly, a known or expected exchange rate revaluation (devaluation) leads to an almost instantaneous decrease (increase) in the spot rate by the arbitrage process outlined above. Usually this rapid adjustment process is omitted from the analysis. What one is left with is the no-arbitrage condition

$$s(t + 1) - s(t) = \varepsilon(t + 1) \qquad E[\varepsilon(t + 1)] = 0 \qquad (11.14)$$

That is, all that can be said about the future spot rate(s) is contained in the current rate:

$$E[s(t + k) \mid s(t)] = s(t) \qquad \text{for any } k > 0 \qquad (11.15)$$

If we add the restriction that $E(\mid s(t) \mid) < \infty$, then the stochastic process $\{s(t)\}$ is said to be a martingale.[6] A stronger assumption is to maintain that the $\varepsilon(t)$ are iid, which produces the random walk. Because of the volatility clusters (fact 10), the random walk is unnecessarily restrictive and hence we concentrate on the unit root property.[7]

An important implication of the no-arbitrage argument is the impossibility of trading rules. It is important because many economists and technical analysts usually have difficulty accepting this feature of efficient markets. To develop the argument suppose that $\{s(t)\}$ is a martingale with $s(0) = \varepsilon(0) = 0$. From (11.14) we have that

$$s(t) = \varepsilon(1) + \cdots + \varepsilon(t) \tag{11.16}$$

Because of equation (11.16) we can replace the conditioning variables in (11.15) by

$$E[s(t+1) | \varepsilon(1), \ldots, \varepsilon(t)] = s(t)$$

In this spirit the more general definition of a martingale allows the conditioning variables to be any stochastic process $\{y(t)\}$ such that

$$E[s(t+1) | y(1), \ldots, y(t)] = s(t) \tag{11.17}$$

Often $\{y(t)\} = \{\varepsilon(t)\}$, but we may want to enlarge the information set by other random variables from the past. By the law of iterated expectations[8]

$$E[s(t+1) | y(1), \ldots, y(t-1)]$$

$$= E\{E[s(t+1) | y(1), \ldots, y(t)] | y(1), \ldots, y(t-1)\}$$

$$= E[s(t) | y(1), \ldots, y(t-1)]$$

$$= s(t-1)$$

By induction we get

$$E[s(t+1) | y(1), \ldots, y(k)] = s(k) \qquad k = 1, \ldots, t$$

It follows that any subsequence, e.g. $\{s(2t)\}$, follows a martingale as well.

This last observation can be used to show the impossibility of trading systems. Let $\{s(t)\}$ again be a martingale with respect to $\{y(t)\}$ (see equation (11.17)). Let $\chi(t) = \chi[y(1), \ldots, y(t)]$ be a function of all past information which takes on the value 1 or 0. The value 1 is associated with playing, say investing one dollar in foreign currency with a return $s(t) - s(t-1)$, and 0 denotes abstention, i.e. skipping the possibility of investment. When $\chi(n) = 1$, the gain at the nth trial is

$$s(n) - s(n-1)$$

and zero otherwise. The accumulated gain $a(n)$ at time n is

$$a(n) = a(n-1) + \chi(n-1)[s(n) - s(n-1)]$$

Because $E[a(1)] = \chi(1) E[s(1)] = 0$ by definition, and using an induction argument, the unconditional expectation $E[a(n)]$ clearly exists, i.e. it is zero. Hence, the conditional expectations can be calculated as well. In particular

$$E[a(n) \mid y(1), \ldots, y(n-1)]$$

$$= a(n-1) + \chi(n-1) \{E[s(n) \mid y(1), \ldots, y(n-1)] - s(n-1)\}$$

$$= a(n-1) \tag{11.18}$$

Thus $\{a(n)\}$ is a martingale, cf. equation (11.17). We have proved the following.

THEOREM 1: IMPOSSIBILITY OF TRADING SYSTEMS   Every sequence of zero–one decision functions $\chi(t)$ changes the martingale $\{s(t)\}$ into a new martingale $\{a(t)\}$.

As a special case consider the option to halt playing altogether. In this case the decision function $\chi(t)$ becomes $\chi(t < t_0) = 1$ and $\chi(t \geq t_0) = 0$ for some t_0. The function tells when to stop investing. By the above theorem it is immediate that corollary 1 holds.

COROLLARY 1   "Optimal" stopping does not affect the martingale property of $\{a(n)\}$.

Theorem 1 and corollary 1 dispel the possibility of devising profitable trading schemes (which are linear in the outcome) such as those proposed by technical analysis. But if there exists structure in the higher moments of $\varepsilon(t)$, then there may exist profitable trading rules (that are nonlinear in the outcome). Thus a risk-averse agent might be able to exploit a scheme like ARCH (see below).

3.1.2   Monetary theory of fundamentals

How can we reconcile the simple scheme in (11.14) and (11.15) with the elaborate fundamentals models that are so common in economics? Consider, for example, the simple monetary model. From the Keynesian money demand or logarithmic quantity equation we have

$$m(t) = p(t) + \phi y(t) - \Psi I(t) \tag{11.19}$$

where $y(t)$ is logarithmic income, $m(t)$ is the logarithm of the money stock, and Ψ is the interest semielasticity of money demand. Equate money demand with money supply and subtract a similar relation (with identical parameters) for the foreign country. This yields

$$m(t) - m^*(t) = p(t) - p^*(t) + \phi[y(t) - y^*(t)] - \Psi[I(t) - I^*(t)] \tag{11.20}$$

Sinning against facts 12 and 11 for the sake of the presentation, invoke PPP

$$s(t) = p(t) - p^*(t) \tag{11.21}$$

and uncovered interest rate parity

$$I(t) - I^*(t) = E_t[s(t+1)] - s(t) \tag{11.22}$$

Solve for the exchange rate from equations (11.20)–(11.22):

$$s(t) = \frac{\Psi}{1+\Psi} E_t[s(t+1)] + \frac{1}{1+\Psi}\{m(t) - m^*(t) - \phi[y(t) - y^*(t)]\} \tag{11.23}$$

For clarity of exposition, we restate this equation as

$$s(t) = \lambda E_t[s(t+1)] + x(t) \qquad 0 < \lambda < 1 \tag{11.24}$$

Through recursive forward substitution the particular (no bubble) solution to equation (11.24) reads

$$s(t) = \sum_{i=0}^{\infty} \lambda^i E_t[x(t+i)] \tag{11.25}$$

If we are willing to make the assumption that the fundamentals' process $\{x(t)\}$ is a martingale, then the no-bubbles forward solution to equation (11.24) implies the martingale model (11.14) and (11.15). Thus the fundamentalist view is not contradictory to the no-arbitrage unit root property. The reason is that rational expectations rule out arbitrage possibilities in the forward-looking model (11.16). Crucial for this result is that the fundamentals are a martingale. This may be more or less plausible for the high frequency returns. Typically the fundamentals, like income, display a high persistence and cannot be observed as frequently as the returns. The no-change view of the fundamentals may therefore not be a bad assumption. (The fundamentals which are regularly observed, such as the interest rates, usually display the martingale property as well.) This would agree with fact 16 and the tests conducted by Meese and Rogoff (1983). When Meese and Rogoff first published their results (see table 11.6 above) these met with incredulity, and many researchers have since tried to beat the martingale model, without much success. Nowadays the nature of the forward solution to equation (11.16) is better understood.

3.1.3 Is the foreign exchange market efficient?

After the demise of the structural models, economists turned to the theory of finance and embarked on large-scale testing of the (weak-form) efficient market hypothesis for the foreign exchange market. The absence of fundamentals on the right-hand side of equation (11.14) does not necessarily imply that the foreign exchange market is efficient. As a simple counterexample, consider the stationary process which is open to arbitrage:

$$s(t+1) = \beta s(t) + \varepsilon(t+1) \qquad |\beta| < 1 \tag{11.26}$$

The test of market efficiency then reduces to a test for the unit root $\beta = 1$. While estimation of the two simple alternatives (11.14) and (11.26) can proceed by ordinary least squares, testing for $H_0: \beta = 1$ against $H_1: |\beta| < 1$ is not so simple. The reason is that, if the process $\{s(t)\}$ in (11.14) has been initiated in the indefinite past, then $\text{var}[s(t)] = \infty$ (even if $\text{var}[\varepsilon(t)]$ is bounded and nonzero). This invalidates the asymptotic normality of $\hat{\beta}$ which obtains if $|\beta| < 1$, and hence impairs the conventional t test. Nevertheless, White (1958) obtained the limiting distribution of $\hat{\beta} - \beta$ appropriately normalized for the cases $\beta = 1$ and $\beta > 1$. On the basis of this Dickey and Fuller constructed the critical values for the t test $(\hat{\beta} - 1)/\hat{s}_\beta$ (see Fuller, 1976, table 8.5.2). For example, for the one-sided test of H_0 against H_1 with a hundred observations the critical value is -1.95 at the 5 percent significance level (the critical value of the usual t test is -1.65). In conducting this test different critical values apply if a constant or time trend is included in the regressions. The test can also be used when the innovations $\varepsilon(t)$ are fat tailed (the critical values differ slightly) (recall table 11.2) or when some serial correlation exists (the augmented Dickey–Fuller procedure).

An awkward property of the above test procedure is the critical difference between the distribution of the t statistic as to whether $\beta < 1$ or $\beta = 1$. To overcome this problem Schotman and van Dijk (1991) proposed using a Bayesian approach which avoids the discontinuity. The discontinuity also disappears if we drop the crucial assumption that the process $\{s(t)\}$ was initiated in the indefinite past. If the process has been initiated at some point $t - k$, k finite, e.g. the time of the breakdown of the Bretton Woods system say, then $s(t)$ has a proper distribution under H_0 and H_1. The question thus arises which assumption provides the better approximation to reality.

To investigate this question further, extend equation (11.26) by adding moving-average (MA) terms. Recently this extension has received considerable attention (e.g. see Christiano and Eichenbaum, 1990) because it points to a methodological problem with the unit root testing procedures. The presence of MA terms raises the possibility of common factors, which means that the classes of unit root and stationary processes are not meaningfully distinct in finite samples. The argument is fully developed by Blough (1989, 1990) and Cochrane (1991a), but we proceed with the simple example of Stock (1990).

Consider the following autoregressive (AR) integrated moving-average model:

$$s(t) - \beta s(t-1) = \varepsilon(t) - \alpha \varepsilon(t-1) \tag{11.27}$$

where the $\varepsilon(t)$ are IID. Setting $\beta = \alpha = 0$ yields the stationary model

$$s(t) = \varepsilon(t) \qquad (11.28)$$

Changing β to $0 < \beta < 1$ gives the stationary model of equation (11.26). But if we set $\beta = 1$ this produces the nonstationary random walk model of equation (11.14). So far, so good. Now introduce α, $0 < \alpha < 1$, and we get the nonstationary model

$$\Delta s(t) = \varepsilon(t) - \alpha\varepsilon(t-1) \qquad (11.29)$$

However, if we choose $\beta = \alpha = 1$, then (11.29) becomes the stationary model

$$\Delta s(t) = \Delta \varepsilon(t) \qquad (11.30)$$

This is just the first differenced version of (11.28) in which the unit roots of the AR and MA parts cancel (the common factor).

Note that in equation (11.26) there is a range of β for which $s(t)$ will be close to the $s(t)$ from (11.14) assuming that both processes have been initiated at some date finitely far back in the past. Conversely, there is a range of α for which $\Delta s(t)$ in (11.29) will be close to $\Delta s(t)$ generated by (11.30). This can be used to show that in finite samples any unit root process can be arbitrarily well approximated by stationary processes, and any stationary process can be arbitrarily well approximated by unit root processes. This result carries over to (continuous) statistics which are based on the data that are generated by these processes. Thus, according to Blough (1990): "There are stationary processes under which statistics have distributions approximating those under a random walk, and there are unit root processes under which statistics have distributions approximating those under white noise." See also Campbell and Perron (1991) and the ensuing discussion. This implies that in finite samples any test of the null hypothesis of a unit root with size ϕ can have power no greater than ϕ against any stationary alternative and vice versa.[9] The implication of this result is not that persistence cannot be detected, or is unimportant, but only that it is not useful with finitely many observations to distinguish between the perfect arbitrage equation (11.14) and the case of almost perfect arbitrage with β slightly less than 1.

Empirically conventional or Dickey–Fuller critical values usually do not reject the null of a unit root. Hence there is ample evidence of a high persistence in $s(t)$. The only thing we cannot say is whether β is exactly 1 or slightly less than 1. A value of β slightly below 1 does not necessarily invalidate the efficient market hypothesis either, because the opportunities for arbitrage may still be too small to be profitable (given transactions costs, available funds etc.). Values above 1 lead to explosive processes, but the data do not show any indication for this. (Even if β were just slightly larger than 1, this would rapidly show up in the data (see note 10 below).)

There have been other univariate tests of market efficiency, especially geared towards the risk premium. Among these are the popular variance bounds tests and the Euler equation tests. Both reduce to tests of particular discount rate models, and their evidence is equivalent to return forecasting regressions like those above (see Cochrane, 1991b). Both models are rejected by the data, but this does not imply market inefficiency – only a rejection of the particular model that is used to test for market efficiency. Thus more elaborate modeling of, for example, risk aversion may yield models which are not rejected by the data.

3.1.4   Cointegration and market efficiency

Apart from univariate tests of efficiency, one can extend the information set to the history of related prices such as spot prices on other currencies and test for efficiency in a multivariate setting. If individual spot rates contain a unit root, i.e. adhere to (11.14) and (11.15), so that efficiency cannot be rejected, a linear combination of the different rates may be stationary. In this case the variables are said to be cointegrated. By way of example, recall the triangular arbitrage condition (fact 2) which states that the difference between two different dollar spot rates approximately yields the cross rate: $s_1(t) - s_2(t) \approx s_3(t)$. Thus there exists a linear dependence between these three rates and hence they are cointegrated. How is this compatible with efficiency of the foreign exchange market? Note that for three currencies there are only two relative prices, i.e. there can be only two independent markets. Hence the cointegrating relation induced by triangular arbitrage does not contradict efficiency. Thus in a multivariate setting, to be consistent with efficiency, cointegration should be present if the prices relate to the same assets, while there should be no cointegration if the prices relate to different assets (see Granger (1986) who originally developed this idea).

Because the concept of cointegration is so important for the study of market efficiency, we shall investigate the issue further for the relation between spot and forward rates. Recall the unit root process (11.14), with $\varepsilon(t)$ stationary. Thus $s(t)$ is nonstationary,[10] while the linear combination $s(t + 1) - s(t)$ is stationary. Now replace $s(t)$ with the forward rate which is known to be nonstationary as well. Then $s(t)$ and $f(t)$ are said to cointegrate if $s(t) - \beta f(t)$ is stationary for some value of β. The idea is that while individual variables may wander off, arbitrage keeps the two variables close to each other, i.e. both variables remain close to the long-run equilibrium relation $s = \beta f$.

To formalize these ideas, we sin again and consider the system

$$s(t + 1) - s(t) = f(t) - s(t) + \theta(t + 1)$$

$$f(t + 1) = s(t + 1) + \mu(t + 1) \tag{11.31}$$

where $\theta(t + 1)$ and $\mu(t + 1)$ are iid random variables. The second equation of the system is the covered interest parity condition (11.5), i.e. $\mu(t)$ is the interest differential.[11] Taking expectations at time t of the first equation variables and using the second equation yields the uncovered interest rate parity equation (11.10). Both $s(t)$ and $f(t)$ are clearly nonstationary. Rewrite (11.31) into first differences using the differences operator $\Delta x(t) = x(t) - x(t - 1)$ as far as possible:

$$\Delta s(t + 1) = [f(t) - s(t)] + \theta(t + 1)$$

$$\Delta f(t + 1) = \theta(t + 1) + \mu(t + 1) \tag{11.32}$$

Note that in the first equation we are left with an expression in levels $f(t) - s(t)$, which is the cointegrating long-run equilibrium relation between $s(t)$ and $f(t)$. The stationarity of $f(t) - s(t)$ directly follows from the bottom equation in (11.31) by moving $s(t + 1)$ to the left-hand side, i.e. $f(t + 1) - s(t + 1) = \mu(t + 1)$ which is stationary by assumption. Also note that all other random variables in the system (11.32) are stationary as well. The presence of $f(t) - s(t)$ in (11.32) means that current deviations from the equilibrium relation $s = f$ are corrected for by future opposite movements. For example, if $s(t) > f(t)$, then subtracting the second equation from the first equation (11.32) and taking expectations gives $E[\Delta s(t + 1) - \Delta f(t + 1)] < 0$. For this reason (11.32) is often referred to as the error correction mechanism. In fact, if some variables are cointegrated, there always exists an error correction representation (see Engle and Granger, 1987). Also note that this implies some kind of predictability. Even though $\Delta f(t + 1)$ is purely random, knowledge of the current levels $s(t)$ and $f(t)$ does help to predict $\Delta s(t + 1)$, because $E[\Delta s(t + 1)|s(t), f(t)] = f(t) - s(t)$. But, recalling fact 5, the predictability will not be very high.

The first equation of (11.32) has often been tested in regression analysis. However, almost always one has to reject the null hypothesis of a unitary coefficient for the error correction term. Most US dollar exchange rates even yield significantly negative coefficients. An extensive literature has developed (see for example Fama, 1984; Baillie and McMahon, 1989; Froot and Thaler, 1990). The book by Hodrick (1987) is entirely devoted to this topic and discusses several reasons for the negativity of $\hat{b}$, but to date the puzzle has not been resolved.

The error correction system contains a warning against a popular device in applied work. If the variables in a vector autoregression (VAR) are found to be nonstationary, then it is common practice to estimate the VAR in first differences. Note, however, that this produces inconsistent estimates if some of the variables are cointegrated, because omitting the levels term $f(t) - s(t)$ in (11.32) leads to the omitted variables problem. To illustrate how severe this problem can be, suppose one is interested in estimating the cointegrating coefficient β by regressing s on f. Assume (θ, μ) are iid uncorrelated bivariate standard normal. Then a regression in levels yields (using $\Sigma f^2/n \rightarrow n(n-1)/2n$)

$$\hat{\beta} = \frac{\Sigma sf}{\Sigma f^2} = \frac{\Sigma (f + \theta)f}{\Sigma f^2} \xrightarrow{p} \frac{(n-1)/2 + 1}{(n-1)/2} \rightarrow 1$$

where superscript p denotes convergence in probability.

The regression in first differences produces

$$\hat{\beta} = \frac{\Sigma \Delta s \Delta f}{\Sigma \Delta f^2} = \frac{\Sigma [\mu(-1) + \theta](\mu + \theta)}{\Sigma (\mu + \theta)^2} \xrightarrow{p} \frac{\Sigma \theta^2/n}{\Sigma \theta^2/n + \Sigma \mu^2/n} \xrightarrow{p} \frac{1}{2}$$

which is clearly downward biased. But note that if var $\mu <$ var θ the bias will be smaller. This observation is important because of fact 5. An example of the case where omitting the error correction term proved to be important is the issue of German dominance. Several researchers have estimated VARs in first differences of European interest rates but found no influence of German interest rates on the other rates. This effect was hypothesized to exist by several analysts of the EMS. However, Kirchgässner and Wolters (1992) recently showed that if error correction terms are included in the regressions the German dominance hypothesis cannot be rejected. Omitting these terms seriously biased the previous estimates.

Stock and Watson (1988) and Sims et al. (1990) provide further details. Johansen (1991) develops a convenient testing procedure for the number of cointegrating relations. An accessible account of estimation procedures in the case of cointegration is given by Lütkepohl (1991), and Campbell and Perron (1991) provide further intuition. A final word of caution concerning testing for cointegration is needed. Because, just as in the univariate case, in finite samples the multivariate setting does not allow one to distinguish between stationary and unit root relations, the absence or presence of cointegrating relations only carries qualitative information about the presence or absence of persistence.

3.2 The unconditional distribution function and extreme value theory

There are at least three reasons for investigating the properties of the unconditional distribution of the returns on speculative investments.

First, the shape of the unconditional distribution places restrictions on the form of the conditional distribution of $\varepsilon(t)$ given $\varepsilon(t-1), \ldots, \varepsilon(t-n)$. These properties can often be ascertained in a more robust manner, for example due to the central limit law, than the peculiarities of the conditional distribution. Second, an important job of the financial analyst is to provide appropriate risk assessments of longer term risky projects. For this purpose statistics based on the unconditional distribution are useful. Third, returns are often employed in statistical procedures such as regression analysis. The unconditional distribution gives a clue about the appropriate minimization criterion and uses of certain test statistics. The importance of these arguments derives from the characteristic fatness of the tails of the empirical distribution of returns (recall fact 7). The tails may be so thick that the second moment is not defined, thus impairing the appropriateness of say the ordinary least squares regression procedure.

The fat tail property serves as an important organizing principle. At first the French mathematician Bachelier (1900) ventured the suggestion that speculative prices follow a Brownian motion (i.e. a random walk in continuous time with normally distributed innovations). But the normality assumption clearly conflicts with the stylized facts. Therefore Mandelbrot (1963a, b) proposed using the other members of the class of stable distributions which, besides being fat tailed, also have the desirable invariance under addition property (recall facts 2 and 9) but fail to have a finite second moment. Less fat-tailed distributions, like the Student t (see Blattberg and Gonedes, 1974) and Engle's (1982) ARCH distributed innovations (see below) have been proposed because these models exhibit a finite variance. Other models exhibiting a higher than normal kurtosis, such as the discrete mixtures of normals studied by Kon (1984), the mixed diffusion jump process advanced by Press (1967) and the power exponential or GED discussed in Baillie and McMahon (1989), Hsieh (1989), and Nelson (1991) have been applied as well. Boothe and Glassman (1987) provide a comprehensive survey.

While these models in one way or another capture the higher than normal kurtosis, there is considerable controversy over the precise amount of probability mass in the tails of the distribution, e.g. whether or not the second moment is finite. Thus one would like to select the best model among these alternatives. Unfortunately, a comparison between the competing hypotheses is hampered by the fact that some of the models are non-nested (due, for example, to an infinite variance). Therefore conventional model selection criteria like the likelihood ratio or Cox tests cannot be used (see Loretan and Phillips, 1992). Moreover, the concept of fat tails used in this literature is not made precise. To overcome these problems, recent advances in the area of extreme value analysis can be usefully exploited, as this analysis focuses explicitly on the tail behavior of the distribution. To see how, consider a stationary sequence $X_1, X_2, \ldots, X_n$ of iid random variables with a common distribution function F. Suppose one is interested in the probability that the maximum

$$M_n = \max(X_1, X_2, \ldots, X_n) \tag{11.33}$$

of the first n random variables is below a certain level x. This probability is given by

$$P(M_n \le x) = F^n(x) \tag{11.34}$$

Extreme value theory studies the limiting distribution of the order statistic M_n scaled by two normalizing constants a_n and b_n:

$$P(M_n - b_n \le a_n x) \xrightarrow{\mathrm{d}} G(x) \tag{11.35}$$

where $G(x)$ is a so-called extreme value distribution and superscript d indicates convergence in distribution. If $1 - F(x)$ is regularly varying at infinity (recall equation (11.6)), choosing $b_n = 0$ and $a_n = F^{-1}(1 - 1/n)$ we have

$$G(x) = \exp(-x^{-\alpha}) \qquad \alpha > 0 \tag{11.36}$$

where α is the tail index. Results for the case when the X_i are dependent are given in Leadbetter et al. (1983, ch. 3) and for example de Haan et al. (1989) for the particular case of ARCH innovations. The tail index is a good indicator of the tail fatness as it is related to the number of moments that exist. In fact a necessary condition for the limit in equations (11.35) and (11.36) is that $F(x) < 1$ for all x and

$$\int_1^\infty x^\beta \, \mathrm{d}F(x) \tag{11.37}$$

is finite for all $\beta < \alpha$ and infinite for $\beta > \alpha$. This condition provides the following intuition concerning the index of regular variation. Loosely speaking the largest integer $n < \alpha$ corresponds to the number of (integer) moments that exist. If the βth moment exists, then (11.37) must certainly be integrable, while if (11.37) is not integrable, then the βth moment does not exist. What about distributions $F(x)$, like the normal, for which all moments do exist? The exponential decline of the tails of a distribution like the normal means that (11.37) is always integrable, and hence the limit (11.36) does not apply (recall that $\exp(x)$ can be expanded as $\Sigma \, x^j/j!$). For these types of distributions the limit law takes a different form:

$$G(x) = \exp[-\exp(-x)] \tag{11.38}$$

It is easily shown by checking the regular variation property (11.6) that the Student t and the heavy-tailed stable model are in the domain of attraction of $G(x)$ in (11.36).[12] For these two particular models the α values correspond to the degrees of freedom and the characteristic exponent respectively. The ARCH model takes more effort as one has to use appropriate mixing conditions (see de Haan et al., 1989). Somewhat surprisingly, given the excess kurtosis, none of the other models discussed above are in the domain of attraction of $G(x)$ because of their exponentially declining tails, but they do belong to the domain of attraction of the thin-tailed extremal limit law (11.38). Thus there is a sharp difference between the two types of distributions: one class is thin tailed and the other has fat tails. Typically, exchange rate returns belong to the latter class.

The advantage of the extreme value approach is that all fat-tailed models are nested with respect to their tail index into one model. The idea is then to estimate this index directly and use the asymptotic confidence interval to discriminate between the competing hypotheses. The tail index, given a number of observations X_i, can be estimated by maximum likelihood (see Smith, 1987) or by a moment estimator. We shall present the latter procedure because it does not require the assumption that the highest observations exactly follow the law in (11.36) and therefore is more efficient. We present the intuitive derivation developed by de Haan (1990). Assume that $X_1, \ldots, X_n$ is a sample of independent realizations from a distribution $F(x)$ with a regularly varying tail. Thus

$$\lim_{t \to \infty} \frac{1 - F(tx)}{1 - F(t)} = x^{-\alpha} \qquad \alpha > 0 \tag{11.6}$$

Suppose the density $f(x)$ exists. Through integration by parts we have the following equivalence:

$$\int_1^\infty \frac{1 - F(tu)}{u} \, du = \log u \left[1 - F(tu)\right] \Big|_1^\infty + \int_1^\infty \log u \, f(tu)t \, du$$

$$= \int_1^\infty \left[\log(tu) - \log t\right] f(tu)t \, du$$

$$= \int_t^\infty (\log x - \log t) f(x) \, dx \tag{11.39}$$

Combine (11.6) and (11.39) and apply the Lebesgue convergence theorem (interchanging the limit of the integral with the integral of the limit):

$$\frac{\int_t^\infty (\log x - \log t) f(x) \, dx}{1 - F(t)} = \int_1^\infty \frac{1 - F(tu)}{1 - F(t)} \frac{du}{u} \to \int_1^\infty u^{-\alpha} \frac{du}{u} = \frac{1}{\alpha} \tag{11.40}$$

Let $X_{(n)} \geq X_{(n-1)} \geq \cdots \geq X_{(1)}$ denote the ascending order statistics from the sample $X_1, \ldots, X_n$. The idea is now to replace the left-hand expression in (11.40) by its sample analog in order to estimate the inverse tail index $\gamma = 1/\alpha$. Let $F_n(.)$ denote the empirical distribution function. Thus, for some m take $t = X_{(n-m)}$ and hence

$$\hat{\gamma} = \frac{1}{\alpha} = \frac{\int_{X_{(n-m)}}^{\infty} (\log x - \log X_{(n-m)}) \, dF_n(x)}{1 - F_n(X_{(n-m)})}$$

$$= \frac{\left(\sum_{i=0}^{m-1} \log X_{(n-i)} - m \log X_{(n-m)}\right) 1/n}{1 - (n-m)/n}$$

so that

$$\hat{\gamma} = \frac{1}{m} \sum_{i=0}^{m-1} \frac{\log X_{(n-i)}}{X_{(n-m)}} \qquad (11.41)$$

is the proposed estimator. This estimator was first developed by Hill (1975). Mason (1982) shows that $\hat{\gamma}$ is a consistent estimator if $m \to \infty$ and $m/n \to 0$. Hall (1982) and Goldie and Smith (1987) have shown that if m increases suitably rapidly and if the X_i are iid, then asymptotically

$$(\hat{\gamma} - \gamma) m^{1/2} \sim N(0, \gamma^2) \qquad (11.42)$$

For an application of this methodology to foreign exchange rates see Koedijk et al. (1990) and Hols and de Vries (1991). Akgiray et al. (1988) employ the maximum likelihood method to estimate γ for black market exchange rate returns. Other uses of extremal analysis can be made as well, e.g. the analysis of stock market crashes in Jansen and de Vries (1991). Loretan and Phillips (1992) employ the Hill estimator (11.41) to pre-test for the existence of the fourth moment in several return series before applying a standard or nonstandard sample split prediction test. The typical values of the tail index found in these studies is regime dependent. For the exchange rates which are more or less freely floating, the tail index hovers around 3 or 4, while intra-EMS rates and other rates which involve some kind of fixity settle around 2, so that the variance may just exist or not exist.

Extremal value analysis also proves a theoretical backing for fact 9. Let X_i be an iid sequence with common distribution function $F(x)$. If $1 - F(x)$ varies regularly at infinity, i.e. satisfies (11.6) with tail index α, then $\max(X_1 + X_2, \ldots, X_{n-1} + X_n)$, or the maximum of any finite convolution, follows the limit law (11.36) (see Feller, 1971, ch. VIII.8). Even though one often finds that the first two unconditional moments of the returns do exist, and hence that the central limit law applies, it does not follow that the tails of the (rescaled) summands become normal. Mandelbrot (1963a, b) based his choice for the (non-normal) sum stable distributions on the preservation of the shape of the empirical distributions under addition. This proved to be too strong a condition on the moments (infinite variance), but tail additivity seems to hold.

3.3   The conditional distribution function

For forecasting purposes the conditional distribution of the dependent variable is of paramount interest, rather than the unconditional distribution. As Bollerslev and Engle (1986) put it: "the use of the conditional mean explains the success of an economic time series model in forecasting." In the field of speculative price movements most research focuses on the first two conditional moments. This follows from the fact that, in any theoretical economic analysis of risk, the mean return and the variance, if defined, are the two parameters of central interest. The variance signifies the risk and the mean indicates the expected return on investment.

If the first two unconditional moments of the innovation in the returns $\varepsilon(t)$ equation (11.1) exist, then the time series analysis may be greatly facilitated by the Wold decomposition.

THEOREM 2 (WOLD)   Let $\{\varepsilon(t)\}$ be a covariance stationary process with $E[\varepsilon(t)] = 0$ and no deterministic components.[13] Then $\varepsilon(t)$ can be written as

$$\varepsilon(t) = \sum_{j=0}^{\infty} \gamma_j x(t-j) \qquad (11.43)$$

where $\gamma_0 = 1$, $\sum_{j=0}^{\infty} \gamma_j^2 < \infty$, $E[x(t)] = 0$, and

$$E[x(t)^2] \geq 0 \qquad E[x(t)\,x(t-j)] = 0 \qquad \text{for } j \neq 0$$

For a lucid proof, see Sargent (1979, p. 257). The usefulness of this decomposition is that it states that any covariance stationary process can be expressed as an infinite MA process. This representation can often be well approximated through some finite ARMA process – hence the popularity of ARMA and VARMA modeling. But one has to keep in mind that this only provides an approximation, the quality of which is restricted by possible nonlinearities in the data-generating mechanism and the finiteness of the available data set.

In the univariate context, and given the Wold decomposition theorem, not surprisingly research at first focused on the autocorrelation pattern of the returns (for example Fama, 1965). Little or no autocorrelation was found even in the highest frequency data (minute to minute or day to day). This was interpreted as a confirmation of market efficiency. To match these empirical observations with theoretical results we ask the question why the Wold decomposition is of no avail for the study of efficient markets. Suppose $\{s(t)\}$ is a martingale and hence satisfies the no-arbitrage condition, or alternatively we say that $\{\varepsilon(t)\}$ is a fair game. From (11.43) we may write (recall that $\gamma_0 = 1$)

$$x(t) = \sum_0^\infty \gamma_j x(t-j) - \sum_1^\infty \gamma_j x(t-j)$$

$$= \varepsilon(t) - E_{t-1}(\varepsilon_t)$$

$$= \varepsilon(t)$$

as $E_{t-k}[\varepsilon(t)] = 0$ for any $k \geq 1$ if $\{s(t)\}$ is a martingale. Moreover, this shows that

$$\gamma_k x(t-k) = \sum_k^\infty \gamma_j x(t-j) - \sum_{k+1}^\infty \gamma_j x(t-j)$$

$$= E_{t-k}(\varepsilon_t) - E_{t-k-1}(\varepsilon_t)$$

$$= 0$$

for any $k \geq 1$. But the decomposition is rather trivial as $\varepsilon(t) = x(t)$. Hence the Wold decomposition is of no use for the study of martingales.[14] Therefore $\gamma_0 = 1$, $\gamma_k = 0$ for $k \geq 1$ is the unique Wold decomposition of the ARCH process for example.

Now recall fact 10 on volatility clusters. This indicates that although univariate speculative price series are typically not autocorrelated in the mean, they are nevertheless characterized by dependence in the second moment. Mandelbrot (1963b) had already noticed that there are clusters of high and low volatility in the return data. Since then many authors registered the presence of a time-varying volatility in different kinds of financial data. Not until the ARCH model introduced by Engle (1982) and the GARCH extension developed by Bollerslev (1986) have economists come to grips with this phenomenon. Traditionally, heteroskedasticity was approached by introducing an exogenous variable to explain the changing variance. The innovation introduced by Engle was not to try to explain the changing variance by an exogenous source, but to describe it on the basis of the own history of the series (which is in the same spirit as the ARMA methodology for modeling the mean).

The ARCH(1) model for the exchange rate specification (11.14) reads

$$s(t) = s(t-1) + \varepsilon(t)$$

$$\varepsilon(t) = X(t)H(t)^{1/2}$$

$$H(t) = \omega + \lambda\varepsilon(t-1)^2 \qquad 0 < \lambda < 1 \tag{11.44}$$

$$X(t) \text{ iid } N(0, 1)$$

Here the conditional distribution of $s(t)$, given $\varepsilon(t-1)$ and $s(t-1)$, is normal with mean $s(t-1)$ and variance $H(t)$. The conditional variance $H(t)$ is a function of the lagged squared innovations. This induces the clusters of high and low variance. To see this, square the innovation function in equation (11.44) and substitute the variance function in this equation:

$$\varepsilon(t)^2 = \omega X(t)^2 + \lambda X(t)^2 \varepsilon(t-1)^2 \tag{11.45}$$

Hence $E[\varepsilon(t)^2 \mid \varepsilon(t-1)^2] = \omega + \lambda\varepsilon(t-1)^2$, and similarly for the conditional variance as $E[\varepsilon(t) \mid \varepsilon(t-1)] = E[X(t)]E\{[\omega + \lambda\varepsilon(t-1)^2]^{1/2}\} = 0$ by the independence of the $X(t)$. The latter argument shows that $\{s(t)\}$ is still a martingale, but not a random walk because the $\varepsilon(t)$ are not iid. As we saw above the martingale property is the crucial no-arbitrage condition for market efficiency, but also renders the Wold decomposition rather useless. Here the ARMA methodology is transferred to modeling the second moment instead of the first moment.

The ARCH scheme also induces the fat tail property on the unconditional distribution of the returns. To see this, recall equation (11.45) which is in fact a first-order stochastic difference equation. From a result in Kesten (1973) it is known that this equation has a solution

$$\varepsilon(t)^2 \overset{d}{\to} \sum_{j=0}^{\infty} \omega X(t-j)^2 \prod_{i=0}^{j-1} \lambda X(t-i)^2 \tag{11.46}$$

which is unique in distribution provided that

$$E[(\lambda X^2)^{\alpha/2}] = 1 \tag{11.47}$$

for some $\alpha > 0$. Given the normality of X, we can solve for α if $0 < \lambda < 1$ by using

$$\Gamma\left(\frac{\alpha}{2} + \frac{1}{2}\right) = \pi^{1/2}(2\lambda)^{-\alpha/2} \tag{11.48}$$

As it turns out the law of $\varepsilon(t)$ in (11.46) is in the domain of attraction of $G(x)$ in equation (11.36) (see de Haan et al., 1989), with tail index

α as computed in (11.48). Thus exactly α moments are finite.[15] Hence the unconditional distribution of $s(t) - s(t - 1)$ is fat tailed.

Specifications like (11.44) have become extremely popular in the area of international finance. The reason is that it conveniently captures both the clustering phenomenon and the fat tail property. It can be used to explain, for example, the existence of a time-varying risk premium (see Baillie and Bollerslev (1990), but also see Frankel and Meese (1987) who note that the variation in the variance is generally still too small to explain the variability of the risk premium). Some straight-forward extensions of the scheme (11.44) are the use of non-normal innovations but fat-tailed distributed $X(t)$. Hence, both the conditional and the unconditional distributions of the returns become fat tailed.[16] There is evidence that this yields a better description of the returns. Bollerslev (1986) suggested adding lagged $H(t)$ terms to the right-hand side of the variance function, e.g.

$$H(t) = \omega + \lambda \varepsilon(t - 1)^2 + \beta H(t - 1) \qquad (11.49)$$

This model can be considered the variance analog of the ARMA model and was dubbed GARCH (generalized ARCH).[17] Of course more than one lag can be considered. In empirical studies one often encounters $\lambda + \beta$ close to 1 (cf. table 11.5). Hence the fourth moment may not exist and one has to exercise care in reporting test statistics that require a finite fourth moment. This is the case in, for example, testing procedures for serial correlation in the presence of ARCH (see Diebold, 1988, p. 26). (Because one estimates parameters of the variance function, in testing one needs the "variance of the variance" for the central limit law to be applicable.) Nelson (1991) considers an extension whereby the logarithm of $H(t)$ is a function of past $X(t)$ which alleviates some of the problems with the ARCH specification (see Hsieh (1989) for an application). De Vries (1991) also uses $X(t)$ rather than $\varepsilon(t)$ in the variance equation, but assumes that $X(t)$ is non-normal stable distributed. This induces the desirable additivity property in the ARCH model. Drost and Nijman (1993) investigate the same issue by weakening the GARCH equation (11.49) to linear least squares projections of $\varepsilon(t)^2$ on $\varepsilon(t - 1)^2$, $\varepsilon(t - 2)^2$ etc. and show that this class of ARCH models is closed under addition.

The success of the ARCH model is that it cogently captures the volatility clusters (fact 10) and exhibits the fat tail phenomenon (fact 7) and is still compatible with the martingale (no-arbitrage) structure of efficient market prices. Just like the ARMA methodology, the ARCH model does not use exogenous or fundamentals variables. This is its strength because of fact 16. At the same time it is the weakness of the ARCH model. Being an economist one would like to know how these clusters come about. To date we must admit that we have little or no idea what causes the ARCH feature in the returns. There are some suggestions in the literature. For example Obstfeld (1987) has suggested that the clusters arise from periodic changes in policy. To make this argument recall equations (11.23)–(11.25) and suppose that without intervention $y(t) - y^*(t)$ is an iid random variable, while $m(t) - m^*(t)$ follows a random walk:

$$m(t+1) - m^*(t+1) = m(t) - m^*(t) + \mu(t) \qquad (11.50)$$

and $\mu(t)$ is iid. It follows that

$$s(t) = m(t) - m^*(t) - \frac{\phi}{1 + \Psi}[y(t) - y^*(t)] \qquad (11.51)$$

One policy rule is not to intervene in the money market. Another policy rule consists of income targeting:

$$m(t+1) - m^*(t+1) = m(t) - m^*(t) + [y(t) - y^*(t)] + \mu(t) \quad (11.52)$$

The solution for $s(t)$ under this alternative policy rule remains as in (11.51). But $\mathrm{var}[s(t+1)|s(t)]$ will be different under the two rules, owing to the extra random variable on the right-hand side of (11.52) vis-à-vis (11.50). Thus if there are clusters in the usage of certain policy variables, this could explain the ARCH feature of the returns. To date, however, there is little evidence for this (see for example Hodrick's (1989) perceptive study). Another suggestion is that the clustering may come from noise traders (see De Long et al., 1990). Frankel and Meese (1987) present some evidence based on survey data. But so far explaining ARCH is one of the more important open questions.

Another question is whether the volatility clusters generated by the ARCH process are compatible with market efficiency. Without some model of market equilibrium in the background this question is hard to address. We showed that the ARCH model (11.44) induces the martingale property on $\{s(t)\}$ and hence there is no room for arbitrage. Now note that $\mathrm{var}[s(t+1)|s(t)] = \omega + \lambda[s(t) - s(t-1)]^2$. Define $y(t) = [s(t) - s(t-1)]^2$. It follows that $E[y(t+1)|y(t)] = \omega + \lambda y(t)$, which shows that $y(t)$ cannot be a martingale. Thus if $\mathrm{var}[s(t+1)|s(t)]$ is part of the utility function, the scheme $\omega + \lambda y(t)$ may leave scope for arbitrage. The static (conditional) CAPM model with the ARCH effect of Bollerslev et al. (1988) seems inadequate to deal with this issue. Dynamic equilibrium asset pricing models with risk-averse agents do exist. (See LeRoy, 1973; Lucas, 1978; Abel, 1988.) Ohlson (1977) has shown that risk aversion may imply that the mean returns are no longer a martingale, but not necessarily so. The implications for the (conditional) variance have not been scrutinized extensively.

Thus an interesting open question is whether empirically ARCH constitutes a refutation of market efficiency or is compatible with efficiency.

Notes

This chapter is based on lecture notes for the MA class in Advanced International Monetary Economics at the Katholieke Universiteit Leuven. I am grateful to Filip Abraham, Hans Dewachter, Jürgen von Hagen, Kees Koedijk, Luc Lauwers, Charles van Marrewijk, Theo Nijman, Rick van der Ploeg, Peter Schotman, Philip Stork, Guy Van Camp, and Jean-Marie Viaene who all gave valuable comments on an earlier version of the chapter. I would also like to thank the students who participated in the course, and the seminar participants at the Universiteit van Amsterdam. Eva Crabbé meticulously typed the entire chapter.

1   The return is often measured as the logarithmic difference of the level. For the relatively small day to day or week to week changes exhibited by most well-traded currencies, this yields a rather good approximation to the exact definition of a return. For example, for black market rates the logarithmic difference may not be appropriate.

2   A stochastic process $\{s(t)\}$, where $s(t)$ is a random variable and $t \in N$, is said to be stationary if for any positive integer k and any points $t_1, \ldots, t_m$ the joint distribution of $\{s(t_1), \ldots, s(t_m)\}$ is the same as the joint distribution of $\{s(t_1 + k), \ldots, s(t_m + k)\}$, i.e. the joint distribution is invariant under a time shift. A process $\{s(t)\}$ is weakly or covariance stationary if $\mathrm{cov}[s(m), s(k)]$ depends only on the time difference $|m - k|$.

3   We may want deliberately to avoid using the concept of variance because the fat tail property may imply that the second moment is not defined, while other measures of scale like the interquartile range always exist.

4   It has also been found that the volatility gets transmitted from one market to another market where the same exchange rate is quoted at different times. In this way uncertainty concerning money market announcements spreads around the world.

5   During the Israeli hyperinflation it became illegal to transact in dollars, but nevertheless the dollar functioned as a unit of account in, for example, housing contracts. In Mexico the dollar has functioned as a means of payment, and Panama has no currency of its own but uses the US dollar.

6   Note that if, for example, the $\varepsilon(t)$ are independent, $E[\varepsilon(t)] = 0$ and $E[\,|\varepsilon(t)|\,] < \infty$ for all t, it follows that the restriction is satisfied because $E[\,|s(t)|\,] \le E[\,|\varepsilon(1)|\,] + \cdots + E[\,|\varepsilon(t)|\,] < \infty$.

7   The random walk model, however, is useful for obtaining intuition about the implications of a unit root. If $\{s(t)\}$ is a random walk, then $s(t)$ returns to $s(0)$ infinitely often, but the expected waiting time for a return is infinite. The persistence of a random walk is also evident from the U-shaped distribution of sojourn times: the percentage of time α that $s(t) > 0$ is distributed as $2 \arcsin \alpha^{1/2}/\pi$. Another interesting feature is that while two independent random walks meet infinitely often with probability one, this probability is less than one for three or more random walks. The interested reader is advised to consult the lucid elementary treatment of Feller (1970).

8 Recall that $E[E(Y \mid X)] = \int\int y f_{y \mid x}(y \mid x) f_x(x) \; dy \; dx = \int\int y f_{y,x}(y, x) \; dy \; dx = E[Y]$.

9 Some caution should be exercised because the two cases α approaching 1 and β approaching 1 are not entirely symmetric. Sargan and Bhargava (1983) show that if $\alpha = 1$, $\hat{\alpha} = 1$ with asymptotic probability 0.65, and this result holds also in small samples with only somewhat smaller probabilities.

10 As $s(t + 1) = \Sigma_{i=0}^{\infty} \varepsilon(t + 1 - i)$, the innovations in the distant past contribute as much to position of $s(t + 1)$ as the more recent innovations. In explosive processes, e.g. $s(t + 1) = \lambda s(t) + \varepsilon(t + 1)$, $\lambda > 1$, the past is more important than the present.

11 Instead of the iid assumption, $\mu(t)$ may follow a stationary AR process.

12 We say that $F(x)$ is in the domain of attraction of $G(x)$ if the limit (11.35) applies.

13 That is, it contains no component which can be predicted arbitrarily well from past realizations through linear least squares projections. If such a component is present, it has to be added to equation (11.1).

14 I am grateful to Luc Lauwers for suggesting this presentation of the proof.

15 The relation between α, λ, the variance, and the fourth moment is as follows. If $\lambda < 1$, then $\alpha > 2$ and the variance is finite. If $\lambda < \sqrt{(1/3)}$, then $\alpha > 4$ and the fourth moment is finite.

16 If, for example, the Student t distribution with v degrees of freedom is used then $\lambda < 1$ is still sufficient for a finite variance, but $\lambda^2 < (v - 4)/(v - 6) < 1/3$ is required for the fourth moment to be finite.

17 The condition for a finite variance if $X(t)$ is normal or Student distributed becomes $\lambda + \beta < 1$.

References

Abel, A.B. (1988) "Stock prices under time-varying dividend risk: an exact solution in an infinite-horizon general equilibrium model," NBER Working Paper 2621, Cambridge, MA.

Akgiray, V., G.G. Booth, and B. Seifert (1988) "Distribution properties of Latin American black market exchange rates," *Journal of International Money and Finance* 7, 37–48.

Bachelier, L.J.B.A.V. (1900) *Théorie de la Spéculation*, Paris, Gauthier-Villars.

Baillie, R.T. and T. Bollerslev (1990) "A multivariate generalized ARCH approach to modeling risk premia in forward foreign exchange rate markets," *Journal of International Money and Finance* 9, 309–24.

—— and P.C. McMahon (1989) *The Foreign Exchange Market: Theory and Econometric Evidence*, Cambridge, Cambridge University Press.

Barro, R.J. (1972) "Inflationary finance and the welfare cost of inflation," *Journal of Political Economy* 80, 978–1001.

Blattberg, R.C. and N.J. Gonedes (1974) "A comparison of the Stable and Student distributions as statistical models for stock prices," *Journal of Business* 47, 244–80.

Blough, S.R. (1989) "The relationship between power and level for generic unit root tests in finite samples," Working Paper in Economics 232, Johns Hopkins

University.

—— (1990) "Unit roots, stationary, and persistence in finite sample macroeconometrics," Working Paper in Economics 241, Johns Hopkins University.

Bollerslev, T. (1986) "Generalized autoregressive conditional heteroskedasticity," *Journal of Econometrics* 31, 307–27.

——, and R.F. Engle (1986) "Modeling the persistence of conditional variances," *Econometric Review* 5, 1–50.

——, R.F. Engle and J.M. Woolridge (1988) "A capital asset pricing model with time-varying covariances," *Journal of Political Economy* 96, 116–31.

Boothe, P. and D. Glassman (1987) "The statistical distribution of exchange rates: empirical evidence and economic implications," *Journal of International Economics* 22, 297–320.

Campbell, J.Y. and P. Perron (1991) "Pitfalls and opportunities: what macroeconomists should know about unit roots," *NBER Macroeconomics Annual*, Cambridge, MA, National Bureau of Economics Research, pp. 141–201.

Christiano, L.J. and M. Eichenbaum (1990) "Unit roots in real GNP: do we know, and do we care?," *Carnegie-Rochester Conference Series on Public Policy* 32, 7–62.

Cochrane, J.H. (1991a) "A critique of the application of unit root tests," *Journal of Economic Dynamics and Control* 15, 275–84.

—— (1991b) "Volatility tests and efficient markets: a review essay," NBER Working Paper 3591, Cambridge, MA.

De Ceuster, M.J.K. (1992) "The relative effectiveness of efficiency criteria," PhD thesis, Universiteit van Antwerpen.

De Grauwe, P. (1989) *International Money, Postwar Trends and Theories*, Oxford, Oxford University Press.

—— and D. Decupere (1992) "Psychological barriers in the foreign exchange markets," *Journal of International and Comparative Economics* 1, 87–101.

De Long, J.B., A. Shleifer, L.H. Summers and R.J. Waldmann (1990) "Noise trader risk in financial markets," *Journal of Political Economy* 98, 703–38.

Diebold, F.X. (1988) *Empirical Modeling of Exchange Rate Dynamics*, Berlin, Springer.

Drost, F.C. and T.E. Nijman (1993) "Temporal aggregation of GARCH processes," *Econometrica* 61, 909–27.

Engle, R.F. (1982) "Autoregressive conditional heteroscedasticity with estimates of the variance of United Kingdom inflations," *Econometrica* 50, 987–1007.

—— and C.W.J. Granger (1987) "Co-integration and error correction, representation, estimation and testing," *Econometrica* 55, 251–76.

Fama, E.F. (1965) "The behaviour of stock market prices," *Journal of Business* 38, 34–105.

—— (1984) "Forward and spot exchange rates," *Journal of Monetary Economics* 14, 319–38.

Feller, W. (1970) *An Introduction to Probability Theory and its Applications*, vol. 1, New York, Wiley.

—— (1971) *An Introduction to Probability Theory and its Applications*, vol. 2, New York, Wiley.

Frankel, J.A. and R. Meese (1987) "Are exchange rates excessively variable?," in S. Fischer (ed.) *NBER Macroeconomics Annual*, Cambridge, MA, National Bureau of Economics Research, pp. 117–62.

Froot, K.A. and R.H. Thaler (1990) "Anomalies: foreign exchange," *Journal of Economic Perspectives* 4, 179–92.

Fuller, W. (1976) *Introduction to Statistical Time Series*, New York, Wiley.

Gielens, G. and C.G. de Vries (1990) "Speculative prices and stochastic processes," *Nieuw Archief voor Wiskunde* 8, 311–23.

Goldie, C.M. and R.C. Smith (1987) "Slow variation with remainder: theory and applications," *Quarterly Journal of Mathematics*, 2nd Series 38, 45–71.

Goldstein, M. and M. Kahn (1985) "Income and price effects in foreign trade," in R.W. Jones and P.B. Kenen (eds) *Handbook of International Economics*, vol. 2, Amsterdam, North-Holland, 1041–1106.

Goodhart, C.A.E. and L. Figliuoli (1991) "Every minute counts in financial markets," *Journal of International Money and Finance* 10, 23–52.

Granger, C.W.J. (1986) "Developments in the study of cointegrated economic variables," *Oxford Bulletin of Economics and Statistics* 48, 213–28.

Haan, L. de (1990) "Fighting the arch-enemy with mathematics," *Statistica Neerlandica* 44, 45–68.

——, S.I. Resnick, H. Rootzen, and C.G. de Vries (1989) "Extremal behaviour of solutions to a stochastic difference equation with applications to ARCH-processes," *Stochastic Processes and their Applications* 32, 213–24.

Hakkio, C.S. and M. Rush (1989) "Market efficiency and cointegration: an application to the sterling and Deutschemark exchange rates," *Journal of International Money and Finance* 8, 75–88.

Hall, P. (1982) "On some simple estimates of an exponent of regular variation," *Journal of the Royal Statistical Society, Series B* 44, 37–42.

Hansen, L.P. and R.J. Hodrick (1980) "Forward exchange rates as optimal predictors of future spot rates: an econometric analysis," *Journal of Political Economy* 88, 829–53.

Hill, B.M. (1975) "A simple general approach to inference about the tail of a distribution," *Annals of Statistics* 3, 1163–73.

Hodrick, R.J. (1987) *The Empirical Evidence on the Efficiency of Forward and Futures Foreign Exchange Markets*, Chur, Harwoord Academic.

——(1989) "Risk, uncertainty, and exchange rates," *Journal of Monetary Economics* 23, 433–59.

Hols, M.C.A.B. and C.G. de Vries (1991) "The limiting distribution of extremal exchange rate returns," *Journal of Applied Econometrics* 6, 287–302.

Hsieh, D.A. (1989) "Modeling heteroskedasticity in daily foreign exchange rates," *Journal of Business and Economics Statistics* 7, 307–17.

Jansen, D. and C.G. de Vries (1991) "On the frequency of large stock returns: putting booms and busts into perspective," *Review of Economics and Statistics* 73, 18–24.

Johansen, S. (1991) "Estimation and hypothesis testing of cointegration vectors in Gaussian vector autoregressive models," *Econometrica* 59, 1581–90.

Kesten, H. (1973) "Random difference equations and renewal theory for products of random matrices," *Acta Mathematica* 131, 207–48.

Kirchgässner, G. and J. Wolters (1992) "Does the DM dominate the Euromarket?," paper presented at the Conference on Financial Markets Econometrics, Mannheim, February.

Koedijk, K.G., M.M.A. Schafgans and C.G. de Vries (1990) "The tail index of exchange rate returns," *Journal of International Economics* 29, 93–108.

——, P. Stork and C.G. de Vries (1992) "Differences between foreign exchange rate regimes: the view from the tails," *Journal of International Money and Finance* 11, 462–73.

Kon, S. (1984) "Models of stock returns: a comparison," *Journal of Finance* 39, 147–65.

Leadbetter, M.R., G. Lindgren and H. Rootzen (1983) *Extremes and Related Properties of Random Sequences and Processes*, New York, Springer.

Leroy, S.F. (1973) "Risk-aversion and the martingale property of stock prices," *International Economic Review* 14, 436–46.

—— (1989) "Efficient capital markets and martingales," *Journal of Economic Literature* 27, 1583–1621.

Levich, R.M. (1985) "Empirical studies of exchange rates: price behavior, rate determination and market efficiency," in R.W. Jones and P.B. Kenen (eds) *Handbook of International Economics*, vol. 2, Amsterdam, North-Holland.

Loretan, M. and P.C.B. Phillips (1992) "Testing the covariance stationarity of heavy-tailed time series: an overview of the theory with applications to several financial datasets," SSRI Paper 9208, University of Wisconsin.

Lucas, R.E. (1978) "Asset prices in an exchange economy," *Econometrica* 46, 1429–45.

Lütkepohl, H. (1991) *Introduction to Multiple Times Series Analysis*, Berlin, Springer.

Mandelbrot, B. (1963a) "New methods in statistical economics," *Journal of Political Economy* 71, 421–40.

—— (1963b) "The variation of certain speculative prices," *Journal of Business* 36, 394–419.

Mason, D.M. (1982) "Laws of large numbers for sums of extreme values," *Annals of Probability* 10, 754–64.

Meese, R. and K. Rogoff (1983) "Empirical exchange rate models of the seventies: do they fit out of the sample?" *Journal of International Economics* 14, 3–24.

Mussa, M. (1979) "Empirical regularities in the behavior of exchange rates and theories of the foreign exchange market," *Carnegie-Rochester Conference Series on Public Policy* 11, 9–57.

Nelson, D.B. (1991) "Conditional heteroskedasticity in asset returns: a new approach," *Econometrica* 59, 347–70.

Obstfeld, M. (1987) "Peso problems, bubbles, and risk in the empirical assessment of exchange-rate behavior," NBER Working Paper 2203, Cambridge MA.

Ohlson, J.A. (1977) "Risk-aversion and the martingale property of stock prices: comments," *International Economic Review* 18, 229–34.

Phillips, P.C.B. (1987) "Time series regression with a unit root," *Econometrica* 55, 277–301.

Press, S.J. (1967) "A compound events model for security prices," *Journal of Business* 40, 317–35.

Rose, A.K. (1991) "The role of exchange rates in a popular model of international trade: does the 'Marshall–Lerner' condition hold?" *Journal of International Economics* 30, 301–16.

Sargan, J.D. and A. Bhargaoa (1983) "Maximum likelihood estimation of regression models with first order moving average errors when the root lies on the unit circle," *Econometrica* 51, 799–820.

Sargent, T.J. (1979) *Macroeconomic Theory*, New York, Academic Press.

Schotman, P. and H.K. van Dijk (1991) "A Bayesian analysis of the unit root in real exchange rates," *Journal of Econometrics* 49, 195–238.

Sims, C.A., J.H. Stock and M.W. Watson (1990) "Inference in linear time series models with some unit roots," *Econometrica* 58, 113–44.

Smith, R.L. (1987) "Estimating tails of probability distributions," *Annals of Statistics* 15, 1174–1207.

Stock, J.H. (1990) "Unit roots in real GNP: do we know and do we care? A comment," *Carnegie-Rochester Conference Series on Public Policy* 32, 63–82.

—— and M.W. Watson (1988) "Variable trends in economic time series," *Journal of Economic Perspectives* 2, 147–74.

Taylor, S. (1986) *Modelling Financial Time Series*, Chichester, Wiley.

Viaene, J.M. and C.G. de Vries (1992) "International trade and exchange rate volatility," *European Economic Review* 36, 1311–21.

de Vries, C.G. (1988) "Theory and relevance of currency substitution with case studies for Canada and the Netherlands Antilles," *Review of Economics and Statistics* 70, 512–15.

—— (1991) "On the relation between GARCH and stable processes," *Journal of Econometrics* 48, 313–24.

Wasserfallen, W. (1989) "Flexible exchange rates: a closer look," *Journal of Monetary Economics* 23, 511–21.

Westerfield, J.M. (1977) "An examination of foreign exchange risk under fixed and floating rate regimes," *Journal of International Economics* 7, 181–200.

White, J.S. (1958) "The limiting distribution of the serial correlation coefficient in the explosive case," *Annals of Mathematical Statistics* 29, 1188–97.

12 Currency Substitution

ALBERTO GIOVANNINI AND BART TURTELBOOM

1 Introduction

The concept of currency substitution is one of the most ambiguous in economics. Indeed, our dissatisfaction with it has tempted us to discard it completely. We keep on referring to currency substitution because we do not want, in this chapter, to reject altogether a literature that, despite its vagueness, has provided a number of important insights and valuable contributions. Our aim, therefore, is to provide a way to read this vast literature and make sense of an often ill-defined concept. The most important constraint we are working under is of course the state of monetary theory. As Tobin (1983) vehemently put it:

> Why fiat currency, intrinsically useless paper, has positive real value at all and how its value is determined are questions that continue to puzzle economic theorists. . . . A fortiori, the determination of the relative prices of several fiat currencies seems to be a subject on which the utility technology-resource endowment paradigm of basic microeconomic theory has nothing to say.

We disagree with Tobin on the view that "the utility technology-resource endowment paradigm of basic microeconomic theory has nothing to say" on the determinants of the demands for different currencies, and indeed our discussion below makes use of that paradigm and does, in our opinion, illuminate the issues to some extent. However, we think that Tobin raised an important point. The difficulties of monetary theory are in some sense multiplied when one attempts to understand the demand for different currencies.

Our confusion on the definition of currency substitution has been shared by many authors. McKinnon (1985) states that "currency substitution is also treacherous semantically because people differ on its proper interpretation." In his review of Canto and Nickelsburg (1987), Cuddington (1989) refers to "the imprecision regarding the definition of currency substitution [which] plagues . . . most of the previous work on the topic." Canzoneri and Diba (1990) admit that they do not have a "deep theory of currency substitution." Those authors who did try to define currency substitution came up with very different definitions.

A closer look at the way currency substitution has been defined in the literature brings little clarity. Its definition has varied from a very narrow to a broad view of the role of money. At one extreme, Calvo and Végh (1992), following Cuddington (1989), limit currency substitution to the use of different currencies as media of exchange. At the other end of the spectrum, McKinnon (1985) solves the "semantic problem" by distinguishing between direct and indirect currency substitution. "*Direct currency substitution* means that two (or more) currencies compete as a means of payment within the same commodity domain. . . . *Indirect currency substitution* refers to investors switching between non-monetary financial assets. . . ." As has been pointed out (by among others, Spinelli, 1983), the latter form of currency substitution is hardly distinguishable from the concept of capital mobility. Between these two poles, one finds all sorts of variations. Gros and Thygesen (1992), Clements and Schwartz (1992), Agénor and Khan (1992), El-Erian (1988), and Fasano-Filho (1986) define currency substitution as a situation in which foreign money substitutes for domestic money in its three traditional roles. Others – e.g. Handa (1988), Kim (1985), and Elkhafif and Kubursi (1991) – limit their interpretation to the store of value role of money. McKenzie and Thomas (1984) talk about the substitutability between domestic and foreign primary securities.

Many authors abstract from this discussion altogether and define currency substitution as a situation in which domestic money demand is influenced by foreign economic variables. Most often, the relative opportunity cost of holding both currencies is treated as the crucial variable – see Bana and Handa (1990), Marquez (1985a, b, 1992), Neldner (1987), Rogers (1990), Poloz (1984), and Tanzi and Blejer (1982). Miles (1978) stresses the importance of the responsiveness of the demand for both currencies to other economic variables, cautioning that "the mere ownership of foreign currency-denominated balances by domestic residents is not a sufficient condition for currency substitution to occur." Ramirez-Rojas (1985) defines currency substitution as the demand for foreign fiat currency by domestic residents. Khan and Ramirez-Rojas (1986), alternatively, define currency substitution as "the ability of domestic residents to switch between domestic and foreign fiat money." In an end note, they mention that "in actual fact, the definition of currency substitution covers a wide variety of possibilities, such as foreign currency deposits in the domestic financial system, deposits held abroad by domestic residents, and foreign currency notes circulating within the boundaries of the country."

A similar broad range of different interpretations characterizes the definition of *dollarization*, a concept often used to refer to currency substitution in a Latin American context. Lamdany and Dorlhiac (1987) define dollarization as a "replacement, by the monetary authorities, of the national currency with a reserve currency (for example), the dollar, as legal tender," stressing its institutional aspects. Melvin (1988), in contrast, sees dollarization as a market-enforced monetary reform, a somewhat contradictory term referring to "demand-based substitutions away from domestic currency into foreign currency." He defines dollarization as the use of US dollars by Latin Americans in place of domestic currency. Ortiz (1983b) defines dollarization as "the degree to which real and financial transactions are actually performed in dollars relative to those performed in domestic currency" and links it to currency substitution. Calvo and Végh (1992) exclude dollarization, as used in most studies, from their definition of currency substitution since it primarily deals with the unit of account and store of value function of money. Hence, "currency substitution is normally the late stage of the dollarization process."

The first problem of currency substitution is the use of the term "substitution," which is rather uncommon in economics. Webster's *Seventh New Collegiate Dictionary* confirms our concerns. *Substitution* is there defined as the noun corresponding to the verb *to substitute*. The latter, according to the dictionary, is "1: to put in the place of another: EXCHANGE 2: REPLACE." In particular, it is not clear from the term substitution whether it refers to a characteristic of currencies, in which case "substitutability" is to be preferred, or to an equilibrium outcome, in which case "substitution" could be acceptable. Interestingly, the two alternative concepts lead to opposite kinds of research. The study of currency substitutability would naturally explore its potential effects, domestically and internationally, on variables of interest to economists and policymakers. By contrast, the study of substitution would explore the size and the potential causes of the (partial) replacement of one currency with another, and from them extract a better understanding of the mechanics of money demand.

In this chapter we want to discuss both the concept of substitutability and the phenomenon of substitution, its origins and consequences. This separation makes sense because there are no reasons to believe that substitutability implies substitution, or vice versa.[1]

Consider now the determinants of currency substitutability. For that purpose, it is useful to distinguish between the three traditional functions of money: unit of account, provider of transactions services, and provider of store of value services.

Little is known about the unit of account function of monies, except for the fact that making calculations of relative prices using different units of measurement is always a very cumbersome task. Anybody who has traveled to a foreign country knows this problem very well. We suspect that habit, both in its spatial (i.e. market thickness) and temporal dimensions, is an important factor determining the substitutability of unit of account services. The more people are used to operating in different currencies to settle transactions, the more these currencies' unit of account services will be substitutable. Similarly, the longer people have been used to operating in different currencies to settle transactions, the more these currencies' unit of account services will be substitutable.

Store of value substitutability is one of the key theoretical issues in the chapter. It is well known that, as stores of value, currencies are usually dominated by interest-bearing nominal assets, and also by real assets. Yet non-interest-bearing currencies often take up significant shares of portfolios, ostensibly for store of value purposes (the money-under-the-mattress phenomenon). In order to explain this phenomenon, we need to discuss liquidity services in great detail. Since the seminal contribution of Tobin (1958) it is well understood that only if money provides liquidity services will it be held in portfolios together with interest-bearing and other assets.

Such liquidity services, however, are likely to be very different from country to country and to depend on the degree of financial sophistication and capital market liberalization that is present in each country. As we shall note in our discussion below, the concept of store of value substitutability is often intimately linked with the concept of international capital mobility. We think that this linkage has very often led to undue confusion, and we attempt in this chapter to clarify as much as possible the distinction between the two concepts.

Medium of exchange substitutability is what economists have most often in mind when discussing currency substitution, possibly because of the previous observation that money is often dominated by other assets as a store of value.

In discussions of money's transaction services, externalities are often mentioned. A currency is more acceptable when more individuals use it as a means of settlement of private transactions. Indeed, the theory of vehicle currencies in international financial markets (see below) has relied on the concept of substitutability of medium of exchange functions of money to explain the establishment of an internationally acceptable money.

In section 2 of this chapter we attempt to clarify the mechanics of the substitutability of transactions and store of value services of different currencies. We also discuss the macroeconomic implications of currency substitution. Section 3 both reviews the evidence on currency substitution – by discussing the data on circulation of foreign monies during the historical episodes of hyperinflation in Germany and in Russia, in Latin American countries, and in Western European countries – and surveys the econometric studies which have attempted to estimate the substitutability of different currencies. Section 4 explores the implication of currency substitutability and substitution for economic policy. Finally, section 5 contains a few concluding observations.

2   Theoretical models

A discussion of the theoretical underpinnings of currency substitution is just a discussion of the theory of money demand in a multi-currency economy – a country where different currencies circulate, or different countries where several currencies can circulate in each.

The models of money demand that have been developed can be easily cataloged into three major classes: cash-in-advance models, transactions costs models and *ad hoc* models (i.e. models in which the demand for different currencies and the nature of their substitutability is specified *a priori*). In what follows, we discuss in some detail the first two classes of models. Using a cash-in-advance model we ask the basic question: what determines the substitutability of two currencies? This question is further refined using a transactions costs model, which is suitable for illustrating liquidity services of money.[2]

The discussion of the available theoretical models leads us to a review of the implications of currency substitutability. Currency substitutability affects the stability of monetary aggregates, the dynamics of exchange rates, and the government revenue from inflation. Each of these effects raises questions for economic policy, which are discussed in the next section.

2.1   Cash-in-advance models

2.1.1   *Applying the cash-in-advance constraint to specific goods*

The simplest cash-in-advance model can be used to ask the most basic question of currency substitution. Agents maximize utility subject to a budget constraint – which we do not need to specify – and a

cash-in-advance constraint.[3] How should the cash-in-advance constraint be specified? Suppose we just stack two closed economy
cash-in-advance constraints:

$$\frac{M}{P} \geq C \qquad (12.1)$$

$$\frac{M^*}{P^*} \geq C^* \qquad (12.2)$$

where M, C, and P denote nominal money supply, real consumption,
and the price level of the home country, respectively, and asterisks
denote the corresponding variables of the foreign country. This
assumption does not allow any substitution between the two currencies
for the purpose of acquiring the two goods in the consumption basket.
In this model, the cash-in-advance constraint always binds (agents do
not want to employ resources to accumulate an asset, money, which is
dominated by all other assets), and therefore the domestic and foreign
price levels are determined by the quantity equations, obtained by
replacing the inequalities in (12.1) and (12.2) with equals signs.

The relative price of the two goods is determined by goods market
equilibrium. For simplicity assume exogenous supplies of the two goods
and a representative agent. Under these assumptions the marginal rate
of substitution is an exogenous variable fluctuating with the output of
the two goods and so is their relative price:

$$\frac{eP^*}{P} = \frac{U_1(C, C^*)}{U_2(C, C^*)} \qquad (12.3)$$

where e denotes the nominal exchange rate and subscripts 1 and 2
indicate, respectively, the partial derivatives of the utility function U
with respect to its first and second argument.

How can we talk about currency substitution in this model? While
the two cash-in-advance constraints do not allow any substitution, the
way the two goods enter the representative agent's utility function
affects, though indirectly, the substitutability of the two currencies. If
the utility function is constant elasticity of substitution (CES), with
elasticity parameter σ, the relative price of the two goods is

$$\frac{eP^*}{P} = \left(\frac{y}{y^*}\right)^{1/\sigma} \qquad (12.4)$$

where y denotes real output. Substituting the quantity equations, we
find an expression for the nominal exchange rate:

$$e = \left(\frac{y}{y^*}\right)^{(1-\sigma)/\sigma} \frac{M}{M^*} \qquad (12.5)$$

An increase in domestic output y brings about an increase in money demand, which calls for an appreciation of the national currency – a decrease in e. At the same time, however, the relative price of domestic goods falls, with elasticity $1/\sigma$. The larger the elasticity of substitution of the two goods, the smaller the change in their relative price in response to a change in their supply. In particular, if σ is greater than 1, the money demand effect on the nominal exchange rate prevails: an increase in domestic output brings about a nominal exchange rate appreciation.

As pointed out before, the specification of the cash-in-advance constraint in this model is very special, and difficult to justify: why could agents not use any currency to purchase any one of the two goods? After all, transactions costs in international money markets are a fraction of transactions costs in goods markets. In this model, the arbitrariness of the version of the cash-in-advance constraint used matches the arbitrariness of the cash-in-advance constraint itself. Nevertheless, it is useful, in this context, to ask what determines the substitutability of the two currencies.

Substitutability can here be determined by two things: the parameter of the utility function and the specification of the cash-in-advance constraint. Consider the utility function first. If the two goods become ever more substitutable, the two currencies become themselves more substitutable, since the goods they purchase become indistinguishable in agents' tastes. What happens when the two goods are more substitutable? For a given covariance matrix of exogenous shocks, equation (12.5) implies that a higher value of σ, when $\sigma > 1$, increases the volatility of the nominal exchange rate.

This occurs because when the two goods are highly substitutable a change in their supplies brings about pressure on the exchange rate through the money demand effect, but relative prices are insensitive and hence do not provide the dampening effect described above.

2.1.2 Exchange rate indeterminacy

What happens when we change the specification of the cash-in-advance constraint? Consider the extreme case when either currency can be used to buy either good, but – as before – currencies are always needed to buy goods. The cash-in-advance constraint is now

$$\frac{M}{P} + \frac{eP^*}{P}\frac{M^*}{P^*} \geq y + \frac{eP^*}{P} y^* \tag{12.6}$$

Figure 12.1 illustrates the determination of equilibrium in this case. The two functions used in the figure, f and g, are respectively the relative price of foreign (starred) goods and the value, in domestic

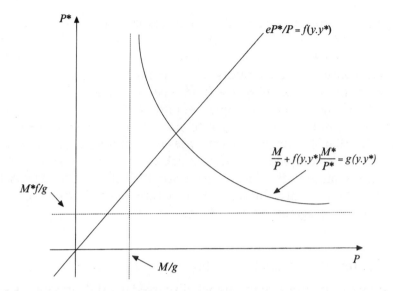

Figure 12.1   The problem of multiple exchange rate equilibria.

currency terms, of output at home and abroad, i.e. the value of total purchases (the right-hand side expression in equation (12.6)). Both are functions of just domestic and foreign output, which are assumed exogenous. This model has an infinity of equilibria, represented in the figure by the points on the downward-sloping schedule, each characterized by a certain triplet (P, P^*, e). This triplet is determined by the intersection of the array crossing the origin and the curve. The slope of the array equals the known function f divided by the exchange rate. Hence each of the infinite equilibrium triplets is characterized by a different value of the nominal exchange rate.

The multiplicity of exchange rates displayed in this model is the result of Kareken and Wallace (1981), who obtained it in a different set-up. The result highlights the potential instabilities caused by currency substitution. In this model, as in Kareken and Wallace's, the implications of exchange rate indeterminacy are limited, however, for two reasons. First, indeterminacy is mirrored by the equivalence, from a welfare viewpoint, of all equilibria. Agents do not care about the different exchange rate equilibria. Second, multiple exchange rates are in this model a knife-edge property, in the sense that an arbitrarily small constraint on the use of national monies would immediately pin down the exchange rate. In this respect, an especially realistic constraint is that adopted by Giovannini and Turtelboom (1992), who postulate that taxes have to be paid with the currency of the government which levies them.[4]

These problems, however, are in part an artifact of the assumption of a single representative agent that characterizes the model used here. King et al. (1992) demonstrate that the exchange rate indeterminacy result can be obtained in a model where a fringe of agents does not face cash-in-advance type constraints. In their model, characterized by the presence of three types of agents (one type being the speculative fringe and each of the other two types bound to the use of a particular currency), the multiple exchange rate equilibria can have real effects, to the extent that financial markets are not complete. This result is intuitive, since complete financial markets are often regarded as the dual of the representative agent assumption. With incomplete markets, random exchange rate fluctuations generate redistribution of wealth among the three agents, which affects welfare.

2.2 Transactions costs models

The simple cash-in-advance model discussed in the previous section helps to illuminate a number of questions regarding the concept of substitutability of different currencies but does not explain how different monies can work as stores of value. Every instant, agents can costlessly acquire the cash they need for their purchases. For this reason they will never want to carry "idle" cash balances in their portfolio. Whatever cash they need to purchase goods they can obtain immediately by liquidating part of their portfolio of bonds or other assets. Indeed, in the model described in the previous section, money does not serve as a store of value.

Casual empiricism, however, suggests that – to different degrees in different countries – money still has an important role as a store of value. This role stems from the transactions costs incurred in transforming other assets instantaneously into goods, or into money. These transactions costs make money more "liquid" than other assets.

To illustrate the store of value services of money, we use a model where such transactions costs are described as follows: money facilitates purchases of goods, and every period agents need to acquire the cash balances they plan to use next period for goods purchases.[5] The inability of agents to acquire cash instantaneously to facilitate goods purchases makes money more liquid than other assets. Once again we resort to the useful concept of a representative agent. The agent solves the following problem:

$$\max \sum_{t=0}^{\infty} \beta^t U(C_t, C_t^*) \qquad (12.7)$$

subject to

$$\frac{B_{t+1}}{P_t} + \frac{e_t B^*_{t+1}}{P_t} + \frac{M_{t+1}}{P_t} + \frac{e_t M^*_{t+1}}{P_t}$$

$$= y_t + \frac{e_t P^*_t y^*_t}{P_t} - C_t - \frac{e_t P^*_t C^*_t}{P_t} - \Phi\left(C_t, C^*_t, \frac{M_t}{P_t}, \frac{M^*_t}{P^*_t}\right) +$$

$$\frac{B_t(1 + i_{t-1})}{P_t} + \frac{e_t B^*_t(1 + i^*_{t-1})}{P_t} + \frac{M_t}{P_t} + \frac{e_t M^*_t}{P_t}$$

$$+ \frac{Z_t}{P_t} + \frac{e_t Z^*_t}{P_t} \tag{12.8}$$

where y and y^* are the endowments of the two goods, B and B^* are domestic and foreign bonds, and Φ represents transactions costs. The function Φ is increasing in C and C^* and decreasing in the stocks of real money balances M/P and M^*/P^*. We do not impose any other constraints on Φ since they are not needed for what follows, but it should be noted here that the nature of the substitutability of currencies depends crucially on the form of the Φ function. Z and Z^* are exogenous transfers of domestic and foreign cash balances. Every period t, the agent chooses the amount of bonds B_{t+1} and B^*_{t+1} maturing at time $t+1$ and the cash M_{t+1} and M^*_{t+1} that he wants to hold. A domestic bond maturing a time $t+1$ has a known interest rate i_t.

Let λ_t represent the Lagrange multiplier associated with the budget constraint. The first-order conditions with respect to C and C^* yield the following:

$$U_C(C_t, C^*_t) = \lambda_t(1 + \Phi_{t,C}) \tag{12.9}$$

$$U_{C^*}(C_t, C^*_t) = \frac{e_t P^*_t}{P_t} \lambda_t\left(1 + \frac{P_t}{e_t P^*_t} \Phi_{t,C^*}\right) \tag{12.10}$$

The subscripts to the symbol Φ_t denote partial derivatives of the Φ function, evaluated at time t, with respect to the variables in the subscripts. Equations (12.9) and (12.10) show an important feature of this model. The presence of liquidity costs induces a potential wedge between the marginal rate of substitution of the two goods and the marginal rate of transformation, represented by their relative price (the real exchange rate). This wedge depends on the form of the liquidity function. It could equal zero if the two partial derivatives were identical: this would happen, for example, if the C and C^* were perfectly substitutable in the function Φ.

Taking derivatives with respect to the two monies and the stock of domestic bonds we get

$$\frac{\lambda_t}{P_t} = \beta E_t \left[\frac{\lambda_{t+1}}{P_{t+1}} (1 - \Phi_{t+1,M/P}) \right] \tag{12.11}$$

$$\frac{e_t \lambda_t}{P_t} = \beta E_t \left[\frac{e_{t+1} \lambda_{t+1}}{P_{t+1}} \left(1 - \frac{P_{t+1}}{P^*_{t+1} e_{t+1}} \Phi_{t+1,M^*/P^*} \right) \right] \tag{12.12}$$

$$\frac{\lambda_t}{P_t} = \beta E_t \left[\frac{\lambda_{t+1}}{P_{t+1}} (1 + i_t) \right] \tag{12.13}$$

Equations (12.11), (12.12), and (12.13) are the traditional first-order conditions from asset-pricing models. They yield the usual "β representation" of *ex ante* rates of return, whereby the return on an asset, in excess of the risk-free rate, equals the excess return over the risk-free rate of a benchmark asset multiplied by a factor of proportionality determined by the covariance of the individual asset with the benchmark portfolio. In this model, the benchmark portfolio is perfectly conditionally correlated with the multiplier associated with the budget constraint, λ.[6] Consider the first-order condition with respect to domestic-currency bonds. Rearranging it we get

$$1 = (1 + i_t)\beta E_t \left(\frac{\lambda_{t+1}}{\lambda_t} \frac{P_{t+1}}{P_t} \right) \tag{12.14}$$

Since the nominal interest rate is known at the time the one-period bond is acquired, the familiar relation between the expectation of a product of random variables and the product of their expectations implies that the return on the domestic-currency bond is determined by the covariance between the rate of deflation and the rate of growth of the marginal utility of wealth (λ).

Notice that, in the case of the domestic and foreign money, the payoff is determined by the liquidity services that they offer, represented by the partial derivative of the liquidity function with respect to the real money stocks (the sign of that partial derivative and the minus sign in front of it cancel).

After imposing a specific functional form on the function Φ, one can solve the system (12.11), (12.12), and (12.13), augmented with the first-order condition with respect to the foreign bond, and obtain demand correspondences for domestic and foreign money. We do not undertake this exercise because the final result is, not surprisingly, entirely determined by the assumed functional form for the liquidity function. Alternatively, one can obtain portfolio-balance-like equations (relating demand for bonds and money, domestic and foreign, to wealth and expected returns) by finding the functional form relating λ to the representative agent's wealth. This is straightforward in a two-period setting, and yields the static capital asset pricing model as well as the traditional portfolio balance asset demand equations,[7] but it is much less straightforward in the infinite-horizon model discussed here.

In summary, the model of liquidity discussed in this section has shown that the demand for domestic and foreign currency is determined by their expected liquidity services, and that agents trade off money and other assets in their portfolio by comparing their expected returns and their covariance matrix. These liquidity services, however, are not directly related to rates of return on bonds, but are determined – at least in the specific model used here – by the amount of consumption purchases and the amount of real balances available to consumers.

The liquidity model of money demand illustrates the determinants of the demand for different currencies for store of value purposes. It is of crucial importance, especially for those countries where the liquidity services of money are significant because underdeveloped financial markets do not permit easy purchases and sales of financial assets by individuals. With illiquid financial assets, the liquidity services of money increase and so does the demand for money for store of value purposes. If the domestic currency has low expected returns (as is the case in high-inflation countries), the foreign currency becomes a significant liquid investment for domestic residents.

The liquidity model is also suited to illustrate another important aspect of the substitution and the substitutability of different currencies, sometimes referred to – in the international economics literature – as the "vehicle currency" phenomenon (see Krugman, 1980; Black, 1991; Matsuyama et al., 1991).[8]

Suppose that the optimization problem of this section pertains to one atomistic individual, identical to all others in the economy, and that the liquidity cost function is not only defined over the holdings of real cash balances and the flows of consumption by the individual, but also over the shares of domestic and foreign currency in the total stock of money balances in the economy. The larger the aggregate share of the domestic currency, the more likely it is for a consumer to find a counterparty willing to accept it in payment for a good or a service. Thus, the cross partial derivative of the liquidity function with respect to, say, domestic real money balances and the aggregate share of domestic real money balances in the economy is negative.

This model displays multiple equilibria since, in the aggregate, the cost of using either one of the two currencies is decreasing in the proportion of that currency in private portfolios. This property of the model has been used to explain the establishment of an international currency, and its lingering even after the economic conditions for it to be a vehicle currency do not exist anymore (Krugman, 1980). The externality can also be employed to explain other hysteresis-type phenomena, such as for example the persistence of large holdings of foreign cash balances even after the end of inflationary episodes, documented by Guidotti and Rodriguez (1991).

2.3   Implications of currency substitutability

In this section we describe some of the implications of the coexistence of different monies in agents' portfolios and of the substitutability among them.

2.3.1   Gresham's law

The natural point of departure is the classic proposition on the effects of the coexistence of different monies. Gresham's law, one of the best known propositions in monetary economics, says that "bad money drives out good," or that the less valuable currency substitutes for the more valuable currency in monetary circulation. To understand Gresham's law it is important to keep in mind that it is a description of monetary instabilities under a bimetallic standard. In a bimetallic standard the central bank freely exchanges at a fixed nominal price two metals (say gold and silver) for money. Fixing the nominal value of gold and silver coins means fixing also their relative price. Gold and silver are traded in the nonmonetary market (industrial market) as well, where newly mined ore is also sold originally. A condition of equilibrium between the monetary and nonmonetary markets is that the official parity equals the relative price of the two metals in the industrial market.

Consider now what happens when some exogenous shock (say an increase in silver ore production that tends to make silver cheaper in the industrial market, gold more expensive) drives the relative price of the two metals away from the official parity. Private agents would find it profitable to buy gold from the central bank at the official parity to resell it in the industrial market. This would produce a progressive disappearance of gold from monetary circulation. In other words, the "bad" money has driven out the "good": hence Gresham's law.

This discussion clearly implies that Gresham's law cannot apply in a world of fiat currencies, because there is no industrial market to arbitrage national different currencies to. It is still possible, however, to consider the effects of a change in two currencies' relative valuation caused by a change in their relative monetary services: transactions services and store of value services. Suppose, for example, that private agents expect a devaluation to occur over some future horizon: in this case the store of value services of a currency increase relative to those of another. Agents would bring the "bad" currency to central banks in exchange for the "good" one. The "good" currency drives out the "bad" from monetary circulation. The same would occur with a change in transactions services originating, for example, when one currency gets increasingly used to make payments and therefore – as we argued above – becomes more acceptable in private transactions. Also in this case the "good" currency would drive out the "bad." Hence, the kind of shocks in money demand that can occur in a fiat currency system imply that Gresham's law can only occur in reverse (we have taken the foregoing discussion from Giovannini, 1991b).[9] The general lesson of Gresham's law is that, whenever different currencies coexist in an integrated economy under fixed exchange rates, fluctuations of their relative valuation affect their circulation. This in turn can give rise to instabilities, usually caused by the inability of monetary authorities and the banking system to accommodate these demand fluctuations fully: there is always a limit beyond which central banks cannot run down their reserves or cannot increase their borrowing from other central banks and the banking system.

2.3.2   Effects on the real exchange rate and the inflation tax

Two other questions on the effects of currency substitution have had a prominent role in the literature: the effects of currency substitution on real exchange rate fluctuations in a flexible exchange rate regime, and the effects of currency substitution on the inflation tax.

The first question was first analyzed by Calvo and Rodriguez (1977). These authors consider a model where foreign currency provides store of value services, presumably because financial assets are illiquid. This occurs, as we have argued in the previous section, in all those economies where financial markets, perhaps because of pervasive government regulations, are repressed or underdeveloped. Because in Calvo and Rodriguez's (1977) model foreign cash balances are the only internationally traded asset, the accumulation of foreign cash balances can only occur through current account surpluses. Hence, in their model, a change in the rate of growth of the domestic money stock leads domestic residents to want to accumulate foreign assets (foreign cash balances), which they can only accomplish through a current account surplus. The equilibrium response is a depreciation of the real exchange rate, which produces enough of a current account surplus to permit the desired accumulation of foreign cash balances. Hence, in the model of Calvo and Rodriguez (1977), a monetary disturbance leads to fluctuations of the real exchange rate associated with the phenomenon of currency substitution.[10]

The second question concerns the effects of currency substitutability on inflationary financing of government deficits. Intuitively, the higher the substitutability of domestic and foreign currency is, the more difficult it is for the government to finance deficits by printing money. On the one hand, seigniorage is taken up by the foreign money holdings, and on the other hand the demand for domestic currency would probably become more sensitive to the inflation tax rate.

Hence, for any given level of the inflation tax rate, the revenue from the inflation tax would be lower in the presence of currency substitution.[11]

3   Empirical evidence

3.1   A first glance

There are many data problems which prevent a clean measurement of the actual amount of currency substitution. The ideal measurement would include foreign banknotes circulating as medium of exchange and store of value in the economy, as well as checking accounts and short-term deposits denominated in foreign currencies in the domestic banking system and abroad.

Given the obvious difficulties in estimating foreign currency notes in the economy, this part of currency substitution is generally excluded from its measurement. Even in industrial countries, data on cross-border credit-card and check payments are not, to our knowledge, publicly available. Melvin and Afcha de la Parra (1989) developed a method to estimate the amount of dollar banknotes circulating in Bolivia, based on a ratio of check clearings to total demand deposits. However, their methodology does not seem to be easily transferable to other countries. Kamin and Ericsson (1993) employ data on shipments of US dollar notes to Argentina in the latter half of the 1980s and find it to be a significant and growing component of currency substitution in Argentina.

3.1.1   Foreign currency deposits

The data on foreign currency deposits (FCDs) have to be interpreted carefully. Quite often, the maturity structure of these deposits is not available. Hence, one can only guess which part of these series actually cover the currency substitution phenomenon. Whereas data on FCDs in the domestic banking system are often available, FCDs held by residents abroad are harder to measure. Indeed, all flows through third countries and third currencies are very hard to detect. Data on deposits held abroad in the care of a nonresident – commonly used in some developing countries – are also not available. In addition, data on deposits held in offshore banking centers are often unreliable.

To summarize, it is reasonable to treat the available data as a lower bound on the actual amount of currency substitution. This underestimation will be more severe in a situation of extreme economic instability, when the risk that the FCDs in the domestic economy will be confiscated, or their prohibition, makes them both attractive and hidden.

What do the available data tell us? Figure 12.2 describes the

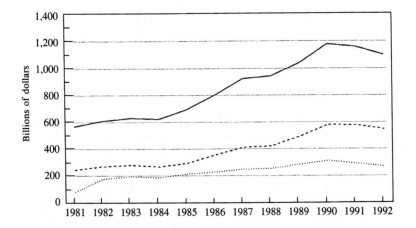

Figure 12.2   Foreign currency deposits: ——— , world; - - -, industrial countries; . . ., developing countries. Cross-border deposits are according to the residence of the depositor, in billions of 1981 US dollars.

Source: International Financial Statistics

evolution of FCDs worldwide, in the industrialized world and in developing countries. These series are estimates of the deposits in major international banking centers. They should be interpreted with caution since little is known about the maturity of the deposits included. In constant US dollars, the figure shows a worldwide increase from 600 billion to around 1100 billion dollars during the 1980s, an increase which was more pronounced in industrialized countries than in developing countries.

Most of the voluminous empirical work on currency substitution concentrates on Europe and the western hemisphere.[12] Figure 12.3 depicts the extent of currency substitution in Mexico, Peru, Bolivia, and Uruguay. The solid line shows the proportion of FCDs, held at home and abroad, in the extended monetary aggregate – M2 plus these FCDs (except for Bolivia, where only FCDs in the domestic banking

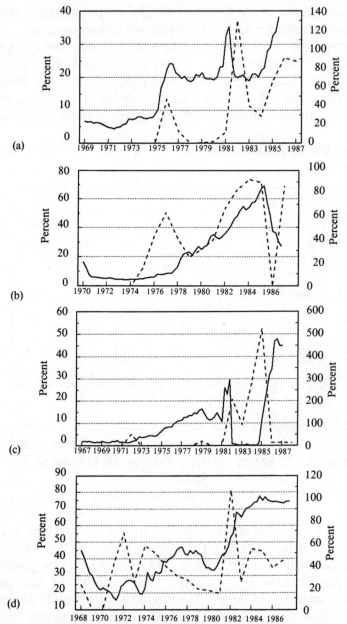

Figure 12.3 Dollarization and macroeconomic instability in Latin America: (a) Mexico; (b) Peru; (c) Bolivia; (d) Uruguay; ———, FCD/(M2 + FCD); - - -, exchange rate change. FCDs are dollar deposits held in the domestic banking system and abroad, except for Bolivia where only dollar deposits in the domestic banking sector are included. Their ratio to an extended money aggregate is on the left scale; the annual exchange rate change is on the right scale.

Sources: Savastana, 1992; Sachs, 1989; *International Financial Statistics*

system are included).[13] As the figure shows, these four countries have experienced, in the last twenty years, a dramatic increase in the use of foreign currency by domestic residents.[14] The degree of currency substitution appears to be related to macroeconomic instability. In all four countries FCDs rise with currency depreciation, although towards the end of the 1980s they remain at relatively high levels despite the introduction of stabilization packages.[15]

Figure 12.4 provides more information on the breakdown of foreign

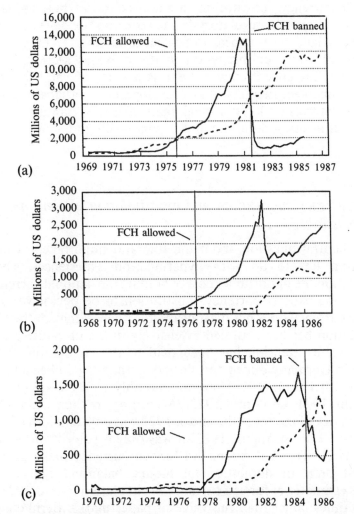

Figure 12.4 Dollar deposits in Latin America: (a) Mexico; (b) Uruguay; (c) Peru; ——, FCH; ---, FCA. FCH are dollar deposits held in the domestic banking system. FCA are dollar deposits held in the USA. Vertical lines indicate when FCHs were allowed and eliminated.

Source: Savastano, 1992

408 ALBERTO GIOVANNINI AND BART TURTELBOOM

currency holdings for Mexico, Peru, and Uruguay, by reporting FCDs held in the domestic banking system and abroad. Notice that the substitution of FCDs at domestic banks with FCDs held abroad occurred mostly after FCDs were banned in the domestic banking system. This substitution, however, was not instantaneous.

The experience of Latin American countries shows the importance of macroeconomic instability in the development of currency substitution. It is beyond the scope of this chapter to explain the differences in the degree of currency substitution in these countries but, as Savastano (1992) points out, the regulatory framework and the development stage of the financial system appear to be crucial factors.[16] This observation is consistent with our discussion in the previous section, where we argued that foreign currency is held as a store of value in countries where the financial markets' underdevelopment, perhaps coupled with pervasive controls on international financial assets' transactions, makes all financial assets – domestic and foreign – illiquid.

3.1.2 Currency substitution and hyperinflation in Germany and Russia

Another natural question about the role and importance of currency substitution has to do with hyperinflation experiences. During a hyperinflation the opportunity cost of holding the national currency is so high that one expects currency substitution to be pervasive. Yet, the domestic currency does not disappear altogether. Although the German hyperinflation has been studied extensively in the literature on money demand, scant attention has been paid to the circulation of foreign currency in Germany during this period, perhaps again because of data problems. Abel et al. (1979) provide monthly data on the real money stock from 1921 until mid-1923. According to their data, the real domestic stock of money at the end of 1922 was only one-fifth of its value in January 1921. In August 1923, it was only 4 percent of its value in January 1921. To what extent did foreign currency make up for this exorbitant drop in domestic real money balances? Beusch (1928) mentions estimates of foreign currency in circulation in mid-1923 which were ten times larger than the value of paper marks. Bernholz (1989) estimates that in mid-1923 there were about 4 billion gold-marks of "value-stable" money in circulation. This includes 2–3 billion gold-marks of foreign currency and 1.1 billion gold-marks of "emergency money." The rest was made up of commodity-backed money: notes representing specified amounts of rye, coal, and other commodities. Together with 4 billion gold-marks of value-stable currency, Bernholz estimates a circulation of 80–800 gold-marks' worth of inflating currency after June 1923.[17]

These very dramatic fluctuations of monetary aggregates suggest two preliminary observations. First, when inflation reaches extremely high values, the economy naturally adopts substitutes to the depreciating currency. And, second, the inflating currency does not completely disappear. This stubbornness of the hyperinflating money is an unexplored phenomenon. It could be due both to legal enforcement of its use for some transactions (i.e. taxes to be paid in cash) and/or to the hysteresis-type phenomena described in section 2.2.

Russia went through a hyperinflationary cycle and stabilization during 1922–3. However, as Rostowski (1992) mentions, the Russian authorities introduced a second stable currency, the *Chervontsy*, circulating together with the inflating currency, the *Sovznaki*, fifteen months before the stabilization. Figure 12.5 shows that the *total* real

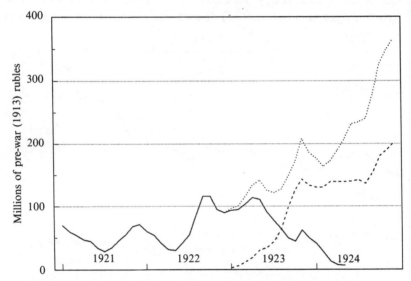

Figure 12.5 Currency substitution during the Russian hyperinflation, 1921–4: ——— , *Sovznaki*; ---, *Chervontsy*; . . ., total. The total also includes transport certificates and treasury notes.
Source: Rostowski, 1992

money stock had a positive trend, despite the collapse of the value of the *Sovznaki*. At the end of 1922 the stock of *Sovznaki* stood at 90 million pre-war rubles. By the end of 1923, the total money stock, *Sovznaki* plus *Chervontsy* and transport certificates, stood at 186.7 million pre-war rubles. Although the real stock of *Sovznaki* had fallen to 50 million, the circulation of the new currency had more than made up for this decline. During 1924, the real value of *Sovznaki* all but evaporated, and the *Chervontsy* almost completely replaced it. The total stock kept growing rapidly throughout 1924, to reach 365.2 million of pre-war rubles in December 1924.

3.1.3   Cross-border deposits in Europe

Currency substitution is an issue of interest not only in countries characterized by significant macroeconomic instabilities like those mentioned so far, but also in countries where, even with low rates of inflation, the opening up of financial markets and the degree of integration with the rest of the world make the definition of a domestic monetary aggregate a difficult exercise (with attendant difficulties in monetary targeting). This is the case in Europe, where during the second half of the 1980s many countries have opened up their financial markets to a very substantial extent, and where – as a result – the holdings of foreign-currency deposits have increased noticeably. Figure 12.6 (from Angeloni et al., 1991) shows the evolution of cross-border

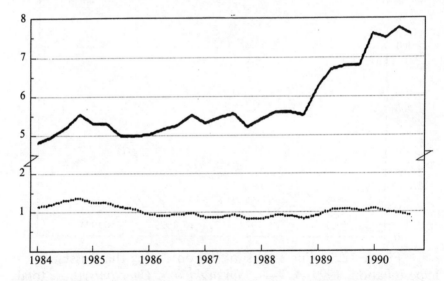

Figure 12.6   Cross-border deposits in the European Community: ——, gross; . . ., net. Gross CBDs are the sum of European residents' deposits held outside their own country. Net CBDs are the difference between gross CBDs and European residents' CBDs held in Europe.
Source: Angeloni et al., 1991

deposits (CBDs) as a percentage of a broad monetary aggregate in the European Community (EC) during 1983–90. Gross CBDs – defined as deposits held by European residents outside their own country – were fairly constant during 1983–8 at around 5 percent of the stock of broad money, but in the following two years they increased to about 8 percent. Net CBDs, defined as deposits held by European residents outside the EC, remained constant at around 1 percent of the aggregate broad money stock.

Figure 12.7 (also from Angeloni et al., 1991) describes the evolution of CBDs in France, Germany, Italy, and the UK. For each country, the figure reports three concepts of CBDs: deposits held by residents with foreign banks, denominated in domestic and foreign currencies (residence of the holder); deposits with domestic banks held by nonresidents in domestic and foreign currencies (residence of the bank); and, finally, deposits denominated in national currency held by nonresidents with domestic or foreign banks plus deposits denominated in national currency held by residents in foreign banks minus deposits denominated in foreign currencies held by residents with domestic banks (currency of denomination). The figure shows the importance of foreign deposits with domestic banks in a country, like the UK, with a major international financial center in it, as well as the importance of changes in regulations. In Germany the government abolished, in December 1985, the exemption for reserve requirements of short-term bank deposits, and the result was a big jump in CBDs.[18] A sizeable increase in CBDs is also observable in correspondence to the introduction of the withholding tax in January 1989, subsequently abolished in June 1989. The increase of CBDs in France and Italy occurs, for each of the two countries, after changes in regulations affecting foreign exchange controls and reserve requirements. In general, CBDs have increased after the relaxation of foreign exchange controls. In summary, while the size of CBDs for the UK dwarfs that of France and Italy, the acceleration of CBDs in the last two countries is a very remarkable phenomenon, and possibly a more serious source of money demand instabilities.

3.2   Econometrics

In the empirical literature currency substitutability has been defined and estimated in many different ways, often difficult to reconcile with each other or with theoretical models. Yet, three categories of empirical models can be identified.[19] In the first, demand functions for domestic and foreign monies are part of a static (two-period) portfolio balance model, where optimal holdings of domestic and foreign assets are chosen together with currencies. This strand of the literature treats domestic and foreign interest rates, together with exchange rate changes, as jointly determined in a general financial equilibrium.

In the second category currency substitutability is estimated in a narrower set-up. In these models, agents first decide on the optimal mix

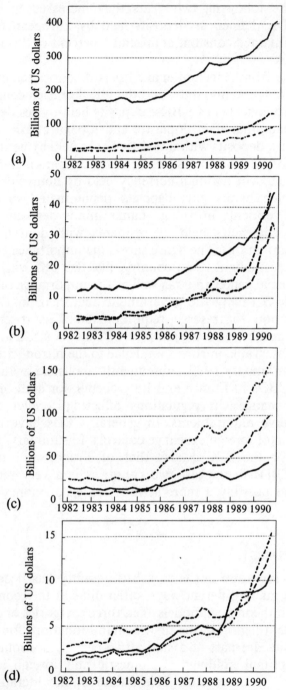

Figure 12.7   Deviation between M2 and extended monetary aggregates: (a) UK; (b) France; (c) Germany; (d) Italy. Cross-border deposits according to national currency (— – —), residence of holders (- - -), and residence of banks (——).

Source: Angeloni et al., 1991

of monetary and nonmonetary assets. In a second stage, they decide how to allocate the monetary assets between the different currencies in their portfolio. The latter decision is based only on the degree to which both currencies contribute to delivering money services and on the relative opportunity cost between the two currencies.

Finally, a more recent strand of literature starts from the first-order conditions of a representative agent's dynamic optimization problem and, with some auxiliary assumptions, recovers the parameters of interest, which allow the estimation of the substitutability of different currencies.

3.2.1   The portfolio balance model

Consider the two-period portfolio balance model first. Investors choose among domestic money M, foreign money M^*, domestic bonds B, and foreign bonds B^*. The derivation of the asset demand equation was pointed out in the previous section. In the first-order necessary conditions for optimization – from equations (12.11), (12.12), (12.13) – the marginal utility of wealth equals, in equilibrium, the marginal utility of the end-of-period value of the portfolio, i.e. the sum of the holdings of each asset multiplied by the value of each asset – including its own income – at the end of the period. Hence, from these first-order conditions it is possible to solve for the desired holdings of each of the available assets.

In the illustration below, we follow Branson and Henderson (1983), where – without the explicit solution of an optimization problem – the *domestic* demand for assets is postulated to depend on their relative returns:

$$M = M\left[\overset{-}{i}, \overset{-}{(i^* + e^e)}, \overset{-}{e^e}, \overset{+}{PY}, \overset{+}{P^c}, \overset{+}{W}\right] \tag{12.15}$$

$$eM^* = M^*\left[\overset{-}{i}, \overset{-}{(i^* + e^e)}, \overset{+}{e^e}, \overset{+}{PY}, \overset{+}{P^c}, \overset{+}{W}\right] \tag{12.16}$$

$$B = B\left[\overset{+}{i}, \overset{-}{(i^* + e^e)}, \overset{-}{e^e}, \overset{-}{PY}, \overset{-}{P^c}, \overset{+}{W}\right] \tag{12.17}$$

$$eB^* = B^*\left[\overset{-}{i}, \overset{+}{(i^* + e^e)}, \overset{-}{e^e}, \overset{-}{PY}, \overset{-}{P^c}, \overset{+}{W}\right] \tag{12.18}$$

satisfying the usual wealth constraints. The first argument i in equations (12.15)–(12.18) is the return on holding bonds denominated in domestic currency relative to the return on domestic money (minus the rate of domestic inflation). It is assumed that all four assets are substitutes in the portfolio. Hence, an increase in i raises the demand for domestic bonds but lowers the demand for their substitutes in the portfolio. The nominal return on bonds in foreign currency is i^*. Expressed in domestic currency, this return becomes $i^* + e^e$, with e^e the expected change in the exchange rate. It affects the demand for foreign securities positively and the other asset demands negatively. Once again, this second argument is in fact a real return differential, where the return on domestic money is minus the rate of inflation.[20] Similarly, the third argument e^e is the return on foreign money, converted into domestic currency.[21]

The fourth argument, PY, is the home-currency value of domestic output and affects demand for all assets positively. P^c is the price of the domestic consumer's consumption bundle expressed in home currency. An increase in P^c increases the demand for both monies and lowers the demand for bonds denominated in domestic and foreign currency. The positive effect of domestic wealth W, the last argument, reflects the assumption that all assets are "normal assets."

The discussion of the theoretical models of liquidity and the demand for domestic and foreign monies as stores of value suggests a possible source of misspecification in this model. In the portfolio balance equations derived in section 2.2 the real returns from holding the domestic and foreign currencies, i.e. their liquidity services, have to be added to minus the rate of inflation, and are distinct from the domestic and foreign interest rates and the rate of change of the exchange rate. Yet, they do not appear in the equations written above, thus raising questions about specification biases.

Indeed, in the absence of such liquidity services, it is not clear why domestic and foreign money are held at all. One potential way out is to assume that such liquidity services are constant and thus independent of the other returns in the equations. Such an assumption, however, is never invoked in the empirical papers we have surveyed.

For estimation purposes, equations (12.15)–(12.18) can be approximated in log-linear form:[22]

$$\log\left(\frac{M}{P}\right) = \alpha_0 + \alpha_1 \log Y + \alpha_2 i + \alpha_3(i^* + e^e) + \alpha_4 e^e \qquad (12.19)$$

$$\log\left(\frac{eM^*}{P^*}\right) = \beta_0 + \beta_1 \log Y + \beta_2 i + \beta_3(i^* + e^e) + \beta_4 e^e \qquad (12.20)$$

$$\log\left(\frac{B}{P}\right) = \gamma_0 + \gamma_1 \log Y + \gamma_2 i + \gamma_3(i^* + e^e) + \gamma_4 e^e \qquad (12.21)$$

$$\log\left(\frac{eB^*}{P^*}\right) = \delta_0 + \delta_1 \log Y + \delta_2 i + \delta_3(i^* + e^e) + \delta_4 e^e \qquad (12.22)$$

In the literature, currency substitutability is defined as the extent to which residents replace domestic money in their portfolio with foreign money in response to a change in their relative rate of return.[23] In equation (12.19) this is reflected in the term α_4. Substitution between bonds, which McKinnon called *indirect currency substitution* is measured by γ_3 and δ_2.[24] When estimating this set of equations, the inclusion of both $i* + e^e$ and e^e allows one, according to some, to distinguish between capital mobility and currency substitutability.[25]

In addition to the conceptual problem raised above on the estimation of these money and asset demand equations, there are two other issues that often surface in empirical work based on these equations: multicollinearity and partial adjustment. In these portfolio balance models rates of return are highly collinear (and indeed perfectly collinear when uncovered interest parity is assumed by those researchers who take the expected future spot exchange rate to be proxied by the forward exchange rate).[26] Precise estimation of the parameters of interest is thus difficult. Finally, the assumption of partial adjustment (not written out in the illustration above), which amounts to introducing the lagged dependent variable on the right-hand side of the regressions, is difficult to justify, since it is hard to identify costs of adjustment of private financial portfolios. The lagged dependent variable picks up any serial correlation of the estimated residuals in the original equation. Even accepting the presence of slow adjustment due to adjustment costs, the estimated coefficients of the lagged dependent variables often indicate that these costs of adjustment are implausibly high, and imply implausibly slow adjustment.[27]

In the sequential portfolio balance approach, the choice between the two currencies is made after the shares of monetary and nonmonetary assets have been determined (Miles, 1978). In Miles's model, domestic and foreign money are both inputs in a CES function that produces money services (MS):

$$\frac{MS}{P} = \left[\lambda_1 \left(\frac{M}{P}\right)^{-\rho} + \lambda_2 \left(\frac{M*}{P*}\right)^{-\rho} \right]^{-1/\rho} \qquad (12.23)$$

This money services function is maximized subject to the following constraint:

$$M_0 = \frac{M}{P}(1 + i) + \frac{M*}{P*}(1 + i*) \qquad (12.24)$$

where M_0 is the desired level of money services fixed at the previous stage of the portfolio maximization problem. The agent allocates these money services between the two monies depending on their relative opportunity costs (expressed in the asset constraint) and their relative efficiency in providing money services (expressed in the money services production function). The resulting first-order condition expresses the relative demand for both currencies as a function of the interest rate differential, assuming that purchasing power parity holds continuously:

$$\log\left(\frac{M}{eM^*}\right) = \eta_0 + \eta_1[\log(1 + i^*) - \log(1 + i)] \qquad (12.25)$$

In this set-up, η_0 is the ratio of the weight of domestic real money over the weight of foreign real money in the money services function (12.23), λ_1/λ_2. $\eta_1 = \rho/(1 + \rho)$ and, according to Miles, measures the degree of currency substitutability. With perfect currency substitutability, η_1 goes to infinity. This implies that ρ goes to -1 and the money services function (12.23) becomes the weighted sum of domestic and foreign real money.[28] In equation (12.25) the log-difference of domestic and foreign interest rates is equal, in the presence of international capital mobility, to the forward premium (by the interest rate parity condition). The forward premium is in turn assumed to be equal to the expected rate of change of the exchange rate – i.e. perfect asset substitutability is assumed as well. This specification could be viewed as a special case of the two-period model described above, where the expected rate of change of the exchange rate represents the relative real return of foreign money over domestic money.

Bordo and Choudhri (1982) modify the model of Miles by adding output to the maximization problem. Hence output also enters the equations to be estimated. For variations on Bordo and Choudhri's model, see Neldner (1987), Bana and Handa (1990), and Batten and Hafer (1984). Other authors use different variables to measure the opportunity cost of money.

Abel et al. (1979), studying the German hyperinflation, use a proxy for expected inflation (actual inflation, instrumented) instead of the domestic interest rate. Frenkel (1977) uses the forward premium as a measure of anticipated inflation. For similar exercises in a different context, see Agénor (1990), Agénor and Khan (1992), and Ghosh (1989).

3.2.2   Utility of money services and estimation of Euler equations

Finally, the last category of empirical models of the demand for different currencies includes the dynamic models of İmrohoroğlu (1991) and Bufman and Leiderman (1992). Instead of directly estimating money demand equations, these authors exploit the orthogonality restrictions stemming from the first-order conditions for optimization, as well as from the assumption of rational expectations. İmrohoroğlu (1991) develops a model in which a representative agent derives instantaneous utility from consumption and from money services. The latter are produced by both domestic and foreign real money through a CES technology. The problem is to maximize the present discounted value of instantaneous utilities subject to a standard budget constraint. Among the first-order necessary conditions for optimization are a set of Euler equations specifying the equilibrium dynamics for marginal utilities. One such Euler equation in İmrohoroğlu's model is the following:

$$U_{c,t} = U_{M/P,t} + \beta(1 + i_t)E_t\left(U_{c,t+1} \frac{P_t}{P_{t+1}}\right) \qquad (12.26)$$

where subscripts indicate the arguments of partial derivatives of the utility function evaluated at different time periods. Equation (12.26) says that the utility obtained from holding cash balances drives a wedge between the expected rate of growth of marginal utility and the expected real interest rate. That wedge is the marginal utility of cash balances. A similar result is obtainable from the model discussed in section 2.2 by combining equations (12.9) and (12.13). After proper parametrization, these equations can be estimated using Hansen's GMM technique. Bufman and Leiderman (1993) extend this framework by incorporating nonexpected utility to disentangle behavior towards risk and intertemporal preferences.

Clearly, the empirical models of İmrohoroğlu and Bufman and Leiderman are much closer to the underlying theoretical models than those that have been used more frequently in the literature so far. However, their models, like most models of money demand, are subject to criticism on the services that domestic and foreign money are assumed to perform, and in particular on the inclusion of money balances in agents' utility function.

3.3   Parameter estimates

Despite the controversies that theoretical models of the demand for different monies can stimulate, and the more bitter controversies on their empirical applications, a look at the estimated values of the parameters of the equations described in the previous section provides a more complete evaluation of the phenomenon of currency substitution. Even if these parameters might not actually give a precise quantification of the substitutability of different monies, they provide useful information on the correlations in the data.

In order to keep the discussion manageable, we shall concentrate on the "classic" case studies of currency substitution: Latin American countries and Canada.[29]

For Latin American countries, most studies find significant currency substitutability. Ramirez-Rojas (1985) estimates a variant of equation

(12.25) for Argentina, Mexico, and Uruguay. He finds the coefficient of the inflation differential *vis-à-vis* the USA to be negative and significant in the case of Argentina and Mexico, and ranging from -1.5 to -3.2. The earlier work of Ortiz (1983b) on Mexico yielded comparable results.

Canto and Nickelsburg (1987) project the rate of change in the ratio of domestic real money to foreign real money in Argentina on the change in the (log) exchange rate over the 1956–9 and 1979–81 periods, obtaining coefficients that are comparable with those of the previous authors.

Canada is certainly the country which generated most controversy in the debate on currency substitutability. Miles (1978) estimated equation (12.25) and claimed to find high currency substitutability. His estimate of the interest rate differential was -5.4 during 1960–75. Bordo and Choudhri's (1982) estimates of the coefficient on the interest rate differential were no longer significantly different from zero when they included income in Miles's equation.[30]

Other papers claiming negative results on the substitutability between US and Canadian dollars in Canada include Brillembourg and Schadler (1979) and Cuddington (1983). Similarly, İmrohoroğlu's (1991) GMM estimates of the elasticity of substitution of US and Canadian money balances range from -0.2926 to -0.4337 (depending on the instruments used).

4   Policy questions

Currency substitutability has received most attention since the mid-1970s. While the breakdown of the Bretton Woods system seemed to have revived hopes of pursuing independent monetary policies, the macroeconomic instabilities following the oil shock had shattered those hopes in many industrial countries.

Exchange rate movements were far beyond what had been expected at the time Bretton Woods collapsed, and inflation rates were beyond anything seen during the Bretton Woods period.

Towards the end of the 1970s, these problems were accompanied by a suspicion that traditional money demand equations were failing because velocity had become more unstable, thus making monetary targeting a more difficult task.[31] This perceived instability in velocity functions led some authors, like Brittain (1981) and McKinnon (1982), to attribute it to currency substitution and to advocate greater international monetary cooperation.

Figure 12.8 plots residuals from standard money demand equations

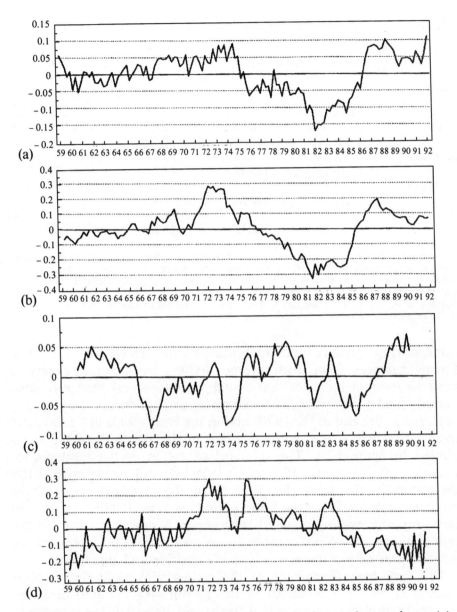

Figure 12.8   Residuals of standard money demand equations: (a) USA; (b) Canada; (c) Germany; (d) Japan.

Source: Own calculations

for the USA, Canada, Germany, and Japan; the estimates are reported in table 12.1. We regressed real narrow money (M1) on a constant, real output and the change in the GDP deflator in log-linear form. Our sample is quarterly and the data are from *International Financial Statistics*. The residual from the money demand equation is the excess of actual real money balances over real money balances predicted from

Table 12.1   Cross-country regressions for money demand

$$\ln\left(\frac{M_t}{P_t}\right) = \alpha_0 + \alpha_1 \ln(y_t) + \alpha_2 \pi_t + \alpha_3 D_{1,t} + \alpha_4 D_{2,t} + \alpha_5 D_{3,t} + u_t$$

	α_0	α_1	α_2	R^2	DW
USA	4.02	0.30	− 5.85	0.64	0.21
	(25.01)	(14.67)	(− 6.79)		
Canada	− 5.82	1.20	− 1.93	0.85	0.07
	(− 16.18)	(26.48)	(− 1.37)		
Germany	− 3.72	1.13	− 0.52	0.98	0.23
	(− 33.39)	(82.13)	(− 1.39)		
Japan	− 7.34	2.26	5.37	0.96	0.40
	(− 20.87)	(52.45)	(5.28)		

The variables labeled D are seasonal dummies. t statistics in parentheses; DW, Durbin–Watson statistic. Money is IFS line 34 (M1) and y is real GDP (except for Germany, for which GNP is used), also from IFS. π is measured by the log-difference in the GDP deflator. All data are quarterly.
Samples: USA 59:1–92:1; Canada, 59:2–91:4; Germany, 60:2–90:1 (after that date there is a break in the data due to German unification); Japan, 59:1–91:1.

our estimated velocity function. Since – by the velocity identity – real money balances equal real income divided by income velocity, a positive residual indicates that actual velocity is less than estimated velocity, and vice versa. The "missing money" phenomenon is clearly apparent at the end of the 1970s and in the early 1980s in Canada and the USA. There is also some increase in the volatility of the series plotted in figure 12.8. The standard deviation of the residuals for Canada is 0.049 in the 59:2 to 69:4 period, and increases to 0.159 thereafter. In the USA the increase in the standard error of the estimated residual over the same periods is from 0.029 to 0.069. In Germany, the missing money phenomenon is not so marked. In the case of Japan, we do not observe any special pattern but note that the inflation elasticity of money demand is positive and significant.

The very high persistence of the estimated velocity innovations (measured by the low values of the Durbin–Watson statistics), the apparent correlation of velocity disturbances, as well as the increase in their volatility in the 1970s (in the case of the USA and Canada), raised questions about monetary stability under flexible exchange rates. Currency substitutability emerged as a major, albeit controversial, explanation for some of these anomalies. McKinnon (1982) argued this point forcefully and suggested that, although currency substitutability makes the demand for national monies more unstable, worldwide demand for money was more stable and hence a better predictor of domestic inflation. On the basis of this observation, he argued that all countries should set monetary targets compatible with zero inflation, assuming no shocks in money demand. After having set these targets, all countries would pursue a policy of symmetric nonsterilized intervention to accommodate demand shocks. This would prevent monetary authorities from destabilizing the world money supply which could then be used to guide domestic inflation.

This idea has been discussed widely in the literature. For example, Spinelli (1983) argues that standard money demand equations with a scale variable and domestic interest rates leave little variation in money demand unexplained. Moreover, the empirical evidence we survey in the previous section is not conclusive in establishing the influence of foreign interest rates or expected exchange rate changes on domestic money demand. Where statistically significant cross-elasticities have been found, they are usually much smaller than the elasticity with respect to the domestic interest rate. Finally, even the evidence assembled here only suggests the presence of instabilities in the USA and Canada: estimated residuals for Germany and Japan do not display easily detectable breaks in the sample.[32]

McKinnon's idea has recently been explored in the context of the European Monetary System. As mentioned in section 2, cross-border deposits have risen steadily throughout the 1980s in EC countries. Kremers and Lane (1990) show that a narrow measure of money demand in the European exchange rate mechanism (ERM) has a more stable relation with ERM-wide income, inflation, interest rates, and the ECU–dollar exchange rate than national money demand equations.[33] Angeloni et al. (1991) estimate the information content of traditional money demand equations and those extended with cross-border deposits. They conclude that narrow monetary aggregates provide most information but that their informational content has diminished recently. Some extended monetary aggregates dominate traditional aggregates in terms of information content.

Instead of looking for a proper redefinition of national monetary aggregates, Bayoumi and Kenen (1992) went back to McKinnon's original approach and tested the hypothesis that ERM-wide money is as good a predictor of inflation as national money supplies since 1987. They ran Granger causality tests of inflation in ERM countries and domestic and ERM-wide money over 1983–90 and 1987–90. They found ERM-wide money to Granger-cause inflation in several countries for both sample periods.[34]

A more radical policy implication of currency substitutability is that discussed and advocated by Hayek:

> the countries of the Common Market ... mutually bind themselves by formal treaty not to place any obstacles in the way of the free dealing throughout their territories in one another's currencies (including gold

coins) or of a similar free exercise of the banking business by any
institution legally established in any of their territories.

(1976, p. 17)

The effect of this plan is

to impose upon existing monetary and financial agencies a very much
needed discipline by making it impossible for any of them, and for any
length of time, to issue a kind of money substantially less reliable and
useful than the money of any other.

(1976, p. 17)

Hayek's policy proposition is predicated on the assumption that
monetary authorities use their monopoly on note issuance, sustained by
legal tender rules and other regulations, to maximize their own income
or the income of their governments. Increasing the competition among
monetary authorities would thus eliminate this behavior and increase
economic efficiency. Hayek's proposition is extremely attractive from a
theoretical perspective, but its basic premise is likely to be faulty: the
objective of national monetary authorities – at least in most industrial
countries – is not to maximize the revenue from inflation.

In connection with the debate on European monetary unification, the
UK government (HM Treasury, 1989) has adopted Hayek's views by
putting forth a proposal for an evolutionary approach to currency
unification, based on the idea of currency competition, to be achieved
through "the complete removal of all unnecessary restrictions on the
use of Community currencies [and] . . . by tackling remaining barriers,
including those affecting the development of appropriate technology,
the use of relatively cheap and convenient means of payments" (HM
Treasury, 1989, paras 21, 22).

The British proposal, seemingly in the same vein as Hayek's, is
actually far from it. The achievement of a monetary union, even by the
adoption of the most stable and efficient currency, is equivalent to the
evolution from a regime of monopolistic competition to a monopoly:
all the virtues of competition, under Hayek's maintained assumption,
are lost (see Giovannini (1992a), and the discussions of the British
proposal in Weil (1991), Woodford (1991) and Flemming (1991)).[35]

In developing countries, the policy issues arising from currency
substitutability are rather different. Two major concerns stand out: first,
the effect of currency substitutability on the effectiveness of stabilization programs; second, the effects of currency substitutability on the
revenue from inflation.

Calvo and Végh (1992) discuss the effects of currency substitutability
on stabilization packages. One of the difficult problems faced by

countries trying to stabilize stems from the credibility of the policy change. Recently, many stabilization packages have been characterized by the fixing of the nominal exchange rate, or the establishment of a crawling peg which ensured progressive appreciations of the real exchange rate. The question is whether dollarization – or the circulation in the economy of the currency the government is pegging to – facilitates the stabilization, by improving credibility. In principle, credibility could be strengthened if the circulation of foreign currency in the economy largely eliminates the incentives that the government has to manipulate the national currency. In practice, however, such effect has never been tested. An additional question on the effects of currency substitutability in stabilization plans regards the choice of fixed versus flexible exchange rates. The discussion in section 2 points out, rather unambiguously, that in the presence of currency substitutability there is higher volatility of exchange rates, with potential distributional effects in the economy. These observations lead one to advocate fixed exchange rates in a stabilization whenever currency substitutability is of significant importance.[36]

The effect of currency substitutability on inflationary finance and seigniorage has been discussed above in section 2. We would like to mention here the theoretical contributions of Végh (1989a), Hercowitz and Sadka (1987) (who discuss the relation between currency substitution, the inflation tax, and foreign exchange restrictions), and Khan and Ramirez-Rojas (1986), as well as the empirical work of Bufman and Leiderman (1992, 1993) (on Israel), İmrohoroğlu (1991) (on Canada), Savastano (1992), McNelis and Asilis (1992), and Rojas-Suarez (1992) (on Latin America), and Sturzenegger (1992) who analyzes the regressivity of the inflation tax. These explorations often lead to surprising results. For example, Bufman and Leiderman find that modest increases in dollarization have a large impact on the revenue from seigniorage. Their simulations reveal that a 10 percent increase in the dollarization ratio (from 30 to 40 percent) halves the seigniorage–GNP ratio for a wide variety of inflation rates (their calculations are based on the model described above, estimated on Israeli data).

Finally, currency substitutability also has implications for the optimal rate of inflation. Note that, in general, equations (12.9) and (12.10) above imply that the marginal rate of transformation between two goods deviates from the marginal rate of substitution because of liquidity costs. Such liquidity costs, in turn, are affected by the rates of inflation in the two currencies. Hence, the model implies an optimal *relative* rate of inflation, such that the marginal rate of transformation of different goods equals their marginal rate of substitution.[37] This result, as Végh (1989a) has also pointed out, dramatically alters the analysis of the optimal inflation rate in a small country in the presence of currency substitution.[38] Given the foreign rate of inflation, the domestic rate of inflation should be chosen to minimize the distortions in relative goods prices mentioned above.

5   Concluding observations

We conclude this survey of currency substitution with a brief list of the questions, raised in this chapter, which we think represent significant challenges for future research.

The first regards the specification of the money demand equation. The boom of the empirical literature on currency substitution has shown the variety of alternative specifications of the money demand equation that could be generated by alternative theoretical models, as well as the difficulty of behavioral interpretations of its parameters. The instabilities of standard money demand equations that we have documented suggest that finding a generally acceptable and stable relation between monetary aggregates and other macroeconomic variables remains one of the main challenges of monetary theory, with major implications for monetary policy.

The second question left open by our survey regards the empirical importance of the transactions externality in money demand. Its importance is suggested by four kinds of evidence: casual empiricism *cum* introspection (e.g. US dollars are generally acceptable by hotels and taxicabs in big cities outside the USA), the nondisappearance of hyperinflating currencies (discussed in section 3), the persistence of foreign-currency deposits in economies that have completed stabilization programs (also discussed in section 3), and the international vehicle currency phenomenon, which we mentioned in section 2. Understanding the transactions externality, as well as its implications on the behavior of velocity and monetary management, is in our view an important area for future research.

Finally, in this chapter we have discussed in several places the effects of capital market liberalization. The traditional view on the liberalization of capital markets and of international capital flows is that it makes monetary management more difficult, since free international capital flows are highly sensitive to rate of return differentials and, in particular, to expectations of exchange rate fluctuations. On the other hand, we have pointed out that restricted capital markets make financial assets illiquid, and provide a boost for the demand for money for store of value purposes. Whenever domestic-currency inflation is high, restricted financial markets are likely to increase the demand for more stable foreign cash. The phenomenon of currency substitution might therefore be more pervasive in countries where financial assets are illiquid and domestic money loses purchasing power fast. Thus it is not clear what is worse for monetary management: restricted financial markets with currency substitution or free capital markets with high international capital mobility. In general, the question of whether free international capital movements are to be advocated or rejected *per se* has not received satisfactory answers so far in international monetary theory.

Notes

We are grateful to Jaime Marquez and Miguel Savastano for helpful comments and to Benedict Clements and Miguel Savastano for providing some of the data. We acknowledge financial support from the Belgian National Science Foundation and Columbia University (travel grant).

1   We do not expect, *a priori*, that high currency substitutability necessarily implies large fluctuations in holdings of domestic and foreign currency by the public: we come to this conclusion bearing in mind the standard demand-and-supply diagram (where, as is customary, higher substitutability means flatter demand curves) and observing that in such diagrams large fluctuations in quantities, even when demand (or relative demand) curves are highly elastic, can only be produced by the right combination of shocks. Of course, at this stage we are unable to argue which price, or relative price, belongs to the diagram, and what are the determinants of supply functions and – for that matter – demand functions. This is indeed the whole problem that we want to tackle in the chapter. Conversely, it is possible to observe large movements in domestic and foreign-currency holdings without highly substitutable currencies.

2   A version of the cash-in-advance model could generate the same liquidity effects.

3   See, for example, Lucas (1982). Boyer and Kingston (1987) employ a similar model which incorporates cash and credit goods to analyze the effects of currency substitution on exchange rate volatility and the transmission of inflation.

4   Girton and Roper (1981) also find this exchange rate indeterminacy when currencies are perfectly substitutable. However, when they endogenize monetary policy, the result on the variability is reversed. Giovannini (1989) finds increased exchange rate volatility in a currency substitution model. Canzoneri and Diba (1992), however, find that currency substitution will have a stabilizing effect on exchange rates in the European Community. For other studies on the relation between currency substitution and exchange rate volatility, see Boyer and Kingston (1987), Canzoneri et al. (1990), Chand and Onitsuka (1985), Daniel (1985), Henderson (1989), Isaac (1989), King et al. (1986), Koustas and Ng (1991), Lapan and Enders (1983), Marquez (1984), Park (1987), and Saurman (1986).

5   See, for example, Marshall (1987). Poloz (1986) also uses a transaction cost model.

6   See Richard (1981) and Hansen et al. (1981).

7   Since wealth is just the value of the holdings of different assets, asset demand equations can be obtained by solving the first-order conditions.

8   See Thomas and Wickens (1991) for an attempt at quantifying the vehicle currency effect in the context of money demand estimation.

9   However, it is easy to verify that an increase in the monetary services of a specific currency increases its monetary circulation both under a commodity standard and under a fiat standard: see Giovannini (1991b). Indeed Bernholz (1989) refers to the opposite phenomenon – "good" money driving out "bad" money – as *Thiers' law* after the French historian Louis A. Thiers who identified cases in which "specie, which was supposed to be hoarded or carried abroad, found its way into circulation. That which had been hidden came forth; that which had quitted France returned. The southern provinces are full of piasters, which came from Spain . . ." during the French revolution (Thiers (1840), quoted in Bernholz (1989)). Bernholz also refers to other historical episodes where "good" money drove out "bad" money: the USA during 1776–81, Peru in 1875–87, and Mexico in 1913–17. See also Guidotti and Rodriguez (1991).

10 The original result of Calvo and Rodriguez (1977) was subsequently extended and refined by various authors, including Liviatan (1981), Calvo (1985), and Végh (1988). See Calvo and Végh (1992) for a careful discussion of this strand of the literature. The interest of this literature stems also from the fact that, in the traditional Mundell–Fleming–Dornbusch model of flexible exchange rates with sticky prices, the extent of overshooting is inversely proportional to the interest elasticity of money demand, a parameter that has often been assumed to represent the elasticity of substitution of different currencies.

11 This discussion will be taken up further in section 3.

12 Little is known about the extent of currency substitution in Asia and Africa, although there is casual evidence of dollarization in some African countries. Agénor and Khan (1992) give evidence for some African and Asian countries.

13 This explains the sudden fall of FCDs in 1982–5 in Bolivia when FCDs were outlawed. This sudden fall did not occur in the other three countries at the time when FCDs at home were outlawed, because there was a substitution between FCDs held in the domestic banking system and those held abroad. See figure 12.3.

14 For an in-depth analysis of the Latin American experience, see Savastano (1992). See also Dornbusch et al. (1990).

15 Guidotti (1989, 1993) and Clements and Schwartz (1992) deal more in depth with the limited effectiveness of stabilization policies in reversing currency substitution.

16 One issue not addressed here is the effect of the drug trade on dollarization in Latin America. The available evidence suggests that it does affect the degree of dollarization in Peru and Bolivia, but not so much in Colombia. Melvin and Ladman (1991) did find evidence of the significance of the drug trade. Loans in informal loan markets in the Cochabamba Upper Valley in Bolivia were more likely to be denominated in dollars during the coca harvest than at other times of the year.

17   As Holtfrerich (1980) points out, the adoption of foreign currency by the German economy induced the government to push ahead with a monetary reform to recapture the inflation tax. See also Dornbusch (1987).

18   For more detail, see Angeloni et al. (1991).

19   While most of the empirical papers can be classified in the three categories that follow, some do not fit our classification method. See, for instance, Girton and Roper (1981), El-Erian (1988), and Clements and Schwartz (1992).

20   Indeed, the real return on the foreign bond, in terms of domestic goods, equals the own real rate of interest on the foreign bond plus the expected rate of change of the real exchange rate – the expected rate of change of the nominal exchange rate plus the expected foreign price inflation minus the expected domestic price inflation. Subtracting the real return on the domestic currency, we obtain the nominal return in the equation.

21   Again, the real return on the foreign money, expressed in terms of foreign goods, is minus the expected foreign rate of inflation. This can be transformed into a real return expressed in domestic goods by adding the expected rate of change of the exchange rate. Finally, adding the expected domestic rate of inflation (i.e. subtracting the return on the domestic money stock expressed in terms of domestic goods) we are left with the expected change in the nominal exchange rate.

22   Under suitable assumptions, described in detail in Branson and Henderson (1983), the price of the consumption bundle and nominal wealth drop out of these equations.

23   This section looks at currency substitutability from the perspective of the domestic resident. A similar set of equations can be written for the foreign resident.

24   An intermediate case is the substitution between money denominated in one currency and bonds denominated in the other currency, measured by α_3, β_2, and γ_4. See also Thomas (1985).

25   The most thorough application of this model that we know of is Cuddington (1983), who estimates equation (12.19) in this general portfolio balance framework to test for currency substitutability in the UK, Canada, and Germany.

26   See, for example, Cuddington (1983).

27   In this portfolio balance approach, several different versions of equation (12.19) have been estimated. Marquez (1992) described a slightly different set-up:

$$\log\left(\frac{M}{P}\right) = v_0 + v_1 \log y + v_2 i + v_3 i^* + v_4 e^e$$

again in a partial adjustment context. According to the author, v_3 measures capital mobility and $v_4 - v_3$ indicates currency substitutability. Examples of other portfolio balance models are in Miles and Stewart (1980) and Brittain (1981).

28   Numerous authors have built upon this specification. Ortiz (1983a, b) estimated a partial adjustment version for Mexico, incorporating foreign exchange risk and political risk. Ramirez-Rojas adapted equation (12.25) to study currency substitutability in Argentina, Mexico, and Uruguay. Other extensions can be found in Rojas-Suárez (1992), Elkhafif and Kubursi (1991),

Savastano (1992), Joines (1985), Bergstrandt and Bundt (1990), Melvin (1988), Boon et al. (1988), and de Vries (1988).

29 For the reader interested in specific countries, we would like to draw attention to the following studies: Argentina (Fasano-Filho, 1986; Kamin and Ericsson, 1993; Ramirez-Rojas, 1985), Bolivia (Clements and Schwartz, 1992; Melvin, 1988; Melvin and Afcha de la Parra, 1989), Costa Rica (Camacho and Gonzalez-Vega, 1985), Dominican Republic (Canto, 1985), Dutch Antilles (de Vries, 1988), Egypt (Boutros-Ghali, 1980; El-Erian, 1988; Elkhafif and Kubursi, 1991), Finland (Virén, 1990a), Germany (Baade and Nazmi, 1989; Miles, 1981; Miles and Stewart, 1980; Laney et al., 1984; Neldner, 1987), Mexico (Laney, 1981; Gruben and Lawler, 1983; Ortiz, 1983a, b; Ramirez-Rojas, 1985; Rogers, 1992), the Netherlands (Traa, 1991), Peru (Beckerman, 1987; McNelis and Nickelsburg, 1990; Rojas-Suarez, 1992), UK (McKenzie and Thomas, 1984), USA (McKinnon, 1982; McKinnon and Tan, 1983; Ross, 1983; Radcliffe et al., 1984, 1985; Daniel and Fried, 1985; Marquez, 1985b; Batten and Hafer, 1984, 1985; Willett, 1987; Virén, 1989, 1990b), Uruguay (Ramirez-Rojas, 1985), Venezuela (Marquez, 1984, 1987), Yemen (El-Erian, 1988).

30 See also Bana and Handa (1990) who extended the Bordo–Choudhri model with a variable measuring the cost of switching from one currency into the other. They found more evidence of currency substitutability during the flexible exchange rate period than Bordo and Choudhri did. Ghosh (1989) also found significant substitutability. Other estimates are reported by Gregory and MacKinnon (1980), de Vries (1988), and Daniel and Fried (1983) (who point to the omission of a variable measuring postal strikes in Bordo–Choudhri's specification).

31 See Goldfeld and Sichel (1990).

32 McKinnon's empirical arguments have also been re-examined. Ross (1983) points out that the evidence that McKinnon used could actually support an opposite conclusion and claims that ignoring foreign influences on domestic money is not too important. Goldstein and Haynes (1984) run "St Louis regressions" to refute McKinnon's conjecture on the superiority of world money as a predictor of US inflation.

33 For a similar analysis, see Monticelli and Strauss-Khan (1992).

34 As the authors point out, these tests should be seen as indicative and should be interpreted with caution. Their results show that both ERM-wide and national money seem to be weakly correlated with inflation in the Granger sense.

35 For related studies on the European Monetary System, see Giovannini (1990, 1991a, c, 1992b) and Gros and Thygesen (1992).

36 Some Latin American countries promoted foreign-currency deposits in their economy after the stabilization package was put into place. Note also that a big repatriation of foreign-currency deposits in the domestic banking system enhances the credibility of the stabilization package. Melvin and Fenske (1992) argue, on the other hand, that the absence of dedollarization in Bolivia might be related to the low credibility of the stabilization package.

37 See Canzoneri et al. (1992) for a discussion of this problem in the context of a different model.

38 See Friedman (1969), Guidotti and Végh (1992), Kimbrough (1986, 1991), Phelps (1973), and Végh (1989b).

References

Abel, A., R. Dornbusch, J. Huizinga, and A. Marcus (1979) "Money demand during hyperinflation," *Journal of Monetary Economics* 5, 97–104.

Agénor, P.R. (1990) "Stabilization policies in developing countries with a parallel market for foreign exchange: a formal framework," *IMF Staff Papers* 37 (3), 560–92.

—— and M.S. Khan (1992) "Foreign currency deposits and the demand for money in developing countries," IMF Working Paper WP/92/1, Washington, DC.

Angeloni, I., C. Cottarelli, and A. Levy (1991) "Cross-border deposits and monetary aggregates in the transition to EMU," presented at the conference on Monetary Policy in Stage Two of EMU, Milan.

Baade, R.A. and N. Nazmi (1989) "Currency substitution and money demand in the United States, West Germany and Japan," *Kredit und Kapital* 3, 363–74.

Bana, I.M. and J. Handa (1990) "Currency substitution and transactions costs," *Empirical Economics* 15 (3), 231–43.

Batten, D.S. and R.W. Hafer (1984) "Currency substitution: a test of its importance," *Federal Reserve Bank of St Louis Review* 66 (7), 5–11.

—— and —— (1985) "Money, income, and currency substitution: evidence from three countries," *Federal Reserve Bank of St Louis Review* 67 (5), 27–35.

—— and —— (1986) "The impact of international factors on U.S. inflation: an empirical test of the currency substitution hypothesis," *Southern Economic Journal* 53 (2), 400–12.

Bayoumi, T.A. and P.B. Kenen (1992) "Using an EC-wide monetary aggregate in stage two of European monetary union," IMF Working Paper WP/92/56, Washington, DC.

Beckerman, P. (1987) "Inflation and dollar accounts in Peru's banking system, 1978–84," *World Development* 15 (8), 1087–1106.

Bergstrand, J.H. and T.P. Bundt (1990) "Currency substitution and monetary autonomy: the foreign demand for U.S. demand deposits," *Journal of International Money and Finance* 9 (3), 325–34.

Bernholz, P. (1989) "Currency competition, inflation, Gresham's law and exchange rate," *Journal of Institutional and Theoretical Economics* 145 (3), 465–88.

Beusch, P. (1928) *Währungszerfall und Währungsstabilisierung*, Berlin, Julius Springer.

Black, S.W. (1991) "Transactions costs and vehicle currencies," *Journal of International Money and Finance* 10, 512–26.

Boon, M., C. Kool, and C. de Vries (1988) "Simulating currency substitution bias," *Economic Letters* 28 (3), 269–72.

Bordo, M. and E. Choudhri (1982) "Currency substitution and demand for money: some empirical evidence for Canada," *Journal of Money, Credit and Banking* 14, 48–57.

Boutros-Ghali, Y. (1980) "Foreign exchange, black markets and currency substitution: the case of Egypt," mimeo, International Monetary Fund.

Boyer, R.S. and G.H. Kingston (1987) "Currency substitution under finance constraints," *Journal of International Money and Finance* 6 (3), 235–50.

Branson, W.H. and D.W. Henderson (1983) "The specification and influence of assets markets," in R.W. Jones and P.B. Kenen (eds) *Handbook of International Economics*, Amsterdam, North-Holland, pp. 749–806.

Brillembourg, A. and S.M. Schadler (1979) "A model of currency substitution in exchange rate determination, 1973–78," *IMF Staff Papers* 26 (3), 513–42.

Brittain, B. (1981) "International currency substitution and the apparent instability of velocity in some Western European economies and in the United States," *Journal of Money, Credit and Banking* 13, 135–55.

Bufman, G. and L. Leiderman (1992) "Simulating an optimizing model of currency substitution," *Revista de Analisis Economico* 7 (1), 109–24.

—— and —— (1993) "Currency substitution under nonexpected utility: some empirical evidence," *Journal of Money, Credit, and Banking*, 25, 320–5.

Calvo, G.A. (1985) "Currency substitution and the real exchange rate: the utility maximization approach," *Journal of International Money and Finance* 4 (2), 175–88.

—— and C.A. Rodriguez (1977) "A model of exchange rate determination under currency substitution and rational expectations," *Journal of Political Economy* 85, 617–24.

—— and C.A. Végh (1992) "Currency substitution in developing countries: an introduction," *Revista de Analisis Economico* 7 (1), 3–28.

Camacho, A.C. and C. Gonzalez-Vega (1985) "Foreign exchange speculation, currency substitution, and domestic deposit mobilization: the case of Costa Rica," in M.B. Connolly and J. McDermott (eds) *The Economics of the Caribbean Basin*, New York, Praeger, pp. 251–83.

Canto, V.A. (1985) "Monetary policy, 'dollarization', and parallel market exchange rates: the case of the Dominican Republic," *Journal of International Money and Finance* 4, 507–21.

—— and G. Nickelsburg (1987) *Currency Substitution: Theory and Evidence from Latin America*, Boston, MA, Kluwer Academic.

Canzoneri, M.B. and B.T. Diba (1990) "Currency substitution in the European Community," Department of Economics Working Paper 90–15, Georgetown University.

—— and —— (1992) "The inflation discipline of currency substitution," *European Economic Review* 36 (4), 827–46.

——, ——, and A. Giovannini (1990) "Two concepts of currency substitution and their implications for exchange rate volatility," mimeo, Columbia University.

——, ——, and —— (1992) "Currency substitution: from the policy questions to the theory and back," mimeo, Columbia University.

Chand, S.K. and Y. Onitsuka (1985) "Stocks, flows, and some exchange rate dynamics for the currency substitution model," *Journal of International Money and Finance* 4 (1), 61–82.

Clements, B. and G. Schwartz (1992) "Currency substitution: the recent experience of Bolivia," IMF Working Paper, Washington, DC.

Cuddington, J. (1983) "Currency substitutability, capital mobility and money demand," *Journal of International Money and Finance* 2, 111–33.

—— (1989) "Review of *Currency Substitution: Theory and Evidence from Latin America*," by V.A. Canto and G. Nickelsburg," *Journal of Money, Credit and Banking* 21, 267–71.

Daniel, B.C. (1985) "Monetary autonomy and exchange rate dynamics under currency substitution," *Journal of International Economics* 19 (1–2), 119–39.

—— and H.O. Fried (1983) "Currency substitution, postal strikes, and Canadian money demand," *Canadian Journal of Economics* 16 (4), 612–24.

—— and —— (1985) "Currency substitution and U.S. money demand: a theoretical and empirical study," Department of Economics Discussion Paper 194, State University of Albany.

Dornbusch, R. (1987) "Lessons from the German experience of the 1920s," in R. Dornbusch and S. Fischer (eds) *Macroeconomics and Finance*, Cambridge, MA, MIT Press.

——, F. Sturzenegger, and H. Wolf (1990) "Extreme inflation: dynamics and stabilization," *Brookings Papers on Economic Activity* 2, 1–84.

El-Erian, M. (1988) "Currency substitution in Egypt and the Yemen Arab Republic: a comparative quantitative analysis," *IMF Staff Papers* 35 (1), 85–103.

Elkhafif, M.A. and A.A. Kubursi (1991) "Currency substitution and exchange rate instability: which comes first?" QSEP Research Report 277, McMaster University.

Fasano-Filho, U. (1986) "Currency substitution and the demand for money: the Argentine case, 1960–1976," *Weltwirtschaftliches Archiv* 122 (2), 327–39.

Flemming, J. (1991) "Discussion" of Weil, P. "Currency competition and the transition to monetary union: currency competition and the evolution of multicurrency regions," and Woodford M., "Currency competition and the transition to monetary union: does competition between currencies lead to price level and exchange rate stability?" in A. Giovannini and C. Maier (eds) *European Financial Integration*, Cambridge, Cambridge University Press, pp. 302–4.

Frenkel, J.A. (1977) "The forward exchange rate, expectations and the demand for money: the German hyperinflation," *American Economic Review* 67 (4), 653–70.

Friedman, M. (1969) *The Optimum Quantity of Money*, Chicago, IL, Aldine.

Ghosh, S.K. (1989) "Currency substitution and demand for money in Canada: further evidence," *Journal of Macroeconomics* 11 (1), 81–93.

Giovannini, A. (1989) "Currency substitution and monetary policy," paper written for the conference on *Managing Change in the European Monetary System*, Ministerio de Economia y Hacienda, Madrid.

—— (1990) "The transition to European monetary union," Essays in International Finance 178, Princeton University.

—— (1991a) "Currency substitution and the fluctuations of foreign-exchange reserves with credibly fixed exchange rates," NBER Working Paper 3636, Cambridge, MA.

—— (1991b) "Money demand and monetary control in an integrated European economy," *European Economy, Special Edition* 1, 93–106.

—— (1991c) "Currency substitution and monetary policy," in C. Wihlborg, M. Fratianni, and T.D. Willett (eds) *Financial Regulation and Monetary Arrangement, after 1992, Gothenburg*, Amsterdam, North-Holland, pp. 203–16.

—— (1992a) "Central banking in a monetary union: reflections on the proposed statute of the European central bank," mimeo, Columbia University.

—— (1992b) "The currency reform as the last stage of economic and monetary union: some policy questions," *European Economic Review* 36 (4), 433–44.

—— and B. Turtelboom (1992) "A simple model of money and taxes and an illustration on Brazilian data," mimeo, Columbia University.

Girton, L. and D. Roper (1981) "Theory and implications of currency substitution," *Journal of Money, Credit, and Banking* 13, 12–30.

Goldfeld, S. and D. Sichel (1990) "The demand for money," in B. Friedman and F. Hahn (eds) *Handbook of Monetary Economics*, Amsterdam, North-Holland.

Goldstein, H.N. and S.E. Haynes (1984) "A critical appraisal of McKinnon's world money supply hypothesis," *American Economic Review* 74 (1), 217–24.

Gregory, A. and J.G. MacKinnon (1980) "Where's my cheque? A note on postal strikes and the demand for money in Canada," *Canadian Journal of Economics* 14, 488–95.

Gros, D. and D. Thygesen (1992) *European Monetary Integration*, London, Longman.

Gruben, W.C. and P.J. Lawler (1983) "Currency substitution: the use of dollar coin and currency in the Texas border area of Mexico," *Federal Reserve Bank of Dallas Economic Review* 10–20.

Guidotti, P.E. (1989) "Exchange rate determination, interest rates, and an integrative approach to the demand for money," *Journal of International Money and Finance* 8 (1), 29–45.

—— (1993) "Currency substitution and financial innovation," *Journal of Money, Credit, and Banking* 25 (1), 109–24.

—— and C.A. Rodriguez (1991) "Dollarization in Latin America: Gresham's law in reverse?" IMF Working Paper 91/117, Washington, DC.

—— and C.A. Végh (1992) "Currency substitution and the optimal inflation tax," mimeo, International Monetary Fund.

Handa, J. (1988) "Substitution among currencies: a preferred habitat hypothesis," *International Economic Journal* 2 (2), 41–61.

Hansen, L.P., S.F. Richard, and K.J. Singleton (1981) "Econometric implications of the intertemporal capital asset pricing model," mimeo, Graduate School of Industrial Administration, Carnegie-Mellon University.

Hayek, F.A. (1976) *Denationalization of Money*, London: Institute of Economic Affairs.

Henderson, D.W. (1989) "Liberalization of financial markets and the volatility of exchange rates," in R.M. Stern (ed.) *Trade and Investment Relations among the United States, Canada and Japan*, Chicago, IL, Chicago University Press, pp. 365–73.

Hercowitz, Z. and E. Sadka (1987) "On optimal currency substitution policy and public finance," in A. Razin and E. Sadka (eds) *Economic Policy in Theory and Practice*, New York, St Martin's Press.

HM Treasury (1989) "An evolutionary approach to economic and monetary union," Discussion Paper.

Holtfrerich, C.-L. (1980) *Die Deutsche Inflation*, Berlin, de Gruyter.

İmrohoroğlu, S. (1991) "An empirical investigation of currency substitution," mimeo, University of Southern California.

Isaac, A.G. (1989) "Exchange rate volatility and currency substitution," *Journal of*

International Money and Finance 8 (2), 277–84.

Joines, D.H. (1985) "International currency substitution and the income velocity of money," *Journal of International Money and Finance* 4 (3), 303–16.

Kamin, S. and N. Ericsson (1993) "Dollarization in Argentina," mimeo, Federal Reserve Board, Washington, DC.

Kareken, J. and N. Wallace (1981) "On the indeterminacy of equilibrium exchange rates," *Quarterly Journal of Economics* 96, 207–22.

Khan, M. and C.L. Ramirez-Rojas (1986): "Currency substitution and government revenue for inflation," *Revista de Analisis Economico* 1, 79–88.

Kim, K.S. (1985) "Currency substitution in a production economy," *Journal of International Economics* 18 (1–2), 141–58.

Kimbrough, K. (1986) "The optimum quantity theory of money rule in the theory of public finance," *Journal of Monetary Economics* 18, 277–84.

——(1991) "Optimal taxation and inflation in an open economy," *Journal of Economic Dynamics and Control* 15, 179–96.

King, D.T., B.H. Putnam, and S.D. Wilford (1986) "A currency portfolio approach to exchange rate determination: exchange rate stability and independence of monetary policy," in B.H. Putnam and S.D. Wilford (eds) *The Monetary Approach to International Adjustment*, New York, Praeger.

King, R., N. Wallace, and W.E. Weber (1992) "Nonfundamental uncertainty and exchange rates," *Journal of International Economics* 32, 83–109.

Koustas, Z. and K.S. Ng (1991) "Currency substitution and exchange rate dynamics: a note," *Atlantic Economic Journal* 19 (2), 47–50.

Kremers, J.J.M. and T.D. Lane (1990) "Economic and monetary integration and the aggregate demand for money in the EMS," *IMF Staff Papers* 37 (4), 777–805.

Krugman, P. (1980) "Vehicle currencies and the structure of international exchange," *Journal of Money, Credit and Banking* 13 (3), 513–26.

Lamdany, R. and J. Dorlhiac (1987) "The dollarization of a small economy," *Scandinavian Journal of Economics* 89 (1), 91–102.

Laney, L.O. (1981) "Currency substitution: the Mexican case," *Voice of the Federal Reserve Bank of Dallas* 1–10.

——, C.D. Radcliffe and T.D. Willett (1984) "Currency substitution: comment," *Southern Economic Journal* 50 (4), 1196–1200.

Lapan, H.E. and W. Enders (1983) "Rational expectations, endogenous currency substitution, and exchange rate determination," *Quarterly Journal of Economics* 98 (3), 427–39.

Liviatan, N. (1981) "Monetary expansion and real exchange rate dynamics," *Journal of Political Economy* 89, 1218–27.

Lucas, R. (1982) "Interest rates and currency prices in a two-country world," *Journal of Monetary Economics* 10, 335–59.

Marquez, J.R. (1984) "Currency substitution, duality, and exchange rate indeterminacy: an empirical analysis of the Venezuelan experience," International Finance Discussion Papers 242.

——(1985a) "Currency substitution and the new divisia monetary aggregates: the U.S. case," International Finance Discussion Paper 257.

——(1985b) "Currency substitution and economic monetary aggregates: the U.S. case," *Economic Letters* 19 (4), 363–7.

——(1987) "Money demand in open economies: a currency substitution model for Venezuela," *Journal of International Money and Finance* 6 (2), 167–78.

—— (1992) "Currency substitution," mimeo, Federal Reserve Board; in P. Newman, M. Milgate, and J. Eatwell (eds) *The New Palgrave Dictionary of Money and Finance*, New York, Stockton Press, pp. 565–6.

Marshall, D.A. (1987) "Inflation and asset returns in a monetary economy with transactions costs," Doctoral Dissertation, Carnegie-Mellon University.

Matsuyama, K., N. Kiyotaki, and A. Matsui (1991) "Toward a theory of international currency," mimeo, Northwestern Unversity.

McKenzie, G. and S. Thomas (1984) "Currency substitution, monetary policy and international banking," Department of Economics Discussion Paper 8403, University of Southampton.

McKinnon, R.I. (1982) "Currency substitution and instability in the world dollar standard," *American Economic Review* 72 (3), 320–33.

—— (1985) "Two concepts of international currency substitution," in M.D. Connolly and J. McDermott (eds) *The Economics of the Caribbean Basin*, New York, Praeger, pp. 101–13.

—— and D. Mathieson (1981) "How to manage a repressed economy," Princeton Essays in International Finance.

—— and K.Y. Tan (1983) "Currency substitution and instability in the world dollar standard: reply," *American Economic Review* 73 (3), 474–6.

McNelis, P.D. and C. Asilis (1992) "A dynamic simulation analysis of currency substitution in an optimizing framework with transactions costs," *Revista de Analisis Economico* 7 (1), 139–52.

—— and G. Nickelsburg (1990) "Money, prices and dollarization: evidence from Ecuador and Peru," *Revista de Analisis Economico* 5.

Melvin, M. (1988) "The dollarization of Latin America as a market-enforced monetary reform: evidence and implications," *Economic Development and Cultural Change* 36, 543–57.

—— and G. Afcha de la Parra (1989) "Dollar currency in Latin America: a Bolivian application," *Economic Letters* 31, 393–7.

—— and K. Fenske (1992) "Dollarization and monetary reform: evidence from the Cochabamba region of Bolivia," *Revista de Analisis Economico* 7 (1), 125–38.

—— and J. Ladman (1991) "Coca dollars and the dollarization of South America," *Journal of Money, Credit and Banking* 23, 752–63.

Miles, M.A. (1978) "Currency substitution, flexible exchange rates, and monetary independence," *American Economic Review* 68, 428–36.

—— (1981) "Currency substitution: some further results and conclusions," *Southern Economic Journal* 48, 78–86.

—— and M.B. Stewart (1980) "The effects of risk and return on the currency composition of money demand," *Weltwirtschaftliches Archiv* 116, 613–25.

Monticelli, C. and M.O. Strauss-Kahn (1992) "European integration and the demand for Broad Money," mimeo, Bank for International Settlements, Basle.

Neldner, M. (1987) "Currency substitution in West Germany. An empirical estimation of the substitution effect using Slutsky-elasticities," *Journal of Institutional and Theoretical Economics* 143 (4), 630–42.

Ortiz, G. (1983a) "Currency substitution in Mexico: the dollarization problem," *Journal of Money, Credit and Banking* 15 (2), 174–85.

—— (1983b) "Dollarization in Mexico: causes and consequences," in P. Armella,

R. Dornbusch, and M. Obstfeld (eds) *Financial Policies and the World Capital Market: The Problem of Latin American Countries*, Chicago, IL, University of Chicago Press, pp. 71–94.

Park, W.A. (1987) "Crawling peg, inflation hedges, and exchange rate dynamics," *Journal of International Economics* 23 (1–2), 131–50.

Phelps, E. (1973) "Inflation in the theory of public finance," *Swedish Journal of Economics* 75, 67–82.

Poloz, S.S. (1984) "Transactions demand for money in a two-currency economy," *Journal of Monetary Economics* 14, 241–50.

—— (1986) "Currency substitution and the precautionary demand for money," *Journal of International Money and Finance* 5 (1), 115–24.

Radcliffe, C., A.D. Warga, and T.D. Willett (1984) "Currency substitution and instability in the world dollar standard: comment," *American Economic Review* 74 (5), 1129–31.

——, ——, and —— (1985) "International influences on U.S. national income: currency substitution, exchange rate changes, and commodity shocks," in S.W. Arndt, R.J. Sweeney, and T.D. Willett (eds) *Exchange Rates, Trade, and the U.S. Economy*, Cambridge, MA, Harper & Row, Ballinger, pp. 213–26.

Ramirez-Rojas, C.L. (1985) "Currency substitution in Argentina, Mexico, and Uruguay," *IMF Staff Papers* 32 (4), 629–67.

Richard, S.F. (1981) "Asset prices in an exchange economy," mimeo, Carnegie-Mellon University.

Rogers, J.H. (1990) "Foreign inflation transmission under flexible exchange rates and currency substitution," *Journal of Money, Credit, and Banking* 22 (2), 195–208.

—— (1992) "Convertibility risk and dollarization in Mexico: a vectorautoregressive analysis," *Journal of International Money and Finance* 11, 188–207.

Rojas-Suárez, L. (1992) "Currency substitution and inflation in Peru," *Revista de Analisis Economico* 7 (1), 153–76.

Ross, M.H. (1983) "Currency substitution and instability in the world dollar standard: comment," *American Economic Review* 73 (3), 473.

Rostowski, J. (1992) "The benefits of currency substitution during high inflation and stabilization," *Revista de Analisis Economico* 7 (1), 91–108.

Sachs, J.D. (ed.) (1989) *Developing Country Debt and the World Economy*, Chicago, IL, and London, University of Chicago Press, for the National Bureau of Economic Research.

Saurman, D.S. (1986) "Currency substitution, the exchange rate, and the real interest rate (non) differential: shipping the bad money in: a note," *Journal of Money, Credit and Banking* 18 (4), 512–18.

Savastano, M.A. (1992) "The pattern of currency substitution in Latin America: an overview," *Revista de Analisis Economico* 7 (1), 29–72.

Spinelli, F. (1983) "Currency substitution, flexible exchange rates, and the case for international monetary cooperation: discussion of a recent proposal," *IMF Staff Papers* 30 (4), 755–83.

Sturzenegger, F. (1992) "Currency substitution and the regressivity of the inflation tax," *Revista de Analisis Economico* 7 (1), 177–92.

Tanzi, V. and M. Blejer (1982) "Inflation, interest rates and currency substitution in developing countries: a discussion of the major issues," *World Development* 10 (9), 781–90.

Thiers, L.A. (1840) *History of the French Revolution*, 3 vols, Philadelphia, PA, Carey & Hart.

Thomas, L.R. (1985) "Portfolio theory and currency substitution," *Journal of Money, Credit and Banking* 17, 347–57.

Thomas, S.H. and M.R. Wickens (1991) "Currency substitution and vehicle currencies: tests of alternative hypotheses for the dollar, DM and yen," CEPR Discussion Paper 507.

Tobin, J. (1958) "Liquidity preference as behavior towards risk," *Review of Economic Studies* 25 (2), 65–86.

—— (1983) "The state of exchange rate theory: some sceptical observations," in R.N. Cooper, P.B. Kenen, J.B. de Macedo, and J. van Ypersele de Strihou (eds) *The International Monetary System under Flexible Exchange Rates*, New York, Ballinger.

Traa, B.M. (1991) "Money demand in the Netherlands," IMF Working Paper WP/91/57, Washington, DC.

Végh, C.A. (1988) "Effects of currency substitution on the response of the current account to supply shocks," *IMF Staff Papers* 35 (4) 574–91.

—— (1989a) "The optimal inflation tax in the presence of currency substitution," *Journal of Monetary Economics* 24 (1), 139–46.

—— (1989b) "Government spending and inflationary finance: a public finance approach," *IMF Staff Papers* 36, 657–77.

Virén, M. (1989) "How does domestic and foreign money growth affect the U.S. Economy?" Bank of Finland Discussion Paper 19/89.

—— (1990a) "Currency substitution, financial innovations and money demand: a note," *Applied Economics* 22, 1591–6.

—— (1990b) "McKinnon's currency substitution hypothesis: some new evidence," *Economia Internazionale* 43 (2–3), 226–34.

de Vries, C.G (1988) "Theory and relevance of currency substitution with case studies for Canada and the Netherlands Antilles," *Review of Economics and Statistics* 70 (3), 512–15.

Weil, P. (1991) "Currency competition and the transition to monetary union: currency competition and the evolution of multicurrency regions," in A. Giovannini and C. Maier (eds) *European Financial Integration*, Cambridge, Cambridge University Press, pp. 290–304.

Willett, T.D. (1987) "Currency substitution, US money demand, and international interdependence," *Contemporary Policy Issues* 5 (3), 76–82.

Woodford, M. (1991) "Currency competition and the transition to monetary union: does competition between currencies lead to price level and exchange rate stability?" in A. Giovannini and C. Maier (eds) *European Financial Integration*, Cambridge, Cambridge University Press, pp. 257–89.

PART V

DEBT, DEFICITS, AND GROWTH

13 Sovereign Immunity and International Lending

KENNETH M. KLETZER

1 Introduction

Respect for sovereign immunity is an important constraint on the international mobility of financial capital. The absence of a supranational legal authority to enforce the terms of agreements between governments or between nationals of one country and the government or nationals of another restricts the opportunities for intertemporal exchange. The history of lending to sovereigns demonstrates the consequences of lender's inabilities to enforce the repayment obligations of debtors specified in loan contracts.[1] Repayments of loans to sovereigns during the nineteenth and twentieth centuries have not approached the contractual obligations in an overwhelming number of cases. Many loans went into default as identified by historians.

Although debt repayments have not come close to meeting formal contractual obligations, the inability of lenders to use collateral to enforce loan contracts does not seem to have disabled them from recovering principal on average. Recently, economic historians have shown that, overall, lending to sovereign nations has been very profitable with returns comparing well with the average returns on contemporaneous creditor country government public debt issues. Eichengreen and Portes (1989a, b) examined samples of UK and US foreign bond issues floated in the 1920s and found that the overall internal rates of return exceeded the yields on medium-term contemporaneous public debt issued by the respective creditor countries. The rates of return on both sets of foreign bond issues were substantially below the interest rates set in the initial loan agreements. Lindert and Morton (1989) found a similar pattern in their sample of 1552 external loans to the largest ten borrowing countries (as of the last thirty years) between 1850 and 1970. The average yield was 0.42 percent above the yield on domestic government bonds, while the *ex ante* contracts offered a return on average of 2 percent over the same bond rates.

Default, while very frequent, did not necessarily lead to losses for lenders of either principal or interest. Eichengreen and Portes (1989b), for example, find that, for their sample, default led to a fall in the average rate of return but that this remained positive for both UK and US issues. In particular, all sterling loans issued to Brazil in the 1920s that they sample went into default, and the internal rate of return on these bonds ranged between 1.1 and 2.3 percent.[2]

Historically, when breach of contract, or default, has occurred there has been no abrupt termination of the relationship that is often associated with domestic bankruptcy. Instead, there is much evidence that these are ongoing relationships that continue through renegotiation, settlement of past debts, and subsequent lending. Settlement has been achieved in almost all cases on an individual case basis through bilateral negotiations.[3] Renegotiation has taken on any number of aliases, including rescheduling, partial payment, involuntary lending, debt repurchase, and new loans. A loan contract may be viewed by the trading parties to be a supporting document and not a complete description of what they expect to unfold over time. Default and subsequent renegotiation may well be an expected part of the equilibrium behavior, as suggested by Wallich (1943). That is, they are part of a complex event-contingent relationship governed by an implicit contract.

This chapter surveys theoretical models of international portfolio lending when sovereign immunity is respected. A sequence of three approaches to modeling capital flows under potential sovereign repudiation and the renegotiation of long-term debtor–creditor relationships is presented. This is not intended to be a comprehensive survey of the literature on sovereign debt, even restricted to theoretical modeling. Instead, what are presented are three general models that provide a framework within which the theoretical literature can be set. The approach taken in this restricted survey is game-theoretic. The view here is that game theory provides an explicit formal language that is extremely useful for presenting a versatile bare-bones structure for theoretical models of debt. The presentation of this chapter is an introduction to this approach to thinking about intertemporal exchange between sovereign nations.

To a large extent the literature that is discussed below is recent and succeeds some thorough literature surveys in print. The coverage of the surveys by Cardoso and Dornbusch (1989), Eaton et al. (1986), Eaton and Taylor (1986), Eaton (1989a), and Kletzer (1987) is not reiterated. For reasons of space, no discussion of the closely related issue of foreign direct investment under sovereign immunity is offered. The literature on foreign direct investment and expropriation risk also uses game-theoretic models that are similar in essential ways to those discussed in this chapter.

2 Repayment incentives and sovereign borrowing

The first issue that needs to be addressed is the nature of the motivation for sovereign borrowers to repay lenders. In the common case for domestic credit transactions, the lender has the legal right to appeal to a court to confiscate the borrower's collateral in the event of contract breach. Contracts can be agreed upon between a creditor and debtor that rely on the power of the state for enforcement. Typically, loan contracts list particular assets of the borrower (often those acquired with the borrowed funds) that can be attached in the event of default. Contracts (or the law in general) specify the contingencies in which the creditor can threaten to seize collateral. In the case of sovereign borrowing, the assets that lie outside a debtor's borders and so could be subject to seizure have always been very limited and not come close in value to the amounts lent.

Foreign governments or private agents do have the ability to cease trading with a sovereign or her subjects. One form of threat often suggested to enforce repayment is the imposition of contemporaneous sanctions such as interference with current commodity trade (e.g. through embargoes or suspension of trade preferences). For example, Diaz-Alejandro (1983) discusses the differential treatment of the USA and Great Britain by Brazil and Argentina in the 1930s. Each debtor repaid the country with which she had a large net trade surplus and, presumably, a greater concern for maintaining market access. Bulow and Rogoff (1989a) present several other cases. However, both historically and in the experience of Brazil, Ecuador, and Peru during the 1980s, there is evidence that lenders or their governments have been reluctant to threaten trade disruption in response to nonperformance on foreign loans (Eichengreen and Portes, 1989b; Sachs, 1989).

An alternative motive for repayment is the threat that intertemporal, rather than contemporaneous, trade will be disrupted. Eaton and Gersovitz (1981) propose that the threat of an embargo on future credit inflows from private sources can serve to motivate repayments by a debtor continuing to seek to smooth her aggregate consumption over time; the borrower has an incentive to maintain a reputation for repayment.[4] Conceptually, what matters for sustaining international capital flows is that some trading opportunity can be credibly disrupted, be it intratemporal or intertemporal. More generally, unilateral aid flows, military aid, and the like can be included in the set of opportunities for foreign trade that might be suspended in the event of a default.

Given that actual repayments and formal contractual obligations have so often diverged, one of the objects of this survey is to present a model of the equilibrium relationship that underlies the formal contract. The concern here is with the pattern of net resource transfers that occur in equilibrium and the punishments or incentives that support these flows. A major concern is whether or not the capital-exporting-country governments must enforce threatened punishments on the borrowing countries on behalf of private lenders to sustain intertemporal trade. This issue is addressed in the context of two models, one using contemporaneous trade sanctions and the other suspension of cooperation in smoothing the debtor's consumption to enforce equilibrium resource transfers.

The threat of suspending, in whole or in part, some international trading opportunity for the debtor can support lending in essentially the same way that the threat of seizure of assets does. In many cases, both types of enforcement amount to the ability of the creditor to impair the debtor's use of her assets. In both domestic and international lending, contracts may serve to secure for the lender in exchange for initial payment a right to threaten an action in some events. The value of these rights may not be fully specified in the contracts for all contingencies that might arise with positive probability and may be established in subsequent negotiations between debtor and creditor. Renegotiation of payment streams away from amounts specified in debt contracts can be interpreted as bargaining over the value of the punishment threat in some event. Likewise, the sovereign country has the ability to deny future net resource transfers to foreigners. If the motive for borrowing is to smooth consumption over time, then her threat of not cooperating in intertemporal exchange can be used in symmetric fashion to the same threat for the lender. The value of this threat can also be negotiated, leading to payments by foreigners to the country.[5] This is a view of renegotiation of sovereign debt that is elaborated below.

One of the historical differences observed between foreign and domestic lending is the length of the relationship following breach of formal contract. Departures from the formal contract could just as well be part of the equilibrium plan in an uncertain world for domestic debt secured by collateral enforced by courts as for sovereign debt enforced by some form of sanctions. In fact, renegotiation of debt is not infrequent for many firms in the USA. However, bankruptcy and foreclosure are common outcomes. This may be best explained by introducing incomplete information about the characteristics of the market participants. In this chapter, only models of complete information are presented. These can serve as frameworks that can be extended to games of imperfect information to examine how unobservable characteristics of borrowers change things.[6]

3   Potential repudiation and willingness to repay

3.1   Lending and the threat of sanctions

The first modern analytic model of lending with respect for sovereign immunity was presented by Eaton and Gersovitz (1981). They formalize the notion that a borrower only pays as much as it is worth to her to avoid some threatened sanctions. The borrower faces the possibility that some trading opportunity will be suspended or impaired if she fails to service her external debt. Eaton and Gersovitz argue that the disruption of contemporaneous commodity trade or interruption of future intertemporal trade (credit inflows) might serve as punishment threats.

Eaton and Gersovitz argue that it is not debtor solvency that determines the magnitude of foreign capital inflows but rather the sovereign's willingness to make payments. The country's willingness to make payments to foreign creditors is determined by the social welfare she believes that she will attain if sanctions are imposed. If the threat of sanctions is credible, then the sovereign compares her social welfare under repayment to what she realizes by refusing to meet her external obligation.

The first version of the Eaton and Gersovitz model assumes that sanctions are imposed in every future period whenever the borrower fails to repay the gross interest obligation she incurred. The country seeks to maximize a discounted stream of utility from current consumption given by

$$U = \sum_{t=0}^{\infty} \beta^t u(c_t) \qquad 0 < \beta < 1$$

where c_t denotes consumption at time t and β stands for the discount factor. The debtor has an endowment of a nonstorable good equal to y each period. The punishment is expressed in terms of the consumption cost of sanctions each period. For example, if contemporaneous trade is disrupted, then part of the value of the endowment every period is lost owing to trading on inferior terms. The loss due to trade sanctions is then given by P_t, which is assumed constant for convenience only. If the borrower faces a repayment obligation of R_t, then she compares the utility attained with repudiation

$$U_t^d = \sum_{i=t+1}^{\infty} \beta^{i-t} u(y - P) \tag{13.1}$$

with the utility received with repayment

$$U_t^r = u(y - R_0) + \sum_{i=t+1}^{\infty} \beta^{i-t} u(c_i) \tag{13.2}$$

where $\{c_i\}_{i=t+1}^{\infty}$ is the equilibrium path for consumption that follows repayment. This depends on what repayment obligations are imposed or will be incurred in future periods.

Suppose that the lender seeks to maximize a stream of repayments net of lending discounted using a discount factor $\gamma > \beta$. The maximum amount that he will lend is given by

$$l = \frac{\gamma}{1 - \gamma} P$$

since P is the maximum that he can demand in every period $t > 0$. Bulow and Rogoff (1989a) present a model which assumes that trade sanctions are used to enforce repayments and endogenizes the value of these sanctions. That is, they present an explicit model to calculate P. When the value of the debtor's endowment is random, the amount repaid is negotiated each period. The Bulow and Rogoff model of renegotiation is presented in section 4.

3.2   Threat of a permanent embargo on new loans

In a second version of their model, Eaton and Gersovitz (1981) adopt the punishment threat that a permanent embargo on new loans is imposed whenever the borrower fails to make a payment as contracted. The endowment for the borrower is assumed to follow a stochastic process with a nontrivial support every period (for simplicity, assume that the distribution is independently and identically distributed (iid) and the support is finite). For $u(c)$ strictly concave, this ensures that the sovereign will always want to smooth her consumption across states of nature. Maintaining access to international capital markets is valuable.

Assume that lenders maximize expected profits and that in equilibrium if the country has not yet defaulted lenders earn zero expected profit on any loan they make (to represent free entry). If the borrower repays an outstanding obligation, then she is assumed to be able to take a new loan that same period from those offered by lenders. Given the strategies for lenders, if the country has not defaulted at any time up to date t, then her pay-offs to any choice of action are given by

$$U_t = u(y_t - A_t) + E\left[\sum_{i=t+1}^{\infty} \beta^{i-t}u(y_i)\right] \qquad (13.3)$$

if $A_t < R_t$ and

$$U_t = U_t^r(R_t) = \max_{(l_t, R_{t+1})} \{u(y_t - R_t + l_t) + \beta E \max[U_{t+1}^d, U_{t+1}^r(R_{t+1})]\} \qquad (13.4)$$

if she pays R_t, where (l_t, R_{t+1}) satisfies

$$l_t \le \gamma E(A_{t+1} | R_{t+1}) \qquad (13.5)$$

In equilibrium, the country either pays R_t or nothing. The gains from consumption-smoothing are lost to both parties when a default occurs in this model. Given the restrictions assumed on the strategy space for lenders, these strategies form a subgame perfect equilibrium. After default has occurred, the lender will never make a positive payment to the borrower and the borrower will never make a positive payment to the lender. Therefore, the path of actions taken by each is a Nash equilibrium response to the strategy chosen by the other in every subsequent event.[7] These are trigger strategy punishments. The maximum amount that will be lent in any event reached without prior default (repudiation in the equilibrium for this model) can be calculated from the solution to the problem for the debtor and lender expressed in equations (13.3)–(13.5).

Two constraints are imposed in the Eaton and Gersovitz model. The first is that the loan contract is not renegotiable. This is expressed as a restriction on the lenders' strategy spaces: they always respond to payments from the debtor that fall short of the gross interest specified in simple one-period debt contracts by switching to the punishment path. The second is that although the punishment of a permanent credit embargo is subgame perfect, meaning that no single agent can raise his or her utility by unilaterally deviating, there are alternative paths of actions yielding utilities to all agents which Pareto dominate permanent loan autarky. An example of such a path is the initial equilibrium path. The possibility that the players cannot commit to forgo mutually beneficial renegotiation of the punishment by abandoning it would raise doubts about the credibility of such a threat. In section 5, this possibility is raised in a model of lending and repayment motivated by gains from consumption-smoothing which also allows for renegotiation of formal contractual obligations. Support is given for self-enforcement of consumption-smoothing transfers to a sovereign.

4 Bargaining over payments

In the absence of a supranational authority to enforce contract terms binding on a sovereign borrower, payments between creditors and debtors may be negotiated at each date. A natural way to begin to model the payments that are made by a country to foreign creditors is to suppose that at each date the parties bargain the resource transfer to be made in exchange for the nonexercise of penalties.

4.1 Foreign creditors' ability to disrupt commodity trade

Bulow and Rogoff (1989a) propose just this type of approach. They suppose that a foreign creditor possesses the ability to disrupt the sovereign's current commodity trade in each period. In their model economy, there are gains for the country from trading current output for importable consumables. The creditor can impose an embargo on trade period by period. He bargains with the sovereign over the amount that she pays to avoid these sanctions, i.e. over the terms of trade for the current period.

Suppose that the country produces only bananas and faces a given world relative price q for bananas in terms of a single importable good. Under free trade given q, the country will export its entire crop of bananas realizing positive gains from trade. However, it is assumed that the creditor can impose an embargo on the country's trade allowing the creditor to demand (possible) payment from the country. Any payments that are made to attain access to foreign trade are identified by Bulow and Rogoff with debt service payments. To set this up in the popular framework of Rubinstein's (1982) approach to the noncooperative Nash bargaining problem, assume that the country seeks to maximize the utility of a risk-neutral representative agent who discounts future consumption at a given constant rate of time preference. The objective function for the government is given by

$$U = \sum_{t=0}^{\infty} \exp(-\delta t)(b_t + m_t) \tag{13.6}$$

where $\delta > 0$ and b_t and m_t are home consumption of bananas and the importable respectively. It is assumed that q exceeds unity. Likewise, the creditor is assumed to be risk neutral and discounts future payments at the rate r, his opportunity rate of interest. Bananas are storable but depreciate at a constant proportionate rate λ.

Each period after harvest, bargaining follows a simple extensive form game in which the creditor first offers an amount of bananas that the sovereign pays for the ability to export her crop at that date. The country accepts this proposal or rejects it immediately making a counterproposal, which the creditor then considers. If a proposal is accepted by one of the parties, then trade takes place immediately. Trade in this case is an exchange of bananas for the trade sanctions. That is, the creditor forgoes his ability to disrupt trade that period. Bananas and sanctions are traded simultaneously. To assure that some amount is paid for forgoing trade disruption in a subgame perfect equilibrium, Bulow and Rogoff need to assume that there is an opportunity cost associated with trade disruption for the creditor (it is worth something; i.e. it costs something to provide). Otherwise, a subgame perfect equilibrium will exist in which nothing is paid for the sanctions by the country and sanctions are never imposed. They assume that the creditor will be able to receive some small (relative to equilibrium payments) benefit if they choose to impose the trade sanctions. Denote this opportunity cost by c.

This set-up is just the Rubinstein problem for bargaining over the price for the sale and purchase of one unit of an indivisible good, where the payment will be made simultaneously with transfer of the good when agreement is reached. What is being traded here are current sanctions for bananas. Two interpretations that faithfully describe the situation modeled help clarify this. One is that the creditor possesses a monopoly franchise on trade with the sovereign. That is, he has the monopsony right to import bananas from the country, and at each date they bargain over the price for the banana harvest. The subgame perfect equilibrium for the extensive form game yields the bilateral monopoly price for bananas and the division of the gains from trade. The opportunity cost for the buyer is just the market price for bananas from other sources. The second interpretation is that the creditor is able to extort "protection money" payments from the country by threatening to destroy part of the value of the national harvest. The ability to threaten credibly to harm the country is enforced by a third party, in the model of Bulow and Rogoff, who for some reason does not already use it to extort payments.

4.2 Subgame perfect equilibrium division of the gains from trade

The model as described has a unique subgame perfect equilibrium division of the gains from trade. In Rubinstein's version delay to agreement is costly, so that under complete and perfect information agreement is reached with the first offer by the creditor and the outcome is Pareto efficient (the order of moves can be reversed without qualitatively changing the results). With a depreciating harvest, the equilibrium amount paid by the country to the creditor in the limit as the time between offers and counteroffers approaches zero is given by

$$P = \min\left[\frac{\delta + \lambda}{(\delta + \lambda) + (r + \lambda)} Y, \frac{q-1}{q} Y\right] \qquad (13.7)$$

where Y is the value of the current harvest at world prices.[8] This assumes that the opportunity cost c to the creditor of selling his ability to impose sanctions, i.e. of trading the sanctions for bananas or of purchasing bananas from other suppliers under the interpretation of a monopoly franchise, is less than P so that the option of not trading has no effect on the subgame perfect pay-offs. The first term in brackets gives the subgame perfect equilibrium division of the value of the country's harvest in the Rubinstein model when the alternative is delayed trade. The second term is the most that the creditor can assure himself when the country is better off consuming bananas than exchanging them for importables at the terms of trade defined by the Nash bargaining solution. If the second term is smaller, the country gets the same utility as she would under autarky but still exports the entire crop in equilibrium.

Impatience plays a role in the equilibrium division of the surplus here. If one player in the bargaining game becomes more impatient, then the amount that player can assure that he or she receives in the subgame reached by refusing an offer made by the other bargainer falls. The amount the player could receive by refusing and having the counterproposal it makes accepted one stage later is discounted more heavily. An increase in the rate of discount for the creditor, interpreted here as an increase in his opportunity rate of interest, leads to a fall in the "price" that the country pays to purchase the one-period trade sanctions. Likewise, an increase in the sovereign's discount rate leads to a decrease in the fraction of the gains from trade she enjoys. An increase in the depreciation rate for bananas leads to a rise in P if r exceeds δ and a fall in P if r is less than δ. This follows because P falls if the ratio of the gross rate of impatience for the creditor to that for the country rises, and conversely.

4.3   Interpretation of trade between exportables and sanctions

So far, it should be clear that the fact that the model is set up as a multi-period economy (infinite horizon in this presentation) has no bearing on the amounts that are paid by the indebted country to her creditors. This is an important point about the Bulow and Rogoff model: there is no intertemporal exchange associated with the equilibrium for the bargaining model. We have to go to a separate transaction to argue that these payments have to do with debt, as opposed to say monopoly and monopsony power in international trade.

Bulow and Rogoff assume that the party identified here as the creditor purchased the right to impose trade sanctions by making a transfer of resources to the country in an initial period. The bargaining game is a model of how repayments are made and therefore of how a value for the stream of privileges to impose sanctions for some given number of periods is calculated. The creditor pays the (expected) discounted present value of the equilibrium payments P for the stream of units of sanctions to sell each period. Why the creditor must pay the country for this property right is not addressed. Other sovereign states, the creditor countries, have the ability to enforce contemporaneous trade sanctions. For some reason, they are not already exercising this power. That is, the banana-importing countries are not already exercising their market power in world trade in bananas (or whatever commodities the less developed capital-importing countries export). Further, rather than sell this unexploited market power to private agents, the creditor country governments have chosen implicitly to grant these gains to the potential debtor countries themselves. In this example, they have given the banana exporter the present value of the monopoly franchise on developed country exports to her. The less developed country then sells the right to import bananas under monopoly franchise for its competitive market value.[9]

The initial transaction labeled as a loan is not intrinsically tied to the stream of payments made by the country to avoid trade sanctions. The ability to impose trade sanctions, or, equivalently, exercise market power in international trade, exists before any transfer is made by private agents to the sovereign country. The creditor/importing country governments that are capable of imposing such sanctions choose to forgo exploiting these opportunities. The separate transaction occurs when the creditor country governments transfer in some fashion a stream of these privileges to the debtor country. The right that is transferred to the less developed country is the guarantee that the sanctions will be enforced, so that they are worth something. The banana-exporting country just trades this property (the guarantee that sanctions will be imposed by the importing country governments on behalf of whoever owns them) for goods. Note that when the importing country governments give this stream of sanctions to the exporter, they are guaranteeing that the sanctions will be imposed on behalf of the current possessor. Of course, the exporter does not want them imposed on her trade. As long as she retains possession by not selling the privilege to invoke sanction, the guarantee is that she does not have to make any payments to trade each harvest at world prices. If the opportunity cost to the country of the sanctions (the reduction in her utility from making the stream of payments P) is less than or equal to the value of the sanctions to a third party (the private creditor), then the country should choose to sell the right to impose sanctions. The guarantee comes into play because it assures that the sanctions have value, to the purchaser and therefore to the seller. The decision of the importing countries to forgo demanding payments in exchange for not imposing trade sanctions while guaranteeing that they will enforce the same sanctions on behalf of the less developed country or her assignee is a form of foreign aid.

Bulow and Rogoff assume that the debtor's representative agent's discount rate exceeds the creditor's opportunity interest rate to motivate the initial loan. This just assures that the sovereign will gain by selling the privilege to threaten trade sanctions (equivalently, to monopsony purchase of her harvest). Otherwise, she is better off using the right to impose trade sanctions herself, selling her exports at the current world price every period rather than selling them for a lower price and obtaining higher consumption in the first period.

This model is called one of constant recontracting in its title. The usual way to think about contracting in a multi-stage game is to envision that the players communicate at the start of the game and agree on the strategies they will follow. Often, it is assumed that the strategies chosen form a subgame perfect equilibrium (or satisfy a further refinement). In each period, the unique subgame perfect equilibrium is played for the division of the surplus available for that period alone in the Bulow and Rogoff model. In the repetition of this game for a finite number of periods, the unique subgame perfect equilibrium is just repetition of the unique equilibrium for each period (it is useful to think of the Nash bargaining game for division of the harvest in each period as the stage game). There is no gain from agreeing to play a particular pair of strategies in the multi-period game. Each date the division of surplus in the remainder of the game is bargained, but this is just the division of the current intra-period surplus. In the infinitely repeated version of this game, it can be shown that multiple equilibria can exist, some of which involve departures from the Nash bargaining division of the harvest.[10] However, with both parties possessing linear utilities in current consumption, all such equilibria are Pareto unranked. There is no cost to spot contracting for bananas because there are no gains from intertemporal trade.

The role for a contract here is to serve as an instrument to establish current ownership of the privilege to threaten trade sanctions before the creditor country governments, the third parties who enforce the threat. Suppose that the value of the harvest, Y, is stochastic, owing either to demand or supply shocks, and that the contracts that are used to establish ownership of sanctions are standard debt contracts specifying non-state-contingent repayments. Then the equilibrium value for the sanctions, P, is stochastic. In equilibrium for δ exceeding r, the creditor will acquire the right to demand payments equal to each possible value of P. Using simple one-period debt contracts, we see that the gross interest owed under the contract each period will equal the maximum possible value for P in the support. In every other event, the actual payment will be less than the amount listed in the formal document.

Several bargaining models have appeared in the literature. Fernandez and Rosenthal (1990) model a bargaining game over settlement of an existing debt obligation where completion of negotiations results in an end to the creditor's ability to extract future payments. Fernandez and Kaarat (1988) discuss the role of lender heterogeneity in a bargaining framework, and Ozler (1989a) adopts Nash's bargaining solution to motivate an empirical analysis of renegotiation of sovereign debts. Kletzer (1989a, b) discusses inefficiencies in strategic Nash bargaining models when there is asymmetric information.

5   Intertemporal exchange and sovereignty

5.1   A consumption-smoothing model of sovereign borrowing

This section analyzes a simple model of international borrowing and lending for the purpose of smoothing national consumption over time. The model contrasts with the Nash bargaining model of the previous section in two important ways. The first is that while the problem is well described as a bargaining situation following the recent literature on multi-stage games, the Nash bargaining framework is not a suitable analytic description of it.[11] The second is that lenders are assumed not to have access to enforcement of some threat to punish the borrower by a third party. Punishment and consequently sustainability of lending and repayment are internal to the relationship between the creditor and debtor. The model is developed as one of intertemporal barter between a pair of sovereigns and then interpreted in terms of lending by private agents to a sovereign country. This section presents a simple deterministic representation of the model analyzed by Kletzer and Wright (1990a, b).[12]

We begin with a very simple model of an infinite-horizon economy in which there are two agents, labeled for reasons of convenience rather than substance as a debtor and a creditor, who have preferences over streams of consumption of a single nonstorable good representable by the following pair of utility functions:

$$U = \sum_{t=0}^{\infty} \beta^t u(c_t) \qquad (13.8)$$

for the debtor and

$$V = \sum_{t=0}^{\infty} \beta^t v(c_t) \qquad (13.9)$$

for the creditor, where $0 < \beta < 1$, and $u(c)$ and $v(c)$ are both increasing, strictly concave, and twice continuously differentiable for non-negative c.

The global endowment each period is constant and normalized to equal unity. The debtor country's share of this endowment (harvest) in period t is y_t, where $0 < y_t < 1$. Consumption in period t for the creditor country is equal to $1 - c_t$, where c_t denotes the debtor country's consumption in period t for the remainder. We are just assuming that the two agents are risk averse and have negatively correlated endowments to motivate gains from intertemporal trade. For simplicity, let the debtor's share of the global harvest follow a deterministic process alternating between a low fraction y_1 in even-numbered periods and a high fraction y_2 in odd-numbered periods ($y_1 < y_2$).

Next, we just assume that sovereign immunity is respected in the sense that no part of the endowment of each country can be confiscated through force by the other country. A country might willingly consume less than its current (nonstorable) harvest giving part of the output to its counterpart in exchange for future return of the favor. In every period, each country always has the option of choosing to consume its current endowment.

This leads to a simple repeated game in which the stage game is as follows. For later notational convenience, the debtor country will be referred to as country 0 and the creditor country as country 1. The action space for country 0 is the interval $[0, y_t]$, where the action is the amount of her endowment transferred to country 1. Likewise, the action space for country 1 is the interval $[0, 1 - y_t]$, and his action is the amount of his endowment given to country 0.[13] The stage-game pay-off for the debtor and the creditor are given by $u(c_t) - u(y_t)$ and $v(1 - c_t) - v(1 - y_t)$ respectively. This single-shot game has a unique Nash equilibrium in which both players consume their endowments, since giving anything to the other reduces own consumption for any given strategy chosen by the opponent.

If this game is repeated an infinite number of times with the oscillating harvest, then an infinity of subgame perfect equilibrium outcomes is possible if the discount factor β is large enough (but still less than unity). This is the Folk Theorem for repeated games with discounting under perfect (equivalently, complete) information.[14] The set of equilibrium paths for consumption and international transfers supportable through subgame perfect equilibrium strategy pairs can be described using permanent repetition of the single-shot Nash equilibrium as a punishment path. That is, the minimum payoff one player can assure that the other obtains in this game (the minmax pay-off) is zero. This is the pay-off each receives by permanently playing the Nash equilibrium action for the stage game. One subgame perfect equilibrium is for both countries never to give the other country any of the national harvest no matter what either of them has done in the past.

The repeated game pay-offs are defined as functions of the paths of transfers made by the two players. A path is a sequence of pairs of transfers $a_t \equiv (a_t^0, a_t^1)$, for $t = 0, 1, 2, \ldots$; $s \equiv \{a_t\}_{t=0}^{\infty}$. The pay-offs are given by

$$\Pi_t^0(s) = [u(y_t - a_t^0 + a_t^1) - u(y_t)] + \beta\Pi_{t+1}^0(s) \qquad (13.10)$$

and

$$\Pi_t^1(s) = [v(1 - y_t - a_t^1 + a_t^0) - v(1 - y_t)] + \beta\Pi_{t+1}^1(s) \qquad (13.11)$$

A subgame perfect equilibrium for this game is a pair of strategies for the repeated game that specify the action that each player takes at each date as a function of the history of all past actions for both players. Following Abreu (1988), it suffices to find all paths that are supportable by some subgame perfect equilibrium to restrict attention to those that specify just three paths: one to be followed from date 0 on until one player alone deviates from it; a path, denoted q^0, to be initiated whenever the debtor alone deviates; and a path q^1 to be initiated whenever the creditor alone deviates. The paths q^0 and q^1 are started whenever the respective player takes an action that is different from that specified in the last path initiated, whether that is s or one of the punishment paths.

All subgame perfect equilibria satisfy the following inequalities:

$$[u(y_t - a_t^0 + a_t^1) - u(y_t)] + \beta\Pi_{t+1}^0(s) \geq [u(y_t + a_t^1) - u(y_t)] + \beta\Pi_{t+1}^0(q^0)$$

$$(13.12)$$

and

$$[v(1 - y_t - a_t^1 + a_t^0) - v(1 - y_t)] + \beta\Pi_{t+1}^1(s) \geq [v(1 - y_t + a_t^0) - v(1 - y_t)]$$
$$+ \beta\Pi_{t+1}^1(q^1)$$

$$(13.13)$$

These inequalities hold where s is the initial path as written or is replaced by any punishment path (in which case the current action a_t is that specified by the ongoing punishment). Since it suffices for finding all of the equilibrium transfer paths to adopt the worst punishments available, which are permanent repetition of the Nash equilibrium for the stage game, the following inequalities are satisfied by an equilibrium path:

$$[u(y_t - a_t^0) - u(y_t)] + \beta \Pi_{t+1}^0(s) \geq 0 \qquad (13.14)$$

and

$$[v(1 - y_t - a_t^1) - v(1 - y_t)] + \beta \Pi_{t+1}^1(s) \geq 0 \qquad (13.15)$$

This is because only the net resource transfer from one country to the other matters for utilities. Therefore it does not affect anything of substance to assume that in equilibrium only one country makes a positive transfer to the other at any date (unless both happen to consume their endowments).

The set of subgame equilibrium intertemporal trading paths for this economy can be derived using inequalities (13.14) and (13.15). This is done by deriving the paths that support the utility possibility frontier for the two countries generated by subgame perfect equilibria. These are found by maximizing the surplus for country 0 subject to providing country 1 with some feasible level of surplus and the constraints expressed by inequalities (13.14) and (13.15). This is the following simple dynamic programming problem where the notation is changed to denote the surplus possibility frontier as $\Pi_t^0(\Pi_t^1)$:[15]

$$\underset{c_t,\, \Pi_{t+1}^1}{\text{maximize}} [u(c_t) - u(y_t) + \beta \Pi_{t+1}^0(\Pi_{t+1}^1)]$$

$$\text{subject to } \hat{\Pi}_t^1 \leq (1 - c_t) + \beta \Pi_{t+1}^1 \qquad (13.16)$$

$$\Pi_{t+1}^0(\Pi_{t+1}^1) \geq 0$$

$$\Pi_{t+1}^1 \geq 0$$

It is straightforward that this is a concave dynamic programming problem and that the surplus possibility frontier $\Pi_t^0(\Pi_t^1)$ is continuously differentiable. It is also downward sloping in Π_t^1.

Using the first-order conditions for a maximum and the envelope condition, necessary conditions for an efficient subgame perfect equilibrium are given by

$$u'(c_t) = (1 + \phi_{t+1})u'(c_{t+1}) - \psi_{t+1}$$

$$\phi_{t+1} \geq 0 \qquad \Pi_{t+1}^0 \geq 0 \qquad \phi_{t+1}\Pi_{t+1}^0 = 0 \qquad (13.17)$$

$$\psi_{t+1} \geq 0 \qquad \Pi_{t+1}^1 \geq 0 \qquad \psi_{t+1}\Pi_{t+1}^1 = 0$$

where ϕ_{t+1} and ψ_{t+1} are the multipliers on the last two constraints for the program.

Equation (13.17) implies that consumption will be fully smoothed for both countries between any two dates as long as the perfection constraints are not binding in the second period for either country. If a constraint binds, then consumption will not be fully smoothed, but a subgame perfect equilibrium may still exist that differs from permanent repetition of the single-shot Nash equilibrium, so that some degree of cooperation is sustainable.

First, there exists a number $\bar{\beta} < 1$ such that, for $\beta \geq \bar{\beta}$, complete smoothing of the consumptions for each country is possible in some equilibrium. This $\bar{\beta}$ solves the two equations along with c between y^1 and y^2:

$$u(c)(1 + \beta) = u(y^2) + \beta u(y^1)$$

and

$$v(1 - c)(1 + \beta) = v(1 - y^1) + \beta v(1 - y^2)$$

Because at least one of $u(c)$ or $v(c)$ is strictly concave, a solution exists in the domain claimed.

Next, there exists a number $\hat{\beta} > 0$ such that if $\beta \leq \hat{\beta}$ then the only equilibrium outcome is permanent autarky. This value satisfies

$$\frac{u'(y^2)}{\beta u'(y^1)} = \frac{\beta v'(1 - y^2)}{v'(1 - y^1)}$$

Concavity of $u(c)$ and $v(c)$ with strict concavity of at least one implies that $0 < \hat{\beta} < \bar{\beta} < 1$. If the discount factor is in the interval $[\hat{\beta}, \bar{\beta}]$, then the necessary conditions for the efficient equilibrium paths imply that consumption for the debtor country is given by

$$0 \leq c_t \leq \bar{c}^1 \quad \text{for } t = 0,$$

$$c_t = \underline{c}^2 \quad \text{for } t = 1, 3, 5, \ldots$$

$$c_t = \bar{c}^1 \quad \text{for } t = 2, 4, 6, \ldots$$

where $v(1 - \bar{c}^1) + \beta v(1 - \underline{c}^2) = v(1 - y^2) + \beta v(1 - y^1)$ and $u(\underline{c}^2) + \beta u(\bar{c}^1) = u(y^2) + \beta u(y^1)$. The initial transfer (equivalently, c in period 0) depends on the division of surplus for the entire infinite-horizon game. If all the surplus goes to the debtor (an assumption that would represent free entry by lenders in an extended model), then the initial transfer from creditor country to the debtor would be $\bar{c}^1 - y^1$, leaving the creditor with the same utility from the equilibrium path as he would attain by consuming his endowment every period.

If β is greater than or equal to $\bar{\beta}$, then the initial consumption is again between y^1 and $\bar{c}^1$ for country 0, but consumption for every period thereafter equals the maximum of c_0 and $\underline{c}^2$, where c^1 and $\bar{c}^2$ are as defined above. A Pareto-optimal intertemporal allocation is achieved only if the surplus in the relationship is divided so that $\bar{c}^1 \leq c_0 \leq \underline{c}^2$.[16]

In deriving the set of utilities and intertemporal transfer paths that can be achieved using subgame perfect equilibria, deviation by either country from the equilibrium path leads to a continuation pay-off (the surplus for the repeated game received starting in the next period) for that country of zero, the same as it attains under permanent autarky. If permanent autarky (trigger strategy punishment) is invoked as the punishment threat to sustain cooperative behavior in equilibrium, then the credibility of this threat should be considered. In the context of sovereign borrowing, worries that such an embargo on future consumption-smoothing inflows of resources will not be credible, in that it is likely to be abandoned, have been raised frequently. The point of these concerns is that under such punishments the gains from intertemporal trade in the relationship are unexploited; both countries can gain by stopping the punishment and starting over. If they do renegotiate the punishment (i.e. renegotiate, or "recontract," the strategy pair that they are following) after a history that includes a deviation by one player from the equilibrium path, then that punishment no longer has any bite. If it is required to sustain cooperation, then cooperation will not be viable under potential mutually advantageous renegotiation.

This model has the property that there exist equilibrium paths that give one of the countries a continuation pay-off of zero and are efficient in the set of all subgame perfect equilibrium paths. The punishments described below have the same "strength" as do permanent embargoes but do not forsake the gains from trade. They have the interpretation of short-lived moratoria on payments to a deviant player immediately after he or she deviates. The equilibrium that incorporates this type of punishment is a strong subgame perfect (Nash) equilibrium in the terminology of Rubinstein (1980). After every history of actions for the two countries, the pay-offs in the repeated game from that time forward are Pareto efficient in the set of all pay-offs for subgame perfect equilibria. This equilibrium satisfies all the different notions of renegotiation-proofness that have been proposed in the literature. An equilibrium is renegotiation-proof if the two players cannot recontract, i.e. communicate after play has commenced and choose to play a new pair of subgame perfect equilibrium strategies, to their mutual benefit. Alternative definitions of renegotiation-proof equilibria entertain different restrictions on the set of new candidate equilibria.[17]

Suppose that the discount factor exceeds $\hat{\beta}$ and the debtor country deviates from an ongoing efficient equilibrium path at an odd date t. This is a date that her endowment is y^2 and so she is expected to make a payment to country 1. At date $t+1$, country 1 pays the debtor nothing in place of the maximum of $\{c_0 - y^1, \bar{c}^1 - y^1\}$ which is the amount he would pay if a deviation had never occurred. This is the start of an efficient path for the subgame beginning at date $t+1$ with an endowment for the debtor country of y^1 in which the creditor gets all the surplus from cooperation. In period $t+2$, the debtor's endowment is y^2, and she pays the creditor $y^2 - c^2$, attaining the same utility from date $t+2$ as that she would get from consuming her endowment in every remaining period. Her surplus starting in period $t+2$ is zero, so that the maximum surplus she can obtain by deviating from the equilibrium path at date t is also zero:

$$\Pi_t^0 = \max_{a_t} \{[u(y^2 - a_t) - u(y^2)] + \beta[u(y^1) - u(y^1)] + \beta^2 \Pi_{t+2}^0\} = 0$$

$$(13.18)$$

when a_t is less than the action required by the ongoing path because $c_{t+1} = y^1$ and $\Pi_{t+2}^0 = 0$.

This is a credible punishment by a reasonable criterion because the only way that the creditor cannot punish is to make a positive transfer to the debtor, consuming less than his endowment and reducing his stage-game pay-off. That is, he only deviates from a strategy that benefits him in the long run by taking an action that reduces his current stage-game pay-off. However, myopic, he will not want to do this. The debtor country is expected to cooperate in her own punishment here. She can do no better, since if she deviates from this punishment path it will just be restarted in period $t+3$ ($y_{t+3} = y^1$) by another single-period moratorium on transfers from country 1.

If country 1 deviates from the initial path at some even-numbered date t', then his punishment is started in period $t'+1$. The debtor does not pay him the amount that the equilibrium path prescribes: the maximum of $\{y^2 - c_0, y^2 - c^2\}$. In period $t'+2$, when the debtor country's endowment is again y^1, country 1 pays the debtor $\bar{c}^1 - y^1$ under the punishment q^1. This is the amount that starts off a new efficient equilibrium path with all of the surplus going to the debtor country. If the creditor country deviates again by making a smaller payment, then the debtor responds by consuming her endowment y^2 at date $t'+3$ rather than giving part of it to the creditor. She imposes a moratorium on repayments to the creditor after he deviates. This moratorium lasts for only one period in the equilibrium for the subgame reached through the deviation.

There is no need for credit embargoes for multiple periods, much less for an infinite horizon. Intertemporal barter is sustained using punishment paths that are Pareto undominated by any subgame perfect equilibrium path. These punishments also have the appealing interpretation that a moratorium on net resource transfers to a country that departs from the equilibrium path is imposed until the deviant makes an adequate payment to the other country. Below, an argument will be given that these are enforceable punishments when there are many potential creditors or debtors.

A question one might ask of this argument is why the debtor or the creditor ever needs to accept zero surplus along the equilibrium path. Whenever β is large enough to allow some smoothing, the share of the total surplus (gains from trade) received by each country varies across dates. For example, if the discount factor is between $\hat{\beta}$ and $\bar{\beta}$ then both countries get zero surplus on the respective dates that they make positive transfers to the other country. Recontracting as in the Bulow and Rogoff model through bargaining over the division of surplus in the remainder of the game leads to an equilibrium that is not renegotiation-proof.[18]

The problem studied by Rubinstein (1982) and other papers on noncooperative Nash bargaining is one in which trade takes place simultaneously. The seller accepts payment at the same moment that he gives up the commodity. In the consumption-smoothing problem, on an odd date the debtor country has a good harvest ($y_t = y^2$) and makes a unilateral transfer to the creditor. The creditor gives her nothing at the same time. If she attempts to make a payment that would give her half of the surplus (the Rubinstein solution with common discount rates as the time between offers goes to zero), the creditor can simply take it, consume in excess of his current endowment, and still be able to punish her the next period. Nash bargaining works because there is an opportunity cost to agreement for both parties. For the seller, this is what he would get in the next round discounted. In the consumption-smoothing game, there is no opportunity cost to the creditor of accepting whatever he is given in an odd period.

It should be noted that only one strong subgame perfect equilibrium was described above. There are many for this game, in general. Since a player might deviate when his or her surplus in the equilibrium path is positive, the punishment does not necessarily have to assure that the deviant attains zero continuation surplus. In many cases, the punishment can be a new efficient path that begins with a positive, rather than zero, transfer from the other player.

5.2   Self-enforcing lending

This simple model of intertemporal barter can be interpreted as a model of lending by risk-neutral creditors to a sovereign country seeking to smooth her consumption over time. The first modification is the introduction of many potential creditors, labeled $j = 1, 2, \ldots, J$, having the same utility function. For simplicity, each of the potential creditors is assumed to be risk neutral, so that $v(c) = c$. Further, each of them is assumed to have an endowment of the nonstorable good equal to unity every period. The debtor country (country 0) has the alternating stream of endowments as before $(0 < y^1 < y^2 < 1)$.

First, if there is only one lender $(J = 1)$, then there exist values $\hat{\beta}$ and $\bar{\beta}$ as before and an equilibrium strategy pair that gives efficient pay-offs to the debtor and the creditor (within the set achievable using subgame perfect equilibria) for every history of actions for the players. The punishment chosen if the country deviates from some cooperative path is the one-shot moratorium on repayments. This is repeated as long as she continues to deviate (by not following the punishment path).

If there are other potential (intertemporal) trading partners for the country, then the punishments need to be extended to specify how each player behaves in each path or punishment and what punishments are invoked when a lender (new or old) deviates from an ongoing path, notably, punishment of the debtor. The Folk Theorem continues to hold, and there are subgame perfect equilibria that sustain pay-offs Pareto dominating permanent autarky for sufficiently large discount factors $(\beta \geq \hat{\beta})$. However, a natural concern is whether an equilibrium exists that is not disrupted by renegotiation within subsets of players. In particular, can the country refuse to pay one lender and start up a new smoothing relationship with another lender?

In this model, there exists a strong subgame perfect equilibrium for $J > 1$. One such equilibrium is described here. A formal proof of existence is given in a stochastic model in Kletzer and Wright (1990b). A strong perfect equilibrium is constructed by finding strategies assuring that if the country deviates in a smoothing relationship with one lender then she cannot improve upon her pay-off under autarky by forming a new relationship with another lender.

When there are more than two players, the definition of a strong subgame perfect equilibrium needs to be restated. Let σ_c denote the c-tuple of strategies followed by players in the coalition C of size c. The $(J + 1 - c)$-tuple of strategies for the players not in C is denoted σ_{-c} (σ_i is player i's strategy). Holding σ_{-c} fixed (recall that strategies tell how each player acts as a function of the past actions of all players) induces a repeated game for the coalition C. An equilibrium σ will be strong if for every nonempty coalition C of the players σ_c sustains a Pareto-undominated pay-off vector for the members of C in the set of pay-offs attainable using subgame perfect equilibria for the game induced by σ_{-c}, in each feasible history of actions for all players. What this means is that no coalition can find an alternative set of strategies for its members, taking as given the strategies chosen by the rest of the players, that increases the pay-off for each of its members in some history of actions that could occur. This extends the idea behind subgame perfect equilibrium to coalitions. As pointed out by Bernheim et al. (1987), this is a very strong notion of coalition-proofness for repeated games, and often strong subgame perfect equilibria do not exist.[19]

The equilibrium described here supports an efficient subgame perfect equilibrium path of transfers between the country and lender 1. At date 0, all the gains from trade are assumed to go to the debtor, and the lender receives zero surplus. A strategy is constructed for lender 1 with the following property: if the country deviates from the equilibrium path, autarky is the only subgame perfect equilibrium outcome for the game played by a coalition of the debtor and other lenders and induced by this strategy. A consequence of this strategy is that the equilibrium pay-offs to all lenders other than lender 1 are zero in any subgame (i.e. after any feasible history). This is a very strong property that, as explained below, follows from symmetry in the availability of commitment opportunities for the lenders and the debtor.

The equilibrium path for the strategy profile constructed follows the dynamics given already for the two-player version letting $v(c) = c$. If lender 1 ever deviates, paying the country less than he should along the initial path, then his punishment is the punishment q^1 extended so that the action for the other lenders is to consume their endowments (as they do in the initial path). If the country deviates, then her punishment is a moratorium by all lenders until she makes the transfer to lender 1 that re-initiates an efficient equilibrium path giving up all of the surplus to lender 1. This is not the full specification of the equilibrium strategies. Punishments must be given that are adopted when a lender j, $j > 1$, deviates from an ongoing punishment of the debtor.

A lender j, $j > 1$, deviates from the punishment of the country if he makes a positive transfer to her while she is under a moratorium on payments from lender 1. Suppose that the country deviates from the initial path by refusing to make a transfer to lender 1 at date t when her endowment is y^2. Under the punishment q^0, the debtor receives no transfer at date $t + 1$ and makes a transfer to lender 1 leaving her zero surplus in $t + 2$ (when her endowment is again y^2). Instead, she might try to reach an agreement with lender j under which the two of them initiate a different smoothing path and split the gains from trade. In such an agreement the country pays lender j less in period $t + 2$ than she is expected to pay lender 1. This amount should only be positive if lender j will make a positive payment to the debtor in some future period, say $t + 3$ (when y is y^1), in the equilibrium path for the strategies they agree to follow. Lender j will only make a payment at $t + 3$ if, in equilibrium, he will receive at least as much from the debtor in present value thereafter.

Lender 1 can assure that that type of arrangement will not work by relying on the inability of every agent to commit his or her future actions. Suppose that the country and lender j have made such an agreement in which the country pays a positive amount to lender j in period $t + 2$. Lender j then makes the agreed-upon payment to the debtor on date $t + 3$ when her endowment is y^1, thereby deviating from the punishment. If this is rational, then the agreement calls for the country to pay lender j in some future period; without loss of generality, assume that this is $t + 4$ (when her endowment is y^2). Lender 1 responds by offering the borrower an alternative (efficient) smoothing path starting in period $t + 4$ that gives the country more surplus looking forward from then on than she would attain honoring the agreement with lender j. This alternative path begins with the country making a smaller payment to lender 1 than she has agreed to make to lender j. Lender 1 will always want to make this offer since the proposed path starts with a payment to him, giving him a positive stage-game pay-off and therefore positive surplus in the repeated game looking forward from date $t + 4$. The offer increases the country's surplus over what it would be in the relationship with lender j, so that the debtor will not choose to pay lender j in period $t + 4$.

At date $t + 3$, lender j recognizes that he will receive nothing in return for any payments made to the debtor. Therefore, in equilibrium he never makes a transfer to the country when she is being punished; if he does, his equilibrium surplus in period $t + 3$ is negative. The debtor also recognizes that making payments to anybody other than lender 1 can only reduce her surplus (including a payment to lender j in period $t + 2$). After deviating, the most she can attain is zero surplus – what she receives if she cooperates in the punishment.

This equilibrium exists because no player can commit his or her future actions. The country cannot commit to repay lender j and will not when she is offered an alternative path giving her more surplus by lender 1. Lender j also cannot commit to make a future payment to the country. Because he recognizes that his pay-off will be zero in equilibrium for a subgame reached if he makes a payment, he never makes one. This means that the moratorium type of punishment is credible and an efficient subgame perfect equilibrium path of consumption-smoothing transfers can be supported.

Bulow and Rogoff (1989b) (see also Cohen, 1991) claim that reputations alone cannot support intertemporal trade. They argue that third party enforcement is necessary if any lending is to take place, so that the threat of a credit embargo is only useful if it is enforced by creditor country governments through mechanisms such as seniority clauses. They set up a proof of this claim in a model that assumes that lenders can commit to make positive resource transfers in future events even if when those events are reached doing so is not in their best interests. These commitments require explicit enforcement by third parties.[20]

Adding the third party enforcement assumed by Bulow and Rogoff to this model allows lender j ($j > 1$) to commit to make a payment to the country at date $t + 3$ (when her endowment is y^1) in exchange for a payment from the country in period $t + 2$. On date $t + 3$, lender j must follow through whether or not he expects ever to receive another payment from the borrower. The possibility of lender commitment allows the country and lender j to reach an agreement in period $t + 2$ (when her endowment is y^2) that gives each of them positive surplus. If only this commitment opportunity is introduced, then the argument of Bulow and Rogoff holds, as they prove. Some lender can always offer a profitable contract to the country whenever she is expected to repay another lender, so she will never make a repayment. The addition of a third party that enforces lender commitment destroys the possibility of intertemporal trade unless the third party also enforces the claim of lender 1.

What Bulow and Rogoff (1989b) prove is that, if the lenders are committed to repay the loans they receive, then without further third party intervention no lending takes place in equilibrium. They claim, however, that this proves that reputation alone cannot support lending to a sovereign country. That is, they argue that the threat of noncooperation cannot sustain intertemporal trade in an infinitely repeated game of smoothing a sovereign's consumption. The argument above shows that this is not a correct implication, as one might infer already from the extensive literature on repeated games.[21] If lenders and debtors are treated symmetrically with respect to their access to commitment opportunities, then intertemporal trade is self-enforcing in the very strong sense that it is supported using a strong subgame perfect equilibrium. This symmetric treatment is automatic when we assume anarchy as in the model of intertemporal barter adopted here: there is no third party present. It is the presence of the third party in the first place that creates the need for the third party to support consumption-smoothing transfer paths.[22]

The argument given for self-enforcement (coalition and renegotiation-proofness) of an efficient subgame perfect equilibrium path relied on a simple idea. This is that anyone is not only allowed to cheat a cheater but is expected to do so. If a deviant debtor ever makes a transfer to another lender, then he should (in equilibrium for the subgame reached through that history of actions) keep it and never follow through on his agreement to play new strategies with the debtor.

If he deviates from the embargo of her, then he becomes the cheater and she is expected to cheat him. In fact, she is encouraged to do so, since her "slate" is cleaned with lender 1 who offers her part of the surplus from then on. This has intuitive appeal.

The possibility of intertemporal trade relies on the existence of gains from intertemporal trade between the country and the lenders. As pointed out by Eaton and Gersovitz (1981) and reiterated in several surveys,[23] this requires that at every date the country faces future variability in her endowment and that she has concave preferences. Capital accumulation can be introduced into these models as long as a point cannot be reached with certainty after which the borrower makes but never receives positive payments.

5.3   Debt contracts

The path of transfers to and from the sovereign country in the simple alternating endowments model can be interpreted in terms of standard one-period debt contracts. It is assumed that the lender attains zero surplus from initiating an efficient equilibrium path with the borrower. This assumption can be called free entry (it is made to avoid the need explicitly to model entry).

On the first date, the creditor (lender 1) pays the debtor the amount $l = \bar{c}^1 - y^1 > 0$ (for $\beta > \hat{\beta}$). The next period her endowment is y^2, and the country pays the lender $R = y^2 - \max(\underline{c}^2, \underline{c}^1)$.[24] In equilibrium for this endowment stream, the lender's surplus (profit) is just

$$\Pi_0^1 = -l + \beta R + \beta^2 \Pi_2^1$$

The assumption of free entry and the necessary conditions for efficiency of the subgame perfect equilibrium path imply that $\Pi_0^1 = \Pi_2^1 = 0$. Therefore $R = \beta^{-1} l$. The repayment is made at a gross rate of interest equal to the creditor's discount rate plus one because there is no uncertainty about the endowment for period 1.[25] The maximum amount that is lent is constrained by what the debtor is willing to pay out of her endowment in period 1 looking forward, given the equilibrium strategies.

This is not the same as solvency which must be defined in terms of the capacity of the debtor country government to tax the resources of the private economy. If the debtor can imose lump-sum taxes subject to leaving the representative household with non-negative consumption in every period, then the country will be solvent in any planned sequence of transfers less than or equal to y_t for all $t > 0$. Full smoothing would be feasible under such a solvency criterion for any β between 0 and 1.

5.4   Renegotiation and the role of debt contracts

When the endowments of the agents follow a deterministic process, a simple debt contract suffices to describe the agreed-upon equilibrium actions for participants. If the endowments of risk-averse agents are stochastic, then the payments made at each date in the equilibrium will generally depend on the states of nature as well as on histories of actions. Standard debt contracts specifying the amounts lent and noncontingent gross interest payments to be made will not be sufficient descriptions of the equilibrium behavior.

A number of authors have suggested that debt renegotiation, in its various guises as rescheduling, involuntary lending, debt rollovers, and other aliases, is part of implicit state-contingent contracting between lenders and borrowers. Grossman and van Huyck (1988) adopt a consumption-smoothing model of borrowing by a sovereign and propose that some defaults (defined as breaches of simple one-period debt contracts by the borrower) are "excusable." The debtor's output is independently and identically distributed over dates. They propose that, although the debt contract is written as non-state-contingent, it is actually an implicit contract in which renegotiation yields the contingent payments.

Like Bulow and Rogoff (1989b), Grossman and van Huyck implicitly assume that the lender is able to commit his future actions.[26] Worrall (1990) explicitly solves a model of consumption-smoothing along the lines of Grossman and van Huyck (1988). He assumes that the sovereign country's endowment of nonstorable output is iid, the borrower faces a trigger strategy penalty for deviating from the equilibrium path, and the risk-neutral lender can commit to make payments at future dates. Third party enforcement of lender commitments is explicit. The surplus (expected profit) for a lender looking forward at any time later than the initial date can be negative in equilibrium.

The idea behind the proposal that renegotiation of simple debt contracts serves to implement an implicit state-contingent contract is that the formal debt service obligation $\bar{R}$ is at least as large as the maximum repayment that occurs with positive probability in equilibrium. The lender and the borrower renegotiate the actual amount to be repaid, but implicitly this amount is thought to be positive. The lender receives a non-negative payment and chooses whether or not to offer a new loan (i.e. a gross resource transfer) in the same period. Unless the lender is coerced to make payments to the country by a third party, then any new loan should provide non-negative expected profits. The assumptions that lenders renegotiate repayments owed to them and can choose not to make new loans are equivalent to the explicit assumption that lenders cannot commit to accept negative surpluses looking forward at any date. This point is elaborated below.

To discuss the renegotiation of standard debt contracts, the simple model of intertemporal barter is extended to allow the country's endowment to follow a stochastic process with finite support. Kletzer and Wright (1990a, b) do this for an iid endowment process, although all the dynamics discussed in that paper apply for a general class of autocorrelated endowment processes.

Let the support for the country's endowment of the nonstorable good each period be given by $\{y^1, \ldots, y^S\}$, and the cumulative distribution function for y_{t+1} conditional on past endowments be given by $F(y_{t+1} \mid y_0, \ldots, y_t)$. Ignoring some needed technical assumptions (these are standard), the problem for finding the surplus possibility frontier is now given by

$$\underset{c_t, \{\Pi^1_{t+1,s}\}^S_{s=1}}{\text{maximize}}\{[u(c_t) - u(y_t)] + \beta E_t \Pi^0_{t+1,s}(\Pi^1_{t+1,s})\} \qquad (13.19)$$

subject to

$$\Pi^1_t \le [y_t - c_t] + \beta E_t \Pi^1_{t+1,s} \qquad (13.19a)$$

$$\Pi^0_{t+1,s}(\Pi^1_{t+1,s}) \ge 0 \qquad \text{for all } s = 1, \ldots, S \qquad (13.19b)$$

$$\Pi^1_{t+1,s} \ge 0 \qquad \text{for all } s = 1, \ldots, S \qquad (13.19c)$$

where the expectation E_t is taken with respect to the distribution $F(. \mid y_0, \ldots, y_t)$. The information available to both players at date t is the history of endowments through date t.

With a continuity restriction on the distribution function, it can be proved that the set of surplus pairs that are sustainable using subgame perfect equilibria is compact and convex with a continuously differentiable and strictly concave frontier, so that this is a concave dynamic programming problem. Using the envelope condition and first-order conditions, one of the necessary conditions for a path of payments to be efficient is given by

$$u'(c_t) = (1 + \phi_{t+1,s}) u'(c_{t+1,s}) - \psi_{t+1,s} \qquad (13.20)$$

where $\phi_{t+1,s}$ and $\psi_{t+1,s}$ are the non-negative multipliers for the constraints (13.19b) and (13.19c) respectively for each state s. These depend on the history of endowments for the country up through date t.

The net payment made by the lender to the country in an efficient equilibrium path at any date t depends on the history of endowment realizations through time t, $\omega_t \equiv (y_0, \ldots, y_t)$, and the initial division of the surplus between the lender and the country. It can be shown that this net payment lies in an interval $[\underline{\tau}, \overline{\tau}]$, where $\underline{\tau} \le 0$ and $\overline{\tau} \ge 0$. The limits of these intervals depend upon ω_t to the extent that $F(y_{t+1}|\omega_t)$ does, so that $\underline{\tau}$ and $\overline{\tau}$ depend on y_t alone if the endowment process is iid. Within the interval, the amount of the net payment depends on ω_t and the initial division of surplus even in the iid case, in general.[27] This implies that the same type of punishments defined for the simple deterministic model can be used in the more general stochastic model (see Kletzer and Wright, 1990a, b). The punishment that the lender imposes on the borrower if she deviates from an ongoing path is a moratorium on new net resource transfers to her until after she has made a transfer that initiates a new efficient path with all of the surplus going to the lender. This transfer is $-\underline{\tau}$, determined by the history of endowments at the time she pays it. If the lender deviates, then the borrower imposes a moratorium on net resource transfers to him (repayments) until he pays $\overline{\tau}$, the amount that gives the country all the surplus from a new efficient path. Intertemporal barter is self-enforcing if, for example, punishments of other potential lenders adopted when they interfere with punishment of the borrower are analogous to those proposed for the deterministic model.

The efficient subgame perfect equilibrium path of payments can be replicated using one-period loan contracts with state-contingent repayments.[28] These are written as a loan l_t and repayment schedule $R_{t+1,s}$. The country's consumption at date t in state q is given by

$$c_t = y_t - R_{t,q} + l_t \tag{13.21}$$

The lender's surplus in the date–state pair (t, q) is the expected discounted stream of net payments he receives from time t onwards. This is given by

$$\Pi_{t,q}^1 = R_{t,q} + E_t \left[\sum_{i=t+1}^{\infty} \beta^{i-t}(-l_i + \beta R_{i+1,s}) \right] \tag{13.22}$$

It can be assumed that each loan made after date 0 (the initial date) earns zero expected profit, without loss of generality. That is,

$$-l_t + \beta E_t R_{t+1,s} = 0 \tag{13.23}$$

so that

$$\Pi_{t,q}^1 = R_{t,q} \qquad \text{for all } t \geq 0 \tag{13.24}$$

The surplus for the lender in the entire relationship is the expected profit for the first contract. Under the assumption of free entry, this would be zero.

A simple example illustrates. Suppose that the country's endowment process is iid and can assume two possible values $y^1 < y^2$, each with probability one-half. The solution for a constrained efficient equilibrium yields values $\bar{c}^1 \geq y^1$ and $\underline{c}^2 \leq y^2$, as in the deterministic example. There exist $\underline{\beta}$ and $\bar{\beta}$ such that $0 < \underline{\beta} < \bar{\beta} < 1$. If $\bar{\beta} > \beta > \underline{\beta}$, then $\bar{c}^1 < \underline{c}^2$ so that consumption is incompletely smoothed over states. The following equalities hold:

$$(2 - \beta)(\bar{c}^1 - y^1) = \beta(y^2 - \bar{c}^2) \qquad \text{since } \Pi^1_{t,1} = 0$$

and

$$u(\underline{c}^2) - u(y^2) = \frac{\beta}{1 - \beta}\frac{1}{2}\{[u(\bar{c}^1) + u(\underline{c}^2)] - [u(y^1) + u(y^2)]\}$$

In the steady state for the equilibrium path, the country consumes $\bar{c}^1$ in state 1 and $\underline{c}^2$ in state 2. The steady-state consumption and payments between the borrower and the lender can be supported using the following one-period loan contracts with state-contingent repayment schedules:

$$l_t = l^* = \bar{c}^1 - y^1$$

for both states 1 and 2,

$$R_{t+1,1} = R^*_1 = 0$$

and

$$R_{t+1,2} = R^*_2 = \frac{2}{\beta}(\bar{c}^1 - y^1)$$

If simple one-period debt contracts with possible renegotiation of repayments are used in this steady state, these will specify the principal l^* and gross interest payment R^*_2.

The constraint that the lender's surplus is non-negative in every event (t, q) means that the contingent repayment $R_{t,q}$ is always non-negative. If the state-contingent repayment is interpreted as the outcome of renegotiation of a standard one-period debt contract, then lender noncommitment is simply the assumption that lenders are only willing to negotiate repayments down to zero and make new loans (payments) that earn non-negative profits in expectation.

If lenders are able to commit their future actions (the non-negativity constraint on $\Pi^1_{t+1,s}$ is not imposed), then they can commit to receive negative repayments in some events. Relaxing the constraint implies that risk-neutral lenders will in general offer contracts specifying negative repayments for events that occur with positive probability. In these events, the lender would prefer to renege and suffer the harshest punishment that the country can inflict on him by herself (giving him zero surplus), but commitment rules out this option. Because a third party is needed to enforce the lender's commitment, an implicit contract is inadequate. The third party needs to know how much the lender is required to pay the borrower in such events, so that an explicit (state-contingent) contract is necessary.

Worrall (1990) solves for the efficient smoothing path under the commitment assumption made by Bulow and Rogoff (1989b) and implicitly by Grossman and van Huyck (1988) when y_t is iid. The constraint that $\Pi^1_{t+1,s} \geq 0$ for each state and every date $t \geq 0$ is not imposed, although Π^1_0 is restricted to be non-negative. The efficient path is given by solving the following problem (see Worrall, 1990, for details):

$$\underset{c_t, \Pi^1_{t+1}}{\text{maximize}} \; [u(c_t) - u(y_t) + \beta \sum_{s=1}^{S} p_s \Pi^0_{t+1,s}(\Pi^1_{t+1,s})] \qquad (13.25)$$

subject to

$$(y_t - c_t) + \beta \sum_{s=1}^{S} p_s \Pi^1_{t+1,s} \geq \Pi^1_{t,k} \qquad \text{for all } k = 1, \ldots, S$$

$$\Pi^0_{t+1,s}(\Pi^1_{t+1,s}) \geq 0 \qquad \text{for all } s = 1, \ldots, S$$

$$\Pi^1_0 \geq 0$$

where p_s is the (positive) probability that state s occurs.

Worrall shows that consumption is always fully smoothed in the steady state for every value of $\beta > 0$, and that as the steady state is approached consumption for the sovereign is monotonically rising.[29] Consumption is not smoothed over all dates, but the steady state is reached in finite time.[30]

This solution path for transfers can also be replicated using one-period loan contracts with state-contingent repayments. Again, it can be assumed that every loan made after date 0 earns zero expected profit, so that the surplus for the lender at date t in state s is given by

$$\Pi^1_{t,s} = R_{t,s}$$

In general, assuming lender commitment makes a difference, and some repayments will be negative in equilibrium. As Kletzer et al. (1992) point out, whenever the country's consumption is not completely smoothed over all dates from date 0 onward,[31] the steady-state state-contingent contract specifies a negative repayment by the borrower in the second period of the contract for the lowest endowment state. When the lender makes a loan in period t, he commits himself also to make a payment to the borrower if the worst state of nature occurs in period $t + 1$ (although he receives payments in good states of nature). Once such a payment is made, the contract is fulfilled, and the borrower owes him nothing more. A new one-period debt contract will be offered in equilibrium that achieves zero expected profit. These contracts offer more insurance for the country than do implicit state-contingent debt contracts. The commitment assumption made in Bulow and Rogoff (1989b), Grossman and van Huyck (1988), and Worrall (1990) makes an explicit contract necessary whenever the constraint that the country attains at least zero surplus is binding for some state.[32]

Atkeson (1991) extends the problem considered by Worrall (1990) to allow for an unobservable action by the country.[33] In his model of repeated moral hazard, lenders are explicitly assumed to commit to a repayment schedule. These contracts are insurance contracts subject to moral hazard and to the noncommitment constraints for the country. They cannot be interpreted as implicit contracts achieved through renegotiation of simple one-period debt contracts. Equilibrium is supported by punishments given by Abreu et al. (1990). These are short-lived punishments similar to ones proposed above for the simpler case of observable actions. Imperfect information could be introduced into the model of lending with renegotiation (i.e. without lender commitment), or, similarly, the noncommitment constraint could be added to the model of Atkeson (1991). Under general assumptions there should exist punishments sustaining payoffs on the frontier of the surplus possibility set for subgame perfect equilibria. With imperfect information about debtor policies that affect the distribution for her endowment each period, it is expected that punishments will be invoked in equilibrium with positive probability.[34]

6   Conclusion: some implications for policymaking

During the 1980s a large number of authors addressed the potential need for policy intervention in international capital markets. This concern arose from the effect of external indebtedness on the macro-economic performance of a number of developing countries. One of the primary policy proposals pursued by several countries was the repurchase of outstanding debt obligations at discount.

Bulow and Rogoff (1988) argue that if the debtor country's own resources are used to repurchase debt the country will not gain, in general. Their argument is that when the formal outstanding debt exceeds the expected present value of future payments by the country, a reduction of the external debt will not coincide with an equal fall in the discounted value of payments. Since payments are made to avoid sanctions, the value of these is unlikely to change in proportion to the formal external claims. By selling a debt claim a creditor forgoes his share of the future payments to be made by the debtor after the repurchase. If all debt has the same seniority, then the opportunity cost for creditors is the price of debt after the deal. This is the average value of all outstanding debt claims, while the fall in the expected present value of payments is the marginal value of the total debt.

The Nash bargaining model of Bulow and Rogoff (1989a) helps to illustrate. The maximum expected present value of payments supported by the threat of trade disruption is independent of how much debt is on record. If formal debt claims exceed this amount (they trade at discount), then a marginal reduction in outstanding debt will not reduce the payments made by the country. Any resources used to repurchase debt provide a lump-sum transfer to creditors with no benefit for the country. When debt no longer trades at a discount, then the country just pays the present value of the reduction in payments it attains. The country prefers not to repurchase debt if its discount rate is higher than the discount rate for creditors. In consumption-smoothing models with perfect information, as van Wijnbergen (1990) points out, the borrower will only be worse off paying to reduce her future transfers to the lender. Payment of an amount that leaves a risk-neutral lender just indifferent will reduce the surplus of the risk-averse debtor (the risk premium measures her loss). In the consumption-smoothing model presented above, debtor-financed repurchases of debt will only be welfare reducing.

The argument in favor of debt repurchase was the claim that reduction of outstanding debt obligations could raise the surplus of both lenders and debtors (see, for example, Krugman, 1988, 1989; Sachs, 1990). One argument is that it is costly to transfer resources from the private sector to the public sector for debt repayment so that the existence of external public debt implies distortionary taxation of private sector activity. This is likely to lead to taxation of capital income, inhibiting investment in the country. In a repeated game of perfect information, these costs would go into the calculation of the subgame perfect equilibrium strategies for lenders and borrowers. Such costs can be added to the models presented above. If the costs are convex, then efficient self-enforcing equilibria exist and can be attained through mutually beneficial negotiation as outlined. While nonconvex costs of distortionary taxation can create difficulties, it is not clear how debt reduction would be useful for assuring that creditors and debtors coordinate on an efficient equilibrium path. Intervention is not justified unless there are other distortions.[35]

In an economy with pre-existing market failures, foreign loans might be sought and made willingly that lead to overall welfare losses. This is an application of the general theory of the second best. Under such circumstances, external debt can affect domestic saving and investment, inhibiting or encouraging growth. For example, foreign indebt-edness can affect household saving adversely because of implied future tax burdens or positively if aggregate saving rises to attain a long-run wealth target. An interesting topic along these lines is the analysis of the effects of external borrowing opportunities and debt on growth in the presence of externalities associated with domestic investment. Two papers on endogenous growth under perfect international capital mobility indicate how identifying the source of growth externalities is crucial for drawing policy inferences. Alogoskoufis and van der Ploeg (1991) study the effects of public sector debt in a two-country model with overlapping generations in which investment by one firm raise the productivity of capital for other firms as in Romer (1986) (see also chapter 16 in this volume). An increase in national public debt reduces the rate of growth through financial crowding out. Buiter and Kletzer (1991) study an overlapping generations model incorporating external effects in the accumulation of human capital by households following Razin (1972) and Lucas (1988). In that model, the issue of public debt leads to an increase in the accumulation of human capital by the young by reducing their lifetime resources. This leads to an increase in the rate of growth. In chapter 14 of this volume Cohen elaborates on the effects of external debt on growth.

The presence of incomplete information can lead to a case for policy intervention, possibly including debt repurchase or forgiveness.[36] In the Atkeson (1991) model of repeated insurance with moral hazard, the equilibrium path is efficient given the asymmetry of information and the country's sovereignty. Unobservable actions by the government are not enough to find a basis for debt repurchase. However, if private agents are unsure of how the government will respond in the future to external debt obligations, then the presence of the debt burden itself can induce overall efficiency losses in equilibrium. This is the case if households and firms are uncertain of the objective function of the government so that they do not know the government's pay-offs for different feasible choices of strategies. Policy uncertainty is an impor-tant potential theoretical basis for intervention in international capital markets. Benchmark models with complete information and either observable or (perhaps partially) unobservable actions can help to clarify the source of imperfections that can be addressed by multi-lateral policies or by unilateral debt reduction.

Imperfect observability of actions does lead to welfare losses in many cases, leading to a basis for multi-lateral policy reform. Kletzer (1984) presents a simple model in the spirit of Eaton and Gersovitz (1981) to compare equilibria when lenders can observe the market behavior of other lenders with when they cannot. With repudiation of debt possible, unobservability of other lender actions leads to a third-best equilibrium that is Pareto dominated by one in which lenders are able to reveal their actions to other lenders. What they need to reveal is the amount they have lent. This set-up was motivated by the frequent press reports that lenders did not know how much had been lent to large debtor countries after the repayments crises of the 1980s began. The results of the model apply when the asymmetry of information is switched to the other side of the market, so that the debtor country government does not observe how much debt it is incurring. This happened in a number of countries in the 1970s and 1980s because private and parastatal firms, as well as separate government ministries, were able to borrow from abroad under explicit or implicit government guarantees.[37] If the borrowing government does not know its contingent debt liability, then the same third-best equilibrium allocation arises. This model could be extended to the repeated game framework surveyed above. The implications would be that debt is built up too fast. There will be too much consumption in early periods and less intertemporal smoothing of the debtor's consumption.

Notes

1   An interesting statement of the difficulties posed by sovereignty for foreign investors is given by Keynes (1924).
2   In addition to the papers mentioned in the text, other papers that present and discuss the historical record on lending, default, and repayment since 1920 include Eichengreen (1989) and Eichengreen and Portes (1990).
3   See Eichengreen and Lindert (1989).
4   Ozler (1989b, 1992) presents empirical evidence that past behavior by sovereign countries in international credit markets affects access to loans and the terms on which credit is offered.
5   There are controversies concerning this notion (see Cohen, 1991). The skeptical reader is invited to read the presentation of consumption-smoothing models of renegotiation of repayments and new loans given here or in Kletzer and Wright (1990a, b).
6   Many authors have studied models that analyze lending with imperfect information. The references include a nonexhaustive list. Examples are Asilis (1989), Atkeson (1991), Cole and English (1987), Cole et al. (1991), Cole and Kehoe (1992), Detragiache (1990), Gale and Hellwig (1989), Kehoe and Levine (1990), Kletzer (1984, 1989a, b), and Suarez (1988).
7   Other reputations-based models of sovereign borrowing include Kletzer (1984, 1989a, b), Manuelli (1986), O'Connell (1987), Suarez (1988), Grossman and van Huyck (1988), Bulow and Rogoff (1989b), Asilis (1989), Gale and Hellwig (1989), Atkeson (1991), Kletzer and Wright (1990a, b), Eaton (1989b), Kehoe and Levine (1990), Kahn (1989), Craig (1991), and Cole and Kehoe (1992).

8   Bulow and Rogoff make the assumption that if a trade embargo is imposed the country will still be able to trade but will obtain only a fraction $1 - \beta$ of the imports that it would in the absence of the embargo. Here, it is assumed for simplicity that the country can only consume bananas under embargo, so that β is unity.

9   An answer to the question of why the creditor countries do not already demand payments from the debtor country is that they have other interests at stake that would be sacrificed by doing so. If this is the case, then the question becomes why creditor country governments defend the claims of private lenders when it is not in their best interest. Alexander (1987) gives a lengthy discussion of how public interests are likely to take legal precedence over private interests under "state doctrine."

10 In their original article, Bulow and Rogoff point out that they assume a finite horizon to avoid the possibility of other equilibria arising in an infinitely repeated game. Alternative subgame perfect equilibria that can be found support equilibrium paths in which the division of surplus departs from the stage-game (Rubinstein) pay-offs but switches back and forth between favoring each party (and always continues to do so). Punishments that can support any of these other subgame perfect equilibria are reversions to permanent repetition of the Nash bargaining solution, the Bulow and Rogoff equilibrium.

11 This terminology is emphasized by Abreu et al. (1989) in the context of renegotiation-proof equilibria for repeated games. Kletzer and Wright (1990a) propose renegotiation-proofness as a notion of bargaining equilibrium for the sovereign borrowing problem in consumption-smoothing models.

12 Craig (1991) discusses a similar model in which labor productivity for the borrowing country fluctuates deterministically over time in an infinite-horizon model.

13 For convenience, the debtor is called she (in keeping with the tradition for countries) and the creditor is called he.

14 See, for example, Fudenberg and Tirole (1991, section 5.1).

15 The surplus possibility frontier is just the utility possibility frontier with the origin moved to the autarky utility levels.

16 This is consistent with the Folk Theorem which tells us that a Pareto-optimal allocation can be sustained by some subgame perfect equilibrium if the discount factor is large enough. It does not imply that all the efficient subgame perfect equilibria (ones sustaining pay-offs Pareto undominated by the pay-offs for any other subgame perfect equilibrium) provide Pareto-optimal allocations.

17 Definitions of renegotiation-proofness current to the literature on repeated games include those given by Abreu et al. (1989), Asheim (1988), Farrell (1984), Farrell and Maskin (1989), and Pearce (1987) for infinitely repeated games. See also Evans and Maskin (1989) and Bernheim and Ray (1989) on efficient renegotiation-proof equilibria of infinitely repeated games.

18 An equilibrium path can be constructed dividing the surplus for the remainder of the infinite-horizon path using the Nash bargaining solution shares every period. A path other than just repetition of the Nash equilibrium for the stage game may be supported by the one-shot moratorium type of punishment used here. However, this type of equilibrium would not survive

renegotiation to a strong subgame perfect Nash equilibrium. In every stage, the pay-offs will be Pareto dominated by those sustained by the strategies proposed. By the definitions of Farrell and Maskin, this *ad hoc* application of some Nash bargaining division would yield an equilibrium that is not strongly renegotiation-proof.

19 Bernheim et al. (1987) propose an alternative, weaker definition of coalition-proofness. Their definition requires that any candidate equilibrium used for ruling out some subgame perfect equilibrium cannot be ruled out in turn. The definition is given recursively, so that it applies to finitely repeated games. It is the most established definition of renegotiation-proofness in finitely repeated games.

20 See Bulow and Rogoff (1989b, p. 45, lines 12–16).

21 Cole and Kehoe (1992), Cole et al. (1991), and Eaton (1989b) all present models in which international lending is sustained by reputations. In each of these papers, lenders do not know the debtor's type. That is, these are games of incomplete information. Reputations concern the pay-offs for debtors. Bulow and Rogoff (1989b) raise the possibility that their argument will not go through if the borrower must worry about the reputation she earns for other market relationships she might have. This is the case dealt with by Cole and Kehoe. Eaton sets up a production-smoothing model with multiple types of borrowers. The borrower is only concerned with her reputation in the one relationship, as in Bulow and Rogoff (1989b) and Kletzer and Wright (1990b).

22 Cohen (1991) uses a consumption-smoothing model and imposes the constraint that in period $t + 1$ the debtor will be just indifferent between autarky and repayment if she repays in period t. Therefore, any repayment this period reduces her surplus below zero (see p. 94). This argument is not an analysis of the question of whether lending and repayment are self-enforcing since continuation values are fixed rather than derived from equilibria for the subgames reached.

23 See, for example, Eaton et al. (1986) or Kletzer (1987).

24 Recall that $\bar{c}^1 > \underline{c}^2$ for $\beta > \bar{\beta}$ and that $\bar{c}^1 < \underline{c}^2$ for $\beta < \bar{\beta}$.

25 Note that if the lender is risk-averse, as in the initial presentation of the example model, then the interest rate is less than the common rate of discount. When $v(c) \equiv u(c)$ the equilibrium rate of interest (net) is zero.

26 Grossman and van Huyck (1988) are somewhat unclear about the assumptions being made. The description of the model and analysis are inconsistent with the assumption that the lender cannot commit. The equilibrium path for the model presented in Grossman and van Huyck (1988) is fully derived in Worrall (1990).

27 This dynamic programming problem is set up and solved by Thomas and Worrall (1988) in a model of implicit wage contracts with iid spot market wages.

28 It can be seen from the constraints to problem (13.19) and equation (13.22) below that short-term contracts suffice and that the opportunity to contract over longer horizons would not increase the set of attainable plans.

29 The necessary conditions for a solution include

$$u'(c_t) = (1 + \phi_{t+1,s})u'(c_{t+1}) \qquad \phi_{t+1,s} \geq 0 \qquad \text{for all } s = 1, \ldots, s$$

This implies monotonicity. The finite support and iid endowment process ensure that consumption is fully smoothed in a steady state that exists and is reached with probability one in finite time.

30 Grossman and van Huyck (1988) assert the solution to the dynamic programming problem implied by their model. They do not assert the solution demonstrated by Worrall (1990).

31 This happens whenever at least one of the constraints $\Pi_{t,s}^0 \geq 0$ is binding.

32 Worrall (1990) states on page 1102:

> However, since the contract is not enforceable it makes no difference whether the repayments are specified in advance as state contingent or whether there is a state independent repayment followed by *ex post*, fully anticipated renegotiations or reschedulings so as to make the repayments state contingent.

In his conclusion, he recognizes that the assumptions allow repayments to be negative and points out that restricting them to be non-negative would lead to incompletely smoothed steady states as derived in Thomas and Worrall (1988). He does not recognize that the absence of these constraints implies that renegotiation of non-state-contingent contracts will not achieve the equilibrium. He also points out that Grossman and van Huyck (1988) argue that, if the self-enforcement constraint for the borrower is binding in some states, then the lender will not fully indemnify the borrower in the lowest income state. As pointed out above, their discussion presumes that lenders can commit. Worrall shows that complete smoothing is not possible across all dates for their set-up even though it is achieved in the steady state when the borrower's constraint is binding in some states.

Grossman and van Huyck raise an interesting related issue when they allow investment at home by the debtor. They assume that the country cannot commit to invest and argue that the country's consumption will not be completely smoothed in a constrained efficient equilibrium if investment reduces the riskiness of her income stream.

33 There are many other papers that analyze models of lending with asymmetries of information. A nonexhaustive listing includes Asilis (1989), Cole et al. (1991), Cole and English (1987), Cole and Kehoe (1992), Detragiache (1990), Gale and Hellwig (1989), Kehoe and Levine (1990), Kletzer (1984, 1989a, b), and Suarez (1988).

34 Several papers show that this is a general result for subgame perfect equilibria in repeated games with imperfect information. See Fudenberg and Tirole (1991, ch. 5).

35 Eaton (1987) considers a model of lending with potential capital flight in which there can be multiple equilibria. One of these equilibria involves capital flight with default while the other entails repayment without capital flight. The possibility of high rates of taxation of the income earned from investment at home and evasion of home taxes of investment earnings from abroad leads to the existence of these equilibria. Coordination on one equilibrium (the one with home investment and repayment) leads to a Pareto-superior allocation. This is an interesting example of how little one might need to add to sharpen the discussion of the case for intervention and also of the information requirements for policymakers.

36 Games of incomplete information and of imperfect information are treated in formally the same fashion (see Fudenberg and Tirole, 1991). The phrase incomplete information is used here to indicate that participants do not know characteristics, including beliefs, of other agents.

37 Carlos Diaz-Alejandro (1984) notes how foreign debt incurred by private Chilean banks was explicitly not guaranteed by the Chilean government but that lenders were able to persuade the government to assume these obligations when the banks went bankrupt. Foreign lenders appear to have assumed that an implicit guarantee existed in equilibrium.

References

Abreu, D. (1988) "On the theory of infinitely repeated games with discounting," *Econometrica* 55, 383–96.

——, D. Pearce, and E. Stacchetti (1989) "Renegotiation and symmetry in repeated games," mimeo, Harvard University.

——, ——, and —— (1990) "Toward a theory of discounted repeated games with imperfect monitoring," *Econometrica* 58, 1041–64.

Alexander, L.S. (1987) "Three essays on sovereign default and international lending," PhD Dissertation, Yale University.

Alogoskoufis, G. and F. van der Ploeg (1991) "On budgetary policies, growth, and external deficits in an interdependent world," *Journal of the Japanese and International Economies* 5, 305–24.

Asheim, G. (1988) "Extending renegotiation-proofness to infinite horizon games," mimeo, Norwegian School of Economics and Business Administration.

Asilis, C.M. (1989) "Recurrent debt crisis in an optimal dynamic strategic model of sovereign lending," mimeo, Georgetown University.

Atkeson, A. (1991) "International lending with moral hazard and risk of repudiation," *Econometrica* 59, 1069–89.

Bernheim, B.D. and D. Ray (1989) "Collective dynamic choice in repeated games," *Games and Economic Behavior* 1, 295–326.

——, B. Peleg, and M.D. Whinston (1987) "Coalition-proof Nash equilibrium 1: concepts," *Journal of Economic Theory*, 42, 1–12.

Buiter, W.H. and K.M. Kletzer (1991) "Persistent differences in national productivity growth rates with a common technology and free capital mobility: the roles of public debt, capital taxation and policy towards human capital formation," *Journal of the Japanese and International Economies* 5, 325–53.

Bulow, J. and K. Rogoff (1988) "The buyback boondoggle," *Brookings Papers on Economic Activity* 2, 675–98.

—— and —— (1989a) "A constant recontracting model of sovereign debt," *Journal of Political Economy* 97, 155–78.

—— and —— (1989b) "LDC debt: is to forgive to forget?" *American Economic Review* 79, 43–50.

Cardoso, E.A. and R. Dornbusch (1989) "Foreign private capital flows," in H.B. Chenery and T.N. Srinivasan (eds) *Handbook of Development Economics*, Amsterdam, North-Holland.

Cohen, D. (1991) *Private Lending to Sovereign States*, Cambridge, MA, MIT Press.

Cole, H.L. and W.B. English (1987) "Two-sided sovereign default and international equity contracts," mimeo, University of Pennsylvania, August.

—— and P. Kehoe (1992) "Reputational spillover across relationships with enduring and transient benefits: reviving reputation models of debt," mimeo, Federal Reserve Bank of Minneapolis Research Department (revised, January).

——, J. Dow, and W.B. English (1991), "Default, settlement and signaling: lending resumption in a reputational model of sovereign debt," Federal Reserve Bank of Minneapolis Research Department Working Paper 488.

Craig, B. (1991) "The role of heterogeneity in supporting international credit market transactions in the presence of sovereign risks," mimeo, Oberlin College.

Detragiache, E. (1990) "Bankruptcy and debt forgiveness in credit markets with asymmetric information," mimeo, Johns Hopkins University.

Diaz-Alejandro, C.F. (1983) "Stories of the 1930s for the 1980s," in P.A. Armella, R. Dornbusch, and M. Obstfeld (eds) *Financial Policies and the World Capital Market: The Problem of Latin American Countries*, Chicago, IL, University of Chicago Press.

—— (1984) "Goodbye financial repression, hello financial crash," *Journal of Development Economics* 19, 1–24.

Eaton, J. (1987) "Public debt guarantees and private capital flight," *World Bank Economic Review* 1, 337–95.

—— (1989a) "Foreign public capital flows," in H.B. Chenery and T.N. Srinivasan (eds) *Handbook of Development Economics*, Amsterdam, North-Holland.

—— (1989b) "Sovereign debt, reputation and credit terms," mimeo, University of Virginia, October.

—— and M. Gersovitz (1981) "Debt with potential repudiation: theory and estimation," *Review of Economic Studies* 48, 289–309.

—— and L. Taylor (1986) "Developing country finance and debt," *Journal of Development Economics* 22, 209–65.

——, M. Gersovitz, and J.E. Stiglitz (1986) "The pure theory of country risk," *European Economic Review* 30, 481–513.

Eichengreen, B. (1989) "The U.S. capital market and foreign lending, 1920–1955," in J.D. Sachs (ed.) *Developing Country Debt and Economic Performance*, Chicago, IL, University of Chicago Press.

—— and P.H. Lindert (1989) "Overview," in B. Eichengreen and P.H. Lindert (eds) *The International Debt Crisis in Historical Perspective*, Cambridge, MA, MIT Press.

—— and R. Portes (1989a) "After the deluge: default, negotiation, and readjustment during the interwar years," in B. Eichengreen and P.H. Lindert (eds) *The International Debt Crisis in Historical Perspective*, Cambridge, MA, MIT Press.

—— and —— (1989b) "Setting defaults in the era of bond finance," *World Bank Economic Review* 3 (2), 211–39.

—— and —— (1990) "Foreign lending and default: the experience since the 1920s," mimeo, Debt and International Finance Division, The World Bank.

Evans, R. and E. Maskin (1989) "Efficient renegotiation-proof equilibria in repeated games," *Games and Economic Behavior* 1, 361–9.

Farrell, J. (1984) "Credible repeated game equilibria," mimeo, University of California, Berkeley.

—— and E. Maskin (1989) "Renegotiation in repeated games," *Games and Economic Behavior* 1, 327–60.

Fernandez, R. and D. Kaaret (1988) "Bank size, reputation, and debt renegotiation," NBER Working Paper 2704, Cambridge, MA.

—— and R.W. Rosenthal (1990) "Strategic models of sovereign-debt renegotiations," *Review of Economic Studies* 57, 331–50.

Fudenberg, D. and J. Tirole (1991) *Game Theory*, Cambridge, MA, MIT Press.

Gale, D. and M. Hellwig (1989) "Reputation and renegotiation: the case of sovereign debt," *International Economic Review* 30, 3–22.

Grossman, H.I. and J.B. van Huyck (1988) "Sovereign debt as a contingent claim: excusable default, repudiation, and reputation," *American Economic Review* 78, 1088–97.

Kahn, R.B. (1989) "Borrowers' reputation and the market for international loans," mimeo, Board of Governors of the Federal Reserve System.

Kehoe, T.J. and D.K. Levine (1990) "Debt constrained asset markets," mimeo, Federal Reserve Bank of Minneapolis, Research Department.

Keynes, J.M. (1924) "Foreign investment and national advantage," *The Nation and the Atheneum*, August 9, 584–7.

Kletzer, K.M. (1984) "Asymmetries of information and LDC borrowing with sovereign risk," *Economic Journal* 94, 287–307.

—— (1987) "External borrowing by LDCs: a survey of some theoretical issues," in G. Ranis and T.P. Schultz (eds) *The State of Development Economics: Progress and perspectives*, Oxford, Blackwell.

—— (1989a) "Sovereign debt renegotiation under asymmetric information," in J.A. Frenkel, M.P. Dooley, and P. Wickham (eds) *Analytic Issues in Debt*, Washington, DC, International Monetary Fund.

—— (1989b) "Inefficient private renegotiation of sovereign debt," Discussion Paper 357, Centre for Economic Policy Research, London, December.

—— and B.D. Wright (1990a) "Renegotiation of sovereign debt in a consumption-smoothing model," Economic Growth Center Discussion Paper 610, Yale University, September.

—— and —— (1990b) "Self-enforcement of sovereign lending," mimeo, Yale University, October.

——, ——, and D.M.G. Newbery (1992) "Smoothing primary exporters' price risks: bonds, futures, options and insurance," *Oxford Economic Papers* 44, forthcoming.

Krugman, P.R. (1988) "Financing vs. forgiving a debt overhang," *Journal of Development Economics* 29, 253–68.

—— (1989) "Market-based debt reduction schemes," in J.A. Frenkel, M.P. Dooley, and P. Wickham (eds) *Analytic Issues in Debt*, Washington, DC, International Monetary Fund.

Lindert, P.H. and P.J. Morton (1989) "How sovereign debt has worked," in J.D. Sachs (ed.) *Developing Country Debt and the World Economy*, Chicago, IL, University of Chicago Press.

Lucas, R.E., Jr (1988) "On the mechanics of economic development," *Journal of Monetary Economics* 22, 3–42.

Manuelli, R.E. (1986) "A general equilibrium model of international credit markets," mimeo, Kellogg School of Management, MEDS, Northwestern University.

O'Connell, S.A. (1987) "Moral hazard, reputation, and intertemporal substitution in bankruptcies," Center for Analytic Research in Economics and the Social

Sciences Working Paper 87–18, University of Pennsylvania.

Ozler, S. (1989a) "On the relation between reschedulings and bank value: theory and evidence," *American Economic Review* 79, 1117–31.

——(1989b) "Have commercial banks ignored history?" mimeo, University of California at Los Angeles.

——(1992) "The evolution of credit terms: an empirical study of commercial bank lending to developing countries," *Journal of Development Economics* 38, 79–91.

Pearce, D.G. (1987) "Renegotiation-proof equilibria: collective rationality and intertemporal cooperation," Cowles Foundation Discussion Paper 855, Yale University.

Razin, A. (1972) "Investment in human capital and economic growth," *Metroeconomica* 24, 101–16.

Romer, P.M. (1986) "Increasing returns and long-run growth," *Journal of Political Economy* 94, 1002–37.

Rubinstein, A. (1980) "Strong perfect equilibrium in supergames," *International Journal of Game Theory* 9, 1–12.

——(1982) "Perfect equilibrium in a bargaining model," *Econometrica* 50, 97–109.

Sachs, J.D. (1989) "Introduction," in J.D. Sachs (ed.) *Developing Country Debt and Economic Performance*, vol. 1, Chicago, IL, University of Chicago Press.

——(1990) "A strategy for efficient debt reduction," *Journal of Economic Perspectives* 4, 19–30.

Suarez, J.J.C. (1988) "On debt, defaults and reputation," Department of Economics Working Paper 88-23, Brown University.

Thomas, J. and T. Worrall (1988) "Self-enforcing wage contracts," *Review of Economic Studies* 55, 541–53.

Wallich, H.C. (1943) "The future of Latin American dollar bonds," *American Economic Review* 33 (2), 324–35.

van Wijnbergen, S. (1990) "Cash/debt buy-backs and the insurance value of reserves," *Journal of International Economics* 29 (1–2), 123–31.

Worrall, T. (1990) "Debt with potential repudiation," *European Economic Review* 34 (5), 1099–1109.

14 Growth and External Debt

DANIEL COHEN

1 Introduction

The theory of external debt has been booming over the past decade and a half, under the obvious pressure of events. It essentially went through four stages. The first stage portrayed external debt as a vehicle for smooth intertemporal arbitrages. The last stage investigated how best it should be written off.

The first stage of the literature emphasized the intertemporal nature of a balance of payments. It reflected the view, popular in the 1970s, that world excess savings (brought by the oil shocks) were efficiently recycled to the developing countries. According to this view, current account deficits of the developing countries were an "equilibrium" phenomenon which enabled these countries to raise productive capacities, out of which, it was hoped, their debt could be smoothly repaid.

The 1980s were the decade when external debt became a bitter component of the developing countries' life. World interest rates shot up and the time horizon of the lenders consequently got shorter. The 1980s became the decade during which the developing countries had to transfer (in net terms) resources to the rich countries. Correlatively, theories of debt repudiation became the main tool of analysis of the developing countries' debt (see chapter 13 in this volume for a survey of such theories). Theoretically and empirically, one wondered what was the mix of stick and carrots that the lenders could threaten or attract the debtors with in order to induce them to pay their debt. Whatever the specifics of these instruments, it now appears, a decade later, that the net resources that developing countries were willing to transfer abroad never much exceeded 3 percent of gross domestic product (GDP). This gives an indirect measure of the costs perceived to be associated with debt repudiation.

It soon appeared, in general, that the stock of debt accumulated in the 1970s and in the early 1980s exceeded the present value of expected transfers that the debtor countries were willing to pay. The theory of external debt reflected this situation and investigated the potential effects of the debt crisis on the pattern of growth of the debtor countries. The "debt overhang" was soon to be portrayed as a potential tax on the countries' resources, with its negative effect on capital accumulation. While it is unambiguously the case that, in the great majority of cases, domestic investment of the large debtors went below the levels that were reached in the 1970s, there is a theoretical and an empirical dispute on the chain of causality. Some argued that the countries which were hard hit by external shocks were simultaneously led to reduce their domestic investments and to let their external debt go out of control. One also made the point that the 1970s were not an appropriate benchmark (given the cheap cost of credit during that decade).

Finally, as we moved into the 1990s, the key question became that of efficiently writing down the face value of the debt. Getting the "right" price at which to undertake these deals was one dimension where academic research became quite active. A key distinction between the average price at which *one* individual investor would be willing to sell its debt and the *marginal* price at which lenders as a whole would sell (when internalizing the effects of their decisions on the aggregate value of the debt) set the agenda of the debate in the late 1980s.

This chapter will proceed to follow these four stages of the literature. First, we shall spell out the conditions under which one can view a country's balance of payments in the same fashion as the cash flow of an infinitely lived individual. We then proceed to investigate the consequences of the risk of debt repudiation on the credit constraint that a country is subject to. Third, we investigate the implications of such credit ceilings on the pattern of growth of a debtor country. Finally, we review how the market price of a sovereign nation's debt helps to determine how an efficient write-off of the debt should proceed.

2   Intertemporal budget constraints for individuals and for nations

The analysis of a country's balance of payments in an intertemporal framework was renewed by the work of Bazdarich (1978), Dornbusch and Fischer (1980), Sachs (1981), and Razin and Svensson (1983) (see also chapter 15 in this volume). The guiding line of these papers was to apply the permanent income theory to the case of a nation portrayed as an infinitely lived agent and to interpret the so-called "disequilibria" of the balance of payments as an equilibrium phenomenon. Further models paid specific attention to the problem of aggregating the intertemporal budget constraints of an infinite number of finitely lived agents. Such work has applied the structure of the overlapping generations model to the case of a small open economy. The key papers include Buiter (1981), Dornbusch (1985), Weil (1985), and the work by Frenkel and Razin (1989). Let us now proceed to summarize in an integrated model the issues that are dealt with in these models and specify the cases when it is meaningful to aggregate all individual budget constraints of the agents inhabiting a nation into an aggregated balance of payments.

For any finitely lived individual, the budget constraint which he is subject to is unambiguously defined by the following constraint: at the time when the agent dies, he must leave no unpaid debt. Call i such an individual and let us assume that he has free access to the world financial markets. Call r the riskless rate of interest on these markets. Let W_t^i be the financial wealth of the individual i at time t, call ω_t^i the endowment he receives at time t, and let C_t^i be his consumption during that time. The law of motion of individual i's wealth can be written

$$\dot{W}_t^i = r W_t^i + \omega_t^i - C_t^i \qquad (14.1)$$

(in which a dot represents a time derivative).

Assume that the time horizon of the agent is a deterministic interval $[t_i, T_i]$. Agent i's solvency constraint is then written as

$$W_{T_i}^i = 0 \qquad (14.2)$$

Equation (14.2) should actually be written as an inequality. Assuming no satiation of consumption and that there are no transfers of assets across individuals, it is obviously legitimate to write the budget constraint (in the absence of bequests) as an equality.

On the other hand, writing equation (14.1) in present value terms gives, for all pairs (t, T),

$$W_T^i \exp[-r(T-t)] + \int_t^T C_s^i \exp[-r(s-t)] \, ds$$

$$= \int_t^T \omega_s^i \exp[-r(s-t)] \, ds + W_t^i \qquad (14.3)$$

which together with (14.2) implies that

$$\int_t^\infty C_s^i \exp[-r(s-t)]\, ds = \int_t^\infty \omega_s^i \exp[-r(s-t)]\, ds + W_t^i \qquad (14.4)$$

with the obvious convention that $C_s^i = \omega_s^i = W_s^i = 0$ if the agent is not alive at time s.

Let us now see how the individual agents' intertemporal budget constraints can be aggregated over the economy. Call

$$C_t = \sum_i C_t^i \qquad \omega_t = \sum_i \omega_t^i \qquad W_t = \sum_i W_t^i$$

the aggregate consumption, income, and wealth, respectively, of the country at any time t. W_t (in the absence of domestic government bonds) is just the net external asset of the country. Aggregating all equations (14.3) together, we get

$$W_T \exp[-r(T-t)] + \int_t^T C_s \exp[-r(s-t)]\, ds$$

$$= \int_t^T \omega_s \exp[-r(s-t)]\, ds + W_t \qquad (14.5)$$

If the economy has a finite life, i.e. if all agents die before a given terminal time T, it follows immediately from (14.2) that

$$W_T = 0$$

At the end of the economy's time horizon, all its external debt will have been reimbursed.

What happens instead when the economy has an infinite horizon? Can we proceed to show that

$$\lim_{t \to \infty} W_t \exp(-rt) = 0$$

which is the corresponding budget constraint that an infinitely lived individual is subject to? The answer is: it depends.

When $T \to \infty$, it is always true that (14.5) implies that

$$\lim_{T \to \infty} W_T \exp[-r(T-t)] + \int_t^\infty C_s \exp[-r(s-t)]\, ds$$

$$= \int_t^\infty \omega_s \exp[-r(s-t)]\, ds + W_t \qquad (14.5')$$

and we also know from aggregating (14.4) over all agents that

$$\int_t^\infty C_s \exp[-r(s-t)]\,ds = \int_t^\infty \omega_s \exp[-r(s-t)]\,ds + W_t \quad (14.4')$$

Yet these two equalities do not always imply (by subtraction) that $\lim_{T\to\infty} W_T \exp[-r(T-t)] = 0$. Indeed, one needs to distinguish two cases.

1   When the wealth of the nation is finite, i.e. when

$$\int_t^\infty \omega_s \exp(-rs)\,ds < +\infty$$

then it does follow by subtraction of (14.4') from (14.5') that the "transversality condition"

$$\lim_{t\to\infty} W_t \exp(-rt) = 0 \quad (14.6)$$

is satisfied.

This condition states that the present discounted value of aggregate wealth is zero (i.e. non-negative) in the long run. It is the standard constraint which is imposed on an infinitely lived individual.

2   If the country's wealth is infinite, then (14.4') reads $+\infty = +\infty$ and we cannot proceed to show that (14.6) is satisfied. Consider, for instance, the simple case of an overlapping generations model in which each agent i saves S when young and dissaves $S(1+r)$ when old. Let N_t be the number of young agents and N_{t-1} the number of old agents. Take $N_t = (1+n)^t N_0$. The aggregate external position of the country is the stock of assets accumulated by the young agent, i.e. $N_t S$. When $n > r$, one sees that the present discounted value of the country's external wealth goes to infinity. When $S < 0$ (the young agents borrow) the country – as a whole – does not reimburse its debt (in present value terms) even though each individual agent does.

In the remainder of this chapter, we shall only analyze the case when the wealth of the nation is finite. In that case, aggregating each individual budget constraint does deliver that the country – as a whole – repays its debt to the rest of the world (in present value terms). For all practical matters, the balance of payments follows an intertemporal pattern which mimics the cash flow of an infinitely lived individual which is subject to an intertemporal budget constraint.

3 The risk of debt repudiation

The analysis of the risk of debt repudiation is the second stage of the modern literature on external debt. It has been brought to life by the work of Eaton and Gersovitz (1981). Early work on the topic also includes Kharas (1984), Kletzer (1984), Krugman (1985), Ozler (1986), and Sachs and Cohen (1985). The useful survey by Eaton et al. (1986) as well as the other papers in the special issue of the *European Economic Review* (June 1986) give an overview of the state of the theory in 1985. An earlier useful survey is McDonald (1982). More recently a second generation of models of debt repudiation has applied the tools of modern bargaining theory to the analysis of debt rescheduling. The pioneering paper here is Bulow and Rogoff (1989a). Other early papers in this area include O'Connell (1988), Eaton (1989), and Fernandez and Rosenthal (1990). Chapter 13 in this volume provides a useful survey of the more game-theoretic issues associated with debt repudiation.

The key to all such analyses is to identify the determinants of debt repayment taking account of the risk of debt repudiation. What kind of sanctions are necessary to induce a country to repay its debt? What are the lessons of the debt crisis of the 1980s for assessing their empirical magnitude? These are the questions that I now want to address.

3.1 An infinite horizon benchmark with frictionless access to the world financial market

For simplicity, let us assume from now on that the country is inhabited by a representative consumer who is endowed each period with a quantity $(Q_t)_{t \geq 0}$ of the numeraire. We assume that Q_t is a continuous process whose present discounted value (at world interest rates) is finite. Let us start by assuming that the country (i.e. its representative agent) has free access to the world financial market.

Let us take the utility of the representative agent to be of the following separable form:

$$U = \int_0^\infty \exp(-\delta t) u(C_t) \, dt \qquad (14.7)$$

with $u(C_t) = \frac{1}{\gamma} C_t^\gamma$ if $\gamma \neq 0$ and $u(C_t) = \log C_t$ if $\gamma = 0$, where $\gamma \equiv 1 - 1/\sigma$ and σ denotes the intertemporal elasticity of substitution.

The agent's debt follows the law of motion

$$\dot{D}_t = rD_t + C_t - Q_t \qquad (14.8)$$

and is subject to the transversality condition $\lim_{t \to \infty} \exp(-rt) D_t = 0$.

The first-order condition has the form

$$\dot{C_t}/C_t = \sigma(r - \delta) \qquad (14.9)$$

so that three cases emerge.

3.1.1 $r < \delta$

The country is more "impatient" than the representative investor in the world financial market. In this case, the growth rate of consumption is negative and, asymptotically, the country drives itself to starvation by accumulating an external debt whose services eventually absorb the country's resources.

3.1.2 $r > \delta$

The reverse situation occurs. The country is more patient than the rest of the world and – asymptotically – owns the entire world. The assumption that the country is "small" with respect to the world financial market could obviously not be maintained in this case. It is a case that we shall not investigate here since, in any case, the country is asymptotically a creditor rather than a debtor.

3.1.3 $r = \delta$

This is the threshold case when the country's subjective discount factor coincides with the world rate of interest. The country (i.e. again its representative agent) seeks to maintain a flat pattern of consumption over time.

3.2   The risk of debt repudiation

Let us now assume that the country has the option of repudiating its external debt. We do not investigate, here, the bargaining implications of debt repudiation and simply assume that the country defaults whenever the level of welfare that it would reach by servicing its debt goes below the reservation level of welfare that it would have access to by defaulting. Let us now describe such a reservation level.

When a country defaults, we shall assume that the creditors cut all access of the country to the world financial market either as a debtor or as a creditor. This implies, in particular, that the country cannot accumulate reserves after it has defaulted. This is an important restriction, as the work by Bulow and Rogoff (1989b) has shown (see below). Second, we also assume that a defaulting country loses a fraction λ of its income so that its post-default pattern of consumption is simply

$$C_t = (1 - \lambda)Q_t \qquad (14.10)$$

The particular case $\lambda = 0$ is of interest in its own right and corresponds to the case when the creditors' sanction against a defaulting debtor amounts to imposing financial autarky forever after the debtor has defaulted. We now want to investigate what the equilibrium pattern of consumption is under this threat of potential repudiation.

Let us call $\bar{D}_t$ the credit ceiling that the creditor will have to impose on the country so as to avoid default. Call

$$\underline{U}_t = \int_t^\infty \exp[-\delta(s-t)]\, u[Q_s(1-\lambda)]\, ds \qquad (14.11)$$

the reservation level of welfare that the country has access to by defaulting. $\bar{D}_t$ must be set so as to guarantee that

$$U_t \geq \underline{U}_t \qquad \forall t \geq 0 \qquad (14.12)$$

where

$$U_t \equiv \int_t^\infty \exp[-\delta(s-t)]\, u(C_s)\, ds$$

measures the level of welfare associated with "servicing" the debt. In order to characterize $\bar{D}_t$ (and to define more specifically how the "service" of the debt is optimally spread out by the creditors), we shall prove the following.

PROPOSITION 1   On any time interval $[a, b]$ on which the constraint (14.12) binds, the country services $P_t = \lambda Q_t$ to its creditors.

In the particular case when $\lambda = 0$, proposition 1 shows that the country will not service its debt in those time intervals during which it is rationed. In a different framework (when the country can accumulate reserves after it has defaulted) Bulow and Rogoff (1989b) have shown that short of direct sanctions ($\lambda = 0$) a country will never service its debt. This is not quite what proposition 1 shows. In the framework that we analyze, it can indeed very well be the case that the country will decide to service its debt in those time intervals when it is *not* rationed (see below). In Bulow and Rogoff's analysis, these intervals correspond to the times when the country would accumulate reserves.

PROOF   The proof of proposition 1 is straightforward. Assume that

$$\int_t^\infty \exp[-\delta(s-t)] \, u[Q_s(1-\lambda)] \, ds = \int_t^\infty \exp[-\delta(s-t)] \, u(C_s) \, ds$$

on a time interval $]a, b[$. Differentiating both sides yields

$$u[Q_t(1-\lambda)] = u(C_t)$$

so that

$$C_t = Q_t(1-\lambda). \qquad \square$$

Going from proposition 1 to determining the credit ceiling $\bar{D}_t$ is not in the general case a straightforward exercise and very much depends on the nature of the problem. In cases when the credit ceiling binds forever after the first moment when it started to bind, one knows for sure that

$$\bar{D}_t = \int_t^\infty \exp[-r(s-t)]\lambda Q_s \, ds \qquad (14.13)$$

since the service of the debt will in this case never exceed λQ_s every period. This will typically be the case when δ is large and when Q_t does not exhibit much volatility. In this case indeed the debtor is "impatient" to consume and not too much concerned with the problem of making consumption less volatile than output. Consider instead the other extreme case when $\delta = r$ and when output is volatile. In this case there will be periods when output is high enough that the country will always *voluntarily* want to service its debt so as to leave open the possibility of borrowing when output is low. (On this point, see the useful survey by Eaton (1993); a counterexample, in a model with imperfect information, is offered by Atkeson (1991).) In such circumstances, the service of the debt may exceed $P_t = \lambda Q_t$. Consider, for instance, the case when $\lambda = 0$. In this case, whenever the credit ceiling binds, one knows for sure that the debtor will not transfer anything and will consume $C_t = Q_t$. On the other hand, when the credit ceiling does *not* bind, we know (since $\delta = r$) that the country will consume a flat amount. The pattern of consumption of the country is then a sequence of periods during which consumption equals output and a sequence of time intervals when the country perfectly smooths out the fluctuations of output.

In all cases, however, we know for sure that $\bar{D}_t$ as defined in (14.13) is a lower bound to the credit ceiling imposed on the country. Indeed, for sure, the creditors always know that they can recapture λQ_t every period (since, at worst, the country would then become indifferent between servicing the debt and defaulting).

3.3   The solvency of a growing economy

Take the case of an economy which is exogenously growing at a constant rate $n > 0$: $Q_t = Q_0 \exp(nt)$. If $\delta > r$, we know that the credit ceiling will be binding one day or the other. Indeed, consumption would otherwise fall to zero while the productive capacity of the country would grow exponentially. For any value of $\lambda < 1$, defaulting has to become a superior option. Conversely, when the credit ceiling starts to bind, we also know that it will bind forever. Indeed, given the homogeneity of the utility function it is straightforward to show that the credit ceiling constraint simply grows exponentially at the rate n. We can then characterize the credit ceiling $\bar{D}_t$ through equation (14.13) and get

$$\bar{D}_t = \frac{\lambda Q_t}{r - n} \tag{14.13'}$$

Another simple way to characterize the lenders' behavior in this case is to write (14.13′) as

$$\lambda = (r - n)\frac{D_t}{Q_t}$$

When the credit constraint binds, the net service of the debt (λ) is equal to the amount of resources that are needed to stabilize the ratio of debt to GDP. The equation, which essentially amounts to deflating the interest rate by the growth rate in order to measure the cost of servicing the debt, was the key to the early analyses of the debt crisis carried out by for example Cline (1983) and Cohen (1985). It was coined by Dornbusch (1985) as the Avramovic–Cline model. Dornbusch and Fischer (1985) and Feldstein (1986) offer insightful implications of these dynamics.

Over the years 1983–90, the severely indebted middle-income countries transferred about 3 percent of their GDP to their creditors. Indirectly, this gives us an idea of the value of λ, the (direct) cost of debt repudiation. Domestic budgetary problems, however, should also be taken into account (see Reisen, 1989, and the studies in Sachs, 1989b).

4   Patterns of growth of a debtor country

As the build up of debt during the 1970s unfolded its effects in the 1980s, it soon appeared that the debt was too large to be serviced in full. It is in this context that the idea of a "debt overhang" was applied to the cases of the developing countries (see Sachs, 1989a). Debt becomes a "tax" on the countries' resources. As Krugman (1988) put it, it may give rise to a debt Laffer curve effect. This analogy between debt and tax for analyzing debt–equity swaps was developed by Helpman (1988) and Froot (1989). The implications of the risk of debt repudiation on growth are also examined in Marcet and Marimon (1992).

4.1   A model of growth and external debt

Let us now proceed to analyze explicitly the (endogenous) pattern of growth of a debtor country which is subject to a credit ceiling constraint and investigate the extent to which the Laffer curve effect is potentially important. The model that we use is derived from Cohen and Sachs (1986) and Cohen (1991). It follows the "AK" structure for generating endogenous growth which was popularized by Rebello (1991).

Assume that production in the economy arises from a linear technology of production

$$Q_t = aK_t \tag{14.14}$$

in which Q_t represents output at time t and K_t the stock of installed capital. The law of motion of capital is

$$\dot{K}_t = I_t - dK_t \tag{14.15}$$

where a dot denotes a time derivative, d stands for the depreciation rate and I_t is the flow of newly installed capital. We follow Abel (1979) and Hayashi (1982) and assume that installing I_t new units of capital requires the firms to spend an amount given by

$$J_t = I_t \left(1 + \frac{1}{2} \phi \frac{I_t}{K_t} \right) \tag{14.16}$$

where $\frac{1}{2} \phi I_t^2 / K_t$ represents an installation cost. Because the technology for installing capital and for producing output goods exhibits constant returns to scale, this model yields an endogenous growth equilibrium of the variety examined by Romer (1986).

We continue to assume that the economy is inhabited by a representative consumer whose utility is of the form (14.7). Before analyzing specifically the pattern of growth of a country which is subject to a credit constraint, let us first analyze the two extreme benchmarks when the economy is closed and when it has free access to the world financial markets.

4.2   Financial autarky

When the economy has no access to the world financial markets, domestic saving is the only source of finance for capital accumulation.

One can readily analyze the closed economy equilibrium through the equilibrium value of the domestic interest rate. Call r_0 the financial autarky interest rate. Households determine the equilibrium growth rate of consumption through

$$\dot{C}_t/C_t = \sigma(r_0 - \delta)$$

On the other hand, the firms choose their investment rate so as to maximize the present discounted value of their cash flows:

$$\max_{(J_t)_{t \geq 0}} \int_0^\infty \exp(-r_0 t)(Q_t - J_t)\, dt$$

Given the linearity embedded in the model, this program amounts to determining a domestic investment rate

$$x_0 \equiv \frac{I_t}{Q_t}$$

and – equivalently – a growth rate of GDP

$$n_0 = ax_0 - d$$

from

$$x_0 = \arg\max_x \left[\frac{1 - x(1 + \frac{1}{2}\phi ax)}{r_0 + d - ax} \right]$$

From the producers' side, x_0 is a decreasing function of r_0 and so is n_0, while from the consumer's side the rate of growth of consumption is an increasing function of r_0. The equilibrium is consequently (at best) uniquely determined as the rate for which output and consumption grow at the same rate. We assume, here, that the conditions are satisfied which guarantee such a unique solution.

In this model with a representative consumer and no externality, it is obviously equivalent to solving the social planner problem and getting the equilibrium investment and growth rates directly as the rates which maximize consumer welfare. From the latter perspective, one can directly characterize financial autarky as the solution to the following system:

$$n_0 = ax_0 - d$$

$$x_0 = \arg\max_x \frac{1}{\gamma} \frac{[1 - x(1 + \frac{1}{2}\phi ax)]^\gamma}{\delta - \gamma(ax - d)} \tag{14.17}$$

We assume that n_0 is positive.

4.3   Free access to world financial markets

Let us now assume that the country is unexpectedly open to the world financial markets, on which a constant interest rate r prevails.

If the access to the financial market is totally free, the country obeys the Fisherian maxim and separates its decision to invest from its decision to consume. Focusing here on the decision to invest, the firms will choose their investment strategy so as to maximize the wealth of their shareholders when measured at world interest rates.

Here again one can show that the equilibrium strategy amounts to selecting a fixed investment rate x^* which is a solution to

$$\max_{x} \int_0^{\infty} \exp(-rt)(Q_t - J_t)\, dt$$

subject to (14.15), or equivalently finding a solution to

$$x^* = \arg\max_{x} \left[\frac{1 - x(1 + \tfrac{1}{2}\phi ax)}{r + d - ax} \right] \tag{14.18}$$

Whenever $r < \delta$ (which we shall assume) and when n_0 in (14.17) is positive, one can prove (see appendix 1) by comparison with (14.17) that the equilibrium investment rate and the corresponding growth rate – in (14.18) – are larger in the open economy than in the closed economy.

4.4   Credit rationing

Let us now assume that the access to the world financial market is not entirely free but is subject to an aggregate credit rationing constraint. Following our earlier analysis, let us assume that the country can choose to repudiate its external debt and – subject to a penalty which the creditors impose on its domestic production – return to financial autarky. Let us then assume that the post-default technology of production is characterized by the following:

$$Q_d(t) = a(1 - \lambda)K_t \qquad 0 < \lambda < 1$$

all other things remaining equal. The country which has defaulted would then choose an investment and growth strategy which is a solution to (14.17) when $a(1 - \lambda)$ is substituted for a. In order to avoid default, the banks must impose an aggregate credit ceiling on the country's external debt (since we imposed $r < \delta$). To determine how the credit ceiling constraint is imposed, we need to know how the banks monitor the repayments made by the country at the time when the credit ceiling binds. We shall distinguish two regimes of repayment here. In each case, we shall look for the loosest credit ceiling that the banks may impose without inducing the debtor to default.

4.4.1 Smooth repayments

Let us first assume that, when the credit ceiling binds and is set at the maximum that is compatible with nonrepudiation of the debt, the lenders can monitor the growth strategy of the borrower (subject to the constraint of avoiding default). One can show (see appendix 2) that the banks can reach their constrained first best outcome by requiring the debtor to pay

$$P_t = z^*(r - n)\, Q_t$$

where z^* is a constant which is the maximum that the country can accept without defaulting (and is therefore an increasing function of λ, the cost of debt repudiation); r is the opportunity cost of funds for the banks, and n is the endogenous growth rate that the country selects in response to this rescheduling strategy. The corresponding equilibrium investment rate is chosen by the country so as to

$$\underset{n}{\text{maximize}} \ \frac{1}{\gamma} \frac{[1 - z^*(r - n) - x(1 + \frac{1}{2}\phi ax)]^\gamma}{\delta - \gamma n}$$

subject to $n = ax - d$.

One also shows (in appendix 2) that the new equilibrium investment rate is always *below* the rate that would prevail when the country has free access to capital markets. It is *above* the rate which is obtained in the financial autarky case, however. In fact, investment can be shown to be an increasing function of the transfers z^* which the country has to make. In this case, the service of debt *crowds in* investment above the financial autarky level. When such a regime prevails, the larger λ is, the larger the credit ceiling, the larger the observed debt, and the faster the growth rate! The intuition behind this paradoxical result is simply the following: the creditors are less impatient than the debtors, and they consequently value growth more than the debtor itself. The larger λ is, the larger their command on the domestic economy. In the extreme case when $\lambda = 1$, z^* is at its maximum value and the creditors choose the socially efficient growth rate, the rate which maximizes (at world prices) the country's wealth.

4.4.2 Forced repayments

Assume now that the banks *cannot* monitor the investment strategy of the country nor *commit* their rescheduling strategy to follow a given rule. In this case they can only make the payments they ask contingent upon the country's current resources. They therefore ask for a payment $P_t = b^*Q_t$ in which b^* is small enough to keep the country from defaulting. (This argument is based on the technique of Cohen and Michel (1988) for calculating a "time-consistent" equilibrium.) The country's response to this rescheduling strategy is one in which it chooses investment and growth as a solution to

$$n = ax_{b^*} - d$$

$$x_{b^*} = \arg\max_x \frac{1}{\gamma} \frac{[1 - b^* - x(1 + \frac{1}{2}\phi ax)]^\gamma}{\delta + \gamma d - \gamma ax} \qquad (14.17')$$

The comparison of this equilibrium with the one which is obtained under financial autarky shows that the new growth rate is necessarily below the financial autarky level.

The case of forced repayment may be identified with the "debt overhang" idea. Here, indeed, the larger the "debt tax" (measured by b^*), the lower the investment rate. Neglecting the adjustment cost, one can show that the equilibrium investment rate can be approximated by

$$y_{b^*} = y_0 - \sigma b^* \qquad (14.19)$$

where σ denotes the intertemporal elasticity of substitution, y_0 stands for the investment rate which prevails under financial autarky, and y_{b^*} is the investment rate which prevails when the debtor must pay b^*Q_t to its creditors each period. As can be seen, under this regime the service of the debt *crowds out* domestic investment by a factor which is just the intertemporal elasticity of substitution. Importantly, if $b^* < 0$, i.e. if the country *receives* foreign funds in a constrained fashion, equation (14.18) will also prevail.

Empirically, the work by Warner (1991) challenges the view that debt caused the investment slowdown. He shows indeed that the terms of trade fluctuations go a long way toward explaining that decline. Cohen (1993b) estimates an equation such as (14.19). Compared with a financial autarkic level, one does find that investment was crowded *out* by the net transfers that the countries were asked to perform. The crowding out coefficient was found to be "relatively" small, however, and worth 1/3, which corresponds – along the lines of the interpretation suggested by equation (14.19) – to an identical value for the intertemporal rate of substitution (which is reasonable). Interestingly, one also finds that, in the 1960s, investment was crowded *in* by the *in*flows of foreign finance by a (statistically) identical factor of 1/3. (In quite a different setting, Chenery and Syrkin (1975) found a similar number.)

4.5   The transition to the steady state

Let us now analyze the transition from a starting point where the country has no initial debt to the point where the country has reached its credit ceiling.

The analysis of the equilibrium growth rate is best undertaken through the analysis of the domestic interest rate. As long as the credit ceiling does not bind, the domestic interest rate is simply equal to the world interest rate. When the credit ceiling is hit, it jumps to the level which is consistent with the equilibrium investment rate which is reached in either of the two cases. If the smooth repayment regime prevails the domestic interest rate will be above the world interest rate but below the autarkic rate. If instead the forced repayment regime prevails, the domestic interest rate will be above each of these two rates.

Whichever of these two rates prevails when the credit ceiling binds, the transitional dynamics now simply amount to investigating the effect on capital accumulation of a perfectly anticipated jump of the interest rate. With adjustment costs, investment gradually declines from a level which is necessarily below the "free access" case to a level which is above or below the autarkic rate, depending on which regime of repayment prevails.

From a longitudinal viewpoint it is now necessarily the case that more debt implies less investment (which would not have been the case, in a cross-section analysis, if the smooth repayment regime had prevailed). Time series analyses of the debtor country performed along these lines (e.g. Borensztein, 1991) do find such a negative correlation.

5   How to write off the debt?

Debt repurchases have played an important role in the solution of the debt crisis of the 1930s (see Eichengreen and Portes, 1986; Eichengreen and Lindert, 1989). Secondary markets (or at least secondary market pricing) have now become, once again, the core of many proposals to end the debt crisis (and indeed are already a key part of the Brady plan). (An early proponent of debt write-off was Kenen (1983); in defense of voluntary debt write-off, see Williamson (1988).) We now turn to review briefly their potential role as described in the recent literature on the subject and, in particular, the criticisms of this role put forward in the academic literature by Bulow and Rogoff (1988) or Dooley (1988). We then proceed to give some empirical evidence on the issue.

5.1   A theoretical background: marginal and average prices

To set up the ideas in an explicit model, let us simplify the analysis undertaken thus far and consider a one-period model of a country which owes a debt at the end of the period. Assume that the country always has the option to repudiate its debt and, again, also assume that the banks can (credibly) impose, in retaliation, a sanction that amounts to a fraction λQ of the country's income. Finally, assume that the banks can always get the country to pay that fraction λQ that the country would forgo by defaulting. Call $dF(Q)$ the density of the (random) distribution of the country's income. Let us take the banks to be risk neutral. We can write the (beginning of the period) market value of a debt whose contractual value is D as

$$V(D) = \left[\int_0^{D/\lambda} \lambda Q \, dF(Q) + \int_{D/\lambda}^{\infty} D \, dF(Q) \right]$$

The first term in brackets represents how much the banks can get when the income of the country is so low that the country would rather default than service the debt fully ($\lambda Q \leq D$). The second term measures the expected payments that accrue to the banks when the country honors the contractual value of the debt (an event which has a probability $1 - F(D/\lambda)$).

The market price of the debt (as observed on the secondary market) can simply be written as

$$q(D) = \left[\int_0^{D/\lambda} \frac{\lambda Q}{D} \, dF(Q) + 1 - F\left(\frac{D}{\lambda}\right) \right]$$

If a country were, say, to repurchase one dollar of its debt on the secondary market, this is the price that it would have to pay. If instead the country wants to repurchase an amount B and is *known* to be willing to do so, then – as Dooley (1988) first pointed out – the price at which the transaction will be undertaken can only be the *ex post* equilibrium price. (Otherwise, no lenders will actually sell its claim.) We then get that the price for the transaction has to be

$$q(D - B) = \left[\int_0^{(D-B)/\lambda} \frac{\lambda Q}{D - B} \, dF(Q) + 1 - F\left(\frac{D-B}{\lambda}\right) \right]$$

Obviously, if a debtor country is known to be willing to repurchase *all* of its debt ($B = D$), the only price at which the transaction will be undertaken is $q = 1$.

This crucial remark makes it very undesirable to set up, say, an institution endowed with a given amount of money which would operate openly to repurchase less developed country debt. Such an institution would immediately raise the price and defeat its own purpose.

The point which is made by Bulow and Rogoff radicalizes this criticism. Assume that the country (or an institution acting on its behalf) repurchases a small fraction of the debt so that, say, this measures the benefit that is captured by the country. For the country, what matters is the reduction of the market value of the debt, i.e.

$$p(D) \equiv V'(D) = 1 - F(D/\lambda)$$

which is strictly (perhaps much) lower than $q(D)$. Hence, even if the country was repurchasing a fraction B of its debt one dollar after the other, repeatedly taking the creditors by "surprise" (i.e. they never expect that the next dollar will be repurchased, but they always know at each point in time what is the exact stock of debt), it would still be overpaying its debt as it would pay

$$\rho = \int_{D-B}^{D} q(D) \, \mathrm{d}D$$

which is strictly more expensive than

$$\Delta V = V(D) - V(D - B) = \int_{D-B}^{D} p(D) \, \mathrm{d}D$$

Bulow and Rogoff (1991) concluded that this wedge between the cost of a debt buyback and its real effect on the market value of the debt makes it unlikely to turn buybacks into a profitable investment (see also the survey in Diwan and Claessens, 1989). Does this reasoning apply to the debt crisis of the 1930s and lead us to interpret the large buybacks which were then performed as an unworthy investment? Not necessarily. As we pointed out in Cohen and Verdier (1990) a buyback can be good if it is done *secretly*. If, say, Morgan repurchases Brazil's debt – held by Citicorp – on Brazil's behalf without revealing for whom the purchase is made, there are no limits to the extent of the repurchases which can be made by Morgan at the given price. (It is only when Brazil's actions are discovered that the price rises, since only in that case does the reduction in its outstanding external debt raise the price.) (Another argument in favor of buybacks as an insurance device is provided by van Wijnbergen (1990b).)

Yet, as far as the open buybacks such as those that the Brady deal encourages are concerned, it is obviously crucial to make sure that the price at which the buyback is undertaken is appropriate. This involves a comprehensive *ex ante* agreement with the creditors, so that none of them can free-ride on the others. This is exactly what the Brady deal has done. In a process called "novation," it was agreed that all the previous debt had to be exchanged against one of the three options which were open.

In order to evaluate empirically how the Brady deal has worked I will first analyze how the distinction between average and marginal price can be reconstructed empirically.

5.2   Econometric estimates

Previous econometric estimates of the secondary market involve Purcell and Orlanski (1988), Sachs and Huizinga (1987), Fernandez and Ozler (1990), and Ozler (1989). I will rely here on Cohen (1992).

To the extent that we are interested in distinguishing the average price from the marginal price of the debt, we want to estimate a price equation which yields such a distinction explicitly. In order to do this, I shall use a logistic function of prices to account for the discrepancy. Specifically, I obtain (for 1989 data)

$$\log\left(\frac{q}{1-q}\right) = -2.71 - 1.47 \log\left(\frac{D}{Q}\right) + 5.48\text{HUN} \qquad R^2 = 0.72 \quad (14.20)$$

$$(-3.44) \qquad\qquad (5.31)$$

in which D is the stock of the debt, Q is per capita income (such as measured by Summers and Heston, in percentage of 1980 US per capita income), and HUN is a proxy for Hungary (Hungary is controlled for because it is the only country in the sample which did not reschedule its debt).

By differentiating both sides we get

$$\frac{dq}{q} = -1.47(1-q)\frac{dD}{D}$$

Calling $V = qD$ the market value of debt, we get

$$\frac{dV}{V} = [1 - 1.47(1-q)]\frac{dD}{D} \qquad\qquad (14.21)$$

There is consequently a threshold price for which the elasticity of price with respect to debt is (in absolute value) smaller than unity. The price here is $q^* = 0.32$ cents. In part coincidentally, this price is not significantly different from the average price (0.35) of the representative middle-income debtor at the end of 1989.

One can also rewrite equation (14.21) as

$$\frac{dV}{V} = 1.47(q - q*)\frac{dD}{D}$$

or, equivalently, we can write that the marginal price is

$$p = 1.47(q - q*)q$$

Below the price $q*$ there is a case of the debt Laffer curve: reducing the face value of the debt may *raise* its market value. As I emphasized in my earlier paper, however, there are only very few countries for which – with 95 percent confidence – this mechanism is bound to appear. Around that threshold point we can take the marginal price of the debt to be nil. Lenders, as a whole, are essentially indifferent between one dollar more or less on their books. For countries which would repurchase their debt to the left of the price $q*$, the deal would offer the bankers a "boondoggle," as Bulow and Rogoff have put it for the Bolivian buyback which occurred in 1987. Empirically, using similar tools of analysis the work by Diwan and Kletzer (1990) and by van Wijnbergen (1990a) has shown that the Brady deal did succeed in pricing the debt appropriately.

Another illustration of equation (14.21) is as follows. Consider a debt which is originally priced at 32 cents. Assume that the debt is unilaterally written down by 50 percent. What is the real cost for the bankers of such a write-down? Using equation (14.21), we get that the 50 percent write-off would bring the price to 0.57 so that the market value would go from 0.32 to 0.285. This only represents an 11 percent write-off in real terms. In nominal terms, the result is more spectacular: a 50 percent write-off only cost 3.5 percent of the original value of the debt! With a debt-to-GDP ratio of 100 percent (which is the average middle-income debtor level) this represents 3.5 percent of GDP. (Similar conclusions are reached in the simulation studies of Bartolini and Dixit (1991) and Cohen (1993a).)

6   What will be the fifth stage?

As we moved through the four stages of the debt crisis, we must wonder whether the debt crisis of the 1980s should caution the developing countries against borrowing on the financial markets. Should we consider that capital flows towards the poor countries should only be designed, say, to smooth terms of trade fluctuations, or do we think that there is some scope for capital mobility to help the "poor" countries grow faster? These are the questions that the fifth stage of the literature will have to address. The new literature on growth originating in the work of Romer (1986) and Lucas (1988) will certainly offer the fifth stage its starting point (see chapter 16 in this volume for a survey of the issues). Already, Lucas (1990) has used this approach to challenge the view that capital, even if it were free of sovereign risk, should move from the rich to the poor countries. Similarly, the work by Barro and Sala-i-Martin (1991), comparing the pattern of growth of regions (free, one should think, of sovereign risks) within a nation to the pattern of growth of nations across the world rejected the view that there is much difference between them. Without entering here into this new and promising research agenda, one can postulate hot debates, in the future, on the way we should draw the lessons of the debt crisis of the 1980s.

Appendix 1: Financial autarky, default, and free access to the world financial markets

Let us first characterize the equilibrium which prevails *after* the country has defaulted, i.e. when its production function is $Q_t = a(1 - \lambda)K_t$. Financial autarky will appear as the particular case when $\lambda = 0$. We can write the post-default level of welfare as

$$U_\lambda = C_\lambda Q_0$$

(where $t = 0$ is conventionally set to be the time of default) in which C_λ is defined as

$$C_\lambda = \max_x \frac{1}{\gamma} \frac{[1 - \lambda - x(1 + \frac{1}{2} \phi ax)]^\gamma}{\delta + \gamma d - \gamma ax} \tag{A14.1}$$

The first-order condition for x is

$$\frac{1 + \phi ax}{1 - \lambda - x(1 + \frac{1}{2} \phi ax)} = \frac{1}{\delta + \gamma d - \gamma ax}$$

which can also be written as

$$\gamma(ax - d) + \frac{1 - \lambda - x(1 + \frac{1}{2} \phi ax)}{1 + \phi ax} = \delta \tag{A14.2}$$

The left-hand side of (A14.2) is a decreasing function of x, its derivative is

$$- a(1 - \gamma) - \frac{\phi a[1 - \lambda - x(1 + \frac{1}{2} \phi ax)]}{(1 + \phi ax)^2}$$

It is also a decreasing function of λ. With positive growth $(ax \geq d)$ the left-hand side of (A14.2) increases with γ. It can thus be seen why $\gamma < 1$ and $\delta > r$ will imply that the investment rate is smaller after default ($\lambda > 0$) or under financial autarky ($\lambda = 0$) than under free access to the world financial markets (which is obtained with $\gamma = 1$ and $\delta = r$).

Appendix 2: The smooth repayment case

Because of the linear structure of the model, the lenders who want to extract the maximum repayment from the borrowers must find a payment strategy $P = b^*Q$ and a constant investment rate x^* so as to solve the following problem:

$$V_0^* = \max_{(b,x)} \int_0^\infty \exp(-rt)\, bQ_t\, dt \qquad (A14.3)$$

where $Q_t = \exp(nt)\, Q_0$ and $n = ax - d$, subject to

$$\frac{1}{\gamma} \int_0^\infty \exp(-\delta t)[1 - b - x(1 + \tfrac{1}{2}\phi ax)]^\gamma\, Q_t^\gamma \geq C_\lambda Q_0^\gamma$$

(Because of the linearity of the model this inequality implies that similar ones will hold in the future.)

Define $\omega(x) \equiv 1/(r + d - ax)$ so that the lenders' pay-off can be written

$$V = b\omega(x)Q_0 \qquad (A14.4)$$

The problem faced by the lenders can then be written in the following more compact form. Find z^*, the solution to

$$z^* = \max_{(b,x)} b\omega(x) \qquad (A14.5)$$

subject to

$$\frac{1}{\gamma} \frac{[1 - b - x(1 + \tfrac{1}{2}\phi ax)]^\gamma}{\delta + \gamma d - \gamma ax} \geq C_\lambda$$

By duality this problem is simply that of finding the largest z^* such that

$$\max_x \frac{1}{\gamma} \frac{[1 - z^*\omega(x)^{-1} - x(1 + \tfrac{1}{2}\phi ax)]^\gamma}{\delta + \gamma d - \gamma ax} = C_\lambda$$

$$\equiv \max_x \frac{1}{\gamma} \frac{[1 - \lambda - x(1 + \tfrac{1}{2}\phi ax)]^\lambda}{\delta + \gamma d - \gamma ax} \qquad (A14.6)$$

which is what is stated in the text.

The geometry of the problem can be readily drawn as in figure 14.1 in the space (x, b). The indifference curves of the debtor are

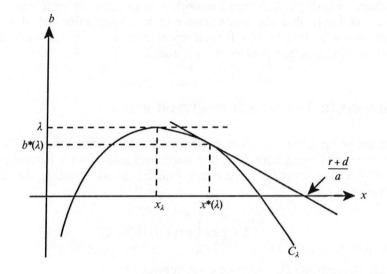

Figure 14.1   As z^* is increased (corresponding to a larger λ) the tangency point shifts towards the northeast: the country invests more and pays more. This also shows why investment is above the financial autarky rate (which corresponds to $\lambda = 0$) and below the socially efficient rate (which corresponds to $\lambda = 1$).

$$\frac{1}{\gamma}\left[1 - b - x\left(1 + \frac{1}{2}\phi ax\right)\right]^{\gamma} = C(\delta + \gamma d - \gamma ax) \qquad (A14.7)$$

and they reach their maxima on a line whose equation is (A14.2) and which is negatively sloped (see appendix 1). The utility C_λ is obtained when the maximum is at $b = \lambda$. When the lenders design the optimal repayment scheme, they choose a point $(b^*(\lambda), c^*(\lambda))$ on the indifference curve C_λ so as to get the largest z^* such that

$$b = z^*(r + d - ax) \qquad (A14.8)$$

The tangency point is to the right of (λ, x_d): it involves a larger investment rate $(x^* > x_d)$ and a lower repayment $(b^* < \lambda)$ than the post-default point.

References

Abel, A. (1979) "Investment and the value of capital," New York, Garland Publishing.

Atkeson, A. (1991) "International lending with moral hazard and risk of repudiation," *Econometrica* 59 (4), 1069–90.

Avramovic, D. and Al. (1964) *Economic Growth and External Debt*, Baltimore, MD, Johns Hopkins University Press.

Barro, R. and X. Sala-i-Martin (1991) "Convergence across states and regions," *Brookings Papers on Economic Activity* 1, 107–82.

Bartolini, L. and A. Dixit (1991) "Market valuation of illiquid debt and implications for conflict among creditors," *IMF Staff Papers* 38, 828–49.

Bazdarich, M. (1978) "Optimal growth and stages in the balance of payments," *Journal of International Economics* 11, 425–43.

Borenzstein, E. (1991) "The debt overhang: an empirical analysis of the Philippines," mimeo, International Monetary Fund.

Buiter, W. (1981) "Time preference and international lending and borrowing in an overlapping generations model," *Journal of Political Economy* 89, 769–97.

Bulow, J. and K. Rogoff (1988) "The buy-back boondoggle," *Brookings Papers on Economic Activity* 2, 675–98.

—— and ——(1989a) "A constant recontracting model of sovereign debt," *Journal of Political Economy* 97, 166–77.

—— and ——(1989b) "LDC: is to forgive to forget?" *American Economic Review* 79, 43–50.

—— and ——(1991) "Debt buy-back: no cure for debt overhang," *Quarterly Journal of Economics* 57, 1219–36.

Chenery, H.B. and M. Syrkin (1975) *Patterns of Development 1950–1970*, London, Oxford University Press.

Cline, W. (1983) *International Debt and the Stability of the World Economy*, Washington, DC, Institute for International Economics.

Cohen, D. (1985) "How to evaluate the solvency of an indebted nation?" *Economic Policy* 1, 139–56.

——(1991) *Private Lending to Sovereign States: A Theoretical Autopsy*, Cambridge, MA, MIT Press.

—— (1992) "The debt crisis: a post mortem," in *NBER Macroeconomics Annual*, vol. 7, Cambridge, MA, MIT Press.

——(1993a) "A valuation formula for LDC debt," *Journal of International Economics* 34, 167–80.

——(1993b) "Low investment and large LDC debt in the eighties: an empirical analysis," *American Economic Review*, 83, 437–49.

—— and P. Michel (1988) "How should control theory be used by a time-consistent government?" *Review of Economic Studies* 55, 263–74.

—— and J. Sachs (1986) "Growth and external debt under risk of debt repudiation," *European Economic Review* 30, 529–60.

—— and T. Verdier (1990) "Secret buy-backs of LDC debt," CEPREMAP 9018 (Centre d'Etudes Prospectives d'Economie Mathématique appliquée à la Planification).

Diwan, I. and S. Claessens (1989) "Market based debt reductions," in M. Husain and I. Diwan (eds) *Dealing with the Debt Crisis*, Washington, DC, World Bank.

—— and K. Kletzer (1990) "Voluntary choices in concerted deal," Working Paper 527, World Bank PPR.

Dooley, M. (1988) "Buy-backs and the market valuation of external debt," *IMF Staff Papers* 35 (2), 215–29.

Dornbusch, R. (1985) "Intergenerational and international trade," *Journal of International Economics* 18, 123–39.

—— and S. Fischer (1980) "Exchange rates and the current account," *American Economic Review* 70, 960–71.

—— and —— (1985) "The world debt problem: origins and prospects," *Journal of Development Planning* 16, 57–81.

Eaton, J. (1989) "Debt relief and the international enforcement of loan contracts," *Journal of Economic Perspectives* 4, 43–56.

—— (1993) "External debt: a primer," *The World Bank Economic Review* 7, 137–72.

—— and M. Gersovitz (1981) "Debt with potential repudiation: theoretical and empirical analysis," *Review of Economic Studies* 48, 289–309.

——, ——, and J. Stiglitz (1986) "The pure theory of country risk," *European Economic Review* 30, 481–513.

Eichengreen, B. and P. Lindert (eds) (1989) *The International Debt Crisis in Historical Perspective*, Cambridge, MA, MIT Press.

—— and R. Portes (1986) "Debt and default in the 1930s: causes and consequences," *European Economic Review* 30, 599–640.

Feldstein, M. (1986) "International debt service and economic growth – some simple analytics," NBER Working Paper 2046, Cambridge, MA.

Fernandez, R. and S. Ozler (1991) "Debt concentration and secondary market prices: a theoretical and empirical analysis," NBER Working Paper 3654, Cambridge, MA.

—— and R. Rosenthal (1990) "Strategic analysis of sovereign debt renegotiations," *Review of Economic Studies* 57, 331–49.

Fischer, S. (1989) "Resolving the international debt crisis," in J. Sachs (ed.) *Developing Country Debt and Economic Performance*, Chicago, IL, University of Chicago Press.

Frenkel, J. and A. Razin (1989) *Fiscal Policy in an Interdependent World*, Cambridge, MA, MIT Press.

Froot, K. (1989) "Buy-backs, exit bonds, and the optimality of debt and liquidity relief," *International Economic Review* 30, 49–70.

Hayashi, F. (1982) "Tobin's marginal q and average q: a neoclassical interpretation," *Econometrica* 50, 213–24.

Helpman, E. (1988) "The simple analytics of debt–equity swaps," *American Economy Review* 79, 440–51.

Husain, M. and I. Diwan (1989) *Dealing with the Debt Crisis*, Washington, DC, World Bank.

Kenen, D. (1983) *New York Times*, March 6.

Kharas, H. (1984) "The long-run creditworthiness of developing countries theory and practice," *Quarterly Journal of Economics* 99, 415–39.

Kletzer, K. (1984) "Asymmetries of information and LDC borrowing with sovereign risk," *Economic Journal* 94, 287–307.

Krugman, P. (1985) "International debt strategies in an uncertain world," in G.W. Smith and J.D. Cuddington (eds) *International Debt and the Developing Countries*, Washington DC, World Bank.

—— (1988) "Financing vs forgiving a debt overhang: some analytical notes, *Journal of Development Economics* 29, 253–68.

Lucas, Robert (1988) "On the mechanics of economic development," *Journal of Monetary Economics* 22, 3–42.

—— (1990) "Why can't capital flow from rich to poor countries?" *American Economic Review, Papers and Proceedings* 83.

Marcet, A. and R. Marimon (1992) "Communication, commitment and growth," *Journal of Economic Theory* 58, 219–49.

McDonald, C. (1982) "Debt capacity and developing country borrowing: a survey of the literature," *IMF Staff Papers* 29, 603–46.

O'Connell, S. (1988) "A bargaining theory of international reserves," mimeo, University of Pennsylvania.

Ozler, S. (1989) "The motives for international bank rescheduling, 1978–1983: theory and evidence," *American Economic Review* 89, 1117–31.

—— (1990) "Have commercial banks ignored history?" mimeo, University of California at Los Angeles.

Purcell, J. and D. Orlanski (1988) "Developing countries loans: a new valuation model for secondary market trading," Corporate Bond Research, Solomon Brothers, June.

Razin, A. and L. Svensson (1983) "The terms of trade and the current account: the Harberger–Laursen–Meltzer effect," *Journal of Political Economy* 91, 97–125.

Rebello, S. (1991) "Long run analysis and long run growth," *Journal of Political Economy* 99, 500–21.

Reisen, H. (1989) "Public debt, north and south," in M. Husain and I. Diwan (eds) *Dealing with the Debt Crisis*, Paris, OECD.

Romer, P. (1986) "Increasing returns and long-run growth," *Journal of Political Economy* 94, 1002–37.

Rubinstein, A. (1982) "Perfect equilibrium in a bargaining model," *Econometrica* 50, 97–110.

Sachs, J. (1981) "The current account and macroeconomic adjustment in the 1970s," *Brookings Papers on Economic Activity* 2, 201–82.

—— (1989a) "The debt overhang of developing countries," in J. de Macedo and R. Findlay (eds) *Debt, Growth and Stabilization: essays in memory of Carlos Dias Alejandro*, Oxford, Blackwell.

—— (ed.) (1989b) *Developing Country Debt and Macroeconomic Performance*, Chicago, IL, University of Chicago Press.

—— and D. Cohen (1985) "LDC borrowing with default risk," *Kredit und Kapital, Special Issue on International Banking* 8, 211–35.

—— and H. Huizinga (1987) "US commercial banks and the developing country debt crisis," *Brooking Papers on Economic Activity* 2, 555–606.

Warner, A. (1991) "Did the debt crisis cause the investment crisis?" *Quarterly Journal of Economics* 67, 1161–86.

Weil, P. (1985) "Essays on the valuation of unbacked assets," PhD thesis, Harvard University.

van Wijnbergen, S. (1990a) "Mexico's external debt restructuring in 1989/90: an economic analysis," *Economic Policy* 12, 13–56.

—— (1990b) "Cash debt buy-backs and the insurance value of reserves," *Journal of International Economics* 29, 123–32.

Williamson, J. (1988) *Voluntary Approach to Debt Relief*, Washington, DC, Institute for International Economics.

World Debt Tables (1989) "External debt of developing countries," Washington, DC, World Bank.

15   Savings, Investment, and the Current Account

PARTHA SEN

1   Introduction

The history of balance of payments theory since the Second World War can be broken up into three periods. The first lasted until the early 1970s and can be broadly identified with Keynesian short-run theory. The second period begins with the advent of rational expectations and, in open economy macroeconomics, the emphasis on asset dynamics. The third phase which began in the early 1980s lays emphasis on deriving the basic relationships from microeconomic foundations while continuing to assume perfect foresight or rational expectations.

We begin with the basic open economy national income identity

$$S^H + S^G \ I + \text{CA}$$

where S^H (S^G) is the saving of the households (the government), I denotes investment, and CA stands for the current account surplus (or equivalently the dissaving by the rest of the world). It would be fair to say that almost all the models before optimizing models came to dominate the scene focused on S^H, S^G, and CA. Investment, if included at all, was always on a back-burner.

The first generation of models, i.e. short-run Keynesian-type models, postulated *ad hoc* specifications of various behavioral relationships. Thus the domestic saving function would be postulated to depend on real disposable income, the real interest rate, and real wealth. For instance, the original Laursen and Metzler (1950) result depended crucially on the way the real income argument in the saving function was defined. Sometimes the saving was written as closing the gap between a given target level of wealth and the current level of wealth (*à la* Metzler).[1]

The definition of wealth in these models included government bonds and the issue of Ricardian equivalence was never raised.

The saving of the government was simply derived from the government budget constraint. In a static model fiscal policy was simply a matter of changing the level either of government expenditure or of taxes. The government was not worried about an explicit maximization exercise (with the attendant problem of time consistency) or its solvency.

The investment function was invariably modeled with the interest rate as its sole argument, as in the Mundell–Fleming model. At best it included output and the capital stock.

In the early models the current account (or equivalently the trade balance, given the interest service account) was a function of output, foreign output, and the relative price of the domestic good. There was an excessive emphasis on exports and imports and the effects of the relative price on these items. By contrast, the recent optimizing models are content to let the current account be determined residually as the difference between domestic saving and investment.

With the advent of rational expectations models in open economy macroeconomics a qualitatively new element was introduced. Even if the specification of savings, investment, and the current account remained unchanged, to the extent that some of the determinants were forward-looking jump variables, an intertemporal element was introduced. For instance, an anticipated depreciation would cause an immediate depreciation which could improve the trade balance through the relative price effect and raise private sector saving by lowering real wealth (the former is true if the Marshall–Lerner condition is satisfied and the latter if the share in wealth of foreign bonds for a creditor country is less than the share of the foreign good in the price index). Moreover, asset dynamics also became important. A surplus in the current account leads to accumulation of foreign assets which in turn affects behavior in the future. In fact, this entire phase of modeling the open economy (which is summarized in the North-Holland *Handbook of International Economics*, vol. 2) can be described as the asset market approach (although this term has often been used for a subset of this general line of thinking).

Despite these advances, it was felt that the behavioral equations lacked theoretical underpinnings and some microeconomic foundations must be provided. A price had to be paid for this. Heterogeneity among agents was almost totally banished. The new monetary models left a lot to be desired, since there is much about the microfoundations of money that we do not know. Whatever the shortcomings of these models, they have been extensively (almost exclusively) used in the last ten years and are surveyed in this chapter.

We first look at the building blocks of the most commonly used general equilibrium models. We then bring these together and survey some of the shocks analyzed in the literature. Finally, we look at some other possible ways of modeling the open economy which have not been used extensively but are promising areas for future research.

2   Household preferences and saving

Households are assumed to maximize an intertemporal additively separable utility function where future utility is discounted at the rate δ.[2] Here three types of specifications are used.

2.1   Two-period models

To start off consider the simplest dynamic problem for the consumer, namely the two-period problem. The consumer maximizes a time-separable utility function subject to an intertemporal budget constraint. The intertemporal budget constraint, which is assumed routinely in the literature, is equivalent to assuming perfect capital markets.

$$\max_{C_0, C_1} V(C_0, C_1) = u(C_0) + (1 + \delta)^{-1} u(C_1) \tag{15.1}$$

subject to

$$C_0 + (1 + r)^{-1} C(1) = W \equiv y_0 + \frac{1}{1+r} y_1 \tag{15.2}$$

where C_i $(i = 0, 1)$ denotes the consumption in period i, $Y_i (i = 0, 1)$ denotes wage income in period i, δ stands for the fixed discount rate or the rate of time preference, r is the interest rate, V is assumed to be increasing and strictly concave in its arguments, and W denotes the given lifetime wealth of the consumer. This maximization gives the usual first-order condition:[3]

$$u'(C_0) = (1 + r)(1 + \delta)^{-1} u'(C_1) \tag{15.3}$$

Equation (15.3) is the familiar Euler equation. It tells us (a) that if the discount rate and the interest rate are equal then $C_0 = C_1$, i.e. the consumer smooths his or her consumption path, and (b) that if $r > \delta$ then $C_0 > C_1$ and vice versa (consumption tilting). For an extensive discussion of these and related issues, see Frenkel and Razin (1987).

Three points need to be noted here. First, we could readily account for uncertainty in the above exercise; second, having determined the path of consumption from (15.2) and (15.3), saving in the first period

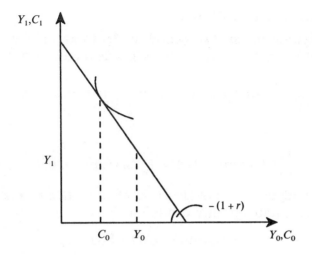

Figure 15.1   Saving and consumption in the two-period model.

would be just $Y_0 - C_0$ (figure 15.1). This is equal to the present value of dissaving in the next period (since there are no bequest motives and the consumer would rather not leave any unspent income).

Finally, the model of equations (15.1) and (15.2) is a single good model but we could as well interpret it as a multi-good problem if we treat C_i as the consumption aggregate in period i. Within-period consumption would be determined by relative prices of goods in this two-part maximization procedure. Care should be taken then to interpret the interest rate variable r as the consumption rate of interest. To illustrate, suppose a small open economy has access to the world capital market and can borrow or lend at an interest rate r on bonds denominated in terms of the traded good. If the relative price of the traded good in terms of the nontraded good changes across periods, then the real interest rate from the consumer's point of view is not constant. See Dornbusch (1983), Obstfeld (1985), Persson and Svensson (1985), and Frenkel and Razin (1987) on this issue.

It is easy to think of an overlapping generations model of consumers who live for two periods. Each period new consumers are born and the old die. The advantage of this formulation (see section 2.3 for a continuous-time analog) is that individuals can choose any profile of consumption and yet society can achieve a steady state. In this framework the young save and thus a rise in the interest rate definitely increases their opportunity set (which is not the case for the borrower). This is discussed in the appendix.

2.2   Infinite-horizon models

The generalization of this two-period model to an infinite horizon is fairly straightforward. We use the continuous-time version

$$\max_{\{C(t)\}} \int_0^\infty u[C(t)] \exp(-\delta t)\, dt \qquad u' > 0,\, u'' < 0 \qquad (15.1a)$$

subject to

$$\int_0^\infty C(t) \exp(-rt)\, dt = \int_0^t Y(t) \exp(-rt)\, dt \qquad (15.2a)$$

The lifetime budget constraint (15.2a) is often written as a flow budget constraint and a transversality condition:

$$\dot{a}(t) = ra(t) - C(t) + Y(t) \qquad (15.2b)$$

$$\lim_{t\to\infty} a(t) \exp(-rt) \geq 0 \qquad (15.2c)$$

where $a(t)$ is the stock of assets at t. The maximization of (15.1a) subject to (15.2b) and (15.2c) gives the following conditions:

$$u'[C(t)] = \lambda(t) \qquad (15.3a)$$

$$\dot{\lambda}(t) = \lambda(t)(\delta - r) \qquad (15.3b)$$

$$\lim_{t\to\infty} \lambda(t) \exp(-\delta t) \geq 0 \qquad (15.3c)$$

where $\lambda(t)$ is the "co-state" variable associated with the state variable $a(t)$. Equation (15.3b) is the continuous-time analog of equation (15.3). Equation (15.3c) is a transversality condition on λ.

In (15.3b) we immediately see a potential problem with the infinite-horizon model that is not present in (15.1). If δ and r are fixed, then the only possibility of a smooth path of consumption is if by chance $\delta = r$. Otherwise (when $r > \delta$), consumption is continuously postponed and assets are accumulated or (when $\delta > r$) consumption is brought forward and the consumer continuously piles up debt (as long as it is possible to do so). Neither of these cases yields a steady state. In these models it is therefore usually assumed that $\delta = r$, but this is not an innocuous assumption since it gives rise to a zero-root problem (by setting $\lambda = 0$, which implies that a temporary shock has a permanent effect; see Giavazzi and Wyplosz, 1985; Sen and Turnovsky, 1990).

Another way out of this impasse is to let the rate of time preference be variable. This modeling strategy has been followed by many (see for example Obstfeld, 1982; Sen, 1984; Devereux and Shi, 1991). The original papers in this literature are by Uzawa (1968) and Epstein and Hynes (1983). Svensson and Razin (1983) provide a good discussion of the problem associated with this class of literature. The unattractive feature of the models is that for stability we require the discount rate to be increasing in instantaneous utility. Loosely speaking, this means that the rich are more impatient. On the other hand, the attractive feature is that it gives rise to a target-wealth type of formulation for a small open economy. To see this, note that in the steady state we require

$$r = \delta(\tilde{U}) \qquad \delta' > 0$$

and this ties down the steady-state level of utility $\tilde{U}$. Hence, any shock which reduces current utility below the steady state will give rise to saving so that in the new steady state utility is restored to its (unchanged) steady-state level. This formulation also enables us to analyze the consequences of a change in the world interest rate which the fixed discount rate models do not allow (although this has been done in the literature, not legitimately in our view, as in Svensson, 1984).

Finally, in a world of capital immobility (or less than perfect mobility) it is the interest rate which adjusts endogenously to equal the predetermined discount rate, much as it would with a closed economy. This structure is potentially important for modeling the (optimal) current account behavior of developing countries where (expected and actual) capital controls are the rule rather than the exception.

Capital immobility implies that the domestic consumers have no access to the world capital markets. Current account surpluses (or deficits) have to be matched by either private capital account deficits or deficits in the official settlements balances. In the former case we may have the domestic private sector accumulating foreign currency (as in a model of currency substitution; see Liviatan, 1981; Sen, 1990). In the latter case the central bank intervenes to target the exchange rate (see for example Michener, 1984; Sen, 1991).

The infinite-horizon representative consumer model has another property, namely that of Ricardian equivalence. It is clear, by appropriately modifying equation (15.2a) to include taxes, that the relevant tax term (for lump-sum taxes) is the present value of all current and future tax obligations. If the government were to finance a given expenditure by debt rather than lump-sum taxes, the consumer's lifetime resources available for consumption would be unchanged and therefore so would be his or her path of consumption.

The other solution to the problem of zero roots and also that of Ricardian equivalence is to introduce heterogeneity among consumers. This is done in the overlapping generations model. The earlier overlapping generations model allows for two generations each of which lives for two periods (as in the appendix). The discount rate need not be equal to the market interest rate and the consumer can tilt his or her consumption towards or away from the first period. If individuals with the same date of birth (of the same "cohort") have identical tastes, then society's consumption profile can remain flat over time despite consumption tilting by individuals (see Buiter, 1981). If individuals live for two periods and have no bequest motives (i.e. they do not "live on" through their descendants), then Ricardian equivalence does not hold. A change in the mix of lump-sum taxes and debt to finance a given government expenditure will have real effects (see Persson, 1985).

The continuous-time infinite-horizon version of the overlapping generations model has also been used extensively (see Frenkel and Razin, 1987; Matsuyama, 1987; Engel and Kletzer, 1989; van der Ploeg, 1991). Initially (as in Blanchard (1985) for the closed economy and Frenkel and Razin (1987) and Matsuyama (1987) for the open economy), it was believed that if, following Yaari (1965), agents have finite lives then Ricardian equivalence will not hold. Agents die and new ones, not altruistically linked to the earlier ones, are born and the mix of debt and lump-sum taxes becomes important. But Weil (1989) clarified that death had nothing to do with the Ricardian equivalence issue. It is new households who have no nonhuman wealth at birth who cause Ricardian equivalence to break down (see Buiter (1988) and chapter 16 of this volume for a discussion).

2.3   Infinite-horizon model with new births

An individual born at time s (his or her vintage or cohort) maximizes the following functional at t ($t > s$):

$$\max_{\{c(V)\}} \int_t^\infty u[c(s,v)] \exp[-\delta(v-t)] \, dv \qquad (15.4a)$$

Since agents are assumed to be heterogeneous and we will be resorting to aggregation below, we assume that $u(.)$ belongs to the constant-relative-risk-aversion family:

$$u(c) = \frac{c^{1-R}}{1-R} \qquad R > 0 \qquad (15.4b)$$

When $R > 1$ the income effect of an increased interest rate dominates whereas when $R < 1$ the substitution effect dominates. $R = 1$ corresponds to the logarithmic utility function for which the income and substitution effects cancel. Note that the intertemporal elasticity of consumption is given by R^{-1}.

The financial assets of the household are $a(s, t)$. The household receives wage $w(t)$ and pays taxes $T(t)$. Note that neither w nor T is cohort specific. The supply of labor is inelastic, say unity. The household's flow budget constraint is given by

$$\dot{a}(s, t) = w(t) - T(t) - c(s, t) + ra(s, t) \tag{15.4c}$$

Finally, there is the transversality condition

$$\lim_{v \to \infty} c(s, v) \exp(-rv) > 0 \tag{15.4d}$$

The transversality condition and the flow budget constraint give us the intertemporal budget constraint:

$$\int_t^\infty c(s, v) \exp(-rv) \, dv \leqslant a(s, t) + h(t) \tag{15.4e}$$

where

$$h(t) \equiv \int_t^\infty [w(v) - T(v)] \exp(-rv) \, dv$$

is the human wealth of the individual. The optimal consumption path is given by

$$c(s, t) = \theta[a(s, t) + h(t)] \tag{15.5a}$$

where

$$\theta \equiv R^{-1}[\delta - (1 - R)r] \tag{15.5b}$$

Note that the marginal propensity to consume out of total wealth, θ, reduces to δ when $R = 1$, i.e. is independent of the interest rate. Consumption grows over time according to

$$\dot{c}(s, t) = \left(\frac{r - \delta}{R}\right) c(s, t) \tag{15.5c}$$

Aggregating over all individuals at time t (for any variable $x(t)$ the aggregate is defined as $X(t) \equiv n \int_{-\infty}^t x(s, t) \exp(nt) \, dt$ where $n > 0$ denotes the growth rate of the population), we have equation (15.6a) corresponding to equation (15.5c) for the individual:

$$C(t) = (r - \delta)R^{-1}C(t) - n\theta A(t) \tag{15.6a}$$

The last term in the above expression is due to the fact that newly born households are not linked altruistically to existing households and they are born with only human wealth but no financial assets. Thus the change in consumption is the average change in consumption $(r - \delta)R^{-1}C$ less the consumption out of assets of the household born at t (see Buiter, 1988; Obstfeld, 1989; Weil, 1989; Nielsen and Sørensen, 1991). In these models Ricardian equivalence does not hold precisely because the average and marginal consumptions diverge.

The other dynamic equation is obtained by aggregating over the individual asset accumulation equations:

$$\dot{A} = (r - n)A(t) + w(t) - T(t) - C(t) \qquad (15.6b)$$

where again the term $nA(t)$ appears because $a(t, t) = 0$.

The steady state of this model is obtained by putting $\dot{A} = \dot{C} = 0$. It is easy to check that r need not equal δ. If, for instance, $r > \delta$, individual consumption is rising over time but per capita consumption can be constant as a result of population growth and the fact that new households are born without financial wealth.

For the two cases $r > \delta$ and $r < \delta$ we have the phase diagrams given in figure 15.2. The slope of the $\dot{C} = 0$ line differs in the two cases and

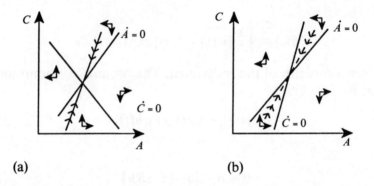

(a)   (b)

Figure 15.2   Saving and consumption with overlapping generations of infinitely lived households: (a) $\delta > r$; (b) $r > \delta$.

the directions in which the vertical arrows point. But the qualitative behaviors are similar in that the stable arm slopes up and the unstable arm slopes down. Note that we have assumed $r - n > 0$, i.e. that the economy is dynamically efficient.

3   Producers and investment

In this section we look at the profit-maximizing firm's behavior when it is faced with a perfect capital market and no (current or expected) sales constraints. There are interesting results when these assumptions do not hold but, by and large, the open economy macroeconomics literature has ignored this and focused entirely on the infinite-horizon competitive firm.

3.1   A two-period model

Suppose a firm produces a homogeneous output and cannot augment capital stock within a given period. It then maximizes profits by choosing current period and future period variable inputs and next period's capital stock. Its problem is to maximize profits:

$$\pi \equiv F(K_0, L_0) + \theta F(K_1, L_1) - w_0 L_0 - \theta w_1 L_1 - I_0 \qquad (15.7)$$

where K_i (L_i) is the ith period capital (labor) input, w_i is the wage rate, I_0 is the investment in period 0, and θ is the discount factor. There is no depreciation, and so the capital stock in period 1 equals $K_1 \equiv K_0 + I_0$.
    The first-order condition for this problem is

$$F_{L_i}(.) = w_i \qquad i = 0, 1 \qquad (15.8a)$$

$$\theta F_{K_1}(.) = 1 \qquad (15.8b)$$

Equation (15.8a) is the usual condition that the marginal product of labor should equal the real wage rate. Equation (15.8b) equates the marginal product to the interest factor:

$$F_{K_1}(.) = 1 + r \equiv \theta^{-1}$$

Equations (15.8) can be inverted to give the usual demand functions for labor, L_1 and L_2, and for investment, I_0.
    Of course, if K is augmentable within the period, the intertemporal problem of the firm becomes a static one in each period (see Sen, 1991).

3.2   Infinite-horizon one-good models

The firm's maximization problem at time 0 now becomes

$$\max_{\{L(t), I(t)\}} \int_t^\infty F[K(t), L(t)] - w(t)L(t) - h[I(t)] \exp(-rt) \, dt \quad (15.9a)$$

subject to the capital accumulation equation

$$\dot{K}(t) = I(t) - \beta K(t) \qquad (15.9b)$$

which is the continuous-time analog of (15.7). The function h representing cost of adjustment is increasing and convex in its argument, i.e. $h' > 0$, $h'' > 0$.[4] This is needed to make the flow of investment I finite. β is the depreciation rate. The literature makes different assumptions about what should be the argument in $h(.)$. For expositional purposes, (15.9a) will do (see Hayashi, 1982; Engel and Kletzer, 1989; Matsuyama, 1987; Brock, 1988; Sen and Turnovsky, 1989a, b; Bevan et al., 1990; Gavin, 1990; Nielsen and Sørensen, 1991).
    The optimality conditions are

$$F_L(K, L) = w \qquad (15.10a)$$

$$h'(I) = q \qquad (15.10b)$$

$$\dot{q} = (r+\beta)q - F_K(K, L) \tag{15.10c}$$

and transversality conditions on K and q. Note that we have dropped the subscripts and introduced a shadow price q associated with (15.9b). Hence, q is the shadow price of capital.

Equation (15.10b) equates the cost of a unit of investment to its gain (see (15.10c′) below) and (15.10c) is the arbitrage equation. We can solve equation (15.10c) forward and impose a terminal condition on q to obtain

$$q(0) = \int_0^\infty F_K(t) \exp(-rt)\, dt \tag{15.10c′}$$

which explicitly equates the shadow price q to the discounted value of the current and future marginal products of K.

Solving for L in terms of the given ws from (15.10a) and of I in terms of q from (15.10b) and substituting in (15.10c) and (15.9b) we can get a system of differential equations in q and K. This is shown in figure 15.3. The stable adjustment path is downward sloping in q–K space.

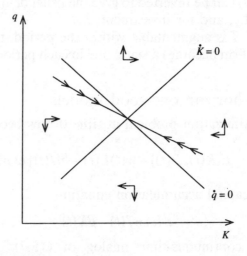

Figure 15.3 Investment and adjustment costs.

3.3   Infinite-horizon two-sector models

Not too many open economy models of this kind exist which look at investment (see Bazdarich, 1978; Murphy, 1986; Matsuyama, 1988; Obstfeld, 1989; Turnovsky, 1991; Brock, 1992; Turnovsky and Sen, 1992; van Wincoop, 1992).

The usual two-sector model in the optimal growth literature with its distinction between a consumption good and a capital good was extended by Bazdarich (1978) to analyze the debt and capital accumulation problem of a small open economy. This type of specification has not proved very popular.

We look at the dependent economy model where a distinction has been made between traded and nontraded goods. Here either good could be the investment good. For a small open economy which can buy or sell traded goods at a given price, we require some costs of adjustment to ensure that investment remains finite, very much like the problem in equation (15.9) (see Obstfeld (1989) where adjustment costs are absent). On the other hand, if investment goods are nontraded goods, then we do not need to impose arbitrary costs of adjustment. We turn to study this case in detail.

In what follows (which draws from Turnovsky and Sen, 1992) some economy-wide implications will of necessity creep in, since the total labor force and capital will be allocated over the two goods and the nontraded goods market has to clear domestically.

$$\max_{\{K_j, L_j, I\}} \int_0^\infty [F(K_T, L_T) + eG(K_N, L_N) - wL - eI] \exp(-rt)\, dt \qquad (15.11a)$$

subject to

$$K_T + K_N = K \qquad (15.11b)$$

$$L_T + L_N = L = 1 \qquad (15.11c)$$

$$\dot{K} = I \qquad (15.11d)$$

where K_j and L_j denote capital and labor employed in the jth sector $(j \equiv N, T)$ and e stands for the price of nontraded goods. We have omitted the time subscripts for notational ease. The functions $F(.)$ and $G(.)$ are increasing and homogeneous of degree one in their respective arguments. The optimality conditions are

$$F_K(K_T, L_T) = eG_K(K_N, L_N) = r \qquad (15.12a)$$

$$F_L(K_T, L_T) = eG_L(K_N, L_N) = w \qquad (15.12b)$$

$$\dot{e}/e + G_K(K_N, L_N) = r \qquad (15.12c)$$

Equations (15.12a) and (15.12b) equate marginal products across sectors and (15.12c) is the arbitrage equation which equates the return from holding capital (in terms of nontraded goods) to the return r on other assets. Note that $\dot{e}/e$ is the capital gain on nontraded goods that are held as capital. In addition, we need a transversality condition on K:

$$\lim_{t \to \infty} K(t) \exp(-rt) \geq 0 \qquad (15.12d)$$

Writing (15.12a), (15.12b), and (15.11b) in the intensive form we obtain

$$f'(k_T) = eg'(k_N) \tag{15.13a}$$

$$f(k_T) - k_T f'(k_T) = e[g(k_N) - k_N g'(k_N)] \tag{15.13b}$$

$$\rho k_T + (1 - \rho)k_N = K \tag{15.13c}$$

where $k_j \equiv K_j/L_j$ is the capital intensity in the jth sector and $\rho \equiv L_T/L$ denotes the share of the labor force in the traded goods sector. Equations (15.13a)–(15.13c) can be solved for k_T, k_N, and r in terms of k and e:

$$k_T = k_T(e) \qquad k_T' = \frac{g}{f''(k_N - k_T)} \tag{15.14a}$$

$$k_N = k_N(e) \qquad k_N' = \frac{f}{e^2 g''(k_N - k_T)} \tag{15.14b}$$

$$\rho = \rho(e, K) \quad \rho_K = (k_T - k_N)^{-1} \quad \rho_e = (k_T - k_N)^{-2} \frac{(1 - e)f}{e^2 g''} + \frac{eg}{f''} < 0 \tag{15.14c}$$

The signs of the derivatives depend on capital intensities in the two sectors. For example, a rise in the price of nontraded goods e causes resources to move to the traded sector. If that sector is capital intensive, relative scarcity of capital increases and the wage–rental ratio falls, inducing substitution of labor for capital in both sectors.

We get the two dynamic equations by substitution of (15.14b) in (15.12c) to obtain

$$\dot{e} = e[r - g'(k_N)] \tag{15.15a}$$

$$\dot{K} = (1 - \rho)g(k_N) - C_N \tag{15.15b}$$

Equation (15.15b) is the nontraded goods market clearing equation, where C_N stands for the consumption of that good (which depends on e, among other things).

We can solve (15.14b) and (15.14c) for k_N and ρ in terms of K and e and substitute these in (15.15a) and (15.15b) to get a system of two differential equations in e and K. Linearizing around the steady state (a tilde denotes a steady state value) we obtain

$$\begin{pmatrix} \dot{e} \\ \dot{K} \end{pmatrix} = \begin{pmatrix} a_{11} & 0 \\ a_{21} & a_{22} \end{pmatrix} \begin{pmatrix} e - \tilde{e} \\ K - \tilde{K} \end{pmatrix} \tag{15.16}$$

where $a_{11} \equiv -f/e(k_N - k_T)$, $a_{22} \equiv g/(k_N - k_T)$, $a_{21} > 0$. It is readily checked that when $k_T > k_N$ the stable solution implies

$$K(t) = \tilde{K} + (K_0 - \tilde{K}) \exp(a_{22}t) \tag{15.17a}$$

$$e(t) = \tilde{e} \tag{15.17b}$$

The relative price is constant during the dynamic evolution of the economy (see figure 15.4).

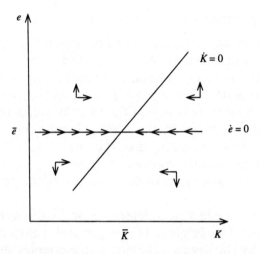

Figure 15.4 Dynamics of the real exchange rate if the traded sector is more capital intensive: $k_T > k_N$.

When $k_N > k_T$, we then have

$$K(t) = \tilde{K} + (K - \tilde{K}) \exp(a_{22}t) \qquad (15.18a)$$

$$e = \tilde{e} + \frac{a_{22} - a_{11}}{a_{21}} (K - \tilde{K}) \qquad (15.18b)$$

and the stable arm is downward sloping in $K - e$ space (see figure 15.5).

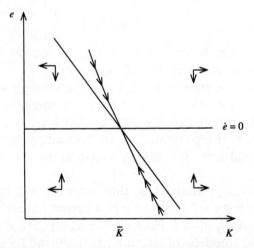

Figure 15.5 Dynamics of the real exchange rate if the nontraded sector is more capital intensive: $k_N > k_T$.

4   Three examples

4.1   The Harberger–Laursen–Metzler effect, oil prices etc.

What happens to an economy's current account if its terms of trade deteriorate? This question, posed first by Harberger (1950) and Laursen and Metzler (1950), has given rise to a substantial literature in the last forty years. The issue, however, is of more than theoretical interest. The world faced two large increases in the price of oil in the 1970s and an equally dramatic collapse in the 1980s. Most non-oil primary-good-exporting countries complain that the prices of exports have been falling over the last twenty years or so. Indeed, this has been one of the major casues of the poor growth performance of the non-oil developing countries.

What then is the effect of a deterioration in the terms of trade that a country faces? The original Harberger and Laursen–Metzler result was generated by the saving behavior of the country in question. They believed that a terms of trade worsening for a given volume of output lowered real income (in terms of either a basket of goods or importables) and led to a fall in saving. Since they did not look at investment, this implied a worsening of the trade balance.

Obstfeld (1982) restarted the debate (there was a voluminous literature in the 1950s and the 1960s on this issue) by suggesting that the saving effect could be exactly the opposite of that claimed by Laursen, Metzler, and Harberger. He used a Uzawa-type utility specification. Now, as we saw above, the foreign interest rate ties down the steady-state utility level of a small open economy:

$$r = \delta(\tilde{u})$$

where r denotes the foreign interest rate, $\tilde{u}$ stands for the level of steady-state utility, and δ is the discount rate.

Now imagine an economy starting off in a steady state. A worsening of the terms of trade would lower its real income and current level of utility. The only way it can get back to $\tilde{u}$ (which is unchanged) is by saving. Hence, a sharp reduction in consumption follows. In the absence of investment this saving is equal to the current account surplus.

The most thorough analysis of this problem was by Svensson and Razin (1983) who started off from a two-period model and then moved to an infinite-horizon model. Here we sketch an outline of their analysis in terms of our models of section 2. This model also includes a discussion of the effects of an increase in the price of intermediate goods.

The representative consumer's optimization problem is a multi-good version of the model represented in equations (15.1) and (15.2):

$$\max V(C_0, C_1) \tag{15.19a}$$

subject to

$$P_0 C_0 + P_1 C_1 (1 + r)^{-1} = W \tag{15.19b}$$

where $V(.)$ is assumed to be homothetic. C_0 and C_1 are now to be interpreted as utilities from consumption of the two goods in each period:

$$C_i = u(X_i, M_i) \qquad i = 0, 1$$

where X is the domestic (exportable) good and M is the importable. The function $u(.)$ is assumed to be homogeneous of degree one, without loss of generality. P_0 and P_1 are the price indexes corresponding to C_0 and C_1 respectively. The price index P_i is the exact price index corresponding to the unit expenditure function. The good Y is the numeraire and r denotes the interest rate.

Wealth W is equal to the present value of the gross domestic product (GDP) of the two periods less the value of investment in period 0:

$$W \equiv p_0 Y_0 + p_1 Y_1 (1 + r)^{-1} - p_0 I_0 \tag{15.20a}$$

with

$$Y_i = \max[F(K_i, L_i, Z_i) - q_i Z_i] \qquad i = 0, 1 \tag{15.20b}$$

and

$$K_1 \equiv K_0 + I_0 \tag{15.20c}$$

where Z_i is the intermediate input (oil) whose price (relative to the domestic good) is q_i, and p_i is the relative price of domestic goods in terms of the foreign good. Investment must be carried out one period in advance. We also assume that labor in each period is supplied inelastically and assume it is equal to L. $F(.)$ is constant returns to scale with positive but diminishing marginal products. The three factors are assumed to be cooperant or Edgeworth complementary (see Svensson, 1984).

The relevant discount factor for the firm is then $p_1[(1 + r)p_0]^{-1}$. Investment is carried to the point where

$$F_{k_1} = \frac{\partial Y_1}{\partial K_1} = (1 + r)p_0 p_1^{-1} \tag{15.21a}$$

Also, the marginal products of labor and Z must equal their respective prices:

$$F_i = \frac{\partial Y_i}{\partial L_i} = w_i \qquad i = 0, 1 \qquad (15.21b)$$

$$F_i = \frac{dY_i}{dZ_i} = q_i \qquad i = 0, 1 \qquad (15.21c)$$

where w_i is the product wage rate.

What are the effects of an increase in q_i or a fall p_i on I_0, Y_0, and Y_1? Before proceeding, note that a fall in p_i corresponds to a deterioration of the final goods terms of trade and a rise in q_i corresponds to a deterioration in the "imported input terms of trade."

A temporary rise in q, i.e. in q_0, lowers Z_0 and Y_0. Note that K_0 is predetermined and labor L_0 is inelastically supplied. It has no effect on either I_0 or Y_1. A rise in q_1 lowers Z_1 (own-price effect). This in turn lowers the marginal product of capital (because $F_{KZ} > 0$). To restore the equality of marginal product with the interest factor (which is unchanged at $(1 + r)p_0/p_1$) K_1 must fall. Hence, private investment I_0 falls. Output in period 1 falls because of a decline in K_1 and Z_1.

A permanent increase in q (i.e. both q_0 and q_1) reduces Y_0, Y_1, and I_0. We see that an increase in the price of oil tends to improve the current account through its effect on investment when that increase is permanent or expected in the future and has no effect on investment when it is temporary.

The effect of a decrease in p_0 or p_1 on investment, given q_i, works through the discount factor. A fall in p_0 lowers the discount factor, *ceteris paribus*, while a fall in p_1 raises it. A fall in p_0 (p_1), therefore, increases (decreases) investment I_0 and raises (lowers) Z_1 because of its effect on the marginal product of Z. Thus a fall in p_0 (or a *rise* in p_1) raises I_0, Z_1, and thus Y_1. A fall in p_0 in addition lowers Y_0 through its effect on Z_0. A permanent worsening of the terms of trade has an ambiguous effect on future production and I_0 since the interest factor could rise, fall, or stay unchanged. But current production definitely falls.

Turning now to the effects on savings, we find that oil price increases are the easiest to analyze. Current period savings fall if the increase in q is temporary and rise if q is expected to rise in the future. Both these effects are due to consumption smoothing. A permanent increase in the price of oil has an ambiguous effect on current saving because both of the above effects are at work.

Svensson (1984) shows that if we make additional assumptions that $dq_0 = dq_1 = dq$ and initial imports of oil are equal, i.e. $Z_0 = Z_1 = Z$, then the change in period 0 trade balance can be written as (assuming $r = \delta$)

$$dt_0 = \left(\frac{\partial C_0}{\partial W} - \frac{\partial C_1}{\partial W}\right)[- Z(1 + r)^{-1} \, dq] - \frac{dI_0}{dq} \, dq$$

This expression is positive if $\partial C_1/\partial W > \partial C_0/\partial W$. If the consumption propensity out of wealth is equal in both periods, then saving is unaffected.

Taking into consideration both the saving and the investment effects of an oil price increase, we see that a temporary increase worsens the current account. (Saving falls and investment is unaffected.) An expected future increase improves the current period current account (saving rises, investment falls). A sufficient condition for a permanent oil price increase to improve the current account is that savings do not change, since investment clearly falls.

The main difference in effect on saving between an intermediate good price change and a final good price change is that the former (as we saw above) does not change the interest factor. The effect of an oil price increase on consumption just works through its effect on wealth. But when p changes we know that the interest factor for the firm will change unless the proportionate change in p_0 is the same as that in p_1.

The interest factor relevant for consumption decisions is, of course, $P_0(1 + r)/P_1$ where P_0 and P_1 are the exact price indexes associated with unit subutility expenditures C_0 and C_1 respectively. These price indexes are increasing and homogeneous of degree one in the respective p_is and the price of the numeraire M, taken to be unity.

In addition to the production effects of changes in p_i, which enter the consumer's problem through a change in W, we now have a wealth and an intertemporal substitution effect of a change in $P_0(1 + r)/P_1$.

The saving effect of a terms of trade shock is uncertain. A decrease in p_0 lowers the real value of domestic output in terms of consumption $p_0 y_0/P_0$ and lowers the real interest rate (via a fall in P_0). The former channel lowers current consumption but the latter channel has ambiguous effects. Therefore the current account effects of a fall in p_0 are also uncertain.

We can similarly work out the effects of a future and a permanent terms of trade shock. For an excellent discussion of these issues, the reader is referred to Persson and Svensson (1985).

We now briefly turn to the infinite-horizon versions of the model studied above. Matsuyama (1987) considers the case of an oil price increase in a model with finite lives and new births (where Ricardian equivalence thus does not hold).

As in the two-period model considered above, investment falls following an unanticipated increase in the price of oil. The saving effect in Matsuyama's model is ambiguous. The effect on the current account can be decomposed into a pure wealth effect which worsens the current account and a portfolio substitution effect which improves it. The net outcome depends on the relative magnitudes of these two effects (see also Bruno and Sachs, 1982b).

Sen and Turnovsky (1989b) look at the decline in the price of a small country's exportable in a model with an endogenous labor supply. The deterioration in the terms of trade has an income and a substitution effect on labor supply. The (negative) wealth effect tends to increase labor supply and the rise in price of the goods aggregate increases the consumption of leisure through a substitution effect. The long-run marginal product of capital has to equal the given world interest rate. Hence, when the income effect dominates, capital is accumulated along the adjustment path, and in the other case it is run down. In their model investment always dominates the saving effect and is accompanied by current account deficits.

In this model temporary shocks have permanent effects because the discount rate is set equal to the world interest rate. A temporary shock has qualitatively the same effect as a permanent shock (see Sen and Turnovsky, 1989a).

We finally consider models with capital immobility. These are important because many of the world's countries which have suffered significant terms of trade deterioration do not have access (or have limited access) to the world capital markets.

If borrowing or lending is forbidden then what would be the counterpart of a current account deficit? In Sen (1990) it is the accumulation of foreign currency by the domestic public which enters the capital account, while in Sen (1991) it is the official settlements balance in a regime of fixed exchange rates which adjusts.

Sen (1990) considers an unanticipated permanent terms of trade deterioration in a model with currency substitution while Sen (1991) looks at an intermediate good price increase. The results are similar for both models. The negative shocks lower new steady-state levels of wealth but dissaving occurs over time through current account deficits. Hence, a Laursen–Metzler type of result is obtained. Recall that the original Laursen–Metzler (1950) model looked at an open economy without capital mobility.

4.2 Fiscal policy

Consider first an economy which takes its terms of trade as given and produces only traded goods. Suppose in such an economy that the government increases its expenditure financed through lump-sum taxes.

Investment is unaffected if the future marginal product does not change (if, for example, there is no increase in labor supply). Lifetime private consumption will fall because of the decline in wealth. Saving and the current account in period 0 will then depend on whether the taxes are levied in period 0 or period 1. The change in welfare will depend on whether government expenditure yields utility or not in addition to the decline in welfare due to the fall in private consumption.

Two-country variants of this model are discussed by, among others, Frenkel and Razin (1987), Devereux (1987), Djajic (1987a), and Greenwood and Kimbrough (1985). These models have one major advantage over the model considered here, namely that the interest rate can be made endogenous.

Let us now consider a two-good version of the above model. We either go the dependent economy way and introduce a nontraded good or analyze the semi-small economy where the domestic economy, though small in the sense of taking foreign variables as given, has some market power in its exportable good. Let us consider the latter extension.

The investment problem of the firm is very much like the one we looked at in our analysis of a terms of trade shock. The firm looks at the profitability of investment:

$$F_K(K, L) = (1 + r)p_0/p_1$$

but now p_0 and p_1 are not exogenous. It seems reasonable to assume that if the fiscal expansion is temporary p_0 will rise if the increased expenditure is directed towards the home good (see below); therefore K_1 will fall. This will imply a decline in I_0. Note that output is unchanged in period 0 and it declines in period 1. This assumes that labor supply is exogenous.

On the other hand if the fiscal expansion occurs in the future and is again directed towards the home good, then p_1 rises. This causes investment to rise in period 0. Output in period 1 will rise.

The effects mentioned in the preceding two paragraphs are reversed if the fiscal expansion is directed towards the foreign good.

If we take the utility function to be the one in section 4.1, i.e. $V(C_0, C_1)$ where V is homothetic as are the subutility functions C_0 and C_1, V definitely falls. C_0 and C_1 will tend to fall because of the wealth effect but there is also an intertemporal price effect which could go either way, as in the case of the terms of trade shock of section 4.1. In addition, there are within-period effects of changes in p_i, X_i, and M_{i0}.

The goods market clearing conditions are given by

$$F(K_0, L) = X_0 + I_0 + X_0^*(p_0) + G_0 \qquad X_i^{*\prime} < 0, i = 0, 1 \qquad (15.22a)$$

$$F(K_0 + I_0, L) = X_1 + X_1^*(p_1) + G_1 \qquad X_i^{*\prime} < 0, i = 0, 1 \qquad (15.22b)$$

where X_i^* is the foreign demand for the domestic good and G_i is the domestic government's demand for the domestic good.

Output in period 0 is predetermined (equation (15.22a)) and an increase in that period creates an excess demand and tends to push p_0 up, which reduces I_0 and X_0^*. C_0 tends to fall because of the reduced wealth and the substitution effect of a rise in the interest rate facing the consumer. The income effect of the interest rate for a lender works in the opposite direction. For a given C_0, a higher p_0 causes a substitution away from X_0.

The infinite-horizon models come in two groups. One follows Uzawa (1968) and Epstein and Hynes (1983) in making the rate of time preference variable. Contributions in this genre include Obstfeld (1982), Devereux and Shi (1991), and Sen (1984). The other takes the rate of time preference to be fixed. This includes Turnovsky and Sen (1991).

In Turnovsky and Sen (1991) it is shown that both a permanent and a temporary increase in government expenditure directed towards the domestic good increases investment, decreases national saving and thus increases the current account deficit. Since the discount rate is set equal to the world interest rate, temporary policy has a permanent effect. When the increased government expenditure falls on the importable, the effects on investment and the current account are likely to be reversed although this is not inevitable.

In the Uzawa-type model of Sen (1984) there is no capital accumulation and increased government expenditure on either good gives rise to a current account surplus. This is due to the target-wealth-type implication of the variable rate of time preference. An increase in (lump-sum) taxes lowers steady-state utility and the representative consumer saves to get back to the original level of utility, as discussed in section 2. This is true irrespective of whether government spending falls on the domestic or the foreign good. The savings take the form of interest-bearing foreign assets.

4.3   The Feldstein–Horioka puzzle

Feldstein and Horioka (1980) started off from the basic model analyzed in section 2. In that model the households maximize utility subject to their intertemporal budget constraint and firms maximize their profits. Savings and investment decisions are made independently of each other. The "domestic firm" need not be owned by domestic residents, but its investment decisions are part of the domestic economy's GDP. In this set-up, Feldstein and Horioka asserted, we should find no correlation between (domestic) saving and investment.

They ran a regression for some industrial countries and found a correlation coefficient of 0.91 between domestic saving and investment. This they took as an indicator of lack of capital mobility – remember that, in a closed economy, saving and investment have to be equal to each other. Later authors modified their econometric specification to take simultaneity etc. into account, but they came up with numbers very close to that of Feldstein and Horioka. The question then arises: does a high correlation between saving and investment indicate low capital mobility?

Obstfeld (1986) gave two examples where a high correlation did not imply the absence of capital mobility. In the first example population growth caused both savings and investment to rise. Savings rise because agents in their youth save in an overlapping generations framework and because of population growth there is more saving by the young than dissaving by the old. Investment takes place to equate the marginal product of capital in the next period to the world interest rate.

The second example essentially reduces to analyzing a temporary unanticipated productivity shock. This will cause investment to rise, and since labor receives wages which are temporarily high there will be saving out of these to smooth consumption.

Wong (1990) gives an example of a two-sector model with nontraded goods where an exogenous decline in the discount rate causes saving to rise. Investment rises to ensure equality of returns across sectors. He also looks at the empirical evidence more carefully and is skeptical about the robustness of the original findings.

From the shocks analyzed above we can generate many examples where saving and investment can be correlated. An expected future fiscal expansion directed towards the domestic good causes investment to rise. If taxes are to be levied in the future, consumers will save today.

Consider another simple example. Suppose the government is planning (or so the private sector believes) to pay a subsidy on capital in place in period 1. Lump-sum taxes will be imposed on the households to pay for this. The households will save in period 0 in a bid to smooth consumption. The firm will undertake investment in period 0. The expectation of policy change may or may not be realized and so there could be a "peso problem" in empirically implementing this.

Hence, from a theoretical point of view, one should not make too much of a relationship between two endogenous variables. But the empirical puzzle remains (see Murphy, 1984; Engel and Kletzer, 1989; Finn, 1990; for more on this issue).

5   Other shocks and some neglected areas

The class of models we have looked at has been applied to study a wide variety of shocks. Commercial policy, distortionary taxation, taste and productivity shocks, natural resource discoveries, the transfer problem, etc. have all been studied.

Commercial policy has been analyzed within intertemporal maximization models and this provides a link between this class of models and models of the pure theory of trade. For instance, Razin and Svensson (1983) find that one of the durable results of trade theory, namely the symmetry between import tariffs and export taxes, does not hold in an intertemporal model unless the tariffs and taxes are permanent. Other papers in this area include Djajic (1987b), Brock (1988), Fender and Yip (1989), Sen and Turnovsky (1989b), and Turnovsky (1991).

Capital taxation, investment tax credits, consumption, and labor taxes have all been analyzed within an explicit intertemporal setting. Sen and Turnovsky (1990), for instance, find that a temporary investment tax credit will lead to a higher steady-state utility level. This is due to the zero-root problem. See also Nielsen and Sørensen (1991), Turnovsky and Bianconi (1992), Bianconi (1992), and Frenkel and Razin (1987).

Taste and productivity shocks form an integral part of the real business cycle literature (see for example Stockman and Tesar, 1991; Finn, 1990; and chapter 3 in this volume). Fiscal policy and input prices are analytically similar to productivity shocks (see Obstfeld (1986) and the references contained therein). The endogenous growth literature also belongs here (Grossman and Helpman, 1991; and chapters 14 and 16 in this volume).

The Dutch disease literature is vast (see for example Fender and Nandkumar, 1987; Neary and van Wijnbergen, 1986; van Wijnbergen, 1985; Bruno and Sachs, 1982b). The transfer problem has been analyzed in an explicit intertemporal framework by Gavin (1990).

Closed economy macroeconomics has seen a resurgence of Keynesian theory with its emphasis on imperfect competition, imperfect information, and involuntary unemployment. No corresponding thinking is discernable in the open economy literature although chapter 2 of this volume makes a start. This is somewhat surprising in that at least in the theory of imperfect competition there are results and frameworks in the pure theory of trade which are ideally suited for application to macro issues (see Svensson and van Wijnbergen (1987) for an early application).

For example, monopolistic competition could provide a more realistic set-up in which to analyze fiscal policy, tariffs, and exchange rate policy. Fixed and sunk costs could explain the effectiveness of policies in ways that are not readily comprehensible in competitive models (see Baldwin, 1988; Das, 1989; Lin, 1989; Sen, 1991).

Take the example of the US current account deficits. Many observers felt that, since a real appreciation had caused the exit of many US firms and sunk costs were involved, the real value of the dollar had depreciated beyond its starting point for US firms to move back (see for example Baldwin, 1988). The point made by Lin (1989) is that while this is the right policy for "re-industrialization" the current account remains in deficit while entry occurs. Lin's model is also a partial equilibrium one and so begs the question of what policy causes the real depreciation.

Another promising area of research is that initiated by Calvo (1986). This looks at the implication of reducing one distortion when others are present. As an example, consider liberalization of trade which is not credible. Lack of credibility acts like a distortion and liberalization is not welfare improving. Since this issue is of fundamental importance in macroeconomic and trade policy, it is surprising that there are not other models looking at other distortions. These could draw upon the game-theoretic trade liberalization models (e.g. Matsuyama, 1992).

An area which should witness a surge of activity in the near future is the introduction of uncertainty in simple general equilibrium models. Some progress has been made in this area by real business cycle theorists but they rely on numerical simulations to "mimic" the data (see chapter 3 of this volume). Recently, Grinols and Turnovsky (1991) have looked at various policies in a continuous-time model with uncertainty. Continuous-time models incorporating uncertainty have been used extensively in studies of the European Monetary System and also in the literature about speculative attack on a fixed exchange rate (see chapter 8 of this volume). However, these are usually models which are not based on maximizing behavior and are partial equilibrium in nature.

The integration of the monetary sector and the real sector remains to be done in a satisfactory way in open economy macroeconomics. A related issue is price stickiness and the real effects of monetary policy. The cash-in-advance constraint is at least conceptually straightforward to model in a closed economy. In an open economy in which cash is to be obtained in advance it is not too clear (see Helpman and Razin, 1984). Putting money in the utility function or in a transactions technology is not a way out. These issues are important because nominal exchange rate changes reflect themselves in changes in competitiveness. While it is not impossible to get a flexible-price model to get nominal and real exchange rates to move together, it is not clear why nominal rigidity should not be examined in greater detail. Here Calvo (1984) provides a tractable way for introducing nominal rigidities (see for example Calvo and Vegh (1990) for an application).

Appendix

Consider the open economy version of two-period overlapping generations models. Assume that the economy produces only traded goods and takes the world interest rate as given. In the first period of a person's life (youth), he or she works and in the second (old age) he or she lives off his or her savings.

For a time-separable utility function we can solve the Euler equation and the budget constraint for the optimal values of C_0 and C_1:

$$U'(C_0) = (1 + r)(1 + \delta)^{-1} U'(C_1)$$

$$w_0 \equiv C_0 + C_1(1 + r)^{-1}$$

where w_0 is the wage earned by a person who is young in period 0 and who supplies one unit of labor inelastically and r is the world interest rate.

The indirect utility function for a person born at time 0 is

$$V_0 = V(w_0, r) \qquad V_1 > 0,\ V_2 > 0$$

The foreign interest rate ties down the rental rate of capital. If technology is linearly homogeneous, this ties down the capital–labor ratio and hence the wage rate.

The balance of trade b_0 per capita is given by

$$b_0 = f(k) - C_0 - \tilde{C}_1(1 + n)^{-1} - nk$$

where $k \equiv K/L$, $\tilde{C}_1$ is the consumption by the old in period 0, and n is the growth rate of the population. For more details of this, see Buiter (1981) and Persson (1985).

Notes

This chapter has benefited from helpful discussions with Phil Brock, Jonathan Eaton, Charles Engel, Nobu Kiyotaki, and Søren Bo Nielsen. The debt to Steve Turnovsky is self-evident to anyone reading it.
1   It is interesting to note that we get a similar formulation from the variable rate of time preference discussed in section 2 below.
2   In this chapter we shall use direct utility functions and not the indirect utility function or the expenditure function, mainly because most infinite-horizon models do not use them.
3   Throughout this chapter a prime will denote the derivative of a function of a single variable and a subscript the partial of a function of several variables; a dot over a variable denotes its time derivative.
4   In addition, $h'(0) = 1$.

References

Baldwin, R. (1988) "Hysteresis in import prices: the beachhead effect," *American Economic Review* 78, 773–85.

Bazdarich, M.J. (1978) "Optimal growth and stages in the balance of payments," *Journal of International Economics* 4, 425–43.

Bevan, D.L., P. Collier, and J.W. Gunning (1990) "Temporary trade shocks and dynamic adjustment," mimeo, University of Oxford.

Bianconi, M. (1992) "Fiscal policy in a simple two-country dynamic model," mimeo, Tufts University.

Blanchard, O.J. (1985) "Debt deficits and finite horizons," *Journal of Political Economy* 91, 589–610.

Brock, P.L. (1988) "Investment, the current account and the relative prices of nontraded goods in a small open economy," *Journal of International Economics* 24, 235–53.

—— (1992) "Nontraded investment, production structure and the current account," mimeo, University of Washington.

Bruno, M. and J. Sachs (1982a) "Input price shocks and the slowdown in economic growth: the case of UK manufacturing," *Review of Economic Studies* 49, 479–505.

—— and —— (1982b) "Energy and resource allocation: a dynamic model of the 'Dutch disease,'" *Review of Economic Studies* 49, 845–59.

Buiter, W.H. (1981) "Time preference and international lending and borrowing in an overlapping generations model," *Journal of Political Economy* 89, 769–97.

—— (1988) "Death, population growth, productivity growth and debt neutrality," *Economic Journal* 98, 279–93.

Calvo, G.A. (1984) "Staggered contracts and exchange rate policy," in J.A. Frenkel (ed.) *Exchange Rates and International Macroeconomics*, Chicago, IL, University of Chicago Press.

—— (1986) "Temporary stabilization: predetermined exchange rates," *Journal of Political Economy* 94, 1319–29.

—— and V. Vegh (1990) "Credibility and the dynamics of stabilization policy: a basic framework," mimeo, International Monetary Fund, Washington, DC.

Das, S.P. (1989) "Open economy macroeconomics in the presence of intraindustry trade and scale economics," mimeo, Indiana University.

Devereux, M. (1987) "Fiscal spending, the terms of trade, and the real interest rate," *Journal of International Economics* 22, 219–32.

—— and S. Shi (1991) "Capital accumulation and the current account in a two-country model," *Journal of International Economics* 30, 1–25.

Djajic, S. (1987a) "Effects of budgetary policies in open economies: the role of intertemporal consumption substitution," *Journal of International Money and Finance* 6, 373–83.

—— (1987b) "Temporary import quota and the current account," *Journal of International Economics* 22, 349–62.

Dornbusch, R. (1983) "Real interest rates, home goods and optimal external borrowings," *Journal of Political Economy* 91, 141–53.

Engel, C. and K. Kletzer (1989) "Saving and investment in an open economy with non-traded goods," *International Economic Review* 30, 735–52.

—— and —— (1990) "Tariffs and saving in a model with new generations,"

Journal of International Economics 28, 71–91.

Epstein, L.G. and J.A. Hynes (1983) "The rate of time preference in dynamic economic analysis," *Journal of Political Economy* 91, 611–28.

Feldstein, M. and C. Horioka (1980) "Domestic saving and international capital flows," *Economic Journal* 90, 314–29.

Fender, J. and P. Nandkumar (1987) "Oil in an intertemporal macroeconomic model," *Greek Economic Review* 9, 38–56.

—— and C.K. Yip (1989) "Tariffs and employment: an intertemporal model," *Economic Journal* 99, 806–17.

Finn, M.G. (1990) "On saving and investment dynamic in an open economy," *Journal of International Economics* 29, 1–22.

Frenkel, J.A. and A. Razin (1987) *Fiscal Policies and the World Economy*, Cambridge, MA, MIT Press.

Gavin, M. (1990) "International transmission of macroeconomic disturbances: the role of equity markets," Discussion Paper 466, Columbia University.

—— (1991) "Tariffs and the current account: on the macroeconomic effect of commercial policy," *Journal of Economic Dynamics and Control* 15, 27–52.

Giavazzi, F. and C. Wyplosz (1985) "The zero root problem: a note on the dynamic determination of the stationary equilibrium in linear models," *Review of Economic Studies* 52, 352–7.

Greenwood, J. and K.P. Kimbrough (1985) "Capital controls and financial policy in the world economy," *Canadian Journal of Economics* 18, 743–65.

Grinols, E.L. and S.J. Turnovsky (1991) "Stochastic equilibrium and exchange rate determination in a small open economy," NBER Working Paper 3651, Cambridge, MA.

Grossman, G.M. and E. Helpman (1991) *Innovation and Growth in the Global Economy*, Cambridge, MA, MIT Press.

Harberger, A.C. (1950) "Currency depreciation, income and the balance of trade," *Journal of Political Economy* 58, 47–60.

Hayashi, F. (1982) "Tobin's q, rational expectations and optimal investment rule," *Econometrica* 50, 213–24.

Laursen, S. and L.A. Metzler (1950) "Flexible exchange rates and the theory of employment," *Review of Economics and Statistics* 32, 281–312.

Lin, H.C. (1989) "Current account dynamics, hysteresis and exchange rate shocks," mimeo, University of Illinois.

Liviatan, N. (1981) "Monetary expansion and the real exchange rate," *Journal of Political Economy* 89, 1218–27.

Matsuyama, K. (1987) "Current account dynamics in a finite horizon model," *Journal of International Economics* 23, 299–313.

—— (1992) "Imperfect competition, foreign trade and the multipliers: Machlup–Metzler fifty years later," Working Paper E-9, Hoover Institution.

Michener, R. (1984) "A neoclassical model of the balance of payments," *Review of Economic Studies* 51, 651–64.

Murphy, R.G. (1984) "Capital mobility and the relationship between saving and investment in OECD countries," *Journal of International Money and Finance* 3, 327–42.

—— (1986) "Productivity shocks, non-traded goods and optimal capital accumulation," *European Economic Review* 30, 1081–95.

Neary, J.P. and S. van Wijnbergen (1986) *Natural Resources and the Macroecon-*

omy, Cambridge, MA, MIT Press.

Nielsen, S.B. and P.B. Sørensen (1991) "Capital income taxation in a growing open economy," *European Economic Review* 34, 179–97.

Obstfeld, M. (1982) "Aggregate spending and the terms of trade: is there a Laursen–Metzler effect?" *Quarterly Journal of Economics* 10, 251–70.

—— (1983) "Intertemporal price speculation and the optimal current account deficit," *Journal of International Money and Finance* 2, 135–45.

—— (1986) "Capital mobility in the world economy: theory and measurement," *Carnegie-Rochester Conference Series* 24, 55–104.

—— (1989) "Fiscal deficits and relative prices in a growing world economy," *Journal of Monetary Economics* 23, 461–84.

Persson, T. (1985) "Deficits and intergenerational welfare in open economies," *Journal of International Economics* 19, 67–84.

—— and L.E.O. Svensson (1985) "Current account dynamics and the terms of trade: Harberger–Laursen–Metzler two generations later," *Journal of Political Economy* 93, 43–65.

van der Ploeg, F. (1991) "Money and capital in interdependent economies with overlapping generations," *Economica* 58, 233–56.

Razin, A. and L.E.O. Svensson (1983) "Trade taxes and the current account," *Economics Letters* 13, 55–7.

Sen, P. (1984) "Fiscal policy and the current account: an optimizing model," mimeo, University of Michigan.

—— (1990) "Terms of trade shock and the current account in a monetary economy," *Economica* 57, 383–94.

—— (1991) "Imported input price and the current account in an optimizing model without capital mobility," *Journal of Economic Dynamics and Control* 15, 91–101.

—— and S.J. Turnovsky (1989a) "Deterioration of the terms of trade and capital accumulation: a re-examination of the Laursen–Metzler effect," *Journal of International Economics* 26, 212–28.

—— and —— (1989b) "Tariffs, capital accumulation and the current account in a small open economy," *International Economic Review* 30, 811–31.

—— and —— (1990) "Investment tax credit in an open economy," *Journal of Public Economics* 42, 277–99.

Stockman, A.C. and L.L. Tesar (1991) "Tastes and technology in a two-country model of the business cycle – explaining international co-movements," NBER Working Paper 1103, Cambridge, MA.

Svensson, L.E.O. (1984) "Oil prices, welfare and the trade balance," *Quarterly Journal of Economics* 99, 649–72.

—— and A. Razin (1983) "The terms of trade and the current account: the Harberger–Laursen–Metzler effect," *Journal of Political Economy* 91, 97–125.

—— and S. van Wijnbergen (1987) "Excess capacity, monopolistic competition and international transmission of monetary disturbances," NBER Working Paper 2262, Cambridge, MA.

Turnovsky, S.J. (1991) "Tariffs and sectoral adjustments in an open economy," *Journal of Economic Dynamics and Control* 15, 53–89.

—— and M. Bianconi (1992) "The international transmission of tax policies in a dynamic world economy," *Review of International Economics*, forthcoming.

—— and P. Sen (1991) "Fiscal policy, capital accumulation and debt in an open economy," *Oxford Economic Papers* 43, 1–24.

—— and —— (1992) "Investment in a two-sector dependent economy," mimeo, University of Washington.

Uzawa, H. (1968) "Time preference, the consumption function and optimum asset holding," in J.N. Wolfe (ed.) *Value, Capital and Growth: papers in honour of Sir John Hicks*, Edinburgh, Edinburgh University Press.

Weil, P. (1989) "Overlapping families of infinitely-lived agents," *Journal of Public Economics* 38, 183–98.

van Wijnbergen, S. (1985) "Optimal capital accumulation and the allocation of investment between traded and non-traded sectors in producing countries," *Scandinavian Journal of Economics* 87, 89–100.

van Wincoop, E. (1992) "Structural adjustment and the construction sector," *European Economic Review*, forthcoming.

Wong, D.Y. (1990) "What do saving–investment relationships tell about capital mobility," *Journal of International Money and Finance* 9, 60–74.

Yaari, M.E. (1965) "Uncertain lifetime, life insurance and the theory of the consumer," *Review of Economic Studies* 32, 137–50.

16 Growth, Deficits, and Research and Development in the Global Economy

FREDERICK VAN DER PLOEG AND PAUL TANG

1 Introduction

In the orthodox neoclassical theory, set out by Solow (1956) and others, the possibility of sustained economic growth is ascribed to an exogenous factor of production, i.e. the passage of time. This result is intimately linked to one of the properties of the neoclassical production function that is employed in this theory. This function relates the output to factor inputs, the stock of accumulated physical capital goods (machinery, computers, and the like), and labor. It displays decreasing returns to scale with respect to the use of each (reproducible) factor of production. It follows that an increase in the stock of capital goods, given the employed amount of labor, yields a less than proportionate increase in output. Expansion of the capital stock implies a decline in the return on a further expansion and for this reason may ultimately cease. Opportunities for profitable investments are limited and will eventually be exhausted. Technical changes, however, that improve the productivity of labor and thus of capital can prevent the rate of return on investment from falling. If the labor force grows at an (exogenous) rate equal to the sum of population growth and labor-augmenting technical progress, capital, output, and consumption will eventually also grow at this exogenous rate on an equilibrium (also called balanced) growth path. Accumulation of capital is in this sense complementary to ongoing technical developments. Neoclassical theory does not provide an economic explanation for these developments, but rather imposes a time trend on the model for the long-run rate of economic growth. Neoclassical theory does attempt to explain the speed of adjustment towards a balanced growth trajectory.

The possibility of exogenous technical progress reconciles the neoclassical theory with Kaldor's 'stylized facts' (1961): a steady growth rate of output (per worker); a more or less constant ratio between output and the capital stock; a constant return on investment; a fairly stable functional distribution of income. However, as technical progress is assumed to be exogenous in the older vintages of growth theory, not much explanatory power is gained from its introduction. Furthermore, when the standard Solow model is calibrated to real data in order to explain the adjustment towards balanced growth paths, the predictions for the speed of convergence or for the national income share of capital income are too high.

Many empirical studies try to attribute the growth of output mainly to quantitative and qualitative changes in the stocks of productive factors. The residual growth in output that cannot be explained by growth in the factors of production is referred to as the Solow residual. The calculation of Solow residuals usually supposes perfect competition in factor and output markets so that the contributions of the growth in capital and in labor to growth in output are weighted by the national income shares of capital and labor respectively. Empirical studies typically find that part of the growth in output cannot be accounted for by growth in the factors of production alone. The resulting Solow residuals are normally ascribed to technical progress and may be of considerable size, as table 16.1 shows.

Table 16.1 Gross domestic product and augmented joint factor productivity (annual average compound growth rate)

	1870–1913	1913–50		1950–73		1973–84	
	GDP	GDP	AJFP	GDP	AJFP	GDP	AJFP
France	1.7	1.1	0.6	5.1	3.1	2.2	0.9
Germany	2.8	1.3	0.2	5.9	3.6	1.7	1.1
Japan	2.5	2.2	0.0	9.4	4.7	3.8	0.4
Netherlands	2.1	2.4	0.5	4.7	2.4	1.6	0.1
UK	1.9	1.3	0.4	3.0	1.5	1.1	0.6
USA	4.2	2.8	1.2	3.7	1.1	2.3	− 0.3

The augmented joint factor productivity (AJFP) equals production growth (GDP) minus the contributions of the changes in quantity and quality of labor and capital.
Source: Maddison, 1987, tables 1 and 11b.

In this chapter we attempt to survey the contributions that have been made in the literature to explain the presence of sizeable Solow residuals and at the same time to provide an understanding of what factors determine the long-run rate of growth of a country in the global economy and how this helps us to understand issues of development. The more policy-oriented aspects of the issues described in this chapter are discussed in van der Ploeg and Tang (1992).

In section 2 we discuss the international implications of the classical theory of economic growth within the context of a macroeconomic model of overlapping generations. Since there is no operational bequest motive, budgetary policy changes have real effects. In section 3 we discuss how a large variety of the new theories of endogenous growth build on the classic work of Uzawa (1965) and Conlisk (1969). The assumption of decreasing returns to a narrow concept of capital is rejected in favor of constant returns to a very broad measure of capital. The long-run rate of growth then depends on a host of supply-side determinants such as learning by doing, intentional investment in human capital, research and development (R&D) in the capital goods and consumption goods industries, and public infrastructure and other public goods. Section 4 applies the new theories of economic growth to obtain a grasp of the issues of catch-up and development and in doing this takes an international perspective. Section 4 deals with the global distribution of welfare. It focuses on the relationship between growth and development, hitherto a neglected subject in the more theoretical literature, and thus analyzes under what conditions rates of economic growth and levels of per capita income will converge or diverge. It also explains why the orthodox theory of economic growth may be somewhat more optimistic about development and catch-up of poor with rich countries than the new theories of endogenous growth.

Section 5 gives a two-country analysis of endogenous growth, based on the notion of learning by doing and government spending affecting the productivity of capital, in the context of overlapping generations. This section explicitly takes into account international knowledge spillovers. Just as in section 2, section 5 allows for departures from Ricardian equivalence between debt issue and taxation; absence of an intergenerational bequest motive and overlapping generations are introduced to show the possible consequences of conventional macro-economic and budgetary policies for private investment. Comparison of the analytical results obtained in sections 2 and 5 clearly reveals the analytical similarities but also the differences between the traditional and the new theories of economic growth and their implications for international macroeconomics. Section 5 thus deals with the effects of demand-side policies on the rate of economic growth; in particular, we analyze the international spillover effects of demand-side policies and stress the importance of international capital mobility. Section 5 thus focuses on the relation between economic growth and budgetary and monetary policy, i.e. government expenditure, public debt, and mon-etary growth. It demonstrates that, once allowance is made for departures from Ricardian debt neutrality, the new theories of eco-nomic growth can explain for the first time that a high national income share of government consumption and high ratios of government debt to national income depress growth prospects and push up real interest rates in the global economy.

Section 6 directs attention to a view on endogenous growth which stresses the role of variety in consumer products as well as R&D, along the lines of Grossman and Helpman (1991). This view is based on the idea that more labor assigned to the R&D sector or to human capital accumulation rather than to the production of goods boosts growth; Grossman and Helpman (1991) focus on knowledge as a nonrival public good and Lucas (1988) focuses on knowledge as a rival public good. We also apply the theory to address the question of growth and trade. Section 7 briefly reviews the scope for growth-promoting government policy, the consequences of trade and integration for the rate of economic growth, and the political economy of growth. Section 8 concludes the chapter.

2   The capital stock and fiscal policy

The familiar framework of optimizing infinitely lived agents often yields Ricardian equivalence between public debt issue and taxation (Barro, 1974). However, this equivalence is violated by the birth of new households (see Weil, 1989). The current stock of public debt is in the hands of the existing households but will in the future be serviced in part by at present nonexisting households. If the former do not value the consumption of the latter, a fraction of the public debt is net wealth to the existing households. This and the following section will also show that as a consequence public debt and government spending may crowd out private investment. Both sections deal with the case of two countries that produce homogeneous perfectly substitutable goods and impose no restrictions on trade. Also, domestic and foreign assets are perfect substitutes and the flow of capital between the countries is unrestricted. The countries are identical with respect to the technology of production, intertemporal preferences of the households, and demographic structure, but may differ in the stock of public debt and in government spending. Households do not have an intergenerational bequest motive. Entry (i.e. the birth) of new households occurs at the rate β and households face a constant instantaneous probability of death λ, so that the growth rate of the population amounts to $n \equiv \beta - \lambda$.

The main difference between this section and section 5 is the modeling of supply. This section relies on the traditional theory of economic growth in which technical progress is exogenous; it presents a simplified version of models used by Giovannini (1988), Obstfeld (1988), and van der Ploeg (1990). Section 5 follows the recent theories (surveyed in sections 3 and 4) in which learning by doing as a side effect of investment constitutes the engine of growth; it builds on work by Alogoskoufis and van der Ploeg (1991a, b, c). This difference mainly shows in the consequences of fiscal policy. Changes in public debt or in government spending affect the level of the capital stock in the traditional theory, but affect the growth rate of the capital stock in the new theories of economic growth.

2.1   An overlapping generations model for two countries

The expected utility of a household born at time v and living at time t can be written as

$$U(v, t) = \int_t^\infty u[c(v, s)] \exp[\, - \,(\rho + \lambda)(s - t)] \, ds \qquad (16.1)$$

where the effective discount rate equals the sum of the subjective rate of time preference ρ and the probability of death λ, u represents instantaneous utility, and c denotes private consumption. Instantaneous utility is an isoelastic function of consumption

$$u[c(v, t)] = \frac{c(v, t)^{1 - 1/\sigma}}{1 - 1/\sigma} \qquad \sigma > 0, \sigma \neq 1$$

$$= \ln[c(v, t)] \qquad \sigma = 1 \qquad (16.2)$$

where σ represents the intertemporal elasticity of substitution. The household maximizes expected utility subject to the budget constraint

$$\frac{da(v, t)}{dt} = [r(t) + \lambda]a(v, t) + w(v, t) - \tau(v, t) - c(v, t) \qquad (16.3)$$

where a, w, and τ denote nonhuman assets, gross wage income, and lump-sum taxes. Households leave their estate contingent on their death to insurance companies, but receive premiums (λa) during their lifetime from these companies. Under the assumption of free entry and perfect competition the payments by and the receipts of the insurance companies exactly match, so that the insurance premium is actuarially fair and no profits are made. Private consumption amounts to a fraction of the sum of nonhuman and human wealth:

$$c(v, t) = \phi(t)[a(v, t) + h(v, t)] \qquad (16.4)$$

where ϕ is the marginal propensity to consume out of wealth,

$$\phi(t) \equiv [\int_t^\infty \exp\{-\int_t^s [(1-\sigma)r(u) + \sigma p + \lambda]\, du\}\, ds]^{-1} \quad (16.5)$$

and human wealth h is the present discounted value of future wage income minus taxes,

$$h(v, t) \equiv \int_t^\infty \exp\{-\int_t^s [r(u) + \lambda]\, du\}\, [w(v, s) - \tau(v, s)]\, ds \quad (16.6)$$

The marginal propensity to consume is also determined by the future path of the real interest rate. The effect of the real interest rate on spending depends on the magnitude of the intertemporal elasticity of substitution. If $\sigma > 1$ the substitution effect dominates and spending is negatively related to the interest rate, because the main effect of a higher interest rate is a reduction in the price of future goods which induces substitution away from current to future goods. However, if $\sigma < 1$ the income effect dominates and spending is positively related to the interest rate, so that the main effect of a higher interest rate is a higher level of real income which induces more consumption of both current and future goods. If the intertemporal elasticity of substitution equals unity, the substitution and income effects exactly cancel and the marginal propensity is constant and equal to the effective discount rate, i.e. the sum of the subjective rate of time preference and the instantaneous probability of death $(p + \lambda)$. Both wage income and taxes are assumed to be independent of age, so that differences in human wealth between households vanish.

The cohort of households born at time v is at time t only a fraction of the initial size, $\beta L(v) \exp[-\lambda(t-v)]$, where $L(v) = \exp(nv)$ denotes the size of the population at time v. This can be used to aggregate variables. Given that newly born households do not inherit nonhuman wealth (i.e. there is an absence of an intergenerational bequest motive), differential equations for total private consumption, total private nonhuman wealth, and the marginal propensity to consume can be obtained (cf. Blanchard and Fischer, 1989, ch. 3):

$$\dot{C}(t) = \{\sigma[r(t) - \rho] + n\}C(t) - \beta\phi(t)A(t) \quad (16.7)$$

$$\dot{A}(t) = r(t)A(t) + W(t) - T(t) - C(t) \quad (16.8)$$

$$\frac{\dot{\phi}(t)}{\phi(t)} = \phi(t) - [(1-\sigma)\tau(t) + \sigma p + \lambda] \quad (16.9)$$

Firms are identical and operate in perfectly competitive goods and factor markets. They produce according to the production function $P(K, ML)$, which displays constant returns to scale with respect to the use of capital K and labor ML, where the latter is measured in units of efficiency. That is, the productivity of labor depends on a technical parameter M that increases exogenously at the constant rate m. The parameter m is also referred to as the rate of labor-augmenting technical progress and in the orthodox theories of economic growth is assumed to be exogenous. Under the assumption of perfect capital mobility the dynamic optimization problem of the firm collapses into a static problem. Maximization of the present discounted value of the firm demands at every point of time that the marginal productivity of capital equals the user cost of capital, i.e. the sum of the interest rate and the depreciation rate δ, and that the marginal productivity of labor equals the wage. The labor market is assumed to clear at any instant and the labor supply is exogenous (and assumed to equal unity for an individual household).

The government finances its consumption G and the interest payments on debt D by lump-sum taxation T and/or the issue of debt:

$$\dot{D}(t) = r(t)D(t) + G(t) - T(t) \tag{16.10}$$

Solvency of the government requires that the sum of the current stock of debt and the present value of future consumption does not exceed the present value of future taxes:

$$D(t) + \int_t^\infty \exp[- \int_t^s r(u)\, du]\, G(s)\, ds \le \int_t^\infty \exp[- \int_t^s r(u)\, du]\, T(s)\, ds \tag{16.11}$$

Suppose the world consists of two countries. As domestic and foreign goods and assets are perfect substitutes and the flows of goods and of assets are unrestricted, the agents in both countries face the same price on the product market and the same real interest rate. The accumulation of external assets F can be deduced from the current account. The accounting identity for an open economy says that the current account matches national income Y, which in this case is the sum of production and interest payments on external debt or receipts from external assets minus domestic absorption:

$$\dot{F}(t) = r(t)F(t) + Y(t) - C(t) - I(t) - G(t) \tag{16.12}$$

where $I(t) = \dot{K}(t) + \delta K(t)$. The trade balance is the excess of domestic production over domestic absorption $(Y - C - I - G)$. Equilibrium on the world goods markets requires that, given that we assume that the law of one price holds throughout the world, total demand for goods by households, firms, and governments in the two countries must equal the total supply of goods by the two countries.

The analysis in this section can more easily be pursued by expressing the variables in terms of efficiency units of labor and denoting these by small letters instead of capitals (e.g. $c \equiv C/ML$). Furthermore, in the following we take the intertemporal elasticity of substitution to equal unity, so that the dynamic analysis for the short run is facilitated. The above equations for the two countries can then be summarized as

$$\dot{c}(t) = [r(t) - \rho - m]c(t) - \beta(\rho + \lambda)[k(t) + d(t) + f(t)] \quad (16.13)$$

$$\dot{d}(t) = [r(t) - (n + m)]d(t) + g(t) - \tau(t) \quad (16.14)$$

$$\dot{f}(t) = [r(t) - (n + m)]f(t) + p[k(t)] - c(t) - i(t) - g(t) \quad (16.15)$$

$$i(t) = \dot{k} + (\delta + n + m)k(t) \quad (16.16)$$

$$r(t) = p'[k(t)] - \delta \quad (16.17)$$

where $p(k) \equiv P(k, l)$ stands for the intensive-form production function.

2.2   Short-run dynamics and long-run equilibrium

2.2.1   *Global effects on the capital intensity of budgetary policy changes*

Since the external assets of one country are matched by the external liabilities of the other country and we assume that the structures of the home and foreign country are symmetric, the (unweighted) average level of consumption c_a and of capital k_a can be determined from the above system of equations. If we assume that public debt has a stationary value, the world economy can be described by two (nonlinear) differential equations (the annotation for time has been deleted for notational simplicity):

$$\dot{c}_a = [p'(k_a) - \rho - (\delta + m)]c_a - \beta(\rho + \lambda)(k_a + d_a) \quad (16.18)$$

$$\dot{k}_a = p(k_a) - (\delta + n + m)k_a - c_a - g_a \quad (16.19)$$

We assume that the condition for (local) saddlepath stability is satisfied. For the long-run level of (average) consumption to be positive the marginal productivity of capital has to exceed the sum of the rate of time preference and the rate of technical progress (except for the very improbable configuration that private wealth is negative).

The evolution of consumption coincides with the familiar Ramsey rule if there is no entry of new generations ($\beta = 0$) and Ricardian equivalence holds. The resulting steady-state capital intensity corresponds to the modified golden rule which sets the marginal product of private capital (net of depreciation) equal to the rate of time preference ρ plus the rate of labor-augmenting technical progress m. Comparison of the case of a positive birth rate ($\beta > 0$) with that of a zero birth rate reveals that in the latter case the marginal productivity of capital is lower than in the former case, so that the absence of an intergenerational bequest motive and entry of new households imply a lower stock of capital and a lower level of consumption than corresponds to the modified golden rule. Figure 16.1 depicts the combinations of con-

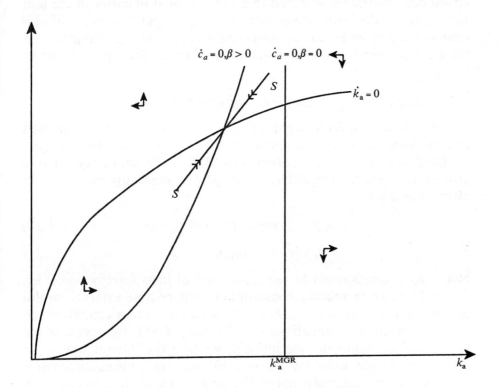

Figure 16.1 Classical growth and overlapping generations.

sumption and capital for which the changes in consumption and capital are zero (see equations (16.18) and (16.19)).

A permanent and unanticipated rise in public debt in either country shifts the $\dot{c}_a = 0$ schedule to the left. Initially private consumption (by current generations) might increase, as public debt is partly serviced by yet unborn generations. Eventually the rise in public debt, however, crowds out investment and lowers the capital stock. Clearly, this effect does not arise if the birth rate is zero as then the associated postponement of taxation is anticipated by households who save now in order to pay for the taxes that are required in the future to service the higher stock of public debt. If the birth rate is positive, private agents who are currently alive anticipate that in the future there will be more shoulders to carry the burden of higher taxes and thus they save less and consume more in the short run.

A permanent increase in government spending shifts the $\dot{k}_a = 0$ schedule to the right. This increase will not totally crowd out private consumption because the rise in taxes is partly paid by new households. Consequently, the sum of public and private consumption will rise and crowd out investment and lead to a lower capital intensity in the long run. Again, if the birth rate is zero, a change in public consumption is counteracted by an exactly opposite change in private consumption, i.e. there is 100 percent crowding out and no effect on the capital intensity.

2.2.2   The current account and budget deficits

As both the level and the evolution of the capital stock and the interest rate are similar in the two countries and as the public debt is again assumed to be constant, equations (16.13)–(16.15) can be rewritten to give expressions for the difference in private consumption c_r and in external assets f_r:

$$\dot{c}_r = (r - \rho - m)c_r - \beta(\rho + \lambda)(d_r + f_r) \qquad (16.20)$$

$$\dot{f}_r = [r - (n + m)]f_r - c_r - g_r \qquad (16.21)$$

Note that f_r corresponds to twice the level of (net) foreign assets, i.e. $f_r = 2f$. Changes in relative consumption and relative external wealth depend on the interest rate, i.e. on the accumulation of capital, which can be derived from equations (16.18) and (16.19). However, as the systems of equations do not interact, we take the interest rate to be constant and equal to its value in equilibrium. Again the equilibrium is supposed to be saddlepath stable. Figure 16.2 shows the combinations of relative consumption and relative external wealth for which the time derivatives of the two variables are zero. The figure corresponds with a situation in which both government spending and public debt in one country exceed those in the other country.

An unanticipated and permanent increase in public debt in the first country or decrease in the second country shifts the $\dot{c}_r = 0$ schedule to the left. Relative consumption will at first rise, but will gradually fall below its initial level. The change in public debt implies a rise in external liabilities of the first country or, in other words, a rise in the external assets of the second country. A permanent increase in relative government spending shifts the $\dot{f}_r = 0$ schedule to the right. Relative consumption undershoots its value in the new equilibrium. Because of its expansionary budgetary policy the country will experience a deficit on the current account, i.e. an accumulation of foreign liabilities, and therefore a further decline of consumption until the equilibrium is restored.

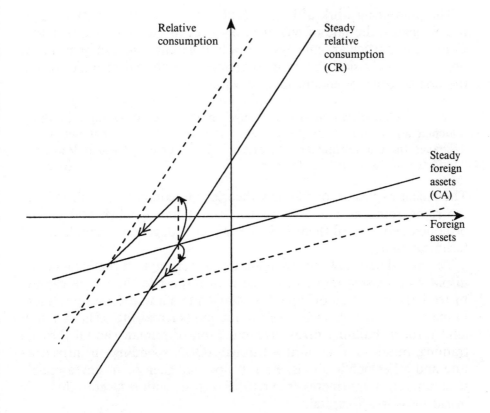

Figure 16.2   Budget deficits and foreign debt.

3   New theories of endogenous growth

Section 2 presented a simple two-country overlapping generations model based on the traditional theory of economic growth. Effectively, the long-run rate of economic growth of variables such as aggregate private consumption, capital, and output corresponds to the natural rate of growth, being the growth in efficiency units. The natural rate of growth corresponds to the sum of population growth n and labor-augmenting technical progress m and is assumed to be *exogenous*. The new theories of growth attempt to explain the long-run growth rate, i.e. try to put flesh and blood to the parameter m. In this section and in section 4 we give a verbal survey of these new theories of growth and examine their implications for issues in international macroeconomics. In sections 5 and 6 we then present analytical models based on endogenous growth and explore some issues to do with the global economy and development.

The pioneering work of Uzawa (1965) and Conlisk (1969) attempts to endogenize the rate of technical progress in the neoclassical model. Conlisk, in particular, conveys radically different conclusions from the orthodox neoclassical theory of economic growth and provides one of the first theories of endogenous growth:

> In the Solow–Swan model a change in the rate of savings, in the depreciation rate or in the constant rate of unemployment will not change the equilibrium growth rate g^* ...; whereas g^* will indeed be affected in the model of this paper (p. 69)

The recent explosion of the new theories of economic growth take up the same route as that set out by Uzawa and Conlisk and amend orthodox neoclassical theory by offering an endogenous formulation of technical change.[1]

The new theories of growth abandon the assumption that production displays decreasing returns to scale with respect to the use of capital. Instead, the definition of capital is enlarged to allow also for investment in many reproducible factors of production (such as the reclamation of land through building dikes, accumulation of human capital through training, build-up of knowhow through R&D, spending on infrastructure and other public goods, etc.). It does not then seem unreasonable to assume constant (increasing) returns to scale with respect to this very broad measure of capital.[2]

3.1 Relationship to old theories of growth

The Harrod–Domar condition says that the warranted growth rate of an economy must be given by the ratio of the aggregate savings rate divided by the capital–output ratio. The natural growth rate of an economy is given by the sum of the rate of population growth and the rate of labor-augmenting technical progress. On a balanced growth path the warranted growth rate must be equal to the natural growth rate. In general, one can think of four main channels by which balanced growth can be ensured and each of these channels is associated with a particular brand of economic growth theory (see van der Ploeg (1984) for a survey).

The first channel is through adjustments in the aggregate savings rate arising from changes in the functional distribution of income. These are the post-Keynesian stories of the symbiotic contradictions of capitalism and the class struggle associated with the names of Michael Kalecki, Joan Robinson, Nicholas Kaldor, Richard Goodwin, and Luigi Pasinetti ("UK Cambridge"). The idea is that workers save a smaller proportion of their income than capitalists so that the savings ratio and the warranted rate of economic growth decline when the national income share of labor increases. The second channel relaxes the post-Keynesian assumption of complementarity between the factors of production and thus arrives at balanced growth through adjustments in the capital–output ratio. This, of course, is achieved by neoclassical substitution between the factors of production and is associated with the names of Robert Solow and others ("US Cambridge"); this was the route emphasized in the traditional theories of economic growth whose international features were highlighted in section 2.[3]

The third and fourth channels arrive at balanced growth through adjustments in the natural rate of growth. The third channel does this through adjustments in the population growth rate and is associated with the name of Robert Malthus. The fourth channel, in contrast, does this by adjustments in the rate of technical progress and is highlighted by the new theories of endogenous growth.

The new theories of endogenous growth adopt the assumption of a constant ratio of a very broad measure of capital to national income. At least four different views on the relevant concept of capital, i.e. on the engine of endogenous growth, have been put forward in the recent literature on economic growth.

3.2   Learning by doing

First, Romer (1986) has revived the work of Arrow (1962) on learning by doing and should get the credit for making theoretical and empirical research into questions of economic growth fashionable again. In many ways one could argue that the new theories of economic growth tackle old and important questions with new tools.

Both Romer and Arrow assume that investment in knowledge by one firm has a positive effect on the production possibilities of other firms, as knowledge cannot perfectly be patented or be hidden from other rival firms in the industry or the economy. Consequently, production of consumption and capital goods may display constant or increasing returns to scale with respect to reproducible productive factors, i.e. physical capital and knowledge, at an aggregate level but decreasing returns to scale at a firm level. Because of the absence of an effective patent market, the stock of knowledge is like a public good. As firms do or cannot fully internalize the effect of their investment on the publicly available stock of knowledge and technology, the rate of economic growth is beneath the socially optimal level. This provides a strong reason for government intervention in order to correct for the absence of patent markets. This provides a justification of why many politicians argue for public subsidies for private expenditures on R&D.

When an effective patent market does exist, however, there may be a danger of over-investment in the sense that the growth rate of a decentralized market economy may then be higher than the socially optimal growth rate. The problem may be that firms are engaged in an R&D race in which each of them tries to win a contest in which the price at the end of the race is an infinitely lived patent (see Beath et al. (1992) for a nice survey of these issues). Of course, the required policy response of the government in such a situation is very different from the case in which patent markets are missing.

3.3   Human capital

The second tack that the literature on endogenous growth has taken is based on Lucas (1988), who has focused on the intentional accumulation of knowledge. Human capital can be increased by devoting time to learning, but naturally this is at the expense of time devoted to work or leisure. Human capital can be considered as an asset, so that the financial return on investment in human capital (i.e. training, education, etc.) must be compared with the return on nonhuman financial assets. Building on the classic work of Uzawa (1965), Lucas (1988) assumes that the accumulation of human capital is subject to constant (or increasing) returns to scale.

Lucas formulates his model for infinitely lived households. He also defends the validity of his model if households have finite lives by arguing that the stock of human capital may be transferred from older generations to younger generations. Like Romer and Arrow, Lucas presupposes that the stock of knowledge, i.e. the stock of human capital, has a positive external effect on the production of goods, though this is not a necessary assumption for a sustainable and endogenous rate of economic growth. Hence, knowledge according to this view is very much a public good. The most striking example of this is language. It is not much use being able to speak a particular language if the people that you have social and economic relations with do not speak the same language as well. Similar arguments hold for the use of computer software and many other skills.

Again it is easy to argue that in a competitive market economy the public good character of intentional accumulation of knowledge yields a growth rate that is lower than the socially optimal growth rate. This provides a strong rationale for government intervention in the form of publicly provided schooling (particularly at the elementary level) and training. One could also think of government subsidies to private training programs in order to achieve an efficient growth rate.

3.4 Research and development

Third, some authors have put R&D central in their analysis of the engine of economic growth (for example, Romer, 1990; Grossman and Helpman, 1990a, b, 1991; Aghion and Howitt, 1992). The output of R&D may be seen as blueprints for new products or for a better quality of products. The initial investment in R&D is counterbalanced by a subsequent stream of profits, because the producer of a differentiated good has at least temporarily a monopolistic position arising from, for example, a patent on the blueprint for this newly developed good.

The Schumpeterian idea that innovative activities depend on the expected profitability is clearly reflected in these models. An increase in monopoly power, in other words an increase in the discounted value of future profits arising from (say) a lower price elasticity for the demand for the product that is being sold, typically implies an increase in R&D. This implication is not at odds with the common belief that competition fosters economic growth. It only emphasizes that urge for and existence of profits are essential for firms to conduct innovative activity.

Consumers benefit from the production and sale of the invented goods both directly and indirectly. The reason is that, on the one hand, consumers value variety or quality while, on the other hand, productivity depends positively on the variety or on the quality of factors of production (e.g. those bought from the capital goods industry). The growth rate of the economy corresponds to the growth in the number of varieties or in the quality of consumer and capital goods.

Technological spillovers play an important role. In the case of expanding product variety, the productivity of R&D is thought to be positively linked to the pool of public knowledge. An increase in the number of varieties decreases profits per brand, as expenditure is spread (evenly) over all varieties, but the higher number of varieties increases productivity of R&D. As both forces tend to cancel each other, investment in R&D remains profitable. In the case of rising product quality the introduction of a product on the market contributes to the stock of knowledge because the attributes of the products can be studied and effort can be directed to improve upon the state of the art. It follows that the revenues of R&D can partly be appropriated by the firms in this sector.

3.5 Public infrastructure

The fourth direction in which the new theories of endogenous growth have progressed is based on the work of Barro (1990) and Barro and Sala-i-Martin (1990). They have exploited the idea that government investments in both the material infrastructure (think of public highways and railways) and the immaterial infrastructure (think of education, protection of property rights, and the like) are essential to economic growth. Effectively, the production function is extended to include government services that raise the productivity of private capital. The idea is that there are constant (or increasing) returns to scale with respect to capital of all the firms in the industry or economy together as well as the spending on public goods. Clearly, the rate of economic growth is boosted by an increase in the national income share of these types of public goods.

However, in as far as the increase in public goods must be financed by distortionary taxes, the after-tax marginal productivity of capital, the rate of interest, and the rate of economic growth are diminished. This part of the literature adds some public finance arguments by examining the optimal tax rate and provision of public goods. For Cobb–Douglas production functions, the tax rate that maximizes social welfare is also the one that maximizes growth. In general, e.g. for constant elasticity of substitution production functions, maximizing growth is not the same as maximizing social welfare.

3.6   Evaluation of various theories of endogenous growth

The recent elaborations of the orthodox neoclassical theory are not mutually exclusive and have many common features. They share the notion that technical progress is not manna from heaven but is related to economic activity. With the exception of the fourth view the intentional accumulation of knowledge is brought to the fore as the driving force behind economic growth. The deliberate search for new and better products or production techniques, the conscious exploration and exploitation of the economic environment – whether this environment is nature to an individual scientist or a market to a particular firm – rather than the duplication of already existing means, methods, and ideas, constitutes the basis of, at least, technical progress.

The level of technology cannot be raised drastically. Technical advancement proceeds gradually, and productivity and augmentation of productivity in the present are conditional on investment (in a broad measure of capital) in the past. The pace of economic growth depends on intertemporal preferences of households, i.e. on the choice between consumption and saving, as is emphasized by the Ramsey (1928) model of economic growth but also by an important precursor of the new theories of growth, namely Conlisk (1969). In the Ramsey model households are thought to choose a consumption path over time. The steepness of this path, i.e. the growth rate of private consumption, depends negatively on the degree of impatience for current consumption and positively on the willingness to substitute current for future consumption and on the real rate of return on savings, particularly so if the elasticity of intertemporal substitution is high.

An increase in the real rate of return induces households to save a greater fraction of their income if the substitution effect dominates the income effect. It also induces households to postpone consumption, so that the rate of growth of private consumption is increased. Many authors, however, think that the decision to save is distorted by the impossibility of collecting the yield of investment fully, as ideas cannot be kept secret and the use of ideas cannot be adequately protected by law. The development of the computer program "Windows" by Microsoft has been inspired by the success of Macintosh. However, the external effect of investment may not be confined to investment in R&D or in education. Obviously, neither France nor the UK would have considered building the Chunnel on its own. Another example of an external effect of investment in public infrastructure are the passes in Switzerland that are crucial to the efficient flow of traffic within the European Community. The downward bias in the return on investment causes the rate of private savings to be too low.

The recent neoclassical theories may differ in their characterization of knowledge. Knowledge can be considered a rival or a nonrival productive factor. Means can be called nonrival if usage for one purpose does not limit usage for other purposes. Clear examples are dikes, television programs, and the principle of the internal combustion engine. Romer (1986, 1990) and Grossman and Helpman (1990a, b; 1991) represent knowledge, especially the contributions of R&D, as a nonrival productive factor. From Lucas (1988), however, can be derived the notion that knowledge and labor may be intangible. A surgeon can devote his attention to only one patient at a time.[4] The same distinction applies to publicly provided goods. Barro (1990) argues that few of these goods are not subject to congestion. This argument can be illustrated by many examples, such as roads or recreation areas (think of traffic jams or of a coastal resort on a sunny day). It also applies to the protection of property rights, as emloyment in the legal system, e.g. the number of criminals, is a function of the size of the population.

Nonrival technology implies that production is subject to economies of scale at an aggregate level. Remember that production is at least linearly related to a broad measure of capital, so that a doubling of both the labor force and the stock of capital amounts to more than a doubling of production. This outcome often incites the criticism that ongoing accumulation of capital and growth of the population therefore imply that the rate of economic growth accelerates rather than approaches a constant value.

The logic of this argument can be questioned. First, Romer (1986) implicitly refers to the traditional idea (see for example Hicks, 1950) that an upper boundary on the rate of economic growth may exist. Second, the argument is partial and has to be extended to include an explanation for the population growth; one may wonder whether the decrease in population growth in the Western world is a mere coincidence or can be partially attributed in a Malthusian fashion to the increase in the standard of living. Besides, Romer (1990) provides rudimentary evidence that the rate of economic growth has risen over the last two centuries.

4 Growth and development: convergence or divergence?

Differences in growth rates between countries may be added to Kaldor's list of stylized facts. The orthodox neoclassical theory clearly predicts that the growth rates of different countries should converge in the long run. The crucial assumption for this convergence in growth rates is diminishing marginal productivity of capital. Poor countries with a dilapidated and low level of capital stock have lots of investment opportunities and face high real interest rates, so that consumers have a strong incentive to postpone consumption and save. This is why neoclassical theory predicts that poor countries have higher growth rates than rich countries on the adjustment path towards the equilibrium growth path. In fact, neoclassical theory also strongly suggests that there is a natural tendency for production per head of different countries to converge, mainly because technology is universally available and applicable.

Neoclassical theory thus has a fairly optimistic view on growth and development. However, the empirical speed of convergence is much slower than the traditional neoclassical theory predicts. This is why Mankiw et al. (1992) include human capital as a separate factor of production in a Solow-style growth model. In this way they explain the observed too low pace of convergence and rehabilitate the main qualities of the Solow (1956) model. However, their extension of the traditional theory does not consider the possibility of capital mobility.

4.1 Saving, investment, and the current account

As the marginal productivity of capital in poor countries is thought to exceed that in rich countries, it is efficient for the poor countries to borrow from the rich countries on a large scale. A flow of funds from north or south could increase the speed of convergence of growth rates considerably and would be an excellent development policy. The theory suggests that, in the absence of any restrictions on the mobility of capital (e.g. irreversibility of investment), the speed of convergence should be infinite. Perfect mobility also implies that domestic saving and domestic investment should be uncorrelated. The "golden rule" says that the optimal level of the current account deficit, being the net increase in the wealth of a nation, should after all be equal to the level of investment *with a market rate of return* (plus any shortfalls of the current level of production from the permanent level of production minus any discrepancies between the current level of public spending and the permanent level of public spending) (e.g. see chapter 15 in this volume).

However, empirical estimates by Feldstein and Horioka (1980) sharply contradict this prediction. Barro et al. (1992) claim that in practice the flow of capital is restrained by imperfections in the market. In particular, they assume that the collateral value of human capital is negligible in practice and the amount of debt is restricted by the collateral value of physical captial. In the case of capital mobility and an operative restriction on borrowing, the speed of convergence is faster than in the case of capital immobility but nevertheless finite. The process of convergence in a partially open economy resembles that of a closed economy. Still, capital is thought to flow during the process of adjustment from rich countries to poor countries. The particular imperfection of the capital market restores the link between domestic saving and domestic investment. It yields a partial explanation of the Feldstein–Horioka puzzle, as only some countries encounter restrictions on borrowing.

4.2   International spillovers of investment

Theories of economic growth are usually formulated and developed for a closed economy. The predictions from the new theories of growth about convergence and development depend on the translation of these theories to the context of open and interdependent economies. Recent literature suggests that international spillovers of investment may provide besides (perfect) capital mobility a strong reason for convergence of growth rates, although differences in levels of output and of consumption between countries may remain (see for example Alogoskoufis and van der Ploeg, 1991c; Grossman and Helpman, 1991). Spillovers of technology cause the marginal productivity of a broad measure of capital in a backward area to exceed that in an advanced area, so that the incentive to invest in the former area is higher than in the latter area. What are the territorial boundaries of the spillovers? Are external effects of investment confined to an area like Silicon Valley or are spillovers international? Although the external effects of investment in R&D are more likely to cross borders than those of investment in human capital, this question has to be answered empirically rather than theoretically. Note, however, that both the older and the newer theories (may) predict convergence between countries, in levels of productivity or in rates of growth, and may be empirically hard to distinguish.

Grossman and Helpman (1991), Buiter and Kletzer (1991), and Alogoskoufis and van der Ploeg (1991a, c) have constructed examples in which growth rates of output differ between countries permanently. Even though international mobility of (physical) capital is perfect, differences can arise in these examples when nontradeable and reproducible inputs are used in the production of a tradeable commodity. The results of Buiter and Kletzer and Grossman and Helpman rely on the assumption that international spillovers of knowledge are absent. Buiter and Kletzer focus on the accumulation of human capital. Differences in intertemporal preferences of households or, more importantly, in public expenditure on schooling may cause countries to grow at disparate rates. Grossman and Helpman show that, under the assumption that invention and production of a variety are intrinsically related, owing to economies of scale a large country can gain an (absolute) advantage in the research for and the development of new varieties. It follows that a large country can specialize in the conduct of R&D at the expense of innovative activity in a small country. Alogoskoufis and van der Ploeg (1992) model international spillovers of knowledge and find convergence of growth rates unless the costs of adjustment for investment projects differs between countries. These adjustment costs can in fact be considered as a nontradeable input.

The point of international spillovers in the production process is that there are decreasing returns to capital at a national level but constant (or increasing) returns to capital at a global level. This means that there is some scope for convergence, particularly if there is capital mobility and the importance of nontraded factors of production is not too large, while at the same time the growth rate of the global economy is endogenous. More analytical details on these arguments may be found in section 5.

4.3   Subsistence, poverty, and growth

These examples do not necessarily imply that the welfare of households in distinct countries develop differently, for the households may face the same possibilities for investing their savings as a result of perfect mobility of capital. However, this has the implication that developing countries are best helped by an unrestricted access to the global capital market. Note that differences in levels of consumption may be persistent. Rebelo (1991) therefore focuses attention on subsistence levels of private consumption. Consumption in poor countries may then grow at a slower rate than in rich countries, for in poor countries resources are devoted to subsistence consumption needs rather than to savings. In the case of a closed or partially open economy this may temporarily reverse the theoretical predictions. In the traditional story a developing country may have abundant opportunities to invest, so that the incentive to save is high and the growth rate can exceed that in a developed country. However, funds for investment may not abound because in developing countries a large part of income is used to satisfy basic needs. For this reason convergence in levels of productivity or in rates of growth, as predicted by the traditional or the recent theory of growth, may be very slow (cf. Kuznets, 1966). In fact, poor countries whose citizens need to devote a large part of their income to subsistence needs may grow at a slower rate than rich countries. This is, of course, in strong contradiction with the orthodox neoclassical theory of economic growth.

5 Knowledge spillovers: an international perspective

This section builds on Alogoskoufis and van der Ploeg (1990, 1991) and incorporates the learning by doing and public infrastructure determinants of economic growth surveyed in sections 3.2 and 3.5 into a mainstream model of open economy macroeconomics. It combines the orthodox theories of economic growth with the new theories of endogenous growth by assuming decreasing returns to capital at the national level but constant returns to a broad measure of capital at the global level. Although many reasons for international trade can be put forward, here attention is focused on international differences in the efficiency of production and budgetary policy stances.

The difference between section 2 and this section is mainly the technology of production. Again firms produce under perfect competition and face constant returns to scale but benefits from both domestic and international spillovers of knowledge and from public investment. Governments spend on two types of public goods, namely (pure Samuelson-style) public consumption goods and growth-promoting public infrastructure (training, R&D, etc.), levy lump-sum taxes, and issue debt. Hence, attention is focused on a world with two main types of externality: (a) production externalities arising from spillovers in production; and (b) consumption externalities because the currently alive cannot trade with generations that will be born in the future. This section thus investigates the analytical implications of endogenous growth and overlapping generations for the international economy.

5.1   Domestic and international spillovers in production

The technology of firm j at time t is given by

$$y(j, t) = P[k(j,t), m(t)l(j, t)]$$

with

$$m(t) = \frac{M[K(t), K^*(t), S(t)]}{L(t)} \tag{16.22}$$

where y, l, S, K^*, and m denote output, employment, public infrastructure, foreign capital, and the efficiency of labor respectively. The economy-wide efficiency of labor (m) increases when the capital (think of R&D, ideas, etc.) of other firms in the domestic economy or abroad increases and when expenditures on public infrastructure increases. The first two effects capture external effects of the type stressed by Arrow (1962) and Romer (1986), whereas the last effect has been stressed by Barro (1990). Note that the productivity of labor depends on a rival public good. The novel feature is that this production function integrates the old and the new theories of growth by allowing for decreasing returns to private capital at the national and *a fortiori* at the firm level ($\eta_1 < \eta_1 + \eta_2 < 1$) but constant returns to capital and public infrastructure at the global level. The production function $P(.)$ is assumed to display constant returns to scale and to have a Cobb–Douglas specification:

$$y(j, t) = \theta k(j, t)^{\eta_1} l(j, t)^{1 - \eta_1} \left[\frac{K(t)^{\eta_2} K^*(t)^{\eta_3} S(t)^{1 - \eta_1 - \eta_2 - \eta_3}}{L(t)^{1 - \eta_1}} \right]$$

$$\theta, \eta_1, \eta_2, \eta_3 \geq 0, \quad \eta_1 + \eta_2 + \eta_3 < 1 \tag{16.23}$$

where θ denotes the efficiency of production. Individual firms maximize profits under perfect competition, and so they ensure that the marginal product of private capital equals the user cost of capital, i.e. the interest rate plus the depreciation rate for capital (δ). In symmetric equilibrium we obtain

$$r(t) + \delta = \eta_1 \left[\frac{y(j, t)}{k(j, t)} \right] = \eta_1 \theta \left[\frac{K^*(t)}{K(t)} \right]^{\eta_3} \left[\frac{S(t)}{K(t)} \right]^{1 - \eta - \eta_3} \qquad \eta \equiv \eta_1 + \eta_2$$

$$\tag{16.24}$$

There is a global capital market. Arbitrage ensures that interest rates are equalized throughout the world $(r = r^*)$. Foreign variables are denoted with an asterisk. It follows that the equilibrium world interest rate and relative capital stock can be rewritten as

$$r = r^* = \eta_1\left[\theta\theta^*\left(\frac{S}{K}\frac{S^*}{K^*}\right)^{1-\eta-\eta_3}\right]^{1/2} - \delta \quad \frac{K}{K^*} = \left[\frac{\theta}{\theta^*}\left(\frac{S/K}{S^*/K^*}\right)^{1-\eta-\eta_3}\right]^{1/2\eta_3} \quad (16.25)$$

The global interest rate increases with the geometric average of the domestic and foreign efficiency of production, and both the home and foreign intensity of public infrastructure. Countries with a higher efficiency of production and a higher intensity of public infrastructure end up with more private capital than other countries. Note that aggregate nonasset income corresponds to the return on domestic and foreign spillovers in production and the return on public infrastructure, all of which individual firms do not have to pay a price for, i.e. $W = (1 - \eta_1)Y$ which corresponds to the wage bill when firms set the marginal productivity of labor equal to the wage. Aggregate home and foreign production can be written as

$$Y = \theta K^\eta K^{*\eta_3} S^{1-\eta-\eta_3}$$
$$= \theta K, \qquad Y^*$$
$$= \theta K^* \qquad \theta \equiv \left[\theta\theta^*\left(\frac{S}{K}\frac{S^*}{K^*}\right)^{1-\eta-\eta_3}\right]^{1/2} \qquad (16.26)$$

Note that the existence of a global capital market ensures that all countries have the same output–capital ratio and that this ratio increases when efficiency of production or public infrastructure at home or abroad increases. Hence, there is international convergence of growth rates of both output and capital:

$$\gamma \equiv \frac{\dot{K}}{K} = \frac{\dot{Y}}{Y} = \gamma^* \qquad \pi \equiv \gamma - n, \pi^* \equiv \gamma - n^* \qquad (16.27)$$

Of course, there is no international convergence in levels of income per capita. Poor countries (low θ, low S/K) have a lower output and capital stock than rich countries. Clearly, countries with a fast growing population must tolerate a lower growth in income per head (π) than other countries.

5.2   Loose budgetary policy stances destroy global growth prospects

The evolution of private consumption, public debt and foreign assets are still described by equations (16.7), (16.10), and (16.12). A glance at equation (16.26) reveals that the marginal propensity to consume out of wealth is constant as the ratio of public investment to the capital stock in the two countries is assumed to be constant at any point of time. In the following the variables will be scaled by private capital rather than by efficiency units of labor as in section 2. Owing to the symmetry of the home and foreign countries, the global and relative effects of budgetary policy can again be analyzed separately. If one denotes global averages of variables with the subscript A (e.g. $C_A \equiv \frac{1}{2}(C/K + C^*/K^*)$), the world economy can be described by

$$\dot{C}_A = [\sigma(r - \rho) + n - \gamma]C_A - \beta[\sigma\rho + (1 - \sigma)r + \lambda](1 + D_A) \quad (16.28)$$

$$\dot{D}_A = (r - \gamma)D_A + G_A + S_A - T_A \quad (16.29)$$

where the global interest rate and the growth rate are given by

$$r = \eta_1\theta - \delta \qquad \gamma = (\theta - C_A - G_A - S_A) - \delta \quad (16.30)$$

The expression for the global growth rate corresponds to the Harrod–Domar condition for balanced growth in the world economy, i.e the net growth rate $\gamma - \delta$ equals the propensity to save (one minus the sum of private and public propensities to consume) divided by the capital–output ratio. It thus defines a negative relationship between the global private consumption C_A and the global growth rate, namely the HD locus in figure 16.3. The HD locus shifts down when government

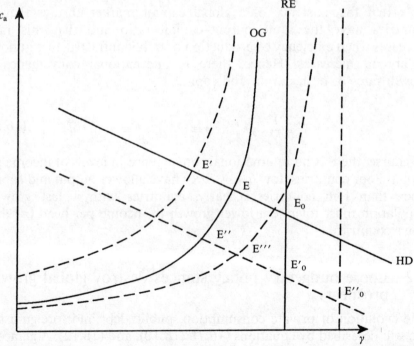

Figure 16.3 Overlapping generations and endogenous growth.

consumption is increased. Public infrastructure also crowds out private savings and investment and reduces growth prospects, but at the same time it raises the productivity of private capital and boosts growth prospects.

The equation for the evolution of private consumption will be called the overlapping generations (OG) locus. When there is no entry of new generations ($\beta = 0$), the OG locus reduces to the Ricardian equivalence (RE) locus. The RE locus is vertical since it defines the global growth rate as the modified golden rule ($\gamma = \sigma(r - \rho) + n$). This RE growth rate is the growth rate stressed by Romer (1986) and others. It increases when the efficiency of production at home or abroad increases, when public infrastructure at home or abroad increases, when the extent of domestic and international spillovers in production is large, and when households become more patient. These effects are large when the elasticity of intertemporal substitution is large. The RE growth rate does not depend on nonproductive budgetary policy stances or intertemporal shifts in taxation, which is a logical consequence of debt neutrality.

The RE growth rate provides an upper bound on the growth rate of a world with consumption externalities ($\beta > 0$), i.e. the RE locus is an asymptote of the OG locus. This is not surprising, because the fact that households are finitely lived and know that they can shift the burden of future taxes to yet unborn generations makes them consume more and save less so that fewer funds are available for investment purposes and growth prospects decline. The OG locus slopes upwards because a higher growth rate of private consumption means that households save a lot of assets and so in equilibrium households can afford to consume more.

Global equilibrium is at the intersection of the HD and OG loci. As long as the ratios of government debt to national income are constant, there are no transitional dynamics. Both private consumption and the growth rate immediately jump to their new equilibrium values. The OG–HD equilibrium induces a lower growth rate and a higher national income share of private consumption than the RE–HD equilibrium (compare E with E_0). Since new generations of households share the burden of servicing the government debt, current generations consume more and save less than in a world with infinite horizons and intergenerational bequest motives. As a result, fewer funds are available for investment and growth is less. Hence, global growth is less than in a first-best outcome on account of both consumption externalities ($\beta > 0$) and domestic and foreign spillovers in production ($\eta_1 < 1$).

In a world characterized by Ricardian debt neutrality ($\beta = 0$) pure demand-side-oriented budgetary policy cannot affect global growth. An increase in government consumption leads to 100 percent crowding out of private consumption (compare E_0 with E_0'), whereas intertemporal shifts in (lump-sum) taxation leave private consumption unaffected. However, supply-side-oriented budgetary policy such as increases in national income shares of public infrastructure at home or abroad raise the marginal productivity of private capital and thus the interest rate so that households find it attractive to postpone consumption and growth prospects improve (cf. Barro, 1990). Naturally, such a supply-side policy leads to more than 100 percent crowding out of private consumption (compare E_0 with E_0''). Note that as a result of the twin assumptions of a global capital market and (imperfect) international knowledge spillovers, it does not matter for the global growth rate in which part of the world the public infrastructure is undertaken.

Now consider a more realistic situation in which there is entry of new generations and debt neutrality does not hold ($\beta > 0$). A rise in the global ratio of government debt to national income may come about through a postponement of taxation. Current generations of households undertake a consumption bonanza, because they know that future taxes will also be shouldered by future, yet unborn, generations. Fewer funds are available for investment purposes and global growth declines. This may be seen from the upward shift of the OG locus (equilibrium moves from E to E').

A balanced-budget increase in the global (national income) share of government consumption (G_A) crowds out private consumption on account of the higher taxes that are required to finance government spending. Since part of the burden of higher taxes in the future is born by future generations, crowding out is less than 100 percent. On balance global savings and investment decline so that the global growth rate falls. The above is confirmed by the inward shift of the HD locus (equilibrium moves from E to E'').

Clearly, a looser (demand-side-oriented) budgetary policy, irrespective of whether it occurs at home or abroad, destroys growth prospects throughout the world. An expansion of supply-side budgetary policies such as public infrastructure has two effects. On the one hand, it suffers from the usual crowding out of private consumption and fall in growth that is associated with any increase in government expenditures. On the other hand, it raises the marginal productivity of private capital and boosts global growth. In addition to the inward shift of the HD locus, there is an outward shift of the OG locus so that the equilibrium moves from E to E'''. Although it is clear that the national income shares of private consumption must fall, it is not possible to say *a priori* whether the global growth rate will decrease or increase.

5.3   External debt and government debt

To complete the solution of the world model, it is necessary to analyze the global differences, which will be denoted by the subscript R (e.g. $C_R \equiv C/K - C^*/K^*$):

$$\dot{C}_R = [\sigma(r - \rho) + n - \gamma]C_R - \beta[\sigma\rho + (1 - \sigma)r + \lambda](D_R + F_R) \qquad (16.31)$$

$$\dot{F}_R = (r - \gamma)F_R - C_R - G_R - S_R \qquad (16.32)$$

where r and γ have already been determined by the global averages. Assume that the world interest rate exceeds the world growth rate $(r > \gamma)$ and that the home country has a higher national income share of government spending than the foreign country $(G_R + S_R > 0)$. It follows that the locus describing equilibrium on the current account (the CA locus) slopes upwards and has a negative intercept with the vertical axis in figure 16.2. The locus describing common growth rates in the national income shares of private consumption (the CR locus) slopes upwards, as $\gamma - n < \sigma(r - \rho)$. Assume the saddlepath condition is satisfied.

An instantaneous increase in the ratio of government debt to national income at home relative to that ratio abroad (higher D_R) shifts the CR locus to the left. The new equilibrium E′ is associated with a decrease in private consumption at home relative to abroad and an accumulation of foreign debt by the home country. On impact relative private consumption misadjusts, i.e. rises on account of the postponement of taxation at home. Along the adjustment path the home country experiences deficits on the current account and builds up foreign debt. In the long run the home country must generate a trade surplus in order to generate sufficient income to service the accumulated foreign debt. The long-run result of an increase in relative government debt must thus be a fall in relative private consumption. The short-run pattern corresponds somewhat to the experience of the USA in the early 1980s, whereas some of the long-run pattern may be occurring in the early 1990s.

An increase in the national income share of government consumption of the home country shifts the CA locus to the right and changes the long-run equilibrium from E to E″. The initial fall in relative consumption undershoots, and so the home country builds up a foreign debt along the adjustment path. Over time the burden of servicing the foreign debt increases, and so relative private consumption falls over time.

Hence, if one country goes for a postponement of taxation, it boosts private consumption in the short run but worsens growth prospects for all other countries in the world, leads to an accumulation of foreign debt, and reduces private consumption in the long run. If one country goes for an increase in government consumption, it must tolerate a build-up of foreign debt and ongoing falls in private consumption, and at the same time it reduces global interest and growth rates.

5.4   Budgetary policies, interest rates, and adjustment costs for investment

An unsatisfactory feature of the analysis so far is that the global interest rate depends on technological parameters and supply-side-oriented policies such as expenditures on public infrastructure, R&D, etc. but not on demand-side-oriented government policies. One would expect the global interest rate to rise when budgetary policies throughout the world become looser. Such an extension may also help to explain an empirical puzzle. The analysis so far predicts a positive correlation between interest rates and growth rates. The source of this correlation is a variety of technology shocks, because it is reasonable to suppose that these shocks dominate preference shocks (in particular shocks in the subjective rate of time preference). Empirically it is hard to detect such a positive correlation – hence the puzzle. These are two good reasons why the analysis must be extended to allow also for an effect of demand-side policies on interest rates. A straightforward way to do this is to allow for adjustments costs for private investment.

Firm j maximizes the present value of future profits:

$$\int_t^{\infty} \left\{ y(j, v) - w(v) l(j, v) - \left[1 + \psi\left(\frac{i(j, v)}{k(j, v)}\right) \right] i(j, v) \right\} \exp\left[- \int_t^v r(u)\, du \right] dv \tag{16.33}$$

where i denotes gross investment and ψ stands for the adjustment cost parameter. It follows that the marginal productivity of capital plus the marginal reduction in adjustment costs arising from an additional unit of capital must equal the user cost of capital and that the investment rate increases when the value of the firm (q) rises. Ignoring the effects of public infrastructure ($\eta_1 + \eta_2 + \eta_3 = 1$, $S = S^* = 0$), aggregation across firms of these optimality conditions yields

$$q = 1 + 2\psi \frac{I}{K} \qquad \eta_1 \theta \left(\frac{K}{K^*}\right)^{\eta - 1} - \psi\left(\frac{I}{K}\right)^2 = \left(r + \delta - \frac{\dot{q}}{q}\right) q \tag{16.34}$$

Perfect capital mobility throughout the world then yields in steady state the global interest rate:

$$r = \frac{\dot{q}}{q} - \delta + \left[\frac{\eta_1 \theta - (q - 1)^2 / 4\psi}{q} \right] \qquad q - 1 = 2\psi(\gamma + \delta) \tag{16.35}$$

Since the value of the firm is the discounted value of future profits, there is a negative relation between the interest rate r and the value of the stock market (q). Since a high value of Tobin's "q" induces a high investment rate and $I/K = \gamma + \delta$, it is clear that the production side of the economy defines a negative relationship between the interest rate and the growth or (net) investment rate. This asset market equilibrium and aggregate supply relationship is represented by the AS locus in figure 16.4. The AS locus slopes downwards and lies entirely below the real

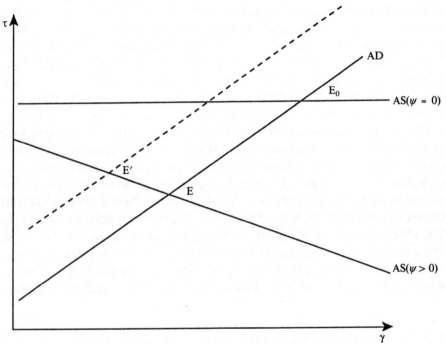

Figure 16.4   Real interest rates and growth rates.

interest rate that would prevail if there were no adjustment costs for investment, i.e. $r = \eta_1\theta - \delta$. The steady-state global consumption function and the Harrod–Domar condition yield the following aggregate demand relationship between growth and interest rate:

$$\gamma = \sigma(r - \rho) + n - \frac{\beta[\sigma\rho + (1 - \sigma)r + \lambda](1 + D_A)}{\theta - G_A - \delta - \gamma} \qquad (16.36)$$

which is represented by the AD locus in figure 16.3. The AD locus slopes upwards, as long as $(\rho + \lambda)/(\gamma - n) > 1 - 1/\sigma$ holds which will definitely be the case if the intertemporal substitution effect is at least as big as the income effect ($\sigma > 1$). In that case, an increase in the global interest rate induces a smaller propensity to consume out of wealth so that households save more and the world economy can grow at a higher rate.

Global equilibrium occurs at the intersection of the AD and AS curves. Clearly, adjustment costs for investment lead, independently of whether debt neutrality holds or not, to a lower global interest rate and lower global growth (compare E with E_0). In general, looser budgetary policies, i.e. a postponement of taxes that induces a rise in the global ratio of debt to national income or an increase in government consumption, cause a rise in global interest rates, a fall in share prices throughout the world, and a reduction in global growth. Those countries that are responsible for the laxer budgetary policies build up foreign debt and eventually have to pay for their effervescent fiscal policies with lower *levels* as well as lower *growth* of private consumption. The other countries build up foreign assets and enjoy higher *levels* of consumption, but have to suffer a lower growth rate.

The extension explains the empirical puzzle mentioned above as long as one allows for departures from Ricardian debt neutrality. If debt neutrality holds, only technical shocks induce shifts in interest rates and growth rates. This results in a positive correlation between interest rates and growth rates. To obtain a negative correlation between interest rates and growth rates, it is necessary to depart from debt neutrality. In that case, changes in budgetary policies induce shifts in the AD curve and a negative correlation between interest and growth rates. If shocks to budgetary policies are of the same order of magnitude as technical shocks, one observes no correlation between interest and growth rates.

5.5   Divergence in growth rates

So far, the assumption of a global capital market ensures that the growth rates of various countries must be the same. This is obviously unrealistic. To get divergent growth rates one could assume different intensities of investment in human capital in different countries (e.g. Buiter and Kletzer, 1991). An alternative that stays within the spirit of the analysis so far is to allow for different costs of adjustment of investment for different countries. It is easy to show that, in steady state, output in each country will be proportional to its capital stock and that, if $\theta > \theta^*$ and $\psi > \psi^*$, steady-state home capital exceeds foreign capital, $K > K^*$. Capital flows to the country in which it has the higher marginal productivity and costs of adjustment are higher. A country with high adjustment costs for investment requires a lower gross investment rate in order for share prices to be equalized throughout the world. If countries start with the same capital, the country with higher adjustment costs has higher share prices and attracts capital until share prices are equalized again. An equilibrium condition is that

$$\psi(\gamma+\delta) = \psi^*(\gamma^*+\delta^*) \tag{16.37}$$

The country, with other things equal, that faces higher adjustment costs for investment or a higher depreciation rate of its capital will end up with a lower growth rate than other countries.

6   Research and development: an engine of growth

An important engine of economic growth is the intentional accumulation of knowledge by the research for and development of new or better products (e.g. Romer, 1990; Grossman and Helpman, 1991; Aghion and Howitt, 1992). The following presents an approach, along the lines of Grossman and Helpman (1991), in which R&D involves a continuous expansion of product variety. It is based on the ideas surveyed in sections 3.3, 3.4, and 4.

6.1   Expanding product variety

The economy consists of two sectors: (a) a monopolistic competitive sector which produces differentiated final goods; (b) a competitive sector which conducts R&D. Labor is the only primary factor of production. Both labor and financial capital are perfectly mobile across sectors. All households are identical. Consumption and savings decisions follow from the life-cycle hypothesis. The preferences of the infinitely lived representative household may be written as

$$U(t) = \int_t^\infty \left[\frac{C(v)^{1-1/\sigma}}{1-1/\sigma} \right] \exp[-p(v-t)] \, dv \tag{16.38}$$

where p is the subjective rate of time preference, σ denotes the elasticity of intertemporal substitution, and C represents an index of private consumption. The representative household has a love for diversity, and so the index depends not only on the consumed amount of each variety (x_j) but also on the number of varieties (N):

$$C \equiv \left(\int_0^N x_j^\eta \, dj \right)^{1/\eta} \qquad 0 < \eta < 1 \tag{16.39}$$

For convenience, the range of available varieties is assumed to be continuous and the integer constraint is not considered.[5] Maximization of utility subject to the household budget constraint yields the Keynes–Ramsey rule:

$$\frac{\dot{C}}{C} = \sigma\left(R - \frac{\dot{P}_C}{P_C} - \rho\right) = \sigma(r - \rho) \qquad r \equiv R - \frac{\dot{P}_C}{P_C} \qquad (16.40)$$

where R is the producer (nominal) interest rate and P_C is the ideal index for the price of consumption, such that the product of the indexes for this price and for private consumption equals household expenditure E. The ideal price index is given by

$$P_C = \left[\int_0^N p_j^{\eta/(\eta-1)} \, dj\right]^{(\eta-1)/\eta} \qquad (16.41)$$

The representative household postpones consumption and thus saves when the consumer (real) interest rate r exceeds the rate of time preference ρ, and particularly if the elasticity of intertemporal substitution σ is high. The household spends a fraction of its expenditure on each available variety:

$$x_i = \frac{p_i^{-\varepsilon}}{\int_0^N p_j^{1-\varepsilon} \, dj} E \qquad \varepsilon \equiv \frac{1}{1-\eta} \qquad (16.42)$$

where ε is the elasticity of substitution between any pair of varieties.

Each variety is produced by a single firm. The monopolistic power of firms is derived from infinitely lived patents.[6] A firm buys a patent from the R&D sector on a free market. This set-up cost is financed by the issue of equity shares. Production of each firm displays constant returns to scale with respect to the use of labor. Each firm maximizes profits subject to the perceived demand function for its products, given total household expenditure, the prices set by other firms, and the wage. As all firms are identical and face the same conditions, firms charge the same price p and supply the same amount x. The price charged to consumers will be a constant mark-up over the wage, and profits π are a fraction of total revenue:

$$p = \frac{1}{1 - 1/\varepsilon} w = \frac{1}{\eta} w \qquad \pi = (1 - \eta)\frac{E}{N} = \frac{1}{\varepsilon}\frac{E}{N} \qquad (16.43)$$

Dividends fully exhaust profits of firms. The return on equity consists of these dividends and the expected change in its stock market value. Arbitrage ensures that the rate of return on equity coincides with the producer interest rate:

$$\frac{\pi}{P_N} + \frac{\dot{P}_N}{P_N} = R \qquad (16.44)$$

In a perfect foresight equilibrium that excludes speculative bubbles in asset prices, the stock market value of a typical firm in the final goods sector (P_N) matches the present discounted value of future profits. As the output of the R&D sector is blueprints for new products and patents are infinitely lived, the share price of such a firm also equals the price of a patented blueprint.

A representative firm in the R&D sector can "add incrementally to the set of available products by devoting a given finite amount of labor to R&D for a brief interval of time," and so the number of varieties cannot be increased instantaneously (Grossman and Helpman, 1991, p. 51). The productivity in the R&D sector depends on the freely accessible economy-wide accumulated stock of knowledge as represented by the number of available varieties. Ideas and information that are contained in new products are instantaneously and costlessly available to current R&D. As a consequence, the output of R&D is only partly appropriable. Knowledge in this form is a nonrival input and its accumulation is given by

$$\dot{N} = ANL_N \tag{16.45}$$

where L_N denotes labor employed by the R&D sector. Profit maximization implies, if demand for labor is positive but bounded, that productivity of labor employed in the R&D sector must equal the relevant producer wage for that sector.

$$P_N AN = w \tag{16.46}$$

The supply of labor by the households (L) is given. Labor can be used either for R&D of new products (L_N) or for the production of differentiated goods. As the firms in the monopolistic competitive sector are alike, the equilibrium condition for the labor market can be written as

$$L = \frac{1}{A}\frac{\dot{N}}{N} + \frac{E}{p} \tag{16.47}$$

where, for simplicity, the labor coefficient for the final goods industry is normalized to unity. To pinpoint nominal magnitudes of variables, private expenditure – rather than a price – is normalized to unity, i.e. $E = 1$ and thus $C = 1/P_C$. For a detailed derivation of the solution, the reader is referred to Grossman and Helpman (1991).

There are no transitional dynamics, and so the economy immediately jumps to a balanced growth path. Along this path the division of labor over both sectors remains constant, so that the number of product varieties expands at the rate γ_N. The balanced growth path is furthermore characterized – because of the chosen normalization – by a constant value for the price of a typical variety, the wage, and the price of a share on the stock market. However, the effective price of private consumption decreases, and thus the index of private consumption increases at a constant rate.

From the equilibrium conditions for the capital market and for the labor market and from the first-order conditions for profit maximization, a negative relationship between the growth rate and the consumer (real) interest rate r can be derived. A change in the latter directly affects the present discounted value of future profits, and therefore the allocation of labor over the R&D and final goods sector. For the same reason, the rate of innovation depends on the elasticity of substitution between consumer varieties. More monopoly power entails higher profits, and boosts R&D at the expense of the production in the final goods sector. Given the interest rate, the size of the labor force influences the level of activity positively in both sectors. The growth in the number of varieties can thus be written as

$$\gamma_N = \frac{1-\eta}{\eta} AL - r = \frac{1}{\varepsilon - 1} AL - r \qquad (16.48)$$

The intertemporal preferences of the household can be summarized by the Keynes–Ramsey rule, which dictates a positive relationship between the rate of innovation and the real interest rate. If the household is more willing to substitute current consumption for future consumption (an increase in σ) or becomes more patient (a decrease in ρ), the desired growth rate in private consumption rises given the interest rate:

$$\gamma_N = \sigma(r - \rho)\left(\frac{\eta}{1 - \eta}\right) \qquad (16.49)$$

It follows that the equilibrium growth rate in the number of varieties is

$$\gamma_N = \frac{\sigma}{1 - \eta(1 - \sigma)} [(1 - \eta AL - \eta\rho] \qquad (16.50)$$

The growth rate of consumption (γ_C) is a constant fraction of the rate of innovation:

$$\gamma_C = \frac{1 - \eta}{\eta} \gamma_N = \frac{1}{\varepsilon - 1} \gamma_N \qquad (16.51)$$

Hence, equilibrium growth rises with the efficiency of labor in the R&D sector (A), the size of the labor force (L), and the degree of monopoly power ($1/\eta$), and growth declines with the degree of impatience (ρ). These effects on growth are amplified when the elasticity of intertemporal substitution rises. Note that a growing population leads in this theory to an ever-increasing growth rate of the economy, so that really what is required to extend the analysis is an endogenous explanation of population growth.

6.2   Knowledge spillovers, redundancy, and international trade

In the above story economic growth is driven by the continuous accumulation of knowledge. Changes in the stock of knowledge facilitate the invention of new products. The introduction of new products on the market or the patenting of an invention adds to the stock of knowledge. So, the exchange of goods and the exchange of ideas are intimately linked. Nevertheless, a strict distinction between trade and communication is made for expositional purposes.[7] The removal of impediments to the flow of ideas and information between countries can increase the rate of innovation. The separate effects of international communication and international trade can be discussed in the context of two countries. Only balanced growth paths are considered. For simplicity, it is assumed that imitation requires as many resources as innovation.

Assume that the exchange of ideas and of information between countries A and B is perfect, but that the exchange of differentiated products is zero. The set of available varieties in the two countries may overlap. The degree to which varieties are produced both in country A and in country B is arbitrary. Although the magnitude of the overlap can change with time it will be taken to be constant. The common stock of knowledge M – as before – is related to past investments in R&D. The possibility of learning from duplicative R&D is ignored. The common stock of knowledge can thus be expressed as a time-invariant fraction of the available varieties, say $M = \zeta(N^A + N^B)$.

The theory developed for a country in autarky can easily be adapted to incorporate the spillover effect. The main difference is that the productivity of the R&D sector also depends on the number of available varieties in the other country, so that the development of countries throughout the world is intertwined. The condition for a balanced growth path is that rates of innovation in the two countries must be the same. If the countries do not differ in preferences or technology, the steady-state set of available varieties is in proportion to the size of the labor force. The rate of innovation γ^k along a balanced growth path of an economy with international R&D spillovers in autarky is given by

$$\gamma^k = \frac{\sigma}{1 - \eta(1 - \sigma)} [\zeta(1 - \eta)A(L^A + L^B) - \eta\rho] \qquad (16.52)$$

Comparison with the growth formula for a closed economy given above reveals that international transmission of knowledge boosts the rate of innovation in both countries. The gains are mitigated, however, by the redundancy of some investments, as only novel products contribute to a reduction in the cost of R&D.

However, international trade of goods will remove the redundancy in R&D because it gives an economic incentive to direct efforts towards the invention of new products rather than towards the imitation of existing products. Both invention and imitation entail costs, but the rewards in the case of a monopoly exceed those in the case of a duopoly.[8] Exchange of the differentiated products induces international competition in R&D, even though the blueprints themselves are not traded.

In comparison with the above expression for γ^k, the expression for the pace of innovation in the steady state (γ^t) is only changed for the value of the parameter ζ. Ultimately the overlap in the varieties produced will virtually vanish because of the introduction of trade:

$$\gamma^t = \frac{\sigma}{1 - \eta(1 - \sigma)} [(1 - \eta)A(L^A + L^B) - \eta p] \qquad (16.53)$$

Apart from dynamic effects international trade also has static effects. The integration of product markets implies that the set of varieties of consumer goods available to households increases. As consumers love variety they will spread their expenditure over as many varieties as possible and their utility (i.e. index) of consumption jumps upwards.

International trade also induces an increased size of the goods market and more severe competition in this market. The first effect tends to increase profits, whereas the second effect will put a downward pressure on profits. In the model those two effects exactly cancel.

Naturally the familiar gains of trade due to sectoral specialization can be added to the list of (static) effects. Models like that described above can be extended to include more than one factor of production. Often the distinction is made between skilled and unskilled labor (see, for example, Romer, 1990; Grossman and Helpman, 1991). R&D is thought to be intensive in the former, so that a country that has a relative abundance of skilled labor specializes in R&D.

Rivera-Batiz and Romer (1991a) point out that one must not conclude that trade can only affect growth if knowledge can freely cross borders. They use a so-called laboratory equipment model to show that flows of goods alone can increase the rate of innovation. However, Grossman and Helpman (1991) show that in the absence of international spillovers trade can cause unequal rates of innovation in the sense that a large country can eventually dominate the market for differentiated goods. The possibility of lasting differences in growth rates relates to the structure of the model – just as in the work of Buiter and Kletzer (1991) a nontraded good or service is used as an input in the production of a traded good.

Countries can, of course, differ in technology as represented by the parameter A. If spillovers of knowledge are international in scope and international trade of goods is allowed, this implies differences in wealth of the households. The number of varieties in relation to the size of the labor force is higher in the more productive country than in the less productive country. In the former country the wages exceed those in the latter country, so that the supplied amount per variety differs between the countries. The country with a comparative advantage "specializes" in the number of varieties rather than in the production of each variety.

7 Investment and trade-promoting policy

A remarkable feature of the recent literature on economic growth is the overwhelming support for the idea that investment has positive external effects on production possibilities. The return on investment cannot be fully reaped and the intertemporal choices by households are biased in favor of consumption at the expense of savings. The assumption of an external effect implies an active role of the government. It may take measures to improve upon the intertemporal allocation of resources, because the outcome of decentralized decisions by the various private agents is not optimal. At a general level of thought an external effect is due to an inadequate definition and protection of property rights. In practice, the cost of defining and protecting these rights may be prohibitive. However, examples in which uncertainty about property rights has inhibited investment abound. One can think of the unsettled claims on land and buildings in former East Germany or of the political instability in South America.[9] Clearly, the system of patents may be crucial to protect the research for and development of new or better products and production methods against "cheap" imitation. After all, firms are only willing to conduct R&D if profits can be earned at least temporarily.

7.1 Monopoly power, public policy, and growth

Monopoly power may imply a distortion of relative prices. The government has to balance the dynamic advantage against the static disadvantage of monopoly power. The government can also change the price of future consumption relative to current consumption in other ways. In view of the proposed engines of growth the government may contemplate supporting R&D and/or directing its expenditure to schooling and investing in public infrastructure. Also the design of the fiscal system, taxes on capital income or the fiscal method of depreciation, may affect the rate of return on savings. The government may have to balance the sometimes inevitable distortion and the revenue of taxes. For example, a tax on capital income on the one hand reduces the after-tax rate of return on investment but on the other hand raises revenue that can be used to finance investment in public infrastructure (see Barro, 1990; Barro and Sala-i-Martin, 1990; Alesina and Rodrick; 1991). In this case, except under the special assumption of a Cobb–Douglas production function and apart from any external effects of investment, promotion of economic growth does not necessarily imply maximization of social welfare. In general, only in a situation when private agents do not fully internalize the benefits of investment can public policy be directed to the enhancement of economic growth. But we like to emphasize that the external effects of investment, and so the role of the government, are theoretically assumed rather than empirically derived.

7.2   Trade and economic integration

Trade and economic integration can clearly affect the dynamic performance of economies. Though the nature of the advantages or disadvantages may be static, changes in efficiency affect the decision to save and invest. As Baldwin (1989) points out, the tumult about Europe 1992 cannot be caused by the prediction of a one-time increase in productivity, but the excitement is based on the presumption of a (temporary) increase in growth. What are the possible effects of trade? The familiar argument emphasizes the possibility of specialization in production between countries. The pattern of inter-industry trade reflects, according to the Heckscher–Ohlin theorem, the relative endowment of, for example, skilled and unskilled labor in countries. International specialization has an ambiguous effect on economic growth, for it may imply that resources are devoted less to innovative activity and more to production of goods (see Grossman and Helpman, 1991). Furthermore, consumers may benefit from an expanded range of available products.

Compare as an experiment of thought a closed economy with an open economy. In the closed economy the price of foreign products relative to domestic products is infinite, whereas in the open economy this price is a finite measure and the presence of intra-industry trade enriches the choice of consumers. Consumers love variety and therefore value the expansion in the range of available products. This gain is static and does not affect the dynamic performance of an economy. Intra-industry trade can also influence the intertemporal choice to save and invest directly. Rivera-Batiz and Romer (1991a, b) conclude that increasing returns to scale in the production function of R&D causes free trade or economic integration to have an effect on growth. The point is that two isolated sectors do not conduct R&D as efficiently as one integrated sector.

Increasing returns can be due to specialization in the use of inputs (custom-made machines, various computer programs, different types of fiber) or to spillovers of knowledge. In the first case intra-industry trade expands the available variety of inputs and enables a higher degree of specialization in the use of these inputs. It thus augments the level of productivity and therefore spurs the rate of economic growth. Consumers benefit now and later from the possibility of trade. In the second case international exchange of knowledge and international exchange of goods have to be distinguished. Only through the international communication of research ideas and results can economies of scale be exploited and the productivity of innovative activity be enhanced.

7.3 Increasing returns and international competition

The possible repercussions of trade are in this case diverse. It induces an increase in the size of the market and in addition increases competition in the goods market. The first effect tends to increase the reward on investment in R&D, whereas the second effect will put a downward pressure on the (temporary) profits. The result of the two forces is therefore ambiguous. Rivera-Batiz and Romer emphasize a different mechanism. International trade of (differentiated) goods removes any redundancy in R&D, because it gives an incentive to direct efforts towards invention of new products rather than towards the imitation of already existing products. Hence, the exchange of goods induces international competition in R&D even though the output of R&D, namely blueprints for new or better products, is itself not traded. Furthermore, the distinction between the exchange of knowledge and the exchange of goods is theoretically convenient, but may be drawn too rigorously.

The international flow of goods and of ideas may be intimately linked; perhaps the international spillovers of knowledge are enhanced by the trade of goods and therefore boost investment. In summary, trade may foster growth as a result of exploitation of economies of scale and the creation of an incentive to innovate rather than to imitate. These positive effects will overwhelm any negative effect of inter-industry specialization as long as countries have identical relative endowments of basic inputs. A reallocation of resources at the expense of R&D may occur if dissimilar countries engage in trade.

What are the gains of international economic integration above those of the free exchange of goods? Clearly they are the elimination of border controls and the standardization of government regulation. More generally, the removal of barriers to competition releases resources and improves overall productivity. The harmonization of VAT rates and excise duties, the open procurement of government spending, and the liberalization of financial markets, as far as trade of goods and mobility of capital are not good (short-run) substitutes, induce a reallocation of resources and imply a gain in efficiency.

7.4   Political economy of growth

The instruments of economic policy may not be in the hands of a benevolent and enlightened dictator but subject to a political struggle. The abolition of subsidies on food in order to finance, for example, investment in infrastructure may promote growth but may also provoke chaos. Politicians or political parties that seek re-election and fight for votes are not solely concerned with economic growth, especially as they do not represent future generations directly. They may have to weigh the demand by voters for transfers from the rich to the poor and the distortion of taxes on (capital) income.

Persson and Tabellini (1992), Alesina and Rodrick (1991), and van Ewijk (1991) have tried to model the political choices on redistribution of and taxes on income in a democracy formally.[10] Typically this yields the outcome that an unequal distribution of income hampers economic growth. For in a country with an unequal distribution of income the decisive (median) voter, i.e. the majority, is likely to be poor and asks for a high tax on capital income to finance transfers, so that the incentive to save and therefore the rate of growth is low. This analysis also implies that a limitation on political participation to wealthy people, that was common practice in European countries in earlier days, enables politicians or political parties to choose a low tax rate and a high growth rate. Except for van Ewijk (1991), who relates differences in income among voters to intertemporal preferences, usually the personal distribution of income is considered to be given. However, Persson and Tabellini (1992) acknowledge the possibility of an interaction between growth and income distribution that could potentially modify their analysis. In any case there is strong empirical evidence for a wide range of democracies that a fairer distribution of income and wealth induces the right political conditions for growth-promoting policies.

8 Concluding remarks

This survey has dealt with several engines of growth: research for and development of new products, learning by doing as a side effect of private investment, and public investment in for example infrastructure. Another, deliberately neglected but important, approach focuses on investment in human capital. Although these views on growth may at first sight appear to be rather different from each other, they are not mutually exclusive and share common features. First, in contrast with the orthodox neoclassical theory savings do matter for the determination of the rate of economic growth. Consequently the design of the fiscal system, the definition and the protection of property rights, and the functioning of financial markets are crucial to economic growth. Taxes on capital income, the fiscal method of depreciation, patents on inventions, uncertainty about property rights (think of the situation in Eastern Europe or of the political stability in South America), the channeling of funds from lenders to borrowers, all these factors affect the rate of return on investment and therefore the willingness to postpone consumption. However, not only structural policies but also ordinary budgetary policies interfere with growth if Ricardian equivalence does not hold. We have shown that an increase in public consumption or in government debt will diminish the funds available for investment; consumption of the current generation will not be totally crowded out as yet unborn generations will partly pay the higher taxes in the future. Second, almost all the views on economic growth relate the accumulation of knowledge to externalities, so that private decisions to save and to invest are not optimal and growth is from a social point of view too low. Naturally, this implies an active role for the government; depending on the engine of growth the government should try to support R&D, improve the channels of international communication, promote investment, maintain and expand the infrastructure, and/or invest in education.

The predictions of the recent theories in an international setting clearly depend on the translation of these theories from the context of a closed economy to that of an open economy and are therefore not clearcut. For example, the theoretical relationship between trade and growth has been thoroughly investigated but is ambiguous; empirical results reveal that it may be positive (Roubini and Sala-i-Martin, 1991).

The orthodox theory of growth has a rather optimistic view on the issue of growth and development. In contrast, the recent theories indicate that differences in levels of and even in growth rates of production and consumption may persist. An interesting avenue for further research is therefore to extend these theories to allow for the international migration of labor (see for example Burda and Wyplosz, 1991). This line of research may provide a real-world perspective on the issue of growth and development.

Notes

1   Scott (1989) is one of the few recent contributions to the literature on growth which acknowledges the classic work of Conlisk (1969).
2   Both Scott (1989) and King and Robson (1989) postulate a technical progress function, somewhat in the spirit of Kaldor (1961), rather than a neoclassical production function. We focus on the use of the neoclassical production functions to explain endogenous growth.
3   The standard Ramsey model achieves balanced growth through adjustments in both the capital–output ratio and the aggregate savings rate. Growth in private consumption occurs when the market rate of interest exceeds the subjective rate of time preference, particularly if the elasticity of intertemporal substitution is high. The aggregate savings rate, however, only increases with the interest rate if the substitution effect dominates the income effects (i.e. if the elasticity of intertemporal substitution exceeds unity).
4   As usual the distinction may be ambiguous in practice: a book can be read by one person at the same time, but by many persons in time.
5   This formulation has also been used in other models of growth as (part of) a production function. The interpretation is naturally different, because then a variety represents an intermediate input (Grossman and Helpman, 1991) or a capital good (Romer, 1990). An increased number of varieties entails an increased factor productivity due to a higher degree of specialization in production.
6   Grossman and Helpman also try to underpin the assumption of a single firm by Bertrand competition between an innovator and an imitator when imitation is costly and both products are perfect substitutes. However, if imitation is not too costly, Bertrand price setting may not be credible.
7   The distinction between a flow of ideas and a flow of goods and services was first introduced by Rivera-Batiz and Romer (1991a, b).
8   This argument is strengthened if Bertrand competition is a viable and credible policy for the incumbent producer.
9   In fact Barro (1990) finds a negative (conditional) correlation between the number of assassinations and the number of revolutions on the one hand and the growth rate on the other hand for South American countries. Though this result nicely illustrates the text, it should not be taken too seriously.
10   Usually the political choices are set in a peculiar institutional framework that has to proxy a representative democracy. Furthermore, a formal solution is subject to stringent conditions; for example the choice has to concern a single issue and the distribution of preferences on this subject has to be single peaked.

References

Aghion, Philippe, and Peter Howitt (1992) "A model of growth through creative destruction," *Econometrica* 2, 323–51.

Alesina, Alberto, and Daniel Rodrik (1991) "Distributive politics and economic growth," CEPR Discussion Paper, 565, London.

Alogoskoufis, George, and Frederick van der Ploeg (1990) "Endogenous growth and overlapping generations," Discussion Paper 26/90, Birkbeck College, University of London.

—— and —— (1991a) "Money and growth revisited," CentER Discussion Paper 9109, Tilburg University.

—— and —— (1991b) "On budgetary policies, growth, and external deficits in an interdependent world," *Journal of the Japanese and International Economies* 5 (4), 305–24.

—— and —— (1991c) "Debts, deficits and growth in interdependent economies," CEPR Discussion Paper 533, London.

Arrow, Kenneth J. (1962) "The economic implications of learning by doing," *Review of Economic Studies* 29, 155–73.

Baldwin, R. (1989) "The growth effects of 1992," *Economic Policy* 9.

Barro, Robert J. (1974) "Are government bonds net wealth?" *Journal of Political Economy* 82 (6), 1095–1117.

—— (1990) "Government spending in a simple model of endogenous growth," *Journal of Political Economy* 98, S103–25.

—— and Xavier Sala-i-Martin (1990) "Public finance in models of economic growth," mimeo, Harvard University.

——, N. Gregory Mankiw, and Xavier Sala-i-Martin (1992) "Capital mobility in neoclassical models of growth," mimeo, CEPR.

Beath, John, Y. Katsoulacos, and David Ulph (1992) "Strategic innovation," in M. Bacharach, M. Dempster, and J. Enos (eds) *Mathematical Models in Economics*, Oxford, Oxford University Press.

Blanchard, Olivier J. and Stanley Fischer (1989) *Lectures on Macroeconomics*, Cambridge, MA, MIT Press.

Buiter, Willem H. and Kenneth M. Kletzer (1991) "Persistent differences in national productivity growth rates with common technology and free capital mobility: the roles of private thrift, public debt, capital taxation and policy towards human capital formation," *Journal of the Japanese and International Economies* 5 (4), 325–53.

Burda, Michael, and Charles Wyplosz (1991) "Human capital, investment and migration in an integrated Europe," CEPR Discussion Paper 614, London.

Conlisk, John (1969) "A neoclassical growth model with endogenously positioned technical change frontier," *Economic Journal* 79, 348–62.

van Ewijk, Casper (1991) "Distribution effects in a small open economy with heterogeneous agents," mimeo, Tinbergen Institute.

Feldstein, M.S. and C. Horioka (1980) "Domestic savings and international capital flows," *Economic Journal* 90, 314–29.

Giovannini, Alberto (1988) "The real exchange rate, the capital stock, and fiscal policy," *European Economic Review* 32, 1747–67.

Grossman, Gene M. and Elhanan Helpman (1990a) "Comparative advantage and long-run growth," *American Economic Review* 80, 796–815.

—— and —— (1990b) "Trade, innovation and economic growth," *American Economic Review, Papers and Proceedings* 80, 86–91.

—— and —— (1991) *Innovation and Growth in the Global Economy*, Cambridge, MA, MIT Press.

Hicks, J.R. (1950) *A Contribution to the Theory of the Trade Cycle*, Oxford, Oxford University Press.

Kaldor, Nicholas (1961) "Capital accumulation and economic growth," in F. Lutz (ed.) *The Theory of Capital*, London, Macmillan.

King, Mervyn A. and Mark Robson (1989) "Endogenous growth and the role of history," NBER Working Paper 3173, Cambridge, MA.

Kuznets, Simon (1966) *Modern Economic Growth: rate, structure and spread*, New Haven, CT, Yale University Press.

Lucas, Robert E. (1988) "On the mechanics of economic growth," *Journal of Monetary Economics* 22, 3–42.

Maddison, Angus (1987) "Growth and slowdown in advanced capitalist economies: techniques of quantitative assessment," *Journal of Economic Literature* 25, 649–98.

Mankiw, N. Gregory, David Romer, and D.N. Weil (1992) "A contribution to the empirics of economic growth," *Quarterly Journal of Economics* 107, 407–38.

Obstfeld, Maurice (1988) "Fiscal deficits and relative prices in a growing world economy," *Journal of Monetary Economics* 23, 461–84.

Persson, Torsten, and Guido Tabellini (1992) "Growth, distribution and politics," in A. Cukierman, Z. Hercowitz, and L. Leiderman (eds) *The Political Economy of Business Cycles and Growth*, Cambridge, MA, MIT Press.

van der Ploeg, Frederick (1984) "Macro-dynamic theories of economic growth and fluctuations," in F. van der Ploeg (ed.) *Mathematical Methods in Economics*, Chichester, Wiley.

—— (1990) "Money and capital in interdependent economies with overlapping generations," *Economica* 58, 233–56.

—— and Paul J.G. Tang (1992) "The macroeconomics of growth: an international perspective," *Oxford Review of Economic Policy* 8 (4), 15–28.

Ramsey, Frank P. (1928) "A mathematical theory of saving," *Economic Journal* 38, 543–59.

Rebelo, Sergio (1991) "Growth in open economies," CEPR Discussion Paper 667, London.

Rivera-Batiz, L.A. and Paul M. Romer (1991a) "Economic integration and endogenous growth," *Quarterly Journal of Economics* 106, 531–56.

—— and —— (1991b) "International trade with endogenous technological change," *European Economic Review* 35, 971–1004.

Romer, Paul M. (1986) "Increasing returns and long-run growth," *Journal of Political Economy* 94, 1002–37.

—— (1987) "Growth based on increasing returns due to specialization," *American Economic Review, Papers and Proceedings* 77, 56–62.

—— (1990) "Endogenous technological change," *Journal of Political Economy* 98, S71–S102.

Roubini, Nouriel, and Xavier Sala-i-Martin (1991) "Financial development, the trade regime and economic growth," NBER Working Paper 3876, Cambridge, MA.

Scott, Maurice F. (1989) *A New View of Economic Growth*, Oxford, Oxford

University Press.

Solow, Robert M. (1956) "A contribution to the theory of growth," *Quarterly Journal of Economics*, 70, 65–94.

Uzawa, H. (1965) "Optimum technical change in an aggregate model of economic growth," *International Economic Review* 6, 18–31.

Weil, P. (1989) "Overlapping families of infinitely lived agents," *Journal of Public Economics* 38 (2) 183–98.

Index